For selected older vintages

ITALY	02									
Barolo, Barbaresco	5	9								
Chianti Classico Ris.	5	9								
Brunello	5	9	8	9	8	10	6	8	6	8
Amarone	5	7	9	7	7	10	6	10	6	8
SPAIN										
Ribera del Duero	4	8	7	8	7	6	9	8	9	4
Rioja (red)	6	8	7	6	6	7	8	8	9	5
PORTUGAL										
South	5	8	9	8	6	8	6	8	7	5
North	5	8	9	7	6	8	8	7	7	4
Port	6	7	9	7	6	8	7	7	10	2
USA										
California Cabernet	7	8	8	9	7	9	7	8	9	7
California Chardonnay	8	8	7	8	7	8	6	8	8	7
Oregon Pinot Noir	8	8	9	9	8	5	7	5	9	7
Wash. State Cabernet	8	7	9	9	8	8	9	8	9	7
AUSTRALIA										
Coonawarra Cabernet	8	7	9	8	10	7	9	5	8	7
Hunter Semillon	8	7	9	8	10	8	9	7	8	7
Barossa Shiraz	9	10	8	8	10	8	10	7	9	7
Marg. River Cabernet	7	10	8	10	8	7	9	10	9	6
NEW ZEALAND										
M'lborough Sauvignon	8	8	9	8	5	8	9	3	8	4
Hawkes Bay Cabernet	9	7	8	8	10	7	8	7	8	5
SOUTH AFRICA										
Stellenbosch Cabernet	6	9	8	7	8	9	6	9	8	5
S'bosch Chardonnay	8	8	6	7	7	8	6	8	6	8

Numerals (1–10) represent an overall rating for each year. ◗ *Not ready*
● *Just ready* ● *At peak* ◖ *Past best* ○ *Not generally declared*

Oz Clarke's

Pocket Wine Book 2004

the world of wine from a-z

WEBSTERS

A TIME WARNER/WEBSTERS BOOK

This edition first published in 2003 by
Time Warner Books UK
Brettenham House
Lancaster Place
LONDON WC2E 7EN
www.TimeWarnerBooks.co.uk

Created and designed by
Websters International Publishers Limited
Axe and Bottle Court
70 Newcomen Street
London SE1 1YT
www.websters.co.uk
www.ozclarke.com

12th edition. First published in 1992.
Revised editions published annually.

A CIP catalogue for this book is available from the
British Library.

ISBN 0-316-72578-1

Printed and bound in China

CORPORATE SALES
**Companies, institutions and other organizations wishing to make
bulk purchases of this or any other Oz Clarke title published by
Time Warner Books UK should contact Special Sales on
+44 (0)20-7911 8933.**

Thanks are due to the following people for their invaluable help with
the 2004 edition and the generous spirit in which they have shared
their knowledge: Nicolas Belfrage MW, Bob Campbell MW, Bill Evans,
Elizabeth Eyre, Giles Fallowfield, Peter Forrestal, Roger Harris, Tom
Hyland, James Lawther MW, John Livingstone-Learmonth, Angela
Lloyd, Dan McCarthy, Dave McIntyre, Richard Mayson, Jasper Morris
MW, Stuart Pigott, Victor de la Serna, Patricio Tapia.

CONTENTS

HOW TO USE THE A–Z

The **A–Z** section starts on page 44 and includes over 1600 entries on wines, producers, grapes and wine regions from all over the world. It is followed on page 289 by a **Glossary** of some of the more common winemaking terms that are often seen on labels.

Detailed **Vintage Charts** with information on which of the world's top wines are ready for drinking in 2004 can be found on the inside front and back covers; the front chart features vintages back to 1993; the back chart covers a selection of older vintages for premium wines.

Glass Symbols These indicate the wines produced.

♥ Red wine   ♥ Rosé wine   ♡ White wine

The order of the glasses reflects the importance of the wines in terms of volume produced. For example:

♥ White followed by rosé wine

♥ Red followed by white wine

♥ Red followed by rosé, then white wine

Grape Symbols These identify entries on grape varieties.

⣿ Red grape   ⣿ White grape

Star Symbols These indicate wines and producers that are highly rated by the author.

★   A particularly good wine or producer in its category
★★   An excellent wine or producer in its category – one especially worth seeking out
★★★ An exceptional, world-class wine or producer

Best Years Recommended vintages are listed for many producer and appellation entries. Those listed in bold, e.g. **2001**, **99**, indicate wines that are ready for drinking now, although they may not necessarily be at their best; those appearing in brackets, e.g. (2002), (01), are preliminary assessments of wines that are not yet ready for drinking.

Cross References To help you find your way round the A–Z, wine names, producers and regions that have their own entries elsewhere in the A–Z are indicated by SMALL CAPITALS. Grape varieties are not cross-referred in this way, but more than 70 varieties, from Albariño to Zinfandel, are included.

Special Features The A–Z section includes special 2-page features on the world's most important wine styles, regions and grape varieties. These features include recommended vintages and producers, as well as lists of related entries elsewhere in the A–Z.

Index The Index, starting on page 297, will help you find over 4000 recommended producers, including all of those that don't have their own entry in the A–Z. Some of the world's most famous brand names are also included.

INTRODUCTION

I knew something was up as I sat in a New York restaurant after a long transatlantic flight and just as I was thinking, I really don't feel like yet another glass of Chardonnay, up popped the wine waiter and said, 'Can I get you a glass of Grüner Veltliner?' Yes, I thought. Yes, that's exactly what I want – ripe, mouthfilling white wine as weighty, as alcoholic as a big, barrel-fermented Napa Valley or South Australian Chardonnay, but so much more interesting, with astonishing peppery aroma and fat but bone-dry texture. And all of this achieved without a single oak barrel in sight.

That was just the first day, the first meal. During the next week on America's East Coast, I drank Austrian Grüner Veltliner every day, often having it offered to me before I'd even made the decision myself. I also drank Riesling, Viognier, Gewürztraminer and others. But no Chardonnay. I wasn't offered any. I didn't order any. And I didn't miss it.

Has Chardonnay peaked? Has the golden goose stopped laying its buttery, tropical fruit-flavoured, creamy, nutty, spicy eggs? And if it has, *why* has it? Well, in simple terms of numbers of glasses drunk, it hasn't peaked. This year will see more of it downed than ever before. But among winedrinkers who think about what they like, and are keen to expand their horizons, the word Chardonnay, which used to draw forth a bright smile of anticipation, now results in barely stifled yawns. In showbiz terms, Chardonnay has become grossly overexposed. At the top end the wines are generally too monolithic and overbearing to be an enjoyable drink any more. In the middle range... is it me, or are Australian and Californian Chardonnays getting sweeter? And at the bottom – well, what does Chardonnay mean these days? Everyone makes it, everywhere in the world, usually with a tawdry splash of oak chips to give it flavour, disturbingly often with a dollop of sugar in it too, and it's always one of the cheapest wines in the shop. Chardonnay, from being lauded as the greatest white wine grape in the world, has become a victim of its own overweening success and is now just another word for 'a glass of white'.

It was Chardonnay's good fortune in the beginning – ooh, way back in the 1980s – to be the grape most associated with the rich vanilla tones of oak barrel aging that seemed to signify superiority and style. But that was then. Oak did rule, then. It doesn't now, not in white wines. Our palates have become blunted by the onslaught of oak, and are crying out for something fresher, more nuanced, more interesting; grape varieties with real personality. That's why Sauvignon Blanc is such a runaway success – that in-yer-face tangy citrus assault is thrillingly modern. That's why Pinot Gris (or Grigio if you want to be truly cool), Verdelho, Albariño, Verdicchio, Riesling – and, yes, Grüner Veltliner – are all leaping up the popularity ladder. They have character. They're refreshing. They *taste* of something other than a wooden plank. Chardonnay's problem is that actually it's rather a neutral variety: unless the grapes are really good, it needs dolling up with oak to taste of anything at all.

Interestingly, as wine drinkers veer away from wooded whites, they've lurched toward wooded reds. Cabernet, Merlot, Shiraz or Syrah, Pinot Noir, Grenache, Sangiovese, Barbera, Tempranillo, Zinfandel, Malbec and Touriga Nacional – all these varieties, with really exciting characters of their own, are now being plastered with rich toffee and vanilla oak. It gets so that I can't actually tell which country a wine comes from, nor can I tell its grape variety – and that's a crying shame. Because, although the barrel is the best vessel in which to age a red wine, overuse of wood simply blots out the flavour of the grape. And that same oak aversion that is turning white wine drinkers away from Chardonnay in droves will eventually affect red wine drinkers too. Oak was never supposed to be the dominant flavour, it was supposed to be the seasoning, the salt and pepper. Wine is made of grapes, not trees. Let's taste the fruit, let's taste the vineyard the wine came from, let's taste the difference between vintage conditions. It's time to take back the wine from the barrel coopers, the plank merchants, the oak chip scientists, and return it to the vineyard and the vine.

And with that in mind, where is my thirst going to take me this year? Well, **Austria**, for a start. Several of the best whites I've had recently were from Austria, so I'll have a lot more this year. And I'll continue to indulge in the thoughtful, crystal clear beauty of **German Mosel** Rieslings and wonder why more of you don't join me.

In **Italy**, the quality revolution in **Tuscany** is now so marked, so self-confident that I'll once more embrace these haughty but beautiful reds – and for more rough-and-tumble pleasures I'll hurl myself into Italy's other red wine revolution in the far south of **Campania**, **Basilicata**, **Puglia**, but above all, **Sicily**.

In **Spain**, to be honest, I'll sit in the sun and sip an ice cold Manzanilla sherry and marvel at how such a unique flavour is so little appreciated. And as **Portuguese** reds get better and better I'll start learning the flavours of their fascinating indigenous grape varieties.

In **France** I shall spend most of my time revelling in the thrills and delights of her two most imaginative regions – the **Rhône Valley** and **Languedoc-Roussillon** – mostly for fantastic, and affordable, reds, but also for scented, sensuous whites. Talking of affordable, I shall drink a bit more **Bordeaux**. The market is forcing down the price of the top wines, but the efforts to improve are also really beginning to bear fruit at the lower level.

There's no doubt I'll go on drinking **South American** wines – mostly reds – because they're packed with ripe, original flavours and they don't overcharge. Too many **California** wineries do overcharge, but the quality of Pinot Noir and, increasingly, Syrah, is so good, I'll have to have some. My Pinot Gris I'll get from **Oregon**, my Merlot and Cabernet I'll get from **Washington**.

The young Turks in **South Africa** show no sign of letting up, so I'll drink both reds *and* whites from here. And it's the same in **New Zealand**: the whites are still stunning, but there's a reassuring amount of Pinot Noir, Merlot and even Syrah to quench my thirst.

And will I drink **Australian**? I drank less last year, I'll drink less again this year as the big brands cheapen their wines and dilute their personality. But the myriad of smaller producers round the nation? They're making the best wines they've ever made – so I'll be drinking as many of them as I can lay my hands on.

Oz Clarke

SOME OF MY FAVOURITES

Deciding what to leave out of a fantasy cellar is *so* much harder than knowing what to include. The following are not definitive 'best wines', but a compilation of new discoveries and world-beating stunners that remain on my wish list year after year. Some are easy to find; others are very rare, but if you get the chance to try them, grab it! You can find out more about them in the A–Z on pages 44 to 288: the cross-references in SMALL CAPITALS will guide you to the relevant entries.

WORLD CLASS WINES THAT DON'T COST THE EARTH

- Tim ADAMS Shiraz, CLARE VALLEY, Australia
- CONO SUR 20 Barrels Reserva Merlot, Chile
- Forrest Estate Sauvignon Blanc, MARLBOROUGH, New Zealand
- HIDALGO La Gitana Manzanilla, Spain
- SANTA RITA Triple C, MAIPO, Chile
- STEENBERG Merlot, CONSTANTIA, South Africa

BEST LOOKALIKES TO THE CLASSICS

Bordeaux-style red wines
- ANDREW WILL Sorella, WASHINGTON STATE, USA
- CULLEN Cabernet Sauvignon-Merlot, Australia
- STONYRIDGE Larose, New Zealand
- VERGELEGEN, South Africa

Burgundy-style white wines
- CA' DEL BOSCO Chardonnay, Italy
- GROSSET, Piccadilly Chardonnay, Australia
- LEEUWIN ESTATE Art Series Chardonnay, Australia
- VELICH, Tiglat Chardonnay, Austria

Champagne-style wines
- IRON HORSE Blanc de Blancs, CALIFORNIA, USA
- PIPERS BROOK Pirie, Australia
- ROEDERER ESTATE L'Ermitage, CALIFORNIA, USA

TOP VALUE WINES

- Argentinian Bonarda
- CAVA fizz from Spain
- FAIRVIEW Pinotage, South Africa
- Heartland Shiraz, LIMESTONE COAST, Australia
- Inycon NERO D'AVOLA, SICILY, Italy
- La Palmeria Merlot, LA ROSA, RAPEL, Chile
- Peter LEHMANN Grenache, Australia
- MONTANA Sauvignon Blanc, New Zealand
- Trincadeira, ALENTEJO, Portugal

REGIONS TO WATCH

- ALENTEJO, Portugal
- COLCHAGUA Valley, Chile
- CORBIERES, France
- COSTIERES DE NIMES, France
- GREAT SOUTHERN, Australia
- Luján de Cuyo, MENDOZA, Argentina
- OKANAGAN VALLEY, Canada
- SICILY, Italy
- WACHAU, Austria
- Waipara, CANTERBURY, New Zealand

PRODUCERS TO WATCH

- CRAGGY RANGE, HAWKES BAY, New Zealand
- José Neiva, D F J VINHOS, Portugal
- Diemersfontein, PAARL, South Africa
- Ferngrove, GREAT SOUTHERN, Australia
- Hewitson, BAROSSA, Australia
- PLANETA, SICILY, Italy
- Rijckaert, BURGUNDY WHITE WINES, France
- Telmo RODRIGUEZ, Spain
- Horst SAUER, Franken, Germany
- La Massa, CHIANTI CLASSICO, Italy

AUSTRALIA

- Tim ADAMS Aberfeldy Shiraz
- CAPE MENTELLE Cabernet Sauvignon
- Freycinet Pinot Noir, TASMANIA
- GROSSET Watervale Riesling
- HENSCHKE HILL OF GRACE Shiraz
- HOUGHTON Gladstones Shiraz
- LEEUWIN ESTATE Art Series Chardonnay
- MORRIS Old Premium Liqueur Tokay
- PETALUMA Tiers Chardonnay
- PLANTAGENET Shiraz
- TYRRELL'S Vat 1 Semillon

BORDEAUX
- Ch. ANGELUS (red)
- Ch. CHEVAL-BLANC (red)
- Ch. DUCRU-BEAUCAILLOU (red)
- Ch. GRAND-PUY-LACOSTE (red)
- Ch. LAFAURIE-PEYRAGUEY (sweet)
- Les Forts de LATOUR (red)
- Ch. LEOVILLE-BARTON (red)
- Ch LYNCH-BAGES (red)
- Ch. PICHON-LONGUEVILLE-LALANDE (red)
- Ch. SMITH-HAUT-LAFITTE (white)

BURGUNDY
- CARILLON, Bienvenues-BATARD-MONTRACHET (white)
- R Chevillon, NUITS-ST-GEORGES les Perrières (red)
- COCHE-DURY, CORTON-CHARLEMAGNE (white)
- Dugat-Py, Charmes-CHAMBERTIN (red)
- J-N GAGNARD, BATARD-MONTRACHET (white)
- Anne GROS, CLOS DE VOUGEOT (red)
- LAFON, VOLNAY Santenots (red)
- D MORTET, GEVREY-CHAMBERTIN Lavaux-St-Jacques (red)
- M Rollin, CORTON-CHARLEMAGNE (white)
- E Rouget, ECHEZEAUX (red)

CALIFORNIA
- AU BON CLIMAT Chardonnay Le Bouge D'à côté
- CAIN Five
- Cline Cellars Small Berry Mourvèdre, SONOMA COUNTY
- LAUREL GLEN Cabernet Sauvignon
- Long Meadow Ranch, NAPA VALLEY
- NEWTON Le Puzzle
- Pahlmeyer Red, NAPA VALLEY
- RIDGE Santa Cruz Mountains Chardonnay
- Saucelito Canyon Zinfandel, SAN LUIS OBISPO COUNTY
- SHAFER Hillside Select Cabernet Sauvignon
- Viader, NAPA VALLEY

ITALIAN REDS
- ALLEGRINI AMARONE
- Fattoria di Basciano CHIANTI RUFINA Riserva
- Caggiano, TAURASI
- GAJA LANGHE Sperss
- ISOLE E OLENA Cepparello
- PLANETA Santa Cecilia
- POLIZIANO Le Stanze
- Le Pupille Saffredi (see SUPER-TUSCANS)
- SELVAPIANA CHIANTI RUFINA Riserva Bucerchiale

RHÔNE AND SOUTHERN FRANCE
- Ch. de BEAUCASTEL Roussanne Vieilles Vignes (white)
- Dom. du Chêne, ST-JOSEPH
- CLOS DES PAPES, CHATEAUNEUF-DU-PAPE
- CUILLERON, CONDRIEU les Chaillets
- GRAILLOT, CROZES-HERMITAGE la Guiraude
- JAMET, COTE-ROTIE
- Dom. de la Janasse, CHATEAUNEUF-DU-PAPE Vieilles Vignes
- Ch. de St-Cosme, CONDRIEU

CABERNET SAUVIGNON
- Clos Quebrada de Macul, Domus Aurea, MAIPO Valley, Chile
- GAJA Darmagi, PIEDMONT, Italy
- Ch. GRAND-PUY-LACOSTE, PAUILLAC, France
- Les Forts de LATOUR, PAUILLAC, France
- Long Meadow Ranch, NAPA VALLEY, CALIFORNIA, USA
- RIDGE Monte Bello, CALIFORNIA, USA
- STAG'S LEAP WINE CELLARS SLV, CALIFORNIA, USA
- Terrazas de los Andes, Gran Cabernet Sauvignon, MENDOZA, Argentina

CHARDONNAY
- AU BON CLIMAT Les Nuits Blanches, CALIFORNIA, USA
- CA DEL BOSCO, FRANCIACORTA, Italy
- CARILLON, Bienvenues-BATARD-MONTRACHET, France
- COCHE-DURY, CORTON-CHARLEMAGNE, France
- CONCHA Y TORO Amelia, Chile
- J-N GAGNARD, BATARD-MONTRACHET, France
- GROSSET Piccadilly, ADELAIDE HILLS, Australia
- KISTLER Kistler Vineyard, CALIFORNIA, USA
- KUMEU RIVER, AUCKLAND, New Zealand

- NEWTON Unfiltered, CALIFORNIA, USA
- M Rollin, CORTON-CHARLEMAGNE, France

MERLOT

- ANDREW WILL, WASHINGTON, USA
- Ch. ANGELUS, ST-EMILION, France
- Ch. AUSONE, ST-EMILION, France
- CASA LAPOSTOLLE Cuvée Alexandre, Chile
- CONO SUR Reserva, Chile
- LEONETTI CELLAR, WASHINGTON, USA
- ORNELLAIA Masseto, TUSCANY, Italy
- Ch. PETRUS, POMEROL, France

PINOT NOIR

- ATA RANGI, MARTINBOROUGH, New Zealand
- R Chevillon, NUITS-ST-GEORGES les St-Georges, France
- Dugat-Py, Charmes-CHAMBERTIN, France
- FELTON ROAD, CENTRAL OTAGO, New Zealand
- Freycinet, TASMANIA, Australia
- Anne GROS, CLOS DE VOUGEOT, France
- LAFON, VOLNAY Santenots, France
- SAINTSBURY Reserve, USA
- E Rouget, ECHEZEAUX, France

RIESLING

- BRUNDLMAYER, Austria
- H DONNHOFF Niederhäuser Hermannshöhle, NAHE, Germany
- GROSSET Watervale, CLARE VALLEY, Australia
- GUNDERLOCH Nackenheimer Rothenberg, RHEINHESSEN, Germany
- Fritz HAAG Brauneberger Juffer Sonnenuhr, MOSEL, Germany
- Dr LOOSEN Erdener Prälat, MOSEL, Germany
- Mount Horrocks, CLARE VALLEY, Australia
- Horst SAUER Escherndorfer Lump, FRANKEN, Germany

SAUVIGNON BLANC

- Lucien Crochet, SANCERRE, France
- Didier DAGUENEAU, POUILLY-FUME, France
- Neil ELLIS Groenekloof, South Africa
- Forrest Estate, MARLBOROUGH, New Zealand

- PALLISER ESTATE, Martinborough, New Zealand
- Ch. SMITH-HAUT-LAFITTE, PESSAC-LEOGNAN, France
- STEENBERG, CONSTANTIA, South Africa
- VERGELEGEN, STELLENBOSCH, South Africa
- VILLA MARIA Reserve Clifford Bay, MARLBOROUGH, New Zealand

SYRAH/SHIRAZ

- Tim ADAMS Aberfeldy, CLARE VALLEY, Australia
- BOEKENHOUTSKLOOF, FRANSCHHOEK, South Africa
- BROKENWOOD Graveyard, HUNTER VALLEY, Australia
- CHAVE, HERMITAGE, France
- HENSCHKE HILL OF GRACE, Eden Valley, Australia
- JAMET, COTE-ROTIE, France
- MONTES Folly, COLCHAGUA, Chile
- Ojai, SANTA BARBARA COUNTY, CALIFORNIA, USA
- PENFOLDS GRANGE, Australia

FORTIFIED WINE

- BARBADILLO Amontillado Principe, Spain
- CHAMBERS Rutherglen Muscat, Australia
- GONZALEZ BYASS Noé Pedro Ximénez, Spain
- GRAHAM's Vintage Port
- HENRIQUES & HENRIQUES Madeira
- NIEPOORT Vintage Port

SPARKLING WINE

- BILLECART-SALMON Cuvée N-F Billecart CHAMPAGNE, France
- CLOUDY BAY Pelorus, MARLBOROUGH, New Zealand
- DEUTZ Blanc de Blancs CHAMPAGNE, France
- Alfred GRATIEN Vintage CHAMPAGNE, France
- Charles HEIDSIECK Mis en Caves CHAMPAGNE, France
- Charles MELTON Sparkling Red, BAROSSA, Australia
- PIPERS BROOK Pirie, TASMANIA, Australia
- POL ROGER Vintage CHAMPAGNE, France
- ROEDERER ESTATE L'Ermitage, CALIFORNIA, USA

MODERN WINE STYLES

Not so long ago, if I were to outline the basic wine styles, the list would have been strongly biased towards the classics – Bordeaux, Burgundy, Sancerre, Mosel Riesling, Champagne. But the classics have, over time, become expensive and unreliable – thus opening the door to other, less established regions, and giving them the chance to offer us wines that may or may not owe anything to the originals. *These* are the flavours to which ambitious winemakers the world over now aspire.

WHITE WINES

Ripe, up-front, spicy Chardonnay Fruit is the key here: round, ripe, apricot, peach, melon, pineapple and tropical fruits, spiced up with the vanilla and butterscotch richness of some new oak – often American oak – to make a delicious, approachable, easy-to-drink fruit cocktail of taste. Australia and Chile are best at this style.

Green, tangy Sauvignon New Zealand was the originator of this style – all zingy, grassy, nettles and asparagus and then green apples and peach – and South Africa now has its own tangy, super-fresh examples. Chile has the potential to produce something similar and there are hopeful signs in southern France. Bordeaux and the Loire are the original sources of dry Sauvignon wines, and at last we are seeing an expanding band of committed modern producers matching clean fruit with zippy green tang. Riesling in Australia is often lean and limy.

Bone-dry, neutral whites This doesn't sound very appetizing, but as long as it is well made it will be thirst-quenching and easy to drink. Many Italian whites fit this bill. Southern French wines, where no grape variety is specified, will be like this; so will many wines from Bordeaux, the South-West, Muscadet and Anjou. Modern young Spanish whites and Portuguese Vinho Verdes are good examples, as are Swiss Fendant (Chasselas) and southern German Trocken (dry) wines. I don't like seeing too much neutrality in New World wines, but cheap South African and California whites are 'superneutral'.

White Burgundy By this I mean the nutty, oatmealy-ripe but dry, subtly oaked styles of villages like Meursault at their best. Few people do it well, even in Burgundy itself, and it's a difficult style to emulate. California makes the most effort. Washington, Oregon and New York State each have occasional successes, as do top Australian and New Zealand Chardonnays.

Perfumy, off-dry whites Gewurztraminer, Muscat and Pinot Gris from Alsace will give you this style and in southern Germany Gewürztraminer, Scheurebe, Kerner, Grauburgunder (Pinot Gris) and occasionally Riesling may also do it. In New Zealand Riesling and Gewürztraminer can be excellent. Irsai Oliver from Hungary and Torrontés from Argentina are both heady and perfumed. Albariño in Spain is leaner but heady with citrus scent.

Mouthfuls of luscious gold Good sweet wines are difficult to make. Sauternes is the most famous, but the Loire, and sometimes Alsace, can also come up with rich, intensely sweet wines that can live for decades. Germany's top sweeties are stunning; Austria's are similiar in style to Germany's, but weightier. Hungarian Tokaji has a wonderful sweet-sour smoky flavour. Australia, California and New Zealand also have some exciting examples.

10

RED WINES

Spicy, warm-hearted reds Australia is out in front at the moment through the ebullient resurgence of her Shiraz reds – ripe, almost sweet, sinfully easy to enjoy. France's Rhône Valley is also on the up and the traditional appellations in the far south of France are looking good. In Italy Piedmont is producing delicious beefy Barbera and juicy exotic Dolcetto. Spain's Ribera del Duero and Toro and Portugal's south also deliver the goods, as does Malbec in Argentina. California Zinfandel made in its most powerful style is spicy and rich.

Juicy, fruity reds This used to be the Beaujolais spot, but there hasn't been much exciting Beaujolais recently. Grenache and Syrah vins de pays are better bets, as are grassy, sharp Loire reds. Modern Spanish reds from Valdepeñas and La Mancha do the trick, as do some Garnachas from Aragón, while in Italy young Chianti and Teroldego hit home. Argentina has some good fresh examples from Sangiovese, Tempranillo and other Italian and Spanish grape varieties.

Blackcurranty Cabernet Chile has climbed back to the top of the Cabernet tree, knocking Australia off its perch, though there are still some good examples from Australia. New Zealand also strikes the blackcurrant bell in a much greener, sharper way. California only sometimes hits the sweet spot, and often with Merlot rather than Cabernet. Eastern Europe, in particular Hungary, is doing well, as is southern France. And what about Bordeaux? Only a few of the top wines reach the target; for the price, Tuscan Cabernet is often more exciting.

Tough, tannic long-haul boys Bordeaux does lead this field, and the best wines are really good after 10 years or so – but don't expect wines from minor properties to age in the same way. It's the same in Tuscany and Piedmont – only the top wines last well – especially Chianti Classico, Barolo and Barbaresco. In Portugal there's plenty of tannin and some increasingly good long-lasting Douro reds.

Soft, strawberryish charmers Good Burgundy definitely tops this group. Rioja in Spain can sometimes get there, as can Navarra and Valdepeñas. Pinot Noir in California, Oregon and New Zealand is frequently delicious, and Chile and Australia increasingly get it right too. Germany hits the spot with Spätburgunder (Pinot Noir) now and then. Italy's Lago di Caldaro often smooches in; and over in Bordeaux, of all places, both St-Émilion and Pomerol can do the business.

SPARKLING AND FORTIFIED WINES

Fizz This can be white or pink or red, dry or sweet, and I sometimes think it doesn't matter what it tastes like as long as it's cold enough and there's enough of it. Champagne can be best, but frequently isn't – and there are lots of new-wave winemakers making good-value lookalikes. Australia is tops for tasty bargains, followed by California and New Zealand. Spain pumps out oceans of good basic stuff.

Fortified wines For once in my life I find myself saying that the old ways are definitely the best. There's nothing to beat the top ports and sherries in the deep, rich, sticky stakes – though for the glimmerings of a new angle look to Australia, California and South Africa. The Portuguese island of Madeira produces fortifieds with rich, brown smoky flavours and a startling acid bite – and don't forget the luscious Muscats made all round the Mediterranean.

MATCHING FOOD AND WINE

Give me a rule, I'll break it – well, bend it anyway. So when I see the proliferation of publications laying down rules as to what wine to drink with what food, I get very uneasy and have to quell a burning desire to slosh back a Grand Cru Burgundy with my chilli con carne.

The pleasures of eating and drinking operate on so many levels that hard and fast rules make no sense. What about mood? If I'm in the mood for Champagne, Champagne it shall be, whatever I'm eating. What about place? If I'm sitting gazing out across the shimmering Mediterranean, hand me anything, just as long as it's local – it'll be perfect.

Even so, there are some things that simply don't go well with wine: artichokes, asparagus, spinach, kippers and mackerel, chilli, salsas and vinegars, chocolate, all flatten the flavours of wines. The general rule here is avoid tannic red wines and go for juicy young reds, or whites with plenty of fruit and fresh acidity. And for chocolate, liqueur Muscats, raisiny Banyuls or Italy's grapy, frothy Asti are just about the only things that work. Don't be afraid to experiment. Who would guess that salty Roquefort cheese and rich, sweet Sauternes would go together? But they do, and it's a match made in heaven. So, with these factors in mind, the following pairings are not rules – just my recommendations.

FISH

Grilled or baked white fish
White Burgundy or other fine Chardonnay, Pessac-Léognan or Graves, Viognier, Australian and New Zealand Riesling.

Grilled or baked oily or 'meaty' fish (e.g. salmon, trout, tuna, swordfish) Alsace or Austrian Riesling, Grüner Veltliner, fruity New World Chardonnay or Semillon, Chinon or Bourgueil, New World Pinot Noir.

Fried/battered fish Simple, fresh whites, e.g. Soave, Mâcon-Villages, Pinot Gris, white Bordeaux, or a Spätlese from the Rheingau or Pfalz.

Shellfish Chablis or unoaked Chardonnay, Pinot Blanc; *clams and oysters* Aligoté, Vinho Verde, Seyval Blanc; *crab* Riesling Spätlese, Viognier; *lobster, scallops* white Burgundy or other fine Chardonnay, Champagne, Viognier; *mussels* Muscadet, Pinot Grigio.

Smoked fish Ice-cold basic fizz, manzanilla or fino sherry, Alsace Gewurztraminer or Pinot Gris, Mosel Riesling Kabinett, New World Riesling.

MEAT

Beef/steak *Plain roasted or grilled* tannic reds, top Bordeaux, New World Cabernet Sauvignon, Ribera del Duero, Super-Tuscans, South African Pinotage.

Lamb *Plain roasted or grilled* top red Burgundy, top red Bordeaux, especially Pauillac or St-Éstephe, Rioja Reserva, fine New World Pinot Noir or Merlot.

Pork *Plain roasted or grilled* full, spicy dry whites, e.g. Alsace Pinot Gris, lightly oaked Chardonnay; smooth reds, e.g. Rioja, Alentejo; *ham and bacon* young, fruity reds, e.g. Beaujolais, Teroldego, unoaked Tempranillo, Mendoza Malbec, Lambrusco; *sausages, salami, pâté* rustic/young reds from Beaujolais, Provence, Puglia, and from Merlot, Zinfandel, Pinotage grapes.

Veal *Plain roasted or grilled* full-bodied whites, e.g. Alsace, German, Austrian Pinot Gris, Grüner Veltliner, Vouvray, Châteauneuf-du-Pape; soft reds, e.g. Dolcetto, Baden Pinot Noir, or mature Rioja, Burgundy or Margaux; *with cream-based sauce* full, ripe whites, e.g.

Alsace Pinot Blanc or Pinot Gris, Vouvray, oaked New World Chardonnay; *with rich red-wine sauce (e.g. osso buco)* young Italian reds, Zinfandel.

Venison *Plain roasted or grilled* Barolo, St-Estèphe, Pomerol, Côte de Nuits, Hermitage, big Zinfandel, Alsace or German Pinot Gris; *with red-wine sauce* Piedmont and Portuguese reds, Pomerol, St-Émilion, New World Syrah/Shiraz or Pinotage, Priorat.

Chicken and turkey *Plain roasted or grilled* fine red or white Burgundy, red Rioja Reserva, New World Chardonnay or Semillon.

Duck *Plain roasted* Pomerol, St-Émilion, Côte de Nuits or Rhône reds, New World Syrah/Shiraz (including sparkling) or Merlot; also full, soft whites such as Austrian Riesling; *with orange* German Riesling Auslese, or Barsac.

Game birds *Plain roasted or grilled* top reds from Burgundy, Rhône, Tuscany, Piedmont, Ribera del Duero, New World Cabernet; also full whites such as New World Semillon.

Casseroles and stews Match the dominant ingredient, e.g. red wine for *boeuf bourguignon* or *coq au vin*, dry whites for a fricassee. The weight of the wine should match the richness of the sauce. For strong tomato flavours see Pasta.

ETHNIC CUISINES

Chinese Riesling or Gewürztraminer, unoaked New World Chardonnay; fruity rosé, light German and Austrian reds.

Indian/Tex-Mex Aromatic whites, e.g. Mosel Kabinett or Spätlese or other Riesling, Sauvignon Blanc, Viognier; non-tannic reds, e.g. Valpolicella, Rioja, Merlot, Cabernet Franc, Grenache, Syrah/Shiraz, Zinfandel.

Thai/South-East Asian Spicy whites, e.g. Alsace or New Zealand Pinot Gris, dry Muscat;

dry or off-dry Riesling, New World Sauvignon Blanc. Rich, oaky Australian or California Chardonnay can cope with coconut.

EGGS

Champagne and traditional-method fizz; light, fresh reds such as Beaujolais or Chinon; full, dry unoaked whites; New World rosé.

PASTA

With tomato sauce Barbera, Soave, Verdicchio, New World Sauvignon Blanc; *with meat-based sauce* north or central Italian reds, French or New World Syrah/Shiraz, Zinfandel; *with cream- or cheese-based sauce* soft, full, dry unoaked whites from northern Italy, light Austrian reds; *with seafood/fish sauce* dry, tangy whites, e.g. Verdicchio, Vermentino, Grüner Veltliner, Muscadet; *with pesto* New World Sauvignon Blanc, Dolcetto, Minervois.

SALADS

Sharp-edged whites, e.g. New World Sauvignon Blanc, Chenin Blanc, dry Riesling, Vinho Verde.

CHEESES

Hard Full reds from Italy, France or Spain, New World Merlot or Zinfandel, dry oloroso sherry, tawny port.

Soft LBV port, rich, fruity Rhône reds, Shiraz, Zinfandel, Alsace Pinot Gris, Gewürztraminer.

Blue Botrytized sweet whites such as Sauternes, vintage port, old oloroso sherry, Malmsey Madeira.

Goats' Sancerre, Pouilly-Fumé, New World Sauvignon Blanc, Chinon, Saumur-Champigny.

DESSERTS

Chocolate Australian Liqueur Muscat, Asti, Banyuls.

Fruit-based Sauternes, Eiswein, Moscatel de Valencia.

MATCHING WINE AND FOOD _____

With very special bottles, when you have found an irresistible bargain or when you are casting around for culinary inspiration, it can be a good idea to let the wine dictate the choice of food.

Although I said earlier that rules in this area are made to be bent if not broken, there are certain points to remember when matching wine and food. Before you make specific choices, think about some basic characteristics and see how thinking in terms of grape varieties and wine styles can point you in the right direction.

In many cases, the local food and wine combinations that have evolved over the years simply cannot be bettered (think of ripe Burgundy with *coq au vin* or *boeuf bourguignon*; Chianti Riserva with *bistecca alla Fiorentina*; Muscadet and Breton oysters). Yet the world of food and wine is moving so fast that it would be madness to be restricted by the old tenets. Californian cuisine, fusion food, and the infiltration of innumerable ethnic influences coupled with the re-invigoration of traditional wines, continuous experiment with new methods and blends and the opening up of completely new wine areas mean that the search for perfect food and wine partners is, and will remain, very much an on-going process.

Here are some of the characteristics you need to consider, plus a summary of the main grape varieties and their best food matches.

Body/weight As well as considering the taste of the wine you need to match the weight or body of the wine to the intensity of the food's flavour. A heavy alcoholic wine will not suit a delicate dish; and *vice versa.*

Acidity The acidity of a dish should balance the acidity of a wine. High-acid flavours, such as tomato, lemon or vinegar, need matching acidity in their accompanying wines. Use acidity in wine to cut through the richness of a dish but for this to work, make sure the wine is full in flavour.

Sweetness Sweet food makes dry wine taste unpleasantly lean and acidic. With desserts and puddings find a wine that is at least as sweet as the food (sweeter than the food is fine). However, many savoury foods, such as carrots, onions and parsnips, taste slightly sweet and dishes in which they feature prominently will go best with ripe, fruity wines that have a touch of sweetness.

Salt Salty foods and sweet wines match, but salty foods and tannin are definitely best avoided.

Age/Maturity The bouquet of a wine is only acquired over time and should be savoured and appreciated: with age many red wines acquire complex flavours and perfumes and a similar degree of complexity in the flavour of the food is often a good idea.

Tannin Rare red meat can have the effect of softening tannic wine. Avoid eggs and fish.

Oak Oak flavours in wine vary from the satisfyingly subtle to positively strident. This latter end of the scale can conflict with food, although it may be suitable for smoked fish (white wines only) or full-flavoured meat or game.

Wine in the food If you want to use wine in cooking it is best to use the same style of wine as the one you are going to drink with the meal (it can be an inferior version though).

RED GRAPES

Barbera Wines made to be drunk young have high acidity that can hold their own with sausages, salami, ham, and tomato sauces. Complex older or oak-aged wines from the top growers need to be matched with rich food such as Piemontese beef casseroles and game dishes.

Cabernet Franc Best drunk with plain rather than sauced meat dishes, or, slightly chilled, with grilled or baked salmon or trout. Try it with Indian food.

Cabernet Sauvignon All over the world the Cabernet Sauvignon makes full-flavoured reliable red wine: the ideal food wine. Cabernet Sauvignon seems to have a particular affinity for lamb but it partners all plain roast or grilled meats and game well and would be an excellent choice for many sauced meat dishes such as *boeuf bourguignon*, steak and kidney pie or rabbit stew and substantial dishes made with mushrooms.

Dolcetto Dolcetto produces fruity purple wines that go beautifully with hearty local north Italian meat dishes such as calves' liver and onions or casseroled game with polenta.

Gamay The grape of red Beaujolais, Gamay, makes wine you can drink whenever, wherever, however and with whatever you want – although it's particularly good lightly chilled on hot summer days. It goes well with pâtés, bacon and sausages because its acidity provides a satisfying foil to their richness. It would be a good choice for many vegetarian dishes. If in doubt you are unlikely to go far wrong with Gamay.

Grenache Generally blended with other grapes, Grenache nonetheless dominates, with its high alcoholic strength and rich, spicy flavours. These are wines readily matched with food: casseroles, charcuterie and grills for concentrated older wines; almost anything – from light vegetarian dishes to *soupe de poissons* – for lighter reds and rosés.

Merlot Merlot makes soft, rounded, fruity wines that are some of the easiest red wines to enjoy without food, yet are also a good choice with many kinds of food. Spicier game dishes, herby terrines and pâtés, pheasant, pigeon, duck or goose all team well with Merlot; substantial casseroles made with wine are excellent with top Pomerol châteaux; and the soft fruitiness of the wines is perfect for pork, liver, turkey, and savoury foods with a hint of sweetness such as honey-roast or Bayonne ham.

Nebbiolo Fruity, fragrant, early-drinking styles of Nebbiolo wine are best with local salami, pâtés, *bresaola* and lighter meat dishes. The best Barolos and Barbarescos need substantial food: *bollito misto*, rich hare or beef casseroles and *brasato al Barolo* (a large piece of beef marinated then braised slowly in Barolo) are just the job in Piedmont, or anywhere else for that matter.

Pinot Noir The great grape of Burgundy has taken its food-friendly complexity all over the wine world. However, nothing can beat the marriage of great wine with sublime local food that is Burgundy's heritage, and it is Burgundian dishes that spring to mind as perfect partners for the Pinot Noir: *coq au vin, boeuf bourguignon*, rabbit with mustard, braised ham, chicken with tarragon, steaks from prized Charolais cattle with a rich red-wine sauce ... the list is endless.

Pinot Noir's subtle flavours make it a natural choice for complex meat dishes but it is also excellent with plain grills and roasts and, in its lighter manifestations from, say, the Loire or Oregon, a good match for salmon or tuna.

In spite of the prevalence of superb cheese in Burgundy, the best Pinot Noir red wines are wasted on cheese.

Sangiovese Tuscany is where Sangiovese best expresses the qualities that can lead it, in the right circumstances, to be numbered among the great grapes of the world. And Tuscany is very much 'food with wine' territory. Sangiovese wines such as Chianti, Rosso di Montalcino, Vino Nobile di Montepulciano, and the biggest of them all, Brunello, positively demand to be drunk with food. Drink them with *bistecca alla Fiorentina*, roast meats and game, calves' liver, casseroles, hearty pasta sauces, *porcini* mushrooms and Pecorino cheese.

Syrah/Shiraz Whether from France (in the Northern Rhône), Australia, California or South Africa, this grape always makes powerful, rich, full-bodied wines that are superb with full-flavoured food. The classic barbecue wine, Shiraz/Syrah also goes with roasts, game, hearty casseroles and charcuterie. It can also be good with tangy cheeses such as Manchego or Cheshire.

Tempranillo Spain's best native red grape makes aromatic wines for drinking young, and matures well to a rich (usually) oaky flavour. Tempranillo is good with game, cured hams and sausages, casseroles and meat grilled with herbs; it is particularly good with lamb. It can partner some Indian dishes and goes well with strong soft cheeses such as ripe Brie.

Zinfandel California's much-planted, most versatile grape is used for a bewildering variety of wine styles from bland, slightly sweet pinks to rich, elegant, fruity reds. And the good red Zinfandels themselves may vary greatly in style. If they aren't too oaky they are good with barbecued meats, venison and roast chicken. The hefty old-style wines are a great match with the spicy, mouthfilling San Francisco cuisine, or with game casseroles. The pale blush style of Zin goes well with tomato sauce.

WHITE GRAPES

Albariño Light, crisp, aromatic with apricots and grapefruit, this goes well with crab and prawn dishes as well as Chinese-style chicken dishes.

Aligoté This Burgundian grape can, at its best, make very versatile food wine. It goes well with many fish and seafood dishes, smoked fish, salads and snails in garlic and butter.

Chardonnay More than almost any other grape Chardonnay responds to different climatic conditions and to the winemaker's art. This, plus the relative ease with which it can be grown, accounts for the marked gradation of flavours and styles: from steely, cool-climate austerity to almost tropical lusciousness. The relatively sharp end of the spectrum is one of the best choices for simple fish dishes; most Chardonnays are superb with roast chicken or other white meat; the really full, rich, New World blockbusters need rich fish and seafood dishes. Oaky Chardonnays are a good choice for smoked fish.

Chenin Blanc One of the most versatile of grapes, Chenin Blanc makes wines ranging from averagely quaffable dry whites to the great sweet whites of the Loire. The lighter wines can be good as apéritifs or with light fish dishes or salads. The sweet wines are good with most puddings and superb with those made with slightly tart fruit.

Gewürztraminer Spicy and perfumed, Gewürztraminer has the weight and flavour to go with such hard-to-match dishes as *choucroute* and smoked fish. It is also a good choice for Chinese or any lightly spiced oriental food.

Grüner Veltliner In its lightest form, this makes a peppery, refreshing apéritif. Riper, more structured versions – with savoury notes of nuts and celery along with the pepper – are particularly good with grilled or baked fish.

Marsanne These rich, fat wines are a bit short of acid so match them with simply prepared chicken, pork, fish or vegetables.

Muscadet The dry, light Muscadet grape (best wines are *sur lie*) is perfect with seafood.

Muscat Fragrant, grapy wines ranging from delicate to downright syrupy. The drier ones are more difficult to pair with food, but can be delightful with oriental cuisines; the sweeties come into their own with most desserts. Sweet Moscato d'Asti, delicious by itself, goes well with rich Christmas pudding or mince pies.

Pinot Blanc Clean, bright and appley, Pinot Blanc is very food-friendly. Classic white wine dishes, modern vegetarian dishes, pasta and pizza all match up well.

Pinot Gris Rich, fat wines that need rich, fat food. Go (in Alsace) for *choucroute*, *confit de canard*, rich pork dishes. The Italian Pinot Gris (Grigio) wines are lighter and more suited to pizza or pasta.

Riesling Good dry Rieslings are delicious by themselves, but also excellent with spicy cuisine. Sweet Rieslings are best enjoyed for their own lusciousness but are suitable partners to fruit-based desserts. In between, those with a fresh acid bite and some residual sweetness can counteract the richness of, say, goose or duck, and the fuller examples can be good with oriental food and otherwise hard-to-match salads.

Sauvignon Blanc This grape makes wines with enough bite and sharpness to accompany quite rich fish dishes as well as being an obvious choice for seafood. The characteristic acid intensity makes a brilliant match with dishes made with tomato, but the best match of all is Sancerre and local Loire goats' cheese.

Sémillon/Semillon Dry Bordeaux Blancs are excellent with fish and shellfish; fuller, riper New World Semillons are equal to spicy food and rich sauces, often going even better with meat than with fish; sweet Sémillons can partner many puddings, especially rich, creamy ones. Sémillon also goes well with many cheeses, and Sauternes with Roquefort is a classic combination.

Viognier Viognier is at its best as an apéritif. It can also go well with spicy Indian dishes.

MAKING THE MOST OF WINE _____

Most wine is pretty hardy stuff and can put up with a fair amount of rough handling. Young red wines can knock about in the back of a car for a day or two and be lugged from garage to kitchen to dinner table without coming to too much harm. Serving young white wines when well chilled can cover up all kinds of ill-treatment – a couple of hours in the fridge should do the trick. Even so, there are some conditions that are better than others for storing your wines, especially if they are on the mature side. And there are certain ways of serving wines which will emphasize any flavours or perfumes they have.

STORING

Most wines are sold ready for drinking, and it will be hard to ruin them if you store them for a few months before you pull the cork. Don't stand them next to the central heating or the cooker, though, or on a sunny windowsill.

Light and extremes of temperature are also the things to worry about if you are storing wine long-term. Some wines, Chardonnay for instance, are particularly sensitive to exposure to light over several months, and the damage will be worse if the bottle is made of pale-coloured glass. The warmer the wine, the quicker it will age, and really high temperatures can spoil wine quite quickly. Beware in the winter of garages and outhouses, too: a very cold snap – say –4°C (25°F) or below – will freeze your wine, push out the corks and crack the bottles. An underground cellar is ideal, with a fairly constant temperature of 10°–12°C (50°–53°F). And bottles really do need to lie on their sides, so that the cork stays damp and swollen, and keeps out the air.

TEMPERATURE

The person who thought up the rule that red wine should be served at room temperature certainly didn't live in a modern, centrally heated flat. It's no great sin to serve a big beefy red at the temperature of your central heating, but I prefer most reds just a touch cooler. Over-heated wine tastes flabby, and may lose some of its more volatile aromas. In general, the lighter the red, the cooler it can be. Really light, refreshing reds, such as Beaujolais, are nice lightly chilled. Ideally, I'd serve Burgundy and other Pinot Noir wines at larder temperature (about 15°C/59°F), Bordeaux and Rioja a bit warmer (18°C/64°F), Rhône wines and New World Cabernet at a comfortable room temperature, but no more than 20°C/68°F.

Chilling white wines makes them taste fresher, emphasizing their acidity. White wines with low acidity especially benefit from chilling, and it's vital for sparkling wines if you want to avoid exploding corks and a tableful of froth. Drastic chilling also subdues flavours, however – a useful ruse if you're serving basic wine, but a shame if the wine is very good. A good guide for whites is to give the cheapest and lightest a spell in the fridge, but serve bigger and better wines – Australian Chardonnays or top white Burgundies – perhaps half-way between fridge and central-heating temperature. If you're undecided, err on the cooler side, for whites or reds. To chill wine quickly, and to keep it cool, an ice bucket is more efficient if filled with a mixture of ice and water, rather than ice alone.

OPENING THE BOTTLE

There's no corkscrew to beat the Screwpull, and the Spinhandle Screwpull is especially easy to use. Don't worry if bits of cork crumble into the wine – just fish them out of your glass. Tight corks that refuse to budge might be loosened if you run hot water over the bottle neck to expand the glass. If the cork is loose and falls in, push it right in and don't worry about it.

Opening sparkling wines is a serious business – point the cork away from people! Once you've started, never take your hand off the cork until it's safely out. Remove the foil, loosen the wire, hold the wire and cork firmly and twist the bottle. If the wine froths, hold the bottle at an angle of 45 degrees, and have a glass at hand.

AIRING AND DECANTING

Scientists have proved that opening young to middle-aged red wines an hour before serving makes no difference whatsoever. The surface area of wine in contact with air in the bottle neck is too tiny to be significant. Decanting is a different matter, because sloshing the wine from bottle to jug or decanter mixes it up quite thoroughly with the air. The only wines that really need to be decanted are those that have a sediment which would cloud the wine if they were poured directly – mature red Bordeaux, Burgundy and vintage port are the commonest examples. Ideally, if you are able to plan that far in advance, you need to stand the bottle upright for a day or two to let the sediment settle in the bottom. Draw the cork extremely gently. As you tip the bottle, shine a bright light through from underneath as you pour in a single steady movement. Stop pouring when you see the sediment approaching the bottle neck.

Contrary to many wine buffs' practice, I would decant a mature wine only just before serving; elderly wines often fade rapidly once they meet with air, and an hour in the decanter could kill off what little fruit they had left. By contrast, a good-quality young white wine can benefit from decanting.

GLASSES

If you want to taste wine at its best, to enjoy all its flavours and aromas, to admire its colours and texture, choose glasses designed for the purpose and show the wine a bit of respect. The ideal wine glass is a fairly large tulip shape, made of fine, clear glass, with a slender stem. When you pour the wine, fill the glass no more than halfway to allow space for aromas. For sparkling wines choose a tall, slender glass, as it helps the bubbles to last longer.

KEEPING LEFTOVERS

Leftover white wine keeps better than red, since the tannin and colouring matter in red wine is easily attacked by the air. Any wine, red or white, keeps better in the fridge than in a warm kitchen. And most wines, if well made in the first place, will be perfectly acceptable, if not pristine, after 2 or 3 days re-corked in the fridge. But for better results it's best to use one of the gadgets sold for this purpose. The ones that work by blanketing the wine with heavier-than-air inert gas are much better than those that create a vacuum in the air space in the bottle.

FRANCE

I've visited most of the wine-producing countries of the world by now, but the one I come back to again and again, with my enthusiasm undimmed by time, is France. The sheer range of its wine flavours, the number of wine styles produced, and indeed the quality differences, from very best to very nearly worst, continue to enthral me, and as each year's vintage nears, I find myself itching to leap into the car and head for the vineyards of Champagne, of Burgundy, of Bordeaux and the Loire. France is currently going through a fascinating period – with an eye on the New World, she's redefining her ideas of what makes a wine great, and what makes her wines different from all the others.

CLIMATE AND SOIL

France lies between the 40th and 50th parallels north, and the climate runs from the distinctly chilly and almost too cool to ripen grapes in the far north near the English Channel, right through to the swelteringly hot and almost too torrid to avoid grapes overripening in the far south on the Mediterranean shores. In the north the most refined and delicate sparkling wine is made in Champagne. In the south, rich, luscious dessert Muscats and fortified wines dominate. In between is just about every sort of wine you could wish for.

The factors that influence a wine's flavour are the grape variety, the soil and climate, and the winemaker's techniques. Most of the great wine grapes, like the red Cabernet Sauvignon, Merlot, Pinot Noir and Syrah, and the white Chardonnay, Sauvignon Blanc, Sémillon and Viognier, find conditions in France where they can ripen slowly but reliably – and slow, even ripening always gives better flavours to a wine. Since grapes have been grown for over 2000 years in France, the most suitable varieties for the different soils and meso-climates have naturally evolved. And since winemaking was brought to France by the Romans, generation upon generation of winemakers have refined their techniques to produce the best possible results from their different grape types. The great wines of areas like Bordeaux and Burgundy are the results of centuries of experience and of trial and error, which winemakers from other countries of the world now use as role models in their attempts to create good wine.

WINE REGIONS

White grapes generally ripen more easily than red grapes and they dominate the northern regions. Even so, the chilly Champagne region barely manages to ripen its red or white grapes on its chalky soil. But the resultant acid wine is the ideal base for sparkling wine, and the acidity of the young still wine can, with good winemaking and a few years' maturing, transform into a golden honeyed sparkling wine of incomparable finesse.

Alsace, on the German border, is warmer and drier than Champagne (the vineyards sit in a rain shadow created by the Vosges mountains that rise above the Rhine Valley) but still produces mainly dry white wines, from grapes such as Riesling, Pinot Gris and Gewurztraminer that are not widely encountered elsewhere in France. With its clear blue skies, Alsace can provide ripeness, and therefore the higher alcoholic strength of the warm south, but also the perfume and fragrance of the cool north.

South-east of Paris, Chablis marks the northernmost tip of the Burgundy region, and the Chardonnay grape here produces very dry wines, usually with a streak of green acidity, but nowadays with a fuller softer texture to subdue any harshness.

It's a good 2 hours' drive further south to the heart of Burgundy – the Côte d'Or, which runs between Dijon and Chagny. World-famous villages such as Gevrey-Chambertin and Vosne-Romanée (where the red Pinot Noir dominates) and Meursault and Puligny-Montrachet (where Chardonnay reigns) here produce the great Burgundies that have given the region renown over the centuries. Lesser Burgundies – but they're still good – are produced further south in the Côte Chalonnaise, while between Mâcon and Lyon are the white Mâconnais wine villages (Pouilly-Fuissé and St-Véran are particularly good) and the villages of Beaujolais, famous for bright, easy-going red wine from the Gamay grape. The 10 Beaujolais Crus or 'growths' are the most important vineyard sites and should produce wine with more character and structure.

South of Lyon in the Rhône Valley red wines begin to dominate. The Syrah grape makes great wine at Hermitage and Côte-Rôtie in the north, while in the south the Grenache and a host of supporting grapes (most southern Rhône reds will include at least Syrah, Cinsaut or Mourvèdre in their blends) make full, satisfying reds, of which Châteauneuf-du-Pape is the most famous. The white Viognier makes lovely wine at Condrieu and Château-Grillet in the north.

21

The whole of the south of France is now changing and improving at a bewildering rate, prompted by a new generation or a change in ownership, often bringing in foreign investment to the region. Provence and the scorched Midi vineyards are learning how to produce exciting wines from unpromising land and many of France's tastiest and most affordable wines now come under a Vin de Pays label from the south. In the Languedoc the red wines from traditional vineyards of Grenache, Syrah, Mourvèdre and Carignan can be exceptional, and in the Roussillon the sweet Muscats and Grenache-based fortifieds are equally fine.

The South-West of France is dominated by the wines of Bordeaux, but has many other gems benefiting from the cooling influence of the Atlantic. Dry whites from Gascony and Bergerac can be exciting. Jurançon down in the Basque country produces some remarkable dry and sweet wines, while Madiran, Cahors and Bergerac produce good to excellent reds.

But Bordeaux is the king here. The Cabernet Sauvignon and Merlot are the chief grapes, the Cabernet dominating the production of deep reds from the Médoc peninsula and its famous villages of Margaux, St-Julien, Pauillac and St-Estèphe on the left bank of the Gironde river. Round the city of Bordeaux are Pessac-Léognan and Graves, where Cabernet and Merlot blend to produce fragrant refined reds. On the right bank of the Gironde estuary, the Merlot is most important in the plump rich reds of St-Émilion and Pomerol. Sweet whites from Sémillon and Sauvignon Blanc are made in Sauternes, with increasingly good dry whites produced in the Entre-Deux-Mers, and especially in Graves and Pessac-Léognan.

The Loire Valley is the most northerly of France's Atlantic wine regions but, since the river rises in the heart of France not far from the Rhône, styles vary widely. Sancerre and Pouilly in the east produce tangy Sauvignon whites and some surprising reds; the centre of the river produces fizzy wine at Vouvray and Saumur, sweet wine at Vouvray and the Layon Valley (Chenin Blanc is used for everything here, from sparkling wines to botrytized ones), red wines at Chinon and Bourgueil, and dry whites virtually everywhere; while down at the mouth of the river, as it slips past Nantes into the Atlantic swell, the vineyards of Muscadet produce one of the world's most famous and often least memorable dry white wines.

CLASSIFICATIONS

France has an intricate but eminently logical system for controlling the quality and authenticity of its wines. The system is divided into 4 broad classifications (in ascending order): Vin de Table, Vin de Pays, VDQS (Vin Délimité de Qualité Supérieure) and AC (Appellation Contrôlée). Within the laws there are numerous variations, with certain vineyards or producers singled out for special mention. The 1855 Classification in Bordeaux or the Grands Crus of Alsace or Burgundy are good examples. The intention is a system which rewards quality. Vin de Pays and VDQS wines can be promoted to AC, for example, after a few years' good behaviour. The AC system is now under increasing attack from critics, both inside and outside France, who feel that it is outmoded and ineffectual and that too many poor wines are passed as of Appellation Contrôlée standard.

2002 VINTAGE REPORT

Saved by the bell! That's the story of the 2002 vintage in Bordeaux. This was up-to-the-wire stuff, with difficult fruit set in spring, the threat of botrytis, and indifferent summer weather boding ill. Then the sun came out for a long, lingering spell of dry, sunny weather in September. It won't be a great year, but will vary from modest to very good, with yields down by around 20% on the yearly average. On the whole the Left Bank, with its later-ripening Cabernet Sauvignon, looks like taking the honours. Some châteaux in Listrac, the Médoc, Côtes de Francs and Entre-Deux-Mers got hit by a hailstorm before the harvest, so they had a difficult time. There's a tiny quantity of top quality sweet wine.

Burgundy escaped the heavy storms which hit the south. In fact, the further north in Burgundy, the better the weather. Most Beaujolais was picked in the rain, so it's not special. Mâcon is not bad, though there was still more rain than they would have liked. The Côte d'Or fared much better, with growers of Chardonnay and Pinot Noir equally happy, reporting for the most part healthy grapes with good sugar levels and thick skins. Chablis, enjoying the excellent weather of late September, promises to be very fine.

In the Rhône, the best wines will be those from Hermitage, Cornas and southern parts of St-Joseph. The north did better than the south, but rot and poor ripening were widespread. The 600mm (24 inches) of rain in early September wrecked many southern Rhône hopes. Extreme selectivity will be needed in a generally dilute year.

A very dry early season and then rain around the harvest made this a difficult vintage in the Languedoc-Roussillon. Quantities are also down on previous years. In the east, part of the Hérault *département* was affected by the floods that hit the southern Rhône in September. Elsewhere, producers had to ride out the weather and look for optimum maturity. The best wines will be similar in style to the 1995s, with fruit, charm and rounded tannins. Carignan looks the best of the varieties, with Mourvèdre having the toughest time.

In the Loire, a potentially lousy year was transformed by a sun-drenched September into the best vintage since 1997. Sancerre was hit by storms and fog at the start of the harvest, which may have caused problems for the less attentive producers, but otherwise picking conditions were ideal, with a small crop of concentrated and healthy grapes. Expect ripe-fruited wines with a good balance of body and freshness. Botrytis developed well for the sweet wines, too.

Alsace delivered another good but not spectacular vintage. After a humid summer, problems with rot meant that selection in the vineyard was vital. A late burst of sun in October repaid the patience of those who picked late. Riesling was the most successful variety.

In Champagne, dry, sunny weather in September helped produce a ripe, average-sized harvest of good to excellent quality. Chardonnay in the Côte des Blancs was particularly fine and some houses predict outstanding vintage wines.

See also ALSACE, BORDEAUX RED WINES, BORDEAUX WHITE WINES, BURGUNDY RED WINES, BURGUNDY WHITE WINES, CHAMPAGNE, CORSICA, JURA, LANGUEDOC-ROUSSILLON, LOIRE VALLEY, MIDI, PROVENCE, RHONE VALLEY, ROUSSILLON, SAVOIE, SOUTH-WEST FRANCE; and individual wines and producers.

ITALY

The cultivation of the vine was introduced to Italy around 3000 years ago, by the Greeks (to Sicily and the south) and by the Etruscans (to the north-east and central zones). Despite their great tradition, Italian wines as we know them today are relatively young. New attitudes have resulted, in the last 30 years or so, in a great change in Italian wine. The whole industry has been modernized, and areas like Tuscany are now among the most dynamic of any in the world. With her unique characteristics, challenging wine styles and mass of grape varieties, Italy is now ready again to take on the role of leadership she has avoided for so long.

GRAPE VARIETIES AND WINE REGIONS

Vines are grown all over Italy, from the Austrian border in the north-east to the island of Pantelleria in the far south, nearer to North Africa than to Sicily. The north-west, especially Piedmont, is the home of many of the best Italian red grapes, like Nebbiolo (the grape of Barolo and Barbaresco), Dolcetto and Barbera, while the north-east (Friuli-Venezia Giulia, Alto Adige and the Veneto) is more noted for the success of native white varieties like Garganega, Tocai and Ribolla, reds like Corvina, and imports like Pinot Grigio, Chardonnay

and Sauvignon. The central Po Valley is Lambrusco country. Moving south, Tuscany is best known for its red Chianti, Brunello di Montalcino and Vino Nobile di Montepulciano wines from the native Sangiovese grape as well as its famed Super-Tuscans. South of Rome, where the Mediterranean climate holds sway, modern winemakers are revelling in the chance to make exciting wines from both traditional and international varieties. The islands too have their own varieties: Nero d'Avola in Sicily, red Cannonau and Carignano and white Vermentino in Sardinia.

CLASSIFICATIONS

Vino da Tavola, or 'table wine', is used for a wine that is produced either outside the existing laws, or in an area where no delimited zone exists. Both cheap, basic wines and inspired innovative creations like Tignanello, Sassicaia and other so-called Super-Tuscans used to fall into this anonymous category. Now the fancy wines have become either DOC (particularly in Piedmont with its Langhe DOC) or IGT (a lot of Super-Tuscans are now IGT). Remaining Vino da Tavola are labelled simply as *bianco*, *rosso* or *rosato* without vintages or geographical indications.

IGT (Indicazione Geografica Tipica) began taking effect with the 1995 vintage to identify wines from certain regions or areas as an equivalent of the French Vin de Pays. A great swathe of both ordinary and premium wines traded their Vino da Tavola status for a regional IGT.

DOC (Denominazione di Origine Controllata) is the main classification for wines from designated zones made following traditions that were historically valid but often outdated. Recently the laws have become more flexible, encouraging producers to lower yields and modernize techniques, while bringing quality wines under new appellations that allow for recognition of communes, estates and single vineyards.

DOCG (Denominazione di Origine Controllata e Garantita) was conceived as a 'super-league' for DOCs with a guarantee of authenticity that promised high class but didn't always provide it. Still, despite some dubious promotions to this élite category, wines must be made under stricter standards that have favoured improvements. The best guarantee of quality, however, remains the producer's name.

2002 VINTAGE REPORT

One of the weirdest vintages in memory, being very poor in some places, excellent in others. The summer was marked by horrific if isolated hailstorms (for instance in Barolo), freak tornadoes (in Chianti), too little rain at the beginning and too much towards the end. Many producers, from Tuscany through to Sicily, will be producing only basic wines, no riservas. Quantity is down, by 20% overall, to the lowest figure for 50 years. 2002 has been written off by the pundits, but punters may find some bargains – not for investment but for consumption. On the other hand, some producers declare themselves forced to raise prices despite the poor vintage, having lost a large part of their crop.

See also ABRUZZO, ALTO ADIGE, BASILICATA, CALABRIA, CAMPANIA, EMILIA-ROMAGNA, FRIULI-VENEZIA GIULIA, LAZIO, LIGURIA, LOMBARDY, MARCHE, PIEDMONT, PUGLIA, ROMAGNA, SARDINIA, SICILY, TRENTINO, TUSCANY, UMBRIA, VALLE D'AOSTA, VENETO; and individual wines and producers.

GERMANY

Dull, semi-sweet wines with names like Liebfraumilch, Niersteiner Gutes Domtal and Piesporter Michelsberg used to dominate the export market, but they are rapidly vanishing off all but the most basic radar screens. Though producers at present find exports difficult, single-estate wines, with a greatly improved quality, are now the focus of sales abroad. Throughout Germany, both red and white wines are year by year, region by region, grower by grower, becoming fuller, better balanced and drier.

GRAPE VARIETIES

Riesling makes the best wines, in styles ranging from dry to intensely sweet. Other white wines come from Grauburgunder/Ruländer (Pinot Gris), Weissburgunder (Pinot Blanc), Gewürztraminer, Silvaner and Scheurebe, although Müller-Thurgau produces much of the simpler wine. In the past decade plantings of red grape varieties have doubled to fully 29% of the nation's vineyard. Good reds can be made in the south of the country from Spätburgunder (Pinot Noir) or blends based on Lemberger.

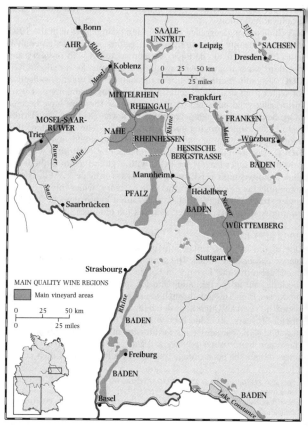

WINE REGIONS

Many of the most delectable Rieslings come from villages such as Bernkastel, Brauneberg, Ürzig and Wehlen on the Mosel, and Kiedrich, Johannisberg and Rüdesheim in the Rheingau. The Nahe makes superb Rieslings in Schlossböckelheim and Traisen, and Niederhausen has the best vineyards in the entire region. Rheinhessen is unfortunately better known for its sugary Niersteiner Gutes Domtal than it is for the excellent racy Rieslings produced on steep slopes in the villages of Nackenheim, Nierstein and Oppenheim. Franken is the one place the Silvaner grape excels, often made in a powerful, dry, earthy style. The Pfalz is climatically similar to Alsace and has a similar potential for well-rounded, dry whites, plus rapidly improving reds. Baden also produces fully ripe wine styles, which appeal to an international market increasingly reared on fuller, drier wines. In Württemberg most of the red wines are thin and dull, but there are a few producers who understand the need for weight and flavour. The other smaller wine regions make little wine and little is exported.

CLASSIFICATIONS

Germany's classification system is based on the ripeness of the grapes and therefore their potential alcohol level.

Tafelwein (table wine) is the most basic term, used for any blended wine, accounting for only a tiny percentage of production.

Landwein (country wine) is a slightly more up-market version, linked to 17 regional areas. These must be Trocken (dry) or Halbtrocken (medium-dry).

QbA (Qualitätswein bestimmter Anbaugebiete) is 'quality' wine from one of 13 designated regions, but the grapes don't have to be very ripe, and sugar can be added to the juice to increase alcoholic content.

QmP (Qualitätswein mit Prädikat) or 'quality wine with distinction' is the top level. There are 6 levels of QmP (in ascending order of ripeness): Kabinett, Spätlese, Auslese, Beerenauslese, Eiswein, Trockenbeerenauslese. The addition of sugar is strictly forbidden.

In 2000, 2 new designations for dry wines were introduced: **Classic** for 'good' varietal wines and **Selection** for 'top quality' varietal wines.

The Rheingau has introduced an official classification – Erstes Gewächs (First Growth) – for its best sites. Other regions are evolving unofficial classifications – currently called Grosses Gewächs or Erste Lage – in the hope that these, too, will become law.

2002 VINTAGE REPORT

In spite of repeated rainfall during the harvest, 2002 looks to be another very good vintage in Germany. Pinot varieties (red and white) seem to have done particularly well, since they were picked before significant rain fell. Though the ripeness of the Riesling grapes was high, generous yields make it unlikely that Rieslings from the Mosel, Mittelrhein, Nahe and Rheingau will equal the great 2001s.

See also AHR, BADEN, FRANKEN, HESSISCHE BERGSTRASSE, MITTELRHEIN, MOSEL-SAAR-RUWER, NAHE, PFALZ, RHEINGAU, RHEINHESSEN, SAALE-UNSTRUT, SACHSEN, WURTTEMBERG; and individual wine villages and producers.

AUSTRIA

I can't think of a European nation where the wine culture has changed so dramatically over a generation as it has in Austria. Austria still makes great sweet wines, but a new order based on world-class medium- and full-bodied dry whites and increasingly fine reds has emerged, including Austria's first territorial appellation, Weinviertel.

WINE REGIONS AND GRAPE VARIETIES

The Danube runs through Niederösterreich, scene of much of Austria's viticulture. The Wachau produces great Riesling and excellent pepper-dry Grüner Veltliner. Next along the Danube are Kremstal and Kamptal, also fine dry white regions with a few good reds. Burgenland, south of Vienna, produces the best reds and also, around the Neusiedler See, superb dessert wines. Further south, in Steiermark, Chardonnay and Sauvignon are increasingly oak-aged.

CLASSIFICATIONS

Wine categories are similar to those in Germany, beginning with **Tafelwein** (table wine) and **Landwein** (country wine, like the French Vin de Pays). **Qualitätswein** must come from one of the 16 main producing regions, or a village or vineyard within the region. Like German wines, quality wines may additionally have a special category: Kabinett, Auslese, Beerenauslese, Ausbruch, Trockenbeerenauslese.

2002 VINTAGE REPORT

Niederösterreich suffered hail in early summer, the worst Danube flood in 150 years in mid-August and rain during the harvest. In spite of this it looks as if 2002 is a very good vintage for dry Riesling and at least a solid one for dry Grüner Veltliner. Life was more difficult for the red wine producers of Burgenland, but Blaufränkisch gave fine results. For dessert wines it may even be a great vintage.

See also BURGENLAND, CARNUNTUM, DONAULAND, KAMPTAL, KREMSTAL, STEIERMARK, THERMENREGION, WACHAU, WIEN; and individual wine villages and producers.

The late 1990s provided a dramatic turnaround in the quality of Spain's long-neglected wines. A drastic modernization of winemaking technology has now allowed regions like Priorat, Ribera del Duero, Rueda, Bierzo, Toro and La Mancha to muscle into the limelight, alongside Rioja and Jerez, with potent fruit-driven wines with the impact and style to convert the modern consumer.

WINE REGIONS

Galicia in the green, hilly north-west grows Spain's most aromatic whites. The heartland of the great Spanish reds, Rioja, Navarra and Ribera del Duero, is situated between the central plateau and the northern coast. Travelling west along the Duero, Rueda produces fresh whites and Toro good ripe reds. Cataluña is principally white wine country (much of it sparkling Cava), though there are some great reds in Priorat and increasingly in Terra Alta and new DO Montsant. Aragón's reds and whites are looking good too. The central plateau of La Mancha makes mainly cheap reds and whites, though non-DO producers are improving spectacularly. Valencia in the south-east can rival La Mancha for fresh, unmemorable but inexpensive reds and whites. Andalucía's specialities are the fortified wines, sherry, Montilla and Málaga.

CLASSIFICATIONS

Vino de Mesa, the equivalent of France's Vin de Table, is the lowest level, but is also used for a growing number of non-DO 'Super-Spanish'.
Vino de la Tierra is Spain's equivalent of France's Vin de Pays.
DO (Denominación de Origen) is the equivalent of France's AC, regulating grape varieties and region of origin.
DOC (Denominación de Origen Calificada) is a super-category. For a long time Rioja was the only region to have been promoted to DOC, but it has now been joined by Priorat.

2002 VINTAGE REPORT

The unusually cool and cloudy (but not necessarily wet) summer did little to ripen the grapes, and then the rains came in late September. Only those producers who avoided grey rot in such early-maturing regions as La Mancha managed to make good wine in what will be remembered as a dismal Spanish vintage.

PORTUGAL

Investment and imagination are paying off in this attractive country, with climates that vary from the mild, damp Minho region in the north-west to the subtropical island of Madeira. Innovative use of native grapes and blending with international varieties means that Portugal is now a rich source of inexpensive yet characterful wines.

WINE REGIONS

The lush Vinho Verde country in the north-west gives very different wine from the parched valleys of the neighbouring Douro, with its drier, more continental climate. The Douro, home of port, is also the source of some of Portugal's best unfortified red wines. In Beiras, which includes Bairrada and Dão, soil types are crucial in determining the character of the wines. Estremadura and Ribatejo use native grape varieties to supply generous quantities of wine from regions either influenced by the maritime climate, or softened by the river Tagus. South of Lisbon, the Terras do Sado and Alentejo produce some exciting table wines – and the Algarve is waking up. Madeira is unique, a volcanic island 850km (530 miles) out in the Atlantic Ocean.

CLASSIFICATIONS

Vinho Regional (8 in number) is equivalent to French Vin de Pays, with laws and permitted varieties much freer than for IPR and DOC.
IPR (Indicação de Proveniência Regulamentada) is the intermediate step for wine regions hoping to move up to DOC status. Many were promoted in 1999, leaving just 5 IPRs. Their wines are referred to as Vinhos de Qualidade Produzidos em Região Determinada (VQPRD).
DOC (Denominação de Origem Controlada) Equivalent to France's AC. Following necessary rationalization, there are now 24 DOC regions.

2002 VINTAGE REPORT

The growing season was very dry throughout the country; fortunately the summer was cool, with no extreme heat. By early September the grapes were in perfect condition and those in the south who were able to pick early made some excellent wines. But in mid-September torrential rain swept in from the Atlantic, drenching the whole country. Small quantities of high-quality Port were made, but for the coastal regions of Bairrada and Vinho Verde 2002 was, with few exceptions, a washout.

See also (SPAIN) ANDALUCIA, ARAGON, BALEARIC ISLANDS, CANARY ISLANDS, CASTILLA-LA MANCHA, CASTILLA Y LEON, CATALUNA, GALICIA; (PORTUGAL) ALENTEJO, ALGARVE, BEIRAS, ESTREMADURA, PORT, RIBATEJO, TERRAS DO SADO, TRAS-OS-MONTES; and individual wines and producers.

USA

The United States has more varied growing conditions for grapes than any other country in the world, which isn't so surprising when you consider that the 50 states of the Union cover an area that is larger than Western Europe; and although Alaska doesn't grow grapes in the icy far north, Washington State does in the north-west, as does Texas in the south and New York State in the north-east, and even Hawaii, lost in the pounding surf of the Pacific Ocean, manages to grow grapes and make wine. Every state, even Alaska (thanks to salmonberry and fireweed), now produces wine of some sort or another; it ranges from some pretty dire offerings which would have been far better distilled into brandy, to some of the greatest and most original wine flavours to be found in the world today.

GRAPE VARIETIES AND WINE REGIONS

California is far and away the most important state for wine production. In its determination to match the best red Bordeaux and white Burgundy, California proved that it was possible to take the classic European role models and successfully re-interpret them in an area thousands of miles away from their home. However, there is more to California than this. The Central Valley produces the majority of the simple beverage wines that still dominate the American market. Napa and Sonoma counties north of San Francisco Bay do produce

great Cabernet and Chardonnay, but grapes like Zinfandel and Merlot are making their mark and Carneros and Russian River Valley are highly successful for Pinot Noir, Chardonnay and sparkling wines. In the north, Mendocino and Lake Counties produce good grapes, while south of San Francisco, in the cool, foggy valleys between Santa Cruz and Santa Barbara, exciting cool-climate flavours are appearing, especially from Chardonnay, Pinot Noir and Syrah.

Oregon, with a cooler and more capricious climate than California, perseveres with Pinot Noir, Chardonnay, Pinot Gris, Pinot Blanc and Riesling with patchy success. Washington, so chilly and misty on the coast, becomes virtual desert east of the Cascade

31

Mountains and it is here, in irrigated vineyards, that superb reds and whites can be made, with thrillingly focused fruit.

New Yorkers are showing that Long Island has all the makings of a classic region: this warm, temperate claw of land to the east of New York City is well suited to Merlot, Cabernet Franc and Chardonnay. Finger Lakes and the Hudson Valley are increasingly turning from hybrid to vinifera grapes and have made a name with Riesling, Chardonnay and sparklers, and improved vineyard management has led to advances with reds, especially Pinot Noir and Cabernet Franc.

Of the other states, Texas has the most widespread plantings of classic vinifera wine varieties, but producers of excellence also exist in Virginia, Maryland and Pennsylvania on the east coast, and Idaho, Arizona and New Mexico in the west.

CLASSIFICATIONS

A rudimentary appellation system was established during the 1970s. AVA (American Viticultural Area) merely defines a spread of land and decrees that at least 85% of the wine's volume must be derived from grapes grown within that AVA. There are currently over 135 AVAs, more than 80 of which are in California.

2002 VINTAGE REPORT

In California, spring rains in the north limited the number of clusters on the vine and pushed back bloom. This ultimately resulted in a late and uneven harvest in many areas (especially Monterey County). It also meant that for many varietals the size of the crop was smaller than normal. Overall the growing season was cool, resulting in a long hang time for the grapes, maintaining natural acidity and increasing intensity. However, a heat spell in mid-September sent temperatures above 38°C (100°F) for three consecutive days in Napa and Sonoma. Look for first-rate Pinot Noirs and excellent Chardonnays, especially from Carneros, Russian River and Monterey, while Cabernets and other reds should be fat and juicy with moderate acidity, although without the intensity of the reds from 1997, 99 or 2001.

In Washington State, some heat spikes in late July caused sugar levels to rise quickly. Warm weather in early September advanced the harvest and some immature fruit was harvested because of high sugar levels. Then a protracted stretch of warm, dry conditions made for one of the longest harvests on record, lasting until early November; resulting in very low acidity and high alcohol levels. In Oregon, dry winter weather caused early flowering under good conditions. Light rain in August and early September was followed by a long, warm, sunny harvest. Intensely aromatic, high-alcohol wines were produced.

After a stellar year in 2001, the Eastern US suffered through a spotty growing season in 2002. A summer drought all along the coast yielded to heavy rains during harvest time. An early winter brought Ontario vintners their earliest icewine harvest on record, raising hopes for an exceptional and plentiful vintage.

See also CALIFORNIA, NEW YORK STATE, OREGON, TEXAS, VIRGINIA, WASHINGTON STATE; and individual wine areas and wineries.

AUSTRALIA

Australian wine today enjoys a reputation still well out of proportion to the quantity of wine produced (total output is about one-tenth of Italy's), though volumes are mushrooming. The heavy, alcoholic wines of the past are long gone; sheer volume of fruit aroma and flavour is the hallmark of today's fine white, red and sparkling styles. Water plays a crucial role in the Australian wine industry: there's more than enough sunshine and not nearly enough rain to grow the grapes, so most growers rely heavily on irrigation. Dynamic and innovative winemakers ensure a steady supply of new wines, wineries and even regions, but consolidation and internationalization of larger operators seems to be causing an unwarranted and unwelcome dumbing down of flavour.

GRAPE VARIETIES
Varietal wines remain more prized than blends. Shiraz has long been a key varietal and is becoming more fashionable than Cabernet Sauvignon, while the position of Chardonnay remains unchallenged. Pinot Noir, Semillon and Riesling lead the pack of alternative varieties.

WINE REGIONS
Western Australia is a vast state, virtually desert except for its southwestern coastal strip. The sun-baked region near Perth was best suited to throaty reds and fortified wines but winery and vineyard expertise is so sophisticated that good dry whites are now being made. The most exciting wines, both red and white, come from Margaret River and Great Southern down towards the coast.

South Australia dominates the wine scene – it grows the most grapes, makes the most wine and is home to most of the nation's biggest wine companies. There is more to it, however, than attractive, undemanding, gluggable wine. The Clare Valley is an outstanding producer of cool-climate Riesling, but some sites in the region produce excellent Shiraz and Cabernet. The Barossa is home to some of the planet's oldest vines, particularly Shiraz and Grenache. Eden Valley, in the hills to the east of Barossa, excels at crisp, steely Rieslings. Coonawarra also makes many thrilling reds.

Victoria was Australia's major producer for most of the 19th century until her vineyards were devastated by the phylloxera louse. It's only recently that Victoria has regained her position as provider of some of the most startling wine styles in the country: stunning liqueur Muscats; the thrilling dark reds of Central Victoria; and the urbane Yarra Valley and Mornington Peninsula reds and whites.

New South Wales was home to the revolution that propelled Australia to the front of the world wine stage (in the Hunter Valley, an area that remains a dominant force). However, the state is a major bulk producer in Riverina, and a clutch of new regions in the Central Ranges are grabbing headlines.

Tasmania, with its cooler climate, is attracting attention for top-quality Pinot Noirs and Champagne-method sparkling wines. Riesling and Gewürztraminer would almost certainly be excellent, if the producers would give them a chance.

CLASSIFICATIONS

Formal appellation control, restricting certain grapes to certain regions, is virtually unknown; regulations are more of a guarantee of authenticity than a guide to quality. In a country so keen on inter-regional blending for its commercial brands, a system resembling France's AC could be problematic. However, the Label Integrity Program (LIP) guarantees all claims made on labels and the Geographical Indications (GI) committee is busy clarifying zones, regions and sub-regions – albeit with plenty of lively, at times acrimonious, debate about where some regional borders should go.

2003 VINTAGE REPORT

Severe drought in winter reduced bunch and berry sizes, and a long hot spell during the summer restricted grape production. Yields were down throughout the country, with the east coast particularly affected. The hotter-than-usual summer brought vintage forward in many areas and created a concertina effect, with too many varieties ripening at the same time: a logistical nightmare for winemakers. Heavy February rains caused some anxious moments in places like the Yarra Valley, Clare, Barossa and Mudgee, and the jury is still out on quality in marginal areas such as parts of Tasmania. In spite of the difficulties, quality has been uniformly high throughout Australia. It's a perfect result given worries about overproduction following the dramatic vineyard expansion of recent years.

See also NEW SOUTH WALES, QUEENSLAND, SOUTH AUSTRALIA, TASMANIA, VICTORIA, WESTERN AUSTRALIA and individual wineries.

NEW ZEALAND _____

New Zealand's wines are characterized by intense fruit flavours, zesty acidity and pungent aromas – the product of cool growing conditions and high-tech winemaking. Styles are diverse due to regional differences, vintage variation and winemaking philosophy.

GRAPE VARIETIES AND WINE REGIONS

Nearly 1600km (1000 miles) separate New Zealand's northernmost wine region from the country's (and the world's) most southerly wine region, Central Otago. In terms of wine styles it is useful to divide the country into two parts. Hawkes Bay and further north, including Gisborne, Auckland and Northland, produce the best Cabernet Sauvignon, Merlot, Cabernet Franc and Syrah. From Martinborough and further south, including Marlborough, Nelson, Canterbury and Central Otago, come the best Sauvignon Blanc, Riesling, Pinot Noir and fizz. Chardonnay and Pinot Gris perform well everywhere, with riper, fleshier styles in the north and finer, zestier styles to the south.

CLASSIFICATIONS

A new system guarantees geographic origin. The broadest designation is New Zealand, followed by North or South Island. Next come the 10 or so regions. Labels may also name specific localities and individual vineyards.

2003 VINTAGE REPORT

Frost, rain and cool weather during flowering have reduced the grape crop to almost half that of 2002's record vintage. Quality is mixed in the North Island, but better in the South Island – and exceptional in Nelson and Central Otago.

NORTH ISLAND
Matakana
AUCKLAND
Kumeu/Huapai
Henderson
Auckland
Waiheke Island
BAY OF PLENTY
WAIKATO
GISBORNE
HAWKES BAY
WELLINGTON
Nelson
NELSON
Blenheim
Martinborough
Wellington
MARLBOROUGH
Waipara
CANTERBURY
Christchurch
SOUTH ISLAND
OTAGO
Dunedin

Main vineyard areas

0   100   200 km
0   100 miles

See also AUCKLAND, CANTERBURY, CENTRAL OTAGO, GISBORNE, HAWKES BAY, KUMEU/HUAPAI, MARLBOROUGH, MARTINBOROUGH, NELSON, WAIHEKE ISLAND; and individual wineries.

35

SOUTH AMERICA

The only two countries to have proved their ability to make fine wine are Chile and Argentina, though clearly Uruguay is going to try to join them. Elsewhere it's largely a story of heat, humidity and the indifference of a local population much keener on spirits than wine.

ARGENTINA

Argentina is the fifth largest producer in the world but, until recently, one of the least known. This was partly because she used to drink all that she produced but also because her political and economic turmoil discouraged foreigners from attempting to do business with her. The economic turmoil took a welcome respite during the 1990s and the Argentine wine industry took the opportunity to modernize, but the collapse of 2002 has once again plunged the country into uncertainty. Mendoza is the hub of wine activity and old plantings of grapes like Malbec, Sangiovese, Tempranillo and Bonarda as well as new ones of Syrah and Cabernet are producing a rich selection of reds. There are good whites too, especially Chardonnay from Uco Valley in Mendoza, aromatic Torrontés from Cafayate in the north, and Sauvignon Blanc and Semillon from the cooler climate of Río Negro in the south.

CHILE

Over the years Chile has boasted of having the world's most perfect conditions for grape growing. Reliable sunshine, no rain, irrigation from the Andes – and almost no disease in the vineyards. Which is all

Main vineyard areas

0   250   500 km
0   250 miles

very well, but most of the world's great wines have been made from grapes grown in far more taxing conditions, and until recently you could accuse Chile of simply having things too easy to excel. Oceans of soft, pleasant reds and whites flooded out, but nothing to make the heart miss a beat. There is now a new generation of wine people in charge here, keen to meet the challenge of upping quality, and results get more exciting every year. Though vineyards extend for over 1100 km (685 miles) north to south, the majority of grapes are grown from just north of Santiago at Aconcagua, down to Maule, with the most important quality areas being cool-climate Casablanca, Maipo and Rapel. Cabernet Sauvignon is the most famous and most widely planted grape, but Merlot, Carmenère (often mislabelled as Merlot), Syrah, Pinot Noir and others perform well here. Whites are more patchy, but Casablanca and, more recently, San Antonio Valley give superb results with Chardonnay and Sauvignon, as do some of the vineyards south of Maule, in Bío-Bío.

URUGUAY

The least-known high-quality South American wine country, Uruguay suffers from relatively high rainfall in a relatively cool climate, and the majority of the vines are on clay soil near Montevideo. This may explain why the thick-skinned, rot-resistant black Tannat grape from South-West France is the leading variety. However, there is a clutch of modern wineries working hard at adapting vineyard practices to the conditions. Expect to see greatly improved, snappy Sauvignon Blanc and full, balanced Chardonnay as well as Merlot, Cabernet Franc, Cabernet Sauvignon – and even Shiraz and Nebbiolo – in the near future. Best producers include Carrau, Castillo Viejo, Filgueira, Irurtia, Juanico, de Lucca, Pisano, Stagnari.

OTHER COUNTRIES

Look at Brazil, how vast it is. Yet in all this expanse, running from 33° South to 5° North, there's nowhere ideal to site a vineyard. The best attempts are made down towards the Uruguayan border. Peru has seemingly good vineyard sites in the Ica Valley south of Lima, but nothing exciting winewise. Bolivia has few vineyards, but they're good, and incredibly high. Venezuela's chief claim to fame is that some of her subtropical vines give three crops a year!

2003 VINTAGE REPORT

In Chile, a hot January and February were followed by a much more moderate April in both the Central Valley and further north in Aconcagua. Dry weather and cool nights allowed slow, steady ripening and a very good balance of sugar and acidity in the wines. Many producers are predicting that 2003 wines, especially the reds, will be both powerful and elegant.

Argentina's Mendoza region saw a welcome drop in temperature in March and early April, allowing the grapes to ripen slowly. Localized hail storms afflicted some vineyards. A classic vintage for Malbec.

See also (ARGENTINA) CAFAYATE, MENDOZA, UCO VALLEY; (CHILE) CASABLANCA, CENTRAL, COLCHAGUA, CURICO, MAIPO, MAULE, RAPEL, SAN ANTONIO; and individual wineries.

SOUTH AFRICA

There is a mood of confidence and optimism in South Africa. The changes being wrought in the vineyards are dramatic and the wines themselves are transformed. Bursting with vibrant fruit, sensitively tempered by oak and actually starting to speak of a sense of place - the French idea of *terroir* is firmly at the heart of the new South African agenda. A flood of new private producers (one opens around every nine days) is also leading the drive for quality. They are still in a minority, however; co-operatives continue to process about 80% of the country's grape crop.

GRAPE VARIETIES AND WINE REGIONS

The Cape's winelands run roughly 400km (250 miles) north and east of Cape Town. The major grape varieties are planted over the entire Cape; Chenin Blanc, though declining, still dominates. Cabernet Sauvignon, Chardonnay, Merlot, Pinotage and Sauvignon Blanc now register more strongly on the dial, though at least 40% of all red vineyards are barely 4 years old. Shiraz would probably top the lot in terms of producers' enthusiasm but there is a shortage of vine material. The swing towards classic, international varieties now includes small quantites of Viognier, Mourvèdre, Malbec, Nebbiolo and Sangiovese. The current vogue for Rhône varieties means that the spotlight is on Grenache, although little is currently grown here, and old bush vine plantings of Cinsaut. There is little typicity of origin, although some areas are historically associated with specific varieties or styles. Stellenbosch currently produces some of the best red wines; Constantia, with its sea-facing slopes, is acknowledged as ideal for Sauvignon Blanc; cooler areas also include Walker Bay in the Overberg district, where the focus is Pinot Noir, and up-and-coming areas such as Durbanville, Darling Hills, Elgin and Elim (at the tip of Africa). The inland, warmer areas are noted for fortifieds, both Muscadel (Muscat) and port styles.

CLASSIFICATION

The Wine of Origin (WO) system – introduced in 1973, with major modifications in 1993 – divides wine-producing areas into regions, districts and wards. Wines can be traced back to their source, but quality is not guaranteed. Varietal wines for export must be made from at least 85% of the named grape. To qualify as an 'estate' wine, the producer's vines must be grown on a single piece of land and the wine vinified, matured and bottled on the property.

2003 VINTAGE REPORT

A favourably cold, wet winter preceded a good spring; floods in the Breede River Valley caused limited damage. The harvest progressed in ideal conditions without the usual searing heatwave. After two low producing years in the major areas, crops reached more normal levels. If winemakers complained about the length of the harvest, quality and quantity should make amends. White wines show balanced acidity, reds good colour and flavour from smaller than normal berries.

See also CONSTANTIA, FRANSCHHOEK, OVERBERG, PAARL, ROBERTSON, STELLENBOSCH; and individual wineries.

OTHER WINE COUNTRIES

ALGERIA The western coastal province of Oran produces three-quarters of Algeria's wine, including the soft but muscular wines of the Coteaux de Tlemcen and dark, beefy reds of the Coteaux de Mascara. Around 80% of the 150,000ha (379,000 acres) of vines are over 40 years old, and with recent substantial replantings there should be great potential here.

BULGARIA After success in the 1980s and disarray in the 90s, the roller coaster seems to have stopped. New World influences in the winery are having some effect, but Bulgaria continues to lose shelf space in the shops, and a new realism is persuading producers to start improvements in their long-neglected vineyards. International varieties (Cabernet Sauvignon, Merlot, Chardonnay) dominate but local grapes – plummy Mavrud, meaty Gamza, deep Melnik, mild-mannered, fruity white Dimiat and Misket – can be good. Best wineries include BOYAR ESTATES, KHAN KRUM and SUHINDOL.

CANADA The strict VQA (Vintners Quality Alliance) maintains high standards in British Columbia and Ontario, and there has been enormous progress in the 2 most important regions – OKANAGAN VALLEY in British Columbia and the NIAGARA PENINSULA in Ontario – where the move from hybrid to vinifera varieties has been rapid. Sweet icewine is still Canada's main trump card. Pinot Gris, Chardonnay, Riesling and Gewürztraminer lead the way in non-sweet whites; Merlot, Cabernet Franc, Cabernet Sauvignon, even Syrah, show potential in red wines.

CHINA Though China officially promotes wine, its potential remains unfulfilled as the Chinese are reluctant to drink it. Plantings, mainly international grapes with some traditional Chinese, German and Russian varieties, are expanding rapidly, yet only 10% of the harvest is crushed for wine. In the next 15 years output could double – or treble – who knows? Major Western and Chinese investment (Beijing Friendship/Pernod Ricard, Dynasty/Rémy-Martin, Great Wall/TORRES, HUADONG/Allied Domecq) has so far led the way.

CROATIA Inland Croatia has an undercurrent of rising potential: bulk whites dominate but small private producers are emerging. Initiatives to sow vines in former minefields are helping to restore Croatia's viticultural heritage. What the country needs now is more investment, more technology in the vineyard and winery and a fair price for the grapes. The best vineyards are on the Dalmatian coast, where international varieties are being planted alongside gutsy Peljesac and Faros reds; deep, tannic Plavac Mali – related to Zinfandel – has long produced the top red wines. GRGICH of California has a winery on the Peljesac peninsula.

CYPRUS This island has not had a high reputation for wine since the Crusades, when COMMANDARIA was reputedly a rich, succulent nectar worth risking your neck for. However, Cyprus is modernizing and, supported by the government, regional press houses and wineries are being built in or near the vineyards. A 3-year restructuring plan and investment by companies like Etko, Keo, Loel and Sodap is at last producing tasty modern reds and whites. For the first time we are seeing varietal wines, and the first efforts with grapes like Cabernet Sauvignon and Sémillon are impressive.

THE CZECH REPUBLIC The vineyards of Bohemia in the north-west and Moravia in the south-east are mainly planted with white varieties

– Grüner Veltliner, Müller-Thurgau, Riesling, Pinot Blanc – with pockets of red such as St-Laurent and Lemberger. Lack of direction is a problem, but Western investment and consultancy are helping.

ENGLAND The wine industry has come of age, with around 1000ha (2470 acres) under vine, 400 vineyards and 115 wineries, though the EU still legislates against the term English wine. Producers have become more focused on what will and will not work in this unpredictable cool climate and in a market where 50% of sales are gate-sales. The Indian summer of 2002 produced an excellent vintage. Some outstanding white and sparkling wines are being produced. The most widely grown grape variety is Müller-Thurgau, the most successful the hybrid Seyval Blanc and German crosses that can hold off disease, such as Bacchus, Huxelrebe, Schönburger. New inter-specific cross-vine varieties must still be labelled table wine. The best white wines are delicate and aromatic, with enough ripeness and depth to balance the crisp acidity. Some excellent late-harvest botrytized dessert wines are made, and red varieties are becoming more popular. The most popular winemaking counties are Kent (Biddenden, NEW WAVE, Davenport), Sussex (BREAKY BOTTOM, Hidden Spring, Nutbourne, NYETIMBER, RIDGEVIEW), Berkshire (VALLEY VINEYARDS), Gloucestershire (THREE CHOIRS), Hampshire (Northbrook Springs, Wickham, Woolings), Oxfordshire (Chiltern Valley), Somerset (Staplecombe) and Surrey (DENBIES).

GEORGIA Georgia faces many challenges – lack of regulation, resistance to change, counterfeiting – but its diverse climates (from subtropical to moderate continental) and soils could produce every style imaginable. International and indigenous varieties abound; the peppery, powerful red Saperavi shows promise. Most wine is still pretty rustic, but investment is beginning to have an effect. GWS (Georgian Wines & Spirits Company, 50% owned by Pernod Ricard) benefits from the flair of Australian winemaker David Nelson.

GREECE There is life beyond the decline of RETSINA. A new generation of winemakers and grape growers, many of them trained in France, Australia or California, have a clear vision of the flavours they want to achieve and their wines are modern but marvellously original too. Polarization between cheap bulk and expensive boutique wines continues, but large companies such as Boutari, Kourtakis and Tsantalis are upping the quality stakes and flavours improve every vintage. More vineyard and marketing work – many labels are still difficult to understand – is needed. International plantings have led to surprising and successful blends with indigenous varieties such as Agiorgitiko, Xynomavro, Assyrtiko, Moschofilero and Roditis. Quality areas: Naousa and Nemea for reds, SAMOS for sweet Muscats, Patras for dessert Mavrodaphne. Wineries to watch include: Aidarinis, ANTONOPOULOS, Gentilini, GEROVASSILIOU, Hatzimichali, Kyr Yanni, Domaine Constantin LAZARIDI, Mercouri, Papaïoannou and Strofilia.

HUNGARY Hungary has an image problem, although superb quality whites abound and red plantings are increasing. Stringent regulations and investment/advice from Australian and western European companies and consultants, particularly in TOKAJI, have put Hungary, with its 22 designated appellations, back on the international wine map. There is renewed interest in native varieties such as Furmint, Irsai Oliver, Kékfrankos and Kadarka, and top Hungarian winemakers –

Tibor Gál, Akos Kamocsay, Vilmos Thummerer and others – are now a solid force. There is a refreshing balance between those who are determined to push individual regional and vineyard potential and those who offer good general quality at an affordable price. 2002 was a difficult vintage; fewer Tokaji Azsú wines may be made.

INDIA This large country has a tiny wine industry, partly due to its climate. Only 1% of the 50,000ha (123,500 acres) of vines is used for wine; both international varieties and ancient Indian ones, such as Arkesham and Arkavati, are planted. CHATEAU INDAGE, with vineyards in the Maharashtra hills east of Mumbai (Bombay), controls 75% of the market and produces still and sparkling wines, in particular Omar Khayyam. Bordeaux superstar Michel Rolland advises Grover Vineyards in Bangalore.

ISRAEL Much of Israel's wine is sweet red, but good dry wines and sparklers are produced at Carmel, the oldest and largest winery, and at GOLAN HEIGHTS, which has been producing international-quality wines since the 1980s. Smaller producers are making Bordeaux-style reds, and there is a move towards Merlot. Some of Israel's most promising wines now come from Castel in the Judean Hills, Galil Mountain in Galilee and Tishbi in Shomron.

JAPAN Wine can be made from locally grown or imported grapes, juice or wine – and the labels don't tell you which is which. Wine is produced in almost every province, though conditions are often too humid. SUNTORY is in the best region, Yamanashi. Other main players are Mercian, Sapporo and Mann, whose Chateau Lumière produces a fine Bordeaux-style red blend.

LEBANON CHATEAU MUSAR, Kefraya and Ksara survived the 25-year war. Peace has brought a new generation of producers and improved quality from the older companies – new releases of wines from Kefraya and Ksara are vastly superior to those produced just a few years ago.

LUXEMBOURG This small, cool country produces pleasant still and sparkling whites from Rivaner, Riesling, Pinot Gris, Pinot Blanc, Auxerrois and Elbling, grown along 42km (26 miles) of the Moselle.

MEXICO In the far north-west of Mexico, in Baja California, some good reds are made by L A CETTO as well as by smaller companies such as Monte Xanic. In the rest of the country, only high-altitude areas such as the Parras Valley and Zacatecas have the potential for quality wines. Casa Madero, in the Parras Valley, has some success with Cabernet Sauvignon. Other promising grape varieties include Nebbiolo, Petite Sirah, Tempranillo, Zinfandel and Barbera, with Viognier and Chardonnay also planted.

MOLDOVA Standards of winemaking and equipment still leave much to be desired, but the quality of fruit is good, and international players, including PENFOLDS and winemakers Jacques Lurton, Hugh Ryman and Alain Thiénot, have worked with local winemakers to produce encouraging whites. However, chaotic social conditions have led to many attempts being abandoned. You may still find an occasional mature Rochu or Negru red from Purkar or, more likely, standard sparkling wines from the Cricova winery.

MONTENEGRO This red-wine-dominated part of the former Yugoslavia shows some potential in the beefy Vranac grape with its bitter cherry flavours.

MOROCCO Known for big, sweet-fruited reds that once found a ready blending market in France. Since the 1990s massive investment by Castel Frères is instigating a rebirth: the first fruits are very tasty Syrah and Cabernet reds at very reasonable prices.

ROMANIA This ancient wineland, of enormous potential, 10th in world production, is slowly getting the message that its strength lies in its *terroir*: Dealul Mare, MURFATLAR and COTNARI all have ancient reputations. International backed ventures are a sign of the mini-revolution, but challenges remain. Huge investment from Halewood, as in the underwhelming Prahova Valley range, may help, but there is a long way to go.

SLOVAKIA The eastern part of the old Czechoslovakia, with its cool-climate vineyards, is dominated by white varieties: Pinot Blanc, Riesling, Grüner Veltliner, Irsai Oliver. Western investment, particularly at the state winery at Nitra and smaller wineries such as Gbelce and Hurbanovo near the Hungarian border at Komárno, is rapidly improving the quality.

SLOVENIA Many of the old Yugoslav Federation's best vineyards are here. On the Italian border, Brda and Vipava have go-ahead co-operatives, and Kraski Teran is a red wine of repute. The Movia range, from the Kristancic family, looks promising. A well-policed quality wine scheme allows only the best to be bottled and exported, and 2003 sees the first real effort to break into the export market since Slovenia's independence. Potential is considerable, and some interesting reds and whites are emerging.

SWITZERLAND Fendant (Chasselas) is the main grape for spritzy but neutral whites from the VALAIS. Like the fruity DOLE reds, they are best drunk very young. German-speaking cantons produce light reds and rosés from Pinot Noir (Blauburgunder), and whites from Müller-Thurgau (Rivaner). Italian-speaking TICINO concentrates on Merlots that have been increasingly impressive since 2000. Serious wines use Cabernet, Chardonnay and traditional varieties like Amigne and Petite Arvine. See also NEUCHATEL and VAUD.

TUNISIA Ancient wine traditions have had an injection of new life from international investment, and results so far are encouraging. Despite lower harvests recently due to drought, exports are on the increase.

TURKEY The world's fifth-largest grape producer, but 97% ends up as raisins. State-owned companies dominate wine production, making basic reds and whites. Producers such as Diren, Kavaklidere, Turasan and Doluca are using modern technology to produce very drinkable wines – in Doluca's case from international varieties.

UKRAINE The Crimea's vineyards, producing hearty reds, are the most important. Muscatels are considered to be a cause for national pride, especially the Massandra brand. The Odessa region is successful with its sparkling wines, the 3 most well-known facilities being the Inkerman winery, Novyi Svet and Zolota Balka. Future European investment is said to be in the pipeline.

ZIMBABWE Despite the present political and economic upheaval, the small wine industry is doing quite well. Summer rain can be more of a problem. There are just two companies: Mukuyu and Stapleford.

A–Z

OF WINES,
PRODUCERS, GRAPES
& WINE REGIONS

In the following pages there are over
1600 entries covering the world's top wines, as well as
leading producers, main wine regions and grape
varieties, followed on page 289 by a glossary of wine
terms and classifications.

*On page 4 you will find a full explanation of
How to Use the A–Z. On page 297 there is an index
of all wine producers in the book, to help you find the
world's best wines.*

ABRUZZO *Italy* East of Rome, this region stretches from the Adriatic coast to the mountainous Apennine interior. White Trebbiano d'Abruzzo DOC is usually dry and neutral; the MONTEPULCIANO D'ABRUZZO DOC is sometimes rosé called Cerasuolo, but generally a strapping, peppery red of real character. Overproduction is a problem, but there are a number of good producers.

ACACIA *Carneros AVA, California, USA* Leading producer of Chardonnay and Pinot Noir from the CARNEROS region for 2 decades. The regular Carneros Chardonnay★ is restrained but attractive. Pinot Noirs include the stunning DeSoto★★★ as well as a Beckstoffer Vineyard★★ and a Carneros★ – the wines have moved to a riper, meatier style of late. Also a voluptuous Carneros Viognier★ and Brut fizz. Best years: (Pinot Noir) (2001) 00 99 **98 97 96 95**.

ACCADEMIA DEI RACEMI *Manduria, Puglia, Italy* Premium venture from the Perrucci family, long-established bulk shippers of basic Puglian wines. Quality, modern-style reds mainly from Primitivo and Negroamaro under various producers' names: Felline (Vigna del Feudo★★), Pervini (PRIMITIVO DI MANDURIA Archidamo★★), Masseria Pepe (Dunico★★). Best years: (reds) 2001 **00 98 97 96**.

TIM ADAMS *Clare Valley, South Australia* Important maker of fine, old-fashioned wine from his own and bought-in local grapes. Classic dry Riesling★★, oaky Semillon★★, and rich, opulent Shiraz★★ (sometimes ★★★) and Cabernet★★. The botrytis Semillon★ can be super, The Fergus★★ is a glorious Grenache-based blend, and minty, peppery Aberfeldy Shiraz★★★ is a remarkable, at times unnerving, mouthful of brilliance from 100-year-old vines growing near WENDOUREE. Best years: (Aberfeldy Shiraz) (2001) (99) 98 97 **96** 95 **94 93 92**.

ADELAIDE HILLS *South Australia* Small and exciting region 30 minutes' drive from Adelaide. High altitude affords a cool, moist climate ideal for fine table wines and superb sparkling wine. Consistently good Sauvignon Blanc and Chardonnay, plus promising Pinot Noir. Best producers: Ashton Hills★, Chain of Ponds, HENSCHKE★★, LENSWOOD VINEYARDS★★, Nepenthe★, PETALUMA★★, SHAW & SMITH★, Geoff WEAVER★★.

ADELSHEIM VINEYARD *Willamette Valley AVA,* 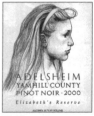 *Oregon, USA* This vineyard first hit the headlines with wine labels depicting various local beauties, including the owner's daughter. Adelsheim has established a reputation for excellent, generally unfiltered, Pinot Noir – especially cherry-scented Elizabeth's Reserve★★ and Bryan Creek Vineyard★ – and rich Chardonnay Stoller Vineyard★★. Also a bright, fresh Pinot Gris★. Best years: (Elizabeth's Reserve) (2002) 01 00 99 98 **96**.

AGE *Rioja DOC, Rioja, Spain* The largest winery in the Bodegas y Bebidas portfolio – now owned by Allied Domecq. The Siglo Saco red Crianza is its best-known wine, perhaps because it comes wrapped in a hessian sack. Best years: (reds) 2000 99 **98 96 95 94**.

AGLIANICO DEL VULTURE DOC *Basilicata, Italy* Red wine from the Aglianico grape grown on the steep slopes of Mt Vulture. Despite being one of Italy's most southerly DOCs the harvest is later than in BAROLO, 750km (470 miles) to the north-west, because the Aglianico grape ripens very late. The best wines are structured, complex and long-lived. Best producers: Basilium★, Consorzio Viticoltori Associati del

Vulture (Carpe Diem★), D'Angelo★★, Cantine del Notaio★★, Paternoster★★, Le Querce★. Best years: (2001) 00 99 98 97 **95 93 90 88**.

AHR *Germany* The Ahr Valley is a small (520ha/1285-acre), mainly red wine region south of Bonn. Chief grape varieties are the Spätburgunder (Pinot Noir) and (Blauer) Portugieser. Most Ahr reds used to be made sweet for the day-trippers from Bonn and Cologne, but this style is on the way out. Meyer-Näkel has achieved a certain international reputation by making serious dry reds.

AIRÉN Spain's – and indeed the world's – most planted white grape can make fresh modern white wines, or thick, yellow, old-fashioned brews. Airén is grown all over the centre and south of Spain, especially in La MANCHA, VALDEPENAS and ANDALUCIA (where it's called Lairén). Any new plantings are now forbidden in the CASTILLA-LA MANCHA region.

ALBAN *Edna Valley AVA, California, USA* A Rhône specialist in the Arroyo Grande district of Edna Valley, John Alban first produced Viognier in 1991. Today he offers 2 bottlings, Estate★★ and Central Coast★. Roussanne★★ from estate vineyards is laden with honey notes. Syrah is represented by 3 bottlings: Reva★★ and the more expensive Lorraine★★ and Seymour's Vineyard★★. Intense Grenache★★ rounds out the line-up. Best years: (Syrah) (2001) (00) 99 98 97 96 **95**.

ALBANA DI ROMAGNA DOCG *Romagna, Italy* In the hills south of Bologna and Ravenna, Italy's first white DOCG was a 'political' appointment that caused outrage among wine enthusiasts because of the totally forgettable flavours of most Albana wine. Though also made in dry and sparkling styles, the sweet *passito* version is the best. Best producers: (passito) Celli, Conti, Ferrucci, Giovanna Madonia (Chimera★), Paradiso, Riva, Tre Monti, Uccellina★, Zerbina (Scacco Matto★★).

ALBARIÑO Possibly Spain's most characterful white grape. It grows in GALICIA in Spain's rainy north-west and, as Alvarinho, in Portugal's VINHO VERDE region. When well made, Albariño wines have fascinating flavours of apricot, peach, grapefruit and Muscat grapes, refreshingly high acidity, highish alcohol – and unrefreshingly high prices.

ALEATICO Rarely seen, ancient, native Italian grape that produces sweet, scented, high-alcohol dessert wines in central and southern Italy. Best producers: AVIGNONESI, Candido (delicious Aleatico di Puglia★).

ALENQUER DOC *Estremadura, Portugal* Maritime-influenced hills north of Lisbon, producing wines from, mostly, local grape varieties, but also Cabernet and Chardonnay. Many wines are simply labelled ESTREMADURA. Best producers: Quinta da Abrigada★, Quinta do Carneiro★, Quinta de Cortezia★, D F J VINHOS★, Quinta de Pancas★★, Casa SANTOS LIMA★. Best years: (reds) 2001 **00 99 97**.

ALENTEJO *Portugal* A large chunk of southern Portugal east of Lisbon and, along with the DOURO, one of Portugal's fastest improving red wine regions. Has had its own DOC since 1999, and there are also 8 DOCs for sub-regions: Borba, Évora, Granja-Amareleja, Moura, Portalegre, Redondo, Reguengos and Vidigueira. Potential is far from realized but already some of Portugal's finest reds come from here. Best producers: (reds) Caves ALIANÇA

(Quinta da Terrugem★★), Fundação Eugénio de Almeida (Cartuxa★, Pera Manca★★), Borba co-op, Quinta do CARMO★, Herdade dos Coelheiros★, CORTES DE CIMA★★, D F J VINHOS★★, Vinha d'Ervideira★, ESPORAO★★, José Maria da FONSECA★, J P VINHOS★, Mouchão★, Quinta do Mouro★, João Portugal RAMOS★★, Reguengos de Monsaraz co-op. Best years: (reds) (2001) 00 **99 97 95 94 91 90 89**.

ALEXANDER VALLEY AVA *Sonoma County, California, USA* Important
AVA, centred on the Russian River, which is fairly warm with only patchy summer fog. Cabernet Sauvignon is highly successful here, with lovely, juicy fruit not marred by an excess of tannin. Chardonnay may also be good but is often overproduced and lacking in ripe, round flavours. Zinfandel and Merlot can be outstanding from hillside vineyards. Best producers: Alexander Valley Vineyards★, Chateau Souverain★, CLOS DU BOIS★, GEYSER PEAK★, JORDAN★, Murphy-Goode★★, SEGHESIO★★, SILVER OAK★★, SIMI★. See also Russian River Valley AVA, Sonoma County. Best years: (reds) (2001) (00) 99 97 **95 94 93 91 90 88**.

ALGARVE *Portugal* Holiday region with feeble-flavoured, mostly red wines in 4 DOCs: Lagoa, Lagos, Portimão and Tavira. The Vinho Regional Algarve classification suffices for D F J VINHOS' ripe-fruited Cataplana★. Look out for the new Vida Nova red from (Sir) Cliff Richard, made by David Baverstock.

ALIANÇA, CAVES *Beira Litoral, Portugal* Based in BAIRRADA, Aliança makes crisp, fresh whites and soft, approachable red Bairradas★. Also made, either from its own vineyards or bought-in grapes or wines, are reds from the DAO and DOURO. The top reds, though, are those from an estate in ALENTEJO, Quinta da Terrugem★★. Aliança also markets varietal Merlot★★, Touriga Nacional★★ and Tinta Roriz★★ (and a Reserva★★ blend of the three) from Quinta da Cortezia in ESTREMADURA.

ALIGOTÉ French grape, found mainly in Burgundy, whose basic characteristic is a lemony tartness. It can make extremely refreshing wine, especially from old vines, but is generally rather dull and lean. In ripe years it can resemble Chardonnay, especially if a little new oak is used. The best comes from the village of Bouzeron in the COTE CHALONNAISE, where Aligoté has its own appellation. Occasionally also found in Moldova and Bulgaria. Drink young. Best producers: (Burgundy) Denis Bachelet★, M Bouzereau★, COCHE-DURY★, A Ente★, JAYER-GILLES★, Denis MORTET★, RION★, TOLLOT-BEAUT★, Villaine★.

ALL SAINTS *Rutherglen, Victoria, Australia* Old winery revived with great flair by Peter Brown of the BROWN BROTHERS family since 1998. Superb fortifieds Rare Tokay★★★ and Rare Muscat★★ have rediscovered past glory. Grand★★ fortifieds are very good but younger. Table wines are big, American oak bruisers.

ALLEGRINI *Valpolicella, Veneto, Italy* High-profile producer in VALPOLICELLA Classico, making single-vineyard La Grola★★ and Palazzo della Torre★★. These are now sold under the regional Veronese IGT – partly to further distance them from the continuing low regard in which much of Valpolicella is held. These, and the barrique-aged La Poja★★★ (made solely with the Corvina grape), show the great potential that exists in Valpolicella. Outstanding AMARONE★★★ and RECIOTO Giovanni Allegrini★★. Best years: (Amarone) (2001) (00) 97 **95 93 90 88 85**.

THIERRY ALLEMAND *Cornas, Rhône Valley, France* Thierry Allemand has a smallholding of some 4ha (10 acres) of vines, some taken over from Noël VERSET. He is determined to keep yields low and to avoid making harsh, tannic wines. With careful vinification he produces 2 intense unfiltered expressions of CORNAS at its dense and powerful best: Chaillot★★ is marginally the lighter; Reynard★★ is from a parcel of very old Syrah. Best years: (Reynard) (2001) 00 99 98 97 96 95 **94 91 90**.

ALLENDE *Rioja DOC, Rioja, Spain* The ebullient Miguel Angel de Gregorio has made his modest, young winery and vineyards in Briones into one of the most admired new names in RIOJA. Scented, uncompromisingly concentrated reds include Aurus★★★, Calvario★★ and the affordable Allende★. There is also a delicate white★. Best years: (reds) (2001) 00 99 **98 97 96**.

ALMAVIVA★★ *Valle del Maipo, Chile* Joint venture between CONCHA Y TORO and Baron Philippe de Rothschild, and currently one of Chile's most expensive reds. Purposeful investment in the winery and a careful choice of vineyard sites are paying dividends as the wines improve with every vintage: 2001 is the best yet and may achieve ★★★. Can be drunk at 5 years but should age for 10. Best years: 2001 00 99 **98 97 96**.

ALOXE-CORTON AC *Côte de Beaune, Burgundy, France* An important village at the northern end of the CÔTE DE BEAUNE producing mostly red wines from Pinot Noir. Its reputation is based on the 2 Grands Crus, CORTON (mainly red) and CORTON-CHARLEMAGNE (white only). Other vineyards in Aloxe-Corton used to be a source of tasty, good-value Burgundy, but nowadays the reds rarely exhibit their former characteristic blend of ripe fruit and appetizing savoury dryness. Almost all the white wine is sold as Grand Cru; straight Aloxe-Corton Blanc is very rare. Best producers: CHANDON DE BRIAILLES★★, M Chapuis★, Marius Delarche★, Dubreuil-Fontaine★, Follin-Arvelet★, Antonin Guyon★, JADOT★, Rapet★, Comte Senard★, TOLLOT-BEAUT★★, Michel Voarick★. Best years: (reds) (2002) (01) 99 98 **97** 96 **95** 93 90.

ALSACE AC *Alsace, France* Tucked away on France's eastern border with Germany, Alsace produces some of the most individual white wines of all, rich in aroma and full of ripe, distinctive flavours. Alsace is almost as far north as Champagne, but its climate is considerably warmer. The best vineyard sites can call themselves Grands Crus; there are currently 50 of these, accounting for 1610ha (3978 acres) or 8% of the total region. Riesling, Muscat, Gewurztraminer and Pinot Gris are generally considered the finest varieties in Alsace and are permitted for Grand Cru wines, as is Sylvaner from 2001. Pinot Blanc can produce good wines, too, but Pinot Noir, the area's only red grape, is usually confined to less well-appointed vineyards. Efforts at dark reds are less successful than the traditional, mildly perfumed style. Alsace was one of the first regions to label its wines by grape variety. Apart from Edelzwicker (a blend), and CREMANT D'ALSACE, all Alsace wines are made from a single grape variety. Best producers: L Albrecht, Barmès-Buecher, J Becker, Léon Beyer, P BLANCK, Bott-Geyl, A Boxler, E Burn, DEISS, Dirler-Cadé, HUGEL, Josmeyer, Kientzler, Kreydenweiss, Kuentz-Bas, S Landmann, Lorentz, A MANN, Meyer-Fonné, MURE, Ostertag, Pfaffenheim co-op, Rolly Gassmann, M Schaetzel, Schlumberger, SCHOFFIT, Bruno Sorg, M Tempé, TRIMBACH, TURCKHEIM co-op, WEINBACH, ZIND-HUMBRECHT. Best years: (2002) 01 00 **99 98 97** 96 **95** 90 89 88 85 83. See also Alsace Vendange Tardive.

ALSACE VENDANGE TARDIVE *Alsace, France* Vendange Tardive
means 'late-harvest'. The grapes (Riesling, Muscat, Pinot Gris or
Gewurztraminer) are picked late and almost overripe, giving higher
sugar levels and potentially more intense flavours. The resulting wines
are usually rich and mouthfilling and often need 5 years or more to
show their personality. A further sub-category of Alsace wines is
Sélection de Grains Nobles – late-harvest wines made exclusively from
super-ripe grapes of the same varieties. Invariably sweet and usually
affected by noble rot, they are among Alsace's finest, but are very
expensive to produce (and to buy). Best producers: Léon Beyer★★, P
BLANCK★★★, Bott-Geyl★★★, E Burn★★★, DEISS★★★, HUGEL★★,
Kientzler★★★, Kreydenweiss★★★, MURE★★, Ostertag★★★, Rolly
Gassmann★★, SCHOFFIT★★, Tempé★★★, WEINBACH★★, ZIND-HUMBRECHT★★★.
Best years: (2002) 01 00 98 97 **96 95 94 93 92 90 89 88 85 76**.

ALTARE *Barolo DOCG, Piedmont, Italy* Elio Altare crafts some of the
most stunning of Alba's wines: excellent Dolcetto d'Alba★★ and
BARBERA D'ALBA★ and even finer BAROLO Vigneto Arborina★★★ and
new Barolo Brunate★★★. Though a professed modernist, his wines
are intense, full and structured while young, but with clearly
discernible fruit flavours, thanks largely to tiny yields. He also makes
3 barrique-aged wines under the LANGHE DOC: Arborina★★★
(Nebbiolo), Larigi★★★ (Barbera) and La Villa★★ (Nebbiolo-Barbera).
Also one of 7 producers that make a version of L'Insieme★★ (a
Nebbiolo-Cabernet-Barbera blend). Best years: (Barolo) (2000) (99) 98
96 95 **93 90 89 88 86 85**.

ALTO ADIGE *Trentino-Alto Adige, Italy* A largely German-speaking
province, originally called Südtirol. The region-wide DOC covers 25 types of
wine. Reds are almost invariably varietal and range from light and perfumed
when made from the Schiava grape, to fruity and more structured from the
Cabernets or Merlot, to dark and velvety if Lagrein is used. Whites include
Chardonnay, Pinot Bianco, Pinot Grigio, Riesling and Sauvignon, and are
usually fresh and fragrant. There is also some good sparkling wine. Much of
the wine comes from well-run co-ops. Sub-zones include the previously
independent DOCs at SANTA MADDALENA and Terlano. Best producers: Abbazia
di Novacella★, Caldaro co-op★, Casòn Hirschprunn★, Colterenzio co-op★★,
Peter Dipoli★, Giorgio Grai★★, Franz Haas★, Hofstätter★★, LAGEDER★★,
Laimburg★, J Niedermayr★, Ignaz Niedriest★, Peter Pliger-Kuenhof★★, Prima
& Nuova/Erste & Neue★, Hans Rottensteiner★, San Michele Appiano co-op★★,
Tiefenbrunner★, Elena Walch★, Baron Widmann★. See also Trentino.

ALVARINHO See Albariño.

AMA, CASTELLO DI *Chianti Classico DOCG, Tuscany, Italy* Model estate
of CHIANTI CLASSICO, with outstanding single-vineyard bottlings★★
(Bellavista and La Casuccia). L'Apparita★★★ is one of Italy's best
Merlots; less impressive Il Chiuso is made from Pinot Nero. Also good
Chardonnay Al Poggio★. Best years: (Chianti Classico) (2001) (00) 99 **98
97 95 93 90 88 85**.

AMARONE DELLA VALPOLICELLA *Valpolicella DOC, Veneto, Italy* A
brilliantly individual, bitter-sweet style of VALPOLICELLA made from
grapes shrivelled on mats for months after harvest. The wine, which
can reach up to 16% of alcohol, differs from the sweet RECIOTO DELLA
VALPOLICELLA in that it is fermented to dryness. Classico is generally the
best, though an exception can be made for DAL FORNO. Best producers:

Stefano Accordini★★, ALLEGRINI★★, Bertani★★, Brigaldara★★, Brunelli★, Tommaso Bussola★★, Michele Castellani-I Castei★★, DAL FORNO★★★, Guerrieri-Rizzardi★★, MASI★, QUINTARELLI★★★, Le Ragose★★, Le Salette★★★, Serègo Alighieri★, Speri★★, Tedeschi★★, Tommasi★, Villa Monteleone★★, Zenato★★. Best years: (2001) (00) 97 **95 93 90 88**.

AMIGNE Swiss grape variety that is virtually limited to the region of Vétroz in the VALAIS. The wine has an earthy, nutty intensity and benefits from a few years' aging. Best producers: Germanier Bon Père, Granges Frères (Escalier de la Dame), Caves Imesch.

AMITY VINEYARDS *Willamette Valley AVA, Oregon, USA* Myron Redford was one of the pioneers in OREGON, opening his winery in 1976. The Gewürztraminer★★ is outstanding and Riesling★ is almost as good. The showpiece is the Pinot Noir, notably the Winemakers Reserve★. Pinot Blanc★ has replaced Chardonnay. Fruity, floral Gamay Noir remains fine value. Best years: (Pinot Noir) (2002) (01) 00 99 **98 97 96**.

ANDALUCÍA *Spain* Fortified wines, or wines naturally so in alcohol that they don't need fortifying, are the speciality of this southern stretch of Spain. Apart from sherry (JEREZ Y MANZANILLA DO), there are the lesser, sherry-like wines of Condado de Huelva DO and MONTILLA-MORILES DO, and the rich, sweet wines of MALAGA DO. These regions also make some modern but bland dry whites; the best are from Condado de Huelva. Red wine is now appearing from producers in Málaga, Granada and Almeria provinces.

ANDERSON VALLEY AVA *California, USA* Small appellation (less than 245ha/600 acres) in western MENDOCINO COUNTY that produces brilliant wines. Most vineyards are within 15 miles of the Pacific Ocean, making this one of the coldest AVAs in California. Delicate Pinot Noirs and Chardonnays, and one of the few places in the state for first-rate Gewürztraminer. Superb sparkling wines with healthy acidity and creamy yeast are highlights as well. Best producers: Greenwood Ridge★, HANDLEY★★, Lazy Creek★, Navarro★★, PACIFIC ECHO★, ROEDERER ESTATE★★.

ANDREW WILL WINERY *Washington State, USA* Winemaker Chris Camarda makes delicious Merlots and powerful Cabernet Sauvignons from a range of older WASHINGTON vineyards. At the top are the complex Champoux Vineyard★★★, the opulent Ciel du Cheval★★★ and the tannic yet ageworthy Klipsun★★★. Wines from the WALLA WALLA vineyards of Pepper Bridge★★ and Seven Hills★ are fruity and drink well early. Sorella★★★, a BORDEAUX blend, is outstanding with age. White wines vary and seem more a pastime than a portfolio. Best years: (reds) (2001) 00 99 97 96 **95 94 93**.

CH. ANGÉLUS★★★ *St-Émilion Grand Cru AC, 1er Grand Cru Classé, Bordeaux, France* One of the best-known ST-EMILION Grands Crus, with an energetic owner and talented winemaker. Increasingly gorgeous wines throughout the 80s and 90s, recognized by promotion to Premier Grand Cru Classé in 1996. Best years: 2001 00 99 98 97 96 95 **94 93 92 90 89 88 85**.

MARQUIS D'ANGERVILLE *Volnay AC, Côte de Beaune, Burgundy, France*
With over half a century's experience and meticulous attention to
detail, Marquis Jacques d'Angerville produces an exemplary range of
elegant Premiers Crus from VOLNAY, the classiest of the COTE DE BEAUNE's
red wine appellations. Clos des Ducs and Taillepieds are ★★★. All
should be kept for at least 5 years. Best years: (top reds) (2002) 99 98
97 96 95 **93 91 90**.

CH. D'ANGLUDET★ *Margaux AC, Cru Bourgeois, Haut-Médoc, Bordeaux,
France* This English-owned château makes a gentle, unobtrusive but
extremely attractive red that is generally of Classed Growth standard
and is never overpriced. It ages well for up to a decade. Best years:
2000 98 **96 95 94 90 89 88 86 85 83 82**.

ANJOU BLANC AC *Loire Valley, France* Ill-defined AC; ranges from bone
dry to sweet, from excellent to dreadful; the best are dry. Up to 20%
Chardonnay or Sauvignon can be added, but many of the leading
producers use 100% Chenin. Best producers: M Angeli★★, Cady,
Fesles★, Montgilet/V Lebreton, Mosse★, Ogereau★, Pierre-Bise★, J
Pithon★★, RICHOU★, Soucherie/P-Y Tijou★, Yves Soulez★. Best years: (top
wines) (2002) 01 **00 99 97 96**.

ANJOU ROUGE AC *Loire Valley, France* Anjou reds (from Cabernets
Sauvignon and Franc or Pineau d'Aunis) are increasingly successful.
Usually fruity, easy-drinking wine, with less tannin than ANJOU-VILLAGES.
Wines made from Gamay are sold as Anjou Gamay. Best producers: M
Angeli★, P Baudouin, Brizé★, Chamboureau, Fesles★, Putille, J Pithon★,
RICHOU★. Best years: (top wines) (2002) 01 **00 97 96 95**.

ANJOU-VILLAGES AC *Loire Valley, France* Since 1985, 46 villages have
been entitled to the AC Anjou-Villages, only for red wine from
Cabernet Franc and Cabernet Sauvignon. Some extremely attractive
dry, fruity reds are emerging in the region, with better aging potential
than ANJOU ROUGE. Anjou-Villages Brissac is a superior sub-appellation.
Best producers: Brizé★, P Delesvaux★, Montgilet/V Lebreton★, de la
Motte, Ogereau★, Pierre-Bise★, Putille★, RICHOU (Vieilles Vignes★★),
Rochelles/J-Y Lebreton★★, Pierre Soulez★, Tigné★, la Varière★. Best
years: (2002) 01 **00 97 96 95 90 89**.

ANSELMI *Soave DOC, Veneto, Italy* Roberto Anselmi (and PIEROPAN) has
shown that much-maligned SOAVE can have personality when
carefully made. Using ultra-modern methods he has honed the fruit
flavours of his San Vincenzo★ and Capitel Foscarino★★ and
introduced small-barrel-aging for single-vineyard Capitel Croce★
and luscious, Sauternes-like I Capitelli★★ (sometimes ★★★). All sold
under the regional IGT rather than Soave DOC. Best years: (I Capitelli)
(2001) (00) 99 **98 97 96 95 93 92 90 88**.

ANTINORI *Tuscany, Italy* World-famous Florentine family firm that has
been involved in wine since 1385, but it is Piero Antinori, the current
head, who has made the Antinori name synonymous with quality
and innovation. The quality of its CHIANTI CLASSICO wines like Badia a
Passignano★ (Riserva★★), Pèppoli★, Tenute Marchese Antinori
Riserva★★ and Villa Antinori is consistently good, but it was its
development of the SUPER-TUSCAN concept of superior wines outside the
DOC that launched a quality revolution during the 1970s.
Introducing small-barrel-aging to Tuscany, TIGNANELLO★★
(Sangiovese-Cabernet) and SOLAIA★★★ (Cabernet-based) can be great
wines. Other Tuscan wines include VINO NOBILE La Braccesca★★,
BRUNELLO DI MONTALCINO Pian delle Vigne★★, BOLGHERI's Guado al

Tasso★★ (Cabernet-Merlot), and Bramasole, a new Syrah-Merlot blend from Cortona DOC. Interests further afield include PRUNOTTO in Piedmont, Tormaresca in PUGLIA, FRANCIACORTA's Monte Nisa, ATLAS PEAK in California and Bátaapáti in Hungary. Best years: (reds) (2001) 00 99 **98 97 95 93 90**. See also Castello della Sala.

ANTONOPOULOS *Patras AO, Peloponnese, Greece*   Boutique winery producing barrel-fermented Chardonnay★★, Cabernet Nea Dris (New Oak)★, a blend of Cabernets Sauvignon and Franc, and Private Collection★, a promising Agiorgitiko-Cabernet blend.

ARAGÓN *Spain*   Most of Aragón, stretching from the Pyrenees south to Spain's central plateau, used to be responsible for much of the country's cheap red wine. There have been improvements, especially in the cooler, hilly, northern SOMONTANO DO. Further south, winemaking is improving in Campo de Borja DO, Calatayud DO and, particularly, CARIÑENA DO; these 3 areas have the potential to be a major budget-price force in a world mad for beefy reds.

ARAUJO *Napa Valley AVA, California, USA*   Boutique winery whose great coup was to buy the Eisele vineyard, traditionally a source of superb Cabernet under the Joseph Phelps label. Araujo Cabernet Sauvignon★★★ is now one of California's most sought-after reds, combining great fruit intensity with powerful but digestible tannins. There is also an attractively zesty Sauvignon Blanc★ and a tiny amount of impressive estate Syrah★★ produced as well.

ARBOIS AC *Jura, France*   The largest of the specific ACs in the Jura region. The whites are made from Chardonnay or the local Savagnin, which can give the wines a sherry-like flavour that is most concentrated in *vin jaune*. There is also a rare, sweet *vin de paille*. Good sparkling CREMANT DU JURA is made mainly from Chardonnay. Best reds and sparklers are from the commune of Pupillin. Best producers: Ch. d'Arlay★, Aviet★, Bourdy★, Désiré★, Dugois★, J Foret★, F Lornet★, H Maire★, P Overnoy★, la Pinte★, J Puffeney★, Pupillin co-op★, Rijckaert★, Rolet★, A & M Tissot★, J Tissot★, Tournelle★. Best years: 2001 **00 99 98 97 96 95**.

ARCHERY SUMMIT *Willamette Valley AVA, Oregon, USA*   Owned by the Andrus family of PINE RIDGE, with more than 40ha (100 acres) in 3 estate vineyards, the focus here is on deeply coloured, heavily oaked Pinot Noir. Single-vineyard Pinot Noirs from Archery Summit Estate★, Red Hills★ and Arcus Estate★ top the list. A white wine labelled Vireton★ is a blend of Pinot Gris, Pinot Blanc and Chardonnay. Best years: (Pinot Noir) (2002) (01) 00 99 98 **96**.

ARGIANO *Brunello di Montalcino DOCG, Tuscany, Italy*   The renaissance begun by a mix of renewed investment and the initial involvement of Giacomo Tachis continues with radically refashioned BRUNELLO★ (Riserva★★) that is both rich and accessible, and scintillating Solengo★★★ (a blend of Cabernet, Merlot, Sangiovese and Syrah). Good ROSSO DI MONTALCINO★, too. Best years: (Brunello) (2001) (00) 99 97 **95 93 90**.

ARGIOLAS *Sardinia, Italy*   Sardinian star making DOC wines Cannonau (Costera★), Monica (Perdera) and Vermentino (Costamolino★) di Sardegna, but the best wines are the IGT Isola dei Nuraghi blends – Turriga★★ and Korem★ are powerful, spicy reds, Angialis★★ a golden, sweet white. All the wines are good value.

ARNEIS Italian grape grown in the ROERO hills in PIEDMONT. Arneis is DOC in Roero, producing dry white wines which, at best, have an attractive nutty, herbal perfume. They can be expensive. Best producers: Araldica/Alasia★, Brovia★, Cascina Chicco★, Correggia★, Deltetto★, GIACOSA★, Malvirà★, Angelo Negro★, PRUNOTTO★, Vietti★, Gianni Voerzio★.

CH. L'ARROSÉE★★ *St-Émilion Grand Cru AC, Grand Cru Classé, Bordeaux, France* This smartly property, just south-west of the small historic town of ST-EMILION, makes really exciting wine: rich, chewy and wonderfully luscious, with a comparatively high proportion (40%) of Cabernet Sauvignon. Drink after 5 years, but may be cellared for 10 or more. Best years: 2000 98 **96 95 94 90 89 88 86 85**.

ARROWOOD *Sonoma Valley AVA, California, USA* Dick Arrowood was the winemaker at CHATEAU ST JEAN during its glory years of Chardonnay. In 1986 he started his own winery, which was purchased in 2000 by MONDAVI. The wines have mostly been tip-top – beautifully balanced Cabernet★★ (Reserve★★), superb Merlot★★, deeply fruity Syrah★★, lovely, velvety Chardonnay★★ and crisp, fragrant Viognier★★. Best years: (Cabernet Sauvignon) (2001) (00) 99 98 97 **96 95 94 91 90**.

ISMAEL ARROYO *Ribera del Duero DO, Castilla y León, Spain* This family bodega was for years one of the best RIBERA DEL DUERO producers, making long-lived, tannic wines, headed by Val Sotillo Reserva★, Gran Reserva★ and Crianza★. A return to previous form would be welcome. Best years: (Val Sotillo Reserva) **1996 95 94 91**.

ARTADI *Rioja DOC, País Vasco, Spain* Under demanding new boss Juan Carlos López de Lacalle, this former co-op is now producing some of RIOJA's deepest, most ambitious reds. These include Grandes Añadas★★★, Viña El Pisón★★★, Pagos Viejos★★ and Viñas de Gain. Best years: (2000) 99 **98 96 95 94 91**.

ASCHERI *Piedmont, Italy* Winemakers in PIEDMONT for at least 5 centuries, the Ascheri style is forward and appealingly drinkable, whether it be BAROLO (Vigna dei Pola★, Sorano★★), Dolcetto d'Alba (Vigna Nirane★) or NEBBIOLO D'ALBA. Montalupa Rosso and Bianco are made from Syrah and Viognier. The Cristina Ascheri MOSCATO D'ASTI is delightful.

ASTI DOCG *Piedmont, Italy* Asti Spumante, the world's best-selling sweet sparkling wine, was long derided as light and cheap, though promotion to DOCG signalled an upturn in quality. Made in the province of Asti south-east of Turin, under the new appellation (which includes the rarer MOSCATO D'ASTI) the wine is now called simply Asti. Its light sweetness and refreshing sparkle make it ideal with fruit, rich cakes and a wide range of sweet dishes. Drink young. Best producers: Araldica, Bera★, Cinzano★, Contero★, Giuseppe Contratto★★, Cascina Fonda★, FONTANAFREDDA, Gancia★, Martini & Rossi★, Cascina Pian d'Or★.

ATA RANGI *Martinborough, North Island, New Zealand* Small, high-quality winery run by 2 families. Stylish, concentrated wines include big, rich Craighall Chardonnay★★, seductively perfumed cherry/plum Pinot Noir★★★ and an impressive Cabernet-Merlot-Syrah blend called Célèbre★★. Young Vines Pinot Noir is not of the same standard, but new Syrah★★ and a concentrated and succulent Sauvignon Blanc★ are exciting. Best years: (Pinot Noir) (2002) 01 00 99 **98 97 96**.

ATLAS PEAK *Atlas Peak AVA, Napa, California, USA* These hillside vineyards, managed by ANTINORI of Italy, are demonstrating a new sense of direction after several years adrift. The 100% Sangiovese has been improving throughout the 1990s, as has Consenso★, a tasty Cabernet-Sangiovese blend. Both can age for 5–10 years. Chardonnay and Cabernet are recent additions. Best years: (reds) (2001) 99 98 97 **96** 95.

AU **BON CLIMAT** *Santa Maria Valley AVA, California, USA* Pace-setting winery in this cool region, run by the talented Jim Clendenen, who spends much time in BURGUNDY and PIEDMONT. The result is lush Chardonnay★★, intense Pinot Noir★★ (Isabelle bottling can be ★★★) and BORDEAUX styles under the Vita Nova label. Watch out for Italian varietals under the Il Podere dell' Olivos label and Cold Heaven Viogniers. QUPÉ operates from the same winery. Best years: (Pinot Noir) (2001) (00) 99 98 **97 96 95 94 91 90**; (Chardonnay) (2001) 00 **99 98 97 95 92**.

AUCKLAND *North Island, New Zealand* Vineyards in the region of Auckland are concentrated in the districts of Henderson, KUMEU/HUAPAI, Matakana and WAIHEKE ISLAND. Clevedon, south of Auckland, is a fledgling area that shows promise. Best producers: Heron's Flight, KUMEU RIVER★. Best years: (Cabernet Sauvignon) (2001) 00 **99 98 96 94 93**.

CH. **AUSONE** ★★★ *St-Émilion Grand Cru AC, 1er Grand Cru Classé, Bordeaux, France* This beautiful property, situated on what are perhaps the best slopes in ST-EMILION, made a much-vaunted return to form in the 1980s, and has maintained high standards. Owner Alain Vauthier's richly textured wines gain added complexity from the high proportion (50%) of Cabernet Franc. Production is a tiny 2000 cases a year. Best years: 2001 00 99 98 97 96 95 **94 90 89 88 86 85 83 82**.

AUXEY-DURESSES AC *Côte de Beaune, Burgundy, France* Auxey-Duresses is a backwater village up a valley behind MEURSAULT. The reds should be light and fresh but can often lack ripeness. At its best, and at 3–5 years, the white is dry, soft, nutty and hinting at the creaminess of a good Meursault, but at much lower prices. Of the Premiers Crus, Les Duresses is the most consistent. Best producers: (reds) Comte Armand★★, J-P Diconne★, Jessiaume Père et Fils, Maison LEROY★, Duc de Magenta★, M Prunier★, P Prunier★; (whites) R Ampeau★, d'Auvenay (Dom. LEROY)★★, J-P Diconne★, DROUHIN★, J-P Fichet★, Olivier LEFLAIVE★, Maison LEROY★, Duc de Magenta★, M Prunier★. Best years: (reds) (2002) 99 **98 96 95**; (whites) (2002) 00 **99 97 96**.

AVIGNONESI *Vino Nobile di Montepulciano DOCG, Tuscany, Italy* The Falvo brothers led Montepulciano's revival as one of TUSCANY's best zones. Although VINO NOBILE★★ is often the best of the dry wines, for a time the international wines, Il Marzocco★ (Chardonnay) and Desiderio★★ (previously Merlot, now Merlot-Cabernet), received more attention. The VIN SANTO★★★ is the most sought-after in Tuscany; there's also a rare red version from Sangiovese, Occhio di Pernice★★★. Best years: (Vino Nobile) (2001) (00) 99 98 97 **95 93 90 88**.

AYL *Saar, Germany* A top Saar village. Its best-known vineyard is Kupp, which produces classy, slaty off-dry and sweet Rieslings on its steep slopes. Best producers: Bischöflicher Konvikt, Peter Lauer★, Dr Heinz Wagner★. Best years: (Riesling Spätlese) (2002) 99 97 **95 94 93 90**.

BABCOCK *Santa Ynez Valley AVA, California, USA* Bryan Babcock has been making wines from SANTA BARBARA fruit since 1984. He focuses on intensely flavoured Pinot Noir★ and Chardonnay★; the Grand Cuvée Chardonnay★★ and Pinot Noir★★ are quite spicy, with evident oak and brisk acidity. The Eleven Oaks Sauvignon Blanc★★ is equally intense and oaky, while the Black Label Syrah★★ highlights jammy black fruit and spice flavours. Best years: Pinot Noir (2001) 00 99 **98 96 95** 94.

BABICH *Henderson, North Island, New Zealand* Family-run winery with some prime vineyard land in MARLBOROUGH and HAWKES BAY. Irongate Chardonnay★ is an intense, steely wine that needs plenty of cellaring, while intense, full-flavoured varietal reds under the Winemakers Reserve label show even greater potential for development. Flagship label The Patriarch features Chardonnay★★ and Cabernet Sauvignon★★, both from Hawkes Bay. Marlborough wines include a stylish Sauvignon Blanc★, a tangy Riesling and a light, fruity Pinot Gris. Best years: (premium Hawkes Bay reds) (2002) 00 99 98 **96**.

BAD DÜRKHEIM *Pfalz, Germany* This spa town has some good vineyards and is the headquarters of the dependable Vier Jahreszeiten Kloster Limburg co-op. Best producers: DARTING★, Fitz-Ritter, Pflüger★, Karl Schaefer★. Best years: (Riesling Spätlese) (2002) 01 99 98 **97 96 93** 92.

BADEN *Germany* Very large wine region stretching from FRANKEN to the Bodensee (Lake Constance). Its dry whites and reds show off the fuller, softer flavours Germany can produce in the warmer climate of its southerly regions. Many of the best non-Riesling German wines of the future will come from here, as well as many of the best barrel-fermented and barrel-aged wines. Good co-operative cellars at Achkarren, Bickensohl, Bötzingen, Durbach, Königsschaffhausen and Sasbach.

BAGA Important red grape in BAIRRADA, which is one of the few regions in Portugal to rely mainly on one variety. Also planted in much smaller quantities in DAO and the RIBATEJO. It can give deep, blackberryish wine, but aggressive tannin is a continual problem.

BAILEYS *North-East Victoria, Australia* Old, traditional winery at Glenrowan, where Australia's most famous bush bandit, Ned Kelly, made his last stand. Now part of Beringer Blass and, after a shaky start, showing real improvement (1920s Block Shiraz★). Also some of Australia's most luscious fortified Muscat and Tokay (Winemakers Selection★★) – still heavenly and irresistible stickies, but I can't help thinking they were better a few years ago.

BAIRRADA DOC *Beira Litoral, Portugal* Bairrada, along with the DOURO and ALENTEJO, is the source of many of Portugal's best red table wines. These can brim over with intense raspberry and blackberry fruit, though the tannin levels are severe and may take quite a few years to soften. The whites are coming on fast with modern vinification methods. With an Atlantic climate, vintages can be very variable. Best producers: (reds) Caves ALIANCA★, Quinta das Bágeiras★, Quinta do Carvalhinho★, Gonçalves Faria★, Caves Messias (Garrafeira★), Caves Primavera (Garrafeira★), Quinta da Rigodeira★, Casa de Saima★★, Caves SAO JOAO★, SOGRAPE, Sidónio de Sousa★★; (whites) Quinta da Rigodeira★, Casa de Saima★, SOGRAPE (Reserva★, Quinta de Pedralvites★). Best years: (reds) 2001 00 **97 96 95 91** 90.

BALATONBOGLÁR WINERY *Transdanubia, Hungary* Premium co-operative, in the Lake Balaton region, that has benefited from heavy investment and the expertise of viticulturist Richard Smart and wine consultant Kym Milne, but still needs to work to improve quality, particularly in the inexpensive, inoffensive range sold under the

Chapel Hill label in the UK. Owned by Henkell & Söhnlein, a large German sparkling wine producer.

BALEARIC ISLANDS *Spain* Medium-bodied reds and soft rosés were the mainstays of Mallorca's 2 DO areas, Binissalem and Plà i Llevant, until the Anima Negra winery began turning out its impressive, deep reds from the native Callet grape. Best producers: Anima Negra★, Franja Roja (J L Ferrer), Hereus de Ribas, Son Bordils★.

BANDOL AC *Provence, France* A lovely fishing port with vineyards high above the Mediterranean, producing some of the best reds and rosés in Provence. The Mourvèdre grape gives Bandol its character – gentle raisin and honey softness with a herby fragrance. The reds happily age for 10 years, sometimes more, but can be very good at 3–4. The rosés, delicious and spicy but often too pricy, should be drunk young. There is a small amount of neutral, overpriced white. Best producers: (reds) Bastide Blanche★★, la Bégude★, Bunan★, Frégate★, le Galantin★, J P Gaussen★★, Gros' Noré★★, l'Hermitage★, Lafran-Veyrolles★, Mas Redorne★, la Noblesse★, PIBARNON★★, Pradeaux★★, Ray-Jane★★, Roche Redonne★, Romassan★, Ste-Anne★, des Salettes★, de Souviou★, la Suffrène★, TEMPIER★★, Terrebrune★, la Tour de Bon★, Vannières★. Best years: 2001 00 99 98 **97 96 95 93 90 89 88**.

BANFI *Brunello di Montalcino DOCG, Tuscany, Italy* High-tech American-owned firm which is now a force in Italy. Noted winemaker Ezio Rivella (here from 1977 to 1999) did much to establish Banfi's reputation. BRUNELLO★, Chardonnay (Fontanelle★), Cabernet (Tavernelle★★) and Merlot (Mandrielle★) are very successful, but even better are Brunello Riserva Poggio all'Oro★★ and SUPER-TUSCANS Summus★★ (a blend of Sangiovese, Cabernet and Syrah) and Excelsus★★ (Cabernet-Merlot). Also has cellars (Vigne Regali) in PIEDMONT for GAVI and fizz. Best years: (top reds) (2001) 99 98 97 **95 93 90**.

BANNOCKBURN *Geelong, Victoria, Australia* The experience gleaned from vintage stints at Burgundy's Dom. DUJAC is reflected in Gary Farr's powerful, gamy Pinot Noir★ and MEURSAULT-like Chardonnay★★, which are among Australia's best or most notorious wines – depending on your view. I prefer the complex and classy Shiraz★★, influenced by Rhône's Alain GRAILLOT. (Note that there was no estate-grown wine in 1998 due to a freak hailstorm.) Best years: (Shiraz) 2001 00 99 98 97 **96 92 91 90 89 88 86**.

BANNOCKBURN
GEELONG
Chardonnay
1999

BANYULS AC *Roussillon, France* One of the best *vins doux naturels*, made mainly from Grenache, with a strong plum and raisin flavour. Rimage – vintaged early bottlings – and tawny styles are the best. Generally served as an apéritif in France and deserves a wider audience. Try sampling it mid-afternoon with some macaroons or plain cake. Best producers: Casa Blanca, Cellier des Templiers★, Clos des Paulilles★, l'Étoile★, Mas Blanc★★, la RECTORIE★★, la Tour Vieille★, Vial Magnères★.

BARBADILLO *Jerez y Manzanilla DO, Andalucía, Spain* The largest sherry company in the coastal town of Sanlúcar de Barrameda makes a wide range of good to excellent wines, in particular salty, dry manzanilla styles (Solear★★) and intense, nutty, but dry amontillados and olorosos, led by Amontillado Principe★★ and Oloroso Cuco★★. Neutral dry white Castillo de San Diego is a best seller in Spain.

BARBARESCO DOCG *Piedmont, Italy* This prestigious red wine, grown near Alba in the LANGHE hills south-east of Turin, is often twinned with its neighbour BAROLO to demonstrate the nobility of the Nebbiolo grape. Barbaresco can be a shade softer and less powerful. The wine usually takes less time to mature and is often considered the more approachable of the two, as exemplified by the international style of GAJA. But, as in Barolo, traditionalists also excel, led by Bruno GIACOSA. Even though the area is relatively compact (575ha/1420 acres), wine styles can differ significantly between vineyards and producers. Best vineyards: Asili, Bricco di Neive, Costa Russi, Crichet Pajè, Gallina, Marcorino, Martinenga, Messoirano, Moccagatta, Montestefano, Ovello, Pora, Rabajà, Rio Sordo, San Lorenzo, Santo Stefano, Serraboella, Sorì Paitin, Sorì Tildìn. Best producers: Barbaresco co-op★★, Piero Busso★, CERETTO★★, Cigliuti★★, Stefano Farina★★, Fontanabianca★★, GAJA★★★, GIACOSA★★★, Marchesi di Gresy★★, Moccagatta★★, Fiorenzo Nada★★, Castello di Neive★★, Oddero★, Paitin★★, Pelissero★★, Pio Cesare★★, PRUNOTTO★, Albino Rocca★★, Bruno Rocca★★, Sottimano★★, La Spinetta★★, Vietti★★. Best years: (2001) 00 99 98 97 96 **95 93 90 89 88 86 85 82**.

BARBERA A native of north-west Italy, Barbera vies with Sangiovese as the most widely planted red grape in the country. When grown for high yields its natural acidity shows through, producing vibrant quaffers. Low yields from the top PIEDMONT estates create intensely rich and complex wines. Oaked versions can be stunning.

BARBERA D'ALBA DOC *Piedmont, Italy* Some of the most outstanding Barbera comes from this appellation. The most modern examples are supple and generous and can be drunk almost at once. More intense, dark-fruited versions require a minimum 3 years' age, but might improve for as much as 8. Best producers: G Alessandria★★, ALTARE★, Azelia★★, Boglietti★★, Brovia★, Cascina Chicco★, CERETTO★, Cigliuti★, CLERICO★, Elvio Cogno★★, Aldo CONTERNO★, Giacomo CONTERNO★, Conterno-Fantino★, Corino★★, Correggia★★, Elio Grasso★, Giuseppe MASCARELLO★, Moccagatta★, M Molino★★, Monfalletto-Cordero di Montezemolo★★, Oberto★★, Parusso★★, Pelissero★, F Principiano★★, PRUNOTTO★★, Albino Rocca★★, Bruno Rocca★, SANDRONE★★, P Scavino★★, La Spinetta★★, Vajra★★, Mauro Veglio★★, Vietti★★, Gianni Voerzio★★, Roberto VOERZIO★★★. Best years: (2001) 00 99 **98 97 96 95**.

BARBERA D'ASTI DOC *Piedmont, Italy* While Dolcetto d'Asti is usually light and simple, wines made from Barbera show a greater range of quality. Unoaked and barrique-aged examples can compete with the best BARBERA D'ALBA and rival some of the better Nebbiolo-based reds. Best examples can be kept for 5–6 years, occasionally longer. Best producers: Araldica/Alasia★, La Barbatella★★, Pietro Barbero★★, Bava★, Bertelli★★, Braida★★, Cascina Castlèt★, Coppo★★, Hastae (Quorum★), Martinetti★★, Il Mongetto★★, PRUNOTTO★★, Cantine Sant'Agata★, Scarpa★★, La Spinetta★★, Vietti★★. Best years: (2001) 00 99 **97 96 95**.

BARDOLINO DOC *Veneto, Italy* Substantial zone centred on Lake Garda, giving, at best, light, scented red and rosé (chiaretto) wines to be drunk young, from the same grape mix as neighbouring VALPOLICELLA. Best producers: Cavalchina★, Corte Gardoni★, Guerrieri-Rizzardi★, MASI, Le Vigne di San Pietro★, Fratelli Zeni.

BAROLO DOCG *Piedmont, Italy* Renowned red wine, named after a village south-west of Alba, from the Nebbiolo grape grown in 1455ha (3595 acres) of vineyards in the steep LANGHE hills. Its status as 'king of wines and wine of kings' for a time proved to be more of a burden than a benefit among Italians, who considered its austere power too much for modern palates, with tough, chewy tannins which took years of cask-aging to soften. But for over a decade, many winemakers have applied new methods to make Barolo that is fresher, cleaner, better balanced and ready sooner, with greater colour, richer fruit and softer tannins yet without sacrificing Barolo's noble character. Distinct styles of wine are made in the zone's villages. Barolo and La Morra make the most perfumed wines; Monforte and Serralunga the most structured; Castiglione Falletto strikes a balance between the two. Barolo is nowadays frequently labelled by vineyards, though the producer's reputation often carries more weight. Best vineyards: Bricco delle Viole, Brunate, Bussia Soprana, Cannubi Boschis, Cerequio, Conca dell'Annunziata, Fiasco, Francia, Giachini, Ginestra, Monfalletto, Monprivato, Rocche dell'Annunziata, Rocche di Castiglione, Santo Stefano di Perno, La Serra, Vigna Rionda, Villero. Best producers: C Alario★★, G Alessandria★★, ALTARE★★, Azelia★★, Boglietti★★, Bongiovanni★★, Brovia★★, CERETTO★★, CHIARLO★★, CLERICO★★, Aldo CONTERNO★★★, Giacomo CONTERNO★★, Conterno-Fantino★★, Corino★★, Luigi Einaudi★★, GAJA★★★, GIACOSA★★★, Elio Grasso★★, M Marengo★★, Bartolo MASCARELLO★★★, Giuseppe MASCARELLO★★★, Monfalletto-Cordero di Montezemolo★★, Oberto★★, Oddero★★, Parusso★★, Pio Cesare★★, Pira★★, E Pira & Figli★★, F Principiano★★, PRUNOTTO★★, Renato RATTI★, Revello★★, Rocche dei Manzoni★★, SANDRONE★★★, P Scavino★★, M Sebaste★★, Vajra★★, Mauro Veglio★★, Vietti★★, Vigna Rionda★★, Gianni Voerzio★★, Roberto VOERZIO★★. Best years: (2001) (00) 99 98 97 96 95 **93 90 89 88 86 85**.

BAROSSA VALLEY See pages 58–9.

BAROSSA VALLEY ESTATE *Barossa, South Australia* Half owned by local grapegrowers, half by industry giant BRL HARDY. Flagship reds are huge, gutsy BAROSSA beauties E&E Black Pepper Shiraz★★, Ebenezer Shiraz★★ and E&E Sparkling Shiraz★★, all of them bursting with ripe plum fruit, spice and plenty of vanilla oak. There's also Ebenezer Cabernet Sauvignon★ and Chardonnay★★ and intense, full-flavoured sparkling Pinot Noir★. The Moculta label offers a good-value range.

JIM BARRY *Clare Valley, South Australia* Formerly more of a white wine outfit, with the famous Florita vineyard as the source of perfumed, classy Rieslings★. However, it is for rich and complex reds such as Cabernet Sauvignon, McCrae Wood Shiraz★ and the heady, palate-busting Armagh Shiraz★★ that it is now known. Best years: (Armagh Shiraz) (2001) (99) 98 96 **95 93 92**.

BARSAC AC *Bordeaux, France* Barsac, largest of the 5 communes in the SAUTERNES AC, also has its own AC, which is used by most, but by no means all, of the top properties. In general, the wines are a little less luscious than other Sauternes, but from good estates they can be marvellous. Best producers: CLIMENS★★★, COUTET★★, DOISY-DAENE★★, Doisy-Dubroca★, DOISY-VEDRINES★★, Myrat★, NAIRAC★★, Piada, Suau★. Best years: (2002) 01 99 **98 97 96 95 90 89 88 86 83**.

BASILICATA *Italy* Obscure southern region specializing in one wine, the potentially excellent, gutsy red called AGLIANICO DEL VULTURE.

BAROSSA

South Australia

The Barossa Valley, an hour or so's drive north of Adelaide in South Australia, is the heart of the Australian wine industry. Penfolds, Orlando, Beringer Blass, Seppelt, Yalumba and other giants have their headquarters here, alongside around 50 or so smaller wineries, producing or processing up to 60% of the nation's wine. However, this percentage is based mostly on grapes trucked in from other regions, because the Barossa's vineyards themselves grow less than 10% of Australia's grapes. Yet Barossa-grown grapes, once rejected as uneconomical for their low yields, are now increasingly prized for those same low yields.

Why? Well, it's highly likely that the world's oldest vines are in the Barossa. The valley was settled in the 1840s by Lutheran immigrants from Silesia, who brought with them vines from Europe, most importantly, as it turned out, cuttings from the Syrah (or Shiraz) variety of France's Rhône Valley. And because Barossa has never been affected by the phylloxera louse, which destroyed much of the world's vineyards in the late 19th century, today you can still see gnarled, twisted old vines sporting just a few tiny bunches of priceless fruit that were planted by refugees from Europe all of a century and a half ago, and are still tended by their descendants. A new wave of winemakers has taken up the cause of the Barossa vines with much zeal and no small amount of national pride, and they now produce from them some of the deepest, most fascinating wines, not just in Australia, but in the world.

GRAPE VARIETIES

Shiraz is prized above all other Barossa grapes, able to conjure headswirling, palate-dousing flavours. Barossa is the main source of Shiraz grapes for Penfolds Grange, the wine that began the revolution in Australian red wine in the 1950s. Cabernet Sauvignon is also excellent and similarly potent, as are the Rhône varieties of heady Grenache and deliciously earthy Mourvèdre; some of the most exciting examples are from the original vines planted in the 19th century. All these varieties are largely grown on the hot, dry, valley floor, but just to the east lie the Barossa Ranges, and in these higher, cooler vineyards, especially in those of the neighbouring Eden Valley, some of Australia's best and most fashionable Rieslings are grown, prized for their steely attack and lime fragrance. But even here you can't get away from Shiraz, and some thrilling examples come from the hills, not least Henschke's Hill of Grace and Mount Edelstone.

CLASSIFICATIONS

The Barossa was among the first zones to be ratified within the Australian system of Geographical Indications and comprises the regions of Barossa Valley and Eden Valley. The Barossa lies within South Australia's collective 'super zone' of Adelaide.

See also GRANGE, SOUTH AUSTRALIA; and individual producers.

BEST YEARS

(Barossa Valley Shiraz) (2001)
99 98 97 **96 94 91 90 88 87**;
(Eden Valley Riesling) **2001 00**
99 98 97 96 95 94 92 91 90 87

BEST PRODUCERS

Shiraz-based reds
BAROSSA VALLEY ESTATE,
Basedow, Bethany, Grant
BURGE, Charles Cimicky
(Signature), Elderton
(Command), Glaetzer,
Greenock Creek (Block Shiraz,
Seven Acres), HENSCHKE,
Hewitson, Jenke, Trevor
Jones, Peter LEHMANN, Charles
MELTON, Miranda (Show
Reserve Old Vine Shiraz),
MOUNTADAM, ORLANDO, PENFOLDS
(RWT, GRANGE), ROCKFORD, ST
HALLETT, Saltram (No. 1 Shiraz),
Three Rivers, Torbreck, Turkey
Flat, VERITAS, The Willows,
YALUMBA (Octavius).

Riesling
Bethany, Grant BURGE, Leo
Buring (Leonay), Heggies
(Botrytis Riesling), HENSCHKE,
Hewitson, Peter LEHMANN,
MOUNTADAM, ORLANDO, Ross
Estate, YALUMBA (Contour).

**Cabernet Sauvignon-based
reds**
Grant BURGE, Greenock Creek,
HENSCHKE, Peter LEHMANN,
ST HALLETT, VERITAS.

**Other reds (containing
Grenache, Mourvèdre,
Shiraz)**
Burge Family (Olive Hill), Grant
BURGE, Charles Cimicky
(Grenache), Elderton (CSM),
Jenke (Mourvèdre), Peter
LEHMANN, Charles MELTON,
PENFOLDS (Bin 138 Old Vine),
Torbreck (Juveniles, The
Steading), Turkey Flat
(Butcher's Block, Grenache
Noir), VERITAS.

Semillon
Basedow, Grant BURGE,
Craneford, HENSCHKE, Jenke,
Peter LEHMANN, ROCKFORD,
Turkey Flat, The Willows.

BASSERMANN-JORDAN *Deidesheim, Pfalz, Germany* Since the arrival o
winemaker Ulrich Mell in 1996, this famous estate has resume
making the rich yet elegant Rieslings of ★ and ★★ quality which long
made its name synonymous with great Deidesheim and FORST wines
Best years: (2002) 01 **00 99** 98 **97 96 90 89 88 86 81 79 76 71**.

CH. BASTOR-LAMONTAGNE★ *Sauternes AC, Cru Bourgeois, Bordeaux*
France Luscious, honeyed sweet wine at a price which allows us
to enjoy high-class SAUTERNES without taking out a second mortgage
Best years: (2002) 01 99 **98 97 96 95 94 90 89 88 86 85 83**.

CH. BATAILLEY AC *Pauillac AC, 5ème Cru Classé, Haut-Médoc, Bordeaux*
France A byword for value for money and reliability among the
Pauillac Classed Growth estates. Marked by a full, obvious blackcurran
fruit, not too much tannin and a luscious overlay of creamy vanilla
Lovely to drink at only 5 years old, the wine continues to age well for
at least 15 years. Best years: 2000 **96 95 94 90 89 88 86 85 83 82**.

BÂTARD-MONTRACHET AC *Grand Cru, Côte de Beaune, Burgundy,*
France This Grand Cru produces some of the world's greatest whites
– they are full, rich and balanced, with a powerful mineral intensity
of fruit and fresh acidity. There are 2 associated Grands Crus
Bienvenues-Bâtard-Montrachet and the minuscule Criots-Bâtard-
Montrachet. All can age for a decade. Best producers: Blain-
Gagnard★★★, CARILLON★★★, DROUHIN★★★, Fontaine-Gagnard★★, J-N
GAGNARD★★★, JADOT★★★, V & F Jouard★★, Louis LATOUR★★, Dom.
LEFLAIVE★★★, Olivier LEFLAIVE★★, Marc Morey★★★, Pierre Morey★★★,
Michel Niellon★★★, RAMONET★★★, SAUZET★★★, VERGET★★★. Best years:
(2002) (01) 00 99 97 96 95 **92 90 89**.

DOM. DES BAUMARD *Coteaux du Layon, Loire Valley, France* Excellent
domaine established nearly 400 years ago. The heart of the domaine
is its sweet wines: sensational QUARTS DE CHAUME★★★ which requires
aging, as well as rich, honeyed, impeccably balanced COTEAUX DU LAYON
Clos de Ste Cathérine★★. Also, a fine steely, mineral-scented
SAVENNIERES Clos du Papillon★★. CREMANT DE LOIRE and ANJOU reds are
OK but a touch unexciting. Best years: (Quarts de Chaume) 2000 99 97
96 95 **93 90 89 88 85 83 81 78 76 71 62 59 47**.

DOM. DE LA BAUME *Vin de Pays d'Oc, Languedoc, France* The French
outpost of BRL HARDY, chiefly making varietal wines. The whites
regularly outperform the reds, but none excel and overall quality is
disappointing given the initial high hopes. Adequate Chardonnay,
Sauvignon Blanc, Merlot, Cabernet Sauvignon and Shiraz are sold
under the La Baume label, and include contract fruit; there are also 2
premium estate wines, a Merlot and a Chardonnay-Viognier blend,
under the Domaine de la Baume label.

LES BAUX-DE-PROVENCE AC *Provence, France* This AC has proved
that organic farming can produce spectacular results mainly due to
the warm dry climate. Good fruit and intelligent winemaking produce
some of the more easily enjoyable reds in Provence. Best producers:
Hauvette★, Mas de la Dame★, Mas de Gourgonnier★, Mas Ste-Berthe★,
Romanin★, Terres Blanches★. Best years: 2001 **00 99 98 97 96 95**.

BÉARN AC *South-West France* While the rest of South-West France has
been busy producing some unusual and original flavours in recent
years, Béarn hasn't managed to cash in. The wines (90% red and
rosé) just aren't special enough, despite some decent grape varieties.
The 2000 vintage saw an upswing in quality. Best producers: Bellocq
co-op, Cauhapé, Guilhemas, Lapeyre★, Nigri.

CH. DE BEAUCASTEL *Châteauneuf-du-Pape AC, Rhône Valley, France*
François Perrin makes some of the richest, most tannic reds★★★ in
CHATEAUNEUF-DU-PAPE, with an unusually high percentage of
Mourvèdre and Syrah, which can take at least a decade to show at
their best. The white Roussanne Vieilles Vignes★★★ is exquisite, too.
Perrin also produces COTES DU RHONE Coudoulet de Beaucastel red★ and
white★ and a range of southern reds, including several good Rhône
villages, under the Domaine Perrin label. Best years: (reds) (2001) 00 99
98 97 96 95 **94 93 90 89 88** 86 85 83 81; (whites) (2001) 00 99 98 97 96
95 94 93 92 90 89 88.

BEAUJOLAIS AC *Beaujolais, Burgundy, France* Famous red wine from a
large area of rolling hills and valleys in southern Burgundy. In the
north, toward Mâcon, most of the reds qualify either as BEAUJOLAIS-
VILLAGES or as a single Cru (10 villages which produce better but more
expensive wine: BROUILLY, CHENAS, CHIROUBLES, COTE DE BROUILLY, FLEURIE,
JULIENAS, MORGON, MOULIN-A-VENT, REGNIE, ST-AMOUR). In the south,
toward Lyon, most of the wine is simple AC Beaujolais, a light red to
be drunk very young, which should be lovely and fresh but is now too
often dilute. Much Beaujolais appears as BEAUJOLAIS NOUVEAU. Beaujolais
Supérieur means wine with a minimum strength of 1% more alcohol
than basic Beaujolais. A little white is made from Chardonnay. Best
producers: (reds) L & J-M Charmet/La Ronze★, DUBOEUF, JADOT (Dom. de
la Madone★), P Sapin (Dom. Père Thomas), Terres Dorées/J-P Brun,
Vissoux/P-M Chermette★.

BEAUJOLAIS NOUVEAU *Beaujolais AC, Burgundy, France* Often known
as Beaujolais Primeur, this is the first release of bouncy, fruity
Beaujolais on the third Thursday of November after the harvest. Once
a simple celebration of the new vintage, then over-hyped and now
enjoyed by the true Beaujolais lover. Quality is generally reasonable
and the wine is delicious until Christmas and the New Year, but
thereafter, while drinkable, is likely to throw a slight sediment.

BEAUJOLAIS-VILLAGES AC *Beaujolais, Burgundy, France* Beaujolais-
Villages can come from one of 38 villages in the north of the region,
many of the best examples rivalling the quality of the BEAUJOLAIS Crus,
having more body, character, complexity and elegance than simple
Beaujolais and representing all the excitement of the Gamay grape at
its best. Best villages in addition to the 10 Crus are Lancié, Quincié
and Perréon. Best producers: (reds) G Descombes★, DUBOEUF, Manoir
du Pavé★, J-C Pivot★, P Sapin (Dom. St-Cyr). Best years: **2002 00**.

BEAULIEU VINEYARD *Napa Valley AVA, California, USA* The late André
Tchelistcheff had a major role in creating this icon for Napa Cabernet
Sauvignon as winemaker from the late 1930s to the late 60s. After he
left, Beaulieu missed a few beats and lived on its reputation for too
long, even though Tchelistcheff continued to consult. However,
recent bottlings of the Private Reserve Cabernet Sauvignon★★ signal
a return to form. A meritage red called Tapestry★★ is also top-
notch. Recent bottlings of Chardonnay★ and Pinot Noir★ from
CARNEROS and Syrah★ have been a pleasant surprise. Best years:
(Private Reserve) (2001) (00) 99 98 97 96 95 94 **92 91 90 87 86 84**.

BEAUMES-DE-VENISE *Rhône Valley, France* Area famous for its sweet
wine, MUSCAT DE BEAUMES-DE-VENISE. The local red wine is also very
good, one of the meatier COTES DU RHONE-VILLAGES, with a ripe,
plummy fruit in warm years. Best producers: (reds) Beaumes-de-
Venise co-op, Bernardins, Cassan, les Goubert★, Redortier.

BEAUNE AC *Côte de Beaune, Burgundy, France* Beaune gives its name to
the southern section of the COTE D'OR, the COTE DE BEAUNE. Most of the
wines are red, with delicious, soft red-fruits ripeness. There are no
Grands Crus but some excellent Premiers Crus, especially Boucherottes,
Bressandes, Clos des Mouches, Fèves, Grèves, Marconnets, Teurons,
Vignes Franches. There's an increasing production of white – DROUHIN
makes an outstandingly good, creamy, nutty Clos des Mouches★★★.
Best producers: (growers) Germain★★, LAFARGE★★, Albert Morot★★,
TOLLOT-BEAUT★★; (merchants) BOUCHARD PERE ET FILS★★ (since 1996),
Champy★, Chanson★, DROUHIN★, Camille Giroud★★, JADOT★★,
JAFFELIN, LABOURE-ROI, THOMAS-MOILLARD★. Best years: (reds) (2002) (01) 99
98 **97** 96 **95** 93 90; (whites) (2002) (01) 00 99 **97** 96 **95**.

CH. BEAU-SÉJOUR BÉCOT★★ *St-Émilion Grand Cru AC, 1er Grand Cru
Classé, Bordeaux, France* Demoted from Premier Grand Cru Classé
in 1986 and promoted again in 1996, this estate is now back on top
form. Brothers Gérard and Dominique Bécot produce firm, ripe,
richly textured wines that need at least 8–10 years to develop. Best
years: 2001 00 98 96 95 **94 90 89 88 86 85**.

BEAUX FRÈRES *Willamette Valley AVA, Oregon,
USA* A venture that has generated much
interest due to the participation of wine
critic Robert Parker; co-owner and winemaker Mike
Etzel is his brother-in-law (hence the name). The
aim has been to make ripe, unfiltered Pinot
Noir★★ that expresses the essence of the grape
and vineyard. Its immediate success has attracted
a cult following. Second label Belles Soeurs★ is
also good. Best years: (2002) 01 00 99 98 **97** 96 94.

GRAHAM BECK WINES *Robertson WO, South Africa* A vibrant two-cellar
operation. In ROBERTSON, Pieter Ferreira concentrates on Cap Classique
sparkling, including an elegant, rich NV Brut from Chardonnay and
Pinot Noir, a toastily fragrant, creamy, barrel-fermented Blanc de
Blancs★ and a quirky sparkling Pinotage★. The Ridge Shiraz★ carries
the flag for reds, while the flavourful, balanced Chardonnay★ does the
same for still white wine; also a promising Viognier. Charles Hopkins
runs the FRANSCHHOEK cellar: his Graham Beck Coastal range – much
from old-vine STELLENBOSCH fruit – is making waves with Shiraz, The
Old Road Pinotage★ and Cabernet Sauvignon★.

J B BECKER *Walluf, Rheingau, Germany* Hajo Becker makes some of the
raciest and longest-living dry Rieslings – usually ★, some Spätlese
trocken ★★ – in the RHEINGAU. He also makes impressive dry
Spätburgunder★ (Pinot Noir) reds matured without any new oak.
Best years: (Riesling Spätlese trocken) (2002) 01 99 98 **97** 96 94 92.

BEDELL CELLARS *Long Island, New York State, USA* Winemaker Kip
Bedell earned a reputation in the 1980s for high-quality, BORDEAUX-
styled Merlot★ (Reserve★★), Cabernet Sauvignon★ and a red blend
called Cupola★★. In the 90s, other wineries began imitating Bedell's
vineyard management techniques, contributing to a quality increase
throughout the region. Bedell sold the winery in 2000, but remains
as winemaker. Best years: (reds) (2001) (00) **98 97** 95.

BEIRAS *Portugal* This large, central Portuguese province includes the
leading DOCs of DAO and BAIRRADA, as well as new DOCs Távora-Varosa
and Beira Interior. A number of important wines are made at the Vinho

Regional level, using Portuguese red and white grape varieties along with international grapes such as Cabernet Sauvignon and Chardonnay. Best producers: Caves ALIANCA (Galeria), D F J VINHOS (Bela Fonte), Figueira de Castelo Rodrigo co-op, Quinta de Foz de Arouce★, Luis PATO★★, Rogenda, Caves SAO JOAO (Quinta do Poço do Lobo).

CH. BELAIR★★ *St-Émilion Grand Cru AC, 1er Grand Cru Classé, Bordeaux, France* Belair is located on ST-EMILION's limestone plateau next to AUSONE. Under the direction of winemaker Pascal Delbeck the estate has been run biodynamically since 1994, and the effects are beginning to be felt with the soft, stylish wines on good form. Best years: 2001 00 98 **95 94 90 89 88 86 85 83 82**.

BELLAVISTA *Franciacorta DOCG, Lombardy, Italy* Winemaker Mattia Vezzola specializes in FRANCIACORTA sparkling wines with a very good Cuvée Brut★★ and 4 distinctive Gran Cuvées★★ (including an excellent rosé). Riserva Vittorio Moretti Extra Brut★★ is made in exceptional years. Also produces lovely still wines, including white blend Convento dell'Annunciata★★★, Chardonnay Uccellanda★★ and red Casotte★ (Pinot Nero) and Solesine★★ (Cabernet-Merlot).

BELLET AC *Provence, France* A tiny AC in the hills behind Nice; the wine, mostly white, is usually overpriced. Ch. de Crémat★ and Ch. de Bellet★ are the most important producers but my favourite is Delmasso★. Best years: **2001 00 99 98 97 96 95**.

BENDIGO *Central Victoria, Australia* Warm, dry, former gold-mining region, which produced some decent wines in the 19th century, and is now home to more than 20 small-scale, high-quality wineries. The best wines are rich, ripe, distinctively minty Shiraz and Cabernet. Best producers: Balgownie, Chateau Leamon, Passing Clouds, Water Wheel. Best years: (Shiraz) (2001) 00 99 98 **97 95 94 93 91 90**.

BERBERANA *Rioja DOC, Rioja, Spain* Now part of one of RIOJA's largest companies, Arco Bodegas Unidas, incorporating Lagunilla, Marqués de Monistrol and MARQUES DE GRINON, Berberana makes a pleasant, lightly oaked Crianza and respectable Reservas and Gran Reservas. Look out for more red wine developments soon. Best years: (Reserva) **1998 96 95 94**.

BERCHER *Burkheim, Baden, Germany* The Bercher brothers run one of the top estates of the KAISERSTUHL. The high points are the powerful oak-aged Spätburgunder★★ (Pinot Noir) reds and Grauburgunder★★ (Pinot Gris) dry whites, which marry richness with perfect balance. Drink young or cellar for 3–5 years or more. Best years: (whites) (2002) 01 **99 98 97 96 94 93**; (reds) (2002) 01 **99 97 96 93**.

BERGERAC AC *South-West France* Bergerac is the main town of the Dordogne and the overall AC for this underrated area on the eastern edge of Bordeaux. The grape varieties are mostly the same as those used in the BORDEAUX ACs. The red is generally like a light, fresh claret, a bit grassy but with a good, raw blackcurrant fruit and hint of earth. Recent vintages have shown more ripe fruit character. Côtes de Bergerac AC wines have a higher minimum alcohol level. In general drink young although a few estate reds can age for at least 3–5 years. The whites are generally lean and dry for quick drinking. Best producers: l'Ancienne Cure★, Bélingard, la Colline★, Court-les-Mûts, Eyssards, Gouyat, la Jaubertie, Moulin Caresse, Panisseau, TOUR DES GENDRES★, Tour des Verdots★, Tourmentine. Best years: (reds) **2000 98 96 95 90**.

BERINGER *Napa Valley AVA, California, USA*   Beringer produces a full range of wine, but, in particular, offers a spectacular range of top-class Cabernet Sauvignons. The Private Reserve Cabernet can be ★★★ and is one of NAPA VALLEY's finest yet most approachable; the Chabot Vineyards★★, when released under its own label, can be equally impressive. The Knight's Valley Cabernet Sauvignon★ is made in a lighter style and is good value. Beringer makes red★★ and white★ Alluvium (meritage wines) from Knight's Valley. The Private Reserve Chardonnay★★ is a powerful wine that ages well. HOWELL MOUNTAIN Merlot★★ from Bancroft Ranch is also very good. Best years: (Cabernet Sauvignon) (2001) (00) 99 98 97 **96 95 94** 93 91 90 87 86 84 81.

BERNKASTEL *Mosel, Germany*   Both a historic wine town in the Middle Mosel and a large Bereich. Top wines, however, will come only from vineyard sites within the town – the most famous of these is the overpriced Doctor vineyard. Many wines from the Graben and Lay sites are as good or better and cost a fraction of the price. Best producers: Hansen-Lauer★, Dr LOOSEN★★, J J PRUM★★, S A PRUM★, Dr H Thanisch★, WEGELER★★. Best years: (2002) 01 **99** 98 **97** 95 **93** 90 88.

BEST'S *Grampians, Victoria, Australia*   Small winery run by Viv Thomson, who makes attractive wines from estate vineyards first planted in 1868. Tasty, clear-fruited Great Western Bin No. 0 Shiraz★ and Great Western Cabernet★ are good, and the Riesling★ shows flashes of brilliance. Tropical-fruity, finely balanced Chardonnay★ is variable, delicious at best; Thomson Family Reserve★★ is a super-Shiraz. Best years: (Thomson Family Reserve) (2001) 99 98 97 96 95 **94 92**.

BETHEL HEIGHTS *Willamette Valley AVA, Oregon, USA*   OREGON winery with a reputation for stylish Pinot Noirs★★ which are delicious young but can also age surprisingly well; the Southeast Block Reserve★★★ is the star. Subtle Chardonnay Reserve★ is gathering acclaim too, and Pinot Gris★★ filled with citrus and mineral scents is crisp and immensely drinkable. Best years: (Pinot Noir) (2002) 01 00 99 98 **96**.

CH. BEYCHEVELLE★ *St-Julien AC, 4ème Cru Classé, Haut-Médoc, Bordeaux, France*   At its best, this beautiful château can make wine of Second Growth quality. The wine has a charming softness even when young, but takes at least a decade to mature into the cedarwood and blackcurrant flavour for which ST-JULIEN is famous. In the best years it is worth its high price and, after a period of inconsistency, quality has become more regular since the late 1990s. Second wine: Amiral de Beychevelle. Best years: 2001 00 99 98 96 **95 90** 89.

BEYERSKLOOF *Stellenbosch WO, South Africa*   Red-wine maestro Beyers Truter co-owns this property – recently merged with nearby Bouwland – in association with the Krige brothers of KANONKOP and a UK-based partner. The striking, supple Cabernet Sauvignon-based Beyerskloof★★ and juicily ripe Pinotage★ remain as good as ever, and have been joined by a succulent, refined Pinotage-Cabernet-Merlot blend called Synergy and flavoursome Pinotage rosé. Best years: (Beyerskloof) 2000 **99 98** 97 96 95 94 93.

BIANCO DI CUSTOZA DOC *Veneto, Italy*   Dry white wine similar to neighbouring SOAVE. Drink young. Best producers: Cavalchina★, Gorgo★, Montresor★, Le Vigne di San Pietro★.

BIENVENUES-BÂTARD-MONTRACHET AC See Bâtard-Montrachet.

BIERZO DO *Castilla y León, Spain*   Sandwiched between the rainy mountains of GALICIA and the arid plains of CASTILLA Y LEON, Bierzo makes mostly commonplace reds. However, the recent arrival of

Alvaro PALACIOS, of PRIORAT fame, with his inspired Corullón★★ red sheds an entirely new and exciting light on the potential of the Mencía grape. Best producers: Pérez Caramés, Estefania, Descendientes de José Palacios★★, Pittacum★, Prada a Tope, Dominio de Tares★, Valtuille★, Castro Ventosa.

JOSEF BIFFAR *Deidesheim, Pfalz, Germany* Gerhard Biffar runs this reliable estate, making dry and sweet Rieslings from top sites in Deidesheim, Ruppertsberg and WACHENHEIM. Consistent ★ quality from recent vintages. Drink young or cellar for 5 years or more. Best years: (Riesling Spätlese) (2002) 01 **99** 98 **97 96 93** 92.

BILLECART-SALMON *Champagne AC, Champagne, France* Top-notch CHAMPAGNE house and one of the few still under family control. The wines are extremely elegant, fresh and delicate, becoming simply irresistible with age. The non-vintage Brut★★, non-vintage Brut Rosé★★, Blanc de Blancs★★★, vintage Cuvée N-F Billecart★★★ and Cuvée Elisabeth Salmon Rosé★★ are all excellent. Best years: (1997) (96) 95 **91 90 89** 88 86 85 82.

BINGEN *Rheinhessen, Germany* This is a small town and also a Bereich, the vineyards of which fall in both the NAHE and RHEINHESSEN. The best vineyard in the town is the Scharlachberg, which produces some exciting wines, stinging with racy acidity and the whiff of coal smoke. Best producer: Villa Sachsen. Best years: (Riesling Spätlese) (2002) 01 **99** 98 **97 96** 90.

BIONDI-SANTI *Brunello di Montalcino DOCG, Tuscany, Italy* Franco Biondi-Santi's Il Greppo estate has, in less than a century, created both a legend and an international standing for BRUNELLO DI MONTALCINO. The modern dynamism of the zone owes more to other producers, however, since quality has slipped over the last 2 decades. Yet the very expensive Riserva★★, with formidable levels of extract, tannin and acidity, deserves a minimum 10 years' further aging after release before serious judgement is passed on it. Franco's son, Jacopo, has created his own range of wines, including Sassoalloro★★, a barrique-aged Sangiovese, and Sangiovese-Cabernet-Merlot blend Schidione★★. Best years: (Riserva) 1990 88 85 **83 82 75 71** 64 55 45 25.

BLAGNY AC *Côte de Beaune, Burgundy, France* The red wine from this tiny hamlet above MEURSAULT and PULIGNY-MONTRACHET can be fair value, if you like a rustic Burgundy. Actually much more Chardonnay than Pinot Noir is grown here, but this is sold as Puligny-Montrachet, Meursault Premier Cru or Meursault-Blagny. Best producers: R Ampeau★, Lamy-Pillot★, Matrot★. Best years: (2002) 99 **97 96** 95.

DOM. PAUL BLANCK *Alsace AC, Alsace, France* Philippe Blanck and his winemaker cousin Frédéric had a run of good vintages in the 1990s and the Blanck wines have become truly exciting. From a huge range, Vieilles Vignes Riesling★★★ and Gewurztraminer★★★ from the Furstentum Grand Cru stand out. Riesling Schlossberg★★★ and Pinot Gris Altenberg★★ also offer depth and finesse. Best years: (Grand Cru Riesling) (2002) 01 00 99 98 **97 96 95** 94 93 92 90 89 88.

BLANQUETTE DE LIMOUX AC *Languedoc-Roussillon, France* Sharp, refreshing fizz from the Mauzac grape, which makes up a minimum 90% of the wine and gives it its striking 'green apple skin' flavour –

the balance is made up of Chardonnay and Chenin Blanc. The traditional (Champagne) method is used to create the sparkle. The more rustic *méthode rurale*, finishing off the original fermentation inside the bottle, is used under a separate appellation – Blanquette Méthode Ancestrale. Best producers: Collin, Fourn★, Guinot Martinolles★, SIEUR D'ARQUES★, les Terres Blanches. See also Créman de Limoux AC and pages 258–9.

WOLF BLASS *Barossa Valley, South Australia*   The Wolf Blass label, with its huge range, is the cornerstone of Beringer Blass, one of the big four Aussie companies. The wines do still faintly reflect the founder's dictum that they must be easy to enjoy, though I think they could do better. The reds show overt oak, sometimes clumsy, and occasionally capture the traditional Blass mint and blackcurrant charm. Whites are on the oaky side, except for the Rieslings, which are good, though sweeter and less vibrant than they used to be, including star Gold Label Riesling★. Black Label★, the top label for reds released at 4 years old, is expensive but good. Regional varietals under the Blass label really should have made more effort at tasting genuinely regional. The Eaglehawk range is reliable quaffing wine. Best years: (Black Label) (2001) 99 98 97 **96 95** 91 90 **88 86**.

BLAUBURGUNDER See Pinot Noir.

BLAUER LEMBERGER See Blaufränkisch.

BLAUFRÄNKISCH Good, ripe Blaufränkisch has a taste similar to raspberries and white pepper or even beetroot. Hungarian in origin, it does well in Austria, where it is the principal red wine grape of BURGENLAND. The Hungarian vineyards (where it is called Kékfrankos) are mostly just across the border on the other side of the Neusiedlersee. Called Lemberger in Germany, where almost all of it is grown in WURTTEMBERG. Also successful in WASHINGTON STATE.

BOEKENHOUTSKLOOF *Franschhoek WO, South Africa*   Perched high in the FRANSCHHOEK mountains, this small winery is named after the surrounding Cape beech trees. Marc Kent's punchy Syrah★★ resonates with black pepper, chocolate, plum and herb savouriness; his Cabernet Sauvignon★★ is deep and powerful and built for the long term. The barrel-fermented Semillon★★, from 100-year-old bush vines, is scented and sophisticated and could become a classic. Second label Porcupine Ridge range offers cheaper but excellent, more fruit-focused drinking. Best years (Cabernet Sauvignon): 2000 **99 98** 97.

BOISSET *Burgundy, France*   Jean Claude Boisset bought his first vineyards in 1964 and began a négociant company whose extraordinary success has enabled him to swallow up many other long-established names such as JAFFELIN, Ponelle, Ropiteau and Heritier Guyot in the COTE D'OR, Moreau in CHABLIS, Cellier des Samsons and Mommessin in BEAUJOLAIS and others elsewhere in France. None of these companies has delivered much in the way of quality wine to date. New projects in LANGUEDOC, Canada and Uruguay. See also Domaine de la Vougeraie.

BOLGHERI DOC *Tuscany, Italy*   In 1994, this zone near the coast south of Livorno extended its DOC beyond simple white and rosé to cover red wines based on Cabernet, Merlot and Sangiovese in various combinations, while creating a special sub-zone category for SASSICAIA. The DOC Rosso Superiore now covers wines from the prestigious estates of Grattamacco★★, Le Macchiole★★, ORNELLAIA★★★, Michele

Satta★★ and ANTINORI's Guado al Tasso★★. Best years (since 1994): (reds) (2001) 00 99 98 97 **96 95 94**.

BOLLINGER *Champagne AC, Champagne, France* One of the great CHAMPAGNE houses, with good non-vintage (Special Cuvée★) and vintage wines (Grande Année★★★), made in a full, rich, rather old-fashioned style that you love or hate. (Bollinger is one of the few houses to ferment its base wine in barrels.) It also produces a range of rarer vintages, including a Vintage RD★★★ and Vieilles Vignes Françaises Blanc de Noirs★★ from ancient, ungrafted Pinot Noir vines. Best years: (Grande Année) (1996) 95 **92 90 89 88 85 82 79**.

CH. LE BON PASTEUR★★ *Pomerol AC, Bordeaux, France* Small château which has established an excellent reputation under the ownership of Michel Rolland, one of Bordeaux's leading winemakers. The wines are expensive, but they are always deliciously soft and full of lush fruit. Best years: 2001 00 99 **98 95 94 93 90 89 88 85 83 82**.

BONNES-MARES AC *Grand Cru, Côte de Nuits, Burgundy, France* A large Grand Cru straddling the communes of CHAMBOLLE-MUSIGNY and MOREY-ST-DENIS. Less famous than many Grands Crus, but commendably consistent over the last few decades. Bonnes-Mares generally has a deep, ripe, smoky plum fruit, which starts rich and chewy and matures over 10–20 years. Best producers: d'Auvenay (Dom. LEROY)★★★, BOUCHARD PERE ET FILS★★, Champy★★, DROUHIN★★, DUJAC★★★, Robert Groffier★★★, JADOT★★★, D Laurent★★, J-F Mugnier★★, ROUMIER★★★, VOGUE★★★, VOUGERAIE★★. Best years: (2002) (01) 00 99 98 97 96 95 **93 90 89 88**.

CH. BONNET *Entre-Deux-Mers AC, Bordeaux, France* This region's pioneering estate for quality and consistency. Large volumes of good, fruity, affordable Entre-Deux-Mers★, and BORDEAUX AC rosé and red, particularly the barrel-aged Merlot-Cabernet Réserve★. Drink this at 3–4 years and the others young. A new special cuvée Dominus★ was launched with the 2000 vintage. Owner André Lurton is also the proprietor of La LOUVIERE and other properties in PESSAC-LEOGNAN.

BONNEZEAUX AC *Loire Valley, France* One of France's great sweet wines, Bonnezeaux is a zone within the larger COTEAUX DU LAYON AC. Like SAUTERNES, the wine is influenced by noble rot, but the flavours are different, as only Chenin Blanc is used. Extensive recent plantings have made quality less reliable. It can age very well in good vintages. Best producers: M Angeli★★★, Fesles★★★, Godineau★★, des Grandes Vignes★★, Petit Val★★, Petits Quarts★★, René Renou★★, Terrebrune★★, la Varière★★. Best years: (2002) 01 00 99 **97** 96 **95 94 93 90 89 88 85 83 79 78 76 71 64 59 47**.

BONNY DOON *Santa Cruz Mountains AVA, California, USA* Iconoclastic operation under Randall Grahm, who revels in the unexpected. He has a particular love for RHONE, Italian and Spanish varietals and for fanciful brand names: Le Cigare Volant★★ is a blend of Grenache and Syrah and is Grahm's homage to CHATEAUNEUF-DU-PAPE. Old Telegram★★ is 100% Mourvèdre. Particularly delightful are his Ca' del Solo Italianate wines, especially a bone-dry Malvasia Bianca★ and a white blend, Il Pescatore★, his answer to VERDICCHIO. He also makes a lovely Syrah★★, Cardinal Zin★ Zinfandel and a pure Riesling from WASHINGTON. Grahm has now spread his net even wider and has 3 new wines from European vineyards: MADIRAN★, a Vin de Pays d'Oc Syrah and an Uva di Troia from PUGLIA. Best years: (Old Telegram) (2001) (00) 99 98 97 **96 95 94 91 90**.

BORDEAUX RED WINES

Bordeaux, France

 This large area of South-West France, centred on the historic city of Bordeaux, produces a larger volume of fine red wine than any other French region. Wonderful Bordeaux-style wines are produced in California, Australia, South Africa and South America, but the home team's top performers still just about keep the upstarts at bay. Around 600 million bottles of red wine a year are produced here. The best wines, known as the Classed Growths, account for a tiny percentage of this figure, but some of their lustre rubs off on the lesser names, making this one of the most popular wine styles.

GRAPE VARIETIES

Bordeaux's reds are commonly divided into 'right' and 'left' bank wines. On the left bank of the Gironde estuary, the red wines are dominated by the Cabernet Sauvignon grape, with varying proportions of Cabernet Franc, Merlot and Petit Verdot. At best they are austere but perfumed with blackcurrant and cedarwood. The most important left bank areas are the Haut-Médoc (especially the communes of Margaux, St-Julien, Pauillac and St-Estèphe) and, south of the city of Bordeaux, the ACs of Pessac-Léognan and Graves. On the right bank, Merlot is the predominant grape, which generally makes the resulting wines more supple and fleshy than those of the left bank. The key areas for Merlot-based wines are St-Émilion and Pomerol.

CLASSIFICATIONS

Red Bordeaux is made all over the region. At its most basic, the wine is simply labelled Bordeaux or Bordeaux Supérieur. Above this are the more specific ACs covering sub-areas (such as the Haut-Médoc) and individual communes (such as Pomerol, St-Émilion or Margaux). Single-estate Crus Bourgeois are the next rung up on the quality ladder, followed by the Crus Classés (Classed Growths) of the Médoc, Graves and St-Émilion. The famous classification of 1855 ranked the top red wines of the Médoc (plus one from Graves) into 5 tiers, from First to Fifth Growths (Crus); there has been only one change, in 1973, promoting Mouton-Rothschild to First Growth status. Since the 1950s the Graves/Pessac-Léognan region has had its own classification, for red and white wines. St-Émilion's classification (for red wines only) has been revised several times, the last modification being in 1996; the possibility of re-grading can help to maintain quality. Curiously, Pomerol, home of Château Pétrus, arguably the most famous red wine in the world, has no official pecking order. Many top Bordeaux châteaux also make 'second wines', which are cheaper versions of their Grands Vins.

See also BORDEAUX, BORDEAUX-COTES DE FRANCS, BORDEAUX SUPERIEUR, CANON-FRONSAC, COTES DE BOURG, COTES DE CASTILLON, FRONSAC, GRAVES, HAUT-MEDOC, LALANDE-DE-POMEROL, LISTRAC-MEDOC, LUSSAC-ST-EMILION, MARGAUX, MEDOC, MONTAGNE-ST-EMILION, MOULIS, PAUILLAC, PESSAC-LEOGNAN, POMEROL, PREMIERES COTES DE BLAYE, PREMIERES COTES DE BORDEAUX, PUISSEGUIN-ST-EMILION, ST-EMILION, ST-ESTEPHE, ST-GEORGES-ST-EMILION, ST-JULIEN; and individual châteaux.

BEST PRODUCERS

Graves, Pessac-Léognan
Dom. de CHEVALIER, HAUT-
BAILLY, HAUT-BRION, la LOUVIERE,
MALARTIC-LAGRAVIERE, la MISSION-
HAUT-BRION, PAPE-CLEMENT,
SMITH-HAUT-LAFITTE.

Margaux BRANE-CANTENAC,
FERRIERE, MALESCOT ST-EXUPERY,
Ch. MARGAUX, PALMER, RAUZAN-
SEGLA.

Pauillac GRAND-PUY-LACOSTE,
LAFITE-ROTHSCHILD,
LATOUR, LYNCH-BAGES,
MOUTON-ROTHSCHILD, PICHON-
LONGUEVILLE, PICHON-
LONGUEVILLE-LALANDE,
PONTET-CANET.

Pomerol le BON PASTEUR,
Certan-de-May, Clinet,
la CONSEILLANTE, l'EGLISE-CLINET,
l'EVANGILE, la FLEUR-PETRUS,
GAZIN, LAFLEUR, LATOUR-A-
POMEROL, PETIT-VILLAGE, PETRUS,
le PIN, TROTANOY, VIEUX-CHATEAU-
CERTAN.

St-Émilion ANGELUS, l'ARROSEE,
AUSONE, BEAU-SEJOUR BECOT,
BELAIR, CANON, CANON-LA-
GAFFELIERE, CHEVAL BLANC, Clos
Fourtet, la Dominique, FIGEAC,
Grand Mayne, MAGDELAINE,
MONBOUSQET, La Mondotte,
PAVIE, PAVIE-MACQUIN, Rol
Valentin, TERTRE-ROTEBOEUF,
TROPLONG-MONDOT, VALANDRAUD.

St-Estèphe CALON-SEGUR, COS
D'ESTOURNEL, HAUT-MARBUZET,
LAFON-ROCHET, MONTROSE.

St-Julien BRANAIRE, DUCRU-
BEAUCAILLOU, GRUAUD-LAROSE,
LAGRANGE, LANGOA-BARTON,
LEOVILLE-BARTON, LEOVILLE-LAS-
CASES, LEOVILLE-POYFERRE,
ST-PIERRE, TALBOT.

BORDEAUX WHITE WINES

Bordeaux, France

This is France's largest fine wine region but, except for the sweet wines of Sauternes and Barsac, Bordeaux's international reputation is based solely on its reds. From 52% of the vineyard area in 1970, white wines now represent only 12% of the present 118,000ha (291,460 acres) of vines. Given the size of the region, the diversity of Bordeaux's white wines should come as no surprise. There are dry, medium and sweet styles, ranging from dreary to some of the most sublime white wines of all. Bordeaux's temperate southern climate – moderated by the influence of the Atlantic and of 2 rivers, the Dordogne and the Garonne, is ideal for white wine production, particularly south of the city along the banks of the Garonne.

GRAPE VARIETIES

Sauvignon Blanc and Sémillon, the most important white grapes, are both varieties of considerable character and are usually blended together. They are backed up by smaller quantities of other grapes, the most notable of which is Muscadelle (unrelated to Muscat), which lends perfume to sweet wines and spiciness to dry.

DRY WINES

With the introduction of new technology and new ideas, many of them influenced by the New World, Bordeaux has become one of France's most exciting white wine areas. The wines have improved beyond recognition over the last decade. At their best, dry Bordeaux whites have fresh fruit flavours of apples, peaches and apricots, balanced by a light grassiness.

SWEET WINES

Bordeaux's most famous whites are its sweet wines made from grapes affected by noble rot, particularly those from Sauternes and Barsac. The noble rot concentrates the flavours, producing rich, honeyed wines replete with pineapple and peach flavours, and which develop a nut-oiliness and greater honeyed richness with age. On the other side of the Garonne river, Cadillac, Loupiac and Ste-Croix-du-Mont also make sweet wines; these rarely attain the richness or complexity of a top Sauternes, but they are considerably less expensive.

CLASSIFICATIONS

The two largest dry white wine ACs in Bordeaux are Bordeaux Blanc and Entre-Deux-Mers. There are plenty of good dry wines in the Graves and Pessac-Léognan regions; the Pessac-Léognan AC, created in 1987, contains all the dry white Classed Growths. The great sweet wines of Sauternes and Barsac were classified as First or Second Growths in 1855.

See also BARSAC, BORDEAUX, BORDEAUX-COTES DE FRANCS, BORDEAUX SUPERIEUR, CADILLAC, CERONS, COTES DE BLAYE, COTES DE BOURG, ENTRE-DEUX-MERS, GRAVES, GRAVES SUPERIEURES, LOUPIAC, PESSAC-LEOGNAN, PREMIERES COTES DE BLAYE, PREMIERES COTES DE BORDEAUX, STE-CROIX-DU-MONT, SAUTERNES; and individual châteaux.

BEST YEARS

(dry) 2001 00 **98 96 95 94 90 89 88 85**; (sweet) (2002) 01 99 **98 97 96 95 90 89 88 86 83**

BEST PRODUCERS

Dry wines

Pessac-Léognan Dom. de CHEVALIER, Couhins-Lurton, FIEUZAL, HAUT-BRION, LATOUR-MARTILLAC, LAVILLE-HAUT-BRION, la LOUVIERE, MALARTIC-LAGRAVIERE, SMITH-HAUT-LAFITTE; *Graves* Ardennes, Brondelle, Chantegrive, Clos Floridène, Dom. la Grave, Magneau, Rahoul, Respide-Médeville, Seuil, Vieux-Ch.-Gaubert, Villa Bel Air.

Entre-Deux-Mers BONNET, de Fontenille, Nardique-la-Gravière, Ste-Marie, Toutigeac, Turcaud.

Bordeaux AC l'Abbaye de Ste-Ferme, CARSIN, DOISY-DAENE (Sec), LYNCH-BAGES, Ch. MARGAUX (Pavillon Blanc), REYNON, Roquefort, Thieuley, Tour de Mirambeau.

Premières Côtes de Blaye Charron (Acacia), Haut-Bertinerie, Cave des Hauts de Gironde co-op, Tourtes (Prestige).

Sweet wines

Sauternes and Barsac CLIMENS, Clos Haut-Peyraguey, COUTET, DOISY-DAENE, DOISY-VEDRINES, FARGUES, GILETTE, GUIRAUD, LAFAURIE-PEYRAGUEY, NAIRAC, Raymond-Lafon, RIEUSSEC, Sigalas-Rabaud, SUDUIRAUT, la TOUR BLANCHE, YQUEM.

Cadillac Cayla, Manos, Mémoires.

Cérons Ch. de Cérons, Grand Enclos du Ch. de Cérons.

Loupiac Clos Jean, Cros, Mémoires.

Ste-Croix-du-Mont Loubens, Pavillon, la Rame.

BORDEAUX AC *Bordeaux, France*   One of the most important ACs in France. It can be applied to reds and rosés as well as to the dry, medium and sweet white wines of the entire Gironde region. Most of the best wines are allowed more specific district or commune ACs (such as MARGAUX or SAUTERNES) but a vast amount of Bordeaux's wine – delicious, atrocious and everything in between – is sold as Bordeaux AC. At its best, straight red Bordeaux is marked by bone-dry grassy fruit and an attractive earthy edge, but far more frequently the wines are tannic and raw – and often overpriced. Good examples usually benefit from a year or so of aging. Bordeaux Blanc, once a byword for flabby, fruitless and oversulphured brews, is joining the modern world with an increasing number of refreshing, pleasant, clean wines. These may be labelled as Bordeaux Sauvignon. Drink as young as possible. Bordeaux Clairet is a pale red wine, virtually rosé but with a little more substance. Best producers: (reds) BONNET★, Dourthe (Numéro 1), Ducla, Sirius, Thieuley★, Tour de Mirambeau, le Trébuchet; (whites) l'Abbaye de Ste-Ferme★, CARSIN★, DOISY-DAENE★, Dourthe (Numéro 1), d:vin★, LYNCH-BAGES★, MARGAUX (Pavillon Blanc★★), Premius, REYNON★, Roquefort★, Sours, Thieuley★, Tour de Mirambeau★. See also pages 68–71.

BORDEAUX-CÔTES DE FRANCS AC *Bordeaux, France*   There's been quite a bit of investment in this tiny area east of ST-EMILION, and the top wines are looking good value. The Thienpont family (Ch. Puygueraud) continues to be the driving force here. Best producers: les Charmes-Godard★, Francs★, Laclaverie★, Marsau, Moulin la Pitié, Pelan★, la Prade★, Puygueraud★★. Best years: 2001 00 **98 97 96 95 94 90**.

BORDEAUX SUPÉRIEUR AC *Bordeaux, France*   This AC covers the same area as the BORDEAUX AC but the wines must have an extra 0.5% of alcohol, a lower yield and a longer period of maturation. Many of the best petits châteaux are labelled Bordeaux Supérieur. Best producers: (reds) l'Abbaye de Ste-Ferme, Barreyre★, de Bouillerot★, de Courteillac★, Laville, Parenchère★, Penin★, le Pin Beausoleil★, Reignac★, de Seguin.

LUIGI BOSCA *Mendoza, Argentina*   Owned by the Arizú family, and located in MENDOZA's Luján de Cuyo, this winery has 400ha (990 acres) planted mainly with Malbec, Cabernet Sauvignon, Syrah, Chardonnay and Sauvignon Blanc. Try the powerful, mineral Finca Los Nobles Chardonnay★ from very old vines at 1300m (4265ft) above sea level; or the dense and chocolaty Finca Los Nobles Malbec-Verdot★★, one of the finest Malbec-based wines in Argentina.

BOSCARELLI *Vino Nobile di Montepulciano DOCG, Tuscany, Italy*   Arguably Montepulciano's best producer, Paola de Ferrari and her sons Luca and Niccolò, with guidance from star enologist Maurizio Castelli, craft rich and stylish reds. VINO NOBILE★★, Riserva del Nocio★★ and the barrique-aged Sangiovese Boscarelli★★ are all brilliant. Best years: (2000) 99 **98 97 96 95 94 93 91 90 88 85**.

BOSCHENDAL *Paarl WO, South Africa*   Red wine production here has shot up in the past 3 years; chief among them are Shiraz, Merlot and a Cabernet Sauvignon-based BORDEAUX blend called Grand Reserve. Flavoursome Chardonnay and Sauvignon Blanc lead the whites. Le Grand Pavillon NV and rich vintage Boschendal Brut remain sound Cap Classique bubblies.

BOUCHARD FINLAYSON *Walker Bay, Overberg WO, South Africa*   Winemaker Peter Finlayson continues to produce dry but classy Pinot Noirs Galpin Peak★ and barrel selection Tête de Cuvée★. Hannibal, a new Sangiovese-Pinot Noir blend reflects his love of Italian varieties.

Chardonnays (Kaimansgaat★ and home-grown Missionvale★) are full, nutty and passably Burgundian. Sauvignon Blanc★ is elegant and fresh. Best years: (Pinot Noir) (2002) 01 **00 99 98 97 96 95**.

BOUCHARD PÈRE ET FILS *Beaune, Burgundy, France* Important merchant and vineyard owner, with vines in some of Burgundy's most spectacular sites, including CORTON, CORTON-CHARLEMAGNE, Chevalier-Montrachet and le MONTRACHET. The firm is owned by Champagne whiz-kid Joseph HENRIOT, who is starting to realize the full potential here. Wines from the company's own vineyards are sold under the Domaines du Château de Beaune label. Don't touch anything pre-1996. Best years: (top reds) (2002) (01) 00 99 98 **97 96**.

BOUCHES-DU-RHÔNE, VIN DE PAYS DES *Provence, France* Wines from 3 areas: the coast, a zone around Aix-en-Provence and the Camargue. Mainly full-bodied, spicy reds, but rosé can be good. Best producers: Ch. Bas, de Boujeu, l'Île St-Pierre, Mas de Rey, TREVALLON★★, Valdition. Best years: (reds) **2001 00 99 98 97 96**.

BOURGOGNE AC *Burgundy, France* Bourgogne is the French name anglicized as 'Burgundy'. This generic AC mops up all the Burgundian wine with no AC of its own, resulting in massive differences in style and quality. The best wines will usually come from a single grower's vineyards just outside the main village ACs of the COTE D'OR. In today's world of high prices such wines may be the only way we can afford the joys of fine Burgundy. If the wine is from a grower, the flavours should follow a regional style. However, if the address on the label is that of a négociant, the wine could be from anywhere in Burgundy. Pinot Noir is the main red grape, but Gamay from a declassified BEAUJOLAIS cru is, absurdly, allowed. Red Bourgogne is usually light, fruity in an upfront strawberry and cherry way, and should be drunk young (within 2–3 years). The rosé (from Pinot Noir) can be pleasant but little is produced. Bourgogne Blanc is a bone-dry Chardonnay wine and most should be drunk within 2 years. Bourgogne Passe-tout-Grains is made from Gamay with a minimum 33% of Pinot Noir, while Bourgogne Grand Ordinaire is the most basic appellation of all – rarely more than a quaffing wine, drunk in local bars. Best producers: (reds/growers) COCHE-DURY★, Dugat-Py★★, J-P Fichet★, Germain★, LAFARGE★, MEO-CAMUZET★★, Pierre Morey★, Patrice RION★★, ROUMIER★; (reds/merchants) DROUHIN★, GIRARDIN★, JADOT★, LABOURE-ROI, Maison LEROY★★, N Potel★★; (reds/co-ops) BUXY★, les Caves des Hautes-Côtes★; (whites/growers) M Bouzereau★, Boyer-Martenot★, COCHE-DURY★, Henri Gouges★★, P Javillier★★, Ch. de Meursault, Guy Roulot★, SAUZET★, TOLLOT-BEAUT★; (whites/merchants) DROUHIN★, FAIVELEY★, JADOT★, Olivier LEFLAIVE, RODET★; (whites/co-ops) BUXY, les Caves des Hautes-Côtes. Best years: (reds) (2002) 01 **00 99**; (whites) (2002) 01 **00 99**. See also pages 76–9.

BOURGOGNE ALIGOTÉ AC See Aligoté.

BOURGOGNE-CÔTE CHALONNAISE AC *Côte Chalonnaise, Burgundy, France* These vineyards have gained in importance, mainly because of spiralling prices on the COTE D'OR to the north. This AC covers vineyards to the west of Chalon-sur-Saône around the villages of Bouzeron, RULLY, MERCUREY, GIVRY and MONTAGNY. Best producers: X Besson, BUXY Co-op★, Villaine★. Best years: (2002) **01 99**.

BOURGOGNE-HAUTES-CÔTES DE BEAUNE AC *Burgundy, France* The hills behind the great COTE DE BEAUNE have been a source of affordable Burgundy since the 1970s. The red wines are lean but drinkable, as is the slightly sharp Chardonnay. Best producers: D & F Clair★, les Caves des Hautes-Côtes★, J-Y Devevey★, L Jacob★, J-L Joillot★, Ch. de Mercey★/RODET, Naudin-Ferrand★, M Serveau★. Best years: (reds) (2002) 01 **00 99**; (whites) (2002) 01 **00 99**.

BOURGOGNE-HAUTES-CÔTES DE NUITS AC *Burgundy, France* Attractive, lightweight wines from the hills behind the CÔTE DE NUITS. The reds are best, with an attractive cherry and plum flavour. The whites tend to be rather dry and flinty. Best producers: (reds) FAIVELEY★, A-F GROS★, M GROS★, A Guyon★, les Caves des Hautes-Côtes★, B Hudelot★, JAYER-GILLES★★, THOMAS-MOILLARD★; (whites) les Caves des Hautes-Côtes★, Y Chaley★, Champy★, J-Y Devevey★, E Hudelot★, JAYER-GILLES★★, Thévenot-le-Brun★, THOMAS-MOILLARD★, A Verdet★. Best years: (reds) (2002) 01 **00 99**; (whites) (2002) 01 **00 99**.

BOURGOGNE-IRANCY AC See Irancy AC.

BOURGUEIL AC *Loire Valley, France* Fine red wine from between Tours and Angers. Made with Cabernet Franc, topped up with a little Cabernet Sauvignon; in hot years results can be superb. Given 5–10 years of age, the wines can develop a wonderful raspberry fragrance. Best producers: (reds) l'Abbaye★, Y Amirault★, Audebort (estate wines★), T Boucard★, P Breton★, la Butte★, la Chevalerie, Max Cognard★, DRUET★★, Forges★, Lamé-Delisle-Boucard★, la Lande/Delaunay★, Nau Frères★, Ouches, Raguenières★. Best years: (2002) 01 00 **97 96 95 90 89**. See also St-Nicolas-de-Bourgueil.

BOUVET-LADUBAY *Saumur AC, Loire Valley, France* Sparkling wine producer owned by the Champagne house TAITTINGER. The basic range (Bouvet Brut, Bouvet Rosé) is good. Cuvée Saphir, the top-selling wine, is over-sweet, but Trésor (Blanc★ and Rosé★), fermented in oak casks, is very good. Weird and wonderful Rubis★ sparkling red is worth trying. The Nonpareils★ range of ANJOU and vin de pays still reds is also good.

BOUVIER Austrian and Slovenian grape short on acidity and so mainly used for sweet to ultra-sweet wines, where it achieves richness but rarely manages to offer any other complexity. Best producers: Weinkellerei Burgenland, KRACHER★, OPITZ★.

BOWEN ESTATE *Coonawarra, South Australia* Doug Bowen can make some of COONAWARRA's best peppery Shiraz★★ and blackcurranty Cabernet★; however, recent releases have seemed less consistent. Chardonnay★ is a good Coonawarra example. Best years: (Shiraz) (2000) **98 97 96 94 93 92 91**.

BOYAR ESTATES *Bulgaria* The leading distributor of Bulgarian wines, selling more than 65 million bottles worldwide each year. It also has extensive vineyard holdings of 1000ha (2470 acres), and wineries at Iambol, Shumen, Sliven (new, state-of-the-art Blueridge) and – following its merger with Vinprom – at Rousse. Its long-term strategy is to have as much control as possible in the vineyards. So far Boyar has stressed its internationalist intentions, with a range of quite attractive young reds led by Cabernet Sauvignon and Merlot, and some decent clean young whites.

BRACHETTO Piedmontese grape revived in dry versions and in sweet, frothy types with a Muscat-like perfume, as exemplified by Brachetto d'Acqui DOCG. Best producers: (dry) Correggia★, Scarpa★; (Brachetto d'Acqui) BANFI★, Braida★, G Marenco★.

CH. BRANAIRE★★ *St-Julien AC, 4ème Cru Classé, Haut-Médoc, Bordeaux, France* After a long period of mediocrity Branaire chose the difficult 93 and 94 vintages to signal its renewed ambition. Subsequent vintages have confirmed a welcome return to full, soft, chocolaty form. Best years: 2001 00 99 98 96 **95 94**.

BRAND'S *Coonawarra, South Australia* COONAWARRA firm, owned by MCWILLIAM'S, with 100ha (250 acres) of new vineyards as well as some ancient vines now over 100 years old. Improved viticulture, greater investment in oak and chief winemaker Jim Brayne's influence have lifted standards dramatically. Ripe Cabernet★★ and Cabernet-Merlot★ are increasingly attractive; Patron's Reserve Cabernet★★ is excellent. New life has been breathed into Shiraz★, and the opulent Stentiford's Reserve★★ shows how good Coonawarra Shiraz can be. Special Release Merlot★★ is among Australia's best examples of the variety. Best years: (reds) (2001) 00 99 98 **97** 96 **94 90**.

CH. BRANE-CANTENAC★★ *Margaux AC, 2ème Cru Classé, Haut-Médoc, Bordeaux, France* After a drab period, Brane-Cantenac returned to form during the late 1990s. Henri Lurton has taken over the family property and is making some superb wines, particularly the 2000. The property now merits its 2nd Growth status, and I am delighted that I can once more enjoy what used to be one of my favourite Bordeaux. Best years: 2001 00 99 98 96 **95 90**.

BRAUNEBERG *Mosel, Germany* Small village with 2 famous vineyard sites, Juffer and Juffer Sonnenuhr, whose wines have a honeyed richness and creamy gentleness rare in the Mosel. Best producers: Bastgen★★, Fritz HAAG★★★, Willi Haag★, Paulinshof★, M F RICHTER★★. Best years: (Riesling Spätlese) (2002) 01 **99** 98 **97** 95 94 **93 90**.

BREAKY BOTTOM *Sussex, England* Small vineyard in the South Downs near Lewes, so badly flooded in 2000 that it is only now getting fully back in action. Peter Hall is a quirky, passionate grower, making dry, nutty Seyval Blanc★ that becomes creamy and BURGUNDY-like after 3–4 years and crisp Müller-Thurgau★ full of hedgerow pungency. Sparkling Seyval Blanc★ is delicious, but there is a shift to fizz made from more classic varieties, using early-ripening clones of Chardonnay.

GEORG BREUER *Rüdesheim, Rheingau, Germany* Medium-sized estate run by Bernhard Breuer, producing quality dry Riesling from vines on the RUDESHEIM Berg Schlossberg★★, Berg Rottland★★ and RAUENTHAL Nonnenberg★★. Also a barrique-aged Pinot Gris and Pinot Noir. Best years: (Berg Schlossberg) (2002) 01 00 99 98 **97** 96 **94 93 90 86 83**.

BRIGHT BROTHERS *Ribatejo, Portugal* The Fiúza-Bright winemaking operation is located in the town of Almeirim in the RIBATEJO and Fiúza-labelled wines are made from local vineyards planted to both Portuguese and French varieties. Australian Peter Bright also sources grapes (exclusively Portuguese varieties) from, chiefly, Palmela (Reserva★) and DOURO (TFN★) for the Bright Brothers label. Bright also makes a range of wines for PENAFLOR in Argentina.

JEAN-MARC BROCARD *Chablis AC, Burgundy, France* Dynamic wine-maker who has built up this 80ha (200-acre) domaine almost from scratch. Except for Premiers Crus (including Montée de la Tonnerre★, Montmains★★) and slow-evolving Grands Crus (les Clos★★ stands out), all the fruit is machine-picked and vinified in steel tanks. Vieilles Vignes★ is usually the best of the regular CHABLIS. Brocard also produces a range of BOURGOGNE Blancs★ from different soil types. Best years: (2002) 01 **99**.

BURGUNDY RED WINES

Burgundy, France

Rich in history and gastronomic tradition, the region of Burgundy (Bourgogne in French) covers a vast tract of eastern France, running from Auxerre, southeast of Paris, down to the city of Lyon. As with its white wines, Burgundy's red wines are extremely diverse. The explanation for this lies partly in the fickle nature of Pinot Noir, the area's principal red grape, and partly in the historical imbalance of supply and demand between growers – who grow the grapes and make and bottle much of the best wine – and merchants, whose efforts originally established the reputation of the wines internationally.

WINE STYLES

Pinot Noir shows many different flavour profiles according to climate, soil and winemaking. The reds from around Auxerre (Épineuil, Irancy) in the north will be light, chalky and strawberry-flavoured. Also light, though more rustic and earthy, are the reds of the Mâconnais in the south, while the Côte Chalonnaise offers solid reds from Givry and Mercurey.

The top reds come from the Côte d'Or, the heartland of Burgundy. Flavours sweep through strawberry, raspberry, damson and cherry – in young wines – to a wild, magnificent maturity of Oriental spices, chocolate, mushrooms and truffles. The greatest of all – the world-famous Grand Cru vineyards such as Chambertin, Musigny, Richebourg and Clos de Vougeot – are in the Côte de Nuits, the northern part of the Côte d'Or from Nuits-St-Georges up toward Dijon. Other fine reds, especially Volnay, Pommard and Corton, come from the Côte de Beaune. Some villages tend toward a fine and elegant style (Chambolle-Musigny, Volnay), others toward a firmer, more tannic structure (Gevrey-Chambertin, Pommard).

The Beaujolais should really be considered as a separate region, growing Gamay on acidic soils rather than Pinot Noir on limestone – though a small amount of Gamay has also crept north to be included in the lesser wines of Burgundy.

CLASSIFICATIONS

A large part of Burgundy has 5 increasingly specific levels of classification: regional ACs (e.g. Bourgogne), specified ACs covering groups of villages (e.g. Côte de Nuits-Villages), village wines taking the village name (Pommard, Vosne-Romanée), Premiers Crus (good village vineyard sites) and Grands Crus (the best individual vineyard sites).

See also ALOXE-CORTON, AUXEY-DURESSES, BEAUJOLAIS, BEAUNE, BLAGNY, BONNES-MARES, BOURGOGNE, BOURGOGNE-COTE CHALONNAISE, BOURGOGNE-HAUTES-COTES DE BEAUNE, CHAMBERTIN, CHAMBOLLE-MUSIGNY, CHASSAGNE-MONTRACHET, CHOREY-LES-BEAUNE, CLOS DE LA ROCHE, CLOS ST-DENIS, CLOS DE VOUGEOT, CORTON, COTE DE BEAUNE, COTE DE NUITS, COTE D'OR, CREMANT DE BOURGOGNE, ECHEZEAUX, FIXIN, GEVREY-CHAMBERTIN, GIVRY, LADOIX, MACON, MARSANNAY, MERCUREY, MEURSAULT, MONTHELIE, MOREY-ST-DENIS, MOULIN-A-VENT, MUSIGNY, NUITS-ST-GEORGES, PERNAND-VERGELESSES, POMMARD, PULIGNY-MONTRACHET, RICHEBOURG, La ROMANEE-CONTI, ROMANEE-ST-VIVANT, RULLY, ST-AUBIN, ST-ROMAIN, SAVIGNY-LES-BEAUNE, La TACHE, VOLNAY, VOSNE-ROMANEE, VOUGEOT; and individual producers.

BEST PRODUCERS

Côte de Nuits B Ambroise, Dom. de l'Arlot, Robert Arnoux, Denis Bachelet, G Barthod, A Burguet, Charlopin, R Chevillon, CLAIR, J-J Confuron, C Dugat, B Dugat-Py, DUJAC, R Engel, Sylvie Esmonin (formerly Michel Esmonin & Fille), Geantet-Pansiot, Gouges, GRIVOT, GROS, Hudelot-Noëllat, JAYER-GILLES, Dom. LEROY, H Lignier, MEO-CAMUZET, Denis MORTET, Mugneret-Gibourg, J-F Mugnier, Perrot-Minot, Ponsot, RION, Dom. de la ROMANEE-CONTI, Roty, E Rouget, ROUMIER, ROUSSEAU, Sérafin, THOMAS-MOILLARD, de VOGUE, VOUGERAIE.

Côte de Beaune Ampeau, d'ANGERVILLE, Comte Armand, J-M Boillot, CHANDON DE BRIAILLES, COCHE-DURY, Courcel, Germain, Michel LAFARGE, LAFON, Montille, Albert Morot, Pousse d'Or, TOLLOT-BEAUT.

Côte Chalonnaise Brintet, H & P Jacqueson, Joblot, M Juillot, Lorenzon, Raquillet, Thénard, Villaine.

Merchants BOUCHARD PERE ET FILS (since 1996), Champy, DROUHIN, DUBOEUF, FAIVELEY, Féry-Meunier, V GIRARDIN, Camille Giroud, JADOT, LABOURE-ROI, D Laurent, Olivier LEFLAIVE, Maison LEROY, Nicolas Potel, RODET.

Co-ops BUXY, les Caves des Hautes-Côtes.

BURGUNDY WHITE WINES

Burgundy, France

White Burgundy has for generations been thought of as the world's leading dry white wine. The top wines have a remarkable succulent richness of honey and hazelnut, melted butter and sprinkled spice, yet are totally dry. Such wines are all from the Chardonnay grape and the finest are generally produced in the Côte de Beaune, the southern part of the Côte d'Or, in the communes of Aloxe-Corton, Meursault, Puligny-Montrachet and Chassagne-Montrachet, where limestone soils and the aspect of the vineyard provide perfect conditions for even ripening of grapes.

WINE STYLES

However, Burgundy encompasses many more wine styles than this, even if no single one quite attains the peaks of quality of those 4 villages on the Côte de Beaune.

Chablis in the north traditionally produces very good steely wines, aggressive and lean when young, but nutty and rounded – though still very dry – after a few years. Modern Chablis is generally a softer, milder wine, easy to drink young, and sometimes enriched with aging in new oak barrels.

There is no doubt that Meursault and the other Côte de Beaune villages can produce stupendous wine, but it is in such demand that unscrupulous producers are often tempted to maximize yields and cut corners on quality. Consequently white Burgundy from these famous villages must be approached with caution. Lesser-known villages such as Pernand-Vergelesses and St-Aubin often provide good wine at lower prices. There are also good wines from some villages in the Côte de Nuits, such as Morey-St-Denis, Nuits-St-Georges and Vougeot, though amounts are tiny compared with the Côte de Beaune.

South of the Côte d'Or the Côte Chalonnaise is becoming more interesting for quality white wine as a result of more widespread use of better equipment for temperature control and now that oak barrels are being used more often for aging. Rully and Montagny are the most important villages, though Givry and Mercurey can produce nice white, too.

The minor Aligoté grape makes some reasonable acidic wine, especially in Bouzeron. Further south, the Mâconnais is a large region, two-thirds planted with Chardonnay. The wine used to be dull and flat and not all that cheap, but there is some fair sparkling Crémant de Bourgogne, and some very good vineyard sites, in particular in St-Véran and in Pouilly-Fuissé. Increasingly stunning wines can now be found, though there's still a lot of dross.

See also ALOXE-CORTON, AUXEY-DURESSES, BATARD-MONTRACHET, BEAUJOLAIS, BEAUNE, BOURGOGNE, BOURGOGNE-COTE CHALONNAISE, CHABLIS, CHASSAGNE-MONTRACHET, CORTON, CORTON-CHARLEMAGNE, COTE DE BEAUNE, COTE DE NUITS, COTE D'OR, CREMANT DE BOURGOGNE, FIXIN, GIVRY, LADOIX, MACON, MARSANNAY, MERCUREY, MEURSAULT, MONTAGNY, MONTHELIE, MONTRACHET, MOREY-ST-DENIS, MUSIGNY, NUITS-ST-GEORGES, PERNAND-VERGELESSES, POUILLY-FUISSE, POUILLY-LOCHE, PULIGNY-MONTRACHET, RULLY, ST-AUBIN, ST-ROMAIN, ST-VERAN, SAVIGNY-LES-BEAUNE, VOUGEOT; and individual producers.

BEST YEARS

(2002) 01 00 99 **97** 96 **95 92**

BEST PRODUCERS

Chablis Barat, J-C Bessin, Billaud-Simon, A & F Boudin/ de Chantemerle, J-M BROCARD, D Dampt, R & V DAUVISSAT, D & E Defaix, Droin, DURUP, W Fèvre, J-P Grossot, LAROCHE, Malandes, Louis MICHEL, G Picq, RAVENEAU, Simonnet-Febvre, Vocoret.

Côte d'Or (Côte de Beaune) G Amiot, R Ampeau, d'Auvenay (LEROY), Blain-Gagnard, Jean Boillot, J-M Boillot, Bonneau du Martray, M Bouzereau, Y Boyer-Martenot, CARILLON, CHANDON DE BRIAILLES, COCHE-DURY, Marc Colin, Colin-Deléger, Arnaud Ente, J-P Fichet, Fontaine-Gagnard, J-N GAGNARD, P Javillier, F Jobard, R Jobard, LAFON, R Lamy-Pillot, Dom. LEFLAIVE, Dom. Matrot, F Mikulski, Bernard Morey, Marc Morey, Pierre Morey, M Niellon, P Pernot, J & J-M Pillot, RAMONET, M Rollin, G Roulot, SAUZET, VERGET.

Côte Chalonnaise S Aladame, H & P Jacqueson.

Mâconnais D & M Barraud, Bonhomme, Corsin, Deux Roches, J A Ferret, Ch. Fuissé, la Greffière, Guffens-Heynen (VERGET), J-J Litaud, O Merlin, Robert-Denogent, Saumaize-Michelin, Soufrandière, Thévenet, Valette.

Merchants BOUCHARD PERE ET FILS, Champy, DROUHIN, FAIVELEY, V GIRARDIN, JADOT, LABOURE-ROI, Louis LATOUR, Olivier LEFLAIVE, Maison LEROY, Rijckaert, RODET, VERGET.

Co-ops BUXY, la CHABLISIENNE, Lugny, Viré.

BROKENWOOD *Hunter Valley, New South Wales, Australia* High-profile winery with delicious aged HUNTER Semillon★★ and Chardonnay★. Best wine is classic Hunter Graveyard Vineyard Shiraz★★★; the MCLAREN VALE Rayner Vineyard Shiraz★★ is also stunning. Cricket Pitch reds and whites are cheerful, fruity ready-drinkers. Best years: (Graveyard Vineyard Shiraz) 2000 99 98 96 **95 94 93 91 90 89 88 86**.

BROUILLY AC *Beaujolais, Burgundy, France* Largest of the 10 BEAUJOLAIS Crus; at its best, the wine is soft, fruity and gluggable. Best producers: Ch. de la Chaize★, DUBOEUF (Ch. de Nevers★), A Michaud★, Ch. Thivin★★. Best years: **2002 00**.

BROWN BROTHERS *North-East Victoria, Australia* Highly successful sizeable family winery, producing a huge range of varietal table wines, which have improved significantly in the past few years. Vintage fizz is consistently good and stickies are superb, especially the Very Old Muscat★★, Port★ and Tokay★★ range. Focuses on cool King Valley and mountain-top Whitlands for its premium grapes.

BRÜNDLMAYER *Kamptal, Niederösterreich, Austria* Willi Bründlmayer makes wine in a variety of Austrian and international styles, but his outstanding dry Riesling (Alte Reben★★★) from the great Heiligenstein vineyard and Grüner Veltliner (Ried Lamm★★★) are the best; high alcohol is matched by superlative fruit and mineral flavours. Good Sekt★. Best years: (Zöbinger Heiligenstein Riesling) (2002) 01 99 **98 97 95 94 93 92 91**.

BRUNELLO DI MONTALCINO DOCG *Tuscany, Italy* Powerful red wine produced from Sangiovese (known locally as Brunello). Traditionally needed over 10 years to soften, but modern practices result in more fruit-rich wines, yet still tannic enough to age spectacularly. Best producers: Altesino★ (Montosoli★★), ARGIANO★ (Riserva★★), BANFI★, Barbi★ (Riserva★★), BIONDI-SANTI★★, Camigliano★★, La Campana★, Caparzo★★, Casanova di Neri★, Casanuova delle Cerbaie★★, Casisano Colombaio★★, CASTELGIOCONDO (Riserva★), Centolani★ (Pietranera★★), Cerbaiona★★, Ciacci Piccolomini d'Aragona★★, Donatella Cinelli Colombini★★, Col d'Orcia★, COSTANTI★, Fuligni★★, La Gerla★★, Le Gode★, Gorelli-Due Portine★, Greppone Mazzi★★, Maurizio Lambardi★★, Lisini★★, Mastrojanni★★, Siro Pacenti★★★, Pian delle Vigne★★/ANTINORI, Pian-cornello★★, Agostina Pieri★★, Pieve Santa Restituta★★, La Poderina★★, Poggio Antico★★, Poggio San Polo★★, Il Poggione★, Salvioni★★, Livio Sassetti-Pertimali★★, Talenti★★, La Togata★★, Valdicava★, Villa Le Prata★★. Best years: (2001) (00) (99) 98 97 **95 93 90 88 85**.

BUCELAS DOC *Estremadura, Portugal* A tiny but historic DOC. The wines are whites based on the Arinto grape (noted for its high acidity). For attractive, modern examples try Quinta da Murta or Quinta da Romeira (Morgado de Santa Catherina★).

VON BUHL *Deidesheim, Pfalz, Germany* Large estate, leased to the Japanese Sanyo group. The wines are rarely subtle, but have full fruit and a confident Riesling character. Drink young.

BUITENVERWACHTING *Constantia WO, South Africa* Time slows down at this beautiful property, part of the Cape's original CONSTANTIA wine farm. The traditional, Old World-style wines also take time to unfold; a ripe, fruit-laden Chardonnay★★, penetrating, zesty Sauvignon Blanc★ and light, racily dry Riesling. Aristocratic red blend Christine★, one of the Cape's most accurate BORDEAUX lookalikes, promises to gain extra dimension from new, virus-free vineyards. Best years: (Christine) 1999 **98 96 95 94 93 92 91**.

BULL'S BLOOD *Hungary* Kékfrankos (Blaufränkisch) grapes sometimes replace robust Kadarka in the blend, thinning the blood; some producers blend with Cabernet Sauvignon, Kékoporto or Merlot. New stringent regulations should improve the quality of Bikavér ('bull's blood') in the 2 permitted regions, Eger and Szekszárd. Winemakers Tibor Gàl (of Egervin) and Vilmos Thummerer are working hard on this front.

GRANT BURGE *Barossa Valley, South Australia* A leading producer in the BAROSSA, making chocolaty Filsell Shiraz★ and Cameron Vale Cabernet★, opulent Summers Chardonnay★, fresh Thorn Riesling★ and oaky Zerk Semillon. Top label is rich Meshach Shiraz★★. Shadrach Cabernet★★, the continually improving RHONE-style blend, Holy Trinity★, and the excellent-value Barossa Vines range are recent additions. Recent vintages have shown a most welcome reduction in oak. Best years: (Meshach) (2001) 99 98 **96 95 94 91 90**.

BURGENLAND *Austria* 4 regions: Neusiedlersee, including Seewinkel for sweet Prädikat wines; Neusiedlersee-Hügelland, famous for sweet wines, now also big reds and fruity dry whites; Mittelburgenland, for robust Blaufränkisch reds; and Südburgenland, for good reds and dry whites. Best producers: FEILER-ARTINGER★★★, Gernot Heinrich★★, Hans Igler★, Juris★, Kollwentz★★, KRACHER★★★, Krutzler★★, M & A Nittnaus★★, OPITZ★, Peter Schandl★, Ernst Triebaumer★★, Umathum★★, VELICH★★, Robert Wenzel★.

BURGUNDY See Bourgogne AC and pages 76–9.

BÜRKLIN-WOLF *Wachenheim, Pfalz, Germany* With nearly 100ha (250 acres) of vineyards, this is one of Germany's largest privately owned estates. Under director Christian von Guradze, a champion of vineyard classification, it has shot back up to the first rank of the region's producers since the 1994 vintage. The powerful, spicy dry Rieslings are now ★ to ★★, with the magnificent dessert wines ★★★. Best years: (Grosses Gewächs Rieslings) (2002) 01 98 **97 96 95**.

BURMESTER *Port DOC, Douro, Portugal* Shipper established since 1730, but now owned by cork giant Amorim. Vintage PORT★★ is much improved, as is the Vintage released under the Quinta Nova de Nossa Senhora do Carmo★ label, a quinta purchased by Burmester in 1991. As well as refined 10- and 20-year-old tawnies, there are some outstanding old colheitas★★ which extend back over 100 years. Also good recent Late Bottled Vintage★ and oak-aged DOURO red, Casa Burmester★. Best years: (Vintage) 2000 97 **95 94**.

BURRWEILER *Pfalz, Germany* Burrweiler is the PFALZ's only wine village with a slate soil like the MOSEL, most notably in the excellent Schäwer site. Elegant dry Rieslings and some fine dessert wines. Best producer: Herbert Messmer★. Best years: (2002) 01 **99 98 97 94 93**.

BUXY, CAVE DES VIGNERONS DE *Côte Chalonnaise, Burgundy, France* Based in the Côte Chalonnaise, this ranks among Burgundy's top co-operatives, producing affordable, well-made Chardonnay and Pinot Noir. The light, oak-aged BOURGOGNE Pinot Noir★ and the red and white Clos de Chenôves★, as well as the nutty, white MONTAGNY★, are all good, reasonably priced, and best with 2–3 years' age.

BUZET AC *South-West France* Good Bordeaux-style red wines from the same mix of grapes and at a lower price. There is very little rosé and the whites are rarely exciting. Best producers: les Vignerons de Buzet (especially Baron d'Ardeuil, Ch. de Gueyze and Cuvée 44), Tissot.

BYRON *Santa Maria Valley AVA, California, USA* After new owner MONDAVI
built a new winery and acquired more vineyards, founder Ken 'Byron'
Brown has been making better-than-ever Pinot Noir and Chardonnay.
His Nielson Vineyard (formerly Estate) Pinot★★ is full of spicy cherry
fruit, and the Nielson Vineyard Chardonnay★★ with mineral notes and
fine balance can age for several years. Regular Chardonnay is often good
value, as is a vibrant Pinot Gris★★. Io★, a robust RHONE blend, is off to
a promising start. Best years: (Nielson Pinot Noir) 2001 00 99 98 **96 95**.

CA' DEL BOSCO *Franciacorta DOCG, Lombardy, Italy* Model estate,
headed by Maurizio Zanella, making some of Italy's finest and most
expensive wines: outstanding sparklers in FRANCIACORTA Brut★★,
Dosage Zero★, Satèn★★ and the prestige Cuvée Annamaria
Clementi★★★; good Terre di Franciacorta Rosso★, remarkably good
Chardonnay★★★, Pinero★★ (Pinot Nero) and a BORDEAUX blend,
Maurizio Zanella★★★. Also promising varietal Carmenère,
Carmenero★.

CABARDÈS AC *Languedoc, France* Next door to MINERVOIS but, as well as
the usual Mediterranean grape varieties, Cabernet Sauvignon and
Merlot are allowed. At best, full-bodied, chewy and rustically
attractive. AC status granted in 1999. Best producers: Cabrol★,
Jouclary, Pennautier★, Salitis, Ventenac. Best years: 2001 **00**.

CABERNET D'ANJOU AC *Loire Valley, France* Can be made from both
Cabernets and generally demi-sec. Now made to drink young, but
there are still a few remarkable old vintages from the 1940s and 50s
around. Best producers: Ogereau, Sablonnettes, Terrebrune.

CABERNET FRANC Often unfairly dismissed as an inferior Cabernet
Sauvignon, Cabernet Franc comes into its own in cool zones or areas
where the soil is damp and heavy. It can have a leafy freshness linked
to raw but tasty blackcurrant-raspberry fruit. In France it thrives in
the LOIRE VALLEY and BORDEAUX, especially ST-EMILION and POMEROL where
it accounts for 19% of the planting. Successful in northern Italy,
especially ALTO ADIGE and FRIULI, although some plantings here have
turned out to be Carmenère, and increasingly preferred to Cabernet
Sauvignon in Tuscany. Experiments with Cabernet Franc on
CALIFORNIA's North Coast and in WASHINGTON STATE show promise. There
are also some good South African, Chilean and Australian examples.

CABERNET SAUVIGNON See pages 84–5.

CADILLAC AC *Bordeaux, France* Sweet wine from the southern half of
the PREMIERES COTES DE BORDEAUX. Styles vary from fresh, semi-sweet to
richly botrytized. The wines have greatly improved in recent vintages.
Drink young. Best producers: CARSIN, Cayla★, Ch. du Juge/Dupleich,
Manos★, Mémoires★, REYNON, Ste-Catherine. Best years: 2001 **99 98**.

CAFAYATE VALLEY *Salta , Argentina* At almost 2000m (6500 ft) above
sea level – a few are even higher – the vineyards of Cafayate are some
of the highest in the world. Located 700km (434 miles) north of
Mendoza, this region is known for its aromatic and intense Torrontés.
Don't miss the perfumed, fruity Malbec and spicy Cabernet Sauvignon.
Best producers: Etchart, San Pedro de Yacochuya, Michel Torino.

CAHORS AC *South-West France* Important South-West red wine region.
This dark, often tannic wine is made from at least 70% Auxerrois
(Bordeaux's Malbec) and has an unforgettable, rich plummy flavour
when ripe and well made – which is less frequent than I'd wish. Ages

well. Best producers: la Caminade★, Cayrou, CEDRE★★, Clos la Coutale★, Clos de Gamot★, Clos Triguedina★, Eugénie, Gaudou, Gautoul★, Haut-Monplaisir, Haute-Serre, les Ifs, LAGREZETTE★, Lamartine★, les Laquets★, les Rigalets★. Best years: 2000 98 **96 95 94 90 89 88 86 85.**

CAIN CELLARS *Napa Valley AVA, California, USA* This Spring Mountain estate appears to be solidly on track. Cain Five★★ is a particularly pleasing, slow-maturing red BORDEAUX blend. Cain Concept★ is a red Bordeaux blend made from hillside vineyards. Also attractive are lower-priced drink-me-now red Cain Cuvée★ and strongly flavoured white Cain Musqué★ (Sauvignon Blanc). Best years: (Cain Five) (2001) (00) 99 97 **95 94 93 91 90 87.**

CALABRIA *Italy* One of Italy's poorest regions. CIRO, Donnici, Savuto and Scavigna reds from the native Gaglioppo grape, and whites from Greco, are much improved thanks to greater winemaking expertise. The leading producers are the Librandi family – who have recently added Magno Megonio★★, from the obscure Magliocco variety, to an already fine range – and Odoardi, with its excellent Scavigna Vigna Garrone.

CALERA *San Benito, California, USA* A pace-setter for California Pinot Noir with 4 different estate wines: Reed Vineyard★★, Selleck Vineyard★★, Jensen Vineyard★★ and Mills★★. They are complex, fascinating wines with power and originality and capable of aging. Mt Harlan Chardonnay★★ is excitingly original too. Small amounts of Viognier★★ are succulent with sensuous fruit. Best years: (Pinot Noir) 2000 99 98 **97 96 95 94 91 90;** (Chardonnay) (2001) 00 99 **98 97 96 95.**

CALIFORNIA *USA* California's importance is not simply in being the leading wine producer in the USA and the fourth largest in the world. Most of the great revolutions in technology and style that have transformed the expectations and achievements of winemakers in every country of the world – including France – were born in the ambitions of a band of Californian winemakers during the 1960s and 70s. They challenged the old order with its regulated, self-serving elitism, democratizing the world of fine wine, to the benefit of every wine drinker. This revolutionary fervour is less evident now. And there are times when Californians seem too intent on establishing their own particular New World old order. A few figures: there are around 200,000ha (500,000 acres) of wine grapes, producing over 500 million gallons of wine annually, about 95% of all wine made in the USA. A large proportion comes from the hot, inland CENTRAL VALLEY. See also Central Coast, Mendocino County, Monterey County, Napa Valley, San Luis Obispo County, Santa Barbara County, Sonoma County.

CALITERRA *Colchagua, Chile* A joint venture between MONDAVI and Chadwick (as is SENA), which has never really lived up to its potential. Few of the wines have expressed any great Chilean character, though Reserva Cabernet Sauvignon and new Arboleda Carmenère aren't bad. I said must try harder last year. Nothing's changed.

CH. CALON-SÉGUR★★ *St-Estèphe AC, 3ème Cru Classé, Haut-Médoc, Bordeaux, France* Long considered one of ST-ESTEPHE's leading châteaux but in the mid-1980s the wines were not as good as they should have been. Recent vintages have been more impressive, with better fruit and a suppler texture. Second wine: Marquis de Ségur. Best years: 2001 00 99 98 96 95 **90 89 86 82.**

83

CABERNET SAUVIGNON

Wine made from Cabernet Sauvignon in places like Australia, California, Chile, Bulgaria, even in parts of southern France, has become so popular now that many people may not realize where it all started – and how Cabernet has managed to become the great, all-purpose omnipresent red wine grape of the world.

WINE STYLES

Bordeaux Cabernet It all began in Bordeaux. With the exception of a clutch of Merlot-based beauties in St-Émilion and Pomerol, all the greatest red Bordeaux wines are based on Cabernet Sauvignon, with varying amounts of Merlot, Cabernet Franc, and possibly Petit Verdot also blended in. The blending is necessary because by itself Cabernet makes such a strong, powerful, aggressive and assertive wine. Dark and tannic when young, the great Bordeaux wines need 10–20 years for the aggression to fade, the fruit becoming sweet and perfumed as fresh blackcurrants, with a fragrance of cedarwood, of cigar boxes mingling magically among the fruit. It is this character which has made red Bordeaux famous for at least 2 centuries.

Cabernet worldwide When winemakers in other parts of the world sought role models to try to improve their wines, most of them automatically thought of Bordeaux and chose Cabernet Sauvignon. It was lucky that they did, because not only is this variety easy to grow in almost all conditions – cool or warm, dry or damp – but that unstoppable personality always powers through. The cheaper wines are generally made to accentuate the blackcurrant fruit and the slightly earthy tannins. They are drinkable young, but able to age surprisingly well. The more ambitious wines are aged in oak barrels, often new ones, to enhance the tannin yet also to add spice and richness capable of developing over a decade or more. Sometimes the Cabernet is blended – usually with Merlot, sometimes with Cabernet Franc, and occasionally with other grapes: Shiraz in Australia, Sangiovese in Italy.

European Cabernets Many vineyards in southern France now produce good, affordable Cabernet Sauvignon. Spain has produced some good Cabernet blends, and Portugal has also had success. Italy's red wine quality revolution was sparked off by the success of Cabernet in Tuscany, and all the leading regions now grow it. Eastern Europe grows lots of Cabernet, but of widely varying quality, while the Eastern Mediterranean (Cyprus, Lebanon, Israel) and North Africa are beginning to produce tasty examples. Germany has tried it but is returning to Pinot Noir. Austria has had more success but is also returning to Blaufränkisch and Zweigelt.

New World Cabernets California's reputation was created by its strong, weighty Cabernets. Recently some producers have eased up, making examples that bring out the fruit flavours and can be drunk young, while others have intensified their styles. Both Australia and New Zealand place more emphasis on upfront fruit in their Cabernets. Chile has made the juicy, blackcurranty style very much her own, and Argentina is showing it wants to join in too. New clones, producing riper fruit and tannins, show South Africa will be capable of mixing with the best.

BEST PRODUCERS

France

Bordeaux Dom. de CHEVALIER, COS D'ESTOURNEL, GRAND-PUY-LACOSTE, GRUAUD-LAROSE, LAFITE-ROTHSCHILD, LATOUR, LEOVILLE-LAS-CASES, LYNCH-BAGES, Ch. MARGAUX, MOUTON-ROTHSCHILD, PICHON-LONGUEVILLE, RAUZAN-SEGLA; *Midi* RICHEAUME, TREVALLON.

Other European Cabernets

Italy BANFI, CA' DEL BOSCO, Col d'Orcia (Olmaia), GAJA, ISOLE E OLENA, LAGEDER, MACULAN, ORNELLAIA, RAMPOLLA, San Leonardo, SASSICAIA, SOLAIA, TASCA D'ALMERITA.

Spain Blecua, MARQUES DE GRINON, TORRES.

New World Cabernets

Australia CAPE MENTELLE, CULLEN, HOWARD PARK, LEEUWIN (Art Series), Majella, MOSS WOOD, MOUNT MARY, PENFOLDS (Bin 707), PENLEY ESTATE, PETALUMA, WENDOUREE.

New Zealand Esk Valley, GOLDWATER, MATUA VALLEY, STONYRIDGE, TE MATA, VILLA MARIA.

USA (California) ARAUJO, BERINGER, Bryant Family, CAYMUS, DALLA VALLE, DIAMOND CREEK, DOMINUS, DUNN, Grace Family, HARLAN, LAUREL GLEN, Long Meadow Ranch, Peter MICHAEL, MINER, MONDAVI, NEWTON, PHELPS, RIDGE, SCREAMING EAGLE, SHAFER, SILVER OAK, SPOTTSWOODE, STAG'S LEAP, Viader; (Washington) ANDREW WILL, LEONETTI, QUILCEDA CREEK, WOODWARD CANYON.

Chile ALMAVIVA, CARMEN (Nativa), CASABLANCA (Santa Isabel), Clos Quebrada de Macul (Domus Aurea), CONCHA Y TORO (Don Melchor, Terrunyo), CONO SUR (20 Barrels).

Argentina CATENA, Terrazas (Gran Cabernet Sauvignon).

South Africa BEYERSKLOOF, BOEKENHOUTSKLOOF, BUITEN-VERWACHTING, Neil ELLIS, KANONKOP, Le Riche, MEERLUST, RUSTENBERG, SAXENBURG, THELEMA, VEENWOUDEN, VERGELEGEN.

CAMBRIA WINERY *Santa Maria Valley AVA, California, USA* The biggest winery in SANTA BARBARA COUNTY. Most of the production is Chardonnay (Katherine's Vineyard★ and Reserve★★), with the remainder devoted to Pinot Noir (Julia's Vineyard★), Syrah★, Viognier and Sangiovese. Best years: (Chardonnay) 2001 00 99 98 97 96 95.

CAMPANIA *Italy* Until recently Italy's south was a desert for the wine lover, but now 3 regions – PUGLIA, SICILY and Campania – lead the revolution there. In Campania moves toward quality have been underpinned by the likes of enologist Riccardo Cotarella. Other producers besides the venerable MASTROBERARDINO have finally begun to realize the potential of its soil, climate and grapes, especially the red Aglianico. DOCs of note are FALERNO DEL MASSICO, Fiano di Avellino, Greco di Tufo, Ischia, TAURASI and VESUVIO. The leading wines are Montevetrano★★★ (Cabernet-Merlot-Aglianico) and Galardi's Terra di Lavoro★★★ (Aglianico-Piedirosso) but also look for top Aglianico reds from Antonio Caggiano★★, De Conciliis★, Feudi di San Gregorio★★, Luigi Maffini★, Orazio Rillo★, Cantina del Taburno★ and others that fall outside the main DOCs.

CAMPILLO *Rioja DOC, País Vasco, Spain* An up-market subsidiary of Bodegas FAUSTINO, producing some exciting new red RIOJAS★. The wines are often Tempranillo-Cabernet Sauvignon blends, with masses of ripe, velvety fruit. Best years: (Reserva) 1999 98 96 95 94.

CAMPO VIEJO *Rioja DOC, Rioja, Spain* The largest producer of RIOJA. Reservas★ and Gran Reservas★ are reliably good, as are the elegant, all-Tempranillo Reserva Viña Alcorta and the barrel-fermented white Viña Alcorta. Albor Tempranillo is a good modern young Rioja, packed with fresh, pastilley fruit. Best years: (Reserva) 1998 96 95 94.

CANARY ISLANDS *Spain* Tacoronte-Acentejo, Lanzarote, La Palma, Hierro, Abona, Valle de Güimar, Valle de la Orotava and Ycoden-Daute-Isora: a total of 8 DOs for the Canaries – there's local politics for you! The sweet Malvasia from Lanzarote or La Palma is worth a try, otherwise stick with the young reds. Best producers: El Grifo, Monje, Viña Norte, Viñátigo.

CANBERRA DISTRICT *New South Wales, Australia* Cool, high altitude (800m/2600ft) may sound good, but excessive cold and frost can be problematic. Lark Hill and Helm make exciting Riesling, Lark Hill and Brindabella Hills some smart Cabernet blends and Clonakilla increasingly sublime Shiraz (with a dollop of Viognier). BRL HARDY is pouring money in here. Best producers: Brindabella Hills★, Clonakilla (Shiraz★★), Doonkuna★, Helm★, Lark Hill★.

DOM. CANET-VALETTE *St-Chinian AC, Languedoc, France* Marc Valette is uncompromising in his quest to make great wine: organic cultivation, low yields, gravity-fed grapes and traditional *pigeage* (foot-stomping) are just some of his methods. The wines offer a fabulously rich expression of ST-CHINIAN's Mediterranean grape varieties and clay-limestone soils. Cuvées include Mille et Une Nuits (1001 Nights)★ and the powerful, complex Syrah-Grenache Le Vin Maghani★★. Best years: (Le Vin Maghani) 2001 00 99 98 97 95.

CANNONAU Sardinian grape variety essentially the same as Spain's Garnacha and France's Grenache Noir. In SARDINIA it produces deep, tannic reds but lighter, modern, dry red wines are gaining in popularity, although traditional sweet and fortified styles can still be found. Best producers: (modern reds) ARGIOLAS, SELLA & MOSCA, Dolianova, Dorgali, Jerzu, Ogliastra, Oliena, Santa Maria La Palma and Trexenta co-ops.

CANOE RIDGE VINEYARD *Columbia Valley AVA, Washington, USA*
Successful WASHINGTON outpost of California's CHALONE group, with reliable and tasty Chardonnay★, fruit-filled Merlot★★ and powerful Cabernet Sauvignon★★. Recent vintages have focused on red wine production and the results are significant, yielding sturdy, ageworthy bottlings. Best years: (reds) 2001 00 99 **98 97**.

CH. CANON★ *St-Émilion Grand Cru AC, 1er Grand Cru Classé, Bordeaux, France* Canon can make some of the richest, most concentrated ST-EMILIONS, but it went into steep decline before being purchased in 1996 by Chanel. Signs are that things are returning to form. The 3.5ha (8.65-acre) vineyard of Grand Cru Classé Ch. Curé-Bon has recently been added to the estate. In good vintages the wine is tannic and rich at first but is worth aging 10–15 years. Second wine: Clos J Kanon. Best years: 2001 00 98 96 95 **90 89 88 86 85 83 82**.

CANON-FRONSAC AC *Bordeaux, France* This AC is the heart of the FRONSAC region. The wines are quite sturdy when young but can age for 10 years or more. Best producers: Barrabaque (Prestige★), Canon de Brem★, Cassagne Haut-Canon★, la Fleur Cailleau, Gaby, Grand-Renouil★, Lamarche Canon Candelaire, Moulin Pey-Labrie★, Pavillon, Vrai Canon Bouché. Best years: 2001 00 98 **97 96 95 94 90 89 88**.

CH. CANON-LA-GAFFELIÈRE★★ *St-Émilion Grand Cru AC, Grand Cru Classé, Bordeaux, France* Owner Stephan von Neipperg has placed this property, located at the foot of the town of ST-EMILION, at the top of the list of Grands Crus Classés. The wines are firm, rich and concentrated. Under the same ownership are Clos l'Oratoire★, Ch. l'Aiguilhe★ in the COTES DE CASTILLON, and the remarkable *micro-cuvée* La Mondotte★★. Best years: 2001 00 99 98 **97 96 95 94 93 90 89**.

CH. CANTEMERLE★ *Haut-Médoc AC, 5ème Cru Classé, Bordeaux, France* With la LAGUNE, the most southerly of the Crus Classés. The wines are delicate in style and excellent in ripe vintages. Second wine: Villeneuve de Cantemerle. Best years: 2001 00 99 96 **95 90 89 83 82**.

CANTERBURY *South Island, New Zealand* The long, cool ripening season of the arid central coast of South Island favours white varieties, particularly Chardonnay, Pinot Gris, Sauvignon Blanc and Riesling, as well as Pinot Noir. The northerly Waipara district produces Canterbury's most exciting wines, especially from Riesling and Pinot Noir. Best producers: GIESEN★, Mountford★, PEGASUS BAY★★, Daniel Schuster★, Waipara West★. Best years: (Pinot Noir) (2002) 01 00 **99 98 96**; (Riesling) (2002) 01 **00 99 98 96**.

CAPE MENTELLE *Margaret River, Western Australia* Leading MARGARET RIVER winery, owned by LVMH. Cape Mentelle's founder, David Hohnen, and winemaker John Durham don't let corporate ownership dull their enthusiasm, and they endlessly and successfully experiment with new grape varieties as well as producing superb, cedary Cabernet★★★, impressive Shiraz★★ and Chardonnay★★, tangy Semillon-Sauvignon Blanc★★ and wonderfully chewy Zinfandel★★. All wines benefit from cellaring – whites up to 5 years, reds 8–15. Best years: (Cabernet Sauvignon) (2000) 99 98 96 95 **94 92 91 90**.

CAPEL VALE *Geographe, Western Australia* Dr Peter Pratten's winery sources fruit from its own vineyards in Geographe, Mount Barker, PEMBERTON and MARGARET RIVER. Many of its CV and White Label wines represent good value, especially Sauvignon Blanc-Semillon★ and Riesling★. The top Connoisseur (Black Label) range has lacked consistency, except for the classy Whispering Hill Riesling★★. Current winemaker Nicole Esdaile has brought far greater focus to the wines and seems determined they should reflect their high-quality vineyard origins. Best years: (Whispering Hill Riesling) **2000 98 97**.

CH. CARBONNIEUX *Pessac-Léognan AC, Cru Classé de Graves, Bordeaux, France* Carbonnieux is the largest of the PESSAC-LEOGNAN Classed Growths. The white★ is a pleasant, mildly oaked wine. The red is well balanced but rarely memorable, and needs some bottle age. Second wine: la Tour-Léognan. Best years: (whites) 2001 00 **99 98 96 95 94 90**; (reds) 2000 98 96 **95 90 89 88 86**.

CARIGNAN The dominant red grape in the south of France is responsible for much boring, cheap, harsh wine. But when made by carbonic maceration, the wine can have delicious spicy fruit. Old vines are capable of thick, rich, impressive reds, with which it is now having the odd success in CALIFORNIA and Chile. There is also some interest in South Africa. Although initially a Spanish grape (as Cariñena or Mazuelo), it is not that widespread there, but is useful for adding colour and acidity in RIOJA and CATALUNA, and has gained unexpected respect in PRIORAT.

CARIGNANO DEL SULCIS DOC *Sardinia, Italy* Carignano is now starting to produce wines of quite startling quality. Rocca Rubia★, a barrique-aged Riserva from the co-op at Santadi, with rich, fleshy and chocolaty fruit, is one of SARDINIA's best reds. In a similar vein, but a step up, is Baie Rosse★★; even better is the more structured and concentrated Terre Brune★★. Best producer: Santadi co-op. Best years: (reds) (2001) 00 99 **98 97 96 95**.

LOUIS CARILLON & FILS *Puligny-Montrachet AC, Côte de Beaune, Burgundy, France* Excellent family-owned estate in PULIGNY-MONTRACHET. The emphasis here is on traditional, finely balanced whites of great concentration, rather than new oak. Look out for the Premiers Crus les Referts★★, Champs Canet★★ and les Perrières★★★, and the tiny but exquisite production of Bienvenues-BATARD-MONTRACHET★★★. Reds from CHASSAGNE-MONTRACHET★, ST-AUBIN★ and MERCUREY★ are good, too. Best years: (whites) (2002) (01) 00 99 **97** 96 **95 92**.

CARIÑENA DO *Aragón, Spain* The largest DO of ARAGON, baking under the mercilessly hot sun in inland eastern Spain, Cariñena has traditionally been a land of cheap, deep red, alcoholic wines from the Garnacha grape. However, a switch to Tempranillo grapes has begun, and some growers now pick earlier. International grape varieties like Cabernet Sauvignon are being planted widely. Best producers: Bodegas San Valero (Monte Ducay, Don Mendo), Señorío de Urbezo.

CARMEN *Maipo, Chile* Sister winery to SANTA RITA, led by Pilar Gonzalez. Both Chardonnay★ and Sauvignon Blanc★ are good, but it is the reds that really shine. Excellent, blackcurrant, organic Nativa Cabernet

Sauvignon★★, throaty, deep Carmenère-Cabernet Sauvignon★★ and Wine Maker's Reserve Red★★ (a blend of 5 varieties) lead the way. Single-vineyard Gold Reserve Cabernet Sauvignon★★ is made only in outstanding years.

CARMENÈRE An important but forgotten constituent of BORDEAUX blends in the 19th century, historically known as Grande Vidure. Planted in Chile, it was generally labelled as Merlot until 1998. When ripe and made with care, it has rich blackberry, plum and spice flavours, with an unexpected but delicious bunch of savoury characters – grilled meat, soy sauce, celery, coffee – thrown in. A true original.

CARMENET *Sonoma Valley AVA, California, USA* Sold to Beringer Blass in 2002, Carmenet sets out to make BORDEAUX-style reds and whites and succeeds brilliantly with its Moon Mountain Estate Reserve★★ and Reserve Sauvignon Blanc★★. Best years: (reds) (2001) (00) 99 98 97 96 95 94 **92 91 90 87 86**.

CARMIGNANO DOCG *Tuscany, Italy* Red wine from the west of Florence, renowned since the 16th century and revived in the 1960s by Capezzana. The blend (85% Sangiovese, 15% Cabernet) is one of Tuscany's more refined wines and can be very long-lived. Although Carmignano is DOCG for its red wine, DOC applies to a lighter red Barco Reale, a rosé called Vin Ruspo and fine VIN SANTO. Best producers: Ambra★ (Vigne Alte★★), Artimino★, Capezzana★★, Le Farnete/E Pierazzuoli★ (Riserva★★), Il Poggiolo★, Villa di Trefiano★. Best years: (2001) 00 99 98 **97 95 90 88 85**.

CARMO, QUINTA DO *Alentejo, Portugal* Well-established estate, part-owned by Domaines Rothschild since 1992. Estate red★ used to be complex and ageworthy, but quality from vintages in the 90s has been very ordinary, especially given its inflated price. However, a large replanting programme does at last seem to be bringing quality up again. Second label: Dom Martinho. Best years: 2000 **99 98 97 94**.

CARNEROS AVA *California, USA* Hugging the northern edge of San Francisco Bay, Carneros includes parts of both NAPA and SONOMA Counties. Windswept and chilly with morning fog off the Bay, it is a top cool-climate area, suitable for Chardonnay and Pinot Noir as both table wine and a base for sparkling wine. Merlot and even Syrah are also coming on well, but vineyard expansion is beginning to worry me. Best producers: ACACIA★★, Buena Vista, Carneros Creek★, DOMAINE CARNEROS★★, David Ramey★★, RASMUSSEN★★, SAINTSBURY★★, Truchard★★. Best years: (Pinot Noir) (2002) 01 00 99 **98 97 96 95 94**.

CARNUNTUM *Niederösterreich, Austria* 890ha (2200-acre) wine region south of the Danube and east of Vienna, with a strong red wine tradition. Best producers: Walter Glatzer, Markowitsch, Pitnauer★.

CH. CARSIN *Premières Côtes de Bordeaux AC, Bordeaux, France* With an Australian winemaker – Mandy Jones – and a winery designed and built by an Australian engineering company, what could you expect other than aromatic and fruity New World-style wines? Carsin delivers the goods with well-oaked, drink-young white Cuvée Prestige★ and red Cuvée Noire★. Also peach and citrus vin de table Etiquette Gris★ and a sweet CADILLAC. Best years: (Cuvée Noire) 2001 **00 98 97 96 95**.

CASA LAPOSTOLLE *Rapel, Chile* Joint venture between Marnier-Lapostolle and Chile's Rabat family, with Michel Rolland at the winemaking helm. Cuvée Alexandre Merlot★★ and Chardonnay★

both have the intensity for several years' aging. Clos Apalta★★★ is a world-class Merlot-Carmenère-Cabernet Sauvignon blend.

CASABLANCA, VALLE DE *Aconcagua, Chile* Coastal valley with a cool-climate personality that is Chile's strongest proof of regional style. Whites dominate, with best results from Chardonnay, Sauvignon Blanc and Gewürztraminer. Even so, the rare reds, Pinot Noir especially but also Merlot and Carmenère, are very good. Best producers: (whites) CASA LAPOSTOLLE★, CASABLANCA★★, CONCHA Y TORO★, ERRAZURIZ★, Morandé★, Veramonte★★, VILLARD ESTATE★. Best years: (whites) 2002 01 99.

CASABLANCA, VIÑA *Casablanca, Chile* This much-acclaimed estate owes its reputation to Ignacio Recabarren, now departed to CONCHA Y TORO, but new Spanish guru Joseba Altuna from GUELBENZU should continue the upward direction. Only top wines use CASABLANCA-sourced fruit. White Label wines use vineyards in Lontué, MAIPO and San Fernando. There is rose- and lychee-filled Gewürztraminer★, excellent tangy, intense Sauvignon Blanc★, quince-edged Santa Isabel Estate Chardonnay★★ and barrel-fermented Chardonnay★ from the same estate. Reds include inky-black Cabernet Sauvignon★ and low-yield White Label Merlot★, together with the minty, exotic Merlot★★ and Cabernet★★ from the Santa Isabel Estate.

DOM. LA CASENOVE *Côtes du Roussillon AC, Roussillon, France* Former photojournalist Étienne Montès, with the help of consultant enologist Jean-Luc COLOMBO, has developed an impressive range of wines, including a perfumed white Vin de Pays Catalan made from Macabeu and Torbat, MUSCAT DE RIVESALTES★, RIVESALTES★ and 2 red COTES DU ROUSSILLON: La Garrigue★ and the predominantly Syrah Commandant François Jaubert★★. Drink this with at least 5 years' bottle age. Best years: (Cdt François Jaubert) 2001 00 98 97 96 95.

CASSIS AC *Provence, France* A picturesque fishing port near Marseille. Because of its situation, its white wine is the most overpriced on the French Riviera. Based on Ugni Blanc and Clairette, the wine can be good if fresh. The red wine is dull but the rosé can be pleasant (especially from a single estate). Best producers: Bagnol★, Clos Ste-Magdelaine★, Ferme Blanche★, Fontblanche, Mas de Boudard, Mas Fontcreuse, Paternel. Best years: 2001 00 99 98 97 96.

CASTEL DEL MONTE DOC *Puglia, Italy* An arid, hilly zone, and an ideal habitat for the Uva di Troia grape, producing long-lived red wine of astonishing character. There is also varietal Aglianico, some good rosé, and the whites produced from international varieties are improving. Best producers: RIVERA★, Santa Lucia, Tormaresca/ANTINORI, Torrevento★. Best years: (2001) 00 99 98 97 96 95 93.

CASTELGIOCONDO *Brunello di Montalcino DOCG, Tuscany, Italy* FRESCOBALDI's estate is the source of merely adequate BRUNELLO, good Brunello Riserva★ and Merlot Lamaione★★. The vineyards are also providing grapes for the much-trumpeted joint venture with MONDAVI, Luce, a Sangiovese-Merlot blend; so far, I'm unimpressed, especially regarding value for money. The second wine, Lucente, is somewhat better from that point of view.

CASTELLARE *Chianti Classico DOCG, Tuscany, Italy* Publisher Paolo Panerai's fine estate in the west of the Classico zone produces excellent CHIANTI CLASSICO★ and deeper, richer Riserva★★. Canonico di Castellare★ (Chardonnay), Coniale di Castellare★★ (Cabernet Sauvignon), and Spartito di Castellare★ (Sauvignon Blanc) are all ripe and fruity. Top wine I Sodi di San Niccolò★★ is an unusual Sangiovese-Malvasia blend, intense but finely perfumed.

CASTILLA-LA MANCHA *Spain* The biggest wine region in the world; hot, dry country with poor clay-chalk soil. The DOs of the central plateau, LA MANCHA and VALDEPENAS, make white wines from the Airén grape, and some good reds from the Cencibel (Tempranillo). Méntrida DO, Manchuela DO and Almansa DO make mostly rustic reds. The most ambitious wines made here are those from MARQUES DE GRINON's Dominio de Valdepusa★★ estate and the Dehesa del Carrizal★ estate, both in the Toledo mountains. Uribes Madero's Calzadilla★ in Cuenca province, Finca Sandoval Syrah★ from Manchuela and Manuel Manzaneque's Cabernet-based reds★★ and Chardonnay from Sierra de Alcaraz in Albacete province are full of promise. Manzaneque now has his own DO, Finca Élez, as does the Marquès de Griñòn: Dominio de Valdepusa DO.

CASTILLA Y LEÓN *Spain* This is Spain's harsh, high plateau, with long cold winters and hot summers (but always cool nights). A few rivers, notably the Duero, temper this climate and afford fine conditions for viticulture. After many decades of winemaking ignorance, with a few exceptions like VEGA SICILIA, the situation has changed radically for the better in 2 of the region's DOs, RIBERA DEL DUERO and RUEDA, and is rapidly improving in the other 3, BIERZO, Cigales and TORO. Dynamic winemakers such as Telmo RODRIGUEZ and Mariano García of MAURO have won huge critical acclaim for the region.

CATALUÑA *Spain* Standards vary among the region's DOs. PENEDES, between Barcelona and Tarragona, has the greatest number of technically equipped wineries in Spain, but doesn't make a commensurate number of superior wines. In the south, mountainous, isolated PRIORAT DOC has become a new icon for its heady, raging reds, and the neighbouring DOs of Montsant and Terra Alta are following in its footsteps. Inland COSTERS DEL SEGRE and CONCA DE BARBERA make potentially excellent reds and whites. Up the coast, Alella makes attractive whites and Ampurdán-Costa Brava (Empordá-Costa Brava), by the French border, is showing signs of life. Cataluña also makes most of Spain's CAVA sparkling wines. The Catalunya DO allows inexpensive blends from anywhere in the region.

NICOLÁS CATENA *Mendoza, Argentina* Argentina's most progressive export-orientated wine producer. Top-end stuff has always been good to excellent, but the basic range was sluggish; it is now greatly improved, if rather rich in a California style, and led by the Argento brand of Chardonnay and Malbec★ – both fresh, modern and perfumed. Catena-owned Esmeralda produces good international-style Chardonnay, oak-aged Cabernet Sauvignon and powerful Agrelo vineyard Malbec, with second-label Alamos providing a rather leaner interpretation. Soft, juicy Malbec and Merlot under the Rutini label, and gob-stopping Bonarda El Mirador★. However, the star wines come from Catena's spectacular Zapata winery in Agrelo. Using a variety of grape sources – from some of Argentina's older Malbec at Lunlunta, right up to new, high-altitude Tupungato fruit – the Alta range of Chardonnay★★, Cabernet★★ and Malbec★★, topped by new Catena Zapata★★, is top-flight. New joint venture with LAFITE-ROTHSCHILD for Caro (Cabernet-Malbec) from the 2000 vintage.

DOM. CAUHAPÉ *Jurançon AC, South-West France* Henri Ramonteu ha
been a major influence in JURANÇON, proving that the area can mak
complex dry whites as well as more traditional sweet wines. Dry
unoaked Jurançon Sec is labelled Chant des Vignes★; the oake
version is Sève d'Automne★. Top wines are sweet Noblesse du
Temps★★ and barrel-fermented Quintessence★★★.

CAVA DO *Spain* Cava, the Catalan and hence Spanish name fo
Champagne-method fizz, is made in 159 towns and villages throughout
Spain, but more than 95% are in CATALUNA. Grapes used are the local tri
of Parellada, Macabeo and Xarel-lo. The best-value, fruitiest Cavas are
generally the youngest, with no more than the minimum 9 months
aging. Some good Catalan Cavas are made with Chardonnay and
maybe Pinot Noir. A number of top-quality wines are now produced
but are seldom seen abroad, since their prices are too close to those of
Champagne to attract international customers. Best producers: Can
Feixes, Can Ràfols dels Caus★, Castellblanch, Castell de Vilarnau,
CODORNIU★, FREIXENET, JUVE Y CAMPS★, Marques de Monistrol, Parxet
RAIMAT, Raventós i Blanc, Rovellats, Agustí Torelló, Jané Ventura.

CAYMUS VINEYARDS *Napa Valley AVA, California, USA* Caymus Caberne
Sauvignon is a ripe, intense and generally tannic style that is good in its
regular bottling★ and can be outstanding as a Special Selection★★★
Conundrum★ is an exotic, full-flavoured blended white. Mer Soleil★★, a
new label for MONTEREY Chardonnay, was an instant success. Best years
(Special Selection) (2001) 00 99 98 97 **95 94 92 91 90 87 86 84**.

DOM. CAZES *Rivesaltes, Roussillon, France* The Cazes brothers make
outstanding MUSCAT DE RIVESALTES★★, RIVESALTES Vieux★★ and the
superb Aimé Cazes★★, but also produce a wide range of red and white
table wines, mainly as COTES DU ROUSSILLON and Vin de Pays des Côtes
Catalanes. Look out for the soft, fruity red Le Canon du Maréchal★
the Cabernet-based Le Credo★ and the small production of barrel-
fermented Chardonnay.

CH. DU CÈDRE *Cahors AC, South-West France* Pascal Verhaegue is the
leader of a new generation of CAHORS winemakers, producing dark,
richly textured wines with a generous coating of chocolaty oak. There
are 3 cuvées: Le Prestige★, the 100% Auxerrois (Malbec) Le Cèdre★★,
which is aged in new oak barrels for 20 months, and from 2000 the
Cuvée JC★ which is fermented and aged in oak. All 3 benefit from at
least 5–6 years' bottle age. Best years: (Le Cèdre) 2001 00 99 98 **97 96**.

CELLIER LE BRUN *Marlborough, South Island, New Zealand*
Champagne-method specialist, with vintage Blanc de Blancs★★, and
tasty blended vintage and non-vintage bubblies. Founder Daniel Le
Brun has now sold up and established a new MARLBOROUGH winery, Le
Brun Family Estate. Best years: (Blanc de Blancs) **1996 95 92 91 90**.

CENCIBEL See Tempranillo.

CENTRAL COAST AVA *California, USA* Huge AVA covering virtually
every vineyard between San Francisco and Los Angeles, with a
number of sub-AVAs, such as SANTA CRUZ MOUNTAINS, Santa Ynez
Valley, SANTA MARIA VALLEY and Monterey, which include some excellent
cooler areas for Pinot Noir and Chardonnay. See also Monterey
County, San Luis Obispo County, Santa Barbara County.

CENTRAL OTAGO *South Island, New Zealand* The only wine region in
New Zealand with a continental rather than maritime climate. Technically
the ripening season is long and cool, suiting Pinot Noir, Gewürztraminer

nd Chardonnay, but there are usually periods of considerable eat during the summer to ntensify flavour. Long autumns ave also produced some excellent Rieslings. There are already well ver 30 wineries and an explosion f plantings, some in good areas

ke Bannockburn and Lowburn, others in areas that could prove decidedly marginal. A region to watch. Best producers: Chard Farm★, FELTON ROAD★★, Gibbston Valley★, Mt Difficulty★, Mount Edward★, Quartz Reef★, Rippon Vineyard★. Best years: (Pinot Noir) (2002) 01 **99 98**.

VALLE CENTRAL *Chile* The heart of Chile's wine industry, encompassing the valleys of MAIPO, RAPEL, CURICO and MAULE. Most major producers are located here, and the key factor determining mesoclimate differences is the distance relative to the coastal and Andean Cordilleras.

CENTRAL VALLEY *California, USA* This vast area grows over 75% of California's wine grapes, used mostly for cheaper styles of wine, along with brandies and grape concentrate. Viewed overall, the quality has improved over the past few years, but it is a hot area, where irrigated vineyards tend to produce excess tonnages of grapes. It has often been said that it is virtually impossible to produce exciting wine in the Central Valley, but in fact the climatic conditions in the northern half are not that unlike those in many parts of Spain and southern France. Growers in the Lodi AVA have expanded vineyards to 26,500ha (65,000 acres), making Lodi the volume leader for Chardonnay, Merlot, Zinfandel and Cabernet. Lodi Zinfandel shows some potential. Other sub-regions with claims to quality are the Sacramento Valley and the Delta area. Best producers: Sutter Home, Woodbridge/MONDAVI.

CENTRAL VICTORIA *Victoria, Australia* Comprising the regions of BENDIGO, Goulburn Valley, HEATHCOTE and the cooler, higher vineyards around the Strathbogie Ranges, the mostly warm conditions of Central Victoria produce powerful and individual wines. The few wineries on the banks of the serene thread of the Goulburn River produce fine RHONE varieties, particularly white Marsanne, while reds from the high country are lean but tasty; whites are delicate and scented. Best producers: DELATITE★★, Jasper Hill★★, MITCHELTON★★, Paul Osicka★★, TAHBILK★, Wild Duck Creek★.

CERETTO *Piedmont, Italy* This merchant house, run by brothers Bruno and Marcello Ceretto, is one of the chief modern producers in BAROLO. With the help of enologist Donato Lanati, Barolo (Bricco Rocche★★, Brunate★★ and Prapò★★), BARBARESCO (Bricco Asili★★), BARBERA D'ALBA Piana★ and white Arneis Blangè are living up to their reputation. Ceretto also produces an oak-aged LANGHE red, Monsordo★★, from Cabernet, Merlot, Pinot Nero and Nebbiolo. An unusual white counterpart, Arbarei, is 100% Riesling. A good sparkler, La Bernardina, is made from Chardonnay and Pinot Noir.

CÉRONS AC *Bordeaux, France* An AC for sweet wine in the GRAVES region of Bordeaux. The soft, mildly honeyed wine is not quite as sweet as SAUTERNES and not so well known, nor so highly priced. Most producers now make dry wine under the Graves label. Best producers: Ch. de Cérons★, Chantegrive, Grand Enclos du Château de Cérons★, Seuil. Best years: 2001 **99 98 97 96 95 90 89**.

L A CETTO *Baja California, Mexico* Mexico's most successful winery relie on mists and cooling Pacific breezes to temper the heat of the Valle de Guadalupe. Italian Camilo Magoni makes ripe, fleshy Petite Sirah, oak aged Cabernet Sauvignon, Zinfandel and Nebbiolo. Whites, led by Chardonnay and Chenin, are greatly improved. Also decent fizz.

CHABLAIS *Vaud, Switzerland* A sub-region of the VAUD, south-east of Lake Geneva. Most of the vineyards lie on the alluvial plains but 2 villages, Yvorne and Aigle, benefit from much steeper slopes and produce tangy whites and good reds. Most of the thirst-quenchingly dry whites are made from Chasselas, or Dorin as it is called locally. The reds are made from Pinot Noir, as is a rosé speciality, Oeil de Perdrix, an enjoyable summer wine. Drink whites and rosés young. Best producers: Henri Badoux, Delarze, Grognuz, J & P Testuz.

CHABLIS AC *Burgundy, France* Chablis, as close to CHAMPAGNE as to the COTE D'OR, is Burgundy's northernmost outpost. When not destroyed by frost or hail, the Chardonnay grape makes a crisp, dry white wine with a steely mineral fruit which can be delicious. Several producers are experimenting with barrel-aging for their better wines, resulting in some full, toasty, positively rich dry whites. Others are intentionally producing a soft, creamy, early-drinking style, which is nice but not really Chablis. The outlying areas come under the Petit Chablis AC and should be drunk young. The better straight Chablis AC should be drunk at 3–5 years, while a good vintage of a leading Chablis Premier Cru may take 5 years to show its full potential. About a quarter of Chablis is designated as Premier Cru, the best vineyards on the rolling limestone slopes being Fourchaume, Mont de Milieu, Montmains, Montée de Tonnerre and Vaillons. Best producers: Barat★, J-C Bessin (Fourchaume★★), Billaud-Simon (Mont de Milieu★★), Pascal Bouchard★, A & F Boudin★★, BROCARD★, la CHABLISIENNE★, Collet★, Dampt★, R & V DAUVISSAT★★, D & E Defaix★, Droin★, DROUHIN★, DURUP★, W Fèvre★, J-P Grossot (Côte de Troesme★★), LAROCHE★★, Malandes (Côte de Léchêt★★), L MICHEL★★, Picq (Vaucoupin★★), Pinson★, RAVENEAU★★, Vocoret★★. Best years: (Chablis Premier Cru) (2002) 00 **99 98 95 90**.

CHABLIS GRAND CRU AC *Burgundy, France* The 7 Grands Crus (Bougros, les Preuses, Vaudésir, Grenouilles, Valmur, les Clos and les Blanchots) facing south-west across the town of Chablis are the heart of the AC. Oak barrel-aging takes the edge off taut flavours, adding a rich warmth to these fine wines. Droin and Fèvre are the most enthusiastic users of new oak, but use it less than they used to. Never drink young: 5–10 years is needed before you can see why you spent your money. Best producers: J-C Bessin★★, Billaud-Simon★★, la CHABLISIENNE★★, J Dauvissat★★, R & V DAUVISSAT★★★, D & E Defaix★★, Droin★★, LAROCHE★★★, Long-Depaquit★★, MICHEL★★★, Pinson★★, RAVENEAU★★★, Servin★, Simonnet-Febvre★★, Vocoret★★. Best years: (2002) 00 99 98 **97** 96 **95 92 90**.

LA CHABLISIENNE *Chablis AC, Burgundy, France* Substantial co-op producing nearly a third of all CHABLIS. The wines are reliable and can aspire to greatness. The best are the oaky Grands Crus – especially les Preuses★★ and Grenouilles (sold as Ch. Grenouille★★) – but the basic unoaked Chablis★, the Vieilles Vignes★★ and the numerous Premiers Crus★ are good, as is the red BOURGOGNE Épineuil. Best years: (whites) (2002) 00 **99 98 97 96**; (reds) (2002) 00 **99**.

CHALONE *Monterey County, California, USA* Producers of full-blown but slow-developing Chardonnay★★ and concentrated Pinot Noir★★ from vineyards on the arid eastern slope of the Coastal Range in mid-

MONTEREY COUNTY. Also very good Pinot Blanc★★ and Chenin Blanc★, as well as Reserve Pinot Noir★★ and Chardonnay★★. Syrah★ is a promising new addition. These are strongly individualistic wines. Best years: (Chardonnay) (2001) 00 99 98 97 **96 95 94 93 92 91 90** 85; (Pinot Noir) 2000 99 98 **96 95 94 92 91 90 88 86**.

CHAMBERS *Rutherglen, Victoria, Australia* Legendary family winery making sheer nectar in the form of Muscat and Tokay. The secret is Bill Chambers' ability to draw on ancient stocks put down in wood by earlier generations. His 'Special'★★ and 'Rare'★★★ blends are national treasures. The Cabernet and Shiraz are good, the whites pedestrian.

CHAMBERTIN AC *Grand Cru, Côte de Nuits, Burgundy, France* The village of GEVREY-CHAMBERTIN, the largest COTE DE NUITS commune, has no fewer than 8 Grands Crus (Chambertin, Chambertin-Clos-de-Bèze, Chapelle-Chambertin, Charmes-Chambertin, Griotte-Chambertin, Latricières-Chambertin, Mazis-Chambertin and Ruchottes-Chambertin), which can produce some of Burgundy's greatest and most intense red wine. Its rough-hewn fruit, seeming to war with fragrant perfumes for its first few years, creates remarkable flavours as the wine ages. Chambertin and Chambertin-Clos-de-Bèze are the greatest sites, but overproduction is a recurrent problem with some producers. Best producers: Denis Bachelet★★, BOUCHARD PERE ET FILS★, Charlopin★, B CLAIR★★★, P Damoy★, DROUHIN★★, Dugat-Py★★★, FAIVELEY★★, R Groffier★★, JADOT★★, D Laurent★★★, Dom. LEROY★★★, Denis MORTET★★★, H Perrot-Minot★★, Ponsot★★, Rossignol-Trapet★, J Roty★★, ROUMIER★★, ROUSSEAU★★★, Trapet★, VOUGERAIE★★. Best years: (2002) (01) 00 99 98 **97 96 95 93 91 90 88**.

CHAMBERTIN-CLOS-DE-BÈZE AC See Chambertin AC.

CHAMBOLLE-MUSIGNY AC *Côte de Nuits, Burgundy, France* AC with the potential to produce the most fragrant, perfumed red Burgundy, when not over-cropped. Encouragingly, more young producers are now bottling their own wines. Best producers: G Barthod★★, DROUHIN★★, DUJAC★★, R Groffier★★, Hudelot-Noëllat★★, JADOT★★, Dom. LEROY★★, Marchand-Grillot★★, D MORTET★★, J-F Mugnier★★, RION★★, ROUMIER★★ VOGUE★★. Best years: (2002) (01) 00 99 98 **97** 96 **95 93 90**.

CHAMPAGNE See pages 96–7.

CHAMPAGNE ROSÉ *Champagne, France* Good pink CHAMPAGNE has a delicious fragrance of cherries and raspberries. The top wines can age well, but most should be drunk on release. Best producers: (vintage) BILLECART-SALMON★★, BOLLINGER★★, Gosset★★, Charles HEIDSIECK★★, JACQUESSON★★, LAURENT-PERRIER (Grand Siècle Alexandra★★★), MOET & CHANDON★★ (Dom Pérignon★★★), POL ROGER★★, Louis ROEDERER★★, RUINART★★★, VEUVE CLICQUOT★★; (non-vintage) Paul Bara★, E Barnaut★★, Beaumont des Crayères★, BILLECART-SALMON★★, Egly-Ouriet★★, Jacquart★, KRUG★★★, LANSON★, LAURENT-PERRIER★, MOET & CHANDON★, PERRIER-JOUET★, RUINART★★, TAITTINGER★, Vilmart★. Best years: (1999) (98) (96) 95 **91 90 89 88 85** 82. See also pages 96–7.

CHANDON DE BRIAILLES *Savigny-lès-Beaune AC, Côte de Beaune, Burgundy, France* The de Nicolays, mother and daughter, combine modern sophistication with traditional values to produce rich but refined reds from SAVIGNY-LES-BEAUNE★, PERNAND-VERGELESSES★★, ALOXE-CORTON★★ and CORTON★★★, and an equally good range of whites from Pernand-Vergelesses★★, Corton★★★ and CORTON-CHARLEMAGNE★★★. Best years: (reds) (2002) (01) 99 98 96 **95 93 90**.

CHAMPAGNE AC

Champagne, France

 The Champagne region produces the most celebrated sparkling wines in the world. East of Paris, it is the most northerly AC in France – a place where grapes struggle to ripen fully. Champagne is divided into 5 distinct areas – the best are the Montagne de Reims where the Pinot Noir grape performs brilliantly, and the Chardonnay-dominated Côte des Blancs south of Épernay. In addition to Chardonnay and Pinot Noir, the only other grape permitted for the production of Champagne is Pinot Meunier.

The wines undergo a second fermentation in the bottle which produces carbon dioxide, dissolved in the wine under pressure. Through this method Champagne acquires its crisp, long-lasting bubbles and a distinctive yeasty, toasty dimension to its flavour. If you buy a bottle of Coteaux Champenois, a still wine from the area, you can see why they decided to make bubbly instead; it usually tastes mean and tart, but is transformed by the Champagne method into one of the most delightfully exhilarating wines of all.

That's the theory anyway, and for 150 years or so the Champenois have persuaded us that their product is second to none. It can be, too, except when it is released too young or sweetened to make up for a lack of richness. When that periodically happens you know that, once again, the powers of marketing have triumphed over the wisdom and skills of the winemaker. But as Champagne expertise begins to turn out exciting sparklers in California, Australia and New Zealand, the Champagne producers must re-focus on quality or lose much of their market for good.

The Champagne trade is dominated by large companies or houses, called négociants-manipulants, recognized by the letters NM on the label. The récoltants-manipulants (recognized by the letters RM) are growers who make their own wine.

STYLES OF CHAMPAGNE

Non-vintage Most Champagne is a blend of 2 or more vintages. Quality varies enormously, depending on who has made the wine and how long it has been aged. Most Champagne is sold as Brut, which is a dry, but rarely bone-dry style. Strangely, Extra Dry denotes a style less dry than Brut.

Vintage Denotes Champagne made with grapes from a single vintage. As a rule, it is made only in the best years, but far too many mediocre years were declared in the 1990s.

Blanc de Blancs A lighter, and at best highly elegant, style of Champagne made solely from the Chardonnay grape.

Blanc de Noirs A white Champagne, but made entirely from black grapes, either Pinot Noir, Pinot Meunier, or a combination of the two. Generally rather solid.

Rosé Pink Champagne, made either from black grapes or (more usually) by mixing a little still red wine into white Champagne.

De luxe cuvée In theory the finest Champagne and certainly always the most expensive, residing in the fanciest bottles.

See also CHAMPAGNE ROSE; and individual producers.

96

BEST YEARS

(1999) (98) 96 **95 90 89 88 85 83 82**

BEST PRODUCERS

Houses BILLECART-SALMON, BOLLINGER, Cattier, Delamotte, Delbeck, DEUTZ, Drappier, Duval-Leroy, Gosset, Alfred GRATIEN, Charles HEIDSIECK, HENRIOT, JACQUESSON, KRUG, LANSON, LAURENT-PERRIER, Bruno PAILLARD, Joseph PERRIER, PERRIER-JOUET, Philipponnat, POL ROGER, POMMERY, Louis ROEDERER, RUINART, Salon, TAITTINGER, VEUVE CLICQUOT.

Growers Michel Arnould, Bara, Barnaut, Beaufort, Beerens, Callot, Charpentier, Chartogne-Taillet, Diebolt Vallois, Daniel Dumont, Egly-Ouriet, René Geoffroy, Gimonnet, André Jacquart, Lamiable, Larmandier, Larmandier-Bernier, Launois, Margaine, Serge Mathieu, G Michel, Moncuit, Alain Robert, Secondé, Selosse, de Sousa, Tarlant, Vilmart.

Co-ops Beaumont les Crayères, Chouilly (Nicolas Feuillatte), Jacquart, Mailly.

De luxe cuvées Belle Époque (PERRIER-JOUET), N-F Billecart (BILLECART-SALMON), Blanc de Millénaires (Charles HEIDSIECK), Clos des Goisses (Philipponnat), Clos de Mesnil (KRUG), Comtes de Champagne (TAITTINGER), Cristal (Louis ROEDERER), Cuvée Josephine (Joseph PERRIER), Cuvée Sir Winston Churchill (POL ROGER), Cuvée William Deutz (DEUTZ), Dom Pérignon (MOET & CHANDON), Dom Ruinart (RUINART), Grand Siècle (LAURENT-PERRIER), Grande Dame (VEUVE CLICQUOT), Noble Cuvée (LANSON), Vintage RD (BOLLINGER).

CHAPEL HILL *McLaren Vale, South Australia* Pam Dunsford makes powerful, classy wines at her hilltop winery. She blends mature McLAREN VALE and COONAWARRA fruit in her Cabernet Sauvignon★★, while Shiraz★★ is all McLaren Vale. Good unwooded Chardonnay★ (Reserve★★), and fascinating, bone-dry, honey-scented Verdelho★★. Best years: (Shiraz) (2001) 00 98 **97 96 95 94 93 91**.

CHAPELLE-CHAMBERTIN AC See Chambertin AC.

LA CHAPELLE LENCLOS *Madiran AC, South-West France* Patrick Ducournau has tamed the savage Tannat grape with controlled oxygenation during barrel aging. The Chapelle Lenclos★★ and Dom. Mouréou★ reds are ripe and concentrated, though they still need at least 5 years to mature. Best years: 2001 00 99 98 **96 95 94 93 90**.

M CHAPOUTIER *Rhône Valley, France* Chapoutier is very much in the vanguard of progress, both in viticulture and in winemaking, and is producing a full range of serious and exciting wines. The HERMITAGE la Sizeranne★★, l'Ermite★★, le Méal★★★ and le Pavillon★★★, white Hermitage Cuvée de l'Orée★★, CROZES-HERMITAGE les Varonniers★★, ST-JOSEPH les Granits★★ and CHATEAUNEUF-DU-PAPE Barbe Rac★★ are all good, but some of them show a surfeit of new oak. Jointly owns Dom. des Béates (Cuvée Terra d'Or★★) in PROVENCE. Best years: (la Sizeranne) (2001) 00 99 98 96 95 **94 91 90 89 88**.

CHARDONNAY See pages 100–101.

CHARMES-CHAMBERTIN AC See Chambertin AC.

CHASSAGNE-MONTRACHET AC *Côte de Beaune, Burgundy, France* Some of Burgundy's greatest white wine vineyards (part of le MONTRACHET and BATARD-MONTRACHET, all of Criots-Bâtard-Montrachet) are within the village boundary. The white Chassagne Premiers Crus are not as well known, but can offer nutty, toasty wines, especially if aged for 4–8 years. Ordinary white Chassagne-Montrachet is usually enjoyable; the red is a little earthy, peppery and plummy and can be an acquired taste. Look out for reds from the following Premiers Crus: Clos de la Boudriotte, Clos St-Jean and Clos de la Chapelle. Best producers: (whites) F d'Allaines★, G Amiot★★, Blain-Gagnard★★, M Colin★★, Colin-Deléger★★, Fontaine-Gagnard★★, J-N GAGNARD★★, V GIRARDIN★★, F & V Jouard★, H Lamy★, Duc de Magenta★, B Morey★★, M Morey★★, M Niellon★★, RAMONET★★; (reds) G Amiot★★, CARILLON★, R Clerget★, V GIRARDIN★★, B Morey★★, RAMONET★. Best years: (whites) (2002) (01) 00 99 **98 97** 96 95 92; (reds) (2002) 99 98 **97** 96 95 93.

CHASSELAS Chasselas is considered a table grape worldwide. Only in BADEN (where it is called Gutedel) and Switzerland (called Dorin, Perlan or Fendant) is it thought to make decent light, dry wines with a slight prickle. A few Swiss examples, notably from DEZALEY, rise above this.

CH. CHASSE-SPLEEN★ *Moulis AC, Cru Bourgeois, Haut-Médoc, Bordeaux, France* Chasse-Spleen is not a Classed Growth – but during the 1980s it built a tremendous reputation for ripe, concentrated and powerful wines under the late proprietor, Bernadette Villars. The château is now run by Villars' daughter Céline, and recent vintages are again finding the form of the old days. Second wine: l'Ermitage de Chasse-Spleen. Best years: 2001 00 99 96 **95 94 90 89 88 86 83 82**.

CHÂTEAU-CHALON AC *Jura, France* The most prized – and pricy – *vin jaune*, it is difficult to find, even in the Jura. But if you do find a bottle, beware – the awesome flavour will shock your tastebuds like no other

French wine. Not released until 6 years after the vintage, it can be kept for much longer. Best producers: Baud★★, Berthet-Bondet★★, Bourdy★★, Chalandard★★, Credoz★, Durand-Perron★★, J Macle★★, H Maire★★. Best years: 1996 95 94 93 **92 91 90 89 88 87 86 85**.

CHÂTEAU-GRILLET AC★★ *Rhône Valley, France*   This rare and *very* expensive RHONE white, made from Viognier and aged in oak, has a magic reek of orchard fruit and harvest bloom when young and can age well. However, many of the top CONDRIEUS consistently make superior wine. Best years: 2001 00 **99 98 95**.

CHATEAU INDAGE *Maharashtra, India*   Winemaker John Locke (ex-BONNY DOON) is building on technology introduced by Champagne consultants PIPER-HEIDSIECK. Dry sparklers are firm, fresh and chunky – though quality is somewhat erratic. Traditional-method Omar Khayyám is produced from a blend of Chardonnay, Ugni Blanc, Pinot Noir and Pinot Meunier. A demi-sec and a remarkably good pink fizz are also produced, plus red and white table wines. Bangalore Purple, an indigenous grape variety of India, is used in a new red blend. A joint venture with Wente of California and the French Taillan group will bring in new investment, and vineyard expansion to 1000ha (2470 acres).

CHATEAU MONTELENA *Napa Valley AVA, California, USA*   Napa winery producing well-balanced Chardonnay★★ and a Cabernet★★ that is impressive, if slow to develop. There is also a fascinating, soft Zinfandel-Sangiovese blend, St Vincent★★. Best years: (Chardonnay) (2001) 00 99 **98 97 96 95 94**; (Cabernet) (2001) (00) 99 98 97 96 **95 94 93 91 90 87 86 85 84.**

CHATEAU MUSAR *Ghazir, Lebanon*   Founded by Gaston Hochar in the 1930s and now run by his Bordeaux-trained son Serge, Musar is famous for having made wine every year bar two (1976 and 84) throughout Lebanon's civil war. From an unlikely blend of primarily Cabernet Sauvignon, Cinsaut and Syrah comes a wine of real, if wildly exotic, character, with sweet, spicy fruit and good aging potential: Hochar says that red Musar★ 'should be drunk at 15 years'. Some recent vintages have not quite lived up to expectations, in part due to 4 successive years of low rainfall, but latest harvests are encouraging. There is also a rosé, and a white from local grape varieties Obaideh and Merwah – Chardonnay and Sémillon lookalikes respectively. Trial plantings of Merlot may result in a Cinsault-Merlot blend. Best years: (red) (1999) (98) (97) **96 95 94 93 91 90 89 88**; (white) **1997**.

CHATEAU ST JEAN *Sonoma Valley AVA, California, USA*   Once known almost entirely for its range of Chardonnays (Belle Terre★★ and Robert Young★★), St Jean has emerged as a producer of delicious reds including a BORDEAUX-style blend called Cinq Cépages★★ and a Reserve Merlot★★. Best years: (Chardonnay) (2001) 00 99 **98 97 96 95 94 91 90**; (Cabernet) (2001) (00) 99 97 96 **95 94**.

CHATEAU STE MICHELLE *Washington State, USA*   A pioneering winery with an enormous range of wines, including several attractive vineyard-designated Chardonnays★, Cabernet Sauvignons★ and Merlots★, especially Cold Creek Vineyard★★ wines. Good Riesling, both dry and sweet, and increasingly interesting red Meritage★ and white Sauvignon. Partnership with Italy's ANTINORI and Germany's Ernst LOOSEN have produced dark, powerful red Col Solare★★, a lovely dry Riesling Eroica★ and a thrilling sweet version, TBA★★★, made in tiny quantities. Best years: (premium reds) 2001 00 99 **98 97 96**.

CHARDONNAY

I never thought I'd see myself write this. Yes, we are getting bored with Chardonnay. Not all Chardonnay there's probably more top Chardonnay being produced right now than ever before. And for millions of wine drinkers the Chardonnay revolution (easy to pronounce, easy to swallow) has only just begun. But in the heart of the wine world – the middle market, where people care about flavour but also care about price – we're getting fed up. Far too much sugary, over-oaked, unrefreshing junk has been dumped into our laps recently, from countries and producers who should know better. Add to this the increasingly desperate dirt-cheap offerings at the rump end of the market, and you'll see why I think the great golden goose of Chardonnay has the carving knife of cynicism and greed firmly held against its neck. It's now the fourth most-planted variety in the world. The next few years will show whether it wishes to be the supremely versatile all-rounder or the sloppy jack of all trades and master of none.

WINE STYLES

France Although a relatively neutral variety if left alone (this is what makes it so suitable as a base wine for top-quality Champagne-method sparkling wine), the grape can ripen in a surprising range of conditions, developing a subtle gradation of flavours going from the sharp apple-core greenness of Chardonnay grown in Champagne or the Loire, through the exciting, bone-dry yet succulent flavours of white Burgundy, to a round, perfumed flavour in Languedoc-Roussillon.

Other regions Italy produces Chardonnay that can be bone dry and lean or fat, spicy and lush. Spain does much the same. California and Australia virtually created their reputations on great, viscous, almost syrupy, tropical fruits and spice-flavoured Chardonnays; the best producers are now moving away from this style. Some of the best New World Chardonnays, dry but ripe and subtly oaked, are coming from South Africa. New Zealand is producing rich, deep, but beautifully balanced Chardonnays, while Chile and Argentina have found it easy to grow and are rapidly learning how to make fine wine from it too. Add Germany, Austria, Canada, New York State, Greece, Portugal, Slovenia, Moldova, Romania, even China, and you'll see it can perform almost anywhere. **Using oak** The reason for all these different flavours lies in Chardonnay's wonderful susceptibility to the winemaker's aspirations and skills. The most important manipulation is the use of the oak barrel for fermenting and aging the wine. Chardonnay is the grape of the great white Burgundies and these are fermented and matured in oak (not necessarily new oak); the effect is to give a marvellous round, nutty richness to a wine that is yet savoury and dry. This is enriched still further by aging the wine on its lees.

The New World winemakers sought to emulate the great Burgundies, planting Chardonnay and employing thousands of oak barrels (mostly new), and their success – and the enthusiasm with which wine drinkers embraced the wine – has caused winemakers everywhere else to see Chardonnay as the perfect variety – easy to grow, easy to turn into wine and easy to sell to an adoring public.

BEST PRODUCERS

France *Chablis* J-C Bessin, A & F Boudin, DAUVISSAT, Droin, LAROCHE, MICHEL, RAVENEAU; *Côte d'Or* G Amiot, R Ampeau, J-M Boillot, Bonneau du Martray, Pascal Bouchard, M Bouzereau, CARILLON, COCHE-DURY, Marc Colin, DROUHIN, Arnaud Ente, J-N GAGNARD, V GIRARDIN, JADOT, F Jobard, R Jobard, LAFON, R Lamy-Pillot, Louis LATOUR, Dom. LEFLAIVE, Bernard Morey, M Niellon, RAMONET, M Rollin, G Roulot, SAUZET, VERGET; *Mâconnais* D & M Barraud, Guffens-Heynen (VERGET), O Merlin, Thévenet, Valette.

Other European Chardonnays
Austria TEMENT, VELICH.

Germany JOHNER, REBHOLZ.

Italy BELLAVISTA, CA' DEL BOSCO, GAJA, LAGEDER, Vie di Romans, Castello della SALA (Cervaro).

Spain ENATE, Manzaneque, TORRES, Señorío de Otazu.

New World Chardonnays
Australia BANNOCKBURN, CULLEN, Giaconda, GROSSET, HOWARD PARK, LEEUWIN, LENSWOOD, MOUNTADAM, PETALUMA, PIERRO, TARRAWARRA, TYRRELL'S.

New Zealand BABICH, CLOUDY BAY, DRY RIVER, FELTON ROAD, ISABEL, KUMEU RIVER, MILLTON, MORTON ESTATE, NEUDORF, PEGASUS BAY, SERESIN, TE MATA, VAVASOUR, Vidal, WITHER HILLS.

USA ARROWOOD, AU BON CLIMAT, BABCOCK, BERINGER, CALERA, CHALONE, CHATEAU ST JEAN, FERRARI-CARANO, FLOWERS, KISTLER, MARCASSIN, MATANZAS CREEK, MERRYVALE, Peter MICHAEL, NEWTON, David Ramey, RIDGE, ROCHIOLI, SAINTSBURY, SANFORD, SHAFER, STEELE, TALBOT.

South Africa BUITENVERWACHTING, Neil ELLIS (Elgin), GLEN CARLOU, HAMILTON RUSSELL, JORDAN, MEERLUST, MULDERBOSCH, THELEMA, VERGELEGEN.

South America CASABLANCA, CATENA, CONCHA Y TORO (Amelia).

101

CHÂTEAUNEUF-DU-PAPE AC *Rhône Valley, France* A large (3350ha/8275-acre) vineyard area between Orange and Avignon. Much Châteauneuf comes from single estates and is one of France's top reds; it's based on Grenache, plus Syrah and Mourvèdre (10 other varieties are also allowed). Always get an estate wine, distinguished by the papal coat of arms embossed on the neck of the bottle. Only 5% of Châteauneuf is white; made mainly from Grenache Blanc, Bourboulenc and Clairette, these wines can be surprisingly good. The top reds, particularly the increasing number of old-vine cuvées, will age for 8 years or more, while the whites are best young. Best producers: (reds) P Autard★, L Barrot★★, BEAUCASTEL★★★, Beaurenard★★, Bois de Boursan★★, H Bonneau★★, Bosquet des Papes★★, du Caillou★★, les Cailloux★★, Chante Perdrix★★, CHAPOUTIER★★, la Charbonnière★★, G Charvin★★, Clos du Mont Olivet★★, CLOS DES PAPES★★★, Font du Loup★★, FONT DE MICHELLE★★, Fortia★★, la Gardine★★, Grand Tinel★★, la Janasse★★, Marcoux★★, Monpertuis★★, Mont-Redon★★, la Nerthe★★, Pégaü★★, RAYAS★★★, la Roquette★★, Roger Sabon★★, Tardieu-Laurent★★, P Usseglio★★, la Vieille-Julienne★★, Vieux Donjon★★, VIEUX TELEGRAPHE★★★, Villeneuve★★; (whites) BEAUCASTEL★★★, CLOS DES PAPES★★, FONT DE MICHELLE★★, Grand Veneur★★, Marcoux★★, RAYAS★★★, St-Cosme★★, VIEUX TELEGRAPHE★★. Best years: (reds) 2001 00 99 98 **97 96 95 94 90 89 88**.

JEAN-LOUIS CHAVE *Rhône Valley, France* Jean-Louis Chave, son of Gérard, has achieved superstar status in his own right. His red HERMITAGE★★★ is one of the world's great wines, surpassed only by the Cuvée Cathelin★★★, produced only in exceptional years. His wonderful, richly flavoured white Hermitage★★★ sometimes even outlasts the reds, as it quietly moves toward its honeyed, nutty zenith. Also produces a small amount of excellent red ST-JOSEPH★★ and an occasional stunning traditional sweet Vin de Paille★★. Expensive, but worth the money. Best years: (reds) (2001) 00 99 98 97 96 95 94 **92 91** 90 89 **88 86 85 83 82 81 79 78**; (whites) (2001) 00 99 98 97 96 95 94 **93 92 91 90 89 88 83**.

CHÉNAS AC *Beaujolais, Burgundy, France* The smallest of the BEAUJOLAIS Crus, Chénas, while little known, offers a range of styles from light and elegant to austere and needing time to develop Burgundian tones. Best producers: (reds) J Benon★★, G Braillon★, L Champagnon★, DUBOEUF (Manoir des Journets★), H Lapierre★, B Santé★. Best years: **2000 99 98**.

CHENIN BLANC One of the most underrated white wine grapes in the world. In the LOIRE VALLEY, where it is also called Pineau de la Loire, it is responsible for the great sweet wines of QUARTS DE CHAUME and BONNEZEAUX, as well as for VOUVRAY, sweet or dry, and much Anjou white. It is also the main grape for the Loire sparkling wines. In South Africa, although vineyards have decreased to 20% of the total area, the best are being identified and retained, making a spectrum of wine styles, from easy-drinking, dryish whites through botrytized desserts to modern barrel-fermented versions. CALIFORNIA, with a few exceptions like Chappellet, only employs it as a blender. New Zealand and Australia have produced good varietal examples.

CH. CHEVAL BLANC★★★ *St-Émilion Grand Cru AC, 1er Grand Cru Classé, Bordeaux, France* Along with AUSONE, the leading ST-EMILION estate. Right on the border with POMEROL, it seems to share some of its sturdy richness, but with an extra spice and fruit that is impressively, recognizably unique. An unusually high percentage (60%) of Cabernet Franc can be used in the blend. Best years: 2001 00 99 98 97 96 95 **94 90 89 88 86 85 83 82.**

CHEVALIER-MONTRACHET AC See Montrachet AC.

DOM. DE CHEVALIER *Pessac-Léognan AC, Cru Classé de Graves, Bordeaux, France* This estate, mainly devoted to red, can produce some of Bordeaux's finest wines. The red★★ always starts out dry and tannic but over 10–20 years gains heavenly cedar, tobacco and blackcurrant flavour. The brilliant white★★★ is both fermented and aged in oak barrels; in the best vintages it will still be improving at 15–20 years. Best years: (reds) 2001 00 99 98 96 95 **90 89 88**; (whites) 2001 00 99 98 97 96 95 **94 90 89 88.**

CHEVERNY AC *Loire Valley, France* A little-known area south of Blois. The local speciality is the white Romorantin grape, which makes a bone-dry wine under the AC Cour-Cheverny, but the best whites are from Chardonnay. Also pleasant Sauvignon, Pinot Noir and Gamay and a bracing Champagne-method fizz. Drink young. Best producers: Cazin, Cheverny co-op, Courtioux, Gendrier★, Gueritte, du Moulin, Salvard, Sauger, C Tessier/la Desoucherie, Tue-Bœuf★.

CHIANTI DOCG *Tuscany, Italy* The most famous of all Italian wines, but there are many styles, depending on what grapes are used, where they are grown, and by which producer. It can be a light, fresh, easy-drinking red wine, but with a characteristic hint of bitterness, or it can be an intense, structured yet sleek wine in the same league as the best BORDEAUX. The vineyards are scattered over central Tuscany, either simply as 'Chianti' or Chianti plus the name of one of the 8 sub-zones: Classico (with its own DOCG), Colli Aretini, Colli Fiorentini, Colli Senesi, Colline Pisane, Montalbano, Montespertoli and Rufina. Sangiovese is the main grape; traditionally it was blended with the red Canaiolo and white Malvasia and Trebbiano. Modern winemakers often make Chianti from Sangiovese alone or blended with 10–15% of Cabernet, Merlot, Syrah or, increasingly, with native grapes like Colorino. See also Chianti Colli Fiorentini, Chianti Colli Senesi, Chianti Rufina, Super-Tuscans.

CHIANTI CLASSICO DOCG *Tuscany, Italy* The original (if slightly enlarged) CHIANTI zone in the hills between Florence and Siena. Classico has led the trend in making richer, more structured and better-balanced wines. Nonetheless, many producers use their best grapes for high-profile SUPER-TUSCANS. Since the 96 vintage, Classico can be made from 100% Sangiovese; the Riserva may now be aged (usually in barrel) for 2 instead of 3 years but must only use red grapes. The finest Riserva wines can improve for a decade or more. Many of the estates also offer regular bottlings of red wine, round and fruity, for drinking about 2–5 years after the harvest. Best producers: Castello di AMA★★, ANTINORI★★, Badia a Coltibuono★★, Brancaia★, Cacchiano★, Capaccia★★, Carpineto★★, Casaloste★★, CASTELLARE★, Castell'in Villa★, Cecchi (Villa Cerna★), Collelungo★, Colombaio di Cencio★, Dievole★, Casa Emma★, FELSINA★★, Le Filigare★, FONTERUTOLI★★, FONTODI★★, ISOLE E OLENA★★, Il Mandorlo★★, La Massa★★, Melini★, Monsanto★★, Monte Bernardi★, Il Palazzino★★, Paneretta★★, Panzanello★★, Poggerino★, Poggiopiano★, Poggio al Sole (Casasilia★★★), Querceto★, QUERCIABELLA★★, Castello dei RAMPOLLA★★, RICASOLI (Castello di Brolio★★), RIECINE★★, Rignana★★, Rocca di Castagnoli★★, RUFFINO★★, San

Felice★★, San Giusto a Rentennano★★, San Polo in Rosso★ Terrabianca★, Vecchie Terre di Montefili★, Verrazzano★, Vignamaggio★ Villa Cafaggio★★, VOLPAIA★★. Best years: (2001) 00 **99 98 97 95 93 90 8**

CHIANTI COLLI FIORENTINI *Chianti DOCG, Tuscany, Italy* Colli Fiorentin covers the hills around Florence. The wines traditionally are made drink young, though some estates make Riservas of real interest. Bes producers: Baggiolino★, Le Calvane, Il Corno, Corzano e Paterno★ Lanciola★, Pasolini dall'Onda★, Poppiano★, La Querce, Sammontan San Vito in Fior di Selva.

CHIANTI COLLI SENESI *Chianti DOCG, Tuscany, Italy* This CHIANTI sub zone consists of a vast area of Siena province (including the towns Montalcino, Montepulciano and San Gimignano). Wines range from everyday quaffers to fairly elegant Riservas. Best producers Campriano★, Carpineta Fontalpino★, Casabianca, Casale-Falchini★ Farnetella★, Ficomontanino★, Pacina★, Paradiso★, Pietraserena.

CHIANTI RUFINA *Chianti DOCG, Tuscany, Italy* Smallest of the CHIANTI sub zones, situated in an enclave of the Apennine mountains to the east o Florence, where wines were noted for exceptional strength, structur and longevity long before they joined the ranks of Chianti. Today th wines, particularly the long-lived Riserva Bucerchiale from SELVAPIAN and FRESCOBALDI's Montesodi, match the best of CHIANTI CLASSICO. Pomin DOC is a small (100ha/250-acre) high-altitude zone almost entirel surrounded by Chianti Rufina; dominated by Frescobaldi, it make greater use of French varieties such as Merlot, Cabernet an Chardonnay. Best producers: (Riservas) Basciano★★, Tenuta di Bossi★ Colognole, FRESCOBALDI★★, Grignano★, Lavacchio★, SELVAPIANA★ Castello del Trebbio★. Best years: (2001) 00 99 **98 97 95 93 90 88 85.**

MICHELE CHIARLO *Piedmont, Italy* From his winery base south of Asti Michele Chiarlo produces stylish wines from several PIEDMONT zones Single-vineyard BAROLOS★★ and BARBARESCOS★ top the list, but BARBERA D'ASTI★ and GAVI★ are reliable, too. The Monferrato DOC embraces Countacc!★, a Nebbiolo-Barbera-Cabernet Sauvignon blend.

CHIMNEY ROCK *Stags Leap District AVA, California, USA* After a shaky start, winemaker Doug Fletcher stepped in to put Chimney Rock on the right track, with powerful yet elegantly shaped Cabernet Sauvignon★★, Reserve Cabernet Sauvignon★★ and a meritage blend called Elevage★. A tangy Fumé Blanc★ is also made. Best years: (Elevage) (2001) 00 99 98 97 **96 95 94 92 91 90.**

CHINON AC *Loire Valley, France* Best red wine of the LOIRE VALLEY, made mainly from Cabernet Franc. Lovely light reds full of raspberry fruit and fresh summer earth to drink young, and heavyweights for keeping; always worth buying a single-estate wine. Best producers: P Alliet★★, B Baudry★★, J & C Baudry★, P Breton★, D Chauveau, Coulaine★, COULY-DUTHEIL★, Delaunay★, DRUET★★, la Grille★, C Joguet★, Noblaie★, la Perrière★, J-M Raffault★, Olga Raffault★, Roncée★, Sourdais★. Best years: (2002) 01 **00 97 96 95 90 89.**

CHIROUBLES AC *Beaujolais, Burgundy, France* The highest in altitude of the BEAUJOLAIS Crus, producing a light, fragrant and juicily delicious Gamay wine capable of exhibiting all the attractions of a youthful Cru. Best producers: Cheysson★, Dom. de la Combe au Loup/Méziat★, Dom. de la Grosse Pierre/A Passot★, J Passot★. Best years: **2002 00.**

CHIVITE *Navarra DO, Navarra, Spain* The longtime leader in exports from NAVARRA, owned and run by the Chivite family. The wine is reliable to good but the reds, in particular, could be a bit more lively. The top range is called Colección 125 and includes a red Reserva★, classy white Blanco★★ made from Chardonnay, and a characterful sweet Vendimia Tardía★★ from Moscatel (Muscat Blanc à Petits Grains).

CHOREY-LÈS-BEAUNE AC *Côte de Beaune, Burgundy, France* One of those tiny, forgotten villages that make good, if not great, Burgundy at prices most of us can still afford, with some committed producers too. Can age for 5–8 years. Best producers: Arnoux Père et Fils★, DROUHIN★, Germain★, Maillard Père et Fils★, TOLLOT-BEAUT★★. Best years: (2002) (01) 99 **98 97 96**.

CHURCH ROAD *Hawkes Bay, New Zealand* Church Road (formerly known as The McDonald Winery) is a premium-wine project owned by MONTANA. There's a dry but balanced Cabernet Sauvignon-Merlot★ and a plummy Reserve Merlot★. Super-premium blend Tom★, first released in 1999, has BORDEAUX-style austerity but good depth. Reserve Chardonnay★ is rich and smooth with flavours of peach, grapefruit and hazelnut. Best years: (Cabernet Sauvignon-Merlot) (2002) 00 **96 95**.

CHURCHILL *Port DOC, Douro, Portugal* Established in 1981, it was the first new PORT shipper for 50 years. The wines are very good, notably Vintage★★, LBV★, Crusted★★, single-quinta Agua Alta★★ and well-aged quirky dry white ports. Quinta da Gricha (purchased in 1999) is a new source of Vintage port. Also new is a red DOURO table wine. Best years: (Vintage) 2000 97 94 **91 85**; (Agua Alta) 1998 **96 95 92 87**.

CINSAUT Also spelt Cinsault. Found mainly in France's southern RHONE, PROVENCE and the MIDI, giving a light wine with fresh, but rather fleeting, neutral fruit. Ideal for rosé wine. Used in the blend for Lebanon's CHATEAU MUSAR. Popular as a bulk blender in South Africa, it is now being rediscovered by enthusiasts of the Rhône style.

CIRÒ DOC *Calabria, Italy* The legend that this was the wine offered to champions in the ancient Olympics has often seemed a more potent reason to buy it than for quality. Yet Cirò Rosso, a full-bodied red from the Gaglioppo grape, has improved remarkably of late. Non-DOC Gaglioppo-based IGTs, like Librandi's Gravello★★ (an oak-aged blend with Cabernet), are genuinely exciting. The DOC also covers a dry white from Greco and a rare dry rosé. Best producers: Caparra & Siciliani★, Librandi★ (Riserva★★), San Francesco★. Best years: (reds) (2000) 99 **97 96 95 93**.

BRUNO CLAIR *Marsannay AC, Côte de Nuits, Burgundy, France* Based in MARSANNAY, Bruno Clair produces a large range of excellent wines from a broad span of vineyards there, as well as in GEVREY-CHAMBERTIN, GIVRY, SAVIGNY and VOSNE-ROMANEE. Most of his wine is red, but there is a small amount of white (CORTON-CHARLEMAGNE★★) and a delicious Marsannay rosé★. Top wines are CHAMBERTIN Clos de Bèze★★★, Gevrey-Chambertin Clos St-Jacques★★★ and vineyard-designated Marsannay reds★★. Best years: (top reds) (2002) (01) 00 99 98 96 **95 93 90**.

CLAIRETTE DE DIE AC *Rhône Valley, France* One of the undeservedly forgotten sparkling wines of France, made from a minimum of 75% Muscat, off-dry with a creamy bubble and an orchard-fresh fragrance.

The *méthode Dioise* is used, which preserves the Muscat scent. Drink young. Best producers: Achard-Vincent★, Clairette de Die co-op★, D Cornillon, J Faure, J-C Raspail★. See also Crémant de Die.

A CLAPE *Cornas, Rhône Valley, France*   The leading estate in CORNAS, Clape's wines★★★ are consistently among the best in the RHONE – dense, tannic and full of rich, roasted fruit. Clape also makes fine COTES DU RHONE, both red★ and white★, and decent ST-PERAY★. Best years: (Cornas) (2001) 00 **99 98 97 96 95 94 92 91 90 89 88 86 85.**

LA CLAPE *Coteaux du Languedoc AC, Languedoc, France*   The mountain of La Clape rears unexpectedly from the flat coastal fields south-east of Narbonne; its vineyards produce some excellent whites from Bourboulenc and Clairette, plus some good reds and rosés, mainly from Grenache, Syrah and Mourvèdre. The whites and reds can age. Best producers: Ferri-Arnaud, l'Hospitalet★, Mire l'Étang, Négly, Pech-Céleyran★, Pech Redon★, Vires. Best years: (reds) 2001 00 99 98 96 95 93 91 90.

CLARE VALLEY *South Australia*   Historic upland valley north of Adelaide with a deceptively moderate climate, able to grow fine, aromatic Riesling, marvellously textured Semillon, rich, robust Shiraz and Cabernet blends and peppery but voluptuous Grenache. Best producers: (whites) Tim ADAMS★★, Jim BARRY★, Wolf BLASS (Gold Label★), Leo Buring (Leonay★★), Crabtree, GROSSET★★★, KNAPPSTEIN★, LEASINGHAM★, MITCHELL★, Mount Horrocks★, PETALUMA★, Pikes, Taylors/Wakefield★; (reds) Tim ADAMS★★, Jim BARRY★★, GROSSET★★, LEASINGHAM★, MITCHELL★, Pikes★, Taylors/Wakefield, WENDOUREE★★★. Best years: (Shiraz) (2001) 99 98 **97 96 94 93 92 91 90 88 86**; (Riesling) 2002 01 **99 98 97 96 95 94 93 92 90.**

CLARENDON HILLS *McLaren Vale, South Australia*   Controversial MCLAREN VALE winery with a name for high-priced, highly extracted, unfined, unfiltered and unobtainable reds. At the top is single-vineyard Astralis (a controversial ★★★), a hugely concentrated Shiraz from old vines aged in 100% French new oak. Other Shiraz★★ labels offer slightly better value, while Merlot★★ and Cabernet Sauvignon★★ aim to rub shoulders with great red BORDEAUX – although I'm not sure which ones. Several cuvées of Old Vines Grenache★★ are marked by saturated black cherry fruit and high alcohol. Best years: (Astralis) 1998 96 **95 94.**

CH. CLARKE *Listrac-Médoc AC, Bordeaux, France*   This property had millions spent on it by the late Baron Edmond de Rothschild during the late 1970s, and from the 98 vintage leading Bordeaux winemaker Michel Rolland has been consultant enologist. The wines can have an attractive blackcurrant fruit, though they never quite escape the typical LISTRAC earthiness. But with a name like Clarke, how could they possibly fail to seduce? There is also a small production of dry white wine, le Merle Blanc. Best years: 2001 00 **99 98 96 95 90 89 88.**

DOMENICO CLERICO *Barolo DOCG, Piedmont, Italy*   Domenico Clerico has been one of the top BAROLO producers for more than a decade. He produces consistently superlative Barolos (Ciabot Mentin Ginestra★★★, Pajana★★★, Per Cristina★★★) and excellent BARBERA D'ALBA (Trevigne★★), all wonderfully balanced. His range also includes LANGHE Arte★★, a barrique-aged blend of Nebbiolo and Barbera. Best years: (Barolos) (2001) (00) (99) 98 97 96 **95 93 90 89 88.**

CH. CLIMENS★★★ *Barsac AC, 1er Cru Classé, Bordeaux, France*   The leading estate in BARSAC, with a deserved reputation for fabulous, sensuous wines, rich and succulent yet streaked with lively lemon acidity. Easy to drink at 5 years, but a good vintage will be richer and more satisfying after 10–15 years. Second wine: les Cyprès (also delicious). Best years: 2002 01 99 98 97 **96 95 90 89 88 86 83 76 75**.

CLOS BAGATELLE *St-Chinian AC, Languedoc-Roussillon, France* Run by siblings Luc and Christine Simon, who produce 5 red cuvées and a MUSCAT DE ST-JEAN-DE-MINERVOIS. Top wine La Gloire de Mon Père★ is made from Syrah, Mourvèdre and Grenache, and aged in 100% new oak barrels; Sélection in only 25%. Unoaked Marie et Mathieu★ is fruit-driven; Cuvée Camille has spicy, herbal aromas; Tradition is a traditional St-Chinian, a Carignan-Cinsaut-Grenache blend.

CLOS DU BOIS *Alexander Valley AVA, California, USA* Winery showcasing gentle, fruit-dominated flavours of SONOMA Chardonnay, Merlot and Cabernet. Top vineyard selections can be exciting, especially the Calcaire★★ and Flintwood★ Chardonnays, as well as the rich, strong Briarcrest Cabernet Sauvignon★★ and Marlstone★★, a red BORDEAUX-style blend. Best years: (reds) (2001) (00) 99 **97 96 95 94 91 90 88 87 86**.

CLOS CENTEILLES *Minervois AC, Languedoc-Roussillon, France* Daniel Domergue and his wife Patricia Boyer are producing excellent MINERVOIS La Livinière and innovative vins de pays. The impressive Clos Centeilles★★ is their top wine; Capitelle de Centeilles★ and Carignanissime★ are 100% Cinsaut and Carignan respectively. Best years: 2001 00 **99 98 97 96 95 94 93**.

CLOS DE LA COULÉE-DE-SERRANT *Savennières AC, Loire Valley, France* Fine estate of only 7ha (17 acres) which merits its own AC within the boundaries of SAVENNIERES. The Joly family runs the property on fervently biodynamic lines, and the estate wine★★ is a concentrated, long-lived, very pricy Chenin Blanc with a honeyed, floral bouquet. Also produces better-value Savennières Roche aux Moines★★ and Becherelle★. Best years: 2001 00 99 **97 96 95 93 90 89 88 85 83 82**.

CLOS ERASMUS★★★ *Priorat DOC, Cataluña, Spain* Daphne Glorian's tiny estate turns out one of the most profound and personal reds in PRIORAT. In her small winery (formerly Alvaro PALACIOS' facility) she also makes a convincing second wine, Laurel★. Best years: (2001) (00) 99 98 **97** 96 **94**.

CLOS MOGADOR★★ *Priorat DOC, Cataluña, Spain* René Barbier Ferrer was one of the pioneers who relaunched the reputation of PRIORAT in the 80s. The wine is a ripe, intense, brooding monster built to age. Best years: (2001) (00) 99 98 97 96 **95 94 93 92 91 90**.

DOM. DU CLOS NAUDIN *Vouvray, Loire Valley, France* Philippe Foreau runs this first-rate VOUVRAY domaine. Depending on the vintage, Foreau produces a range of styles: dry★★, medium-dry★★ and sweet★★ (rare Réserve★★★), as well as Vouvray Mousseux★★ and Pétillant★★. The wines are supremely ageworthy, though in their relative youth are rather softer in style than the more structured Vouvrays of HUET. Best years: (Moelleux Réserve) 1997 96 **95 90 89 88 85 83 78 76 75 70**.

CLOS DES PAPES *Châteauneuf-du-Pape AC, Rhône Valley, France* Paul Avril is one of the outstanding CHATEAUNEUF-DU-PAPE producers. The red★★★ has an unusually high amount of Mourvèdre (20%), which can give greater structure and complexity, and potential longevity. Nevertheless, there is enough Grenache to ensure the wine's approachability in its youth and provide an initial blast of fruit. The white★★ takes on the nutty character of aged Burgundy after 5 or 6 years. Best years: (red) (2001) 00 99 98 97 96 **95 94 93 92 90 89 88 83 81**.

CLOS DE LA ROCHE AC *Grand Cru, Côte de Nuits, Burgundy, France* The best and biggest of the 5 MOREY-ST-DENIS Grands Crus. It has a lovely, bright, red-fruits flavour when young, and should become richly

107

chocolaty or gamy with age. Best producers: DROUHIN★★★, DUJAC★★★, Léchenaut★★★, Dom. LEROY★★★, H Lignier★★★, Henri Perrot-Minot★★, Ponsot★★★, ROUSSEAU★★★. Best years: (2001) 00 99 98 97 96 95 93 **90 89 88**.

CLOS ST-DENIS AC *Grand Cru, Côte de Nuits, Burgundy, France* This small (6.5ha/16-acre) Grand Cru, which gave its name to the village of MOREY-ST-DENIS, produces wines which are sometimes light, but should be wonderfully silky, with the texture that only great Burgundy, so far, can give. Best after 10 years or more. Best producers: Bertagna★★, Charlopin★★, DUJAC★★★, JADOT★★, Ponsot★★★. Best years: (2002) (01) 00 99 98 **97** 96 95 **93 90**.

CLOS UROULAT *Jurançon AC, South-West France* Charles Hours makes stunningly good JURANÇON, but in tiny quantities. Dry Cuvée Marie★★ balances ripe fruit with a deliciously refreshing finish. The richly textured sweet Jurançon★★ pulls together lemon, lime, honey and apricot: enjoyable young, but magnificent when aged. Best years: (sweet) 2001 00 **99 98 96 95** 93 90 89.

CLOS DU VAL *Napa Valley AVA, California, USA* Elegant Cabernet Sauvignon★ (STAGS LEAP DISTRICT bottling★★), Chardonnay★ (Reserve★), Merlot★ and Zinfandel★. The Reserve Cabernet can age well. Ariadne★★, a Semillon-Sauvignon Blanc blend, is a lovely aromatic white. Best years: (Reserve Cabernet) (2001) (00) 99 97 96 **95** **94** 91 90 87 86 84.

CLOS DE VOUGEOT AC *Grand Cru, Côte de Nuits, Burgundy, France* Enclosed by Cistercian monks in the 14th century, and today a considerable tourist attraction, this large (50ha/125-acre) vineyard is now divided among 82 owners. As a result of this division, Clos de Vougeot has become one of the most unreliable Grand Cru Burgundies; the better wine tends to come from the upper and middle parts. When it is good it is wonderfully fleshy, turning dark and exotic after 10 years or more. Best producers: B Ambroise★★, Amiot-Servelle★★, Chopin-Groffier★★, J-J Confuron★★★, R Engel★★★, FAIVELEY★★, GRIVOT★★★, Anne GROS★★★, Haegelen-Jayer★★, JADOT★★★, Dom. LEROY★★★, MEO-CAMUZET★★★, D MORTET★★★, Mugneret-Gibourg★★★, J Raphet★★, VOUGERAIE★★. Best years: (2002) (01) 00 99 98 **97** 96 95 **93 91 90 88**.

CLOUDY BAY *Marlborough, South Island, New Zealand* New Zealand's most successful winery, Cloudy Bay achieved cult status with the first release of its zesty, herbaceous Sauvignon Blanc★★ in 1985. Sauvignon Blanc Te Koko★★ is very different: rich, creamy, oak-matured and bottle-aged. Cloudy Bay also makes Chardonnay★★, a late-harvest Riesling★★, a superb Alsace-style Gewürztraminer★★, Pinot Noir★ and

vintage Pelorus★★, a high-quality old-style Champagne-method fizz. First releases of non-vintage Pelorus★★ are excellent. Best years: (Sauvignon Blanc) (2003) **02 01 00 97**.

J-F COCHE-DURY *Meursault AC, Côte de Beaune, Burgundy, France* Jean-François Coche-Dury is a modest superstar, quietly turning out some of the finest wines on the COTE DE BEAUNE. His best wines are his CORTON-CHARLEMAGNE★★★ and MEURSAULT Perrières★★★, but even his BOURGOGNE Blanc★★ is excellent. His red wines, from VOLNAY★★ and MONTHELIE★, tend to be cheaper than the whites and should be drunk younger. Best years: (whites) (2002) (01) 00 99 97 96 95 **92 90 89**.

COCKBURN *Port DOC, Douro, Portugal* Best known for its Special Reserve ruby, Cockburns has much more than that to offer. Cockburns Vintage★★ is stylishly cedary and Quinta dos Canais★★ is a fine single quinta, while the aged tawnies★★ are famously refined and nutty. Best years: (Vintage) 2000 97 94 **91 83 70 67 63 60 55**; (dos Canais) 2000 99 98 95 **92**.

CODORNÍU *Cava DO, Cataluña, Spain* The biggest Champagne-method sparkling wine company in the world. Anna de Codorníu★ and Jaume Codorníu★ are especially good, but all the sparklers are better than the CAVA average. Drink young for freshness. Codorníu also owns RAIMAT in COSTERS DEL SEGRE, Masía Bach in the PENEDES and Bodegas Bilbaínas in RIOJA, and has purchased 25% of Scala Dei in PRIORAT.

COLCHAGUA, VALLE DE *Rapel, Chile* RAPEL sub-region and home to many exciting estates, such as the acclaimed Apalta vineyard, where CASA LAPOSTOLLE, MONTES and others have plantings. Merlot, Syrah and Carmenère do very well here. San Fernando and Chimbarongo are the best-known sub-zones. Best producers: CASA LAPOSTOLLE★★, Casa Silva★, CONO SUR★★, MONTES★, MONTGRAS★, Viu Manent★.

COLDSTREAM HILLS *Yarra Valley, Victoria, Australia* Founded by Australian wine guru James Halliday, Coldstream Hills has been owned by Southcorp since 1996. Pinot Noir★ is usually good (Reserve★): sappy and smoky with cherry fruit and clever use of all-French oak. Chardonnay★ (Reserve★★) has subtlety and delicacy but real depth as well. Reserve Cabernet★ can be good, though not always ripe. Plans to dramatically increase production don't make a lot of sense in a cool region like YARRA VALLEY. Best years: (Reserve Pinot Noir) 2001 00 **99 98 97 96 94**.

COLLI BOLOGNESI DOC *Emilia-Romagna, Italy* Wines from this zone in the Apennine foothills near Bologna were traditionally slightly sweet and frothy. Today some concessions are made to international taste, resulting in fine Cabernets★★ from Bonzara and Terre Rosse. Other good red wines are produced from Merlot, and increasing amounts of dry white wine are made from Sauvignon, Pignoletto and Pinot Bianco. Best producers: Bonzara (Cabernet★, Merlot★), Santarosa★, Terre Rosse★★, Vallona★. Best years: (reds) (2001) 00 99 98 **97 95 93**.

COLLI ORIENTALI DEL FRIULI DOC *Friuli-Venezia Giulia, Italy* This DOC covers 20 different types of wine. Best known are the sweet whites from Verduzzo in the Ramandolo sub-zone and the delicate Picolit, but it is the reds, from the indigenous Refosco and Schioppettino, as well as imports like Cabernet and dry whites, from Tocai, Ribolla, Pinot Bianco and Malvasia Istriana, that show how exciting the wines can be. Prices are high. Best producers: Ca' Ronesca★, Dario Coos★, Dorigo★, Dri★, Le Due Terre★★, Livio FELLUGA★★, Walter Filiputti★, Adriano Gigante★, Livon★, Meroi★, Miani★, Davide Moschioni★★, Rocca Bernarda★, Rodaro★, Ronchi di Cialla★, Ronchi di Manzano★★, Ronco del Gnemiz★★, Scubla★, Specogna★, Le Vigne di Zamò★★, Zof★. Best years: (whites) (2001) **00 99 98 97**.

COLLI PIACENTINI DOC *Emilia-Romagna, Italy* Home to some of Emilia-Romagna's best wines, this DOC covers 11 different types, the best of which are Cabernet Sauvignon and the red Gutturnio (a blend of Barbera and Bonarda) as well as the medium-sweet white and bubbly Malvasia. Best producers: Luretta★, Lusenti, Castello di Luzzano/Fugazza★, Il Poggiarello★, La Stoppa★ (Cabernet★★), Torre Fornello★, La Tosa (Cabernet Sauvignon★). Best years: (reds) (2001) 00 **99 98 97 95**.

COLLINES RHODANIENNES, VIN DE PAYS DES *Rhône Valley, France*
Region between Vienne and Valence. The best wines are varietal
Gamay and, notably, Syrah, although there are some good juicy
Merlots, too. Best producers: COLOMBO★, P Gaillard★, M Ogier★,
Pochon★, ST-DESIRAT co-op, TAIN-L'HERMITAGE co-op, Vernay★, les Vins de
Vienne (Sotanum)★★. Best years: (reds) 2001 00 **99 98 97**.

COLLIO DOC *Friuli-Venezia Giulia, Italy* These hills are the home of some
of Italy's best and most expensive dry white wines. The zone produces
19 types of wine, including 17 varietals, which range from the local
Tocai and Malvasia Istriana to international types. The best white and
red wines are ageworthy. Best producers: Borgo Conventi★, Borgo del
Tiglio★★, La Castellada★, Damijan★, Livio FELLUGA★★, Marco Felluga★,
Fiegl★, GRAVNER★★★, JERMANN★★, Edi Keber★, Renato Keber★★,
Livon★, Matijaz Tercic★, Primosic★, Princic★, Puiatti★, Russiz
Superiore★, SCHIOPETTO★★, Venica & Venica★★, Villa Russiz★★,
Villanova★. Best years: (whites) (2001) 00 **99 98 97 96 95**.

COLLIOURE AC *Roussillon, France* This tiny fishing port tucked away
in the Pyrenean foothills only a few miles from the Spanish border is
also an AC, and makes a throat-warming red wine that is capable of
aging for a decade but is marvellously rip-roaring when young. Best
producers: (reds) Baillaury★, Casa Blanca, Cellier des Templiers★, Clos
des Paulilles★, Mas Blanc★★, la RECTORIE★★, la Tour Vieille★, Vial
Magnères★. Best years: 2001 00 **99 98 96 95 94 93 91 90**.

COLOMBARD In France, Colombard traditionally has been distilled to
make Armagnac and Cognac, but has now emerged as a table wine
grape in its own right, notably as a Vin de Pays des CÔTES DE GASCOGNE.
At its best, it has a lovely, crisp acidity and fresh, aromatic fruit. The
largest plantings of the grape are in CALIFORNIA, where it generally
produces rather less distinguished wines. South Africa can produce
attractive basic wines and Australia also has some fair examples.

JEAN-LUC COLOMBO *Cornas AC, Rhône Valley, France* Colombo is a
modernist who has caused controversy with his criticism of traditional
methods. His powerful, rich CORNAS has far less tannic grip than some.
Top cuvées are les Ruchets★★ and the lush late-harvest la Louvée★★,
made in tiny quantities. Among négociant wines now produced,
CHATEAUNEUF-DU-PAPE les Bartavelles★, red HERMITAGE★★ and the white
Hermitage le Rouet★★ stand out, although some lesser labels don't
always seem fully ripe. Also produces fragrant, expensive ST-PERAY la
Belle de Mai★★, good COTES DU RHONE★ and vins de pays from the RHONE
and ROUSSILLON. Best years: (Cornas) 2001 00 99 98 **97 95 94 91 90**.

COLUMBIA CREST *Washington State, USA* Offshoot of CHATEAU STE
MICHELLE, producing good-value, good-quality wines. Grand Estates
Merlot★ and Grand Estates Chardonnay★ are strong suits. For fruit
intensity, drink both with 2–3 years' age. Promising, intense Syrah★.

COLUMBIA VALLEY AVA *Washington State, USA* The largest of
WASHINGTON's viticultural regions, covering a third of the landmass in
the state and encompassing both the YAKIMA VALLEY and WALLA WALLA
regions. It produces 98% of the state's wine grapes: Merlot is the most
widely planted variety, with Cabernet Sauvignon and Chardonnay
following close behind. Best producers: ANDREW WILL★★, Cadence★★,
CHATEAU STE MICHELLE★, COLUMBIA CREST★, Matthews Cellars★★, QUILCEDA
CREEK★★. Best years: (reds) 2001 00 99 98 **98 97**.

COLUMBIA WINERY *Columbia Valley AVA, Washington State, USA* Under the guidance of David Lake MW, Columbia produces an assortment of decent wines along with several standouts from Red Willow Vineyard. The best include deeply fruited, built-to-last Cabernet Sauvignon★ and a fruity, smoky-styled Syrah★★. Merlot★ has improved in recent vintages. Best years: (Red Willow reds) (2001) (00) 99 **98** 97.

COMMANDARIA *Cyprus* Dark brown, treacly wine made from red Mavro and white Xynisteri grapes, sun-dried for 2 weeks before vinification and solera aging. Pretty decent stuff but only potentially one of the world's great rich wines. A lighter, drier style is also produced.

CONCA DE BARBERÁ DO *Cataluña, Spain* A quality wine area, but most of its production is sold to CAVA producers. The cool climate here is ideal and TORRES grows excellent Chardonnay, Cabernet Sauvignon, Pinot Noir, Merlot and Tempranillo. Best producers: Sanstravé (Gasset Chardonnay★), TORRES (Milmanda★★, Grans Muralles★).

CONCHA Y TORO *Maipo, Chile* Chile's biggest winery has 3200ha (7900 acres) of vineyards and the talented Ignacio Recabarren (ex-CASABLANCA) behind some of its excellent wines. Top whites include Amelia★★ and Terrunyo★★ Chardonnays and Terrunyo Sauvignon Blanc★. Don Melchor Cabernet Sauvignon★★ (potentially ★★★ from 2001) leads the reds, along with spicy Terrunyo Cabernet Sauvignon★★, excellent Terrunyo Carmenère★★ and new Pinot Noir★. The revitalized Marqués de Casa Concha★ and Casillero del Diablo ranges are also impressive. See also Almaviva.

CONDRIEU AC *Rhône Valley, France* Because of the demand for this wonderfully fragrant wine, made entirely from Viognier, Condrieu is expensive. Ranging from full and opulent to sweet, late-harvested, Condrieu is a sensation everyone should try at least once, but make sure you choose a good producer. Best drunk young. Best producers: G Barge★★, L Betton★★, P & C Bonnefond★★, du Chêne★★, L Chèze★, COLOMBO★★, CUILLERON★★★, DELAS★★, P Dumazet★★, C Facchin★★, Y Gangloff★★, GUIGAL★★, Monteillet★★, R Niero★, A Paret★★, A PERRET★★★, C Pichon★★, ROSTAING★, St-Cosme★, G Vernay★★★, F Villard★★.

CONO SUR *Rapel, Chile* Dynamic sister winery to CONCHA Y TORO, whose Chimbarongo Pinot Noir★ put both grape and region on the Chilean map. The new, largely CASABLANCA-sourced 20 Barrels Pinot★★ is rich and perfumed and the wholly Casablanca 20 Barrels Limited Edition★★ is positively unctuous. Reserva Merlot★★ and Cabernet Sauvignon★★, under both 20 Barrels and Visión labels, are excellent. Isla Negra offers drier, leaner, more 'European' flavours.

CH. LA CONSEILLANTE★★ *Pomerol AC, Bordeaux, France* Elegant, exotic, velvety wine that blossoms beautifully after 5–6 years but can age much longer. Best years: 2001 00 99 98 **96 95 94 90 89 88 86** 85.

CONSTANTIA WO *South Africa* The modern incarnation of this historic heart of South African wine has been epitomized since the mid-1980s by KLEIN CONSTANTIA, BUITENVERWACHTING and Groot Constantia, all part of Simon van der Stel's original 1685 land grant. STEENBERG was also one of the earliest wine farms. Despite the crowding of upmarket houses, many new names and plantings are springing up, some on the steepest slopes. Sauvignon Blanc thrust this cool-climate area into the limelight, but Chardonnays are good and Steenberg also succeeds with reds. Klein Constantia makes unfortified wine based on the 18th-century Constantia. Best producers: BUITENVERWACHTING★, Constantia-Uitsig★, KLEIN CONSTANTIA★, STEENBERG★★. Best years: (whites) **2002** 01 00 99 98.

ALDO CONTERNO *Barolo DOCG, Piedmont, Italy* Arguably BAROLO's finest producer. He makes good Dolcetto d'Alba★, excellent BARBERA D'ALBA Conca Tre Pile★★, a barrique-aged LANGHE Nebbiolo Il Favot★★ blended red Quartetto★★ and 2 Langhe Chardonnays: unoaked Printaniè and Bussiador★, fermented and aged in new wood. Pride of the range, though, are his Barolos from the hill of Bussia. In top vintages he produces Barolos Vigna Colonello★★★, Vigna Cicala★★★ and excellent Granbussia★★★, as well as a blended regular Barolo called Bussia Soprana★★. All these Barolos, though accessible when young, need several years to show their true majesty, but retain a remarkable freshness. Best years: (Barolo) (2000) 99 98 97 96 **95 93 90 89 88 86 85 82**.

GIACOMO CONTERNO *Barolo DOCG, Piedmont, Italy* Aldo's elder brother Giovanni, now followed by his son Roberto, has always taken a more traditional approach to winemaking. His flagship wine is BAROLO Monfortino★★★ (only released after some 6 or 7 years in large oak barrels) but Barolo Cascina Francia★★★ is also superb. An excellent traditional BARBERA D'ALBA★ is also made. Best years: (Monfortino) (2001) (00) (99) (98) (97) (96) (95) 90 **89 88 85 82 79 78 74 71**.

CONTINO *Rioja DOC, Rioja, Spain* An estate on some of the finest RIOJA land, half-owned by CVNE. The wines, including a Reserva★, a single-vineyard Viña del Olivo★★ and an innovative Graciano★ varietal, are made by CVNE. Cellar problems in the late 1980s and early 90s were soon resolved. Best years: (Reserva) 1999 98 **96 95 94 86 85**.

COONAWARRA *South Australia* On a flat limestone belt thinly veneered with terra rossa soil, Coonawarra can produce sublime Cabernet with blackcurrant leafy flavours and spicy Shiraz that age for years. Chardonnay and Riesling can be good. An export-led boom has seen hundreds of new vineyards planted, many of which are outside the legendary terra rossa strip. In view of some disappointing light reds, and a hotly contested boundary dispute, I wonder if Coonawarra's great reputation is not at risk.

Best producers: Balnaves, BOWEN★, BRAND'S★★, HOLLICK★, KATNOOK★, LECONFIELD★, LINDEMANS★★, Majella★★, ORLANDO★, PARKER★, PENFOLDS★★, PENLEY★★, PETALUMA★★, WYNNS★★, Zema★★. Best years: (Cabernet Sauvignon) (2001) 00 99 98 **97 96 94 91 90 86**.

COOPERS CREEK *Auckland, New Zealand* Successful producer of HAWKES BAY Chardonnay★, especially Swamp Reserve Chardonnay★, and tangy MARLBOROUGH Sauvignon Blanc★. Dry Riesling★ and Late Harvest Riesling★ styles are also good. A smart range of Reserve reds from Hawkes Bay includes complex Merlot★ and elegant Cabernet Sauvignon★. Best years: (Chardonnay) (2002) **00 99 98**.

CORBIÈRES AC *Languedoc, France* This huge AC now produces some of the best reds in the LANGUEDOC, with juicy fruit and more than a hint of wild hillside herbs. Excellent young, wines from the best estates can age for years. White Corbières is adequate – drink as young as possible. Best producers: (reds) Baillat★, Bel Eveque★, Caraguilhes★, Ch. Cascadais★, Étang des Colombes★, Fontsainte★, Grand Crès★, Grand Moulin★, Haut-Gléon★, Hélène★, l'Ille★, LASTOURS★, Mansenoble★, MONT TAUCH CO-OP★, les Palais★, St-Auriol★, Vaugelas★, VOULTE-GASPARETS★. Best years: (reds) 2001 **00 99 98 96 95 93**.

CORNAS AC *Rhône Valley, France* Northern Rhône's up-and-coming star, whose pure Syrah wines are especially attractive since those of neighbouring HERMITAGE and COTE-ROTIE have spiralled upward in price. When young, the wine is a thick, impenetrable red, almost black in the ripest years. Many need 10 years' aging. Best producers: ALLEMAND★★, R Balthazar★★, CLAPE★★★, COLOMBO★★, Courbis★★, DELAS★★, E & J Durand★★, Fauterie★, JABOULET★, J Lemenicier★, LIONNET/Rochepertuis★★, TAIN L'HERMITAGE co-op★, Tardieu-Laurent★★, Tunnel★★, VERSET★★, A Voge★. Best years: 2001 00 99 98 97 **96 95 94 91 90 89 88 85 83**.

CORSE AC, VIN DE *Corsica, France* Overall AC for Corsica with 5 superior sub-regions: Calvi, Cap Corse, Figari, Porto Vecchio and Sartène. Ajaccio and Patrimonio are entitled to their own ACs. The most distinctive wines, mainly red, come from local grapes (Nielluccio and Sciacarello for reds, Vermentino for whites). There are some rich sweet Muscats – especially from Muscat de Cap Corse. Best producers: Arena★, Catarelli★, Clos d'Alzeto★, Clos Capitoro, Clos Culombu★, Clos Landry★, Clos Nicrosi★, Gentile★, Leccia★, Maestracci★, Orenga de Gaffory★, Comte Peraldi★, Renucci★, Torraccia.

CORSICA *France* This Mediterranean island has made some pretty dull and undistinguished wines in the past. The last decade has seen a welcome trend toward quality, with co-ops and local growers investing in better equipment and planting noble grape varieties – such as Syrah, Merlot, Cabernet Sauvignon and Mourvèdre for reds, and Chardonnay and Sauvignon Blanc for whites – to complement the local Nielluccio, Sciacarello and Vermentino. Whites and rosés are pleasant for drinking young; reds are more exciting and can age for 3–4 years. See also Corse AC.

CORTES DE CIMA *Alentejo, Portugal* Dane Hans Kristian Jørgensen and his American wife Carrie make excellent modern-style Portuguese reds in the heart of the ALENTEJO. Local grape varieties – Aragonez (Tempranillo), Trincadeira and Periquita – are used for spicy, fruity Chaminé★, oaked red Cortes de Cima★ and a splendid dark, smoky Reserva★★. A little Cabernet, Touriga and Syrah are also grown, the latter for Incógnito★★, a promising gutsy, black-fruited blockbuster. Best years: **2001 00 98**.

CORTESE White grape variety planted primarily in south-eastern PIEDMONT in Italy; it can produce good, fairly acidic, dry whites. Sometimes labelled simply as Cortese Piemonte DOC, it is also used for GAVI.

CORTON AC *Grand Cru, Côte de Beaune, Burgundy, France* This is the only red Grand Cru in the COTE DE BEAUNE and ideally the wines should have the burliness and savoury power of the top COTE DE NUITS wines, combined with the more seductively perfumed fruit of Côte de Beaune. Red Corton should take 10 years to mature, but too many modern examples never get there. Very little white Corton is made. Best producers: B Ambroise★★, Bonneau du Martray★★, CHANDON DE BRIAILLES★★★, Dubreuil-Fontaine★★, FAIVELEY★★, Guyon★★, JADOT★★★, Dom. LEROY★★★, MEO-CAMUZET★★★, Rapet★★, Senard★★, TOLLOT-BEAUT★★★. Best years: (reds) (2002) (01) 00 99 98 **97** 96 95 **93 91 90 89 88**.

CORTON-CHARLEMAGNE AC *Grand Cru, Côte de Beaune, Burgundy, France* Corton-Charlemagne, at the top of the famous Corton hill, is the largest of Burgundy's white Grands Crus. It can produce some of the most impressive white Burgundies – rich, buttery and nutty with a fine mineral quality. The best show their real worth only at 10 years or more. Best producers: B Ambroise★★, Bonneau du Martray★★★, BOUCHARD PERE ET FILS★★, Champy★★, CHANDON DE BRIAILLES★★★, COCHE-DURY★★★, DROUHIN★★, FAIVELEY★★, V GIRARDIN★★★, JADOT★★, P Javillier★★, LATOUR★★, Rapet★★, M Rollin★★★, ROUMIER★★, TOLLOT-BEAUT★★★, VERGET★★. Best years: (2002) (01) 00 99 98 97 96 95 **92 90 89**.

CH. COS D'ESTOURNEL★★ *St-Estèphe AC, 2ème Cru Classé, Haut-Médoc, Bordeaux, France* Top name in ST-ESTEPHE, and one of the leading châteaux in all Bordeaux. Despite a high proportion of Merlot (just under 40%), the wine is classically made for aging and usually needs 10 years to show really well. Recent vintages have been dark, brooding and powerful, but I've found them worryingly sullen and increasingly difficult to judge. Second wine: les Pagodes de Cos. Best years: 2001 00 98 97 96 95 **94 93 90 89 88 86 85 83 82**.

COSTANTI *Brunello di Montalcino DOCG, Tuscany, Italy* One of the original, highly respected Montalcino estates, run by Andrea Costanti, making first-rate BRUNELLO★★ and Rosso★★, as well as a tasty partially barrique-aged Sangiovese called Vermiglio★. The archetypal Brunello of this zone is austere, elegant and long-lived, epitomized by the Costanti Riserva★★. New Calbello wines from the hill of Montosoli include excellent Rosso★★ and promising Merlot-Cabernet blend Ardingo★★. Best years: (Brunello) (2001) (99) (97) 95 93 **90 88 85 82**.

COSTERS DEL SEGRE DO *Cataluña, Spain* DO on the 'banks of the Segre' in western CATALUNA. A great array of grape varieties is grown, with the accent on French varieties. Quality is generally good and prices moderate. Best producers: Celler de Cantonella★, Castell del Remei★, RAIMAT★. Best years: (reds) (2001) 00 99 **98 96 95 94**.

COSTIÈRES DE NÎMES AC *Languedoc, France* Improving AC between Nîmes and Arles. Reds are generally bright and perfumed, rosés are good young gluggers. Whites are usually tasty versions of Marsanne and Roussanne. Best producers: l'Amarine★, Grande Cassagne★, Mas des Bressades★, Mas Carlot, Mourgues du Grès★, Nages★, la Tuilerie★, Vieux-Relais★. Best years: 2001 **00 99 98 96 95**.

CÔTE DE BEAUNE *Côte d'Or, Burgundy, France* Southern part of the COTE D'OR; beginning at the hill of Corton, north of the town of BEAUNE, the Côte de Beaune progresses south as far as les Maranges, with white wines gradually taking over from red.

CÔTE DE BEAUNE AC *Côte de Beaune, Burgundy, France* Small AC for reds and white Burgundy, high on the hill above the city of Beaune, named to ensure confusion with the title for the whole region. Best producers: Allexant, VOUGERAIE★.

CÔTE DE BEAUNE-VILLAGES AC *Côte de Beaune, Burgundy, France* Red wine AC covering 16 villages, such as AUXEY-DURESSES, LADOIX, MARANGES. Most producers use their own village name, but if the wine is a blend from several villages it is sold as Côte de Beaune-Villages. It can also cover the red wine production of mainly white wine villages such as MEURSAULT. Best producers: DROUHIN★, J-P Fichet★, JADOT★. Best years: (2002) 01 99 **98 96**.

CÔTE DE BROUILLY AC *Beaujolais, Burgundy, France* AC for the lower slopes of Mont Brouilly, a small but abrupt volcanic mountain in the south of the BEAUJOLAIS Crus area. The wine is deeper in colour and fruit than wines from BROUILLY. Best producers: Lacondemine★, O Ravier★, Ch. Thivin (Zaccharie Geoffray★★), Viornery★. Best years: (2002) **00 99**.

CÔTE CHALONNAISE See Bourgogne-Côte Chalonnaise.

CÔTE DE NUITS *Côte d'Or, Burgundy, France* This is the northern part of the great COTE D'OR and is *not* an AC. Almost entirely red wine country, the vineyards start in the southern suburbs of Dijon and continue south in a narrow swath to below the town of NUITS-ST-GEORGES. The villages are some of the greatest wine names in the world – GEVREY-CHAMBERTIN, VOUGEOT and VOSNE-ROMANEE etc.

CÔTE DE NUITS-VILLAGES AC *Côte de Nuits, Burgundy, France* This AC is specific to the villages of Corgoloin, Comblanchien and Prémeaux in the south of the COTE DE NUITS and Brochon and FIXIN in the north. Although not much seen, the wines (mostly red) are often good, not very deep in colour but with a nice cherry fruit. Best producers: (reds) D Bachelet★, Chopin-Groffier★, J-J Confuron, JADOT, JAYER-GILLES★, RION★, P Rossignol★. Best years: (reds) (2002) 01 00 99 98 **97 96**.

CÔTE D'OR *Burgundy, France* Europe's most northern great red wine area and also the home of some of the world's best dry white wines. The name, meaning 'golden slope', refers to a 48-km (30-mile) stretch between Dijon and Chagny which divides into the COTE DE NUITS in the north and the COTE DE BEAUNE in the south.

CÔTE ROANNAISE AC *Loire Valley, France* Small AC in the upper Loire producing mostly light reds and rosés from Gamay. A new wave of producers here and in neighbouring Côtes du Forez are on a quality drive. Some of the best wines are non-appellation whites. Best producers: A Demon★, Fontenay★, M Lutz, M & L Montroussier, R Sérol; (Côtes du Forez) Clos de Chozieux, Cave des Vignerons For.eziens, Verdier-Logel.

CÔTE-RÔTIE AC *Rhône Valley, France* The Côte-Rôtie, or 'roasted slope', produces one of France's greatest red wines. The Syrah grape bakes to super-ripeness on these steep slopes, and the small amount of white Viognier sometimes included in the blend gives an unexpected exotic fragrance. Lovely young, it is better aged for 8 years. Best producers: G Barge★★, P & C Bonnefond★★, Bonserine★, B Burgaud★, Clusel-Roch★★, CUILLERON★★, DELAS★★, Duclaux★★, Gallet★★, Garon★, V Gasse★★, J-M Gerin★★, GUIGAL★★, JABOULET★, JAMET★★★, Jasmin★★, M Ogier★, ROSTAING★, Tardieu-Laurent★★, Vidal-Fleury★, F Villard★, Vins de Vienne★★. Best years: 2000 99 98 **96 95 94 91 90 89 88 85**.

COTEAUX D'AIX-EN-PROVENCE AC *Provence, France* This AC was the first in the south to acknowledge that Cabernet Sauvignon can enormously enhance the traditional local grape varieties such as Grenache, Cinsaut, Mourvèdre, Syrah and Carignan. The red wines produced here can age. Some quite good fresh rosé is made, while the white wines, mostly still traditionally made, are pleasant but hardly riveting. Best producers: Ch. Bas★, les Bastides★, des Béates★★, Beaupré★, Calissanne★, Fonscolombe★, des Gavelles★, Revelette★, Vignelaure★. Best years: (reds) 2001 **00 99 98 97 96 95**.

COTEAUX DE L'ARDÈCHE, VIN DE PAYS DES *Rhône Valley, France* Wines from the southern part of the Ardèche. Look out for the increasingly good varietal red wines made from Cabernet Sauvignon, Syrah, Merlot or Gamay and dry, fresh white wines from Chardonnay, Viognier or Sauvignon Blanc. Best producers: Vignerons Ardèchois, Colombier, DUBOEUF, Louis LATOUR, Pradel, ST-DESIRAT co-op.

COTEAUX DE L'AUBANCE AC *Loire Valley, France* Smallish AC north of COTEAUX DU LAYON AC. It is enjoying a renaissance for its sweet or semi-sweet white wines made from Chenin Blanc. Sweet styles can improve for 10–25 years. Best producers: Bablut★★, Deux Moulins★ Haute Perche★, Montgilet/V Lebreton★★, RICHOU★★. Best years: (2002 01 00 **99 97 96 95 93 90**.

COTEAUX CHAMPENOIS AC *Champagne, France* The AC for still wines from Champagne. Fairly acid with a few exceptions, notably from Bouzy and Ay. The best age for 5 years or more. Best producers Bara★, BOLLINGER★, Egly-Ouriet★, LAURENT-PERRIER, Joseph PERRIER, Ch de Saran★ (MOET & CHANDON). Best years: 2002 00 **99 98 96 95 90 89**.

COTEAUX DU LANGUEDOC AC *Languedoc, France* A large and increasingly successful AC situated between Montpellier and Narbonne, producing around 65 million bottles of beefy red and tasty rosé wines. Twelve 'crus', including Montpeyroux, Quatourze and Cabrières, have historically been allowed to append their names to the AC – these are currently being designated by climate and soil type. La CLAPE and PIC ST-LOUP have already been officially recognized. Best producers: Abbaye de Valmagne, l'Aiguelière★★, Aupilhac★, Calage★, Clavel★, la Coste★, Grès St-Paul★, Haut-Blanville, Henry★, Lacroix-Varel★, Mas Cal Demoura, Mas des Chimères★, MAS JULLIEN★, PEYRE ROSE★★, PRIEURE DE ST-JEAN DE BEBIAN★★, Puech-Haut★, St-Martin de la Garrigue★, Terre Megère★. Best years: 2001 **00 99 98 96 95 93 91 90**.

COTEAUX DU LAYON AC *Loire Valley, France* Sweet wine from the Layon Valley south of Angers. The wine is made from Chenin Blanc grapes that, ideally, are attacked by noble rot. In great years like 1996, and from a talented grower, this can be one of the world's exceptional sweet wines. Seven villages are entitled to use the Coteaux du Layon-Villages AC (one of the best is Chaume) and put their own name on the label, and these wines are definitely underpriced for the quality. Two sub-areas, BONNEZEAUX and QUARTS DE CHAUME, have their own ACs. Best producers: P Aquilas★★, P Baudouin★★★, BAUMARD★★, Bergerie★★, Bidet★, Breuil★, Cady★★, P Delesvaux★★★, Forges★★, Guimonière★★, Ogereau★★, Passavant★, Pierre-Bise★★, J Pithon★★★, J Renou★★, Roulerie★★, Sablonnettes★★, Sauveroy★, Soucherie/P-Y Tijou★★, Yves Soulez★★, Touche Noire★. Best years: (2002) 01 99 **97** 96 **95 90 89 88 85 83 76**.

COTEAUX DU LYONNAIS AC *Burgundy, France* Good, light, BEAUJOLAIS-style reds and a few whites and rosés from scattered vineyards between Villefranche and Lyon. Drink young.

COTEAUX DU TRICASTIN AC *Rhône Valley, France* From the southern Drôme, these are bright, fresh reds and rosés with attractive juicy fruit. Only a little of the nutty white is made but is worth looking out for. Drink it young. Best producers: Grangeneuve★, Lônes, St-Luc★, la Tour d'Elyssas, Vieux Micocoulier. Best years: **2001** 00 **99 98 95**.

COTEAUX VAROIS AC *Provence, France* An area to watch, with new plantings of classic grapes. Best producers: Alysses★, Bremond, Calisse★, Deffends★, Garbelle, Routas★, Ch. St-Estève, St-Jean-le-Vieux, St-Jean-de-Villecroze★, Triennes★. Best years: 2001 **00 99 98 97 96 95**.

CÔTES DE BERGERAC AC See Bergerac AC.

CÔTES DE BLAYE AC *Bordeaux, France* AC for white wines from the right bank of the Gironde estuary produced from Colombard and Sauvignon. Almost all the best whites are now dry. Drink young. Best producer: Cave de Marcillac.

CÔTES DE BOURG AC *Bordeaux, France* Mainly a red wine area to the south of the COTES DE BLAYE, where the best producers and the local co-op at Tauriac make great efforts. The reds are earthy but blackcurranty and can age for 6–10 years. Very little white is made, most of which is dry and dull. Best producers: Barbe, Brulesécaille★, Bujan, FALFAS★, Fougas★, Garreau, Guerry, Haut-Guiraud, Haut-Macô★, Macay, Nodoz★, ROC DE CAMBES★, Rousset, Tauriac co-op, Tayac★. Best years: 2001 00 **99 98 96 95 94 90 89**.

CÔTES DE CASTILLON AC *Bordeaux, France* Red wine area just to the east of ST-EMILION. As the price of decent red Bordeaux climbs ever upward, Côtes de Castillon wines have remained a good, reasonably priced alternative – a little earthy but full and round. Depending on the

vintage the wine is enjoyable between 3 and 10 years after the vintage. Best producers: Domaine de l'A★, Aiguilhe★, Belcier★, Cap-de-Faugères★, la Clarière Laithwaite, Clos l'Eglise★, Clos Les Lunelles (from 2001), Clos Puy Arnaud★, Côte-Montpezat★, Lapeyronie★, Poupille★, Robin★, Veyry★, Vieux-Ch.-Champs-de-Mars. Best years: 2001 00 **99 98 96 95**.

CÔTES DE DURAS AC *South-West France* AC between ENTRE-DEUX-MERS and BERGERAC, with 2 very active co-ops which offer good, fresh, grassy reds and whites from traditional BORDEAUX grapes. Drink young. Best producers: Amblard, Clos du Cadaret, Cours, Duras co-op, Grand Mayne, Lafon, Landerrouat co-op, Laulan. Best years: (reds) **2000 98 96 95**.

CÔTES DE FRANCS See Bordeaux-Côtes de Francs.

CÔTES DU FRONTONNAIS AC *South-West France* From north of Toulouse, some of the most distinctive reds – often superb and positively silky in texture – of South-West France. Négrette is the chief grape, but certain producers coarsen it with Cabernet, which rather defeats the object. Best producers: Baudare, Bellevue-la-Forêt★, Cahuzac★, la Colombière, Ferran, Flotis, Laurou, Montauriol, la Palme, Plaisance, le Roc★, St-Louis. Best years: 2001 **00 99 98 97 96 95**.

CÔTES DE GASCOGNE, VIN DE PAYS DES *South-West France* Mainly white wines from the Gers *département*. This is Armagnac country, but the tangy-fresh, fruity table wines are tremendously good – especially when you consider that they were condemned as unfit for anything but distillation not that long ago. Best producers: Aurin, Brumont, GRASSA★, de Joy, Producteurs PLAIMONT★, St-Lannes.

CÔTES DU JURA AC *Jura, France* The regional AC for Jura covers a wide variety of wines, including local specialities *vin jaune* and *vin de paille*. The Savagnin makes strong-tasting whites and Chardonnay is used for some good dry whites and CREMANT DU JURA fizz. Reds and rosés can be good when made from Pinot Noir, but with the local Poulsard and Trousseau the wines can be a bit odd. Drink young. Best producers: Ch. d'Arlay★★, Berthet-Bondet★★, Bourdy★★, Chalandard★, Clavelin★, Durand-Perron★★, Ch. de l'Étoile★, Joly★, A Labet★★, J Maclé★★, Reverchon★, Rijckaert★★, Rolet★★, A & M Tissot★.

CÔTES DU LUBÉRON AC *Rhône Valley, France* Wine production is dominated by the co-ops east of Avignon. The light, easy wines are refreshing and for drinking young. Best producers: Bonnieux co-op, Ch. la Canorgue, la Citadelle★, Fontenille★, Ch. de l'Isolette★, la Tour-d'Aigues co-op, Ch. des Tourettes, Val Joanis, la Verrerie★. Best years: **2001 00 99 98 95**.

CÔTES DU MARMANDAIS AC *South-West France* The red wines are
fairly successful BORDEAUX lookalikes; Syrah is also permitted. Best
producers: Beaulieu, Cave de Beaupuy, Cocumont co-op, Elian Da Ros
(Chante Coucou, Clos Baquey★).

CÔTES DE MONTRAVEL AC See Montravel AC.

CÔTES DE PROVENCE AC *Provence, France* Large AC mainly for fruity
reds and rosés to drink young. Whites are mostly forgettable. Best
producers: Barbanau★, la Bernarde★, Commanderie de Bargemore★,
Commanderie de Peyrassol★, la Courtade★★, Coussin Ste-Victoire★,
Dragon★, Esclans★, Féraud★, des Garcinières★, Gavoty★, Maravenne★,
Ott★, Rabiega★, Réal Martin★, RICHEAUME★, Rimauresq★, Roquefort★,
les Maîtres Vignerons de St-Tropez, Sorin★, Élie Sumeire★, Vannières★.

CÔTES DU RHÔNE AC *Rhône Valley, France* AC for the whole RHONE
VALLEY. Over 90% is red and rosé, mainly from Grenache with some
Cinsaut, Syrah, Carignan and Mourvèdre to add lots of warm, spicy
southern personality. Modern winemaking has revolutionized the
style, and today's wines are generally juicy, spicy and easy to drink,
ideally within 4 years. Most wine is made by co-ops. Best producers:
(reds) Amouriers★, d'Andézon★, les Aphillanthes★, A Brunel★, CLAPE★,
COLOMBO★, Coudoulet de BEAUCASTEL★, Cros de la Mûre★, Fonsalette★,
FONT DE MICHELLE★, Gramenon★, Grand Moulas★, Grand Prebois★,
GUIGAL★, Ch. d'Hugues★, JABOULET, la Janasse★, LIONNET★, J-M
Lombard★, Mas de Libian★, Mont-Redon, la Mordoreé★, REMEJEANNE★,
M Richaud★, ST-GAYAN★, Ste-Anne★, Santa Duc★, Tardieu-Laurent★,
Tours★, Vieux-Chêne★; (whites) CLAPE★, P Gaillard★, REMEJEANNE★, Ste-
Anne★. Best years: (reds) 2001 **00 99 98 95**.

CÔTES DU RHÔNE-VILLAGES AC *Rhône Valley, France* AC for wines
with a higher minimum alcohol content than straightforward COTES
DU RHONE, covering 16 villages in the southern Rhône that have
traditionally made superior wine (especially Cairanne, Rasteau,
Beaumes-de-Venise, Séguret, Valréas, Sablet, Vinsobres, Visan).
Almost all the best are spicy reds that can age well. Best producers:
Achiary★, Alary★, l'Ameillaud★, Amouriers★, Beaurenard★, Bressy-
Masson★, Brusset★, de Cabasse★, Cabotte★, Cave de Cairanne★, D
Charavin★, Charbonnière★, Chaume-Arnaud★, Combe★, Cros de la
Mûre★, Estézargues co-op★, Gourt de Mautens★★, Gramenon★, Grand
Moulas★, les Hautes Cances★, JABOULET★, la Janasse★, l'ORATOIRE ST-
MARTIN★, Pélaquié★, Piaugier★, Rabasse-Charavin★, REMEJEANNE★, M
Richaud★, ST-GAYAN★, Ste-Anne★, la Soumade★, Tours★, Trapadis★,
Verquière★. Best years: (reds) 2001 **00 99 98 95 90**.

CÔTES DU ROUSSILLON AC *Roussillon, France* Large AC covering much
of ROUSSILLON. Mainly red wine; the white is mostly unmemorable.
Production is dominated by the co-ops, some enlightened, but estates
are making their mark. Best producers: (reds) Vignerons Catalans, la
CASENOVE★, CAZES★, Chênes★, J-L COLOMBO★, Ferrer-Ribière★, Força Réal,
GAUBY★★, Jau, Joliette, Laporte★, Mas Crémat★, Piquemal★, Rivesaltes
co-op, Salvat, Sarda-Malet★. Best years: (reds) 2001 **00 99 98 96 95**.

CÔTES DU ROUSSILLON-VILLAGES AC *Roussillon, France* AC for red
wines from the best sites in the northern part of COTES DU ROUSSILLON.
Villages Caramany, Latour-de-France, Lesquerde and Tautavel may add
their own name. Best producers: Agly co-op, Vignerons Catalans,
CAZES★, Chênes★, Clos des Fées★, Fontanel★, Força Réal, Gardiès★,
GAUBY★★, Jau, Joliette, Mas Crémat★, Schistes★. Best years: (reds) 2001
00 **99 98 96 95**.

CÔTES DE ST-MONT VDQS *South-West France* A good VDQS for firm but fruity reds and some fair rosés and dry whites. Best producer: Producteurs PLAIMONT.

CÔTES DE THONGUE, VIN DE PAYS DES *Languedoc, France* Zone north-east of Béziers. Many dull red quaffers, but dynamic estates can produce excellent results. Best producers: l'Arjolle★, Bellevue, les Chemins de Bassac★, Condamine l'Evêque, Croix Belle.

CÔTES DU VENTOUX AC *Rhône Valley, France* Increasingly successful AC, with vineyards on the slopes of Mt Ventoux in the RHONE VALLEY near Carpentras. When the wine is well made from a single estate or blended by a serious merchant, the reds can have a lovely juicy fruit, or in the case of JABOULET and Pesquié, some real stuffing. Best producers: Anges★, Brusset, Champ-Long, La Croix des Pins★, Goult-Cave de Lumières★, JABOULET★, Pesquié★, Valcombe★, Union des Caves du Ventoux, la Verrière, la Vieille Ferme. Best years: (reds) 2001 00 99 98.

CÔTES DU VIVARAIS AC *Rhône Valley, France* In the northern Gard and Ardèche, typical southern Rhône grapes (Grenache, Syrah, Cinsaut, Carignan) produce mainly light, fresh reds and rosés for drinking young. Best producers: Vignerons Ardèchois, Chais du Vivarais, Vigier.

COTNARI *Romania* The warm mesoclimate of this hilly region, close to the border with Moldova, encourages noble rot. Once – but not now – on a footing with TOKAJI, Cotnari's principal local varieties are Grasa, Tamîioasă, Francusa and Fetească Albă.

CÔTTO, QUINTA DO *Douro DOC and Port DOC, Douro, Portugal* Table wine expert in Lower DOURO. Basic red and white Quinta do Côtto are reasonable, and its Grande Escolha★★ is one of Portugal's best reds, oaky and powerful when young, rich and cedary when mature. Best years: (Grande Escolha) 2000 **97 95 94 90 87 85**.

COULY-DUTHEIL *Chinon, Loire Valley, France* Large merchant house responsible for 10% of the CHINON AC. Uses its own vineyards for the best wines, particularly Clos de l'Écho★ (and supercharged Clos de l'Echo Crescendo★) and Clos de l'Olive★. Top négociant blend is la Baronnie Madeleine★, which combines tasty raspberry fruit with a considerable capacity to age. Also sells a range of other Touraine wines. Best years: (reds) (2002) 01 00 **97 96 95 90 89 86 85**.

PIERRE COURSODON *St-Joseph AC, Rhône Valley, France* Family-owned domaine producing rich, oaked ST-JOSEPH★ from very old vines. The red wines need up to 5 years before they show all their magnificent cassis and truffle and violet richness, especially the top wine, La Sensonne★★. Whites are good, too. Best years: (reds) 2001 00 99 98 **97 96 95 94 91 90 89 88 85 83**.

CH. COUTET★★ *Barsac AC, 1er Cru Classé, Bordeaux, France* BARSAC'S largest Classed Growth property has languished behind its neighbour CLIMENS for a generation, but has shown great improvement in recent years. Extraordinarily intense Cuvée Madame★★★ is made in exceptional years. Best years: (2002) 01 99 **98 97 96 95 90 89 88**.

COWRA *New South Wales, Australia* Rapidly emerging district with a reliable warm climate and good water supplies for irrigation. It produces soft, peachy Chardonnay and spicy, cool-tasting Shiraz. Best producers: Cowra Estate, Hamiltons Bluff, Richmond Grove, ROTHBURY★, Charles Sturt University★, Windowrie Estate.

CRAGGY RANGE *Hawkes Bay, North Island, New Zealand* Exciting new venture funded by a wealthy American family and managed by brilliant viticulturist Steve Smith. Extensive vineyards in HAWKES BAY and MARTINBOROUGH are being established. Premium Hawkes Bay wines, made in small quantities, include a stylish Les Beaux Cailloux Chardonnay★★, a bold Cabernet-dominant blend called The Quarry★★, a rich Merlot-dominant blend known as Sophia★★ and the winery's flagship Soler Syrah★★★. Best of the varietal range are restrained yet intense Avery Sauvignon Blanc★ and tangy Rapaura Road Riesling★ from MARLBOROUGH, plus an elegant Chardonnay★ and Merlot★, both from the Seven Poplars Vineyard in Hawkes Bay.

CRASTO, QUINTA DO *Douro DOC and Port DOC, Douro, Portugal* Well situated property belonging to the Roquette family. Very good traditional LBV★★ and Vintage★★ port and thoroughly enjoyable red DOURO★, especially Reserva★★ and varietal Touriga Nacional★★. New flagship reds, Vinha da Ponte★★ and Maria Teresa★★, though first made in the modest 1998 vintage, show further promise. Best years: (port) 2000 99 97 **95 94**; (Reserva red) 2000 **99 98**.

CRÉMANT D'ALSACE AC *Alsace, France* Good Champagne-method sparkling wine from Alsace, usually made from Pinot Blanc. Reasonable quality, if not great value for money. Best producers: BLANCK★, Dopff au Moulin★, Dopff & Irion, J Gross★, Kuentz-Bas, MURE★, Ostertag★, Pfaffenheim co-op, P Sparr★, A Stoffel★, TURCKHEIM co-op★.

CRÉMANT DE BOURGOGNE AC *Burgundy, France* Most Burgundian Crémant is white and is made either from Chardonnay alone or blended with Pinot Noir. The result, especially in ripe years, can be full, soft, almost honey-flavoured – if you give the wine the 2–3 years aging needed for mellowness to develop. The best rosé comes from Chablis and Auxerre in northern Burgundy. Best producers: A Delorme Lucius-Grégoire, Parigot-Richard, Simonnet-Febvre; and the co-ops at Bailly★ (the best for rosé), Lugny★, St-Gengoux-de-Scissé and Viré.

CRÉMANT DE DIE AC *Rhône Valley, France* AC for traditional-method fizz made entirely from the Clairette Blanche grape. Less aromatic than CLAIRETTE DE DIE. Best producers: Clairette de Die co-op, Jacques Faure.

CRÉMANT DU JURA AC *Jura, France* AC for fizz from Jura. Largely Chardonnay-based, with Poulsard for the pinks. Best producers: Ch. de l'Étoile★, de la Pinte, Pupillin co-op★.

CRÉMANT DE LIMOUX AC *Languedoc-Roussillon, France* Sparkling wine made from a blend of Chardonnay, Chenin Blanc, Mauzac and, from 2003, Pinot Noir; the wines generally have more complexity than straight BLANQUETTE DE LIMOUX. Drink young. Best producers: l'Aigle★, Antech, Fourn★, Guinot, Laurens★, Martinolles★, SIEUR D'ARQUES★, Valent.

CRÉMANT DE LOIRE AC *Loire Valley, France* The AC for Champagne-method sparkling wine in Anjou and Touraine, with more fruit and yeast character than those of VOUVRAY and SAUMUR. The wine is good to drink as soon as it is released and can be excellent value. Best producers: BAUMARD★, Berger Frères★, Brizé★, Fardeau★, la Gabillière, Girault, GRATIEN & MEYER★, Lambert★, Langlois-Château★, Michaud★, Oisly-et-Thésée co-op★, Passavant★.

CRIOTS-BÂTARD-MONTRACHET AC See Bâtard-Montrachet AC.

CRISTOM *Willamette Valley AVA, Oregon, USA* Named after the owners' children, Chris and Tom, this winery, nestled in the Eola Hills, makes fine Pinot Noir. Two of the outstanding reserve Pinot Noirs are from Marjorie Vineyard★★ and Jessie Vineyard★★★. Good white wines include Chardonnay from Celilo Vineyard★ (in WASHINGTON), Pinot Gris and Viognier. Best years: (Pinot Noir) (2002) (01) 00 99 **98 97**.

CROFT *Port DOC, Douro, Portugal* Now owned by TAYLOR, these wines are already showing distinct improvements at all levels. Vintage ports ★★ have traditionally been elegant, rather than thunderous. Single-quinta Quinta da Roêda★★ is fine in the most recent vintages. Best years: (Vintage) 2000 94 **91 77 70 66 63 55 45**; (Roêda) 1997 **95 83**.

CROZES-HERMITAGE AC *Rhône Valley, France* The largest of the northern Rhône ACs. Ideally, the pure Syrah reds should have a full colour and a strong, meaty but rich flavour. You can drink them young but in ripe years from a hillside site the wine improves greatly for 2–5 years. The best whites are fresh and clean. In general drink white Crozes young, before the floral perfume disappears. Best producers: (reds) A Belle★★, CHAPOUTIER★, B Chave★ (Tête de Cuvée★★), Colombier★, Combier★ (Clos des Grives★★), DELAS★, O Dumaine★, Entrefaux★, Fayolle★, Ferraton★, GRAILLOT★★, JABOULET★, Pavillon-Mercurol★, Pochon★ (Ch. Curson★★), Remizières★★, G Robin★, M Sorrel★, Tardieu-Laurent★, Vins de Vienne★; (whites) B Chave★, Colombier★, Combier★★, Dard et Ribo★, DELAS★, O Dumaine★, Ferraton★, GRAILLOT★★, JABOULET★, Pochon★ (Ch. Curson★★), Pradelle★, Remizières★★, M Sorrel★. Best years: (reds) 2001 **00 99 98 97 96 95 94 91 90 89 88**.

DR CRUSIUS *Traisen, Nahe, Germany* Dr Peter Crusius produces Rieslings from the Traiser Bastei★ and SCHLOSSBÖCKELHEIMER Felsenberg★ vineyards which manage to be rich, clean and flinty all at the same time. Best within the first 5 years.

YVES CUILLERON *Condrieu AC, Rhône Valley, France* With wines like Cuilleron's you can understand CONDRIEU's fame and perhaps even forgive it its high price. Les Chaillets Vieilles Vignes★★★ is everything wine made from Viognier should be: opulent and rich, with perfumed honey and apricot aromas. La Petite Côte★★ is also exceptional, and the late-harvest les Ayguets★★★ is an extraordinary sweet whirl of dried apricots, honey and barley sugar. Cuilleron also turns a hand to ST-JOSEPH reds★★ and whites★★ and tiny quantities of ripe, dark, spicy CÔTE-RÔTIE★★. A joint venture, les Vins de Vienne, with partners Pierre Gaillard and François Villard, produces a range of wines including Vin de Pays des COLLINES RHODANIENNES Sotanum★★ (100% Syrah) from ancient vineyard terraces in Seyssuel, just north of Vienne. Best years: (Condrieu) **2001 00 99 98 97 96 95**.

CULLEN *Margaret River, Western Australia* One of the original and best MARGARET RIVER vineyards, established by Diana and Kevin Cullen and now run by their daughter Vanya, one of Australia's most talented winemakers. Superb Chardonnay★★★ is one of the region's most complex and satisfying; the Semillon-Sauvignon blend★★, also stellar, marries nectarines with melon and nuts. Their Cabernet Sauvignon-Merlot★★★ is gloriously soft, deep and scented;

this wine is now justifiably regarded as one of Australia's greats, especially since the Reserve bottling was discontinued and all its fruit put into the one blend. Best years: (Cabernet Sauvignon-Merlot) (2001) 00 99 98 97 **96 95 94 92 91 90 86 84 82**.

CURICÓ, VALLE DE *Valle Central, Chile* Most of the big producers here have planted Cabernet Sauvignon, Merlot, Chardonnay and Sauvignon Blanc. The long growing season provides good fruit concentration. Best producers: Canepa★, MONTES★, SAN PEDRO★, Miguel TORRES★, VALDIVIESO★.

CUVAISON *Napa Valley AVA, California, USA* Cuvaison was known fo
brooding red wines in the 1970s. Now, in a more modern style, i
produces tasty, focused Merlot★, sound Cabernet Sauvignon★, delicate
Pinot Noir★ and good Chardonnay. The silky Reserve Chardonnay★ i
worth seeking out. Best years: (Merlot) (2001) 99 98 **97 96 95 94 91 90**

CVNE *Rioja DOC, Rioja, Spain* Compañía Vinícola del Norte de España i
the full name of this firm, but it's usually known as 'coonay'. Viña
Real★ is one of RIOJA's only remaining well-oaked whites; the Viña
Real Reserva★ and Gran Reserva★ reds can be rich and meaty, and
easily surpass the rather commercial Crianzas; the top Imperial Gran
Reserva★★ is long-lived and impressive. Real de Asúa★ is a new
premium red. Best years: (reds) **1996 95 94 91 90 89 87 86 85**.

DIDIER DAGUENEAU *Pouilly-Fumé AC, Loire Valley, France* Didier
Dagueneau is a much-needed innovator and quality fanatic in a
complacent region. His wines generally benefit from 4 or 5 years
aging and, although at times unpredictable, are generally intense and
complex. The range starts with En Chailloux★★ and moves up
through flinty Buisson Renard★★ to top-quality barrel-fermented
Silex★★ and Pur Sang★★. Best years: (2002) 01 00 **99 98 97**.

ROMANO DAL FORNO *Valpolicella DOC, Veneto, Italy* On his small
estate at Illasi, outside the VALPOLICELLA Classico area, Romano Dal
Forno makes one of the most impressive wines of the appellation. His
Valpolicella Superiore★★ from the Monte Lodoletta vineyard is a
model of power and grace, though his RECIOTO DELLA VALPOLICELLA★★★
and AMARONE★★★, from the same source, are even more voluptuous.
Best years: (Amarone) (2001) (00) (97) 96 95 93 **91 90 88 85**.

LUIGI D'ALESSANDRO, TENIMENTI *Cortona DOC, Tuscany, Italy*
Formerly known as the Fattoria di Manzano, the vineyards have
benefited from massive investment and the freedom to plant and
replant with a New World abandon. From the 2000 vintage, Il
Bosco★★ and the 'second' wine, Vescovo II★, are both 100% Syrah.
The white Fontarca★ blends Chardonnay with varying amounts of
Viognier. Best years: (Il Bosco) 2000 **99 98 97 96 95**.

DALLA VALLE *Napa Valley AVA, California, USA* Stunning hillside winery,
producing some of NAPA's most esteemed Cabernets. Foremost among
them is Maya★★★, a magnificent blend of Cabernet Sauvignon and
Cabernet Franc. The straight Cabernet Sauvignon★★★ is almost as
rich. New Pietre Rosse★★ is richly cherryish 100% Sangiovese.
Cabernet-based reds drink well at 10 years, but will keep for 20 or
more. Best years: (Maya) (2001) (00) 99 98 97 96 95 94 **93 91 90**.

DÃO DOC *Beira Alta, Portugal* Dão has steep slopes ideal for vineyards,
and a great climate for growing local grape varieties; yet only in the
last decade have white wines been freshened up, and reds begun to
realize their long-promised potential – but many still have a long way
to go. Best producers: (reds) Caves ALIANÇA, Boas Quintas (Fonte do
Ouro★), Quinta de Cabriz★ (Virgilio Loureiro★★), Quinta das Maias★,
Quinta da Pellada (Tinta Roriz, Touriga Nacional★), Quinta da Ponte
Pedrinha★, Quinta dos ROQUES★★, Quinta de Sães★, Caves SÃO JOÃO★,
SOGRAPE★ (Quinta dos Carvalhais★★); (whites) Quinta de Cabriz, Quinta
das Maias★, Quinta dos ROQUES★, Quinta de Sães★, SOGRAPE★. Best
years: (reds) 2001 00 **99 97 96 95 94** 92.

D'ARENBERG *McLaren Vale, South Australia* Chester Osborn makes
blockbuster Dead Arm Shiraz★★, Footbolt Old Vine Shiraz★, Custodian
Grenache★ and numerous blends from very low-yielding old vines.

These are big, brash, character-filled wines, but seem to have lost a little heft recently. Best years: (Dead Arm Shiraz) 2001 00 99 98 97 **96 95 94**.

DARTING *Bad Dürkheim, Pfalz, Germany* Helmut Darting makes full, richly fruity wines from sites in BAD DÜRKHEIM (Spielberg), Ungstein (Herrenberg) Riesling Spätlese★★) and WACHENHEIM (Mandelgarten), including rich, peachy Kabinett★ from Dürkheim. Best years: (Riesling Spätlese) (2002) 01 99 98 97 96 **93 92**.

RENÉ & VINCENT DAUVISSAT *Chablis AC, Burgundy, France* One of the top domaines in CHABLIS. This is Chablis at its most complex – refreshing, seductive and beautifully structured, with the fruit balancing the subtle influence of mostly older oak. Look out in particular for la Forest★★, the more aromatic Vaillons★★★ and the powerful les Clos★★★. Best years: (2002) 00 99 98 **97** 96 **95 92** 90 89.

MARCO DE BARTOLI *Sicily, Italy* Marco De Bartoli is most noted for a dry but unfortified MARSALA-style wine called Vecchio Samperi; his version of what he believes Marsala was before the first English merchant, John Woodhouse, fortified it for export. Particularly fine are the 20★★- and 30-year-old★★ Riserva wines – dry, intense and redolent of candied citrus peel, dates and old, old raisins. Also excellent is the MOSCATO PASSITO DI PANTELLERIA Bukkuram★★.

DE BORTOLI *Riverina, New South Wales, Australia* Large, family-owned winery producing a truly sublime botrytized Noble One Semillon★★★. Most of the RIVERINA reds and whites are merely decent, but varieties like Petit Verdot, Cabernet Franc and Durif can produce good results. In the YARRA VALLEY De Bortoli is crafting some fine Chardonnay★, Shiraz★, Cabernet★ and Pinot Noir★★. Also good HUNTER Semillon★. Best years: (Noble One) 2000 **99 98 97 96 95 94 93 90 88 87 84 82**.

DEHLINGER *Russian River Valley AVA, California, USA* Outstanding Pinot Noir★★★ from vineyards in the cool RUSSIAN RIVER region a few miles from the Pacific, best at 5–10 years old. Also mouth-filling Chardonnay★★ and bold, peppery Syrah★★. Recent vintages of Cabernet★★ and Bordeaux Blend★★ (Cabernet-Merlot) reflect a surge in quality. Best years: (Pinot Noir) (2001) 00 99 98 97 **96 95 94 91 90**.

MARCEL DEISS *Alsace AC, Alsace, France* Jean-Michel Deiss is fanatical about distinctions of *terroir*, so it was not surprising when in 1998 the estate became biodynamic. The finest wines are Rieslings★★★ from the Grands Crus Altenberg and Schoenenbourg, which in top years also yield stunning Sélection de Grains Nobles★★★. Although Deiss claims to be less interested in Pinot Gris★★, his wines from this variety, as well as his Gewurztraminers★★★, Pinot Noirs★★ and blended Grand Vin d'Altenberg de Bergheim★, are vibrant and delicious. Best years: (Grand Cru Riesling) 2001 00 98 97 96 **95 94 93 92 90 89 88**.

DELAS FRÈRES *Rhône Valley, France* A rapidly improving merchant (owned by DEUTZ) based near Tournon, selling wines from the entire RHÔNE VALLEY, but with its own vineyards in the northern Rhône. Look out for the aromatic CONDRIEU★★, as well as its single-vineyard wines, including dense, powerful red HERMITAGE★★ (les Bessards★★★), which needs a decade or more to reach its peak, perfumed CÔTE-RÔTIE la Landonne★★★ and ST-JOSEPH Ste-Epine★★. The CROZES-HERMITAGE Tour d'Albon★★ is a good bet, as is the CÔTES DU RHÔNE St-Esprit. Best years: (premium reds) 2001 00 99 98 97 **96 95 94** 91 90 89 88 86 85 83 78.

DELATITE *Central Victoria, Australia* The Ritchies' high-altitude vineyard, in sight of VICTORIA's snowfields, grows delicate, aromatic Riesling★★ and Gewürztraminer★★; there is also subtle Chardonnay★

123

and extravagantly fruity reds. The Pinot Noir★ is perfumed, and Devil's River★ is a smart, minty BORDEAUX blend. Best years: (Riesling) 2000 99 **97 96 94 93 87 86 82**.

DELEGAT'S *Henderson, Auckland, North Island, New Zealand* Family winery specializing in Chardonnay, Cabernet-Merlot and Sauvignon Blanc from the HAWKES BAY and MARLBOROUGH (under Oyster Bay★ label) regions. Prices are generally fair and quality is good but not thrilling. Best are Reserve Chardonnay★ and Reserve Merlot★.

DENBIES *Surrey, England* England's largest vineyard, with 107ha (265 acres), is planted on chalky soils outside Dorking. Consultant winemaker John Worontschak encouraged new plantings and created more blends; Nick Patrick is carrying on the good work. Sparkling wines are good; dry whites are enormously improved in recent years; and there have been encouraging releases of dry rosé and decent reds. Having made quite a good reputation for sweet wines up to 1999, wet autumn weather since has wrecked chances.

DEUTZ *Champagne AC, Champagne, France* This small company has been owned by ROEDERER since 1993 and considerable effort and investment have turned a good producer into an excellent one. The non-vintage Brut★★ is now regularly one of the best in Champagne, often boasting a cedary scent, while the top wines are the classic Blanc de Blancs★★ and the weightier Cuvée William Deutz★★. Deutz also makes good fizz in New Zealand. Best years: (1996) **95 93 90 89 88**.

DÉZALEY *Lavaux, Vaud, Switzerland* The top wine commune in the VAUD, making surprisingly powerful, mineral wines from the Chasselas grape. Best producers: Louis Bovard★, Conne, Dubois Fils★, Les Frères Dubois★, J D Fonjallaz (l'Arbalète)★, Pinget★, J & P Testuz.

D F J VINHOS *Portugal* In the early 1990s, UK wine shippers D & F began working with one of Portugal's most innovative winemakers, José Neiva; in 1999 this relationship evolved into D F J Vinhos. The Bela Fonte brand includes varietal reds Baga, Jaen★ and Touriga Franca★ and a white Bical, all from BEIRAS. Other labels include Manta Preta★ from ESTREMADURA, Pedras do Monte★ and Rocha do Monte from TERRAS DO SADO, Senda do Vale★★ from RIBATEJO, and an ALGARVE red, Cataplana★. At the top end are the Grand'Arte reds, including an intensely fruity, peppery Trincadeira★★.

DIAMOND CREEK *Napa Valley AVA, California, USA* Small estate specializing in Cabernet: Volcanic Hill★★★, Red Rock Terrace★★, Gravelly Meadow★★. Traditionally huge, tannic wines that, when tasted young, I swear won't ever come round. Yet there's usually a sweet inner core of fruit that envelops the tannin over 10–15 years; recent releases show wonderful perfume and balance in their youth. Best years: (2001) (00) 99 98 97 96 95 94 92 91 90 **87 86 84 80**.

DIEL, SCHLOSSGUT *Burg Layen, Nahe, Germany* After an iconoclastic youth, Armin Diel has settled down to become one of the leading producers of classic-style Rieslings. Spätlese and Auslese from Dorsheim's top sites are regularly ★★, Eiswein ★★★. Best years: (Riesling Spätlese) (2002) 01 **99 98 97 96 95 93 90 89 88**.

DISTELL *Stellenbosch, South Africa* This company, formed by the merger between Distillers Corporation and South Africa's largest merchant-producer, Stellenbosch Farmers' Winery, controls almost 30% of Cape table wine production and is still finding its feet, but some of the allied individual wineries – such as Neethlingshof★, STELLENZICHT★ and Durbanville Hills★ – are already performing well. The Fleur du Cap range is improving, and other promising labels are Zonnebloem Fine Art and Pongrácz★ Cap Classique fizz. Two wineries in PAARL (Nederburg and Plaisir de Merle★) are run separately. With better vines and a new cellar team, Nederburg is busy reinventing itself; botrytized dessert Edelkeur★ remains the trademark label, and is sold only through an annual auction. Plaisir de Merle, after a great start, lost its way, but signs are that it is on the way back.

CH. DOISY-DAËNE★★ *Sauternes AC, 2ème Cru Classé, Bordeaux, France* A consistently good property in BARSAC (although it uses the SAUTERNES AC for its wines) and unusual in that the sweet wine is made exclusively from Sémillon. It ages well for 10 years or more. The extra-rich Extravagant★★★ is produced in exceptional years. Doisy-Daëne Sec★ is a good, perfumed, dry white. Drink young. Best years: (sweet) (2002) 01 99 **98 97 96 95 90 89 88 86 83**; (dry) 2001 **99 98**.

CH. DOISY-VÉDRINES★★ *Sauternes AC, 2ème Cru Classé, Bordeaux, France* Next door to DOISY-DAENE, Doisy-Védrines is a richly botrytized wine, fatter and more syrupy than most BARSAC wines. Like its neighbour, it also sells its wines under the SAUTERNES AC. Best years: (sweet) (2002) 01 99 **98 97 96 95 90 89 88 86 85 83**.

DOLCETTO One of Italy's most charming native grapes, producing purple wines bursting at the seams with fruit. Virtually exclusive to PIEDMONT, it is DOC in 7 zones, with styles ranging from intense and rich in Alba, Ovada and Dogliani, to lighter, more perfumed versions in Acqui and Asti. Usually best drunk within 1–2 years, traditionally vinified wines can last 10 years or more. Best producers: (Alba) Alario★★, ALTARE★★, Boglietti★★, Bongiovanni★★, Bricco Maiolica★, Brovia★★, Elvio Cogno★★, Aldo CONTERNO★, Conterno-Fantino★★, B Marcarini★, Bartolo MASCARELLO★, Giuseppe MASCARELLO★★, Paitin★, Pelissero★★, PRUNOTTO★, Albino Rocca★★, SANDRONE★★, Vajra★★, Vietti★, Gianni Voerzio★, Roberto VOERZIO★★; (Dogliani) M & E Abbona★, Chionetti★, Luigi Einaudi★★, Pecchenino★★, San Fereolo★★, San Romano★.

DÔLE *Valais, Switzerland* Red wine from the Swiss VALAIS that must be made from at least 51% Pinot Noir, the rest being Gamay. Dôle is generally a light wine – the deeper, richer (100% Pinot Noir) styles have the right to call themselves Pinot Noir. Most should be drunk young, and can be lightly chilled in summer. Best producers: M Clavien, J Germanier, Caves Imesch, Mathier, Caves Orsat.

DOMAINE CARNEROS *Carneros AVA, California, USA* Very successful TAITTINGER-owned sparkling wine house, founded in 1987. The vintage Brut★ now matches, if not surpasses, Taittinger's fizz from Champagne. Also Le Rêve★★ Blanc de Blancs, and some tasty still Pinot Noirs★.

DOMAINE CHANDON *Yarra Valley, Victoria, Australia* MOET & CHANDON's Aussie offshoot makes Champagne-style Pinot Noir-Chardonnay fizz. There are 2 ranges: non-vintage (Brut★ and sparkling red Pinot-Shiraz★) and vintage (Brut★★, Rosé★★, Blanc de Blancs, Blanc de Noirs, Cuvée Riche). There is also an aged Prestige Cuvée, a YARRA VALLEY Brut★★ and half a dozen table wines under the Green Point label. The Green Point name is also used on fizz for export markets.

DOMAINE CHANDON *Napa Valley AVA, California, USA* The first French-owned (MOET & CHANDON) sparkling wine producer in California has shown remarkable consistency and good quality with reasonably priced non-vintage bubblies. The Reserve★ bottlings, rich and creamy are especially good. Blanc de Blancs★ is made entirely from CARNEROS Chardonnay. Étoile★★ is an aged de luxe wine, and is also made as a flavourful Rosé★★. Shadow Creek is the budget line.

DOMAINE DROUHIN OREGON *Willamette Valley AVA, Oregon, USA* Burgundy wine merchant Robert DROUHIN bought 40ha (100 acres) in OREGON in 1987, with plans to make fine Pinot Noir, and this has certainly been achieved. The regular Pinot Noir★ is silky smooth, and the de luxe Pinot Noir Laurène★★ is supple, voluptuous, and one of Oregon's finest. Pinot Noir Louise Drouhin★★, a selection of the finest barrels in the winery, was added in 1999. Chardonnay★ has established itself well since its first release in 1996. Best years: (Pinot Noir) (2002) (01) 00 99 98 **97 96 94 93**.

DOMAINE VISTALBA *Argentina* All the reds from this French-owned company have dark, concentrated fruit, increasing in complexity through the Fabre Montmayou range. The almost black, chocolate-and-damsons Grand Vin★★ is a splendidly topsy-turvy BORDEAUX blend: Malbec plus Cabernet Sauvignon and Merlot. Cuvée Diane★★ (100% Malbec) is denser and richer still. The reds from a second MENDOZA winery, Altos de Temporada, are also potentially excellent. Dual-variety wines from Río Negro, under the Infinitus label, are starting to show some progress.

DOMECQ *Jerez y Manzanilla DO, Andalucía and Rioja DOC, País Vasco, Spain* The largest of the sherry companies, best known for its reliable fino, La Ina★. At the top of the range, dry Amontillado 51-1A★★★, Sibarita Palo Cortado★★★ and Venerable Pedro Ximénez★★ are spectacular. Domecq also makes light, elegant RIOJA, Marqués de Arienzo★.

DOMINUS★★ *Napa Valley AVA, California, USA* Property owned by Christian MOUEIX, director of Bordeaux superstar PETRUS. Wines are based on Cabernet with leavenings of Merlot and Cabernet Franc. Early vintages were mercilessly tannic, but recent ones show great improvement. Best years: (2001) (00) 99 97 96 **95** 94 91 **90**.

DONAULAND *Niederösterreich, Austria* Amorphous 2730ha (6745-acre) wine region on both banks of the Danube stretching from just north of Vienna west to St Polten. Best are the dry Grüner Veltliners from the Wagram area. Best producers: Karl Fritsch★, Bernhard Ott★★, Wimmer-Czerny★.

DÖNNHOFF *Oberhausen, Nahe, Germany* Helmut Dönnhoff is the quiet winemaking genius of the NAHE, conjuring from a string of top sites some of the most mineral dry and naturally sweet Rieslings in the world. The very best are the subtle, long-lived wines from the Niederhäuser Hermannshöhle★★★ vineyard. Eiswein★★★ is equally exciting. Best years: (Hermannshöhle Riesling Spätlese) (2002) 01 00 **99** 98 **97** 96 95 **94 93 90 89 83 76 71**.

DOURO DOC *Douro, Portugal* As well as a flood of port and basic table wine, some of Portugal's top, soft-textured red wines come from here. Quality can be superb when the lush, scented fruit is not too smothered by new oak barrels. Whites are less interesting, and are best young, but reds may improve for 10 years or even more. Best producers: (reds) Caves ALIANÇA (Foral Grande Escolha★), Maria Doroteia Serôdio Borges (Fojo★★), BRIGHT BROTHERS (TFN★), Chryseia★★, Quinta do COTTO (Grande Escolha★★), Quinta do CRASTO★★, FERREIRA★ (Barca Velha★★, Quinta da Leda★★), Quinta da Gaivosa★★, NIEPOORT★★, Quinta do NOVAL★, Quinta do Portal (Grande Reserva★), Quinta de Roriz★★, Quinta de la ROSA★, SOGRAPE, Quinta do Vale Dona Maria★★, Quinta do Vale Meao★★, Quinta do Vale da Raposa (single varietals★★), Vallado★. Best years: (reds) 2001 00 99 **97 95 94 92**.

DOW *Port DOC, Douro, Portugal* The grapes for Dow's Vintage PORT★★★ come mostly from the Quinta do Bomfim, which is also the name of the excellent single quinta★★★. Dow ports are relatively dry compared with those of GRAHAM and WARRE (the 2 other major brands belonging to the Symington family), and there are some excellent aged tawnies★★. Impressive young port has also been produced under the Quinta Senhora da Ribeira★★ label from the 40ha (100-acre) vineyard opposite VESUVIO since 1998. Best years: (Vintage) 2000 97 94 **91 85 83 80 77 70 66 63 60 55 45**; (Bomfim) 1999 98 95 **92 87 86 84**.

DROMANA ESTATE *Mornington Peninsula, Victoria, Australia* In 20 years, Garry Crittenden has built Dromana into one of the MORNINGTON PENINSULA's major producers, with two dozen wines and a growing raft of brands. Winemaking, thankfully, remains on track with fragrant, restrained Pinot Noir★ and Reserve Chardonnay★★ and leafy, fruity Cabernet-Merlot★. Italian varietals under the Garry Crittenden 'i' label, mostly from King Valley grapes, are of special interest, particularly Sangiovese★, Barbera★ and Arneis★. Good-value Schinus label. Best years: (Reserve Chardonnay) **2001 00 99 98 97 95**.

JOSEPH DROUHIN *Beaune, Burgundy, France* One of the best Burgundian merchants, with substantial vineyard holdings in CHABLIS and the COTE D'OR, and DOMAINE DROUHIN OREGON. Drouhin makes a consistently good, if expensive, range of wines from all over Burgundy. Look for BONNES-MARES★★, ROMANEE-ST-VIVANT★★★, BEAUNE Clos des Mouches (red★★ and white★★★), le Musigny★★★ and le MONTRACHET★★★ from the Dom. du Marquis de Laguiche. Drouhin offers fine value in Chablis★ and less glamorous Burgundian ACs, such as RULLY★ and ST-AUBIN★. The BEAUJOLAIS is always good, but overall Drouhin's whites are (just) better than the reds. Quality reds and whites should be aged for at least 5 years, often better nearer 10.

PIERRE-JACQUES DRUET *Bourgueil, Loire Valley, France* A passionate producer of BOURGUEIL and small quantities of CHINON. Druet makes 5 Bourgueils – les Cent Boisselées★, Cuvée Beauvais★★, Cuvée Grand Mont★, Cuvée Reservée★★ and Vaumoreau★★ – each a complex expression of the Cabernet Franc grape. Best aged for at least 3–5 years. Best years: (top cuvées) (2001) 00 99 **97 96 95 90 89 88 85**.

DRY CREEK VALLEY AVA *Sonoma, California, USA* Best known for Sauvignon Blanc, Zinfandel and Cabernet Sauvignon, this valley runs west of ALEXANDER VALLEY AVA, and similarly becomes hotter moving northwards. Best producers: DRY CREEK VINEYARD★, Duxoup★, FERRARI-CARANO★★, GALLO (Zinfandel★, Cabernet Sauvignon★), Michel-Schlumberger★, Nalle★★, Pezzi King★, Preston★, Rafanelli (Zinfandel★★). Best years: (reds) (2001) (00) 99 98 97 **96 95 94 91**.

DRY CREEK VINEYARD *Dry Creek Valley AVA, California, USA* An early advocate of Fumé Blanc, Dave Stare remains faithful to the brisk racy style of Fumé★ and also makes a serious Reserve Fumé Blanc★ which improves with aging. A drink-young Chardonnay (Reserve★) is attractive, but the stars here are red Meritage★, Merlot★ and Old Vine Zinfandel★★. Best years: (Old Vine Zin) (2001) 00 99 **97 96 95 94 93 91**.

DRY RIVER *Martinborough, North Island, New Zealand* Low yields and an uncompromising attitude to quality at Dr Neil McCallum's tiny winery have created some of the country's top Gewürztraminer★★★ and Pinot Gris★★, an intense and seductively smooth Pinot Noir★★★, sleek Chardonnay★★ and powerful, long-lived Craighall Riesling★★★. Excellent Syrah★★ is made in tiny quantities. Best years: (Craighall Riesling) (2002) 01 **00 99 98 96**; (Pinot Noir) 2001 **00 99 96**.

GEORGES DUBOEUF *Beaujolais, Burgundy, France* Known, with some justification, as the King of Beaujolais, Duboeuf is responsible for more than 10% of the wine produced in the region. Given the size of his operation, the quality of the wines is good. Duboeuf also makes and blends wine from the Mâconnais (ST-VERAN★) and the RHONE VALLEY. His BEAUJOLAIS NOUVEAU is usually reliable, but his top wines are those he bottles for independent growers, particularly Jean Descombes★★ in MORGON, Dom. des Quatre Vents★ and la Madone★ in FLEURIE and Dom. de la Tour du Bief★ in MOULIN-A-VENT.

DUCKHORN *Napa Valley AVA, California, USA* Best known for its very chunky, tannic Merlot★ (Estate Merlot★★) – now, thankfully, softer and riper. The Cabernet Sauvignon★ and Sauvignon Blanc★ provide easier drinking. Under the Goldeneye label there is also a ripe, oaky Pinot Noir★. Paraduxx is a Zinfandel-Cabernet blend; Decoy is the budget line. Best years: (Merlot) (2001) 99 **98 97 96 95 94** 91 90 86.

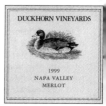

DUCKHORN VINEYARDS

1999
NAPA VALLEY
MERLOT

CH. DUCRU-BEAUCAILLOU★★★ *St-Julien AC, 2ème Cru Classé, Haut-Médoc, Bordeaux, France* Traditionally the epitome of ST-JULIEN, mixing charm and austerity, fruit and firm tannins. Vintages in the mid-1980s and early 90s were flawed, but since 94 Ducru has been back on form. Welcome back to the premier league. Second wine: la Croix de Beaucaillou. Best years: 2001 00 99 98 96 95 **94 85 83 82**.

DUJAC *Morey-St-Denis AC, Côte de Nuits, Burgundy, France* Owner Jacques Seysses is one of Burgundy's most influential winemakers. His estate is based in MOREY-ST-DENIS, and there are also some choice vineyards in CHAMBOLLE-MUSIGNY, ECHEZEAUX and GEVREY-CHAMBERTIN. The wines are all perfumed and elegant, including a small quantity of Morey-St-Denis★ white wine, but the outstanding Dujac bottlings are the Grands Crus – Échézeaux★★★, CLOS DE LA ROCHE★★★, BONNES-MARES★★★ and CLOS ST-DENIS★★★ – all of which will age for a decade or more. From 2000 he and son Jeremy have made some négociant cuvées under the label Dujac Fils et Père. Best years: (Grands Crus) (2002) (01) 00 99 98 96 **95 93 91 90 89**.

DUNN VINEYARDS *Howell Mountain AVA, California, USA* Massive, concentrated, hauntingly perfumed, long-lived Cabernet Sauvignon★★★ is the trademark of Randy Dunn's HOWELL MOUNTAIN wines. His NAPA VALLEY Cabernets★★ are less powerful but still scented. Best years: (2000) 99 97 96 95 94 93 92 91 90 **88 87 86 85 84 82**.

DURIF See Petite Sirah.

JEAN DURUP *Chablis, Burgundy, France* The largest vineyard owner in CHABLIS, Jean Durup is a great believer in unoaked Chablis, which tends to be clean without any great complexity. Best are the Premiers Crus Fourchaume★ and Montée de Tonnerre★★. Wines appear under a variety of labels, including l'Eglantière, Ch. de Maligny and Valéry.

ÉCHÉZEAUX AC *Grand Cru, Côte de Nuits, Burgundy, France* The village of Flagey-Échézeaux, down in the plain away from the vineyards, is best known for its 2 Grands Crus, Échézeaux and the smaller and more prestigious Grands-Échézeaux, which are sandwiched between the world-famous CLOS DE VOUGEOT and VOSNE-ROMANÉE. Few of the 80 growers here have really made a name for themselves, but there are some fine wines with a smoky, plum richness and a soft texture that age well over 10–15 years to a gamy, chocolaty depth. Best producers: R Arnoux★★, BOUCHARD PÈRE ET FILS★★, Cacheux-Sirugue★★★, DROUHIN★★, DUJAC★★★, R Engel★★★, GRIVOT★★★, JAYER-GILLES★★★, Mugneret-Gibourg★★★, Dom. de la ROMANÉE-CONTI★★★, E Rouget★★★. Best years: (2002) (01) 00 99 98 **97** 96 95 **93 90**.

DOM. DE L'ÉCU *Muscadet Sèvre-et-Maine, Loire Valley, France* One of the finest producers in MUSCADET, Guy Bossard's biodynamically run estate also produces GROS PLANT DU PAYS NANTAIS white, a velvety red vin de pays Cabernet blend and a refreshing sparkler, Ludwig Hahn. It is his Muscadet, though, that stands out, especially the top cuvées from different soil types: Gneiss, Orthogneiss★ and fuller-bodied, minerally Granite★★. Best years: (Granite) (2002) 01 **00 99 98**.

EDEN VALLEY See Barossa, pages 58–9.

CH. L'ÉGLISE-CLINET★★★ *Pomerol AC, Bordeaux, France* A tiny 5.5ha (13-acre) domaine in the heart of the POMEROL plateau, l'Église-Clinet has a very old vineyard – one of the reasons for the depth and elegance of the wines. The other is the winemaking ability of owner Denis Durantou. The wine is expensive and in limited supply, but worth seeking out. It can be enjoyed young, though the best examples should be cellared for 10 years or more. Best years: 2001 00 99 98 **97 96 95** 94 93 90 89 86 85.

EIKENDAL *Stellenbosch WO, South Africa* This Helderburg producer makes an understated range of complex and individual wines. There is an elegant, balanced Chardonnay★ with an aging ability uncommon in South Africa, a light-textured but tasty Merlot★, and an occasional Reserve Cabernet★ showing unusual power. Best years: (Chardonnay) **2002 01 00 99 98 97 96**.

ELK COVE *Willamette Valley AVA, Oregon, USA* Dating back to 1973, Elk Cove produces Pinot Noir★★, Cabernet Sauvignon, Pinot Gris★, Chardonnay, Gewürztraminer, Viognier and Riesling★ from its own 27ha (65 acres) of vineyards. The Reserve Pinot Noirs – Roosevelt, Windhill and La Boheme – can now compete with the elite from the state. Best years: (Pinot Noir) (2002) 01 00 99 **98 97**.

NEIL ELLIS *Stellenbosch WO, South Africa* A leading winemaker/négociant, and mentor for many of the Cape's younger winemakers, renowned for powerful, invigorating Groenekloof Sauvignon Blanc★★ and striking STELLENBOSCH reds (blackcurranty Cabernet Sauvignon★★ and supple Cabernet-Merlot★), Ellis has now turned his attention to Shiraz★. Ageworthy single-vineyard Shiraz★ and Cabernet★★ (both from Jonkershoek Valley fruit), and a subtly delicious Chardonnay★★ from cool Elgin confirm his versatility.

ELTVILLE *Rheingau, Germany* Large wine town, making some of the RHEIN-GAU's most racy Riesling wines. Best producers: J B BECKER★, J Fischer, Langwerth von Simmern★. Best years: (2002) 01 00 **99 98 97 96 90**.

EMILIA-ROMAGNA *Italy* Central-eastern region in Italy, divided into the provinces of Emilia (in the west) and ROMAGNA (in the east). It is chiefly infamous for LAMBRUSCO in Emilia. See also Colli Bolognesi, Colli Piacentini.

ENATE *Somontano DO, Aragón, Spain* Enate and VIÑAS DEL VERO seem to be slugging it out for supremacy in the SOMONTANO DO. Barrel-fermented Chardonnay★ is rich, buttery and toasty, Gewürztraminer★ is exotic and convincing. Imported grape varieties also feature in the red Crianza, Reserva★ (100% Cabernet Sauvignon), Reserva Especial★★ (Cabernet-Merlot) and a new blockbuster, Enate Merlot-Merlot★. Best years: (reds) (2001) 00 **99 98 96 95 94**.

ENTRE-DEUX-MERS AC *Bordeaux, France* This AC increasingly represents some of the freshest, snappiest dry white wine in France. In general, drink the latest vintage, though better wines will last a year or two. Sweet wines are sold as PREMIERES COTES DE BORDEAUX, St-Macaire, LOUPIAC and STE-CROIX-DU-MONT. Best producers: Bel Air, BONNET, Castelneau, de Fontenille★, Launay, Moulin-de-Launay, Nardique-la-Gravière★, Ste-Marie★, Tour-de-Mirambeau★, Toutigeac★, Turcaud★.

ERBACH *Rheingau, Germany* Erbach's famous Marcobrunn vineyard is one of the top spots for Riesling on the Rhine. The village wines are elegant, off-dry; those from Marcobrunn more powerful and imposing. Best producers: Jakob Jung★, Knyphausen★, SCHLOSS REINHARTS-HAUSEN★, Schloss Schönborn★. Best years: (Riesling Spätlese) (2002) 01 00 **99 98 97 96 94 93 92**.

ERBALUCE DI CALUSO DOC *Piedmont, Italy* Usually a dry or sparkling white from the Erbaluce grape, but Caluso Passito, where the grapes are semi-dried before fermenting, can be a fine sweet wine. Best producers: (Caluso Passito) Cieck★, Ferrando★, Orsolani★.

ERDEN *Mosel, Germany* Village in the Middle MOSEL, whose most famous vineyards are Prälat and Treppchen. The wines are rich and succulent with a strong mineral character. Best producers: J J Christoffel★★, Dr LOOSEN★★★, Meulenhof★, Mönchhof★★. Best years: (Riesling Spätlese) (2002) 01 **99 97 95 94 93 90**.

ERMITAGE Swiss name for the Marsanne grape of the northern RHONE VALLEY. Mostly found in the central VALAIS, where it produces a range of wines from slightly sweet to lovely honeyed dessert wines. Best producers: Chappaz★, Dom. du Mont d'Or★, Orsat (Marsanne Blanche★).

ERRÁZURIZ *Aconcagua, Chile* American winemaker Ed Flaherty has brought a welcome consistency to this producer's wines. Using grapes from relatively low-yielding Aconcagua slopes north of Santiago, as well as traditional supplies from south of Santiago, there is a uniquely crunchy Merlot★★, reliably powerful Cabernet Sauvignon★ from the Don Maximiano vineyards (also source of SEÑA) and smoky Syrah★. 'Wild Ferment' Chardonnay★★ and Pinot Noir★ from CASABLANCA can excel. New Viñedo Chadwick, from top-quality land in MAIPO, may raise the bar on quality. Best years: (reds) 2002 **01 99 97**.

ESPORÃO *Reguengos DOC, Alentejo, Portugal* Huge estate in the heart of the ALENTEJO, with Australian David Baverstock producing a broad range of wines. The principal labels are Esporão (red★★ and white★ Reservas), Vinha da Defesa★, Monte Velho and Alandra, and there are some delightful varietals: Trincadeira★, Aragonês★★, Cabernet Sauvignon★, Touriga Nacional★ and Syrah★. Best years: (reds) 2001 00 **99 98 97**.

EST! EST!! EST!!! DI MONTEFIASCONE DOC *Lazio, Italy* Modest white accorded its undeserved reputation because of an apocryphal story of a bishop's servant sent ahead to scout out good wines. Getting so excited about this one, he reiterated the thumbs-up code three times. Perhaps it had been a long day. Best producers: Bigi (Graffiti), FALESCO (Poggio dei Gelsi★), Mazziotti (Canuleio★).

CH. DES ESTANILLES *Faugères AC, Languedoc, France* The Louisons know that quality begins in the vineyard. Their best site is the Clos de Fou, with its very steep schistous slope planted with Syrah; the grape 'dominates' the top red cuvée★★ (i.e. 100% – but the AC regulations do not allow them to say so). Also a wood-fermented and aged rosé, plus fine COTEAUX DU LANGUEDOC white★.

ESTREMADURA *Portugal* Portugal's most productive region, occupying the western coastal strip and with an increasing number of clean, characterful wines. The leading area is ALENQUER, promoted to DOC status along with Arruda, Óbidos and Torres Vedras, and there are also the IPRs of Alcobaça and Encostas d'Aire. However, much of the wine, including some of the region's best, is simply labelled as Vinho Regional Estremadura. Spicy, perfumed reds are often based on Castelão, but Cabernet Sauvignon, Syrah, Touriga Nacional and Tinta Roriz contribute to top examples, which can benefit from 4 or 5 years' age. Top producers also make fresh, aromatic whites. Best producers: Quinta da Abrigada★, Companhia Agricola Sanguinhal, Quinta da Cortezia★★/ALIANCA, D F J VINHOS (Grand'Arte Touriga Nacional★, Manta Preta★), Quinta de Pancas★★, Quinta do Monte d'Oiro★★, Casa SANTOS LIMA★. See also Bucelas. Best years: (reds) 2001 00 **99** 97.

L'ÉTOILE AC *Jura, France* A tiny area within the COTES DU JURA which has its own AC for whites, mainly Chardonnay and Savagnin, and for *vin jaune*. Fizz now comes under the CREMANT DU JURA AC. Best producers: Ch. l'Étoile★, Geneletti★, Joly★, Montbourgeau★★, Quintigny★.

CH. L'ÉVANGILE★★ *Pomerol AC, Bordeaux, France* A neighbour to PETRUS and CHEVAL BLANC, this estate has been wholly owned and managed by the Rothschilds of LAFITE-ROTHSCHILD since 1990. The wine is quintessential POMEROL – rich, fat and exotic. Recent vintages have been very good, but expect further improvement as the Rothschild effect intensifies. Best years: 2000 99 98 96 **95 94** 93 90 89 88 85 83 82.

EVANS & TATE *Margaret River, Western Australia* Following the merger (read takeover) with Cranswick, this is now Australia's fifth-largest producer. In spite of the expansion, the quality of the MARGARET RIVER wines has never been better: figgy Chardonnay, crisp Sauvignon-Semillon★, nutty Semillon★★, blackcurranty Cabernet-Merlot★ and concentrated Cabernet Sauvignon★ and Shiraz★. Best years: (Cabernet Sauvignon) (2001) 00 99 **98 96 94**.

EYRIE VINEYARDS *Willamette Valley AVA, Oregon, USA* One of the leading Pinot Noir producers in OREGON, especially the Reserve★, but in poor years the wines can be withdrawn and thin. Chardonnay★ shows nice varietal fruit, while the popular Pinot Gris★ flies off the shelves. Best years: (Pinot Noir Reserve) (2002) 01 00 99 **98 97 96**.

FAIRVIEW *Paarl WO, South Africa* Best known for his many wines from Rhône varieties, owner Charles Back's restless ambition means he also wants to be up with the best in other varieties. Recent land purchases in Darling (for Sauvignon Blanc) and STELLENBOSCH (for other reds) should help him on his way. Fans of Goats do Roam, a spoof on COTES DU RHONE, increase on both sides of the Atlantic; the red★ features Pinotage with Rhône varieties such as Grenache, Cinsaut, Mourvèdre and Syrah; a spicy rosé is lightly oaked; and a lovely white★ is blended from Grenache Blanc, Clairette and Crouchen with a splash of Muscat Apart from the delightfully idiosyncratic Zinfandel-Cinsaut★, Back makes fine Shiraz★★ (Solitude★★ and Beacon Block★★), Carignan★ Malbec★, Merlot★★, Cabernet Sauvignon★ and Pinotage★ (Primo★★) Good whites include Chenin Blanc★, Semillon★ (Oom Pagel★★) and Viognier★. Charles Back also owns the progressive SPICE ROUTE WINE COMPANY and acts as guiding light to the Fair Valley workers empowerment project. Best years: (Shiraz) 2002 01 **00 99 98 97 96 95 93**

JOSEPH FAIVELEY *Nuits-St-Georges AC, Côte de Nuits, Burgundy, France*
This Burgundian merchant makes impressive but rather severely tannic, long-lived red wines (CORTON★★, CHAMBERTIN-Clos-de-Bèze★★★ Mazis-Chambertin★★), principally from its own substantial vineyard holdings. In lesser wines, the fruit may not hold out against the tannin, and even aging may not help. The much cheaper MERCUREY reds★ from the Côte Chalonnaise can be attractive, if on the lean side Whites from Mercurey★ and RULLY★, and the oak-aged BOURGOGNE Blanc represent reasonably good value. Best years: (top reds) (2002) (01) 99 98 97 96 **95 93 90 89**; (whites) (2002) 01 00 99 **97 96**.

FALERNO DEL MASSICO DOC *Campania, Italy* Falernian, from north of Naples, was one of the ancient Romans' superstar wines. The revived DOC, with a white Falanghina and reds from either Aglianico and Piedirosso or from Primitivo, looks promising. Best producers: Michele Moio★, Villa Matilde★ (Vigna Camarato★★). Best years: (reds) (2001) 00 99 **98 97 96 95**.

FALESCO *Lazio, Italy* Property of the phenomenal Cotarella brothers, Renzo and Riccardo; the former is ANTINORI's technical director (so responsible for SOLAIA, TIGNANELLO, etc.), the latter today's most high-profile consultant enologist, working all over Italy from Piedmont to Sicily. Located at Montefiascone, the town of EST! EST!! EST!!!, their Poggio dei Gelsi★ is considered best of the genre, but they are better known for their Merlot Montiano★★, the essence of smooth if somewhat soulless modernity. Best years (Montiano): (2001) (00) 99 98 **97 96 95 94**.

CH. FALFAS★ *Côtes de Bourg AC, Bordeaux, France* Biodynamic estate making concentrated, structured wine that needs 4–5 years to soften. Le Chevalier★ is an old-vines cuvée. Best years: 2001 00 **99 98 96 95 94 90**.

CH. DE FARGUES★★ *Sauternes AC, Cru Bourgeois, Bordeaux, France* Property run by the Lur-Saluces family, who until 1999 also owned Ch. d'YQUEM. The quality of this fine, rich wine is more a tribute to their commitment than to the inherent quality of the vineyard. Best years: 1998 97 **96 95 90 89 88 86 83**.

FAUGÈRES AC *Languedoc, France* Faugères, with its vineyards in the schistous hills north of Béziers in the Hérault, produces red wines whose ripe, soft, rather plummy flavour marks them out from other LANGUEDOC reds. Best producers: Abbaye Sylva Plana★, Alquier★, Léon Barral★, Chenaie★, ESTANILLES★, Faugères co-op, Fraisse, Grézan, Haut-Fabrègues, la Liquière★, Moulin de Ciffre★, Ollier-Taillefer (Cuvée Castel Fossibus★). Best years: 2001 00 **99 98 96 95 94 93**.

FAUSTINO *Rioja DOC, País Vasco and Rioja, and Cava DO, Spain* Family-owned and technically very well equipped, this RIOJA company makes good Reserva V★ and Gran Reserva I★ red Riojas, as well as a more modern, oak-aged red, Faustino de Autor, and pleasant whites and rosés. In 1999 it introduced a fruit-driven Faustino de Crianza. Best years: (reds) 1998 **96 95 94 92 91 90 89 87**.

FEILER-ARTINGER *Rust, Neusiedlersee, Burgenland, Austria* Father and son team Hans and Kurt Feiler make Ausbruch-style dessert wines★★★ of great elegance. Their dry whites are ★. Solitaire★★ is a suave red blend of Merlot with Blaufränkisch and Zweigelt. Best years: (sweet whites) (2002) (01) (00) 99 98 **96 95 94 93 91**; (Solitaire) (2001) 00 **99 97 95 94**.

LIVIO FELLUGA *Colli Orientali del Friuli DOC, Friuli-Venezia Giulia, Italy* A younger generation has continued the great work of Livio Felluga, delivering both quality and quantity from this large Friuli estate. Merlot-Cabernet blend Vertigo★★, raspberryish straight Merlot Riserva Sossò★★ and white Pinot Grigio★, Picolit Riserva★★ and Tocai Friulano★ are all class acts. Sharjs★ combines Chardonnay with Ribolla and oak, but there's more to stimulate the palate in Terre Alte★★, an aromatic blend of Tocai, Pinot Bianco and Sauvignon. Best years: (whites): (2001) **00 99 98 97 96**.

FELSINA, FATTORIA DI *Chianti Classico DOCG, Tuscany, Italy* Full, chunky CHIANTI CLASSICO★★ wines which improve with several years' bottle age. Quality is generally outstanding; most notable are the single-vineyard Riserva Rancia★★★ and Sangiovese Fontalloro★★★. Also good Chardonnay I Sistri★★ and Cabernet Maestro Raro★★. Best years: (Fontalloro) (2001) (00) (99) 98 97 **95 93 90 88 85**.

FELTON ROAD *Central Otago, South Island, New Zealand* Runaway success with vineyards in the old goldfields of Bannockburn. Intensely fruity, seductive Pinot Noir★★ is surpassed by very limited quantities of concentrated, complex Block 3 Pinot Noir★★★ and the equally limited edition Block 5★★★. Three classy Rieslings (all ★★) cover the range from dry to sweet. Mineral, citrus unoaked Chardonnay★★ is one of New Zealand's best; barrel-fermented Chardonnay★★ also impresses. Best years: (Pinot Noir) 2001 **00 99 98 97**.

FENDANT *Valais, Switzerland* Chasselas wine from the steep slopes of the Swiss VALAIS. Good Fendant should be ever so slightly *spritzig*, with a nutty character. However, the average Fendant is thin and virtually characterless. It is best drunk *very* young, but a good example can age for a year or two. Best producers: Chappaz, J Germanier, Gilliard, Caves Imesch, Maye & Fils, Caves Orsat.

FERRARI *Trento DOC, Trentino, Italy* Founded in 1902, the firm is a leader for sparkling wine. Consistent, classy wines include Ferrari Brut★, Maximum Brut★, Perlé★, Rosé★ and vintage Giulio Ferrari Riserva del Fondatore★★, aged 8 years on its lees and an Italian classic.

FERRARI-CARANO *Dry Creek Valley AVA, California, USA* Delightful Chardonnay, with balanced, elegant fruit; the regular bottling★★ has delicious apple-spice fruit, while the Reserve★★ is deeply flavoured with more than a touch of oak. Fumé Blanc★ is also good. Red wines are equally impressive, including Siena★★ (a Sangiovese-Cabernet Sauvignon blend), Trésor★★ (a BORDEAUX blend), Syrah★, Merlot★ and Zinfandel★. Reds can improve for 5–10 years. Best years: (reds) (2001) (00) 99 98 97 **96 95 94 91**.

FERREIRA *Port DOC, Douro DOC, Douro, Portugal* Old port house owned by SOGRAPE. Ferreira is best known for excellent tawny ports: creamy, nutty Quinta do Porto 10-year-old★ and Duque de Braganza

20-year-old★★. The Vintage Port★★ is increasingly good. Ferreira's table wine operation, known as Casa Ferreirinha, produces Portugal's most sought-after red, Barca Velha★★; made from DOURO grape varieties (mainly Tinta Roriz), it is produced only in the finest years – just 12 vintages since 1953. Marginally less good years are now sold as Casa Ferreirinha Reserva★ (previously Reserva Especial). Quinta da Leda reds★★ are also fine. Best years: (Vintage) 2000 97 95 94 **91 85 78 77 70 66 63**; (Barca Velha) **1995 91 85 83 82 81 78**.

CH. FERRIÈRE★★ *Margaux AC, 3ème Cru Classé, Haut-Médoc, Bordeaux, France* The smallest classified growth in MARGAUX, Ferrière was leased to its larger neighbour Ch. LASCOMBES until 1992, when it was purchased by the Merlaut family, owners of Ch. CHASSE-SPLEEN. It is now managed by Claire Villars, and the ripe, rich and perfumed wines are among the best in Margaux AC. Best years: 2001 00 99 98 96 **95**.

FETZER VINEYARDS *Mendocino County, California, USA* Important winery balancing quality and quantity. Basic wines are good, with a tasty Syrah★; Barrel Select bottles are usually ★. Also a leader in organic viticulture with the Bonterra range: Chardonnay★, Viognier★, Merlot★, Roussanne★, Zinfandel★, Cabernet Sauvignon and Sangiovese. Best years: (Barrel Select reds) (2001) 99 98 **97 96 95 94**.

FIANO Exciting, distinctive, low-yielding southern Italian white grape variety. Best producers: (Molise) Di Majo Norante; (Fiano di Avellino DOC in Campania) Colli di Lapio★, Feudi di San Gregorio★★, MASTROBERARDINO★, Terredora di Paolo★, Vadiaperti★; (others) L Maffini (Kràtos★★), PLANETA (Cometa★★).

CH. DE FIEUZAL *Pessac-Léognan AC, Cru Classé de Graves, Bordeaux, France* Recently purchased by Irish businessman Lochlainn Quinn, this is one of the most up-to-date properties in the region. The red★ is drinkable almost immediately, but has the structure to age. Less than 10% of the wine is white★★ but this gorgeous, perfumed (and ageworthy) wine is the star performer here. Second wine (red and white): l'Abeille de Fieuzal. Best years: (reds) 2000 98 96 **95 94 90 89 88 87 86 85 83 82**; (whites) 2001 00 99 **98 96 95 94 93 90 89 88 85**.

CH. FIGEAC★★ *St-Émilion Grand Cru AC, 1er Grand Cru Classé, Bordeaux, France* Leading property whose wine traditionally has a delightful fragrance and gentleness of texture. There is an unusually high percentage of Cabernets Franc and Sauvignon (70%) in the wine, making it more structured than other ST-EMILIONS. After an unconvincing run of vintages from the mid-1980s, recent vintages have been far more like the lovely Figeac of old. Second wine: la Grangeneuve de Figeac. Best years: 2001 00 99 98 95 **90 89 83 82**.

FINGER LAKES AVA *New York State, USA* Cool region in central NEW YORK STATE. Riesling, Chardonnay and sparkling wines are the trump cards here, but Pinot Noir and Cabernet Franc are increasingly successful. Best producers: FOX RUN★, Dr Konstantin FRANK, Glenora, LAMOREAUX LANDING★, Silver Thread, Wagner, Hermann J Wiemer.

FITOU AC *Languedoc-Roussillon, France* One of the success stories of the 1980s. Quality subsequently slumped, but with the innovative MONT TAUCH co-op taking the lead, Fitou is once again an excellent place to seek out dark, herb-scented reds. Best producers: Abelanet, Bertrand-Berge★, Lerys★, Milles Vignes, MONT TAUCH co-op★, Nouvelles★, Rochelière, Rolland, Roudène★. Best years: 2001 00 **99 98 96 95 94 93**.

FIXIN AC *Côte de Nuits, Burgundy, France* Although it's next door to GEVREY-CHAMBERTIN, Fixin rarely produces anything really magical, despite the significant improvement of most red Burgundy over the past decade. The wines are often sold as COTE DE NUITS-VILLAGES. Best producers: Champy★, Pierre Gelin★, Alain Guyard★, Dominique Laurent★★, Naddef★. Best years: (reds) (2002) (01) 00 99 **98 97** 96 95.

FLEURIE AC *Beaujolais, Burgundy, France* The best-known BEAUJOLAIS Cru. Good Fleurie reveals the happy, carefree flavours of the Gamay grape at its best, plus heady perfumes and a delightful juicy sweetness. But demand has meant that too many wines are overpriced and dull. Best producers: J-M Aujoux★, M Chignard★, Clos de la Roilette★, Daumas★, Depardon★, Deprés★, DUBOEUF (single domaines★), H Fessy★, Fleurie co-op★, Metrat★, A & M Morel★, P Sapin (Dom. des Raclets★), Verpoix★, Vissoux/P-M Chermette★★. Best years: (2002) **00 99**.

CH. LA FLEUR-PÉTRUS★★ *Pomerol AC, Bordeaux, France* Like the better-known PETRUS and TROTANOY, this is owned by the dynamic MOUEIX family. Unlike its stablemates, it is situated entirely on gravel soil and tends to produce tighter wines with less immediate fruit but considerable elegance and cellar potential. Among POMEROL's top dozen properties. Best years: 2001 00 99 98 **97 96 95** 94 93 90 89 88 85 82.

FLORA SPRINGS *Napa Valley AVA, California, USA* Best known for red wines such as Cabernet Reserve★★, a BORDEAUX blend called Trilogy★★ and Merlot★★. Chardonnay Reserve★★ tops the whites, and Soliloquy, a barrel-fermented Sauvignon Blanc, offers attractive melon fruit. The winery also works with Italian varietals; a weighty Pinot Grigio★ and a lightly spiced Sangiovese★ are consistent successes. Best years: (Trilogy) (2001) 00 99 97 96 **95 94 93 91**.

FLOWERS *Sonoma Coast AVA, California, USA* Small producer whose estate vineyard, Camp Meeting Ridge, a few miles from the Pacific Ocean, yields wines of great intensity. The Camp Meeting Ridge Pinot Noir★★★ and Chardonnay★★★ are usually made with native yeasts and offer wonderful exotic aromas and flavours. Wines from purchased fruit with a SONOMA COAST designation are ★★ in quality. Best years: (Chardonnay) (2001) **00 99 98 97 96**; (Pinot Noir) (2001) 00 **99 98 97 96**.

FONSECA *Port DOC, Douro, Portugal* Owned by the same group as TAYLOR, Fonseca makes ports in a rich, densely plummy style. Fonseca Vintage★★★ is magnificent, the aged tawnies★★ uniformly superb. Fonseca Guimaraens★★ is the name of the 'off-vintage' wine, but off vintages here are equal to all but the best offerings of other houses. Bin No. 27★ is one of the best examples of a premium ruby port. Best years: (Vintage) 2000 97 94 92 **85 83 77 75 70 66 63 55**.

JOSÉ MARIA DA FONSECA *Terras do Sado, Portugal* Go-ahead company with a new winery (opened in 2001) making a huge range of wines, from fizzy Lancers Rosé to serious reds. Best include Vinya★ (Syrah and Aragonez), Domingos Soares Franco Private Collection★, and Garrafeiras with codenames like CO, RA and TE★★. Optimum★★ is top of the range. Periquita is the mainstay, with Clássico★ made only in the best years. Also SETUBAL made mainly from the Moscatel grape: 5-year-old★ and 20-year-old★★. Older vintage-dated Setúbals are rare but superb, as is Trilogia★★★, a Moscatel de Setúbal blend of 3 outstanding 20th-century vintages (1900, 1934 and 1965).

DOM. FONT DE MICHELLE *Châteauneuf-du-Pape AC, Rhône Valley, France* This much-improved estate is currently among the better performers in CHATEAUNEUF-DU-PAPE. The reds★★, in particular Cuvée

135

Étienne Gonnet★★, and whites★ are stylish but still heady, with richness and southern herb fragrance – and not too expensive. Best years: (Étienne Gonnet red) 2001 00 99 98 **97 95 90 89**.

FONTANAFREDDA *Barolo DOCG, Piedmont, Italy* One of the largest PIEDMONT estates, based in the old BAROLO hunting lodge of the King of Italy. As well as Barolo Serralunga d'Alba★, it also produces a range of Piedmont varietals, several single-vineyard Barolos★ (La Delizia★★), 4 million bottles of ASTI and a good dry sparkler, Contessa Rosa. Best years: (Barolo) (2001) (00) (99) (97) **90 89 88 85**.

FONTERUTOLI, CASTELLO DI *Chianti Classico DOCG, Tuscany, Italy* This eminent estate has belonged to the Mazzei family since the 15th century. Production is now focused on CHIANTI CLASSICO Riserva★★★, which has replaced the fine SUPER-TUSCAN Concerto★★ (Sangiovese with 20% Cabernet) and previously outstanding Riserva Ser Lapo★★. The excellent Siepi★★★ (Sangiovese-Merlot) is being retained. Belguardo★ is a new venture in the southern Maremma, sold under the IGT rather than as MORELLINO DI SCANSANO DOC.

FONTODI *Chianti Classico DOCG, Tuscany, Italy* The Manetti family has built this superbly sited estate into one of the most admired in the CHIANTI CLASSICO area, with excellent *normale*★★, richer Riserva★★ and fine Riserva Vigna del Sorbo★★. SUPER-TUSCAN Flaccianello della Pieve★★★, produced from a single vineyard of old vines, has served as a shining example to other producers of how excellent Sangiovese can be without the addition of other varieties. Two varietals are made under the new Case Via label; of these, the Syrah★★ is most promising. Best years: (Flaccianello) (2001) (00) (99) 98 97 95 **93 90 88 85**.

FORADORI *Teroldego Rotaliano DOC, Trentino, Italy* Producer of dark, spicy, berry-fruited wines, including a regular TEROLDEGO ROTALIANO★ and barrique-aged Granato★★. Foradori's interest in Syrah is producing excellent results, both in the varietal Ailanpa★★ and the smoky, black-cherry lushness of Cabernet-Syrah blend Karanar★. Best years: (Granato) (2001) (00) 99 **97 96 93**.

FORST *Pfalz, Germany* Village with 6 individual vineyard sites, including the Ungeheuer or 'Monster'; wines from the Monster can indeed be quite savage, with a marvellous mineral intensity and richness in the best years. Equally good are the Kirchenstück, Jesuitengarten, Freundstück and Pechstein. Best producers: BASSERMANN-JORDAN★★, von BUHL★, BURKLIN-WOLF★★, MOSBACHER★★, WEGELER★, Werlé★, WOLF★★. Best years: (Riesling Auslese) (2002) 01 99 98 **97 96 94 93 90**.

FOX CREEK *McLaren Vale, South Australia* Impressive, opulent, superripe MCLAREN VALE reds. Reserve Shiraz★★ and Reserve Cabernet Sauvignon★★ have wowed the critics; JSM (Shiraz-Cabernets)★★ is rich and succulent; Merlot★★ is a little lighter but still concentrated and powerful. Vixen sparkling Shiraz★ is also lip-smacking stuff. Whites are comparatively ordinary, albeit fair value for money.

FOX RUN VINEYARDS *Finger Lakes AVA, New York State, USA* A reliable producer of complex ALSACE-style Gewürztraminer★, elegant Reserve Chardonnay★ and a delightfully quaffable semi-dry Riesling. There are also spicy, attractive reds from Pinot Noir and Cabernet Franc and, since 1996, a complex, fruit-forward red Meritage.

FRANCIACORTA DOCG *Lombardy, Italy* A Champagne-method sparkler made from Pinot and Chardonnay grapes. Still whites from Pinot Bianco and Chardonnay and reds from Cabernet, Barbera, Nebbiolo and Merlot are all DOC with the appellation Terre di Franciacorta. Best producers: BELLAVISTA★★, CA' DEL BOSCO★★, Fratelli Berlucchi★, Guido Berlucchi★, Castellino★, Cavalleri★, La Ferghettina★, Enrico Gatti★, Monte Rossa★, Ricci Curbastro★, San Cristoforo★, Uberti★, Villa★.

FRANCISCAN *Napa Valley AVA, California, USA* Consistently good wines at fair prices, from the heart of the NAPA VALLEY. The Cuvée Sauvage Chardonnay★★ is a blockbusting, savoury mouthful, and the Cabernet Sauvignon-based meritage Magnificat★ is very attractive. Estancia is a separate label, with remarkably good-value Chardonnay★ and Pinot Noir★ from CENTRAL COAST and Cabernet Sauvignon★ from ALEXANDER VALLEY, as well as its own Meritage★. Franciscan also owns Mount Veeder Winery, where lean but intense Cabernet Sauvignon★★ of great mineral depth and complexity is made.

DR KONSTANTIN FRANK *New York State, USA* The good doctor was a leading pioneer of vinifera grapes in the FINGER LAKES region of New York State in the 1960s. Now under the direction of his son, Willi, and grandson Fred, the winery continues to spotlight the area's talent with Riesling. There's also some nice Chateau Frank fizz.

FRANKEN *Germany* 6000ha (14,820-acre) wine region specializing in dry wines. Easily recognizable by their squat, green Bocksbeutel bottles (now more familiar because of the Portuguese wine Mateus Rosé). Silvaner is the traditional grape variety, although Müller-Thurgau now predominates. The most famous vineyards are on the hillsides around WURZBURG and IPHOFEN.

FRANSCHHOEK WO *South Africa* A picturesque valley encircled by breathtaking mountain peaks, Franschhoek is a ward within the PAARL district. Huguenot refugees settled here in the 17th century and many of the wineries still bear French names. Semillon is a local speciality (a few vines are close to 100 years old) and the valley is best known for its white wines. However, a diverse range of reds is now showing promise, including Cabrière Pinot Noir★, La Motte Shiraz★ and Stony Brook Cabernet Sauvignon Reserve. Best producers: BOEKEN-HOUTSKLOOF★★, Cabrière Estate★, Jean Daneel Wines, La Motte★, La Petite Ferme, L'Ormarins, Stony Brook. Best years: (reds) **2000 99 98 97**.

FRASCATI DOC *Lazio, Italy* One of Italy's most famous whites, frequently referred to as Rome's quaffing wine. The wine may be made from Trebbiano or Malvasia or any blend thereof; the better examples have a higher proportion of Malvasia. Good Frascati is worth seeking out, most notably Vigna Adriana★, from the revelationary Castel de Paolis. Other light, dry Frascati-like wines come from neighbouring DOCs in the hills of the Castelli Romani and Colli Albani, including Marino, Montecompatri, Velletri and Zagarolo. Best producers: Casale Marchese★, Castel de Paolis★★, Colli di Catone★, Piero Costantini/Villa Simone★, Fontana Candida★, Zandotti★.

FREISA Italian PIEDMONT grape making sweet, foaming, 'happy juice' reds, now sadly rather out of fashion. Some producers are now making a dry style which is very tasty after 3 or 4 years. Best producers: Poderi Colla, Piero Gatti, Giuseppe MASCARELLO, Cantina del Pino, Scarpa★, Vajra★★, Rino Varaldo, Gianni Voerzio.

FREIXENET *Cava DO, Cataluña, Spain* The second-biggest Spanish sparkling wine company (after CODORNIU) makes the famous Cordon Negro Brut CAVA in a vast network of cellars in Sant Sadurní d'Anoia. Freixenet also owns the Castellblanch, Segura Viudas, Conde de Caralt and Canals & Nubiola Cava brands as well as PENEDES winery René Barbier. Its international expansion has gathered pace in recent years with interests in CHAMPAGNE, CALIFORNIA, Australia and BORDEAUX.

FRESCOBALDI *Tuscany, Italy* Florentine company selling large quantities of inexpensive blended CHIANTIS, but from its own vineyards (some 800 ha/1980 acres in total) it produces good to very good wines at Nipozzano (especially CHIANTI RUFINA Castello di Nipozzano Riserva★★ and Montesodi★★★), Tenuta di Pomino★, and CASTELGIOCONDO★ in BRUNELLO DI MONTALCINO. Castelgiocondo is also the early source for the much-ballyhooed new wine, Luce – a joint venture with MONDAVI. Best years: (premium reds) (2001) (00) 99 98 97 **95 93 90 88 85**.

FRIEDRICH-WILHELM-GYMNASIUM *Trier, Ruwer, Germany* New director Helmut Kranich has brought this estate back on song after a serious lapse in performance in the early 1990s. The naturally sweet Rieslings all have an appealing delicacy and lightness, and most Spätlese and Auslese rate ★. Best years: (Riesling Spätlese) (2002) **01 99 98 97 95 90**.

FRIULI GRAVE DOC *Friuli-Venezia Giulia, Italy* DOC in western Friuli covering 19 wine types. Good affordable Merlot, Refosco, Chardonnay, Pinot Grigio, Traminer and Tocai. Best producers: Borgo Magredo★, Le Fredis★, Di Lenardo★, Orgnani★, Pighin★, Pittaro★, Plozner★, Pradio★, Russolo★, Vigneti Le Monde★, Villa Chiopris★, Vistorta★. Best years: (whites) (2001) **00** 98.

FRIULI ISONZO DOC *Friuli-Venezia Giulia, Italy* Classy southern neighbour of COLLIO with wines of outstanding value. The DOC covers 20 styles, including Merlot, Chardonnay, Pinot Grigio and Sauvignon. The best from neighbouring Carso are also good. Best producers: (Isonzo) Borgo San Daniele★, Colmello di Grotta★, Sergio & Mauro Drius★★, Masùt da Rive★ (Silvano Gallo), Lis Neris-Pecorari★★, Pierpaolo Pecorari★★, Giovanni Puiatti★, Ronco del Gelso★★, Tenuta Villanova★, Vie di Romans★★; (Carso) Castelvecchio, Edi Kante★★. Best years: (whites) (2001) **00 99 98 97**.

FRIULI-VENEZIA GIULIA *Italy* North-east Italian region bordering Austria and Slovenia. The hilly DOC zones of COLLIO and COLLI ORIENTALI produce some of Italy's finest whites from Chardonnay, Pinot Bianco, Pinot Grigio, Sauvignon and Tocai, and excellent reds mainly from Cabernet, Merlot and Refosco. The DOCs of Friuli Aquileia, FRIULI ISONZO, Friuli Latisana and FRIULI GRAVE, in the rolling hills and plains, produce good-value wines.

FROMM *Marlborough, South Island, New Zealand* Small winery owned by Austrian George Fromm and managed by the very talented Hätsch Kalberer. Low-yielding vines and intensively managed vineyards are the secret behind a string of winning white wines, including fine Burgundian-style La Strada Reserve Chardonnay★★, German-style Riesling★★ and Riesling Auslese★. Despite its success with whites, Fromm is perhaps best known for intense, long-lived reds, including Clayvin Vineyard Pinot Noir★★, Fromm Vineyard Pinot Noir★★ and a powerful, peppery Syrah★. Best years: (Pinot Noir) (2002) **01 00 99 98**.

FRONSAC AC *Bordeaux, France* Small area west of POMEROL making good-value Merlot-based wines. The top producers have taken note of the feeding frenzy in neighbouring Pomerol and sharpened up their act accordingly, with finely structured wines, occasionally perfumed, and better with at least 5 years' age. Best producers: Carolus, Dalem★, la Dauphine★, Fontenil★, la Grave★, Haut-Carles★, Magondeau Beausite, Mayne-Vieil (Cuvée Aliénas★), Moulin-Haut-Laroque★, Puy Guilhem, la Rivière★, la Rousselle★, Tour du Moulin, les Trois Croix★, la Vieille Cure★, Villars★. Best years: 2001 00 98 **97 96 95 94 90 89 88 86 85**.

FUMÉ BLANC See Sauvignon Blanc.

RUDOLF FÜRST *Bürgstadt, Franken, Germany* Paul Fürst's dry Rieslings★★ are unusually elegant for a region renowned for its earthy white wines, while his Burgundian-style Spätburgunder (Pinot Noir) reds★★ and barrel-fermented Weissburgunder (Pinot Blanc) whites★★ – and Champagne-style sparkler★★ – are some of the best in Germany. Sensual, intellectual wines with excellent aging potential. Best years: (dry Riesling) (2002) 01 **99** 98 **97 94 93 92 90 89 88**; (reds) (2002) 01 00 **99 98 97 94 90**.

JEAN-NOËL GAGNARD *Chassagne-Montrachet AC, Côte de Beaune, Burgundy, France* Now run by daughter Caroline Lestimé, who consistently makes some of the best wines of CHASSAGNE-MONTRACHET. Top wine is rich, toasty BATARD-MONTRACHET★★★, but other whites are first rate, too, particularly Premiers Crus Caillerets★★★ and Morgeot★★. Gagnard's reds★ are not quite as good, but are still among the most enjoyable in Chassagne. All whites are capable of extended cellaring. Best years: (whites) (2002) (01) 00 99 98 **97 96 95**.

GAILLAC AC *South-West France* The whites, mainly from Mauzac with its sharp but attractive green apple bite, are rather stern but, from a decent grower or the revitalized co-ops, can be extremely refreshing. Sweet whites are getting better as well. Some more serious reds are now being made, which require some aging. The star of Gaillac at the moment is the outstanding fizz, ideally not quite dry and packed with fruit. Drink as young as possible. Best producers: Albert, Bosc-Long, Causses-Marines★, Clément Termes, Escausses, de Gineste★, Labarthe★, Labastide-de-Lévis co-op, Mas Pignou, Plageoles★★, Rotier★, Técou co-op★, des Terrisses★.

GAJA *Barbaresco DOCG, Piedmont, Italy* Angelo Gaja brought about the transformation of PIEDMONT from an old-fashioned region that Italians swore made the finest red wine in the world yet the rest of the world disdained, to an area buzzing with excitement. He introduced international standards and charged staggeringly high prices, thus giving other Piedmont growers the chance at last to get a decent return for their labours. Into this fiercely conservative area, full of fascinating grape varieties but proudest of the native Nebbiolo, he introduced French grapes like Cabernet Sauvignon (Darmagi★★), Sauvignon Blanc (Alteni di Brassica★) and Chardonnay (Gaia & Rey★★). He has also renounced the Barbaresco and Barolo DOCGs for his best wines! Gaja's traditional strength has been in single-vineyard wines from the BARBARESCO region: his Sorì San Lorenzo★★★, Sorì Tildìn★★★ and Costa Russi★★★, now sold under the LANGHE DOC, are often cited as Barbaresco's best. Only one premium bottling of Barbaresco★★★ is now made. Sperss★★★ and Conteisa★★★ – from BAROLO, but sold as Langhe DOC wines – are also outstanding. Barbera Sito Rey★ and Nebbiolo-based Langhe Sito Moresco★ are less exciting. Gaja has also invested in BRUNELLO DI MONTALCINO (Pieve Santa Restituta) and BOLGHERI (Cà Marcanda). Best years: (Barbaresco) (2001) (00) 99 98 97 96 **95 93 90 89 88 85 82 79 78 71 61**.

GALICIA *Spain* Up in Spain's hilly, verdant north-west, Galicia is renowned for its Albariño whites. There are 5 DOs: RIAS BAIXAS can make excellent, fragrant Albariño, with modern equipment and serious winemaking; Ribeiro DO has also invested heavily in new equipment, and better local white grapes such as Godello are now being used, as is the case in the mountainous Valdeorras DO. Some young reds from the Mencía grape are also made there and in the Ribeira Sacra DO. Monterrei DO is technically backward but shows some potential with its native white grape variety, Doña Blanca. Most wines are best consumed young.

E & J GALLO *Central Valley, California, USA* Since the release of its Sonoma Estate Chardonnay and Cabernet Sauvignon in the mid-1990s, Gallo, the world's second-biggest winery – known for cheap wines – is at last convincing doubters it can make fine wine. Both limited-production wines came from Gallo's 800ha (2000 acres) of premium vineyards in key SONOMA COUNTY AVAs. Their success led to the establishment of Gallo of Sonoma★★, a new label for varietals such as Zinfandel and Cabernet Sauvignon from DRY CREEK VALLEY and ALEXANDER VALLEY and Chardonnay from several vineyards. New vineyards in RUSSIAN RIVER VALLEY have been planted to Pinot Noir. Yet despite this giant step up in quality, Gallo continues to produce oceans of wine that is at best ordinary, under labels such as Turning Leaf, Gossamer Bay and Garnet Point. More interesting are small-volume brands Anapamu (CENTRAL COAST Chardonnay), Rancho Zabaco (SONOMA COUNTY wines), Marcelina (NAPA wines) and Indigo Hills (MENDOCINO wines).

GALLUCCIO FAMILY WINERIES/GRISTINA *Long Island, New York State, USA* Gristina, a well-regarded LONG ISLAND producer, was acquired in 2000 by Vincent Galluccio, who immediately embarked on expanding facilities and plantings. Stars are the elegant Chardonnay★ and cherry-vanilla Merlot. Best years: (reds) 2001 **00 98**.

GAMAY The only grape allowed for red BEAUJOLAIS. In general Gamay wine is rather rough-edged and quite high in raspy acidity, but in Beaujolais, so long as the yield is not too high, it can achieve a wonderful, juicy-fruit gluggability, almost unmatched in the world of wine. Elsewhere in France, it is successful in the Ardèche and the Loire and less so in the Mâconnais. In Switzerland it is blended with Pinot Noir to create DOLE. In CALIFORNIA, the grape sold under the name of Gamay has now been identified as Valdiguié and the name Gamay is being phased out. There are occasional plantings in Canada, New Zealand, Australia, South Africa and even England, which could become interesting.

GARD, VIN DE PAYS DU *Languedoc, France* Mainly reds and rosés from the western side of the RHONE delta. Most red is light, spicy and attractive. Rosés can be fresh when young, and with modern winemaking, whites can be good. Best producers: des Aveylans★, Baruel★, Cantarelles★, Coste Plane, Grande Cassagne★, Guiot★, Mas des Bressades★.

GARGANEGA Italian white grape from the VENETO in north-east Italy; main component of SOAVE. Grown on hillsides, it can have class, but its reputation is tainted by excessive yields from the Veronese plain.

GARNACHA BLANCA See Grenache Blanc.
GARNACHA TINTA See Grenache Noir.

GATTINARA DOCG *Piedmont, Italy* One of the most capricious of Italy's top red wine areas. The Nebbiolo wines should be softer and lighter than BAROLO, with a delicious, black plums, tar and roses flavour if you're lucky. Drink within 10 years. Vintages follow those for Barolo. Best producers: Antoniolo★, S Gattinara, Nervi★, Travaglini★.

DOM. GAUBY *Côtes du Roussillon-Villages AC, Roussillon, France* Gérard Gauby used to make burly wines in which the fruit was hidden by very hard tannins. Recent vintages have been softer while still retaining concentration, and Gauby is now a hot property in ROUSSILLON. Highlights include powerful COTES DU ROUSSILLON-VILLAGES Vieilles Vignes★★ and Syrah-dominated la Muntada★★ as well as a vin de pays Viognier★★. Best years: (reds) 2001 00 **99 98 97 96 95 94 93**.

GAVI DOCG *Piedmont, Italy* Fashionable and often overpriced, this Cortese-based, steely, lemony white can age up to 5 years, providing it starts life with sufficient fruit. La Scolca's Spumante Brut Soldati★ is an admirable sparkling wine. Best producers: Battistina★, Bergaglio★, Broglia★, La Chiara★, CHIARLO★, FONTANAFREDDA, La Giustiniana★★, Pio Cesare, San Pietro★, La Scolca★, Tassarolo★, Villa Sparina★.

CH. GAZIN★★ *Pomerol AC, Bordeaux, France* One of the largest châteaux in POMEROL, next to the legendary PETRUS. The wine, traditionally a succulent, sweet-textured Pomerol, seemed to lose its way in the 1980s but is now showing real richness and a very individualistic character under the management of owner Nicolas de Bailliencourt. Best years: 2001 00 98 **97 96 95 94 90 89 88**.

GEELONG *Victoria, Australia* Cool-climate, maritime-influenced region revived in the 1960s after destruction by phylloxera in the 19th century. Can be brilliant; potentially a match for the YARRA VALLEY. Impressive Pinot Noir, Chardonnay, Riesling, Sauvignon Blanc and Shiraz. Best producers: BANNOCKBURN★, Idyll, Scotchmans Hill★.

GEISENHEIM *Rheingau, Germany* Village famous for its wine school, founded in 1872. It was here that the Müller-Thurgau grape, now one of Germany's most widely planted grapes, was bred in 1882. Geisenheim's most famous vineyard is the Rothenberg, which produces strong, earthy wines. Best producers: Johannishof, WEGELER, von Zwierlein. Best years: (Riesling Spätlese) (2001) 99 98 **97 96 93 90**.

GEROVASSILIOU *Macedonia AO, Greece* Bordeaux-trained Evángelos Gerovassiliou has 40ha (100 acres) of vineyards and a modern winery in Epanomi in northern Greece. High-quality fruit results in Syrah-dominated Domaine Gerovassiliou red★ and some fresh, modern whites, including a fine Viognier★ that lacks a little perfume but has fantastic fruit, barrel-fermented Chardonnay and Fumé, and the Domaine Gerovassiliou★ white, a most original Assyrtiko-Malagousia blend.

GEVREY-CHAMBERTIN AC *Côte de Nuits, Burgundy, France* There have been periods when the wines of Gevrey-Chambertin too often proved disappointing, but a new generation of growers has restored the reputation of Gevrey as a source of well-coloured, firmly structured, powerful, perfumed wines that become rich and gamy with age. Village wines should be kept for at least 5 years, Premiers Crus and the 8 Grands Crus for 10 years or more, especially CHAMBERTIN and Clos-de-Bèze. Look for the Premier Cru Clos St-Jacques, a wine worthy of promotion to Grand Cru. Best producers: Denis Bachelet★★, L Boillot★, A Burguet★★,

B CLAIR★★, P Damoy★★, DROUHIN★, C Dugat★★, B Dugat-Py★★ DUJAC★★, S Esmonin★★, FAIVELEY★★, Fourrier★★, JADOT★★, Philippe Leclerc★★, Denis MORTET★★★, Rossignol★, J Roty★★, ROUSSEAU★★★ Sérafin★★, J & J-L Trapet★. Best years: (2002) 01 00 99 98 96 **95 93 90**

GEWÜRZTRAMINER *Gewürz* means spice, and the wine certainly can be spicy and exotically perfumed, as well as being typically low in acidity. It is thought to have originated in the village of Tramin, in Italy's ALTO ADIGE, and the name Traminer is used by many producers. In parts of Germany and Austria it is known as Clevner and in Switzerland it is called Heida or Paien. It makes an appearance in many wine-producing countries; quality is mixed and styles vary enormously, from the fresh, light, florally perfumed wines produced in Alto Adige to the rich, luscious, late-harvest ALSACE VENDANGE TARDIVE. Best in France's ALSACE and also good in Austria's Styria (STEIERMARK) and New Zealand.

GEYSER PEAK *Alexander Valley AVA, California, USA* Australian winemaker Daryl Groom's wines tend to be accessible, fruity and fun. Typical are the fruity SONOMA COUNTY Cabernet★ and Merlot★ – ripe, juicy and delicious upon release. The Reserve Alexandre★★, a BORDEAUX-style blend, is made for aging, and the Reserve Shiraz★★ has a cult following. Block Collection features limited production, single-vineyard wines. Best years: (Alexandre) (2001) (00) 99 98 97 **95 94 91**.

BRUNO GIACOSA *Barbaresco DOCG, Piedmont, Italy* One of the great winemakers of the LANGHE hills, and an unashamed traditionalist, leaving his BARBARESCOS and BAROLOS in cask for up to 6 years. Superb Barbarescos Asili★★★, Santo Stefano★★ and Rabaja★★★, and Barolos including Collina Rionda★★★ and Falletto★★. Also excellent Dolcetto d'Alba★, Roero Arneis★, Moscato d'Asti★★ and sparkling Extra Brut★★.

GIESEN *Canterbury, South Island, New Zealand* CANTERBURY's largest winery makes outstanding botrytized Riesling★★, as well as fine dry Riesling★, complex, oaky Chardonnay★, and an intense Sauvignon Blanc★. Best years: (Reserve Chardonnay) (2002) 01 00 **98**.

GIGONDAS AC *Rhône Valley, France* Gigondas wines, mostly red and made mainly from Grenache, have fistfuls of chunky personality. Most drink well with 5 years' age; some need a little more. Best producers: la Boussière★★, Brusset★★, Cassan★★, Cayron★★, Clos des Cazaux★, Clos du Joncuas★★, Cros de la Mûre★★, DELAS★, des Espiers★★, Font-Sane★★, les Goubert★, Gour de Chaule★★, Grapillon d'Or★★, GUIGAL★, JABOULET★, Longue-Toque★, Montvac★★, Moulin de la Gardette★★, les Pallières★, Piaugier★, Raspail-Ay★★, Redortier★★, St-Cosme★★, ST-GAYAN★, Santa-Duc★★, Tardieu-Laurent★★, la Tourade★★, Trignon★★. Best years: 2001 00 **99** 98 **97 95 94 90**.

CH. GILETTE★★ *Sauternes AC, Bordeaux, France* These astonishing wines are stored in concrete vats as opposed to the more normal wooden barrels. This virtually precludes any oxygen contact, and it is oxygen that ages a wine. Consequently, when released at up to 30 years old, they are bursting with life and lusciousness. Best years: **1982 81 79 78 76 75 70 67 61 59 55 53 49**.

GIPPSLAND *Victoria, Australia* Diverse wineries along the southern Victoria coast, all tiny but with massive potential. Results can be erratic, occasionally brilliant. Nicholson River's BURGUNDY-style Chardonnay can sometimes hit ★★. Bass Phillip Reserve★★ and Premium★★ Pinot Noirs are among the best in Australia, with a cult following.

McAlister★, a red BORDEAUX blend, has also produced some tasty flavours. Best producers: Bass Phillip★★, McAlister★, Nicholson River★.

VINCENT GIRARDIN *Santenay AC, Côte de Beaune, Burgundy, France* The best grower in SANTENAY and now a thriving négociant as well, with a new establishment in MEURSAULT★★. Bright, glossy reds from Santenay★★, MARANGES★ and CHASSAGNE-MONTRACHET★★ are surpassed by excellent VOLNAY★★ and POMMARD Grands Épenots★★★. Chassagne-Montrachet whites (Morgeot★★ and Caillerets★★★) are well balanced with good fruit depth. CORTON-CHARLEMAGNE★★★ is exceptional. Best years: (reds) (2002) 01 99 98 **97 96 95**.

GISBORNE *North Island, New Zealand* Gisborne, with its hot, humid climate and fertile soils, delivers both quality and quantity. Local growers have christened their region 'The Chardonnay Capital of New Zealand' and Gewürztraminer and Chenin Blanc are also a success. Good reds, however, are hard to find. Best producers: MILLTON★★, MONTANA, Revington. Best years: (Chardonnay) (2002) **00 98**.

GIVRY AC *Côte Chalonnaise, Burgundy, France* An important CÔTE CHALONNAISE village. The reds have an intensity of fruit and ability to age that are unusual in the region. There are now some attractive, fairly full, nutty whites, too. Best producers: Bourgeon★, Chofflet-Valdenaire★, B CLAIR★, Joblot★★, F Lumpp★★, Parize★, Ragot★, Sarrazin★. Best years: (reds) (2002) **00** 99 98 **97 96 95**; (whites) (2002) **00 99**.

GLEN CARLOU *Paarl WO, South Africa* Extensive new vineyards, mainly Chardonnay, but also some Zinfandel, Tempranillo and Mourvèdre, reveal the bullish mood in this partnership between the Finlaysons and Donald Hess, owner of CALIFORNIA winery The HESS COLLECTION. They also indicate winemaker David Finlayson's versatility: his elegant standard Chardonnay★ and richer toasty Reserve★★ version, the spicy, silky Pinot Noir★, and Grand Classique★★, a red BORDEAUX blend with excellent aging potential, have recently been joined by a rich, spicy Shiraz★★. Best years: (Chardonnay) **2001 00 99 98 97**.

CH. GLORIA★ *St-Julien AC, Cru Bourgeois, Haut-Médoc, Bordeaux, France* An interesting property, created out of tiny plots of Classed Growth land scattered all round ST-JULIEN. Generally very soft and sweet-centred, the wine nonetheless ages well. Second wine: Peymartin. Best years: 2001 00 98 **96 95 90 89 88 86**.

GOLAN HEIGHTS WINERY *Golan Heights, Israel* Israel's leading quality wine producer. Cool summers, high-altitude vineyards and modern winemaking with kosher standards have resulted in good Sauvignon Blanc and Cabernet Sauvignon★, excellent, oaky Chardonnay★ and good bottle-fermented fizz★. Yarden is the top label; Golan and Gamla are mid-range. Expansion to new vineyards in Galilee might offset the threat to the flagship winery as the Middle East crisis evolves.

GOLDMUSKATELLER Moscato Giallo, a strain of Muscat Blanc à Petits Grains, is known as Goldmuskateller in the ALTO ADIGE. Here and elsewhere in Italy's north-east it makes scented wines in dry, off-dry and sweet (*passito*) styles. Best producers: Bolognani★, LAGEDER★, Obermoser.

GOLDWATER ESTATE *Waiheke Island, Auckland, New Zealand* The founding vineyard established by Kim and Jeanette Goldwater on WAIHEKE ISLAND, one of New Zealand's premium red wine districts.

143

Intense, long-lived Cabernet-Merlot★★ and Esslin Merlot★★, made i
an elegant, cedary style with considerable depth and structure. Newl
released Zell Chardonnay★★ from Waiheke looks exciting. Als
attractive MARLBOROUGH Dog Point Sauvignon Blanc★ and Roselan
Chardonnay★ from grapes grown under contract. Best years
(Waiheke reds) 2000 **99** 96.

GONZÁLEZ BYASS *Jerez y Manzanilla DO, Andalucía, Spain* Tio Pepe★
the high-quality fino brand of this huge firm, is the world's biggest
selling sherry. The old sherries are superb: intense, dry Amontillad
del Duque★★★; 2 rich, complex olorosos, sweet Matusalem★★ an
medium Apóstoles★★; treacly Noé Pedro Ximénez★★★. One ste
down is the Alfonso Dry Oloroso★. The firm pioneered the rediscover
of single-vintage (non-solera) dry olorosos★★.

GRAACH *Mosel, Germany* Important Middle MOSEL wine village with
vineyard sites, the most famous being Domprobst (also the best) an
Himmelreich. A third, the Josephshöfer, is wholly owned by the vo
KESSELSTATT estate in Trier. The wines have an attractive fullness t
balance their steely acidity, and great aging potential. Best producers
von KESSELSTATT★★, Dr LOOSEN★★, Markus Molitor★, J J PRUM★★, S A
PRUM★, Max Ferd RICHTER★★, Willi SCHAEFER★★★, SELBACH-OSTER★★
Weins-Prüm★. Best years: (2002) 01 00 **99** 98 97 96 **95** 94 93 90.

GRACIANO Rare, low-yielding but excellent Spanish grape, traditional ir
RIOJA, NAVARRA and, as Parraleta, in SOMONTANO. It makes dense, highly
structured, fragrant reds, and its high acidity adds life when blendec
with low-acid Tempranillo. Two wineries, CONTINO and Viña Ijalba, now
offer varietal examples. Also grown by BROWN BROTHERS in Australia.

GRAHAM *Port DOC, Douro, Portugal* Part of the Symington empire
making rich, florally scented Vintage Port★★★, sweeter than DOW's
and WARRE's, but with the backbone to age. In non-vintage years
makes a fine wine called Malvedos★★. Six Grapes★ is one of the better
premium rubies, and 10-year-old★ and 20-year-old★ tawnies are
consistently good. Used robotic treading machines for the first time in
successful 2000 vintage. Best years: (Vintage) 2000 97 94 91 **85 83 80**
77 75 70 66 63 60; (Malvedos) 1999 95 **92 90 87 86 84**.

ALAIN GRAILLOT *Crozes-Hermitage AC, Rhône Valley, France* This
excellent estate, established in 1985, produces powerfully
concentrated, rich, fruity reds. The top wine is CROZES-HERMITAGE la
Guiraude★★, but the regular Crozes-Hermitage★★ is wonderful too, as
are the ST-JOSEPH★★ and a lovely fragrant white Crozes-Hermitage★★.
Keep top reds for 5 years, though the best will become even finer with
longer aging. Best years: (la Guiraude) 2001 00 **99 96 95 94 91 90 89**.

GRAMPIANS AND PYRENEES *Victoria, Australia* Two adjacent cool-
climate regions in central western VICTORIA. Both produce some of
Australia's most characterful Shiraz, as well as distinguished Riesling,
subtle Pinot Gris and savoury Chardonnay. Best producers: BEST'S★,
Blue Pyrenees, Dalwhinnie★★, MOUNT LANGI GHIRAN★★, Redbank★,
SEPPELT★, TALTARNI★. Best years: (Shiraz) 2001 99 98 97 **96 94 91 90**.

CH. GRAND-PUY-DUCASSE★ *Pauillac AC, 5ème Cru Classé, Haut-Médoc,
Bordeaux, France* After great improvement in the 1980s, form
dipped in the early 90s but recovered again in 95. Approachable after
5 years, but the wines can improve for considerably longer. Second
wine: Artigues-Arnaud. Best years: 2001 00 96 **95 90 89 88 86 85**.

CH. GRAND-PUY-LACOSTE★★ *Pauillac AC, 5ème Cru Classé, Haut-Médoc, Bordeaux, France* Classic PAUILLAC, with lots of blackcurrant and cigar-box perfume. As the wine develops, the flavours mingle with the sweetness of new oak into one of Pauillac's most memorable taste sensations. Second wine: Lacoste-Borie. Best years: 2001 00 99 98 **97** 96 **95 94** 93 90 89 88 86 85 83 82.

GRANDS-ÉCHÉZEAUX AC See Échézeaux AC.

GRANGE★★★ *Barossa Valley, South Australia* In 1950, Max Schubert, chief winemaker at PENFOLDS, visited Europe and came back determined to make a wine that could match the great BORDEAUX reds. Undeterred by a lack of Cabernet Sauvignon grapes and French oak barrels, he set to work with BAROSSA Shiraz and barrels made from the more pungent American oak. Initially ignored and misunderstood, Schubert eventually achieved global recognition for his wine, a stupendously complex, thrillingly rich red that only begins to reveal its magnificence after 10 years in bottle. Produced using only the best grapes, primarily from the Barossa, CLARE and MCLAREN VALE, it is traditionally acknowledged as Australia's greatest red. Best years: 2000 99 98 96 94 92 91 90 **88 86** 84 83 80 76 71 67 66 63 62 55 53 52.

DOM. DE LA GRANGE DES PÈRES *Vin de Pays de l'Hérault, Languedoc, France* Laurent Vaillé's tiny domaine has become a LANGUEDOC legend since its first vintage in 1992. With only 500 cases produced each year, demand is high for the meticulously crafted unfiltered red★★. 1995 was the first vintage of a white★★ which is produced in even smaller quantities. Best years: (red) 2001 00 **99 98 97** 96 **95 94** 93 92.

GRANGEHURST *Stellenbosch WO, South Africa* Boutique winery with a focused 3-wine range. Pinotage★ is modern, the Cabernet-Merlot★★ has a more clarety appeal, while Nikela★, a blend of all 3 varieties, is owner/winemaker Jeremy Walker's answer to the Cape blend. Best years: (Cabernet-Merlot) 2000 99 **98 97** 95 94 93 92.

GRANS-FASSIAN *Leiwen, Mittel Mosel, Germany* LEIWEN owes its reputation largely to Gerhard Grans' success during the late 1980s. His naturally sweet Rieslings have gained in sophistication over the years: Spätlese★★ and Auslese★★ from TRITTENHEIMer Apotheke are  particularly impressive. Eiswein is ★★★ in good vintages. Best years: (Riesling Spätlese, Auslese) (2002) 01 **99** 98 **97 96** 95 93 90.

YVES GRASSA *Vin de Pays des Côtes de Gascogne, South-West France* Innovative COTES DE GASCOGNE producer, who transformed Gascony's thin raw whites into some of the snappiest, fruitiest, almost-dry wines in France. Grassa also makes oak-aged★ and late-harvest★ styles.

ALFRED GRATIEN *Champagne AC, Champagne, France* This small company makes some of my favourite CHAMPAGNE. Its wines are made in wooden casks, which is very rare nowadays. The non-vintage★★ blend is usually 4 years old when sold, rather than the normal 3 years. The vintage★★★ is deliciously ripe and toasty when released but can age for another 10 years. The prestige cuvée, Cuvée Paradis★★, is non-vintage. Best years: (1996) **95** 91 90 89 88 87 85 83.

GRATIEN & MEYER *Loire Valley, France* Owner of Champagne house Alfred GRATIEN, Gratien & Meyer is in turn owned by German sparkling wine company Henkell & Söhnlein. In the Loire the company's reputation rests on its Champagne-method SAUMUR MOUSSEUX, particularly its attractively rich, biscuity Cuvée Flamme★ and the Cuvée Flamme Rosé★. Also a producer of still white Coteaux de SAUMUR, red SAUMUR-CHAMPIGNY and a little CREMANT DE LOIRE★.

GRAVES AC *Bordeaux, France* The Graves region covers the area south of Bordeaux to Langon, but the generally superior villages in the northern half broke away in 1987 to form the PESSAC-LEOGNAN AC. In the southern Graves, a new wave of winemaking has produced plenty of clean, bone-dry white wines with lots of snappy freshness, as well as more complex soft, nutty barrel-aged whites, and some juicy, quick-drinking reds. Sweet white wines take the Graves Supérieures AC; the best make a decent substitute for the more expensive SAUTERNES. Best producers: Archambeau, Ardennes★, le Bonnat, Brondelle★, Chantegrive★, Clos Floridène★★, Dom. la Grave★, l'Hospital, Léhoul, Magence, Magneau★, Rahoul★, Respide-Médeville★, St-Robert★, Seuil★, Vieux-Ch.-Gaubert★, Villa Bel Air★; (sweet) Clos St-Georges, Léhoul. Best years: (reds) 2001 00 **98 96 95 90**; (dry whites) 2001 00 **98 96 95**; (sweet whites) **2001 99 98 97 96 95 90 89**.

GRAVNER *Friuli-Venezia Giulia, Italy* Josko Gravner, FRIULI's most zealous winemaker, sets styles with wood-aged wines of uncommon stature, though some remain outside the COLLIO DOC. Along with prized and high-priced Chardonnay★★, Sauvignon★★ and Ribolla Gialla★, he combines 6 white varieties in Breg★★. Reds are Rosso Gravner★ (predominantly Merlot) and Rujno★★ (Merlot-Cabernet Sauvignon).

GREAT SOUTHERN *Western Australia* A vast, cool-climate region encompassing the sub-regions of Mount Barker, Frankland River, Denmark, Albany and Porongurup. Mount Barker has been particularly successful with Riesling, Shiraz and Cabernet; Frankland River with Riesling, Chardonnay, Shiraz and Cabernet; Denmark with Chardonnay and Pinot Noir; Albany with Pinot Noir; Porongurup with Riesling. There has been frenetic planting of vineyards in the past 5 years, especially in Frankland River. Best producers: Alkoomi★, Ferngrove★, Frankland Estate★★, Gilberts★, Goundrey★, HOUGHTON★★, HOWARD PARK★★, Jingalla★, PLANTAGENET★★, Wignalls★.

GRECHETTO Italian grape centred on UMBRIA, making tasty, anise-tinged dry whites. Also used in VIN SANTO in TUSCANY. Best producers: Antonelli, Barberani-Vallesanta, Caprai, FALESCO★, Palazzone, Castello della SALA.

GRECO See Grechetto.

GRENACHE BLANC A common white grape in the south of France, but without many admirers. Except me, that is, because I love the pear-scented wine flecked with anise that a good producer can achieve. Low-yield examples take surprisingly well to oak. Generally best within a year of the vintage, although the odd old-vine example can age attractively. Grown as Garnacha Blanca in Spain.

GRENACHE NOIR Among the world's most widely planted red grapes – the bulk of it in Spain, where it is called Garnacha Tinta. It is a hot-climate grape and in France it reaches its peak in the southern RHONE, especially in CHATEAUNEUF-DU-PAPE, where it combines great alcoholic strength with rich raspberry fruit and a perfume hot from the herb-strewn hills. It is generally given more tannin, acid and structure by blending with Syrah, Mourvèdre, Cinsaut or other southern French grapes. It can make wonderful rosé in TAVEL, LIRAC and COTES DE PROVENCE, as well as in NAVARRA in Spain. It takes centre stage in ARAGON's Calatayud, Campo de Borja and CARIÑENA, and forms the backbone of the impressive reds of PRIORAT; in RIOJA it adds weight to the Tempranillo. It is also the basis for the *vins doux naturels* of BANYULS and MAURY. Also grown in CALIFORNIA and SOUTH AUSTRALIA, where it has only recently been accorded much respect as imaginative winemakers realized there was a great resource (that no one was taking any notice of) of century-old vines capable of making wild and massively enjoyable reds. There are also stirrings of interest in South Africa. See also Cannonau.

GRGICH HILLS CELLAR *Rutherford AVA, California, USA* Mike Grgich was winemaker at CHATEAU MONTELENA when its Chardonnay shocked Paris judges by finishing ahead of French versions in the famous 1976 tasting. At his own winery he makes ripe, tannic Cabernet★, plummy Merlot★ and a huge, old-style Zinfandel★, but it is his big, ripe, oaky Chardonnay★★ that is one of NAPA's best-selling high-priced wines. Best years: (Chardonnay) (2002) 01 00 99 **98 97 96 95 94 91**.

GRIOTTE-CHAMBERTIN AC See Chambertin AC.

JEAN GRIVOT *Vosne-Romanée AC, Côte de Nuits, Burgundy, France* Étienne Grivot took time to settle down but has now reconciled his father's traditional styles and former consultant Guy Accad's experimentation into a high-quality interpretation of his own. He has made brilliant wines since 1995, especially RICHEBOURG★★★ and NUITS-ST-GEORGES les Boudots★★. Expensive. Best years: (2002) 01 00 99 98 **97** 96 **95**.

GROS *Burgundy, France* Brilliant COTE DE NUITS wines from various members of the family, especially Anne Gros, Michel Gros, Gros Frère et Soeur and Anne-Françoise Gros. Look out for CLOS DE VOUGEOT★★★ and RICHEBOURG★★★ as well as good-value HAUTES-COTES DE NUITS★. Best years: (2002) 01 00 99 98 **97** 96 95 93 90.

GROS PLANT DU PAYS NANTAIS VDQS *Loire Valley, France* From the marshy salt-flats around Nantes, Gros Plant can be searing stuff, but this acidic wine is well suited to the seafood guzzled in the region. Look for a *sur lie* bottling and drink the youngest available. Best producers: Brochet, les Coins, l'ECU, la Grange, Saupin.

GROSSET *Clare Valley, South Australia* Jeffrey Grosset is a perfectionist, crafting tiny quantities of hand-made wines. A Riesling specialist, he bottles Watervale★★★ separately from Polish Hill★★★; both are supremely good and age well. Cabernet blend Gaia★★ is smooth and seamless. Also outstanding Piccadilly (ADELAIDE HILLS) Chardonnay★★★ and very fine Pinot Noir★★ and Semillon-Sauvignon★★. Best years: (Riesling) 2002 01 **00 99 98 97 96 94 93 92 90**.

GROVE MILL *Marlborough, New Zealand* Mid-sized producer with a strong quality focus. Full-bodied Sauvignon Blanc★ is a feature of their range, together with a ripe, rich, remarkably smooth Chardonnay★ and tangy, pungent Riesling. Best years: (Riesling) (2002) 01 **00 99 98**.

CH. GRUAUD-LAROSE★★ *St-Julien AC, 2ème Cru Classé, Haut-Médoc, Bordeaux, France* One of the largest ST-JULIEN estates, now owned by the same family as CHASSE-SPLEEN and HAUT-BAGES-LIBERAL. Until the 1970s these wines were classic, cedary St-Juliens. Since the early 80s, the wines have been darker, richer and coated with new oak, yet have also shown an unnerving animal quality. They're certainly impressive, but it is hard to say whether the animal or the cedar will prevail after 20 years or so of aging in bottle. Second wine: Sarget de Gruaud-Larose. Best years: 2001 00 99 98 **97** 96 **95 94 93 90 89 88 86 85.**

GRÜNER VELTLINER Austrian grape, also grown in Slovakia and Hungary. It is at its best in Austria's KAMPTAL, KREMSTAL and the WACHAU, where the soil and cool climate bring out all the lentilly, white-peppery aromas in the fruit. Styles vary from light and tart to savoury, mouthfilling yet appetizing wines equalling the best in Europe.

GUELBENZU *Spain* Family-owned bodega making good Guelbenzu Crianza★, from Tempranillo, Cabernet and Merlot, and rich concentrated Evo★, made mostly from Cabernet Sauvignon. The new Lautus★★ is made from old vines and incorporates Garnacha in the blend. In 2001, the owners decided to leave the NAVARRA DO and move to a generic *vino de mesa* appellation to protest against existing DO regulations in Spain. Best years: (Evo) 1999 **98 97 96 95 94.**

GUIGAL *Côte-Rôtie AC, Rhône Valley, France* Marcel Guigal is among the most famous names in the RHÔNE, producing wines from his company's own vineyards in CÔTE-RÔTIE under the Château d'Ampuis★★★ label as well as the Guigal range from purchased grapes. Northern Rhône holdings have been tripled with the recent acquisition

of the J-L Grippat and de Vallouit operations. La Mouline, la Turque and la Landonne all rate ★★★ in most critics' opinions, but I have to add the proviso that with all these oaky wines I find the unique beauty and fragrance of Côte-Rôtie difficult to discern. However, many of the top Côte-Rôtie producers have, predictably, decided to follow Guigal's new oak route. I'm more of a fan of the fragrant CONDRIEU★★ (la Doriane★★★). HERMITAGE★★ is also good, as is the cheaper CÔTES DU RHÔNE★. GIGONDAS★ is reasonably chunky. Best years: (top reds) 2001 00 99 98 97 **95 94 91 90 89 88 85 83 82 78.**

CH. GUIRAUD★★ *Sauternes AC, 1er Cru Classé, Bordeaux, France* A property that was hauled up from near extinction by the Canadian Narby family, convinced that Guiraud could be one of SAUTERNES' greatest wines. Selecting only the best grapes and using 50% new oak each year, they have returned Guiraud to the top-quality fold. Keep best vintages for 10 years or more. Second wine (dry): G de Guiraud. Best years: (2002) 01 99 **98 97 96 95 90 89 88 86.**

GUNDERLOCH *Nackenheim, Rheinhessen, Germany* Fritz and Agnes Hasselbach's estate has become one of Germany's best. Sensationally concentrated and luscious Beerenauslese★★★ and Trockenbeerenauslese★★★ dessert Rieslings are expensive for RHEINHESSEN, but worth it. Dry and off-dry Rieslings, at least ★, however, are good value. Late-harvest Spätlese and Auslese are ★★ year in, year out. Best years: (Spätlese, Auslese) (2002) 01 00 **99 98 97 96 95 94 93 92 90 89.**

GUNDLACH-BUNDSCHU *Sonoma Valley AVA, California, USA* Family-owned winery, founded in 1858. From the Rhinefarm Vineyards comes outstanding juicy, fruity Cabernet Sauvignon★★, a rich and tightly structured Merlot★★, a Zinfandel★ and Pinot Noir★. Also produced are 2 Chardonnay★ bottlings and attractive Riesling and

Gewürztraminer★. The Bundschu family has created a small boutique winery, Bartholomew Park.

FRITZ HAAG *Brauneberg, Mosel, Germany*   MOSEL grower with vineyards in the BRAUNEBERGER Juffer and Brauneberger Juffer Sonnenuhr. Pure, elegant Rieslings at least ★ quality, Auslese reaching ★★ or ★★★. Best years: (Auslese) (2002) 01 99 98 **97 96 95 94 93 90 88 85**.

REINHOLD HAART *Piesport, Mosel, Germany*   Theo Haart produces sensational Rieslings – with blackcurrant, peach and citrus aromas – from the great Piesporter Goldtröpfchen★★ vineyard. Ausleses are usually ★★★, but 1999 suffered a bit from heat stress and young vines. Best years: (Spätlese, Auslese) (2002) 01 00 98 **97 96 95 94 93 90 89**.

HAMILTON RUSSELL VINEYARDS *Walker Bay, Overberg WO, South Africa* Anthony Hamilton Russell and winemaker Kevin Grant pursue their goal of classic Pinot Noir and Chardonnay with fierce dedication. From 1999, new Burgundian clones provide a fruitier profile to the Pinot Noir★. The Chardonnay★ maintains the restrained house style. The Southern Right label focuses on Pinotage and Sauvignon Blanc from estate and bought-in grapes. Best years: (Pinot Noir) (2002) **01 00 99 98** 97 96 95; (Chardonnay) **2002** 01 00 99 98 97 96 95.

HANDLEY *Mendocino County, California, USA*   Outstanding producer of sparkling wines, including one of California's best Brut Rosés★ and a delicious Blanc de Blancs★★. An aromatic Gewürztraminer★★ is one of the state's finest. Two bottlings of Chardonnay, from the DRY CREEK VALLEY★ and ANDERSON VALLEY★, are worth seeking out. The Anderson Valley estate Pinot Noirs (regular★, Reserve★★) are in a lighter, more subtle style. Best years: (Pinot Noir Reserve) 2001 00 99 **98 96**.

HANGING ROCK *Macedon Ranges, Victoria, Australia*   Highly individual, gutsy sparkling wine, Macedon Cuvée★★ stands out at John and Anne (née Tyrrell) Ellis's ultra-cool-climate vineyard high in the Macedon Ranges. Tangy estate-grown 'The Jim Jim' Sauvignon Blanc★★ is mouthwatering stuff, while Heathcote Shiraz★★, from a warmer neighbouring region, is the best red.

HARDYS *McLaren Vale, South Australia*   Despite the takeover of BRL Hardy by American giant Constellation, wines under the Hardys flagship label so far still taste reassuringly Australian. Varietals under the Siegersdorf and Nottage Hill labels are among Australia's most reliably good gluggers. Top of the tree are the commemorative Eileen Hardy Shiraz★★★ and Thomas Hardy Cabernet★★★, both dense reds for hedonists. Eileen Hardy Chardonnay★★ is rich, heady, oak-perfumed and complex. Newer releases include the attractively packaged Tintara Shiraz★ and Grenache★, plus 'ecologically aware' Banrock Station★, the inexpensive Insignia wines, good-value Omni sparkling wine and top-quality Arras fizz★★. Best years: (Eileen Hardy Shiraz) 2001 00 98 97 96 95 **93 88 87 81 79 70**.

HARLAN ESTATE *Oakville AVA, California, USA*   Estate in the western hills of OAKVILLE, whose BORDEAUX blend has become one of California's most sought-after reds. Full-bodied and rather tannic, Harlan Estate★★★ offers layers of ripe black fruits and heaps of new French oak. Rough upon release, the wine is built to develop for 10–20 years.

HARTENBERG ESTATE *Stellenbosch WO, South Africa*   After a promising start in 1994, this winery has been marking time of late, but new vineyards should see Hartenberg on the way up again soon. Zinfandel and even the old Pontac vineyards have made way for more Shiraz★, Merlot★★, Cabernet and some Pinotage, all of which perform well in the warm Bottelary Hills. Whites are well served by a firm, flavoursome Chardonnay and, unusually for these north-facing slopes, a vigorous, limy Riesling★. Best years: (premium reds) 2000 98 97 96 95 94.

HARTFORD COURT *Russian River AVA, California, USA* Boutique winery focusing on very limited-production wines from RUSSIAN RIVER and SONOMA COAST fruit. Pinot Noirs include the stylish Marin County★★ bottling and the massive Arrendell Vineyard★★★. Seascape Vineyard Chardonnay★★ has textbook cool-climate intensity and acidity. Hartford Zinfandels include Highwire★ and Fanucchi-Wood Road★★.

HATTENHEIM *Rheingau, Germany* Fine RHEINGAU village with 13 vineyard sites, including a share of the famous Marcobrunn vineyard. Best producers: SCHLOSS REINHARTSHAUSEN★★, Schloss Schönborn★. Best years: (Spätlese, Auslese) (2002) 01 00 99 98 96 95 94 93 92 90.

CH. HAUT-BAGES-LIBÉRAL★ *Pauillac AC, 5ème Cru Classé, Haut-Médoc, Bordeaux, France* Little-known PAUILLAC property that has quietly been gathering plaudits for some years now: loads of unbridled delicious fruit, a positively hedonistic style – and its lack of renown keeps the price just about reasonable. The wines will age well, especially the latest vintages. Best years: 2001 00 99 98 96 95 94 90 89 86 85.

CH. HAUT-BAILLY★★ *Pessac-Léognan AC, Cru Classé de Graves, Bordeaux, France* The softest and most charming among the GRAVES Classed Growths, which has been on good form right through the 1990s. Drinkable very early, but ages well. Second wine: la Parde-de-Haut-Bailly. Best years: 2001 00 99 98 96 95 93 90 89 88 86 85 83 82.

CH. HAUT-BATAILLEY★ *Pauillac AC, 5ème Cru Classé, Haut-Médoc, Bordeaux, France* Despite being owned by the Borie family of DUCRU-BEAUCAILLOU, this estate has produced too many wines that are light, pleasant, attractively spicy, but lacking real class and concentration. Recent vintages have shown improvement and the wine is becoming a bit more substantial. Best years: 2000 99 96 95 90 89 85 83 82.

CH. HAUT-BRION *Pessac-Léognan AC, 1er Cru Classé, Graves, Bordeaux, France* The only Bordeaux property outside the MEDOC and SAUTERNES to be included in the great 1855 Classification, when it was awarded First Growth status. The excellent gravel-based vineyard is now part of Bordeaux's suburbs. The red wine★★★ almost always deserves its exalted status, and there is also a small amount of white★★★ which, at its best, is magically rich yet marvellously dry, blossoming out over 5–10 years. Second wine: (red) Bahans-Haut-Brion. Best years: (red) 2001 00 99 98 96 95 94 93 90 89 88 86 85; (white) 2001 00 99 98 96 95.

CH. HAUT-MARBUZET★★ *St-Estèphe AC, Cru Bourgeois, Haut-Médoc, Bordeaux, France* Impressive ST-ESTEPHE wine with great, rich, mouthfilling blasts of flavour and lots of new oak. Best years: 2001 00 99 98 97 96 95 94 93 90 89 88 86 85 83 82.

HAUT-MÉDOC AC *Bordeaux, France* The finest gravelly soil is here in the southern half of the MEDOC peninsula, and this AC covers all the decent vineyard land not included in the 6 village ACs (MARGAUX, MOULIS, LISTRAC, ST-JULIEN, PAUILLAC and ST-ESTEPHE). The wines vary in quality and style. Best producers: Beaumont, Belgrave★, Bernadotte★, Cambon la Pelouse★, Camensac, CANTEMERLE★, Charmail★, Cissac★, Citran★, Coufran★, la LAGUNE★★, Lanessan★, Malescasse, Maucamps★, Sénéjac★, SOCIANDO-MALLET★★, la Tour-Carnet★, la Tour-du-Haut-Moulin★, Verdignan, Villegeorge. Best years: 2001 00 96 95 94 90 89 88 86 85.

HAUT-MONTRAVEL AC See Montravel AC.

HAUTES-CÔTES DE BEAUNE AC See Bourgogne-Hautes-Côtes de Beaune AC.

150

HAUTES-CÔTES DE NUITS AC See Bourgogne-Hautes-Côtes de Nuits AC.

HAWKES BAY *North Island, New Zealand* One of New Zealand's most prestigious wine regions. The high number of sunshine hours, moderately predictable weather during ripening and a complex array of soil patterns make it ideal for a wide range of winemaking styles. Chardonnay, Cabernet Sauvignon and Merlot are the area's greatest strengths, although Syrah has good potential. Free-draining Gimblett Gravels area is especially promising. Best producers: Alpha Domus★, CHURCH ROAD★, Clearview★, CRAGGY RANGE★★, Esk Valley★★, Matariki★, MATUA VALLEY★★, MORTON ESTATE★, Newton-Forrest★, NGATARAWA★, C J PASK★, Sacred Hill★, SILENI★, TE MATA★★, Trinity Hill, Unison★★, Vidal★★, VILLA MARIA★★. Best years: (premium reds) (2000) 99 **98 96 95 94**.

HEATHCOTE *Central Victoria, Australia* A recent breakaway from the long-established BENDIGO region. Its unique feature is the deep russet Cambrian soil, formed more than 600 million years ago, which is found on the best sites and is proving ideal for Shiraz. Established wineries include Jasper Hill★★, Heathcote and Wild Duck Creek★, while BROWN BROTHERS and TYRRELL'S have extensive new vineyards. Best years: (Shiraz) 2001 00 **97 96 95 94 91 90**.

DR HEGER *Ihringen, Baden, Germany* Joachim Heger specializes in powerful, dry Grauburgunder (Pinot Gris), Weissburgunder (Pinot Blanc) and red Spätburgunder (Pinot Noir)★, with Riesling a sideline. Grauburgunder from the Winklerberg★★ is serious stuff.

CHARLES HEIDSIECK *Champagne AC, Champagne, France* Charles Heidsieck, owned by Rémy Cointreau, is the most consistently fine of all the major houses, with ★★★ vintage Champagne only declared in the very best years. The non-vintage★★, marked with a bottling date (for example, Mis en Cave en 1997), is regularly of vintage quality; these age well for 5 years. Best years: (1995) **90 89 88 85 82**.

HEITZ CELLARS *Napa Valley AVA, California, USA* Star attraction here is the Martha's Vineyard Cabernet Sauvignon★★. Heitz also produces a Bella Oaks Vineyard Cabernet Sauvignon★, a Trailside Vineyard Cabernet★ and a straight Cabernet★ that takes time to understand but can be good. After 1992, phylloxera forced the replanting of Martha's Vineyard and bottling only resumed in 1996. Many believe that early bottlings of Martha's Vineyard are among the best wines ever produced in CALIFORNIA. Grignolino Rosé is an attractive picnic wine. Best years: (Martha's Vineyard) (1997) 96 **92** 91 **86** 85 75.

HENRIOT *Champagne AC, Champagne, France* In 1994 Joseph Henriot bought back the name of his old-established family company. Henriot CHAMPAGNES have an austere clarity – no Pinot Meunier is used. The range includes non-vintage Brut Souverain★ and Blanc de Blancs★, vintage Brut★★ and Rosé★ and deluxe Cuvée des Echanteleurs★★. Best years: (1996) 95 **90 89 88 85**.

HENRIQUES & HENRIQUES *Madeira DOC, Madeira, Portugal* The wines to look for are the 10-year-old★★ and 15-year-old★★ versions of the classic varieties. Vibrant Sercial and Verdelho, and rich Malmsey and Bual are all fine examples of their styles. Henriques & Henriques also has vintage Madeiras★★★ of extraordinary quality.

HENRY OF PELHAM *Niagara Peninsula VQA, Ontario, Canada* Winery making concentrated wines from low-yielding vines. Best are Reserve Chardonnay★, Proprietor's Reserve Riesling★, Riesling Icewine★ and a Cabernet-Merlot blend. Best years: (Riesling Icewine) (2001) 00 99 **98** 97.

HENSCHKE *Eden Valley, South Australia* Fifth-generation winemaker Stephen Henschke and his viticulturist wife Prue make some of Australia's grandest reds from old vines in Eden Valley. Top wine, HILL OF GRACE★★★, is stunning, and Mount Edelstone Shiraz★★★, Cyril Henschke Cabernet★★ and Keyneton Estate★ are also brilliant wines. The whites are full and intensely flavoured too, led by the seductive perfumed Julius Riesling★★, the toasty yet fruity Louis Semillon★★ and Croft Chardonnay★. Best years: (Mount Edelstone) 2001 00 98 97 **96 94 92 91 90 88 86 84 82 80 78**.

HÉRAULT, VIN DE PAYS DE L' *Languedoc, France* A huge region covering the entire Hérault *département*. Red wines predominate, based on Carignan, Grenache and Cinsaut, and most of the wine is sold in bulk. But things are changing. There are lots of hilly vineyards with great potential, and MAS DE DAUMAS GASSAC is merely the first of many exciting reds from the region. The whites are improving, too. Best producers: Bosc, Capion★, la Fadèze, GRANGE DES PERES★★, Jany Limbardié★, MAS DE DAUMAS GASSAC★★, Moulines.

HERMITAGE AC *Rhône Valley, France* Great Hermitage, from steep vineyards above the town of Tain l'Hermitage in the northern RHONE is revered throughout the world as a rare, rich red wine – expensive, memorable and classic. Not all Hermitage achieves such an exciting blend of flavours, but the best growers, with mature red Syrah vines, can create superbly original wine, needing 5–10 years' aging even in a light year and a minimum of 15 years in a ripe vintage. White Hermitage, from Marsanne and Roussanne, is less famous but the best wines, made by traditionalists, can outlive the reds, sometimes lasting as long as 40 years. Best producers: A Belle★★, CHAPOUTIER★★, B Chave★★, J-L CHAVE★★★, Colombier★★, COLOMBO★★, DELAS★★ (les Bessards★★★), B Faurie★★, Fayolle★★, Ferraton★, J-L Grippat★★, GUIGAL★★, JABOULET (la Chapelle★★), Remizières, J-M Sorrel★★, M Sorrel★★★, TAIN L'HERMITAGE co-op★★, Tardieu-Laurent★★, les Vins de Vienne★★. Best years: (reds) 2001 00 99 98 **97 96 95 94 91 90 89 88 85 83 78 71 70**.

JAMES HERRICK *Vin de Pays d'Oc, Languedoc, France* When Herrick and his Aussie partners planted 175ha (435 acres) of Chardonnay between Narbonne and Béziers, many locals thought he was mad. The wines turned out to be a big success, and the brand and vineyards are now part of Southcorp, Australia's leading wine conglomerate. Chardonnay is an attractive blend of tropical fruit and French elegance. A Reserve bottling★ is more concentrated. Syrah-based red blend Cuvée Simone has disappointed.

THE HESS COLLECTION *Mount Veeder AVA, California, USA* NAPA VALLEY producer earning plaudits for its Cabernet Sauvignon★ (Reserve★★), which shows all the intense lime and black cherry originality of its MOUNT VEEDER fruit, without coating it with impenetrable tannins. The Chardonnay★ is ripe with tropical fruit and balanced oak. Budget label is Hess Select. Best years: (Cabernet) (2001) (00) 99 98 97 **96 95 94 91 90**.

HESSISCHE BERGSTRASSE *Germany* Small (455ha/1125-acre), warm wine region near Darmstadt. Much of the winemaking is by the co-op, Bergsträsser Winzer, although the Staatsweingut also makes some good wines. There has been less flirtation with new grape varieties here than elsewhere in Germany, and Riesling is still the most prized grape. Eisweins are a speciality.

HEURIGER *Austria* Fresh, young wine drunk in the many taverns in the Viennese hills. Once the wine is a year old it is called der Alte, or 'old chap'. No really good wine is sold as Heuriger, yet a few swift jugs of it can make for a great evening – but keep the aspirin handy.

HEYL ZU HERRNSHEIM *Nierstein, Rheinhessen, Germany* Historical estate whose main strength is substantial dry whites from the Riesling, Weissburgunder (Pinot Blanc) and Silvaner grapes. However, Auslese and higher Prädikat wines of recent vintages have been of ★★ and – sometimes – ★★★ quality. Only wines from the top sites (Brudersberg, Pettenthal, Hipping, Oelberg) carry the vineyard designation. Other high-quality dry wines are sold under the 'Rotschiefer' name. Best years: (Riesling Auslese) (2001) 99 98 **97 96 93** 90 89.

HEYMANN-LÖWENSTEIN *Winningen, Mosel, Germany* A leading estate of the Lower MOSEL (Terrassenmosel, or terraced Mosel). Its dry Rieslings are unusually full-bodied for the region, those from the Röttgen and Uhlen sites sometimes reaching ★★. Also powerful Auslese. Best years: (Riesling Auslese) (2002) 01 00 **99 98 97** 95 94 93 92 91.

HIDALGO *Jerez y Manzanilla DO, Andalucía, Spain* Hidalgo's Manzanilla La Gitana★★ is deservedly one of the best-selling manzanillas in Spain. Hidalgo is still family-owned, and only uses grapes from its own vineyards. Brands include Mariscal★, Fino Especial and Miraflores, Amontillado Napoleon★★, Oloroso Viejo★★ and Jerez Cortado★.

HILL OF GRACE★★★ *Eden Valley, South Australia* A stunning wine with dark, exotic flavours made by HENSCHKE from a single plot of Shiraz. The Hill of Grace vineyard was first planted in the 1860s, and the old vines produce a powerful, structured wine with superb ripe fruit, chocolate, coffee, earth, leather and the rest. Can be cellared for 20 years or more. Best years: (1999) (98) (97) 96 95 94 **93 92 91 90 88** 86 85 82 78 72.

HILLTOP *Neszmély, Hungary* Chief winemaker Akos Kamocsay is one of Hungary's most respected, and this winery has been Hungary's leader in providing fresh, bright wines, especially white, at friendly prices. The range includes indigenous varieties such as Irsai Oliver and Cserszegi Füszeres as well as Gewürztraminer, Sauvignon Blanc★ and Chardonnay. Hilltop also produces a good but controversial TOKAJI.

HILLTOPS *New South Wales, Australia* Promising high-altitude cherry-growing region with a small but fast-growing area of vineyards around the town of Young. Good potential for reds from Cabernet Sauvignon and Shiraz. Best producers: Demondrille, Grove Estates, MCWILLIAM'S (Barwang vineyard★), Woodonga Hill.

FRANZ HIRTZBERGER *Wachau, Niederösterreich, Austria* One of the WACHAU's top growers. Hirtzberger's finest wines are the concentrated, elegant Smaragd Rieslings from Singerriedel★★★ and Hochrain★★. The best Grüner Veltliner comes from the Honivogl site★★★. Best years: (Riesling Smaragd) (2002) 01 00 99 **98 97 96 95 94** 93 92 90 88.

HOCHHEIM *Rheingau, Germany* Village best known for having given the English the word 'Hock' for Rhine wine, but with good individual vineyard sites, especially Domdechaney, Hölle (hell!) and Kirchenstück. Best producers: Joachim Flick, Franz KUNSTLER★★★, W J Schäfer. Best years: (2002) 01 99 **99 98 97 96 94 93** 92 90 88.

HOGUE CELLARS *Yakima Valley AVA, Washington State, USA* A large winery producing nearly 400,000 cases a year, Hogue Cellars makes a crisp Fumé Blanc, brambly Reserve Cabernet Sauvignon★ and decent Merlot. A peppery Syrah★ and spicy Viognier★ have been added to the mix. Best years: (top reds) 2001 00 99 **97**.

153

HOLLICK *Coonawarra, South Australia* Run by viticulturist Ian Hollick this winery makes a broader range of good wines than is usually found in COONAWARRA: irresistible sparkling Merlot★ (yes, *Merlot*) subtle Chardonnay★, tobaccoey Cabernet-Merlot★ and riche Ravenswood Cabernet Sauvignon★★. Also attractive Sauvignon Semillon and good limy Riesling★. Best years: (Ravenswood) (2001) (00) 99 98 **96 94 93 91 90 88**.

DOM. DE L'HORTUS *Pic St-Loup, Coteaux du Languedoc AC, Languedoc France* From a first vintage in 1990, Jean and Marie-Thérèse Orliac have created one of this region's leading estates. Bergerie de l'Hortus Cuvée Classique★, a ready-to-drink unoaked Mourvèdre-Syrah Grenache blend, has delightful flavours of herbs, plums and cherries. Big brother Grande Cuvée★★ needs time for the fruit and oak to come into harmony. The white Grande Cuvée★ is a Chardonnay-Viognier blend. Best years: (Grande Cuvée red) 2001 00 **99 98 97 96 95 94 93**

HOSPICES DE BEAUNE *Côte de Beaune, Burgundy, France* Scene of theatrical auction on the third Sunday in November each year, the Hospices is an historical foundation which sells wine from its holdings in the CÔTE D'OR to finance its charitable works. The quality of the wine making has increased immeasurably since 1994, partly thanks to a new winery on the outskirts of Beaune. The wines are matured and bottled by the purchaser, which can cause variations in quality, and pricing reflects charitable status rather than common sense.

HOUGHTON *Swan District, Western Australia* WESTERN AUSTRALIA's biggest winery, owned by BRL HARDY, sources fruit from its own outstanding vineyards or from growers in all premium regions of the state. The budget-priced Line range includes the popular, flavoursome 'White Burgundy'★ (called HWB in the EU), good Semillon-Sauvignon Blanc★ and Chenin Blanc; also recently improved Chardonnay and Cabernet. The Moondah Brook Cabernet★★ and Shiraz★★ are a leap up in quality and even better value. Houghton has had enormous success with its new regional range: a Riesling★★ and Shiraz★★ from Frankland River; a MARGARET RIVER Cabernet★★; as well as four of the best wines yet seen from the emerging PEMBERTON region. The dense oaky Gladstones Shiraz★★★ and the powerful, lush flagship Jack Mann Cabernet Sauvignon★★★ have also contributed to the changing profile of Houghton. Best years: (Jack Mann) (2001) 00 99 98 **96 95 94**

VON HÖVEL *Konz-Oberemmel, Saar, Germany* Eberhard von Kunow owns some top sites, including Oberemmeler Hütte. He has always made unusually rich, succulent wines for a region renowned for steely Rieslings, but since 1993 quality has taken another leap; wines are now almost all ★★. Most wines age impressively for 10 years or more. Best years: (Auslese) (2002) 01 99 **97** 96 95 **94 93 90 89 88 85**.

HOWARD PARK *Margaret River, Western Australia* Howard Park now has wineries at Denmark in GREAT SOUTHERN (for whites) and at MARGARET RIVER (for reds). It has been an important player in high-quality Australian Cabernet over the past 15 years. The classic Cabernet Sauvignon-Merlot★★★, built for long cellaring, is matched by intense, floral Riesling★★ and a supremely classy Chardonnay★★. The Scotsdale and Leston Shiraz★ and Cabernet Sauvignon★ are part of an impressive range of regional reds. The Madfish label is good for Shiraz★, Sauvignon-Semillon★ and unwooded Chardonnay★. Best years: (Cabernet-Merlot) 2001 99 98 96 94 93 92 **90 89 88 86**; (Riesling) 2002 01 **00 98 97 96 95 94 93 92 91 90 88 86**.

OWELL MOUNTAIN AVA *Napa Valley, California, USA* NAPA's north-eastern corner is noted for powerhouse Cabernet Sauvignon and Zinfandel as well as exotic, full-flavoured Merlot. Best producers: BERINGER (Merlot★★), DUCKHORN★, DUNN★★, La Jota★, Liparita★, PINE RIDGE (Cabernet Sauvignon★), Viader★★★. Best years: (reds) (2001) (00) 99 98 97 96 **95 94 93 91 90**.

HUADONG WINERY *Shandong Province, China* The first producer of varietal and vintage wines in China, Huadong received massive investment from its former multinational joint owners (Allied Domecq) as well as state support. Money, however, can't change the climate, and excessive moisture from the summer rainy season causes problems. Even so, Riesling and Chardonnay (under the Tsingtao label) are not at all bad and Cabernet Sauvignon and Chardonnay in special 'feng shui' bottles are pretty tasty.

HUET L'ECHANSONNE *Vouvray AC, Loire Valley, France* Complex, traditional Vouvrays that can age for decades, produced using biodynamic methods. Three excellent sites – le Haut-Lieu, Clos du Bourg and le Mont – yield dry★★, medium-dry★★ or sweet★★★ wines, depending on the vintage. Wines from new vineyard Le Vodanis★ are more approachable in their youth. Also very

good Vouvray Mousseux★★. Best years: (2002) 01 **00 99 98 97 96 95 93 90 89 88 85 76 64 61 59 47**.

HUGEL ET FILS *Alsace AC, Alsace, France* Arguably the most famous name in Alsace. As well as wines from its own vineyards, Hugel buys in grapes for basic wines. Best wines are sweet ALSACE VENDANGE TARDIVE★★ and Sélection de Grains Nobles★★★. The Tradition wines are generally rather dull, but the Jubilee wines are often of ★★ quality. Best years: (Vendange Tardive Riesling) (2000) (99) (98) **97 96 95 90 89 88**.

HUNTER VALLEY *New South Wales, Australia* NEW SOUTH WALES' oldest wine region overcomes a tricky climate to make fascinating, ageworthy Semillon and rich, buttery Chardonnay. The reds meet less universal approval. Shiraz is the mainstay, aging well but often developing a leathery overtone; Cabernet can deliver occasional success. Premium region is the Lower Hunter Valley; the Upper Hunter has few wineries but extensive vineyards. Best producers: Allandale★★, BROKENWOOD★★, Kulkunbulla, LAKE'S FOLLY★, LINDEMANS★★, Lowe Family, MCWILLIAM'S★★, Meerea Park★, ROSEMOUNT★, ROTHBURY★, Tower★, TYRRELL'S★★. Best years: (Shiraz) 2001 00 99 98 97 **96 94 91**.

HUNTER'S *Marlborough, South Island, New Zealand* One of MARLBOROUGH's stars, with fine, if austere, Sauvignon★★, savoury, Burgundian Chardonnay★, vibrant Riesling★ and sophisticated Pinot Noir★. Also attractive fizz★. Best years: (Chardonnay) (2002) **01 00 99**.

CH. DU HUREAU *Saumur-Champigny and Saumur, Loire Valley, France* The Vatan family produces an exemplary range of silky SAUMUR-CHAMPIGNY reds in a cellar dug deep into the hillside outside Saumur. The basic red★ (formerly Grande Cuvée) is deliciously bright and fruity. Special cuvées Lisagathe★★ and Fevettes★★ need a bit of time. Jasmine-scented white SAUMUR★★ is exceptional in top years. Decent fizz and occasional sweet Coteaux de Saumur, too. Best years: (top reds) 2001 00 **99 97 96 95**.

INNISKILLIN *Niagara Peninsula, Ontario, Canada* One of Canada's leading wineries, producing good Pinot Noir★ and Cabernet Franc, beautifully rounded Klose Vineyard Chardonnay★ and rich Vidal Icewine★★ and Riesling Icewine★. Another Inniskillin winery is in the OKANAGAN VALLEY in British Columbia. Best years: (Vidal Icewine) (2001) 00 99 **98 97 95 94 92 89**.

IPHOFEN *Franken, Germany* One of the 2 most important wine towns in FRANKEN for dry Riesling and Silvaner. Both are powerful, with a pronounced earthiness. Best producers: JULIUSSPITAL★, Johann Ruck★, Hans Wirsching★. Best years: (2002) 01 **99 98 97 94 93 92 90**.

IRANCY AC *Burgundy, France* Formerly known as Bourgogne-Irancy and labelled simply Irancy from 1996, this northern outpost of vineyards, just south-west of CHABLIS, is an unlikely champion of the clear, pure flavours of the Pinot Noir grape. But red Irancy can be delicate and lightly touched by the ripeness of plums and strawberries and can age well. There is also a little rosé. Best producers: Bienvenu, J-M BROCARD, Cantin, A & J-P Colinot★, Delaloge, Patrice Fort★, Simonnet-Febvre. Best years: (2002) 01 **00 99**.

IRON HORSE VINEYARDS *Sonoma County, California, USA* Outstanding sparkling wines with vintage Brut★★ and Blanc de Blancs★★ delicious on release but highly suitable for aging. The Brut LD★★★ (Late Disgorged) is a heavenly mouthful of sparkling wine – yeasty and complex. Wedding Cuvée★ blanc de noirs and Brut Rosé★ complete the line-up. Table wines include a lovely Pinot Noir★★, a barrel-fermented Chardonnay★ and a seductive Viognier★★.

IROULÉGUY AC *South-West France* A small AC in the Basque Pyrenees. Cabernet Sauvignon, Cabernet Franc and Tannat give robust reds that are softer than MADIRAN. Whites are made from Petit Courbu and Manseng. Best producers: Arretxea★, Brana★, Etxegaraya, Ilarria★, Irouléguy co-op (Mignaberry★). Best years: (reds) 2001 00 **98 97 96 95**.

ISABEL ESTATE *Marlborough, New Zealand* Grapegrowers (for CLOUDY BAY) turned award-winning winemakers Michael and Robyn Tiller are blazing a trail with Sauvignon Blanc★★ that equals the country's best. Aromatic, plum-and-cherry Pinot Noir★★, stylish, concentrated Chardonnay★★, and aromatic Riesling★ and Pinot Gris★ complete the impressive line-up. Best years: (Pinot Noir) (2002) 01 **00 99 98**.

ISOLE E OLENA *Chianti Classico DOCG, Tuscany, Italy* Paolo De Marchi has long been one of the pacesetters in Chianti Classico. His CHIANTI CLASSICO★★, characterized by clean, elegant and spicily perfumed fruit, excels in every vintage. The powerful SUPER-TUSCAN Cepparello★★★ made from 100% Sangiovese, is the top wine. Excellent Syrah★★, Cabernet Sauvignon★★★, Chardonnay★★, and VIN SANTO★★★. Best years: (Cepparello) (2001) (00) 99 98 97 **96 95 93 90 88**.

CH. D'ISSAN★ *Margaux AC, 3ème Cru Classé, Haut-Médoc, Bordeaux, France* This lovely moated property has disappointed me far too often in the past but pulled its socks up in the 90s. When successful, the wine can be one of the most delicate and scented in the MARGAUX AC. Best years: 2001 00 99 98 96 **95 90 89 85**.

PAUL JABOULET AÎNÉ *Rhône Valley, France* During the 1970s, Jaboulet led the way in raising the world's awareness of the great quality of RHONE wines, yet during the 80s the quality faltered, and though many of the wines are still good, they are no longer the star in any appellation. Best wines are top red HERMITAGE la Chapelle★★ and white Chevalier de Stérimberg★★. CROZES-HERMITAGE Thalabert★ is famous, but occasional release Vieilles Vignes★★ is much better nowadays, as are whites Mule Blanche★ and Raymond Roure★. Attractive CORNAS Dom. St-Pierre★, good value COTES DU VENTOUX★, and sweet, perfumed MUSCAT DE BEAUMES-DE-VENISE★★. Best years: (la Chapelle) 2001 00 99 98 97 96 95 **94 91 90 89 88 78**.

ACKSON ESTATE *Marlborough, South Island, New Zealand* An established grapegrower with vineyards in MARLBOROUGH's most prestigious district, Jackson Estate turned its hand to winemaking in 1991, making appley Sauvignon Blanc★ that improves with a little age, restrained Chardonnay and Pinot Noir★ and complex traditional-method fizz★. Best years: (Sauvignon Blanc) **2002 01 00**.

ACQUESSON *Champagne AC, Champagne, France* Venerable Champagne house founded in 1798. The ultra-reliable non-vintage Brut★ and Rosé★ are rather presumptuously called Perfection. The vintage Blanc de Blancs★★ is a classic example of this style, and vintage Signature Brut★★★ is a full-bodied biscuity Champagne of class and longevity. Best years: 1995 **93 90 89 88 85**.

LOUIS JADOT *Beaune, Burgundy, France* A leading merchant based in Beaune with a broad range matched only by DROUHIN, and with rights to some estate wines of the Duc de Magenta★★. Jadot has extensive vineyard holdings for red wines, but it is the firm's whites which have earned its reputation. Excellent in Grands Crus like BATARD-MONTRACHET★★★ and CORTON-CHARLEMAGNE★★ but Jadot also shows a more egalitarian side by producing good wines in lesser ACs like ST-AUBIN★ and RULLY★. Recent developments have included the purchase of top vineyards in the Beaujolais, such as Ch. de Jacques in MOULIN-A-VENT. Best years: (top reds) (2002) 01 00 99 98 **97 96 95 93 90**.

JAFFELIN *Beaune, Burgundy, France* Owned by BOISSET, Jaffelin produces a large range of wines from the COTE D'OR, the COTE CHALONNAISE and BEAUJOLAIS, including a sound range of Village wines.

JAMET *Côte-Rôtie AC, Rhône Valley, France* Jean-Paul and Jean-Luc Jamet are 2 of the most talented growers of COTE-ROTIE. If anything, the wines★★★ from this excellent estate have improved since they took over from their father, Joseph. The wines age well for a decade or more. Best years: 2001 00 99 98 97 96 **95 94 91 90 89 88 85 83**.

JARDIN See Jordan, South Africa.

JARDIN DE LA FRANCE, VIN DE PAYS DU *Loire Valley, France* This vin de pays covers most of the LOIRE VALLEY, and production often exceeds 80 million bottles – mostly of white wine, from Chenin Blanc and Sauvignon Blanc, and usually fairly cheap to buy. There is an increasing amount of good Chardonnay made here, as well as one or two pricy appellation-busting reds. Is the era of the super-Loires dawning? Best producers: BOUVET-LADUBAY, Adéà Consules, l'ECU, Henry Marionnet, RAGOTIERE.

JASNIÈRES AC *Loire Valley, France* Tiny AC north of Tours making long-lived, bone-dry whites from Chenin Blanc. Sweet wine may be made in good years. Best producers: Bellivière★★, J Gigou★★. Best years: (2002) 01 00 **99 97 96 95 93 92 90 89**.

ROBERT JAYER-GILLES *Côte de Nuits, Burgundy, France* Robert Jayer-Gilles produces expensive but sought-after wines, heavily dominated by new oak. Good ALIGOTE★, wonderful HAUTES-COTES DE NUITS Blanc★★, and sensuous reds, including ECHEZEAUX★★★ and NUITS-ST-GEORGES les Damodes★★. Best years: (top reds) (2002) 01 00 99 98 **97 96 95 93**.

JEREZ Y MANZANILLA DO/SHERRY See pages 158–9.

157

JEREZ Y MANZANILLA DO/SHERRY

Andalucía, Spain

The Spanish now own the name outright. At least i the EU, the only wines that can be sold as sherr come from the triangle of vineyard land between th Andalucian towns of inland Jerez de la Frontera, an Sanlúcar de Barrameda and Puerto de Santa María by the sea. Nev agreements signed by the EU are phasing out such other appella tions as South African Sherry.

The best sherries can be spectacular. Three main factor contribute to the high quality potential of wines from this region the chalky-spongy albariza soil where the best vines grow, th Palomino Fino grape – unexciting for table wines but potential; great once transformed by the sherry-making processes – and natural yeast called flor. All sherry must be a minimum of years old, but fine sherries age in barrel for much longer Sherries must be blended through a solera system. About a thir of the wine from the oldest barrels is bottled, and the barrel topped up with slightly younger wine from another set of barrel and so on, for a minimum of 3 sets of barrels. The idea is that th younger wine takes on the character of older wine, as well a keeping the blend refreshed.

MAIN SHERRY STYLES

Fino and manzanilla Fino sherries derive their extraordinary tangy, pungent flavours from flor. Young, newly fermented wine destined for these styles of sherry are deliberately fortified very spar ingly to just 15–15.5% alcohol before being put in barrels for thei minimum of 3 years' maturation. The thin, soft, oatmeal-coloured mush of flor grows on the surface of the wines, protecting then from the air (and therefore keeping them pale) and giving them a characteristic sharp, pungent tang. The addition of younger wine each year feeds the flor, maintaining an even layer. Manzanillas are fino-style wines that have matured in the cooler seaside conditions of Sanlúcar de Barrameda, where the flor grows thickest and the fine, salty tang is most accentuated.

Amontillado True amontillados are fino sherries that have contin ued to age after the flor has died (after about 5 years) and so finish their aging period in contact with air. These should all be bone dry Medium-sweet amontillados are concoctions in which the dry sherry is sweetened with mistela, a blend of grape juice and alcohol

Oloroso This type of sherry is strongly fortified after fermentatior to deter the growth of flor. Olorosos therefore mature in barrel ir contact with the air, which gradually darkens them while they develop rich, intense, nutty and raisiny flavours.

Other styles Manzanilla pasada is aged manzanilla, with greater depth and nuttiness. Palo cortado is an unusual, deliciously nutty, dry style somewhere in between amontillado and oloroso. Sweet oloroso creams and pale creams are almost without exception enriched solely for the export market. Sweet varietal wines are made from sun-dried Pedro Ximénez or Moscatel.

See also individual producers.

BEST PRODUCERS
AND WINES

Argüeso (Manzanilla San León, Manzanilla Fina Las Medallas).

BARBADILLO (Manzanilla Eva, Solear Manzanilla Fina Vieja, Amontillado Príncipe, Amontillado de Sanlúcar, Cuco Oloroso Seco, Palo Cortado Obispo Gascon).

Delgado Zuleta (Manzanilla Pasada La Goya).

Díez Mérito (Don Zoilo Imperial Amontillado, Imperial Fino, Victoria Regina Oloroso).

DOMECQ (Amontillado 51-1A, Sibarita Palo Cortado, Fino La Ina, Venerable Pedro Ximénez).

Garvey (Palo Cortado, Amontillado Tio Guillermo, Pedro Ximénez Gran Orden).

GONZALEZ BYASS (Tio Pepe Fino, Matusalem Oloroso Muy Viejo, Apóstoles Oloroso Viejo, Amontillado del Duque Seco y Muy Viejo, Noé Pedro Ximénez Muy Viejo, Oloroso Viejo de Añado).

HIDALGO (Amontillado Napoleon, Oloroso Viejo, Manzanilla La Gitana, Manzanilla Pasada, Jerez Cortado).

LUSTAU (Almacenista single-producer wines, Old East India Cream, Puerto Fino).

OSBORNE (Amontillado Coquinero, Fino Quinta, Bailén Oloroso, Solera India Oloroso, Pedro Ximénez).

Sánchez Romate (Pedro Ximénez Cardenal Cisneros).

VALDESPINO (Amontillado Coliseo, Amontillado Tio Diego, Amontillado Don Tomás, Cardenal Palo Cortado, Inocente Fino, Oloroso Don Gonzalo, Pedro Ximénez Solera Superior).

Williams & Humbert (Pando Fino, Manzanilla Alegria).

159

JERMANN *Friuli-Venezia Giulia, Italy* Silvio Jermann, in the COLLIO zone o
north-east Italy, produces non-DOC Chardonnay★, Sauvignon Blanc★
Pinot Bianco★ and Pinot Grigio★. Deep, long-lived Vintage Tunina★★
is based on Sauvignon-Chardonnay but includes Ribolla, Malvasia an
Picolit. Barrel-fermented Chardonnay★★ was called 'Where th
dreams have no end' but has, incredibly, been renamed 'Were dreams
now it is just wine'. Vinnae★ is based on Ribolla; Capo Martino★ is als
a blend of local varieties. The wines are plump but pricy.

JOHANNISBERG *Rheingau, Germany* Probably the best known of all th
Rhine wine villages, with 10 vineyard sites, including the famous Schlos
Johannisberg. Best producers: Prinz von Hessen★, Johannishof★★
Schloss Johannisberg★★. Best years: (2002) 01 **99** 98 **97** 96 93 90.

KARL H JOHNER *Bischoffingen, Baden, Germany* Johner specializes in
new oak-aged wines from his native BADEN. The vividly fruity Pino
Noir★ and Pinot Blanc★ are excellent, the Chardonnay SJ★ is one o
Germany's best examples of this varietal, and the rich, silky Pinot Noi
SJ★★ can be one of Germany's finest reds. Best years: (Pinot Noir SJ
(2002) 01 00 99 98 **97** 96 93 90.

JORDAN *Alexander Valley AVA, Sonoma, California, USA* Ripe, fruity
Cabernet Sauvignon★ with a cedar character rare in California. The
Chardonnay★ is balanced and attractive. J★ fizz is an attractive
mouthful, now made independently by Judy Jordan's J Wine Co. Bes
years: (Cabernet) (2001) (00) 99 **97** 96 95 94 91 86.

JORDAN *Stellenbosch WO, South Africa* Meticulously groomed hillside
vineyards, with a variety of aspects and soils, offer favourable sites to
a number of premium varieties. A strong white range is headed by a
nutty Chardonnay★★. Cabernet Sauvignon★, Merlot★ and Cobblers
Hill★, a BORDEAUX blend, show elegant understatement but deepen
with a little age. Sold under the Jardin label in the USA. Best years:
(Chardonnay) **2001** 00 99 98 97 96; (Cobblers Hill) 2000 99 **98** 97.

TONI JOST *Bacharach, Mittelrhein, Germany* Husband and wife team
Peter and Linde Jost have put the MITTELRHEIN on the map. From the
Bacharacher Hahn site come some delicious, racy Rieslings★
including well-structured Halbtrockens★; Auslese★★ adds creaminess
without losing that pine-needle scent. Best years: (Riesling Spätlese)
(2002) 01 99 98 **97** 96 94 93 92 90 89.

J P VINHOS *Terras do Sado, Portugal* Forward-looking operation, using
Portuguese and foreign grapes with equal ease. Quinta da Bacalhôa is
an oaky, meaty Cabernet-Merlot blend; Tinto da Ânfora★ a rich and
figgy ALENTEJO red (Grande Escolha★★ version is powerful and cedary);
and Cova da Ursa★ a toasty, rich Chardonnay, if now more subdued
than previously. Portugal's finest sparkling wine, vintage-dated Loridos
Extra Bruto★, is a pretty decent Champagne lookalike, made from
Chardonnay. New is SÓ (which means 'only' in Portuguese, as in 'only
Syrah'), characterful if atypical. Also decent Moscatel de SETUBAL★.

JULIÉNAS AC *Beaujolais, Burgundy, France* One of the more northerly
BEAUJOLAIS Crus, Juliénas is attractive, 'serious' Beaujolais which can
be big and tannic enough to develop in bottle. Best producers: G
Descombes★, DUBOEUF★, P Granger★, Ch. de Juliénas★, J P Mar-
gerand★, R Monnet★, Pelletier★, B Santé★. Best years: (2002) **00** 99 98.

JULIUSSPITAL *Würzburg, Franken, Germany* A 16th-century charitable
foundation known for its dry wines – especially Silvaners from IPHOFEN
and WURZBURG. Look out for the Würzburger Stein vineyard wines,
sappy Müller-Thurgau, grapefruity Silvaners★★ and petrolly

Rieslings★★. Back on form in 1999, after curiously disappointing 1998 and 97 vintages. Best years: (2002) 01 00 **99 94 93 92 90**.

JUMILLA DO *Murcia and Castilla-La Mancha, Spain* Jumilla's reputation in Spain is for big alcoholic reds. Reds and fruity rosés are made from Monastrell (Mourvèdre), so the potential is there. Whites are mostly boring. Best producers: Casa de la Ermita★, Induvasa (Finca Luzón★), Agapito Rico, Julia Roch (Casa Castillo★★). Best years: 2001 **00 99 98 96**.

JURA See Arbois, Château-Chalon, Côtes du Jura, Crémant du Jura, l'Étoile.

JURANÇON AC *South-West France* The sweet white wine made from late-harvested and occasionally botrytized grapes can be heavenly, with floral, spicy, apricot-quince flavours. The dry wine, Jurançon Sec, can be ageworthy. Best producers: Bellegarde★, Bru-Baché★★, Castera★, CAUHAPE★★, Clos Lapeyre★, Clos Thou★, CLOS UROULAT★★, Larrédya★, Souch★. Best years: (sweet) 2001 00 **99 98 96 95**.

JUVÉ Y CAMPS *Cava DO and Penedès DO, Cataluña, Spain* Juvé y Camps is ultra-traditional – and expensive. Unusually among the Catalan companies, most of the grapes come from its own vineyards. Fruitiest CAVA is Reserva de la Familia Extra Brut★, but the rosé and the top brand white Cava Gran Juvé are also good. Ermita d'Espiells is a neutral, dry white wine.

KAISERSTUHL *Baden, Germany* A 4000ha (10,000-acre) volcanic stump rising to 600m (2000ft) and overlooking the Rhine plain and south BADEN. Best producers: BERCHER★★, Bickensohl co-op, Dr HEGER★★, Karl H JOHNER★, Franz Keller★, Königsschaffhausen co-op, Salwey★★. Best years: (dry whites) 2002 01 **99 98 97 96 93**.

KALLSTADT *Pfalz, Germany* A warm climate combined with the excellent Saumagen site results in the richest dry Rieslings in Germany. These, and the dry Weissburgunder (Pinot Blanc) and Muskateller (Muscat), can stand beside the very best from ALSACE. Pinot Noir is also showing it likes the chalk soil. Best producer: KOEHLER-RUPRECHT★★★. Best years: (2002) 01 00 **99 98 97 96 95 93 92 90 89 88**.

KAMPTAL *Niederösterreich, Austria* 3870ha (9560-acre) wine region centred on the town of Langenlois, making some impressive dry whites, particularly Riesling and Grüner Veltliner. Best producers: BRUNDLMAYER★★, Ehn★★, Hiedler★, Hirsch★, Fred Loimer★★, Schloss Gobelsburg★★. Best years: 2001 00 99 **98 97 95 94 93**.

KANONKOP *Stellenbosch WO, South Africa* This senior-statesman estate produces traditional, long-lived red wines: the muscular, savoury red BORDEAUX blend Paul Sauer★★ and Auction Reserve★★ version really do mature for 10 years or more. A straight Cabernet Sauvignon★ adds to this enviable red wine reputation, and Pinotage★★ (standard and Auction Reserve), from 50-year-old vines, is indelibly associated with the estate. Owned by the Krige brothers, who are also partners, with Beyers Truter, in nearby BEYERSKLOOF. Best years: (Paul Sauer) **1999 98 97 96 95 94 92 91**.

KARTHÄUSERHOF *Trier, Ruwer, Germany* Top Ruwer estate which has gone from strength to strength since Christoph Tyrell and winemaker Ludwig Breiling took charge in 1986. Rieslings combine aromatic extravagance with racy brilliance. Since 1993 most wines are ★★, some Auslese and Eiswein ★★★. Best years: (2002) 01 99 **97** 95 **94** 93 90 89 88.

KATNOOK ESTATE *Coonawarra, South Australia* Chardonnay★★ has consistently been the best of the fairly expensive whites here, though the Riesling★ and Sauvignon★ are pretty good, too. Reds are led by well-structured Cabernet Sauvignon★★ and treacly Shiraz★, with flagship reds, Odyssey Cabernet Sauvignon★★ and Prodigy Shiraz★★, reaching a higher level. Best years: (Odyssey) 2000 99 98 97 96 **94 92 91**.

KÉKFRANKOS See Blaufränkisch.

KELLER *Flörsheim-Dalsheim, Rheinhessen, Germany* Klaus Keller and son Klauspeter are the leading winemakers in the hill country of RHEINHESSEN, away from the Rhine riverbank. They produce a range of varietal dry wines and naturally sweet Rieslings, including succulent Spätlese★ and Auslese★★ from the Dalsheimer Hubacker site. Best years: (Riesling Auslese) (2002) 01 **99 98 97 95**.

KENDALL-JACKSON *Sonoma County, California, USA* Jess Jackson founded KJ in bucolic Lake County in 1982 after buying a vineyard there; the operation has since grown to over 2 million cases. Early success was driven by off-dry Vintner's Reserve Chardonnay, but lately the wines have become more challenging. Today's Chardonnays are barrel fermented and oak aged. Grand Reserve wines are blends from several AVAs. Kendall-Jackson owns other wineries in California, including La Crema (Chardonnay★, Pinot Noir★) and Pepi, as well as Chile (Calina), Argentina (Tapiz) and Australia (Yangarra Park).

KENWOOD *Sonoma Valley AVA, California, USA* Owned by Gary Heck of Korbel sparkling wine fame, this winery has always represented very good quality at reasonable prices. The Sauvignon Blanc★ highlights floral and melon flavours with a slightly earthy finish, while the new Massara Merlot★ offers nice complexity in a subtle style. The range of Zinfandels is impressive (Jack London★★, Mazzoni★, Nuns Canyon★), while the flagship red remains the long-lived Artist Series Cabernet Sauvignon★★. Best years: (Zinfandel) (2001) 00 99 **98 97 96 95 94**.

VON KESSELSTATT *Trier, Mosel, Germany* Good Riesling Kabinett★ and rich, fragrant Spätlese★ and Auslese★★ wines from some top sites at GRAACH (Josephshöfer) in the MOSEL, Scharzhofberg in the Saar and at Kasel in the Ruwer. Best years: (Riesling Spätlese) (2002) 01 99 98 **97 96 95 94 93**.

KHAN KRUM *Black Sea Region, Bulgaria* An all-Bulgarian team makes some of Bulgaria's best modern whites, such as the oaky Reserve Chardonnay and perfumed, apricotty Riesling-Dimiat Country Wine.

KIEDRICH *Rheingau, Germany* Small village whose top vineyard is the Gräfenberg, giving extremely long-lived, mineral Rieslings. Wines from Sandgrub and Wasseros are also often good. Best producers: Knyphausen★, WEIL★. Best years: (Riesling Spätlese, Auslese) (2002) 01 **99 98 97 96 95 94 93 92 90**.

KING ESTATE *Oregon, USA* OREGON's biggest producer of Pinot Gris★ and Pinot Noir. Both are made in a user-friendly style but the Pinot Noir is inconsistent. Reserve Pinot Gris★ and Reserve Pinot Noir offer greater depth. Domaine Pinot Noir is a selection of the best barrels and can be quite good. Best years: (Reserve Pinot Noir) (2002) 01 00 99 **98 96**.

KIONA *Yakima Valley AVA, Washington State, USA* A small operation in sagebrush country, Kiona has a reputation for its barrel-fermented Chardonnay★, big, full Cabernet Sauvignon★, brambly Lemberger★ and delightful dry Rieslings★. Its forte is in the production of good-value late-harvest wines, notably Chenin Blanc★, Riesling★★ and Gewürztraminer★★. Best years: (Late Harvest wines) 2000 99 97.

KISTLER *Sonoma Valley AVA, California, USA* One of California's hottest Chardonnay producers. Wines are made from many different vineyards (Kistler Vineyard, Durell Vineyard and Dutton Ranch can be ★★★; McCrea Vineyard and the ultra-cool-climate Camp Meeting Ridge Vineyard ★★). All possess great complexity with good aging potential. Kistler also makes a number of single-vineyard Pinot Noirs★★ that go from good to very good. Best years: (Kistler Vineyard Chardonnay) (2002) (01) 00 99 **98** 97 **95 94 91 90**.

KLEIN CONSTANTIA *Constantia WO, South Africa* Since 1980, the Jooste family have turned this winery into a South African show-piece. Sauvignon Blanc★, usually crisp and tangy, though sometimes a little ripe, benefits from winemaker Ross Gower's experience in New Zealand. A decent Chardonnay, attractive, off-dry Riesling★ and Vin de Constance★, a Muscat dessert wine based on the 18th-century CONSTANTIA examples, highlight the area's aptitude for white wine. Of the reds, New World-style Shiraz★ looks promising. Best years: (Vin de Constance) **1997 96 95 94 93 92 91 90**.

KNAPPSTEIN *Clare Valley, South Australia* In 1995 Tim Knappstein quit the company, now part of PETALUMA, to focus on his own LENSWOOD VINEYARDS, high in the ADELAIDE HILLS. However, the Knappstein brand is still a market leader, with fine Riesling★★ and Gewürztraminer★, subtly-oaked Semillon-Sauvignon★, Cabernet-Merlot and Chardonnay, plus the premium Enterprise pair, Shiraz★ and Cabernet Sauvignon★. Former Petaluma winemaker Andrew Hardy took charge in 1996, and he has pumped new enthusiasm into the wines. Best years: (Enterprise Cabernet Sauvignon) 2001 00 99 98 **97**.

EMMERICH KNOLL *Unterloiben, Wachau, Niederösterreich, Austria* Since the late 1970s publicity-shy Emmerich Knoll has made some of the greatest Austrian dry white wines. His Riesling and Grüner Veltliner are packed with fruit and are rich and complex. They rarely fail to reach ★★ quality, with Grüner Veltliner and Riesling from both the Loibenberg and Schütt sites ★★★. They repay keeping for 5 years or more. Best years: (Riesling Smaragd) (2002) 01 00 99 **98** 97 **96 95 94 93 92 90 89 88 86 85**.

KOEHLER-RUPRECHT *Kallstadt, Pfalz, Germany* Bernd Philippi makes powerful, very concentrated dry Rieslings★★★ from the Kallstadter Saumagen site, the oak-aged botrytized Elysium★★ and, since 1991, Burgundian-style Spätburgunder (Pinot Noir)★. Philippi is also co-winemaker (with Bernhard Breuer) at Mont du Toit in South Africa, where they produce blockbuster blended reds. Best years: (Riesling Auslese trocken) (2002) 01 00 **99** 98 **97 96** 95 93 90 89 88.

ALOIS KRACHER *Illmitz, Burgenland, Austria* Arguably Austria's greatest sweet winemaker. Nouvelle Vague wines are aged in barriques while Zwischen den Seen wines are spared oak. The Scheurebe Beerenauslesen and TBAs, and the Welschrieslings, Chardonnay-Welschrieslings and Grande Cuvée are all ★★★. The Bouviers★ (often labelled Kracher Beerenauslese) are also good. Since 1997 Kracher has also made first-rate red wines. Best years: (whites) (2002) (01) 00 99 98 **96 95 94 93 91 89 86 81**.

KREMSTAL *Niederösterreich, Austria* 2175ha (5375-acre) wine region on both sides of the Danube around the town of Krems, producing some of Austria's best whites, particularly dry Riesling and Grüner Veltliner. Best producers: Mantlerhof★, Sepp Moser★, Nigl★★,

NIKOLAIHOF★★, Franz Proidl★, Salomon Undhof★★. Best years: (2002) (01) 00 99 **98 97 95 94 93**.

KRUG *Champagne AC, Champagne, France* Serious CHAMPAGNE house, making seriously expensive wines. The non-vintage, Grande Cuvée★, used to knock spots off most other de luxe brands in its rich, rather over-the-top traditional style. Under new owners LVMH, the style seems to have changed dramatically: it's fresher, leaner, more modern – good, but that's not why I buy Krug. Also an impressive vintage★★, a rosé★★ and ethereal single-vineyard Clos du Mesnil★★★ Blanc de Blancs. Best years: (1990) **89 88 85 82 81 79**.

PETER JAKOB KÜHN *Oestrich, Rheingau, Germany* During the late 1990s Kühn was the rising star of the RHEINGAU, frequently making headlines with his substantial dry Rieslings and full, juicy Spätlese. These wines are usually ★, sometimes ★★. Best years: (2002) 01 99 98 **97 96 94 93 92**.

KUMEU/HUAPAI *Auckland, North Island, New Zealand* A small but significant viticultural area north-west of Auckland. The 11 wineries profit from their proximity to New Zealand's largest city. Most producers make little or no wine from their home region. Best producers: COOPERS CREEK★, Harrier Rise, KUMEU RIVER★★, MATUA VALLEY★★, NOBILO. Best years: (reds) (2002) 01 00 **99 98 96 94 93**.

KUMEU RIVER *Kumeu, Auckland, North Island, New Zealand* This family winery has been transformed by New Zealand's first Master of Wine, Michael Brajkovich, who has created a range of adventurous, high-quality wines: a big, complex, award-winning Chardonnay★★★ (Maté's Vineyard★★★), softly stylish Merlot★, complex oak-aged Pinot Gris★ and a newly released premium Merlot-Malbec blend called Melba★★. Only Pinot Noir disappoints so far. Best years: (Chardonnay) (2002) **00 99 98 96**.

KUNDE ESTATE *Sonoma Valley, California, USA* The Kunde family have grown wine-grapes in SONOMA COUNTY for at least 100 years; in 1990 they started producing wines, with spectacular results. The Chardonnays are all impressive – Kinneybrook★★, Wildwood★★ and the powerful, buttery Reserve★★. The Century Vines Zinfandel★★ gets rave reviews, as does the peppery Syrah★★ and the explosively fruity Viognier★★. Best years: (Zinfandel) (2001) 00 99 97 **96 95 94**.

FRANZ KÜNSTLER *Hochheim, Rheingau, Germany* Gunter Künstler makes some of the best dry Rieslings in the RHEINGAU. They are powerful, mineral wines★★, with the Hölle wines often worthy of ★★★. In 1996 he bought the run-down Aschrott estate, which more than doubled his vineyard area. The sweet wine quality has been erratic lately, but the best are fantastic. Best years: (Riesling Spätlese trocken, Auslese trocken) (2002) 01 **99** 98 **97** 96 **94 93 92 90 89 88**.

KWV *Paarl WO, South Africa* The flagship Cathedral Cellar line-up has been enlarged and overall quality improved in recent years. Best are the bright-fruited, well-oaked Triptych★ (Cabernet-Merlot-Shiraz), rich bold Cabernet Sauvignon★ and modern-style Pinotage. Among whites, barrel-fermented Chardonnay shows pleasing fruit/oak balance. Topping everything, and made in very limited quantities, is the single-vineyard Perold; the second release is a very ripe, slick, international-style Shiraz lavishly adorned with new American oak. Port-style fortifieds remain superb value, particularly Vintage★★.

LA AGRÍCOLA *Mendoza, Argentina*   One of Argentina's great success stories. Dynamic owner José Zuccardi saw the potential for export before his compatriots and set about creating a range of utterly enjoyable easy-drinking wines. La Agrícola now exports about 70% of its wine under a number of labels, including Santa Julia and Picajuan Peak. Its greatest success is its basic reds★, often from Italian or Spanish grape varieties. Reserves and top-of-the-range 'Q'★ are improving dramatically with a new barrel-aging facility from the 2001 vintage. Whites are good but less exciting.

LA ROSA *Cachapoal, Rapel, Chile*   Old family operation rejuvenated by La Palmeria and its talented winemaker José Ignacio Cancino. Unoaked Chardonnay★ is pure apricots and figs, and the Merlot★ is a delightful easy-drinking RAPEL style. Reserva and Gran Reserva wines (often ★★) are a step up in quality.

CH. LABÉGORCE-ZÉDÉ★ *Margaux AC, Bordeaux, France*   Although not situated on the best MARGAUX soil, this property has been carefully cherished and improved by Luc Thienpont from POMEROL. The wine isn't that perfumed but the balance between concentration and finesse is always good. Age for 5 years or more. Second wine: Domaine Zédé. A third wine, Z de Zédé, is a simple BORDEAUX AC. Best years: 2001 00 99 98 96 **95 94 90 89 88**.

LABOURÉ-ROI *Nuits-St-Georges AC, Burgundy, France*   Price-conscious and generally reliable merchant, yet no longer so consistent as before as supply struggles to keep up with demand. The CHABLIS★ and MEURSAULT★ are very correct wines, and NUITS-ST-GEORGES★, CHAMBOLLE-MUSIGNY★, GEVREY-CHAMBERTIN★, BEAUNE★ and VOLNAY★ are usually good.

LADOIX AC *Côte de Beaune, Burgundy, France*   Most northerly village in the COTE DE BEAUNE and one of the least known. The village includes some of the Grand Cru CORTON, and the lesser vineyards may be sold as Ladoix-Côte de Beaune or COTE DE BEAUNE-VILLAGES. There are several good growers, and Ladoix wine, mainly red, quite light in colour and a little lean in style, is reasonably priced. Best producers: (reds) P André★, Cachat-Ocquidant★, E Cornu★, Prince Florent de Merode★, A & J-R Nudant★; (whites) P André★, E Cornu★, R & R Jacob★, VERGET★. Best years: (reds) (2002) 01 **99 98 96**.

MICHEL LAFARGE *Côte de Beaune, Burgundy, France*   The doyen of VOLNAY, Michel Lafarge, and his son, Frédéric, produce some outstanding red wines, notably Volnay Clos des Chênes★★★, Volnay Clos du Château des Ducs★★★ (a monopole) and less fashionable BEAUNE Grèves★★. BOURGOGNE Rouge★ is good value. Top wines are accessible when young but can age up to 10 years or more. Best years: (top reds) (2002) 99 98 **97** 96 95 **93 91 90 89 88**.

CH. LAFAURIE-PEYRAGUEY★★★ *Sauternes AC, 1er Cru Classé, Bordeaux, France*   One of the most improved SAUTERNES properties of the 1980s and now frequently one of the best Sauternes of all, sumptuous and rich when young, and marvellously deep and satisfying with age. Best years: (2002) 01 99 **98 97 96 95 90 89 88 86 85 83**.

CH. LAFITE-ROTHSCHILD★★★ *Pauillac AC, 1er Cru Classé, Haut-Médoc, Bordeaux, France*   This PAUILLAC First Growth is frequently cited as the epitome of elegance, indulgence and expense. If vintages of the late 1980s were excellent, those of the late 90s have been superb, with added depth and body to match the wine's traditional finesse. Second wine: les Carruades de Lafite-Rothschild. Best years: 2001 00 99 98 97 96 95 **94 90 89 88 86 85 82**.

CH. LAFLEUR★★★ *Pomerol AC, Bordeaux, France* Using some of POMEROL's most traditional winemaking, this tiny estate can seriously rival the great PETRUS for sheer power and flavour, and indeed in certain years has nudged ahead of Pétrus for hedonistic richness and concentration. Best years: 2001 00 99 98 97 96 **95 94 93 90 89 88**.

LAFON *Meursault AC, Côte de Beaune, Burgundy, France* A leading producer in MEURSAULT and one of Burgundy's current superstars, with a reputation and prices to match. From biodynamic viticulture Dominique Lafon produces rich, powerful Meursaults that spend as long as 2 years in barrel and age superbly in bottle. As well as excellent Meursault, especially Clos de la Barre★★, les Charmes★★★ and les Perrières★★★, Lafon makes a tiny amount of le MONTRACHET★★★ and some really individual and exciting red wines from VOLNAY★★ (Santenots du Milieu★★★) and MONTHELIE★★. Since 1999 the Lafons also own the MACON★ domaine. Best years: (whites) (2002) 01 00 99 97 96 95 **93 92**; (reds) (2002) 99 98 97 96 95 93 **92 91**.

CH. LAFON-ROCHET ★ *St-Estèphe AC, 4ème Cru Classé, Haut-Médoc, Bordeaux, France* Good-value, affordable Classed Growth claret. Recent vintages have seen an increase of Merlot in the blend, making the wine less austere. Delicious and blackcurranty after 10 years. Best years: 2001 00 99 98 96 **95 94 90 89 88 86 85**.

LAGEDER *Alto Adige DOC, Trentino-Alto Adige, Italy* Leading producer in ALTO ADIGE, making good, medium-priced varietals and pricy estate and single-vineyard wines such as Löwengang Cabernet★ and Chardonnay★★,

Sauvignon Lehenhof★★, Cabernet Cor Römigberg★★, Pinot Bianco Haberlehof★★ and Pinot Grigio Benefizium Porer★★. Also owns the historic Casòn Hirschprunn estate, source of excellent Alto Adige blends. Premium white Contest★★ is based on Pinot Grigio and Chardonnay but also includes small amounts of Marsanne and Roussanne. The red equivalent, Casòn★★, is Merlot-Cabernet based; a second red, Corolle★, and white Etelle★ show similar style.

LAGO DI CALDARO DOC *Trentino-Alto Adige, Italy* At its best a lovely, barely red, youthful glugger from the Schiava grape, tasting of strawberries and cream and bacon smoke. However, far too much Caldaro is overproduced. Known in German as Kalterersee. Kalterersee Auslese (Lago di Caldaro Scelto) is not sweet, but has 0.5% more alcohol. Best producers: Caldaro co-op★, LAGEDER★, Prima & Nuova/Erste & Neue★, San Michele Appiano co-op, Schloss Sallegg★.

CH. LAGRANGE★★ *St-Julien AC, 3ème Cru Classé, Haut-Médoc, Bordeaux, France* Since the Japanese company Suntory purchased this large estate in 1983, the leap in quality has been astonishing. No longer an amiable, shambling ST-JULIEN, this is now a single-minded wine of good fruit, meticulous winemaking and fine quality. Second wine: les Fiefs de Lagrange. Best years: 2001 00 99 98 96 **95 94 93 90 89 88 86 85**.

LAGREIN Highly individual black grape variety, planted only in Italy's Trentino-Alto Adige region, producing deep-coloured, brambly, chocolaty reds called Lagrein Dunkel, and full-bodied yet attractively scented rosé (known as Kretzer). Best producers: Colterenzio co-op (Cornell★), Graziano Fontana★, Franz Gojer★, Gries co-op★, Hofstätter★,

LAGEDER★, Laimburg★, Muri-Gries★, J Niedermayr★, I Niedriest★, Plattner-Waldgries★, Hans Rottensteiner★, Santa Maddalena co-op★, Simoncelli★, Terlano co-op★★, Thurnhof★★, Tiefenbrunner★, Zemmer★.

CH. LAGREZETTE *Cahors AC, South-West France* Splendid CAHORS estate owned by Alain-Dominique Perrin, boss of luxury jewellers Cartier. Since 1991, wines have been made in a modern cellar under the eye of enologist Michel Rolland. There's supple, fruity Moulin Lagrezette, oak-aged Chevaliers and Ch. Lagrezette★. In some years, Cuvée Dame Honneur★★ and le Pigeonnier★★ are also produced, mainly from Auxerrois. Best years: 2001 00.

CH. LA LAGUNE ★★ *Haut-Médoc AC, 3ème Cru Classé, Haut-Médoc, Bordeaux, France* Wine from this Classed Growth, the closest in the MEDOC to Bordeaux city, has been consistently good. The best vintages are full of the charry, chestnut warmth of good oak and a deep, cherry-blackcurrant-plum sweetness which, after 10 years or so, becomes outstanding claret. Second wine: Moulin de la Lagune. Best years: 2001 00 98 96 **95 94 90 89 88 86 85 83 82**.

LAKE'S FOLLY *Hunter Valley, New South Wales, Australia* Charismatic founder Dr Max Lake sold out to Perth businessman Peter Fogarty in 2000. In best years, austere Chardonnay★★ ages slowly to a masterly antipodean yet Burgundy-like peak. The red is generally ★, but not consistent. Best years: (red) 2001 00 99 98 97 **96 93 91 89 85 83 81**; (white) 2001 00 99 98 **97 96 94 92 91**.

LALANDE-DE-POMEROL AC *Bordeaux, France* To the north of its more famous neighbour POMEROL, this AC produces full, ripe wines with an unmistakable mineral edge that are very attractive to drink at 3–4 years old, but age reasonably well too. Even though they lack the concentration of top Pomerols, the wines are not particularly cheap. Best producers: Annereaux★, Belles-Graves, Bertineau St-Vincent★, Borderie Mondésir★, Clos de l'Église, la Croix-St-André★, les Cruzelles, la Fleur de Boüard★★, Garraud★, Grand Ormeau★, Haut-Chaigneau, Haut-Surget, les Hauts Conseillants, Perron-La-Fleur, Sergant, la Sergue★, Tournefeuille, Viaud. Best years: 2001 00 **99 98 96 95 94 90 89**.

LAMBRUSCO *Emilia-Romagna, Italy* Lambrusco is the name of a black grape variety, grown in 3 DOC zones on the plains of Emilia, and 1 around Mantova in LOMBARDY, but it is the screwcap bottles of non-DOC Lambrusco that have made the name famous, even though some of them may contain no wine from the Lambrusco grape at all. Originally a dry or semi-sweet fizzy red wine, whose high acidity partnered the rich local food, good dry Lambrusco (especially Lambrusco di Sorbara and Grasparossa di Castelvetro) is worth trying. Best producers: Barbieri, Barbolini, F Bellei★, Casali, Cavicchioli★, Chiarli, Vittorio Graziano★, Oreste Lini, Stefano Spezia, Venturini Baldini.

LAMOREAUX LANDING *Finger Lakes AVA, New York State, USA* One of the most important wineries in FINGER LAKES. Its Chardonnay Reserve★ is a consistent medal winner, and the Pinot Noir★ is arguably the region's best. Merlot★ and Cabernet Franc★ are also attractive, as are Riesling★ and good, quaffable fizz. Best years: 2001 **00 99 98**.

LANDMARK *Sonoma County, California, USA* This producer concentrates on Chardonnay and Pinot Noir. Chardonnays include Overlook★★ and the oakier Damaris Reserve★★ and Lorenzo★★. Pinot Noirs – from Kastania Vineyard★★ in the SONOMA COAST AVA and Grand Detour★★ from Sonoma Mountain AVA – are beautifully focused.

LANGHE DOC *Piedmont, Italy* Important DOC covering wines from the
Langhe hills around Alba. The range of varietals such as Chardonnay,
Barbera and Nebbiolo embrace many former vino da tavola blends of
the highest order. Best producers: (reds) ALTARE★★, Boglietti (Buio★★),
Bongiovanni (Falletto★★), CERETTO★★, CHIARLO★, Cigliuti★★, CLERICO★★,
Aldo CONTERNO★★, Conterno-Fantino (Monprà★★), Luigi Einaudi★,
GAJA★★★, A Ghisolfi★★, Marchesi di Gresy (Virtus★★), F Nada
(Seifile★★), Parusso (Bricco Rovella★★), Rocche dei Manzoni (Quatr
Nas★), Vajra★, Gianni Voerzio (Serrapiu★★), Roberto VOERZIO★★. Best
years: (reds) (2001) 00 99 **98 97 96 95 93 90**.

CH. LANGOA-BARTON ★★ *St-Julien AC, 3ème Cru Classé, Haut-Médoc,
Bordeaux, France* Owned by the Barton family since 1821, Langoa-
Barton is usually lighter in style than its ST-JULIEN stablemate LEOVILLE-
BARTON, but it is still extremely impressive and reasonably priced. Drink
after 7 or 8 years, although it may keep for 15. Second wine: Réserve
de Léoville-Barton (a blend from the young vines of both Barton
properties). Best years: 2001 00 99 98 96 **95 90 89 88 86 85 83 82**.

LANGUEDOC-ROUSSILLON *Midi, France* This vast area of southern
France, running from Nîmes to the Spanish border and covering the
départements of the GARD, HERAULT, Aude and Pyrénées-Orientales, is still a
source of undistinguished cheap wine, but is also one of France's most
exciting wine regions. The transformation is the result of better grape
varieties, temperature-controlled vinification and ambitious producers, from
the heights of MAS DE DAUMAS GASSAC to very good local co-ops. The best
wines are the reds, particularly those from CORBIERES, FAUGERES, MINERVOIS
and PIC ST-LOUP, and some new-wave Cabernets, Merlots and Syrahs, as well
as the more traditional *vins doux naturels*, such as BANYULS, MAURY and MUSCAT
DE RIVESALTES; but we are now seeing exciting whites as well, particularly as
new plantings of Chardonnay, Marsanne, Roussanne, Viognier and
Sauvignon Blanc mature. See also Bouches-du-Rhône, Collioure, Costières
de Nîmes, Coteaux du Languedoc, Côtes du Roussillon, Côtes du Roussillon-
Villages, Côtes de Thongue, Fitou, Muscat de Frontignan, Muscat de
Mireval, Oc, Rivesaltes, Roussillon, St-Chinian.

LANSON *Champagne AC, Champagne, France* Owners Marne &
Champagne are the dominant force in own-label cheap Champagne,
producing 20 million bottles each year under numerous labels.
Fortunately they seem determined to maintain Lanson as their quality
flagship. Non-vintage Black Label ★ is reliable stuff and, like the rosé ★
and vintage ★★ wines, especially de luxe Noble Cuvée ★★, improves
greatly with aging. Best years: 1996 95 **93 90 89 88 85 83 82**.

MICHEL LAROCHE *Chablis AC, Burgundy, France* Dynamic CHABLIS
producer, with good St Martin Vieilles Vignes★ and impressive Grand
Cru Les Clos★★★. Has now branched out with effective LANGUEDOC
operation, Dom. La Chevalière★. Best years: (Chablis) (2002) 00 **99 96**.

CH. LASCOMBES *Margaux AC, 2ème Cru Classé, Haut-Médoc, Bordeaux,
France* One of the great underachievers in MARGAUX, with little worth
drinking in the 1980s and 90s. New American ownership and
investment might make the difference – at least the 2000 is the best in
many years. Best years: 2001 00 96 **95 90 89**.

CH. DE LASTOURS *Corbières AC, Languedoc, France* Large CORBIERES
estate, with some exciting wines. The top white is Blanc de Blancs, but
the best wines are the reds – particularly concentrated old Grenache-

Carignan Ch. de Lastours★, fruity Cuvée Simone Descamps★ and oaky la Grande Rompue. Best years: (reds) 2001 00 **99 98 96 95 94**.

CH. LATOUR ★★★ *Pauillac AC, 1er Cru Classé, Haut-Médoc, Bordeaux, France* Latour's reputation is based on powerful, long-lasting classic wines. Throughout the 1950s, 60s and 70s the property stood for consistency and refusal to compromise in the face of financial pressure. Strangely, in the early 80s there was an attempt to make lighter, more fashionable wines, with mixed results. The late 80s saw a return to classic Latour, much to my relief. Its reputation for making fine wine in less successful vintages is well deserved. After 30 years in British hands, it returned to French ownership in 1993. Second wine: les Forts de Latour. Best years: 2001 00 99 98 97 96 95 **94 93 90 89 88 86**.

LOUIS LATOUR *Beaune, Burgundy, France* Merchant almost as well known for his COTEAUX DE L'ARDECHE Chardonnays as for his Burgundies. Latour's white Burgundies are much better than the reds, although the red CORTON-GRANCEY ★★ can be very good. Latour's oaky CORTON-CHARLEMAGNE ★★, from his own vineyard, is his top wine, but there is also good CHEVALIER-MONTRACHET ★★, BATARD-MONTRACHET ★★ and le MONTRACHET ★★. Even so, as these are the greatest white vineyards in Burgundy, there really should be more top performances. Best years: (top whites) (2002) 01 00 99 **97 96 95 92**.

CH. LATOUR-MARTILLAC *Pessac-Léognan AC, Cru Classé de Graves, Bordeaux, France* A GRAVES Classed Growth that for many years positively cultivated an old-fashioned image but which is now a property to watch. Good value as well. The vineyard is strictly organic, and has many ancient vines. In the past, the reds★ were deep, dark and well structured but they lacked charm. Things improved considerably in the 90s. The whites★ are thoroughly modern and of good quality. Best years: (reds) 2001 00 98 96 **95 90 88 86 85 83**; (whites) 2001 00 **99 98 96 95 94 93 90 89 88**.

CH. LATOUR-À-POMEROL ★★ *Pomerol AC, Bordeaux, France* Directed by Christian MOUEIX of PETRUS fame, this property makes luscious wines with loads of gorgeous fruit and enough tannin to age well. Best years: 2001 00 99 98 96 **95 94 90 89 88 85 83 82**.

LATRICIÈRES-CHAMBERTIN AC See Chambertin AC.

LAUREL GLEN *Sonoma Mountain AVA, California, USA* Owner/wine-maker Patrick Campbell makes only Cabernet★★ at his mountaintop winery. This is rich wine with deep fruit flavours, aging after 6–10 years to a perfumed, complex BORDEAUX style. Counterpoint is a label for wine that does not make it into the top-level Cabernet. Terra Rosa is made from bought-in wine and bargain-label Reds has been made from wines from Chile and Argentina. Best years: (2001) 99 98 97 96 **95 94 93 91 90**.

LAURENT-PERRIER *Champagne AC, Champagne, France* Large, family-owned CHAMPAGNE house, offering flavour and quality at reasonable prices. Non-vintage★ is a bit lean and dry, but the vintage★★ is delicious, and the top wine, Cuvée Grand Siècle★★★, is among the finest Champagnes of all. Good rosé, as non-vintage★ and vintage Grand Siècle Alexandra★★★. Best years: (1996) 95 **93 90 88 85 82**.

L'AVENIR *Stellenbosch WO, South Africa* Ten years on, owner and former sugar broker Marc Wiehe and winemaker and former pharmacist François Naudé continue to have fun and turn out increasingly stylish wines. Pinotage★ and Chenin Blanc★ are Naudé's passion, but Cabernet★ and Chardonnay★ are also elegant and well made. Best years: (Pinotage) **2001 00 99 98 97 96 95**.

CH. LAVILLE-HAUT-BRION★★★ *Pessac-Léognan AC, Cru Classé de Graves, Bordeaux, France* The white wine of la MISSION-HAUT-BRION, one of the finest white PESSAC-LEOGNANs, with a price tag to match. Fermented in barrel, it needs 10 years or more to reach its savoury but luscious peak. Best years: 2001 00 99 98 97 96 **95 94 93 90 89 85**.

DOMAINE CONSTANTIN LAZARIDI *Drama, Greece* At this state-of-the-art, Bordeaux-inspired winery, winemaker Vasilis Tsaktsarlis makes good use of indigenous and international varieties. Wines range from the fresh gooseberry Amethystos white★ (Sauvignon, Semillon and Assyrtiko) to a fascinatingly intense experimental Viognier★ with a stunning, oily, peach kernel finish, tasty Château Julia Chardonnay★ and the fine Amethystos Cava★, an oak-aged Cabernet Sauvignon from very low yields.

LAZIO *Italy* Region best known for FRASCATI, Rome's white glugger. There are also various bland whites from Trebbiano and Malvasia, such as EST! EST!! EST!!! DI MONTEFIASCONE. The region's best are red table wines based on Cabernet and Merlot or Sangiovese from the likes of Castel de Paolis (Quattro Mori★★), Paolo di Mauro (Vigna del Vassallo★★), Cerveteri co-op (Tertium★), Falesco (Montiano★★) as well as wines from Casale del Giglio★, Pietra Pinta★ and Trappolini★.

LEASINGHAM *Clare Valley, South Australia* A wing of BRL HARDY, Leasingham is one of CLARE VALLEY's largest wineries, and is well respected. Bin 56 Cabernet-Malbec★ and Bin 61 Shiraz★, once bargains, are rising in price, while recently minted Classic Clare Shiraz★★ and Cabernet★ are high-alcohol, heavily oaked, overpriced blockbusters; Bastion Shiraz-Cabernet★ is better value. Riesling★★ can be among Clare's best; respectable Chardonnay★ and Semillon-Sauvignon. Sparkling Shiraz★★ is excellent.

L'ECOLE NO 41 *Columbia Valley AVA, Washington State, USA* The velvety and deeply flavoured Seven Hills Merlot★ from this winery can be good, as can the Cabernet Sauvignon★; a BORDEAUX blend called Apogee★★ from the Pepper Bridge vineyard in WALLA WALLA is more interesting. The best wines are the Semillons: a rich, woody, barrel-fermented★ version and exciting single-vineyard Fries Vineyard Semillon★★ and Seven Hills Vineyard Semillon★★. The Chardonnay★ is pleasant, if simple. Best years: (top reds) 2001 00 99 **97 96**.

LECONFIELD *Coonawarra, South Australia* Leconfield's popular appeal continues under winemaker Phillippa Treadwell. Cabernet★ is finely crafted, Merlot★ is delightful, and peppery Shiraz★★ is set to hit the heights in years to come. Best years: (Shiraz) 2000 99 98 **96 95 94 91**.

LEDA *Castilla y León, Spain* Small winery launched by a bunch of young, enthusiastic wine professionals, including the sons of Mariano García (of VEGA SICILIA and MAURO fame). It has taken the country by storm with its profound red Viñas Viejas★★ from very old Tempranillo vines in small plots throughout the Duero region. Best years: 2000 99 98.

LEEUWIN ESTATE *Margaret River, Western Australia* MARGARET RIVER's high flier, with pricy Chardonnay (Art Series★★★) that gets Burgundy lovers drooling into their bibs. Art Series Cabernet Sauvignon★★ (sometimes ★★★) has improved dramatically since 1998 and exhibits superb blackcurrant and cedar balance. Art Series Riesling★★★ is complex and fine, and look out for exceptional Shiraz★★ to come. New labels Prelude and Siblings give Leeuwin pleasure at lower prices. Best years: (Art Series Chardonnay) (2001) 00 99 **98 97** 96 95 94 92 90 87 86 85 83 82 81 80.

DOM. LEFLAIVE *Puligny-Montrachet AC, Côte de Beaune, Burgundy, France* Famous white Burgundy producer, with extensive holdings in some of the world's greatest vineyards (including, since 1990, le MONTRACHET). The price of the wines is correspondingly high, although 1986–92 produced many disappointing wines. A new winemaking team, led by Anne-Claude Leflaive and including the talented Pierre Morey, and the adoption of biodynamic growing soon turned things around. The top wines here – les Pucelles★★★, CHEVALIER-MONTRACHET★★★, BATARD-MONTRACHET★★★ and Bienvenues-Bâtard-Montrachet★★★ – are consistently delicious and can age for up to 20 years. Best years: (2002) 01 00 99 98 **97** 96 **95** 94.

OLIVIER LEFLAIVE FRÈRES *Puligny-Montrachet AC, Côte de Beaune, Burgundy, France* Former co-manager of Dom. LEFLAIVE, négociant Olivier Leflaive specializes in crisp, modern white wines from the COTE D'OR and the COTE CHALONNAISE, but standards are far from consistent. Lesser ACs – ST-ROMAIN, MONTAGNY★, ST-AUBIN★ and RULLY★ – offer good value, but the rich, oaky BATARD-MONTRACHET★★★ is the star turn of winemaker Franck Grux. Best years: (top whites) (2002) 01 00 99 **97** 96 **95**.

PETER LEHMANN *Barossa Valley, South Australia* BAROSSA doyen Lehmann buys grapes from many local growers and owns the superb Stonewell plot, source of his best Shiraz★★★. Splendidly juicy, old-fashioned, fruit-packed reds include Grenache★, Mentor★★ and Eight Songs Shiraz★★. Also lemony Semillon★★ and dry, long-lived Riesling★★ from Eden Valley. Best years: (Stonewell Shiraz) (2001) 99 98 96 **94 93 92** 91 90 89.

JOSEF LEITZ *Rüdesheim, Rheingau, Germany* The Leitz family makes some of the best dry and off-dry Rieslings in RUDESHEIM, especially from the Berg Rottland★★ and Berg Schlossberg★★ sites. Many wines offer excellent value for money. Best years: (Riesling Spätlese) (2002) 01 00 **99** 98 **97** 96 **94 93** 92 90 89.

LEIWEN *Mosel, Germany* This unspectacular village, once a mass producer of cheap wines, has become a hotbed of the MOSEL Riesling revolution. Nowhere else in the region is there such a concentration of dynamic estates and new ideas. Best producers: GRANS-FASSIAN★★, Carl Loewen★★, Josef Rosch★, St Urbans-Hof★, Heinz Schmitt★.

LEMBERGER See Blaufränkisch.

LENSWOOD VINEYARDS *Adelaide Hills, South Australia* Tim and Annie KNAPPSTEIN quickly established a fine reputation for Sauvignon Blanc★★, Chardonnay★★ and Pinot Noir★★. The Palatine★★ red blend was introduced in 1997 and is proving popular. Best years: (Pinot Noir) **2000** 99 98 97 96 95.

LENZ WINERY *Long Island AVA, New York State, USA* A leading LONG ISLAND winery going from strength to strength. The Merlot★ is elegant and powerful with soft, balanced tannins; dry Gewürztraminer★ is spicy and tasty. In good vintages the Pinot Noir★ has deep, ripe fruit. Chardonnay★ is mostly good and Cabernet Franc is appealing. Brut-style sparkling wine★ is hard to find, but worth the search. Best years: (Merlot) (2000) 99 98 **97** 96 95.

LEONETTI CELLAR *Washington State, USA* The Cabernet Sauvignon★★★ and Merlot★★ produced here are immense, with concentrated fruit and enough tannin to chew on but not be blasted by. The tiny production is usually sold out within hours. Sangiovese★ is also pretty interesting. Best years: (Cabernet) 2001 00 99 **98 97 96 95**.

CH. LÉOVILLE-BARTON★★★ *St-Julien AC, 2ème Cru Classé, Haut-Médoc, Bordeaux, France* Made by Anthony Barton, whose family has run this ST-JULIEN property since 1826, this fine claret is a traditionalist's delight. Dark, dry and tannic, and not overly oaked, the wines are often underestimated, but over 10–15 years they achieve a lean yet sensitively proportioned beauty rarely equalled in Bordeaux. Moreover, they are never overpriced. Second wine: Réserve de Léoville-Barton. Best years: 2001 00 99 98 96 95 **94 93 90 89 88 86 85 83 82**.

CH. LÉOVILLE-LAS-CASES★★★ *St-Julien AC, 2ème Cru Classé, Haut-Médoc, Bordeaux, France* The largest of the 3 Léoville properties, with the highest profile of all the ST-JULIENs, making wines of startlingly deep, dark concentration. I now find them so dense and thick in texture that it is difficult to identify them as St-Julien. Second wine: Clos du Marquis. The death of Michel Delon, the genius behind the property, in 2000, may have an effect on the wine style. We shall see. Best years: 2001 00 99 98 96 95 **94 93 90 89 88 86 85 83 82**.

CH. LÉOVILLE-POYFERRÉ★★ *St-Julien AC, 2ème Cru Classé, Haut-Médoc, Bordeaux, France* Since the 1986 vintage Didier Cuvelier has gradually increased the richness of the wine without wavering from its austere style. A string of excellent wines in the 90s frequently show more classic ST-JULIEN style than those of illustrious neighbour LEOVILLE-LAS-CASES. Second wine: Moulin-Riche. Best years: 2001 00 99 98 96 **95 94 90 89 86 85 83 82**.

DOM. LEROY *Vosne-Romanée AC, Côte de Nuits, Burgundy, France* In 1988 Lalou Bize-Leroy bought the former Dom. Noëllat in VOSNE-ROMANÉE, renaming it Domaine Leroy, which should not be confused with her négociant house, Maison LEROY, or the Dom. d'Auvenay, her personal estate. Here she produces fiendishly expensive, though fabulously concentrated, wines with biodynamic methods and almost ludicrously low yields from top vineyards such as CHAMBERTIN★★★, CLOS DE VOUGEOT★★★, MUSIGNY★★★, RICHEBOURG★★★ and ROMANEE-ST-VIVANT★★★. Best years: (top reds) (2002) (01) 00 99 98 97 96 95 90 **89**.

MAISON LEROY *Auxey-Duresses AC, Côte de Beaune, Burgundy, France* Négociant tucked away in the back streets of AUXEY-DURESSES, Leroy co-owns Dom. de la ROMANEE-CONTI, though is no longer involved in its management. However, its own cellar contains an extraordinary range of gems, often terrifyingly expensive, dating back to the beginning of the century. Best years: (reds) **1990 85 71 59 49 47 45**.

LIEBFRAUMILCH *Pfalz, Rheinhessen, Nahe and Rheingau, Germany* Sweetish and low in acidity, Liebfraumilch now has a down-market image and sales are plummeting. It can come from the PFALZ, RHEINHESSEN, NAHE or the RHEINGAU and must be made of 70% Riesling, Silvaner, Müller-Thurgau or Kerner grapes.

LIGURIA *Italy* Thin coastal strip of north-west Italy, running from the French border at Ventimiglia to the Tuscan border. Best-known wines are the Cinqueterre, Colli di Luna, Riviera Ligure di Ponente and Rossese di Dolceacqua DOCs.

LIMESTONE COAST *South Australia* Newly defined zone for the south-east of South Australia, taking in PADTHAWAY, COONAWARRA, Wrattonbully and exciting new regions along the coast at Mount Benson and Robe. Many of the new vineyards in this far-flung area have Coonawarra-like terra rossa soil with great potential for quality. Southcorp, Beringer Blass, YALUMBA, BRL HARDY and EVANS & TATE are all involved.

LIMOUX AC *Languedoc, France* The first AC in the LANGUEDOC to allow producers to use Chardonnay and Chenin Blanc, which must be vinified in oak. Production is dominated by the SIEUR D'ARQUES co-op. From 2003 there will be a red Limoux AC, made from a minimum 50% Merlot as well as Syrah, Grenache, Carignan and Malbec. Best producers: Dom. de l'Aigle★ (RODET), Dom. Begude★, SIEUR D'ARQUES.

LINDEMANS *Murray Darling, Victoria, Australia* Large, historic company that is a key part of Southcorp – but showing worrying signs of losing its way amid the corporate shenanigans bedevilling that conglomerate. Wines come from various regions. Best include HUNTER VALLEY Shiraz (Steven Vineyard★); classic Hunter Semillon★★; mineral COONAWARRA St George Cabernet★; spicy Limestone Ridge Shiraz-Cabernet★★; and Pyrus★★ – a BORDEAUX blend. Also an impressive, if oaky, PADTHAWAY Chardonnay★ and the mass-market Bin 65 Chardonnay. Best years: (Hunter Shiraz) (2001) 00 99 98 96 **94 91 87 86 83 82 80 79**; (Hunter Semillon) 2002 01 00 99 98 97 96 94 91 **90 89 87 86 80 79**; (Coonawarra reds) (2001) (00) 99 98 96 **94 91 90 88 86**.

JEAN LIONNET *Cornas, Rhône Valley, France* Jean Lionnet produces dense, tannic CORNAS★★ in a fairly modern style. The emphasis here is on new oak aging. Because the wines can seem closed when young, it's worth waiting for 6–7 years, especially for his Dom. de Rochepertuis★★. Lionnet also produces impressive COTES DU RHONE★ from his younger Cornas vines, and a little white ST-PERAY★. Best years: (Rochepertuis) 2001 00 99 98 **97 96 95 94 92 91 90 89 88 85**.

LIRAC AC *Rhône Valley, France* An excellent but underrated AC between TAVEL and CHATEAUNEUF-DU-PAPE. The reds have the dusty, spicy fruit of Châteauneuf without quite achieving the intensity of the best examples. They age well but are delicious young. The rosé is refreshing, with a lovely strawberry fruit, and the white can be good – drink them young before the perfume goes. Best producers: Amido★, Aquéria★, Bouchassy★, la Genestière, Joncier★, Lafond-Roc-Epine★, Maby, Mont-Redon★, la Mordorée★★, Pélaquié★, Roger Sabon★★, St-Roch★, Ségriès★, Tavel co-op★. Best years: 2001 00 **99 98 97 96 94 91 90**.

LISTRAC-MÉDOC AC *Haut-Médoc, Bordeaux, France* Set back from the Gironde and away from the best gravel ridges of the HAUT-MEDOC, Listrac wines can be good without ever being thrilling, and are marked by solid fruit, a slightly coarse tannin and an earthy flavour. More Merlot is now being used to soften the style. Best producers: Cap Léon Veyrin, CLARKE, Ducluzeau, Fonréaud, Fourcas-Dupré★, Fourcas-Hosten, Fourcas-Loubaney, Grand Listrac co-op, Mayne-Lalande★, Saransot-Dupré. Best years: 2001 00 **96 95 90 89 88 86 85**.

LOIRE VALLEY *France* The Loire river cuts right through the heart of France. The middle reaches are the home of world-famous SANCERRE and POUILLY-FUME. The region of TOURAINE makes good Sauvignon Blanc and Gamay, while at VOUVRAY and MONTLOUIS the Chenin Blanc makes some pretty good fizz and still whites, ranging from sweet to very dry. The Loire's best reds are made in SAUMUR-CHAMPIGNY, CHINON and BOURGUEIL, mainly from

173

Cabernet Franc, with ANJOU-VILLAGES improving fast. Anjou is famous for rosé, but the best wines are white, either sweet from the Layon Valley or very dry from SAVENNIERES. Near the mouth of the river around Nantes is MUSCADET. See also Anjou Blanc, Anjou Rouge, Bonnezeaux, Cabernet d'Anjou, Cheverny, Côte Roannaise, Coteaux de l'Aubance, Coteaux du Layon, Crémant de Loire, Gros Plant du Pays Nantais, Jardin de la France, Jasnières, Menetou-Salon, Pouilly-sur-Loire, Quarts de Chaume, Quincy, Reuilly, Rosé de Loire, St-Nicolas-de-Bourgueil, Saumur, Saumur Mousseux.

LOMBARDY *Italy* Lombardy is a larger consumer than producer. Many of the best grapes go to provide base wine for Italy's *spumante* industry. However, there are some interesting wines in OLTREPO PAVESE, VALTELLINA, LUGANA and high-quality sparkling and still wines in FRANCIACORTA.

LONG ISLAND AVA *New York State, USA* Long Island, which celebrated 30 years of winegrowing in 2003, encompasses 2 AVAs: the Hamptons, and North Fork, which has more maritime exposure. A long growing season means that concentration of fruit in the wines can be wonderful in a good year – but hurricanes have ruined some vintages. Best grapes are Chardonnay, Merlot and Cabernet Franc. Best producers: BEDELL★★, Castello di Borghese/Hargrave, GALLUCCIO/GRISTINA★, LENZ★, Palmer★, Pellegrini★, Pindar, Schneider★. Best years: (2001) 00 98 97 95.

DR LOOSEN *Bernkastel, Mosel, Germany* Loosen's estate has portions of some of the MOSEL's most famous vineyards: Treppchen and Prälat in ERDEN, Würzgarten in URZIG, Sonnenuhr in WEHLEN, Himmelreich in GRAACH and Lay in BERNKASTEL. Most of the wines achieve ★★, and Spätlese and Auslese from Wehlen, Ürzig and Erden frequently ★★★. One of Germany's foremost protagonists of organic methods, his simple Riesling is excellent, year in year out. A joint venture with CHATEAU STE MICHELLE in WASHINGTON is proving exciting. Best years: (2002) 01 99 98 97 96 95 **94 93 92** 90 89 88 85 76. See also J L Wolf.

LÓPEZ DE HEREDIA *Rioja DOC, Rioja, Spain* Family-owned RIOJA company, still aging wines in old oak casks. Younger red wines are called Viña Cubillo★, and mature wines Viña Tondonia★ and Viña Bosconia★. Good, oaky whites, especially Viña Gravonia★. Best years: (Viña Tondonia) 1995 **94 93** 91 87 86 85.

LOUPIAC AC *Bordeaux, France* A sweet wine area across the Garonne river from BARSAC. The wines are attractively sweet without being gooey. Drink young in general, though they can age. Best producers: Clos Jean★, Cros★, Loupiac-Gaudiet, Mémoires★, Noble★, Ricaud, les Roques. Best years: 2001 **99 98 97 96** 95 90 89 88 86.

CH. LA LOUVIÈRE *Pessac-Léognan AC, Bordeaux, France* The star of PESSAC-LEOGNAN's non-classified estates, its reputation almost entirely due to André Lurton. Well-structured reds★★ and fresh, Sauvignon-based whites★★ are excellent value. Best years: (reds) 2001 00 99 98 **96 95** 94 93 90 89 88 86 85; (whites) 2001 00 99 **98 96** 95 94 93 90 89 88.

LUGANA DOC *Lombardy, Italy* Dry white (occasionally sparkling) from the Trebbiano di Lugana grape. Well-structured wines from the better producers can develop excitingly over a few years. Best producers: Ca' dei Frati★★, Ottella★, Provenza★, Visconti★, Zenato★.

LUNA *Napa Valley, California, USA* Led by winemaker John Kongsgaard (ex-NEWTON), Luna has attracted attention with its ambitious SUPER-TUSCAN-style Sangiovese★, stylish Pinot Grigio★ and attractive Merlot★. Best years: (reds) (2001) 99 **98 97** 96.

LUNGAROTTI *Torgiano DOC, Umbria, Italy* Leading producer of TORGIANO. The Torgiano Riserva (Vigna Monticchio★★) is now DOCG. Also makes red San Giorgio★ (Cabernet-Sangiovese) and Chardonnay Palazzi★.

LUSSAC-ST-ÉMILION AC *Bordeaux, France* Much of the wine from this AC, which tastes like a lighter ST-EMILION, is made by the first-rate local co-op and should be drunk within 4 years of the vintage; certain properties are worth seeking out. Best producers: Barbe-Blanche★, Bel-Air, Bellevue, Courlat, la Grenière, Lyonnat★, Mayne Blanc, des Rochers★, Vieux-Ch.-Chambeau. Best years: 2001 00 **98 96 95 90 89**.

EMILIO LUSTAU *Jerez y Manzanilla DO, Andalucía, Spain* Specializes in supplying 'own-label' wines to supermarkets. Quality is generally good, and there are some real stars at the top, especially the Almacenista range★★: very individual sherries from small, private producers.

CH. LYNCH-BAGES *Pauillac AC, 5ème Cru Classé, Haut-Médoc, Bordeaux, France* I am a great fan of Lynch-Bages red★★★ – with its almost succulent richness, its gentle texture and its starburst of flavours, all butter, blackcurrants and mint, and it is now one of PAUILLAC's most popular wines. Because of its Fifth Growth status, it was inclined to be underpriced; I couldn't say that now, but it's still worth the money. It is impressive at 5 years, beautiful at 10 and irresistible at 20. Second wine: Haut-Bages-Avérous. White wine: Blanc de Lynch-Bages★. Best years: (reds) 2001 00 99 98 96 **95 94 90 89 88 86 85 83 82**.

MÂCON AC *Mâconnais, Burgundy, France* The basic Mâconnais AC, but most whites in the region are labelled under the superior MACON-VILLAGES AC. The wines are rarely exciting. Chardonnay-based Mâcon Blanc, especially, is a rather expensive basic quaffer. Drink young. Mâcon Supérieur has a slightly higher minimum alcohol level. Best producers: Bertillonnes, Bruyère, DUBOEUF, LAFON★. Best years: (2002) **01** 00.

MÂCON-VILLAGES AC *Mâconnais, Burgundy, France* Mâcon-Villages should be an enjoyable, fruity, fresh wine for everyday drinking, but because it is made from Chardonnay, the wines are often overpriced. The name can be used by 43 villages, which may also append their own name, as in Mâcon-Lugny. Co-ops dominate production. Best villages: Chaintré, Chardonnay, Charnay, Clessé, Davayé, Igé, Lugny, Prissé, la Roche Vineuse, St-Gengoux-de-Scissé, Uchizy, Viré. Best producers: D & M Barraud★★, A Bonhomme★★, Deux Roches★, E Gillet★, la Greffière★★, LAFON★, J-J Litaud★, Jean Manciat★, O Merlin★★, Rijckaert★, Roally★, Robert-Denogent★★, Saumaize-Michelin★, la Soufrandière★, J Thévenet★★, Valette★★, VERGET★★, J-J Vincent★. Best years: (2002) 01 **00** 99. See also Viré-Clessé.

MACULAN *Breganze DOC, Veneto, Italy* Fausto Maculan makes an impressive range under the Breganze DOC, led by Cabernet-Merlot blend Fratta★★ and Cabernet Palazzotto★, along with excellent reds★★ and whites★★ from the Ferrata vineyards, but his most impressive wines are sweet Torcolato★★ and outstanding Acininobili★★★, made mainly from botrytized Vespaiolo grapes.

MADEIRA DOC *Madeira, Portugal* The subtropical holiday island of Madeira seems an unlikely place to find a serious wine. However, Madeiras are very serious indeed and the best can survive to a great age. Internationally famous by the 17th century, modern Madeira was shaped by the phylloxera epidemic 100 years ago, which wiped out the vineyards. Replantation was with hybrid and non-vinifera vines greatly inferior to the 'noble' and traditional Malvasia (or Malmsey), Boal (or Bual), Verdelho and Sercial varieties. There are incentives to replant with noble grapes, but progress is slow (having now crept up to 15% of total plantings). The typically burnt, tangy taste of inexpensive Madeira comes from the process of heating in huge vats. The better wines are aged naturally in the subtropical warmth. All the wines are fortified early on and may be sweetened with fortified grape juice before bottling. Basic 3-year-old Madeira is made mainly from Tinta Negra Mole, whereas higher-quality 5-year-old (Reserva), 10-year-old (Reserva Velha), 15-year-old (Extra Reserva) and vintage wines (from a single year, aged in cask for at least 20 years) tend to be made from 1 of the 4 'noble' grapes. Best producers: Barbeito, Barros e Souza, H M Borges, HENRIQUES & HENRIQUES, Vinhos Justino Henriques, MADEIRA WINE COMPANY, Pereira d'Oliveira.

MADEIRA WINE COMPANY *Madeira DOC, Madeira, Portugal* This company ships more than half of all Madeira exported in bottle. Among the brand names are Blandy's, Cossart Gordon, Leacock and Miles. Now controlled by the Symington family from the mainland. Big improvements are taking place in 5-, 10- and 15-year-old wines.

MADIRAN AC *South-West France* In the gentle hills of Vic-Bilh, north of Pau, there has been a steady revival of the Madiran AC. Several of the best producers are now using new oak and micro-oxygenation, and this certainly helps to soften the rather aggressive wine, based on the tannic Tannat grape. Best producers: Aydie★★, Barréjat★, Berthoumieu★, Bouscassé★★, Capmartin★, CHAPELLE LENCLOS★★, du Crampilh★, Caves de Crouseilles, Laffitte-Teston★, MONTUS★★, Mouréou★,

Producteurs PLAIMONT. Best years: 2001 00 98 **97 96 95 94 90 89**.

CH. MAGDELAINE★★ *St-Émilion Grand Cru AC, 1er Grand Cru Classé, Bordeaux, France* Owned by the quality-conscious company of MOUEIX, these are dark, rich, aggressive wines, yet with a load of luscious fruit and oaky spice. In lighter years the wine has a gushing, easy, tender fruit and can be enjoyed at 5–10 years. Best years: 2001 00 99 98 96 95 **90 89 88 85 82 75**.

MAIPO, VALLE DEL *Valle Central, Chile* Birthplace of the Chilean wine industry and increasingly encroached upon by Chile's capital, Santiago. Cabernet is king and many of Chile's premium-priced reds come from here. Good Chardonnay is produced from vineyards close to the Andes. Best producers: ALMAVIVA★★, CARMEN★, Clos Quebrada de Macul★★, CONCHA Y TORO★, El Principal★, Haras de Pirque★, SANTA CAROLINA, SANTA INES/DE MARTINO★, SANTA RITA★, TARAPACA.

MÁLAGA DO *Andalucía, Spain* Málaga is a curious blend of sweet wine, alcohol and juices (some boiled up and concentrated, some fortified, some made from dried grapes) and production is dwindling. The label generally states colour and sweetness. The best are intensely nutty, raisiny and caramelly. A 'sister' appellation, Sierras de Málaga, was created in 2001 to include wineries outside the city limits of Málaga. Best producers: Gomara★, López Hermanos★★, Telmo RODRIGUEZ★★.

CH. MALARTIC-LAGRAVIÈRE★ *Pessac-Léognan AC, Cru Classé de Graves, Bordeaux, France* A change of ownership in 1997 and massive investment in the vineyard and cellars has seen a steady improvement here since the 1998 vintage. The tiny amount of white★ is made from 100% Sauvignon Blanc and usually softens after 3–4 years into a lovely nutty wine. Best years: (reds) 2001 00 99 98 **97 96 90 89**; (whites) 2001 00 99 **98 96 95 94**.

MALBEC A red grape, rich in tannin and flavour, from South-West France. A major ingredient in CAHORS wines, it is also known as Côt or Auxerrois. At its best in Argentina and Chile, where it produces lush-textured, ripe, perfumed, damsony reds. In CALIFORNIA, Australia and New Zealand it sometimes appears in BORDEAUX-style blends. In South Africa it is used both in blends and for varietal wines.

CH. MALESCOT ST-EXUPÉRY★ *Margaux AC, 3ème Cru Classé, Haut-Médoc, Bordeaux, France* Once one of the most scented, exotic reds in Bordeaux, a model of perfumed MARGAUX. In the 1980s Malescot lost its reputation as the wine became pale, dilute and uninspired, but since 1995 it has begun to rediscover that cassis and violet perfume and return to its former glory. Best years: 2001 00 99 98 96 **95 90**.

MALVASIA This grape is widely planted in Italy and is found there in many guises, both white and red. In Fruili, it is known as the Malvasia Istriana and produces light, fragrant wines of great charm, while in TUSCANY, UMBRIA and the rest of central Italy it is used to improve the blend for wines like ORVIETO and FRASCATI. On the islands, Malvasia is used in the production of rich, dry or sweet wines in Bosa and Cagliari (in SARDINIA) and in Lipari off the coast of SICILY to make really tasty, apricotty sweet wines. As a black grape, Malvasia Nera is blended with Negroamaro in southern PUGLIA and with Sangiovese in CHIANTI. The name is derived from Monemvasia, the port in Greece's Peloponnese from which it is said to have been shipped in medieval times. Variants of Malvasia also grow in Spain and mainland Portugal. On the island of MADEIRA it produces sweet, varietal fortified wine, usually known by its English name: Malmsey.

LA MANCHA DO *Castilla-La Mancha, Spain* Spain's vast central plateau is Europe's biggest delimited wine area. Since 1995, DO regulations have allowed for irrigation and the planting of new grape varieties, including Viura, Chardonnay, Cabernet Sauvignon, Merlot and Syrah. Whites are never exciting but nowadays are often fresh and attractive. Reds can be light and fruity, or richer – and there is still some rough, old-style wine. Best producers: Ayuso, Vinícola de Castilla (Castillo de Alhambra, Señorío de Guadianeja★), la Magdalena co-op, Nuestra Señora de la Cabeza co-op (Casa Gualda), Parra Jiménez★, Rodriguez & Berger (Santa Elena), Torres Filoso (Arboles de Castillejo★), Casa de la Viña.

DOM. ALBERT MANN *Alsace AC, Alsace, France* Powerful, flavoursome and ageworthy wines from a range of Grand Cru vineyards, including intense, mineral Rieslings from Furstentum★★ and Rosenberg★★ and rich Furstentum Gewurztraminer★★. An impressive range of Pinot Gris culminates in astonishingly concentrated Sélection de Grains Nobles from Furstentum★★★. Best years: (Sélection de Grains Nobles Gewurztraminer) 1998 97 94 **89**.

MARANGES AC *Côte de Beaune, Burgundy, France* AC in the southern COTE DE BEAUNE. Slightly tough red wines of medium depth, sometimes sold as COTE DE BEAUNE-VILLAGES. Less than 5% of production is white. Best producers: B Bachelet★, M Charleux★, Contat-Grangé★, DROUHIN, GIRARDIN★. Best years: (reds) (2002) 01 99 **97 96 95**.

MARCASSIN *Sonoma County, California, USA* Helen Turley focuses on cool-climate Chardonnay and Pinot Noir. Incredible depth and restrained power are the hallmarks here. Tiny quantities of single-vineyard Chardonnays from Gauer Ranch Upper Barn, Hudson Vineyard, Lorenzo Vineyard and Marcassin Vineyard (the last two both SONOMA COAST) often rank ★★★. Best years: (2001) 00 99 98 **97 96 95**.

MARCHE *Italy* Adriatic region producing increasingly good white VERDICCHIO and reds from Montepulciano and Sangiovese led by ROSSO CONERO and ROSSO PICENO. Good wines from international varieties such as Cabernet, Chardonnay and Sauvignon Blanc and sold under the Marche IGT are becoming more common. Still others may add Merlot, Sangiovese or even Syrah to Montepulciano. The best include Boccadigabbia's Akronte★★ (Cabernet), Oasi degli Angeli's Kurni★★ (Montepulciano), Umani Ronchi's Pelago★★ (Montepulciano-Cabernet-Merlot), La Monacesca's Camerte★★ (Sangiovese-Merlot) and Le Terrazze's Chaos★★ (Montepulciano-Merlot-Syrah).

MARCILLAC AC *South-West France* Strong, dry red wines (and a little rosé), largely made from a local grape, Fer. The reds are rustic but full of fruit and should be drunk at 2–5 years old. Best producers: Michel Laurens, Marcillac-Vallon co-op, Jean-Luc Matha, Philippe Teulier.

MARGARET RIVER *Western Australia* Planted on the advice of agronomist John Gladstones from the late 1960s, this coastal region quickly established its name as a leading area for Cabernet, with marvellously deep, BORDEAUX-like structured reds. Now Chardonnay, concentrated and opulent, vies with Cabernet for top spot, but there is also fine grassy Semillon, often blended with citrus-zest Sauvignon. Neglected Shiraz is attracting support. Best producers: Amberley Estate★, Brookland Valley★, CAPE MENTELLE★★, CULLEN★★★, Devil's Lair★, EVANS & TATE★, Gralyn★, HOWARD PARK★★, LEEUWIN ESTATE★★, MOSS WOOD★★★, PIERRO★★, Suckfizzle★, VASSE FELIX★, Voyager Estate★, Xanadu★. Best years: (Cabernet-based reds) (2001) 00 99 98 96 **95 94 91 90**.

MARGAUX AC *Haut-Médoc, Bordeaux, France* AC centred on the village of Margaux but including Soussans and Cantenac, Labarde and Arsac. Gravel banks dotted through the vineyards mean that the wines are rarely heavy and should have a divine perfume when mature at 7–12 years. Best producers: (Classed Growths) BRANE-CANTENAC★★, Dauzac★, FERRIERE★★, Giscours★, ISSAN★, Kirwan★, LASCOMBES, MALESCOT ST-EXUPERY★★, MARGAUX★★★, PALMER★★, PRIEURE-LICHINE★, RAUZAN-SEGLA★★, Tertre★; (others) ANGLUDET★, Bel-Air Marquis d'Aligre★, la Gurgue★, LABEGORCE-ZEDE★, Monbrison★, SIRAN★. Best years: 2001 00 99 96 **95 90**.

CH. MARGAUX★★★ *Margaux AC, 1er Cru Classé, Haut-Médoc, Bordeaux, France* The greatest wine in the MEDOC. Has produced almost flawless wines since 1978, and inspired winemaker Paul Pontallier continues to produce the best from this great *terroir*. There is also some delicious white, Pavillon Blanc★★, made from Sauvignon Blanc, but it must be the most expensive BORDEAUX AC wine by a mile. Second wine: (red) Pavillon Rouge★★. Best years: (reds) 2001 00 99 98 96 95 94 **93** 90 **89 88 86 85 83 82**; (whites) 2001 00 99 98 **96 95 94 90**.

MARLBOROUGH *South Island, New Zealand* Marlborough has enjoyed such spectacular success as a quality wine region that it is difficult to imagine that the first vines were planted as recently as 1973. Its long, cool and relatively dry ripening season and free-draining stony soils are the major assets. Its snappy, aromatic Sauvignon Blanc first brought the region fame worldwide. Fine-flavoured Chardonnay, steely Riesling, elegant Champagne-method fizz and luscious botrytized wines are other successes. Pinot Noir is improving every year. Best producers: CELLIER LE BRUN, Clifford Bay Estate★, CLOUDY BAY★★, Forrest Estate★★, FROMM★★, GROVE MILL★, HUNTER'S★★, ISABEL★★, JACKSON ESTATE★, Lawson's Dry Hills★, MONTANA, Nautilus★, SAINT CLAIR, SERESIN★★, Stoneleigh, VAVASOUR★★, VILLA MARIA★★, WITHER HILLS★★. Best years: (Chardonnay) (2002) **01 00 99 98 97**; (Pinot Noir) (2002) **01 00 99 98 97**.

MARQUÉS DE CÁCERES *Rioja DOC, Rioja, Spain* Go-ahead RIOJA winery making crisp, aromatic, modern whites★ and rosés★, and fleshy, fruity reds (Reservas★) with the emphasis on aging in bottle, not barrel. There is a new luxury red, Gaudium★. Best years: (reds) 1999 **98 96 95 94 92 91 90 89 87 85 82 78**.

MARQUÉS DE GRIÑÓN *Rioja DOC, Rioja and Rueda DO, Castilla y León, Spain* From his own estate at Malpica, near Toledo, now with its own Dominio de Valdepusa DO, Carlos Falcó (the eponymous Marqués de Griñón) has expanded into the Duero and now into RIOJA, after selling a stake in his company to BERBERANA. Minty Dominio de Valdepusa Cabernet Sauvignon★★ and Durius red (blended from TORO and RIBERA DEL DUERO) have been joined by Petit Verdot★★, Syrah★★ and the top blend, Eméritus★★, from his own estate, 2 Marqués de Griñón red Riojas (a lightly oaked young wine★ and a Reserva★), and white non-DO Durius★. Best years: (Eméritus) 1998 **97**.

MARQUÉS DE MURRIETA *Rioja DOC, Rioja, Spain* The RIOJA bodega that most faithfully preserves the traditional style of long aging. Ultra-conservative, yet sporting glistening new fermentation vats and a Californian bottling line. The splendidly ornate Castillo de Ygay★★ label now includes wines other than the Gran Reserva. A more modern-styled, up-market cuvée, Dalmau★★, was introduced in 1999. Whites are dauntingly oaky, reds packed with savoury mulberry fruit. Best years: (reds) 1999 **96 95 94 92 91 89 87 85 68 64**.

MARQUÉS DE RISCAL *Rioja DOC, País Vasco and Rueda DO, Castilla y León, Spain* A producer which has restored its reputation for classic pungent RIOJA reds (Reserva★). The expensive, Cabernet-based Barón de Chirel★★ cuvée is made only in selected years. Increasingly aromatic RUEDA whites★. Cellar problems during the 1990s look as though they have now been corrected. Best years: (Barón de Chirel) **1996 95 94**.

MARSALA DOC *Sicily, Italy* Fortified wines, once as esteemed as sherry or Madeira. A taste of an old Vergine (unsweetened) Marsala, fine and complex, will show why. Today most is sweetened. Purists say this mars its delicate nuances, but DOC regulations allow for sweetening Fine and Superiore versions. Best producers: DE BARTOLI★★, Florio (Baglio Florio★, Terre Arse★), Pellegrino (Soleras★, Vintage★).

MARSANNAY AC *Côte de Nuits, Burgundy, France* Village almost in Dijon, best known for its rosé, pleasant but quite austere and dry. But the reds are much better, frequently proving to be one of Burgundy's most fragrant wines. There is a little white. Best producers: R Bouvier★, P Charlopin★★, B CLAIR★★, Collotte★, Fougeray de Beauclair★, Geantet-Pansiot★★, JADOT, D MORTET★★, J & J-L Trapet★. Best years: (reds) (2002) 01 **00 99 97 96**.

MARSANNE Undervalued grape yielding rich, nutty wines in the northern Rhône (HERMITAGE, CROZES-HERMITAGE, ST-JOSEPH and ST-PERAY), often with the more lively Roussanne. Also used in PIC ST-LOUP and other Languedoc wines, and performs well in Australia at MITCHELTON and TAHBILK★★. As Ermitage, it produces some good wines in Swiss VALAIS.

MARTINBOROUGH *North Island, New Zealand* A cool, dry climate, free-draining soil and a passion for quality are this region's greatest assets. Mild autumn weather promotes intense flavours balanced by good acidity in all varieties: top Pinot Noir and complex Chardonnay, intense Cabernet, full Sauvignon Blanc and honeyed Riesling. Best producers: ATA RANGI★★, DRY RIVER★★★, MARTINBOROUGH VINEYARD★★, Nga Waka★, PALLISER ESTATE★★, Te Kairanga★. Best years: (Pinot Noir) 2001 **00 99 98 97 96**.

MARTINBOROUGH VINEYARD *Martinborough, North Island, New Zealand* Famous for Pinot Noir★★ but also makes impressive Chardonnay★★, spicy Riesling★, creamy Pinot Gris★ and luscious botrytized styles★★ when vintage conditions allow. Winemaker Claire Mulholland has brought added elegance to the often-blockbuster wines of this high-flying producer. Best years: (Pinot Noir) 2001 **00 99 98 97**.

MARTÍNEZ BUJANDA *Rioja DOC, País Vasco, Spain* Family-owned firm that makes some of the best modern RIOJA. Whites and rosés are young and crisp, reds★ are full of fruit *and* age well. The single vineyard Finca Valpiedra★★ is a major newcomer. The family has now purchased a large estate in La MANCHA, Finca Antigua. Best years: (reds) **1998 96 95 94 92 91 90 87 86 85**.

MARZEMINO This red grape of northern Italy's TRENTINO province makes deep-coloured, plummy and zesty reds that are best drunk within 3–5 years. Best producers: Battistotti★, La Cadalora★, Cavit★, Concilio Vini★, Isera co-op★, Letrari★, Mezzacorona, Eugenio Rosi★, Simoncelli★, Spagnolli★, De Tarczal★, Vallarom★, Vallis Agri★.

MAS BRUGUIÈRE *Pic St-Loup, Coteaux du Languedoc AC, Languedoc, France* One of the top domaines in this quality-oriented region. The basic red★ has rich, spicy Syrah character, while top-of-the-range La Grenadière★★ develops buckets of black fruit and spice after 3 years. Calcadiz is an easy-drinking red from young vines. The Roussanne white Les Mûriers★ is aromatic, fruity and refreshingly crisp.

MAS DE DAUMAS GASSAC *Vin de Pays de l'Hérault, Languedoc, France* Aimé Guibert proves that the HERAULT, normally associated with cheap table wine, is capable of producing great, ageworthy red wines. The tannic yet rich Cabernet Sauvignon-based red★★ and the fabulously scented white★★ (Viognier, Muscat, Chardonnay and Petit Manseng) are usually impressive, if expensive. Sweet Vin de Laurance★★ is a new triumph. Best years: (reds) 2001 00 99 98 **97 96 95 94 93 90**.

MAS JULLIEN *Coteaux du Languedoc AC, Languedoc, France* Olivier Jullien makes fine wines from traditional MIDI varieties. The red Mas Jullien at best can rate ★★★, while the États d'Ame★ is more forward and fruit driven. White★ is also good stuff. Also late-harvest Clairette Beudelle. Best years: (reds) 2001 00 99 98 **97 96 95 94 93 91**.

BARTOLO MASCARELLO *Barolo DOCG, Piedmont, Italy* One of the great old-fashioned producers of BAROLO★★★, yet the wines have an exquisite perfume and balance. The Dolcetto★ and Barbera★ can need a little time to soften. Best years: (Barolo) (2001) (00) (99) 98 97 96 95 **93 90** 89 88 86 85 82 78.

GIUSEPPE MASCARELLO *Barolo DOCG, Piedmont, Italy* The old house of Giuseppe Mascarello (now run by grandson Mauro) is renowned for dense, vibrant Dolcetto d'Alba (Bricco★★) and intense Barbera (Codana★★), but the pride of the house is BAROLO from the Monprivato★★★ vineyard. A little is now produced as a Riserva, Cà d'Morissio★★★, in top years. Small amounts of Barolo are also made from the Bricco, Santo Stefano di Perno and Villero vineyards. Best years: (Monprivato) (2001) (00) (99) 98 97 96 **95 93 91 90 89 88 85 82 78.**

MASI *Veneto, Italy* Family firm, one of the driving forces in VALPOLICELLA. Brolo di Campofiorin★ (effectively if not legally a *ripasso* Valpolicella) is worth looking out for, as is AMARONE (Mazzano★★ and Campolongo di Torbe★★). Valpolicella's Corvina grape is also used in red blends Toar★ and Osar★. The wines of Serègo Alighieri★★ are also produced by Masi. Best years (Amarone): (2001) (00) 97 **95 93 90 88 85.**

MASTROBERARDINO *Campania, Italy* This family firm has long flown the flag for CAMPANIA in southern Italy, though it has now been joined by others. Best known for red TAURASI★★ and white Greco di Tufo★ and Fiano di Avellino★. Best years: (Taurasi Radici) (2001) (99) 97 96 95 **93 90 89 88 85 83 82 81 79 68.**

MATANZAS CREEK *Sonoma Valley AVA, California, USA* Sauvignon Blanc★ is taken seriously here, and the results show in a complex, zesty wine; Chardonnay★★ is rich and toasty but not overblown. Merlot★★ has a high reputation, with its silky, mouthfilling richness. Limited-edition Journey Chardonnay★★ and Merlot★★ are opulent but pricy. In 2000 Jess Jackson (of KENDALL-JACKSON) gained control of the winery. Best years: (Chardonnay) (2001) 00 99 **98 97 96 95 94 91 90**; (Merlot) (2001) (00) 99 97 96 **95 94 93 91 90.**

MATUA VALLEY *Auckland, North Island, New Zealand* In 2001 Matua became part of the Beringer Blass empire; the change in ownership (but not in management) is unlikely to affect the adventurous range of wines, at least in the short term. Best are the sensuous, scented Ararimu Chardonnay★★, lush and strongly varietal Gewürztraminer★, a creamy oak-aged Sauvignon Blanc★, tangy MARLBOROUGH Sauvignon Blanc★ (Shingle Peak), fine Merlot★ and Ararimu Merlot-Cabernet Sauvignon★★. Best years: (Ararimu Merlot-Cabernet) 2000 **98 96 94.**

CH. MAUCAILLOU★ *Moulis AC, Cru Bourgeois, Haut-Médoc, Bordeaux, France* Maucaillou shows that you don't have to be a Classed Growth to make high-quality claret. Expertly made by the Dourthe family, it is soft but classically flavoured. It is accessible early on but ages well for 10–12 years. Best years: 2000 99 98 **96 95 90 89.**

MAULE, VALLE DEL *Valle Central, Chile* The most southerly sub-region of Valle CENTRAL, with wet winters and a large day/night temperature difference. White varieties (mostly Chardonnay and Sauvignon Blanc) outnumber red by nearly 2 to 1, but Merlot's success on clay soils looks set to shift the balance. Best producers: (whites) J Bouchon, Calina★ (KENDALL-JACKSON), Terra Noble.

MAURO *Castilla y León, Spain* After making a name for himself as VEGA SICILIA's winemaker for 30 years, Mariano García has propelled his family's estate to the forefront in Spain and abroad. Wines include

Crianza★★, Vendimia Seleccionada★★ and Terreus★★★. Best years 2000 **99 98 97 96 95 94**.

MAURY AC *Roussillon, France* A *vin doux naturel* made mainly from Grenache Noir. This strong, sweetish wine can be made in either a young, fresh style (vintage) or the locally revered old *rancio* style. Best producers: Mas Amiel★★, la Coume du Roy★, Maury co-op★, Maurydoré★, la Pleiade★.

MAXIMIN GRÜNHAUS *Grünhaus, Ruwer, Germany* The best estate in the Ruwer valley and one of Germany's greatest. Dr Carl von Schubert vinifies separately the wines of his 3 vineyards (Abtsberg, Bruderberg and Herrenberg), making chiefly dry and medium-dry wines of great subtlety. In good vintages the wines are easily ★★★ and the Auslese will age for decades; even QbA and Kabinett wines can age for many years. Best years: (2002) 01 00 97 96 95 **94 93 92** 90 **89 88 85 83** 79 76 75 71.

MAZIS-CHAMBERTIN AC See Chambertin AC.

MAZOYÈRES-CHAMBERTIN AC See Chambertin AC.

McLAREN VALE *South Australia* Sunny maritime region south of Adelaide, producing full-bodied wines from Chardonnay, Sauvignon Blanc, Shiraz, Grenache and Cabernet. About 50 small wineries, plus big boys HARDYS, Southcorp and Beringer Blass. Best producers: Cascabel, CHAPEL HILL★★, CLARENDON HILLS★★, Coriole★, D'ARENBERG★★, FOX CREEK★, Andrew Garrett, HARDYS★★, Kangarilla Road★, Maxwell★, Geoff MERRILL★, REYNELL★★, ROSEMOUNT★, Tatachilla★, WIRRA WIRRA★★.

McWILLIAM'S *Riverina, New South Wales, Australia* Large family winery, whose Hanwood brand is now a joint venture with California's E & J GALLO. Best wines are the Mount Pleasant range from the Lower HUNTER VALLEY: classic bottle-aged Semillons (Elizabeth★★, Lovedale★★), buttery Chardonnays★★ and special-vineyard Shirazes★ – Old Paddock & Old Hill, Maurice O'Shea (★★ in the best years) and Rosehill. Classy liqueur Muscat★★ from RIVERINA, and good table wines from their HILLTOPS Barwang★ vineyard. The Hanwood range (especially Chardonnay and tasty reds) proves that high-volume 'brands' can deliver good flavours at a fair price. Best years: (Elizabeth Semillon) 1997 95 94 93 **91 89 86 83 82 81 79**.

MÉDOC AC *Bordeaux, France* The Médoc peninsula north of Bordeaux on the left bank of the Gironde river produces a good fistful of the world's most famous reds. These are all situated in the HAUT-MEDOC, the southern, more gravelly half of the area. The Médoc AC, for reds only, covers the northern part. Here, in these flat clay vineyards, the Merlot grape dominates. The wines can be attractive in warm years: dry but juicy. Best at 3–5 years old. Best producers: la Cardonne, Escurac, les Grands Chênes★, Greysac, Lacombe-Noaillac, Lafon★, Loudenne, les Ormes-Sorbet★, Patache d'Aux, POTENSAC★★, Ramafort, Rollan-de-By★, la Tour-de-By★, la Tour-Haut-Caussan★, la Tour-St-Bonnet, Vieux-Robin. Best years: 2001 00 **96 95 90 89 88 86 85 82**.

MEERLUST *Stellenbosch WO, South Africa* Owner Hannes Myburgh maintains his late father's faith in the BORDEAUX varieties: his complex Rubicon★★ was one of the Cape's first Bordeaux blends. Italian cellarmaster Giorgio Dalla Cia's passion is refined Merlot★; there's also impressive Chardonnay★★ and ripe Pinot Noir★. Best years: (Rubicon) **1999 98 97 96 95 94 92 91**; (Chardonnay) **2000 99 98 97 96**.

ALPHONSE MELLOT *Sancerre AC, Loire Valley, France* Long-established grower and négociant. The négociant business includes decent wines from POUILLY-FUME and MENETOU-SALON, but the most interesting come from the family's own vineyards in SANCERRE, made with obsessive attention to detail. Dom. la Moussière★ is unoaked, with fresh, intense citrus flavours; the oaked Cuvée Edmond★★ needs a few years to mature to a fascinating rich flavour. Red Génération XIX★★ is outstanding. Best years: (Cuvée Edmond) 2001 00 **99 98 97 96 95 90 89**.

CHARLES MELTON *Barossa Valley, South Australia* One of the leading lights in the renaissance of hand-crafted Shiraz, Grenache and Mourvèdre in the BAROSSA. Fruity Grenache rosé Rose of Virginia★, RHONE blend Nine Popes★★, varietal Grenache★★ and smoky Shiraz★★ have all attained cult status. Cabernet Sauvignon is variable, but ★★ at best. Best years: (Nine Popes) (2001) 99 98 **96 95 94 93 92 91 90**.

MENDOCINO COUNTY *California, USA* The northernmost county of the North Coast AVA. It includes the cool-climate ANDERSON VALLEY AVA, excellent for sparkling wines and the occasional Pinot Noir; and the warmer Redwood Valley AVA, with good Zinfandel and Cabernet. Best producers: FETZER, Fife★, Goldeneye, HANDLEY★★, Husch, Lazy Creek★, McDowell Valley★, Navarro★★, PACIFIC ECHO★, Parducci, ROEDERER★★. Best years: (reds) (2001) (00) 99 **97 96 95 94 93 91 90**.

MENDOZA *Argentina* The most important wine region in Argentina, accounting for about 75% of fine wine production. Situated in the eastern foothills of the Andes, the region's bone-dry climate produces powerful, high-alcohol red wines. Just south of Mendoza city, Maipú and Luján de Cuyo are ideal for Malbec, Syrah and Cabernet Sauvignon. High-altitude sub-regions nearer the Andes, such as Tupungato, produce better whites, particularly Chardonnay. Best producers: Luigi BOSCA★, CATENA★★, DOMAINE VISTALBA★, Finca El Retiro★, Finca La Celia★, LA AGRICOLA★, Nieto Senetiner (Cadus★★), NORTON★, Salentein★, Terrazas de los Andes★★.

MENETOU-SALON AC *Loire Valley, France* Extremely attractive, chalky-clean Sauvignon whites and cherry-fresh Pinot Noir reds and rosés from west of SANCERRE. Best producers: Chatenoy★, Chavet★, J-P Gilbert★, H Pellé★, du Prieuré, J-M Roger★, J Teiller★, Tour St-Martin★.

MÉO-CAMUZET *Vosne-Romanée AC, Côte de Nuits, Burgundy, France* Super-quality estate, run by Jean-Nicolas Méo. New oak barrels and luscious, rich fruit combine in superb wines, which also age well. CLOS DE VOUGEOT★★★, RICHEBOURG★★★ and CORTON★★ are the grandest wines, along with the VOSNE-ROMANEE Premiers Crus, aux Brulées★★, Cros Parantoux★★★ and les Chaumes★★. Also fine NUITS-ST-GEORGES aux Boudots★★ and aux Murgers★★, and now also offering some less expensive négociant wines. Best years: (2002) 01 00 99 97 96 95 93 **90**.

MERCUREY AC *Côte Chalonnaise, Burgundy, France* Most important of the 4 main COTE CHALONNAISE villages. The red is usually pleasant and strawberry-flavoured, sometimes rustic, and can take some aging. There is not much white but I like its buttery, even spicy, taste. Best at 3–4 years old. Best producers: (reds) FAIVELEY★, E Juillot★, M Juillot★★, Lorenzon★★, F Raquillet★, RODET★, de Suremain★★, de Villaine★★; (whites) FAIVELEY (Clos Rochette★), Genot-Boulanger★, M Juillot★, O LEFLAIVE★, Ch. de Chamirey★/RODET. Best years: (reds) (2002) **99 97 96**.

MERLOT See pages 184–5.

GEOFF MERRILL *McLaren Vale, South Australia* High-profile winemaker with an instinctive feel for wine. There's a nicely bottle-aged Reserve Cabernet★ in a light, early-picked, slightly eccentric style, Reserve Shiraz★ and Chardonnay★ (Reserve★★). Also a moreish Grenache rosé under the Mount Hurtle label.

MERLOT

Red wine without tears. That's the reason Merlot has vaulted from being merely Bordeaux's red wine support act, well behind Cabernet Sauvignon in terms of class, to being the red wine drinker's darling, planted like fury all over the world. It is able to claim some seriousness and pedigree, but – crucially – can make wine of a fat, juicy character mercifully low in tannic bitterness, which can be glugged with gay abandon almost as soon as the juice has squirted from the press. Yet this doesn't mean that Merlot is the jelly baby of red wine grapes. Far from it.

WINE STYLES

Bordeaux Merlot The great wines of Pomerol and St-Émilion, on the Right Bank of the Dordogne, are largely based on Merlot and the best of these – for example, Château Pétrus, which is almost 100% Merlot – can mature for 20–30 years. In fact there is more Merlot than Cabernet Sauvignon planted throughout Bordeaux, and I doubt if there is a single red wine property that does not have some growing, because the variety ripens early, can cope with cool conditions and is able to bear a heavy crop of fruit. In a cool, damp area like Bordeaux, Cabernet Sauvignon cannot always ripen, so the soft, mellow character of Merlot is a fundamental component of the blend even in the best, Cabernet-dominated, Médoc estates, imparting a supple richness and approachability to the wines, even when young.

Other European Merlots The south of France has briskly adopted the variety, producing easy-drinking, fruit-driven wines, but in the hot Languedoc the grape often ripens too fast to express its full personality and can seem a little simple and even raw-edged. Italy has long used very high-crop Merlot to produce a simple, light quaffer in the north, particularly in the Veneto, though Friuli and Alto Adige make fuller styles and there are some very impressive Tuscan examples. The Italian-speaking Swiss canton of Ticino is often unjustly overlooked for its intensely fruity, oak-aged versions. Eastern Europe has the potential to provide fertile pastures for Merlot and so far the most convincing, albeit simple, styles have come from Hungary and Bulgaria, although the younger examples are almost invariably better than the old. Spain has developed good Merlot credentials since the mid-1990s.

New World Merlots Youth is also important in the New World, nowhere more so than in Chile. Chilean Merlot, mostly blended with Carmenère, has leapt to the front of the pack of New World examples with gorgeous garnet-red wines of unbelievable crunchy fruit richness that cry out to be drunk virtually in their infancy. California Merlots often have more serious pretensions, but the nature of the grape is such that its soft, juicy quality still shines through. The cooler conditions in Washington State have produced some impressive wines, and the east coast of the US has produced good examples from places such as Long Island. With some French input, South Africa is starting to get Merlot right, and in New Zealand, despite the cool, damp conditions, some gorgeous rich examples have been made. Only Australia seems to find Merlot problematic, but there are some fine exceptions from cooler areas, including some surprisingly good fizzes – red fizzes, that is!

184

BEST PRODUCERS

France

Bordeaux (St-Émilion) ANGELUS, AUSONE, BEAU-SEJOUR BECOT, Clos Fourtet, MAGDELAINE, la Mondotte, TERTRE-ROTEBOEUF, TROPLONG-MONDOT; (Pomerol) le BON PASTEUR, Certan-de-May, Clinet, la CONSEILLANTE, l'EGLISE-CLINET, l'EVANGILE, la FLEUR-PETRUS, GAZIN, LATOUR-A-POMEROL, PETIT-VILLAGE, PETRUS, le PIN, TROTANOY.

Other European Merlots

Italy (Friuli) Livio FELLUGA; (Tuscany) AMA, AVIGNONESI, CASTELGIOCONDO, Ghizzano, Le Macchiole, ORNELLAIA, Petrolo, San Giusto a Rentennano, Tua Rita; (Lazio) FALESCO.

Spain (Penedès) Can Ràfols dels Caus; (Somontano) ENATE.

Switzerland Gialdi (Sassi Grossi), Daniel Huber, Werner Stucky, Christian Zundel.

New World Merlots

USA (California) ARROWOOD, BERINGER, CHATEAU ST JEAN, DUCKHORN, FERRARI-CARANO, MATANZAS CREEK, MERRYVALE, NEWTON, Pahlmeyer, SHAFER, STERLING; (Washington) ANDREW WILL, CANOE RIDGE, LEONETTI; (New York) BEDELL, LENZ.

Australia BRAND'S, CLARENDON HILLS, Elderton, James Irvine, KATNOOK ESTATE, PARKER COONAWARRA ESTATE, PETALUMA, Tatachilla.

New Zealand Esk Valley, GOLDWATER, C J PASK, VILLA MARIA.

South Africa MORGENHOF, SAXENBURG (Private Collection), STEENBERG, THELEMA, VEENWOUDEN, VERGELEGEN.

Chile CARMEN, CASA LAPOSTOLLE (Cuvée Alexandre, Clos Apalta), CASABLANCA, CONO SUR (20 Barrels, Reserva), ERRAZURIZ, LA ROSA (La Palmeria), VALDIVIESO.

MERRYVALE *Napa Valley AVA, California, USA* A Chardonnay powerhouse (Reserve★★, Silhouette★★★, Starmont★★), but reds are not far behind, with BORDEAUX-blend Profile★★ and juicy Reserve Merlot★★. Best years: (Chardonnay) (2001) 00 99 **98 97 96 95**.

MEURSAULT AC *Côte de Beaune, Burgundy, France* The biggest and most popular white wine village in the CÔTE D'OR. There are no Grands Crus, but a whole cluster of Premiers Crus, of which Perrières, Charmes and Genevrières stand out. The general standard is better than in neighbouring Puligny. The golden wine is lovely to drink young but better aged for 5–8 years. Virtually no Meursault red is now made. Best producers: R Ampeau★★, M Bouzereau★★, Boyer-Martenot★★, Coche-Debord★★, COCHE-DURY★★★, DROUHIN★, A Ente★★★, J-P Fichet★★, V GIRARDIN★★, JADOT★★, P Javillier★★, François Jobard★★, Rémi Jobard★★, LAFON★★★, Matrot★★, Pierre Morey★★, G Roulot★★★. Best years: (2002) 01 00 99 **97** 96 **95 92 89**.

CH. MEYNEY★ *St-Estèphe AC, Cru Bourgeois, Haut-Médoc, Bordeaux, France* One of the most reliable ST-ESTÈPHES, producing broad-flavoured wine with dark, plummy fruit. Second wine: Prieur de Meyney. Best years: 2001 00 99 96 **95 94 90** 89 88.

PETER MICHAEL WINERY *Sonoma County, California, USA* British-born Sir Peter Michael caught the wine bug and turned a country retreat into an impressive winery known for its small-batch wines. Les Pavots★★ is the estate red BORDEAUX blend, and Mon Plaisir★★ and Cuvée Indigène★ are his top Chardonnays, both noted for their deep, layered flavours. Best years: (Les Pavots) 1999 97 **96 95 94 93 91 90**.

LOUIS MICHEL *Chablis AC, Burgundy, France* The prime exponent of unoaked CHABLIS. The top Crus – Montmains★★★, Montée de Tonnerre★★★ and les Clos★★★ – are wonderfully fresh, mineral and they age triumphantly. Best years: (top crus) (2002) 00 99 **97** 96 **95 90**.

MIDI *France* A loose geographical term, virtually synonymous with LANGUEDOC-ROUSSILLON, covering the vast, sunbaked area of southern France between the Pyrenees and the RHÔNE VALLEY.

MILLTON *Gisborne, North Island, New Zealand* Organic vineyard using biodynamic methods, whose top wines include the sophisticated Clos St Anne Chardonnay★★, botrytized Opou Vineyard Riesling★★ and complex barrel-fermented Chenin Blanc★. Chardonnays and Rieslings both age well. Best years: (whites) (2002) **00 98** 96.

MINER FAMILY VINEYARDS *Oakville AVA, California, USA* Dave Miner has 32ha (80 acres) planted on a ranch 305m (1000 feet) above the OAKVILLE valley floor. Highlights include yeasty, full-bodied Chardonnay★ (Oakville Ranch★★, Wild Yeast★★) as well as intense Merlot★★ and Cabernet Sauvignon★★ that demand a decade of aging. A stylish Viognier★★ from purchased fruit is also made.

MINERVOIS AC *Languedoc, France* Attractive, mostly red wines from north-east of Carcassonne, made mainly from Syrah, Carignan and Grenache. The local co-ops produce good, juicy, quaffing wine at reasonable prices, but the best wines are made by the estates: full of ripe, red fruit and pine-dust perfume, for drinking young. It can age, especially if a little new oak has been used. Since 1997, a village denomination, La Livinière, covering 4 communes, can be appended to the Minervois label. Best producers: (reds) Aires Hautes★★, CLOS CENTEILLES★★, Coupe-Roses★, Pierre Cros★, Fabas★, Gourgazaud★, la Grave, Maris★, Oupia★, Piccinini★, Pujol, Ste-Eulalie★, TOUR BOISÉE★, Vassière, Villerambert-Julien★, Violet★. Best years: 2001 **00 99 98** 96 95.

CH. LA MISSION-HAUT-BRION★★★ *Pessac-Léognan AC, Cru Classé de Graves, Bordeaux, France* Traditionally I have found la Mission's wines long on power but short on grace, but in the difficult years of the 1990s they showed consistency allied to challenging intensity and fragrance. Best years: 2001 00 99 98 96 95 **94 93 90 89 88 85**.

MISSION HILL *British Columbia, Canada* Spring 2001 saw the expansion of Mission Hill's winery, allowing it to process grapes from its extensive vineyard holdings in the OKANAGAN VALLEY. Kiwi winemaker John Simes has strengthened the winery's red wines of late: excellent Chardonnay★★, Pinot Blanc★ and Pinot Gris★ are joined by Merlot★, Cabernet Sauvignon, Shiraz★, including separate bottlings from 100% estate-grown grapes, and a red meritage blend, Oculus★★.

MITCHELL *Clare Valley, South Australia* Jane and Andrew Mitchell turn out some of CLARE VALLEY's most ageworthy Watervale Riesling★★ and a classy barrel-fermented Growers Semillon★. Growers Grenache★ is a huge unwooded and spirity lump of fruit, but if you're in the mood... Peppertree Shiraz★★ and Sevenhill Cabernet Sauvignon★ are plump, chocolaty and typical of the region.

MITCHELTON *Goulburn Valley, Central Victoria, Australia* VICTORIA's most consistently fine Riesling (Blackwood Park★★), but Rhône varieties are also specialities here, alone (Viognier★) or in blends (Airstrip Marsanne-Roussanne-Viognier). Print Label Shiraz★★ and the Crescent Shiraz-Mourvèdre-Grenache are increasingly deep and structured. Best years: (Print Label) 1998 96 **95 92 91 90**.

MITTELRHEIN *Germany* Small (525ha/1300-acre), northerly wine region. Almost 75% of the wine here is Riesling but, unlike other German regions, the Mittelrhein has been in decline over the last few decades. The vineyard sites are steep and difficult to work – although breathtaking. The best growers (like Toni JOST★★) cluster around Bacharach in the south and Boppard in the north, and produce wines of a striking mineral tang and dry, fruity intensity. Best years: (Riesling Spätlese) (2002) 01 99 98 **93 90**.

MOËT & CHANDON *Champagne AC, Champagne, France* Moët & Chandon dominates the CHAMPAGNE market (more than 25 million bottles a year), and has become a major producer of sparkling wine in CALIFORNIA, Argentina and Australia too. Non-vintage★ can be delightful – soft, creamy and a little spicy – and consistency is pretty good. The vintage★★ usually has considerable style, while the vintage rosé★★ can show a Pinot Noir floral fragrance depressingly rare in modern Champagne. Dom Pérignon★★★ is the de luxe cuvée. It can be one of the greatest Champagnes of all, but you've got to age it for a number of years or you're wasting your money. Best years: (1996) **95 93 92 90 88 86 85 82**.

MONBAZILLAC AC *South-West France* BERGERAC's leading sweet wine. Most is light, pleasant, but forgettable, from the efficient co-op. This style won't age, but a truly rich, late-harvested Monbazillac can last 10 years. Best producers: l'Ancienne Cure★, Bélingard (Blanche de Bosredon★), la Borderie★, Grande Maison★, Haut-Bernasse, Hébras, Theulet★, Tirecul-la-Gravière★★, Tour des Verdots★, Treuil-de-Nailhac★. Best years: 2001 99 **98 97 96 95 90**.

CH. MONBOUSQUET★★ *St-Émilion Grand Cru AC, Bordeaux, France* Gérard Perse, who also owns Ch. PAVIE, has transformed this struggling estate on the Dordogne plain into one of ST-EMILION's 'super-crus'. Rich, voluptuous and very expensive, the wine is drinkable from 3–4 years but will presumably age longer. There is also a tiny volume of white. Best years: 2001 00 99 98 **97 96 95 94**.

ROBERT MONDAVI *Napa Valley, California, USA* Robert Mondavi is a Californian institution, based in NAPA. Best known for the regular Cabernet Sauvignon★, open and fruity with the emphasis on early drinkability, and the Reserve Cabernet★★★, possessing enormous depth and power. A regular★ and a Reserve★ Pinot Noir are velvety smooth and supple wines with style, perfume and balance. For many years the Mondavi trademark wine was Fumé (Sauvignon Blanc) (Reserve Fumé★), but in recent years Chardonnay★ (Reserve★★) has become the winery leader, although, as with most of the wines, I'd like a little more personality to shine through. Mondavi also owns ARROWOOD in SONOMA, BYRON in SANTA BARBARA COUNTY, OPUS ONE in Napa in partnership with the Rothschilds, as well as the Mondavi Woodbridge winery, where inexpensive varietal wines are produced. The La Famiglia range, made in Napa, is based chiefly on Italian varietals. Mondavi is involved in SENA in Chile, and in Italy has associations with FRESCOBALDI (CASTELGIOCONDO), producing a mediocre SUPER-TUSCAN named Luce, and with ORNELLAIA. Best years: (Cabernet Sauvignon Reserve) (2001) (00) 99 98 97 96 95 94 **92 91 88 87 86 85 84**.

MONT TAUCH, LES PRODUCTEURS DU *Fitou, Languedoc-Roussillon, France* A big, quality-conscious co-op producing a large range of MIDI wines, from good gutsy FITOU★ and CORBIERES to rich MUSCAT DE RIVESALTES★ and light but gluggable Vin de Pays du Torgan. Top wine: Terroir de Tuchan★. Best years: (Terroir de Tuchan) 2001 00 **99 98 97**.

MONTAGNE-ST-ÉMILION AC *Bordeaux, France* A ST-EMILION satellite which can produce rather good red wines. The wines are normally ready to drink in 4 years but age quite well in their slightly earthy way. Best producers: Calon, Corbin, Croix Beauséjour★, Faizeau★, Laurets, Montaiguillon, Négrit, Roc-de-Calon, Rocher Corbin, Roudier, Vieux-Ch.-St-André. Best years: 2001 **00 98 96 95 90 89 88**.

MONTAGNY AC *Côte Chalonnaise, Burgundy, France* Wines from this Côte Chalonnaise village can be rather lean, but are greatly improved now that some producers are aging their wines for a few months in new oak. Generally best with 2–5 years' bottle age. Best producers: S Aladame★★, BOUCHARD PERE ET FILS★, BUXY co-op★, Davenay★, FAIVELEY, LATOUR★, O LEFLAIVE★, A Roy★, J Vachet★. Best years: (2002) 01 **00 99**.

MONTALCINO See Brunello di Montalcino DOCG.

MONTANA *Auckland, Gisborne, Hawkes Bay and Marlborough, New Zealand* Montana is owned by Allied Domecq. Since purchasing Corbans in 2001 the company has produced a staggering 50% of New Zealand's wine in addition to importing bulk wine and bottling it for the low price end of the market. Montana's MARLBOROUGH Sauvignon Blanc★ and GISBORNE Chardonnay are in a considerable way to thank for putting New Zealand on the international wine map. To show that it can be the best, the company established CHURCH ROAD★, a small (by Montana standards) winery in HAWKES BAY. Estate bottlings, particularly Ormond Estate Chardonnay★★, also bode well. Makes consistent Lindauer fizz and, with the help of the Champagne house DEUTZ, austere yet full-bodied Deutz Marlborough Cuvée NV Brut★. Montana is now one of the world's biggest producers of Pinot Noir, although they have yet to produce a wine of top quality. Corbans brands include the top-selling Stoneleigh Sauvignon Blanc★ and Riesling★ from Marlborough.

MONTECARLO DOC *Tuscany, Italy*   Both reds (Sangiovese with Syrah) and whites (Trebbiano with Sémillon and Pinot Grigio) are distinctive. Non-DOC wines can include Cabernet, Merlot, Pinot Bianco, Roussanne and Vermentino. Best producers: Buonamico★, Carmignani★, Montechiari★, Wandanna★. Best years: (reds) (2001) **00 99 98 97 96 95 93**.

MONTEFALCO DOC *Umbria, Italy*   Sangiovese-based Montefalco Rosso, often good, is outclassed by dry Sagrantino di Montefalco (now DOCG) and Sagrantino Passito, a glorious sweet red made from dried grapes. Best producers: (Sagrantino) Adanti★, Antonelli★, Caprai★★ (25 Anni★★★), Colpetrone★★. Best years: (Sagrantino) (2001) (00) 99 98 97 96 95 **93 90 88**.

MONTEPULCIANO   Grape, grown mostly in eastern Italy (unconnected with TUSCANY's Sangiovese-based wine VINO NOBILE DI MONTEPULCIANO). Can produce deep-coloured, fleshy, spicy wines with moderate tannin and acidity. Besides MONTEPULCIANO D'ABRUZZO, it is used in ROSSO CONERO and ROSSO PICENO in the MARCHE and also in UMBRIA, Molise and PUGLIA.

MONTEPULCIANO D'ABRUZZO DOC *Abruzzo, Italy*   The Montepulciano grape's most important manifestation. Quality varies from the insipid or rustic to the concentrated and characterful. Best producers: Cataldi Madonna★, Cornacchia★, Filomusi Guelfi★, Illuminati★, Marramiero★, Masciarelli★★, A & E Monti★, Montori★, Nicodemi★, Cantina Tollo★, Umani Ronchi★, Roxan★, La Valentina★, Valentini★★★, L Valori★, Ciccio Zaccagnini★. Best years: (2001) 00 **98 97 95 94 93 90**.

MONTEREY COUNTY *California, USA*   Large CENTRAL COAST county south of San Francisco Bay in the Salinas Valley. The most important AVAs are Arroyo Seco, Chalone, Carmel Valley and Santa Lucia Highlands. Best grapes are Chardonnay, Riesling and Pinot Blanc, with some good Cabernet Sauvignon, Merlot in Carmel Valley and Pinot Noir in the Santa Lucia Highlands in the cool middle of the county. Best producers: Bernardus★★, CHALONE★★, Estancia★, Heller★, Jekel★, Mer Soleil★★, Morgan★, TALBOTT★★, Testarossa★★. Best years: (reds) (2001) (00) 99 **97 96 95 94 91 90**.

MONTES *Curicó, Chile*   One of Chile's pioneering wineries in the modern era, notable for innovative development of top-quality vineyard land on the steep Apalta slopes of COLCHAGUA and the virgin country of Marchihue out towards the Pacific. Sauvignon Blanc★ and Chardonnay★ are good and fruit-led; all

the reds are more austere and need bottle age. Top-of-the-line Montes Alpha M★ is now beginning to shine, but the best wines are Montes Alpha Syrah★★ and an even better Syrah called Montes Folly★★.

MONTEVERTINE *Tuscany, Italy*   Based in the heart of CHIANTI CLASSICO, Montevertine is famous for its non-DOC wines, particularly Le Pergole Torte★★★. This was the first of the SUPER-TUSCANS made solely with Sangiovese, and it remains one of the best. A little Canaiolo is included in the excellent Il Sodaccio★★ and Montevertine Riserva★★. Best years: (Le Pergole Torte) (2001) (00) (99) 98 97 96 **95 93 90 88 85**.

MONTGRAS *Rapel, Chile*   Reds are, so far, well ahead of the whites at this superbly equipped new winery in COLCHAGUA. Reserva Merlot★ and Cabernet★ are oaky but with good plum and berry fruit. New plantings on Ninquén hill, with much lower yields, are now appearing, including Syrah and spicy Cabernet Sauvignon★.

MONTHELIE AC *Côte de Beaune, Burgundy, France* Attractive, mainly red wine village lying halfway along the COTE DE BEAUNE behind MEURSAULT and VOLNAY. The wines generally have a lovely cherry fruit and make pleasant drinking at a good price. Best producers: COCHE-DURY★, Darviot-Perrin★, P Garaudet★, R Jobard★, LAFON★★, Olivier LEFLAIVE★, Monthelie-Douhairet★, Potinet-Ampeau★, G Roulot★★, de Suremain★. Best years: (reds) (2002) 99 **98 97 96**; (whites) (2002) 01 **00 99**.

MONTILLA-MORILES DO *Andalucía, Spain* Sherry-style wines that are sold almost entirely as lower-priced sherry substitutes. However, the wines *can* be superb, particularly the top dry amontillado, oloroso and rich Pedro Ximénez styles. Best producers: Alvear (top labels★★), Aragón, Gracia Hermanos, Pérez Barquero★, Toro Albalá★★.

MONTLOUIS AC *Loire Valley, France* On the opposite bank of the Loire to the VOUVRAY AC, Montlouis wines are made from the same Chenin grape and in similar styles (dry, medium, sweet and Champagne-style fizz) but often a touch more rustic. Two-thirds of the production is Mousseux, a green, appley fizz which is best drunk young. Still wines need aging for 5–10 years, particularly the sweet (Moelleux) version. Best producers: L Chatenay, Chidaine★, Delétang★★, Levasseur-Alex Mathur★, des Liards/Berger★ (Vendange Tardive★★), Moyer★, Taille aux Loups★★. Best years: (2002) 01 00 **99 98 97 96 95 90 89**.

MONTRACHET AC *Côte de Beaune, Burgundy, France* This world-famous Grand Cru straddles the boundary between the villages of CHASSAGNE-MONTRACHET and PULIGNY-MONTRACHET. Produces wines with a unique combination of concentration, finesse and perfume; white Burgundy at its most sublime. Another Grand Cru, Chevalier-Montrachet, immediately above it on the slope yields a slightly leaner wine that is less explosive in its youth, but good examples will become ever more fascinating over 20 years or more. Best producers: G Amiot★★, Colin★★★, DROUHIN (Laguiche)★★★, LAFON★★★, LATOUR★★, Dom. LEFLAIVE★★★, RAMONET★★★, Dom. de la ROMANÉE-CONTI★★★, SAUZET★★, Thénard★★. Best years: (2002) (01) 00 99 97 96 95 **92 90 89 86 85**.

MONTRAVEL AC *South-West France* Dry, medium-dry and sweet white wines from the western end of the BERGERAC region. Sweet ones from Côtes de Montravel AC and Haut-Montravel AC. Red Montravel, from 2001, is made from a minimum 50% Merlot. Best producers: le Bondieu, Gourgueil, Moulin Caresse★, Perreau, Pique-Sègue, Puy-Servain★, le Raz. Best years: (sweet) 2001 00 **98 96 95**.

CH. MONTROSE★★ *St-Estèphe AC, 2ème Cru Classé, Haut-Médoc, Bordeaux, France* A leading ST-ESTEPHE property, once famous for its dark, brooding wine that would take around 30 years to reach its prime. In the late 1970s and early 80s the wines became lighter, but Montrose has now returned to a powerful style, though softer than before. Recent vintages have mostly been extremely good. Second wine: la Dame de Montrose. Best years: 2001 00 99 98 96 95 90 **89 86**.

CH. MONTUS *Madiran AC, South-West France* Alain Brumont has led MADIRAN's revival, using 100% Tannat and deft public relations. The top wine is aged in new oak. He has 3 properties: Montus (Cuvée Prestige★★), Bouscassé (Vieilles Vignes★★) and Meinjarre. Montus and Bouscassé also make enjoyable dry PACHERENC DU VIC-BILH★, while Bouscassé has fine Moelleux★★. Best years: (Cuvée Prestige) 2001 00 99 98 **97 96 95 94 93 91 90 89 88 85**.

MORELLINO DI SCANSANO DOC *Tuscany, Italy* Morellino is the local name for the Sangiovese grape in the south-west of TUSCANY. The wines can be broad and robust, but more and more delightfully perfumed examples are appearing. Best producers: E Banti★, Belguardo★/ FONTERUTOLI, Carletti/Poliziano (Lohsa★), Cecchi★, Il Macereto★, Mantellassi★, Morellino di Scansano co-op★, Moris Farms★★, Poggio Argentaria★★, Le Pupille★★. Best years: (2001) 00 99 **98 97 96 95 93** 90.

MOREY-ST-DENIS AC *Côte de Nuits, Burgundy, France* Morey has 5 Grands Crus (Clos des Lambrays, CLOS DE LA ROCHE, CLOS ST-DENIS, Clos de Tart and a share of BONNES-MARES) as well as some very good Premiers Crus. Basic village wine is sometimes unexciting, but from a quality grower the wine has good fruit and acquires an attractive depth as it ages. A tiny amount of startling nutty white wine is also made. Best producers: Pierre Amiot★, Arlaud★★, Dom. des Beaumonts, CLAIR★★, DUJAC★★★, Dom. des Lambrays★★, H Lignier★★★, H Perrot-Minot★, Ponsot★★, Rossignol-Trapet★, ROUMIER★★, ROUSSEAU★★, Sérafin★★. Best years: (2002) 01 00 99 98 **97** 96 **95 93** 90.

MORGENHOF *Stellenbosch WO, South Africa* A 300-year-old Cape farm grandly restored and run with French flair by owner Anne Cointreau-Huchon. Winemaker Rianie Strydom's equally stylish range spans Cap Classique sparkling to port styles. Best are a well-oaked, muscular Chenin Blanc, structured Merlot★ and the dark-berried, supple Première Sélection★, a BORDEAUX-style blend.

MORGON AC *Beaujolais, Burgundy, France* The longest-lasting of BEAUJOLAIS Crus, wines that should have structure, tannin and acidity to age well – the best normally come from the slopes of the Côte du Py. There are, however, many more Morgons, made in a commercial style for early drinking, which are nothing more than a pleasant, fruity – and pricy – drink. Best producers: N Aucoeur★, G Brun★, DUBOEUF (Jean Descombes★★), M Jonchet★, M Lapierre★. Best years: (2002) **00 99 98**.

MORNINGTON PENINSULA *Victoria, Australia* Exciting cool-climate maritime region dotted with small vineyards. Chardonnay runs the gamut from honeyed to harsh; Pinot Noir can be very stylish indeed in warmer years. Best producers: DROMANA★, Kooyong, Main Ridge★, Moorooduc★, Paringa Estate★, Port Phillip Estate★, STONIER★★, T'Gallant★, Tuck's Ridge. Best years: (Pinot Noir) 2001 00 99 **98 97 95 94**.

MORRIS *Rutherglen, Victoria, Australia* Historic winery, ORLANDO-owned, making traditional favourites like Liqueur Muscat★★ and Tokay★★ (Old Premium★★★), 'ports', 'sherries' and robust table wines from Shiraz★, Cabernet★, Durif★ and Blue Imperial (Cinsaut).

DENIS MORTET *Gevrey-Chambertin AC, Côte de Nuits, Burgundy, France* Denis Mortet joined the ranks of great producers with brilliant 1993s. Early vintages are deep coloured and powerful. Now he is adding finesse. Various cuvées of GEVREY-CHAMBERTIN★★ and tiny amounts of CHAMBERTIN★★★ itself. Best years: (2002) 01 00 98 **97** 96 95 **93**.

MORTON ESTATE *Katikati, North Island, New Zealand* Morton started in the tiny town of Katikati, but has since established a second winery in HAWKES BAY, its principal grape source. It produces New Zealand's most expensive Chardonnay, Coniglio★★★, a Burgundy dead-ringer that is made in minute quantities. Other good wines are the robust, complex Black Label Chardonnay★★, a rich and gamy Black Label Merlot★, the best Hawkes Bay Pinot Noir★ yet, berries and cedar Black Label Merlot-Cabernet Sauvignon★★ and good fizz★★. Best years: (Black Label Chardonnay) **1998 96 95**.

GEORG MOSBACHER *Deidesheim, Pfalz, Germany* This small estate makes dry white and dessert wines in the village of FORST. Best of all are the dry Rieslings★★ from the Forster Ungeheuer site, which are among the lushest in Germany. Delicious young, but worth cellaring for more than 3 years. Best years: (2002) 01 **99** 98 **97 96 94 93 90**.

MOSCATO D'ASTI DOCG *Piedmont, Italy* Utterly beguiling, delicately scented, gently bubbling wine, made from Moscato Bianco grapes grown in the hills between Acqui Terme, Asti and Alba in north-west Italy. The DOCG is the same as for ASTI, but only select grapes go into this wine, which is frizzante (semi-sparkling) rather than fully sparkling. Drink while they're bubbling with youthful fragrance. Best producers: Araldica/Alasia★, ASCHERI★, Bava★, Bera★, Braida★, Cascina Castlèt★, Caudrina★★, Giuseppe Contratto★, Coppo★, Cascina Fonda★, Forteto della Luja★, Icardi★, Marenco★, Beppe Marino★, La Morandina★, Marco Negri★, Perrone★, Cascina Pian d'Or★, Saracco★★, Scagliola★, La Spinetta★★, I Vignaioli di Santo Stefano★.

MOSCATO PASSITO DI PANTELLERIA DOC *Sicily, Italy* Powerful dessert wine made from the Muscat of Alexandria, or Zibibbo grape. Pantelleria is a small island south-west of SICILY, closer to Africa than it is to Italy. The grapes are picked in mid-August and laid out in the hot sun to dry and shrivel for a couple of weeks. They are then crushed and fermented to give an amber-coloured, intensely flavoured sweet Muscat. The wines are best drunk within 5–7 years of the vintage. Best producers: Benanti★, D'Ancona★, DE BARTOLI★★, Donnafugata (Ben Ryé★), MID (Tanit), Murana, Nuova Agricoltura co-op★, Pellegrino.

MOSEL-SAAR-RUWER *Germany* A collection of vineyard areas on the Mosel and its tributaries, the Saar and the Ruwer. The region is shrinking fast as a major restructuring takes place; it now has 10,392ha (25,668 acres), compared with 13,000ha (32,110 acres) a decade ago. The Mosel river rises in the French Vosges before forming the border between Germany and Luxembourg. In its first German incarnation in the Upper Mosel the light, tart Elbling grape holds sway, but with the Middle Mosel begins a series of villages responsible for some of the world's very best Riesling wines: PIESPORT, BRAUNEBERG, BERNKASTEL, GRAACH, WEHLEN, URZIG and ERDEN. The wines are not big or powerful, but in good years they have tremendous slatiness and an ability to blend the greenness of citrus leaves and fruits with the golden warmth of honey. Great wines are rarer in the lower part of the valley as the Mosel swings round into Koblenz, although Winningen is an island of excellence. The Saar can produce wonderful, piercing wines in villages such as Serrig, AYL, OCKFEN and Wiltingen. The Ruwer produces slightly softer wines; the estates of MAXIMIN GRUNHAUS and KARTHAUSERHOF are on every list of the best in Germany.

MOSS WOOD *Margaret River, Western Australia* Seminal MARGARET RIVER winery at the top of its form. Supremely good, scented Cabernet★★★ needing 5 years' age to blossom, classy Chardonnay★★, pale, fragrant Pinot Noir★ and crisp, fruity but ageworthy Semillon★★. Range is expanding with Ribbon Vale★★ and Glenmore★ single-vineyard wines. Best years: (Cabernet) (2001) (00) 99 98 96 95 **94 91 90 85**.

J P MOUEIX *Bordeaux, France* As well as owning PETRUS, la FLEUR-PETRUS, MAGDELAINE, TROTANOY and other properties, the Moueix family runs a thriving merchant business specializing in the wines of the right bank, particularly POMEROL and ST-EMILION. Quality is generally high.

MOULIN-À-VENT AC *Beaujolais, Burgundy, France* Potentially the greatest of the BEAUJOLAIS Crus, taking its name from an ancient windmill that stands above Romanèche-Thorins. The granitic soil yields a majestic wine that with time transforms into a rich Burgundian style more characteristic of the Pinot Noir than the Gamay. Best producers: L Champagnon★, DUBOEUF (single domaines★), Ch. des Jacques★, Ch. du Moulin-à-Vent★, Dom. Romanesca★, P Sapin (Le Vieux Domaine). Best years: (2002) **00 99 98 97 96 95**.

MOULIS AC *Haut-Médoc, Bordeaux, France* Small AC within the HAUT-MEDOC. Much of the wine is excellent – delicious at 5–6 years old, though good examples can age 10–20 years – and not overpriced. Best producers: Anthonic, Biston-Brillette, Brillette, CHASSE-SPLEEN★, Duplessis, Dutruch-Grand-Poujeau, Gressier-Grand-Poujeaux, MAUCAILLOU★, Ch. Moulin-à-Vent, POUJEAUX★★. Best years: 2001 00 **96 95 94 90 89 88 86 85 83 82**.

MOUNT LANGI GHIRAN *Grampians, Victoria, Australia* This winery made its reputation with remarkable dark plum, chocolate and pepper Shiraz★★. Delightful Riesling★, honeyed Pinot Gris★ and melony unwooded Chardonnay★. Joanna★★ Cabernet is dark and intriguing. Best years: (Shiraz) 2001 99 98 97 96 95 **94 93 90 89 86**.

MOUNT MARY *Yarra Valley, Victoria, Australia* Classic property using only estate-grown grapes along BORDEAUX lines, with dry white Triolet★★ blended from Sauvignon Blanc, Semillon and Muscadelle, and Quintet (★★★ for committed Francophiles), from all 5 Bordeaux red grapes, that ages beautifully. The Pinot Noir★★ is almost as good. Best years: (Quintet) (2001) (00) 99 98 97 96 95 **94 93 92 91 90 88 86 84**.

MOUNT VEEDER AVA *Napa Valley, California, USA* Small AVA in south-west NAPA, with Cabernet Sauvignon and Zinfandel wines in a typical rough-hewn style. Best producers: Chateau Potelle★, Robert Craig★★, HESS COLLECTION★, Lokoya★★, Mayacamas★, Mount Veeder Winery★.

MOUNTADAM *Eden Valley, South Australia* The late David Wynn and his Bordeaux-educated son Adam planted this property from scratch. It is now a subsidiary of CAPE MENTELLE. Rich, buttery Chardonnay★★ has a worldwide reputation. There is also sumptuous Pinot Noir★, bold Cabernet-Merlot blend The Red★, and the fruity David Wynn wines. Patriarch★★ is a rich, fruit-laden premium Shiraz. Best years: (Patriarch) 2000 99 98 97 96 95 **94 93 91 90 87**; (Chardonnay) 2001 **00 98 97 94 93 92 91 90**.

MOURVÈDRE The variety originated in Spain, where it is called Monastrell. It dominates the JUMILLA DO and also Alicante, Bullas and Yecla. It needs lots of sunshine to ripen, which is why it performs well on the Mediterranean coast at BANDOL. It is increasingly important as a source of body and tarry, pine-needle flavour in the wines of CHATEAUNEUF-DU-PAPE and parts of the MIDI. It is beginning to make a reputation in Australia and CALIFORNIA, where it is sometimes known as Mataro, and is just starting to make its presence felt in South Africa.

MOUTON-CADET *Bordeaux AC, Bordeaux, France* The most widely sold red BORDEAUX in the world was created by Baron Philippe de Rothschild in the 1930s. Blended from the entire Bordeaux region, the wine is a reliably decent drink – but never cheap. Also a white and rosé.

CH. MOUTON-ROTHSCHILD★★★ *Pauillac AC, 1er Cru Classé, Haut-Médoc, Bordeaux, France* Baron Philippe de Rothschild died in 1988 having raised Mouton from a run-down Second Growth to its promotion to First Growth in 1973, and a reputation as one of the greatest wines in the world. It can still be the most magnificently opulent of the great MEDOC reds, although there were signs of inconsistency through the 90s. Recent vintages seem back on top form. When young, this wine is rich and indulgent on the palate, aging after 15–20 years to a complex bouquet of blackcurrant and cigar box. There is also a white wine, Aile d'Argent. Second wine: Petit-Mouton. Best years: (red) 2001 00 99 98 96 95 **90 89 88 86 85 83 82 70**.

MUDGEE *New South Wales, Australia* Small, long-overlooked region neighbouring HUNTER VALLEY, with a higher altitude and marginally cooler temperatures. Major new plantings are giving it a fresh lease of life; ROSEMOUNT is leading the charge with generally impressive but overpriced Mountain Blue Shiraz-Cabernet★★ and the Hill of Gold range of varietals. Other producers are beginning to make the best use of very good fruit. Best producers: Farmer's Daughter, Andrew Harris★, Huntington Estate★, Miramar★, ORLANDO★, ROSEMOUNT★, Thistle Hill.

MUGA *Rioja DOC, Rioja, Spain* A traditional family winery making high-quality, rich red RIOJA★, especially the Gran Reserva, Prado Enea★★. It is the only bodega in Rioja where every step of red winemaking is still carried out in oak containers. Whites and rosés are good too. The modern Torre Muga Reserva★ marks a major stylistic change. Best years: (Torre Muga Reserva) 1998 **96 95 94**.

MULDERBOSCH *Stellenbosch WO, South Africa* Consistency is the hallmark of both the almost entirely white range and of winemaker Mike Dobrovic's tenure. The sleek, gooseberry-infused Sauvignon Blanc★★ is deservedly a cult wine; drink young and fresh. Purity and intensity are the distinguishing features of Chardonnay★★ and Steen-op-Hout★ (Chenin Blanc brushed with oak). Faithful Hound, a Cabernet-Merlot blend and the sole red, is BORDEAUX-like, though easy-drinking. Best years: (Chardonnay) 2001 00 99 98 97 96 95.

MÜLLER-CATOIR *Neustadt-Haardt, Pfalz, Germany* This PFALZ producer makes wine of a piercing fruit flavour and powerful structure unsurpassed in Germany, including ★★★ Riesling, Scheurebe and Rieslaner; ★★ Gewürztraminer, Muskateller and Pinot Noir; Weissburgunder★. Best years: (Riesling Spätlese) (2002) 01 **99 98 97 96 94 93 92 90 88**.

EGON MÜLLER-SCHARZHOF *Scharzhofberg, Saar, Germany* Some of the world's greatest – and most expensive – sweet Rieslings are this estate's Auslese, Beerenauslese, Trockenbeerenauslese and Eiswein, all ★★★. Regular Kabinett and Spätlese wines are pricy but classic. Best years: (Auslese) (2002) 01 99 97 95 **93** 90 **89 88 83 76 75 71**.

MÜLLER-THURGAU The workhorse grape of Germany, largely responsible for LIEBFRAUMILCH, with 18% of the country's vineyards (second to Riesling, with 21%). When yields are low it produces pleasant floral wines; but this is rare since modern clones are all super-productive. It is occasionally better in England – though the odd good examples with a slightly green edge to the grapy flavour, come from Austria, Switzerland, Luxembourg and Italy's ALTO ADIGE and TRENTINO. New Zealand used to pride itself on making the world's best Müller-Thurgau, but acreage is in terminal decline.

G H MUMM *Champagne AC, Champagne, France* Mumm's top-selling non-vintage brand, Cordon Rouge, usually disappointing in the 1990s, has improved since Dominique Demarville took over as winemaker in 1998. New owners Allied Domecq are apparently supporting his efforts at raising quality. Let's hope so, because there's a long way to go. Best years: 1996 **95 90 89 88 85 82**.

MUMM NAPA *Napa Valley AVA, California, USA* The French Champagne house MUMM and Seagram Classic Wines of California started Mumm Napa in 1983, and the bubbly coming out of California has been very good indeed. The style has now become leaner and drier, which is a pity, but both Cuvée Napa Brut Prestige and Vintage Reserve★ are good. Blanc de Noirs★ is better than most pink Champagnes; also elegant vintage-dated Blanc de Blancs★ and the flagship DVX★.

RENÉ MURÉ *Alsace AC, Alsace, France* This domaine owns much of the best vineyard around the village of Rouffach and is starting to make the best of it. Its pride and joy is the Clos St-Landelin, a parcel within the Grand Cru Vorbourg. The Clos is the source of lush, concentrated wines from all the major varieties, with particularly fine Riesling★★ and Pinot Gris★★. The Muscat Vendange Tardive★★ is rare and remarkable, as is the opulent old-vine Sylvaner Cuvée Oscar★. The Vendange Tardive★★ and Sélection de Grains Nobles★★★ wines are among the best in Alsace. Best years: (Clos St-Landelin Riesling) (2002) 01 00 **99 97 96 95 94 92 90 89 88**.

MURFATLAR *Romania* Region to the west of the Black Sea, producing excellent late-harvest wines (including botrytized versions) from Pinot Gris★, Chardonnay and Muscat Ottonel. Sparkling wines are being made, too. Murfatlar can also be a source of ripe, soft, low-acid reds.

ANDREW MURRAY VINEYARDS *Santa Barbara County, California, USA* Working with RHONE varieties, winemaker Andrew Murray has created an impressive array of wines since the initial 1994 vintage. Rich, aromatic Viognier★ and Roussanne★★ as well as several Syrahs, including Roasted Slope★★ and Hillside Reserve★★. Esperance★ is a spicy blend patterned after a serious COTES DU RHONE. Best years: (Syrah) (2000) 99 98 97 96 **94**.

MUSCADET AC *Loire Valley, France* Muscadet is the general AC for the region around Nantes in north-west France, with 3 better-quality zones: Muscadet Coteaux de la Loire, Muscadet Côtes de Grand Lieu and Muscadet Sèvre-et-Maine. Producers who make basic Muscadet AC are allowed higher yields but cannot use the term *sur lie* on the labels. Generally inexpensive and best drunk young and fresh, a perfect match for the local seafood – but the best can age several years. Best producers: Serge Bâtard★, Chéreau-Carré★, Dorices★, l'ECU★, Gadais, Jacques Guindon, Hautes-Noëlles, Herbauges★, l'Hyvernière★, Luneau-Papin★, Metaireau★, la Preuille, Quatre Routes★, RAGOTIERE★, Sauvion★, la Touché★. Best years: (*sur lie*) (2002) **01 00 99 98**.

MUSCAT See pages 196–7.

MUSCAT OF ALEXANDRIA Muscat of Alexandria rarely shines in its own right but performs a useful job worldwide, adding perfume and fruit to what would otherwise be dull, neutral white wines. It is common for sweet and fortified wines throughout the Mediterranean basin and in South Africa (where it is also known as Hanepoot), as well as being a fruity, perfumed bulk producer there and in Australia, where it is known as Gordo Blanco or Lexia.

MUSCAT

 It's strange, but there's hardly a wine grape in the world which makes wine that actually tastes of the grape itself. Yet there's one variety which is so joyously, exultantly grapy that it more than makes up for all the others – the Muscat, generally thought to be the original wine vine. In fact there seem to be about 200 different branches of the Muscat family worldwide, but the noblest of these and the one that always makes the most exciting wine is called Muscat Blanc à Petits Grains (the Muscat with the small berries). These berries can be crunchily green, golden yellow, pink or even brown – as a result Muscat has a large number of synonyms. The wines they make may be pale and dry, rich and golden, subtly aromatic or as dark and sweet as treacle.

WINE STYLES

France Muscat is grown from the far north-east right down to the Spanish border, yet is rarely accorded great respect in France. This is a pity because the dry, light, hauntingly grapy Muscats of Alsace are some of France's most delicately beautiful wines. It pops up sporadically in the Rhône Valley, especially in the sparkling wine enclave of Die. Mixed with Clairette, the Clairette de Die Tradition is a fragrant grapy fizz that should be better known. Muscat de Beaumes-de-Venise is another well-known version, this time fortified, fragrant and sweet. Its success has encouraged the traditional fortified winemakers of Languedoc-Roussillon, especially in Frontignan and Rivesaltes, to make fresher, more perfumed wines rather than the usual flat or syrupy ones they've produced for generations.

Italy Muscat, mainly Moscato Bianco, is grown in Italy for fragrantly sweet or (rarely) dry table wines in the north and for *passito*-style wines in the south (though Muscat of Alexandria is sometimes preferred below Rome). The most delicate Muscats in Italy are those of Asti, where the grape is called Moscato di Canelli. As either Asti or Moscato d'Asti, this brilliantly fresh fizz can be a blissful drink. Italy also has red varieties: the Moscato Nero for rare sweet wines in Lazio, Lombardy and Piedmont; and Moscato Rosa/Rosenmuskateller and Moscato Giallo/Goldmuskateller for delicately sweet wines in Trentino-Alto Adige and Friuli-Venezia Giulia.

Other regions Elsewhere in Europe, Muscat is a component of some Tokajis in Hungary, Crimea has shown how good it can be in the Massandra fortified wines, and the rich golden Muscats of Samos and Patras are among Greece's finest wines. As Muskateller in Austria and Germany it makes primarily dry, subtly aromatic wines. In Spain, Moscatel de Valencia is sweet, light and sensational value, Moscatel de Grano Menudo is on the resurgence in Navarra and it has also been introduced in Mallorca. Portugal's Moscatel de Setúbal is also wonderfully rich and complex. California grows Muscat, often calling it Muscat Canelli, but South Africa and Australia make better use of it. With darker berries, and called Brown Muscat in Australia and Muscadel in South Africa, it makes some of the world's most sweet and luscious fortified wines, especially in the north-east Victoria regions of Rutherglen and Glenrowan in Australia.

197

BEST PRODUCERS

Sparkling Muscat

France (Clairette de Die) Achard-Vincent, Clairette de Die co-op, Georges Raspail.

Italy (Asti) G Contratto, Gancia; (Moscato d'Asti) Fratelli Bera, Braida, Caudrina, Saracco, La Spinetta.

Dry Muscat

Austria (Muskateller) Lackner-Tinnacher, TEMENT.

France (Alsace) J Becker, Dirler-Cadé, Kientzler, Kuentz-Bas, Rolly Gassmann, Schléret, SCHOFFIT, Sorg, WEINBACH, ZIND-HUMBRECHT.

Germany (Muskateller) BERCHER, Dr HEGER, MULLER-CATOIR, REBHOLZ.

Spain (Alicante) Bocopa co-op; (Penedès) TORRES (Viña Esmeralda).

Italy (Goldmuskateller) LAGEDER.

Sweet Muscat

Australia (Liqueur Muscat) ALL SAINTS, BAILEYS, BROWN BROTHERS, Buller, Campbells, CHAMBERS, MCWILLIAM'S, MORRIS, SEPPELT, Stanton & Killeen, YALUMBA.

France (Alsace) E Burn, René MURE, SCHOFFIT; (Beaumes-de-Venise) Bernardins, DELAS, Durban, Fenouillet, Paul JABOULET, Vidal-Fleury; (Frontignan) la Peyrade; (Rivesaltes) CAZES, Jau, Laporte.

Greece SAMOS co-op.

Italy (Goldmuskateller) Viticoltori Caldaro, Thurnhof; (Pantelleria) DE BARTOLI, Murana.

Portugal (Moscatel de Setúbal) J M da FONSECA, J P VINHOS.

South Africa KLEIN CONSTANTIA.

Spain (Navarra) Camilo Castilla, CHIVITE; (Alicante) Gutiérrez de la Vega, Enrique Mendoza, Primitivo Quiles; (Málaga) Telmo RODRIGUEZ; (Valencia) Gandía; (Terra Alta) Vinos Piñol.

MUSCAT DE BEAUMES-DE-VENISE AC *Rhône Valley, France* Delicious
♀ Muscat *vin doux naturel* from BEAUMES-DE-VENISE in the southern Rhône.
It has a fruity acidity and a bright fresh feel, and is best drunk young
to get all that lovely grapy perfume at its peak. Best producers:
Baumalric★, Beaumes-de-Venise co-op, Bernardins★, CHAPOUTIER★,
Coyeux★, DELAS★, Durban★★, Fenouillet★, JABOULET★★, Vidal-Fleury★.

MUSCAT BLANC À PETITS GRAINS See Muscat.

MUSCAT DE FRONTIGNAN AC *Languedoc, France* Well-known Muscat
♀ *vin doux naturel* on the Mediterranean coast. With colours ranging from
bright gold to deep orange, it is quite impressive but can seem rather
cloying. Muscat de Mireval AC, a little further inland, can have a touch
more acid freshness, and quite an alcoholic kick. Best producers:
(Frontignan) Cave du Muscat de Frontignan, la Peyrade★, Robiscau;
(Mireval) la Capelle★, Mas des Pigeonniers, Moulinas.

MUSCAT DE MIREVAL AC See Muscat de Frontignan AC.

MUSCAT DE RIVESALTES AC *Roussillon, France* Made from Muscat
♀ Blanc à Petits Grains and Muscat of Alexandria, the wine can be very
good indeed, especially since several go-ahead producers are now
allowing the aromatic skins to stay in the juice for longer periods,
thereby gaining perfume and fruit. Most delicious when young. Best
producers: Cave de Baixas (Dom Brial★, Ch. les Pins★), la CASENOVE★,
CAZES★★, Chênes★, Fontanel★, Força Réal★, Jau★, Lafage★, Laporte★,
Mas Rous, MONT TAUCH co-op★, Piquemal★, Sarda-Malet★.

MUSCAT DE ST-JEAN-DE-MINERVOIS AC *Languedoc, France* Up in
♀ the remote Minervois hills, a small AC for fortified Muscat made from
Muscat Blanc à Petits Grains. Less cloying than some Muscats from
the plains of LANGUEDOC-ROUSSILLON, more tangerine and floral. Best
producers: Barroubio★, CLOS BAGATELLE, Vignerons de Septimanie.

MUSIGNY AC *Grand Cru, Côte de Nuits, Burgundy, France* One of a
🍷 handful of truly great Grands Crus, combining power with an exceptional
depth of fruit and lacy elegance – an iron fist in a velvet glove.
Understandably expensive. A tiny amount of white Musigny is produced
by de VOGUE. Best producers: DROUHIN★★★, JADOT★★★, D Laurent★★★,
Dom. LEROY★★★, J-F Mugnier★★★, J Prieur★★, ROUMIER★★★, VOGUE★★★,
VOUGERAIE★★. Best years: (2002) 01 00 99 98 97 96 95 93 **90 89 88**.

NAHE *Germany* 4385ha (10,835-acre) wine region named after the
River Nahe which rises below Birkenfeld and joins the Rhine by BINGEN, just
opposite RUDESHEIM in the RHEINGAU. Riesling, Müller-Thurgau and Silvaner
are the main grapes, but the Rieslings from this geologically complex region
are considered some of Germany's best. The finest vineyards are those of
Niederhausen and SCHLOSSBOCKELHEIM, situated in the dramatic, rocky Upper
Nahe Valley, and at Dorsheim and Münster in the lower Nahe.

CH. NAIRAC★★ *Barsac AC, 2ème Cru Classé, Bordeaux, France* An
♀ established star in BARSAC which, by dint of enormous effort and considerable investment, produces a wine sometimes on a par with the
First Growths. The influence of aging in new oak casks, adding spice
and even a little tannin, makes this sweet wine a good candidate for
aging 10–15 years. Best years: (2002) 01 99 98 97 **96 95 90 89 88**.

NAPA VALLEY See pages 200–1.

NAPA VALLEY AVA *California, USA* An AVA designed to be so inclusive
🏠 that it is almost completely irrelevant. It includes vineyards that are
outside the Napa River drainage system – such as Pope Valley and

Chiles Valley. Because of this a number of sub-AVAs have been and are in the process of being created; a few such as CARNEROS and STAGS LEAP DISTRICT are discernibly different from their neighbours, but many are similar in nature, and many fear that these sub-AVAs will simply dilute the magic of Napa's name. See also Howell Mountain, Mount Veeder, Napa Valley, Oakville, Rutherford.

NAVARRA DO *Navarra, Spain* This buzzing region has increasing numbers of vineyards planted to Cabernet Sauvignon, Merlot and Chardonnay in addition to Tempranillo, Garnacha and Moscatel (Muscat). This translates into a wealth of juicy reds, barrel-fermented whites and modern sweet Muscats, but quality is still more haphazard than it should be. Best producers: Camilo Castilla (Capricho de Goya Muscat★★), CHIVITE★, Magaña★, Vicente Malumbres, Alvaro Marino★, Castillo de Monjardin★, Vinícola Navarra, Nekeas co-op, Ochoa, Palacio de la Vega★, Piedmonte Olite co-op, Príncipe de Viana★, Señorío de Otazu★. Best years: (reds) 2001 **99 98 96 95 94 93**.

NEBBIOLO The grape variety responsible for the majestic wines of BAROLO and BARBARESCO, found almost nowhere outside north-west Italy. Its name derives from the Italian for fog, *nebbia*, because it ripens late when the hills are shrouded in autumn mists. It needs a thick skin to withstand this fog, so often gives very tannic wines that need years to soften. When grown in the limestone soils of the Langhe hills around Alba, Nebbiolo produces wines that are only moderately deep in colour but have a wonderful array of perfumes and an ability to develop great complexity with age – rivalled only by Pinot Noir and Syrah. Barolo is usually considered the best and longest-lived of the Nebbiolo wines; the myth that it needs a decade or more to be drinkable has been dispelled by new-style Barolo, yet the best of the traditional styles are more than worth the wait. Barbaresco, Barolo's neighbour, also varies widely in style between the traditional and the new. NEBBIOLO D'ALBA and ROERO produce lighter styles. The variety is also used for special barrique-aged blends, often with Barbera and/or Cabernet and sold under the LANGHE DOC. Nebbiolo is also the principal grape for reds of northern PIEDMONT – Carema, GATTINARA and Ghemme. In LOMBARDY it is known as Chiavennasca and is the main variety of the Valtellina DOC and VALTELLINA SUPERIORE DOCG wines. Outside Italy, rare good examples have been made in Australia and CALIFORNIA.

NEBBIOLO D'ALBA DOC *Piedmont, Italy* Red wine from Nebbiolo grown around Alba, but excluding the BAROLO and BARBARESCO zones. Vineyards in the LANGHE and ROERO hills, by the Tanaro river, are noted for sandy soils that produce a fragrant, fruity style for early drinking, though some growers make wines that improve for 5 years or more. Best producers: Alario★, ASCHERI, Bricco Maiolica★★, CERETTO, Cascina Chicco★, Correggia★★, GIACOSA★, Giuseppe MASCARELLO★, PRUNOTTO★, RATTI, SANDRONE★, Vietti★. Best years: (2001) 00 **99 98 97 96 95**.

NELSON *South Island, New Zealand* A range of mountains separates Nelson from MARLBOROUGH at the northern end of South Island. Nelson is made up of a series of small hills and valleys with a wide range of mesoclimates. Pinot Noir, Chardonnay, Riesling and Sauvignon Blanc do well. Best producers: Greenhough★, NEUDORF★★, SEIFRIED★/Redwood Valley. Best years: (whites) (2002) **01 00 99 98**.

NAPA VALLEY

California, USA

From the earliest days of California wine, and through all its ups and downs, the Napa Valley has been the standard-bearer for the whole industry and the driving force behind quality and progress. The magical Napa name – derived from an Indian word for plenty – applies to the fertile valley itself, the county in which it is found and the AVA for the overall area, but the region is so viticulturally diverse that the appellation is virtually meaningless.

The valley was first settled by immigrants in the 1830s, and by the late 19th century Napa, and in particular the area around the communities of Rutherford and Oakville, had gained a reputation for exciting Cabernet Sauvignon. Despite the long, dark years of Prohibition, this reputation survived and when the US interest in wine revived during the 1970s, Napa was ready to lead the charge.

GRAPE VARIETIES

Most of the classic French grapes are grown and recent replantings have done much to match varieties to the most suitable locations. Cabernet Sauvignon is planted in profusion and Napa's strongest reputation is for varietal Cabernet and Bordeaux-style (or meritage) blends, mostly Cabernet-Merlot. Pinot Noir and Chardonnay, for both still and sparkling wines, do best in the south, from Yountville down to Carneros. Zinfandel is grown mostly at the north end of the valley. Syrah and Sangiovese are relatively new here.

SUB-REGIONS

The most significant vine-growing area is the valley floor running from Calistoga in the north down to Carneros, below which the Napa River flows out into San Pablo Bay. It has been said that there are more soil types in Napa than in the whole of France, but much of the soil in the valley is heavy, clayish, over-fertile and difficult to drain and really not fit to make great wine. Some of the best vineyards are tucked into the mountain slopes at the valley sides or in selected spots at higher altitudes.

There is as much as a 10° temperature difference between torrid Calistoga and Carneros at the mouth of the valley, cooled by Pacific fog and a benchmark for US Pinot Noir and cool-climate Chardonnay. About 20 major sub-areas have been identified along the valley floor and in the mountains, although there is much debate over how many have a real claim to individuality. Rutherford, Oakville and Yountville in the mid-valley produce Cabernet redolent of dust, dried sage and ultra-ripe blackcurrants. Softer flavours come from Stags Leap to the east. The higher-altitude vineyards of Diamond Mountain, Spring Mountain and Mount Veeder along the Mayacamas mountain range to the west produce deep Cabernets, while Howell Mountain in the north-east has stunning Zinfandel and Merlot.

See also CARNEROS AVA, HOWELL MOUNTAIN AVA, MOUNT VEEDER AVA, NAPA VALLEY AVA, OAKVILLE AVA, RUTHERFORD AVA, STAGS LEAP DISTRICT AVA; and individual producers.

BEST PRODUCERS

Cabernet Sauvignon and meritage blends

Abreu, Altamura, Anderson's Conn Valley, S Anderson, ARAUJO, Barnett (Rattlesnake Hill), BEAULIEU, BERINGER, Bryant Family, Buehler (Reserve), Burgess Cellars, Cafaro, CAIN CELLARS, Cakebread, CAYMUS, CHATEAU MONTELENA, Chateau Potelle (VGS), CHIMNEY ROCK, CLOS DU VAL, Clos Pegase, Colgin, Conn Creek (Anthology), Corison, Cosentino, Robert Craig, DALLA VALLE, Del Dotto, DIAMOND CREEK, DOMINUS, DUCKHORN, DUNN, Elyse, Etude, Far Niente, Fisher, FLORA SPRINGS, Forman, Freemark Abbey, Frog's Leap, Grace Family, Groth, HARLAN ESTATE, Hartwell, HEITZ, HESS, Jarvis, La Jota, Lewis Cellars, Livingston, Lokoya, Long Meadow Ranch, Long Vineyards, Markham, Mayacamas, MERRYVALE, Peter MICHAEL, MINER, MONDAVI, Monticello, Mount Veeder Winery/FRANCISCAN, NEWTON, NIEBAUM-COPPOLA, Oakford, Oakville Ranch (MINER), OPUS ONE, Pahlmeyer, Paradigm, Robert Pecota, Peju Province (HB Vineyard), PHELPS, PINE RIDGE, Plumpjack, Pride Mountain, Quintessa, Raymond, Rombauer (Meilleur du Chai), Rudd Estate, Saddleback, St Clement, SCREAMING EAGLE, Seavey, SHAFER, SILVER OAK, SILVERADO, SPOTTSWOODE, Staglin Family, STAG'S LEAP WINE CELLARS, STERLING, Swanson, The Terraces, Philip Togni, Turnbull, Viader, Villa Mt Eden (Signature Series), Vine Cliff, Vineyard 29, Von Strasser, Whitehall Lane, ZD.

201

NERO D'AVOLA The name of SICILY's great red grape derives from the town of Avola near Siracusa, although it is now planted all over the island. Its deep colour, high sugars and acidity make it useful for blending, especially with the lower-acid Nerello Mascalese, but also with Cabernet, Merlot and Syrah. On its own, and from the right soils, it can be brilliant, with a soft, ripe, spicy black-fruit character. Examples range from simple quaffers to many of Sicily's top reds.

NEUCHÂTEL *Switzerland* Swiss canton with high-altitude vineyards, mainly Chasselas whites and Pinot Noir reds. **Best producers:** Ch. d'Auvernier, Thierry Grosjean, Montmollin, Porret.

NEUDORF *Nelson, South Island, New Zealand* Owners Tim and Judy Finn produce some of New Zealand's most stylish and sought-after wines, including gorgeous, honeyed Chardonnay★★, rich but scented Pinot Noir★★, Sauvignon Blanc★ and Riesling★. **Best years:** (Chardonnay) (2002) 01 00 **99 98 96**; (Pinot Noir) (2001) **00 99 98 97**.

NEW SOUTH WALES *Australia* Australia's most populous state is responsible for about 23% of the country's grape production. The largest centres of production are the irrigated areas of RIVERINA and Murray Darling, Swan Hill and Perricoota on the Murray River, where better viticultural and winemaking practices and lower yields have led to significant quality improvements. Smaller premium-quality regions include the old-established HUNTER VALLEY, COWRA, and higher-altitude MUDGEE, Orange and HILLTOPS. CANBERRA is an area of tiny vineyards at chilly altitudes, as is Tumbarumba at the base of the Snowy Mountains.

NEW WAVE WINES *Kent, England* The merger between Chapel Down and Carr Taylor (including Lamberhurst) has created a major player on the UK scene, with Owen Elias as chief winemaker. Grapes are from their own vineyards in Kent, and bought in from 25 vineyards across southern England. The Chapel Down range includes good, inexpensive sparkling wines (Brut non-vintage, Brut Rosé and Vintage). The Curious Grape range of still wines includes fruity white blends, varietal Bacchus and Pinot Noir and a wood-aged red, Epoch I.

NEW YORK STATE *USA* Wine grapes were first planted on Manhattan Island in the mid-17th century but it wasn't until the early 1950s that a serious wine industry began to develop in the state as vinifera grapes were planted to replace natives such as *Vitis labrusca*. The most important region is the FINGER LAKES in the north of the state, with the Hudson River also showing some form, but LONG ISLAND is the most exciting area. Quality has increased markedly in recent years, as improved vineyard practices help growers cope with the sometimes erratic weather. **Best producer:** (Hudson Valley) Millbrook★.

NEWTON *Napa Valley AVA, California, USA* Spectacular winery and vineyards above St Helena, now owned by LVMH. Cabernet Sauvignon★★, Merlot★★ and Claret★ are some of California's most ageworthy examples. Even better is the single-vineyard Cabernet Sauvignon Le Puzzle★★★. Newton pioneered the unfiltered Chardonnay★★★ style and this lush mouthful remains one of California's best. Age the Chardonnays for up to 5 years, reds for 10–15. **Best years:** (Cabernet Sauvignon) (2001) (00) 99 97 96 **95 94 91 90**.

NGATARAWA *Hawkes Bay, North Island, New Zealand* Viticulture here is organic, with Chardonnay, botrytized Riesling and Cabernet-Merlot produced under the premium Alwyn Reserve label. The Glazebrook range includes attractive Chardonnay★ and Cabernet-Merlot★, both of which are best drunk within 5 years. Best years: (reds) (2002) **00 98**.

NIAGARA PENINSULA *Ontario, Canada* Sandwiched between lakes Erie and Ontario, the Niagara Peninsula benefits from regular through-breezes created by the Niagara escarpment, the cool climate bringing out distinctive characteristics in the wine. Icewine, from Riesling and Vidal, is the showstopper, with growing international acclaim. Chardonnay leads the dry whites, with Pinot Noir, Merlot and Cabernet Franc showing most promise among the reds. Best producers: Cave Spring★, Chateau des Charmes★, HENRY OF PELHAM★, INNISKILLIN★, Konzelmann★, Marynissen, Reif Estate★, Southbrook★, Stoney Ridge, THIRTY BENCH★. Best years: (icewines) (2002) 00 99 **98**.

NIEBAUM-COPPOLA ESTATE *Rutherford AVA, California, USA* Movie director Coppola has turned the historical Inglenook Niebaum winery into an elaborate tourist destination. Rubicon★★, a BORDEAUX blend, lacked grace in the early vintages but with Coppola's greater involvement in the 1990s the wine has taken on a more exciting personality. It still needs 5–6 years of aging. Coppola offers Zinfandel★ under the Edizione Pennino label and Cabernet Franc★ under Coppola Family Wines. Diamond series (especially Syrah and Claret) are good buys. Best years: (Rubicon) (2001) (00) (99) 97 96 95 **94 91 86**.

NIEPOORT *Port DOC, Douro, Portugal* Remarkable small PORT shipper of Dutch origin, run by the widely respected Dirk van der Niepoort. Outstanding Vintage ports★★★, old tawnies★★★ and Colheitas★★★ and a single-quinta wine: Quinta do Passadouro★★. Unfiltered LBVs★★ are among the best in their class – intense and complex. He also produces fine red★★ and white★★ DOURO Redoma and red Passadouro★★ and Batuta★★. Best years: (Vintage) 2000 97 94 92 91 **87 85** 82 80 77 70 66 63 58 55 45 42 27; (Passadouro) 2000 97 **95 94 92**.

NIERSTEIN *Rheinhessen, Germany* Both a small town and a large Bereich which includes the infamous Grosslage Gutes Domtal. The town boasts 23 vineyard sites and the top ones (Pettenthal, Bruders-berg, Hipping, Oelberg and Orbel) are some of the best in the whole Rhine Valley. Best producers: Heinrich Braun★, GUNDERLOCH★★, HEYL ZU HERRNSHEIM★★, ST ANTONY★★. Best years: (2002) 01 99 98 **97 96 93**.

NIKOLAIHOF *Wachau, Niederösterreich, Austria* The Saahs family makes some of the best wines in the WACHAU as well as in nearby Krems-Stein in KREMSTAL, including steely, intense Rieslings from their small plot in the famous Steiner Hund vineyard, always ★★. Best years: (Steiner Hund Riesling Spätlese) (2002) 01 99 98 **97 95 94** 92 91 90 86 79 77.

NOBILO *Kumeu/Huapai, Auckland, North Island, New Zealand* New Zealand's second-largest winery produces a wide range of wines, from popular medium-dry White Cloud to single-vineyard varietals. Lush, intensely flavoured Dixon Vineyard Chardonnay★★ is made only in selected years. Tangy though restrained Sauvignon Blanc★ and a vibrant Chardonnay★ are Nobilo's top wines from the MARLBOROUGH region. In 1998 Nobilo bought Selaks, a mid-sized company with wineries in AUCKLAND and Marlborough; since then they have sold the snappy Selaks Marlborough Sauvignon Blanc★★ alongside the intense Drylands Marlborough Sauvignon Blanc★★, Chardonnay★ and Riesling★. Nobilo is now owned by Australian giant BRL HARDY.

NORTON *Luján de Cuyo, Mendoza, Argentina* Austrian-owned winery
which is investing heavily in new equipment and vineyards. Chief
winemaker, Jorge Riccitelli, works hard at the ever-improving line-up.
Reds impress more than whites, but Torrontés★ can be delightful,
while snappy Sauvignon Blanc★ and 100% barrique-fermented and
oak-aged Reserva Chardonnay★ show potential. In reds, the Porteño
label Sangiovese-Malbec is excellent value, and new Lo Tengo Malbec
is good fruity stuff. Under the Norton label there is good, chocolaty
Sangiovese, soft, rich Merlot★ and good Barbera. Reserva Merlot★ and
Malbec★ are ripe and full; Perdriel del Centenario, from Luján de Cuyo
old vines, is chewy and approachable; top-of-the-line Privada★★ is
approachable young but worthy of aging.

NOVAL, QUINTA DO *Port DOC, Douro, Portugal* Owned by AXA-
Millésimes, this immaculate property is the source of extraordinary
Quinta do Noval Nacional★★★, made from ungrafted vines – some say
the best vintage PORT made, but virtually unobtainable except at
auction. Other Noval ports (including Noval Vintage★★★ and single-
quinta Silval★★) are excellent too. Also fine Colheitas★★ and some
stunning 40-year-old tawnies★★★. Best years: (Nacional) 2000 97 94 87
85 **70 66 63 62 60 31**; (Vintage) 2000 97 95 94 91 **87 85 70 66 63 60**.

NUITS-ST-GEORGES AC *Côte de Nuits, Burgundy, France* This large AC
is one of the few relatively reliable 'village' names in Burgundy.
Although it has no Grands Crus, many of its Premiers Crus (it has 38!)
are extremely good. The red can be rather slow to open out, often
needing at least 5 years. Minuscule amounts of white are made by
Gouges★, l'Arlot, Chevillon and RION. Best producers: l'Arlot★★,
R Arnoux★★, J Chauvenet★, R Chevillon★★, J-J Confuron★★,
FAIVELEY★★, H Gouges★★★, GRIVOT★★, JAYER-GILLES★★, D Laurent★★,
MEO-CAMUZET★★, A Michelot★, Mugneret★★, N Potel★★, RION★★,
THOMAS-MOILLARD★★. Best years: (reds) (2002) 01 00 99 98 **97** 96 **95 93** 90.

NYETIMBER *West Sussex, England* After a stellar start, producing
thrilling sparkling wines capable of matching top CHAMPAGNES,
Nyetimber has been less consistent and less starry of late. Stuart and
Sandy Moss, who started the project, now only retain a consultancy
role, but I very much hope the fantastic quality of their early releases
will soon be repeated. Classic Cuvée, a Chardonnay-Pinot blend, spends
at least 6 years on its lees. Aurora Cuvée Blanc de Blancs is good too.

OAKVILLE AVA *Napa Valley, California, USA* This region is cooler than
RUTHERFORD, which lies immediately to the north. Planted primarily to
Cabernet Sauvignon, the area contains some of the best vineyards,
both on the valley floor (MONDAVI, OPUS ONE, SCREAMING EAGLE) and
hillsides (HARLAN ESTATE, DALLA VALLE), producing wines that display lush,
ripe black fruits and firm tannins. Best years: (Cabernet Sauvignon)
(2001) 99 97 96 95 94 **91** 90.

OC, VIN DE PAYS D' *Languedoc-Roussillon, France* Important Vin de
Pays covering LANGUEDOC-ROUSSILLON. Problems of overproduction and
consequently underripeness have dogged attempts to smarten up its
reputation. Occasional fine red or white shows what can be done. Best
producers: l'Aigle★, la BAUME (whites), Clovallon★, HERRICK, J Lurton,
Maris, Mas Cremat★, Ormesson★, Pech-Céleyran (Viognier★), Quatre
Sous★, St-Saturnin★, SKALLI-FORTANT, VAL D'ORBIEU (top reds★), Virginie.

OCKFEN *Saar, Germany* Village with one famous individual vineyard
site, the Bockstein. The wines can be superb in a sunny year, never
losing their cold steely streak but packing in delightful full-flavoured

fruit as well. Best producers: Dr Fischer, Dr Heinz Wagner★★, St Urbans-Hof★, ZILLIKEN★★. Best years: (2002) 01 99 **97 95 93 90**.

OKANAGAN VALLEY *British Columbia, Canada* The oldest and most important wine-producing region of British Columbia and first home of Canada's rich, honeyed icewine. The Okanagan Lake helps temper

BURROWING OWL
Estate Winery
Chardonnay
2000

the bitterly cold nights but October frosts can be a problem. Chardonnay, Pinot Blanc, Pinot Gris and Pinot Noir are the top-performing grapes. South of the lake, Cabernet, Merlot and even Shiraz are now being grown successfully. Best producers: Blue Mountain★, Burrowing Owl★, Gehringer★, INNISKILLIN, MISSION HILL★, Quail's Gate, SUMAC RIDGE★, Tinhorn Creek. Best years: (reds) (2001) **00 98**.

OLTREPÒ PAVESE DOC *Lombardy, Italy* Oltrepò Pavese is Italy's main source of Pinot Nero, used mainly for sparkling wines that may be called Classese when made by the Champagne method here, though base wines supply *spumante* industries elsewhere. The region supplies Milan's everyday wines, often fizzy, though still reds from Barbera, Bonarda and Pinot Nero and whites from the Pinots, Riesling and Chardonnay can be impressive. Best producers: Cà di Frara★, Le Fracce★, Frecciarossa★, Fugazza, Mazzolino★, Monsupello★, Montelio★, Vercesi del Castellazzo★, Bruno Verdi★. Best years: (reds) (2001) 00 99 **98 97 96 95**.

WILLI OPITZ *Neusiedlersee, Austria* The eccentric and publicity-conscious Willi Opitz produces a remarkable, unusual range of dessert wines from his tiny 2ha (5-acre) vineyard, including red Eiswein. The best are ★★, but dry wines are simpler and less consistent.

OPUS ONE★★ *Oakville AVA, California, USA* Joint venture between Robert MONDAVI and the late Baron Philippe de Rothschild of MOUTON-ROTHSCHILD. The first vintage (1979) of the BORDEAUX-blend wine was released in 1983. At that time, the $50 price was the most expensive for any California wine, though others have reached way beyond it now. The various Opus bottlings have been in the ★★ range but have rarely reached the standard of the Mondavi Reserve Cabernet. Best years: (2001) (00) 99 98 97 96 **95** 94 **93 92 91 90 86 85 84**.

DOM. DE L'ORATOIRE ST-MARTIN *Côtes du Rhône AC, Rhône Valley, France* Careful fruit selection in the vineyard is the secret of Frédéric and François Alary's concentrated COTES DU RHONE-VILLAGES reds and whites. The Haut-Coustias white★ is ripe with aromas of peach and exotic fruits, while the red★★ is a luscious mouthful of raspberries, herbs and spice. Top red Cuvée Prestige★★ is deep and intense with darkly spicy fruit. Best years: (Cuvée Prestige) 2001 00 **99** 98 **97 96 95 94 90 89**.

OREGON *USA* Oregon shot to international stardom in the early 1980s following some perhaps overly generous praise of its Pinot Noir, but it is only with the release of 5 fine vintages in a row – 1998 to 2002 – and some soul-searching by the winemakers about what style they should be pursuing that we can now begin to accept that some of the hype was deserved. Chardonnay can be quite good in an austere, understated style. The rising star is Pinot Gris which, in Oregon's cool climate, can be delicious, with surprising complexity. Pinot Blanc is also gaining momentum. The WILLAMETTE VALLEY is considered the best growing region, although the more Bordeaux-like climate of the Umpqua and Rogue

Valleys can produce good Cabernet Sauvignon and Merlot. Best producers (Rogue, Umpqua) Abacela★, Bridgeview★, Calahan Ridge, Foris★, Henry Estate, Valley View Winery. Best years: (reds) (2002) 01 00 99 **98 96**.

ORLANDO *Barossa Valley, South Australia* Australia's third-biggest wine company and the force behind export colossus Jacob's Creek is owned by Pernod-Ricard. It encompasses MORRIS, Russet Ridge, Wickham Hill, Gramp's, Richmond Grove and Wyndham Estate, and MUDGEE wines Craigmoor, Poet's Corner, Henry Lawson and Montrose. Top wines under the Orlando banner include COONAWARRA reds St Hugo★ and Jacaranda Ridge★, and individualistic Eden Valley Rieslings St Helga★ and Steingarten★★, but Orlando has lacked strength at the premium end. Rich Centenary Hill Barossa Shiraz★★ might change that, as might renewed efforts in Mudgee. Jacob's Creek Reserve and Limited Release★★ wines are excellent, though basic Jacob's Creek in popular lines like Cabernet and Semillon-Chardonnay seems a bit stretched as Australia's most successful export brand. Best years: (St Hugo Cabernet) 2000 99 **98 96 94 92 91 90 88 86**.

ORNELLAIA, TENUTA DELL' *Bolgheri, Tuscany, Italy* This beautiful property was developed by Lodovico Antinori, brother of Piero, after he left the family firm, ANTINORI, to strike out on his own. The red Ornellaia★★★, a Cabernet-Merlot blend, bears comparison with neighbouring SASSICAIA. The white Poggio alle Gazze★★ is made solely with Sauvignon. An outstanding Merlot, Masseto★★★, is produced in small quantities. Bought by MONDAVI and FRESCOBALDI in 2002 – let's hope quality stays up. Best years: (Ornellaia) (2001) (00) 99 98 97 **96 95 94 93 90 88**.

ORTENAU *Baden, Germany* A chain of steep granitic hills between Baden-Baden and Offenburg, which produce the most elegant (generally dry) Rieslings in BADEN, along with fragrant, fruity, medium-bodied Spätburgunder (Pinot Noir) reds. Best producers: Laible★★, Nägelsförst★, Schloss Neuweier★.

ORVIETO DOC *Umbria, Italy* Traditionally a lightly sweet *abboccato* white wine, Orvieto is now usually dry and characterless. In the superior Classico zone, however, the potential for richer, more biscuity wines exists. Not generally a wine for aging. There are also some very good botrytis-affected examples. Best producers: (dry) Barberani-Vallesanta★, La Carraia★, Decugnano dei Barbi★, Palazzone★, Castello della SALA★, Salviano★, Conte Vaselli★, Le Velette★; (sweet) Barberani-Vallesanta★, Decugnano dei Barbi★, Palazzone★, Castello della SALA★★.

OSBORNE *Jerez y Manzanilla DO, Andalucía, Spain* The biggest drinks company in Spain, Osborne does most of its business in brandy and other spirits. Its sherry arm in Puerto de Santa María specializes in the light Fino Quinta★. Amontillado Coquinero★, rich, intense Bailén Oloroso★★ and Solera India Oloroso★★ are very good indeed.

OVERBERG WO *South Africa* One of South Africa's most southerly wine districts, prized for cool-climate viticulture, embracing the upland area of Elgin as well as the coastal ward of Walker Bay. In Elgin, more apple orchards are being turned over to vines; Sauvignon, Chardonnay, Riesling and Pinot Noir vindicate this decision. In Walker Bay, Pinot Noir is the holy grail of the majority, although Chardonnay and Pinotage are also doing well. Best producers: (Elgin) Paul Cluver★, Neil ELLIS★; (Walker Bay) BOUCHARD FINLAYSON★, HAMILTON RUSSELL★, Newton Johnson★. Best years: (Pinot Noir) 2001 **00 99 98 97**.

PAARL WO *South Africa*   Paarl is South Africa's second most densely planted district after Worcester, accounting for 16.3% of all vineyards. There is great diversity of soil and climate here, favouring everything from Cap Classique sparkling wines to sherry styles, but reds are setting the quality pace, especially Shiraz. Its white RHONE counterpart, Viognier, is also performing well. Wellington and FRANSCHHOEK are smaller designated areas (wards) within the Paarl district. Best producers: (Paarl) BOSCHENDAL, DISTELL (Plaisir de Merle★, Nederburg), FAIRVIEW★★, GLEN CARLOU★★, Rupert & Rothschild★, VEENWOUDEN★★, Welgemeend★; (Wellington) Diemersfontein★, Mont du Toit★. Best years: (premium reds) 2001 **00 99 98 97**.

PACHERENC DU VIC-BILH AC *South-West France*   Individual whites from an area overlapping the MADIRAN AC in north-east Béarn. The wines are mainly dry but there are some medium-sweet/sweet late-harvest wines. Most Pacherenc is best drunk young. Best producers: Aydie★, Berthoumieu★, Brumont (Bouscassé★, MONTUS★), du Crampilh★, Damiens, Laffitte-Teston★, Producteurs PLAIMONT★, Sergent★. Best years: 2001 **00 97 96 95**.

PACIFIC ECHO *Anderson Valley AVA, California, USA*   Known until 1998 as Scharffenberger Cellars, this winery produced a string of attractive, toasty sparklers. POMMERY's investment has consolidated this performance. The non-vintage Brut★★, with lovely toasty depth, the exuberant Rosé★★, and the vintage Blanc de Blancs★★ are all excellent.

PADTHAWAY *South Australia*   This wine region has always been the alter-ego of nearby COONAWARRA, growing whites to complement Coonawarra's reds. Padthaway Sauvignon Blanc is some of Australia's tastiest, and LINDEMANS' Padthaway Chardonnay★ is a serious white. But today some excellent reds are made; even GRANGE has included some Padthaway grapes. ORLANDO's premium Lawson's Shiraz★ is 100% Padthaway, HARDYS' Eileen Hardy Shiraz★★★ is half Padthaway. Best producers: Browns of Padthaway, HARDYS★★, Henry's Drive★★, LINDEMANS★, ORLANDO★, Padthaway Estate, SEPPELT.

BRUNO PAILLARD *Champagne AC, Champagne, France*   Bruno Paillard is one of the very few individuals who has created a new CHAMPAGNE house over the past century. Paillard still does the blending himself. The non-vintage Première Cuvée★ is lemony and crisp, the Réserve Privée★ is a blanc de blancs; the vintage Brut★★ is a serious wine, and in 2000 he launched a de luxe cuvée, Ne Plus Ultra★★, a barrel-fermented blend of Grands Crus from the 1990 vintage. Best years: 1995 **90 89 88**.

ALVARO PALACIOS *Priorat DOC, Cataluña, Spain*   The young Alvaro Palacios was already a veteran with Bordeaux and Napa experience when he launched his boutique winery in the rough hills of southern CATALUÑA in the late 1980s. He is now one of the driving forces of the area's sensational rebirth. His expensive, highly concentrated reds (L'Ermita★★★, Finca Dofi★★, Les Terrasses★) from old Garnacha vines and a dollop of Cabernet Sauvignon, Merlot and Syrah have won a cult following. Best years: 2000 **99 98 97 96 95 94 93**.

PALETTE AC *Provence, France*   Tiny AC just east of Aix-en-Provence. Even though the local market pays high prices, I find the reds and rosés rather tough and charmless. However, Ch. Simone manages to achieve a white wine of some flavour from basic southern grapes. Best producers: Crémade, Ch. Simone★.

PALLISER ESTATE *Martinborough, North Island, New Zealand* State-of-the-art winery producing some of New Zealand's best Sauvignon Blanc★★ (certainly the best outside MARLBOROUGH) and Riesling★, with some impressive, rich-textured Pinot Noir★★. Exciting botrytized dessert wines appear in favourable vintages. Méthode★ fizz is also impressive. Best years: (Pinot Noir) (2002) 01 **00 99 98**.

CH. PALMER★★ *Margaux AC, 3ème Cru Classé, Haut-Médoc, Bordeaux, France* This estate was named after a British major-general who fought in the Napoleonic Wars, and is one of the leading properties in MARGAUX AC. The wine is wonderfully perfumed, with irresistible plump fruit. The very best vintages can age for 30 years or more. Second wine: Alter Ego (previously Réserve-du-Général). Best years: 2001 00 99 98 96 95 91 **90 89 88 86 85 83 82**.

PANTHER CREEK *Willamette Valley AVA, Oregon, USA* Sourcing wine from well-placed vineyards in OREGON and WASHINGTON, Panther Creek specializes in cherryish Pinot Noir★★. Single-vineyard wines Shea★★★, Bednarik★★, Freedom Hill★ and Nysa★ have extra complexity and length. Small amounts of Chardonnay from Celilo Vineyard (in Washington), Melón, Pinot Gris and a frothy traditional-method bubbly round out the range. Best years: (Pinot Noir) (2002) 01 00 99 **98 97 96**.

CH. PAPE-CLÉMENT *Pessac-Léognan AC, Cru Classé de Graves, Bordeaux, France* The expensive red wine★★ from this GRAVES property has not always been as consistent as it should be – but things settled down into a high-quality groove during the 1990s. In style it is mid-way between the refinement of HAUT-BRION and the firmness of la MISSION-HAUT-BRION. Also a small production of a much-improved white wine★★. Second wine: (red) Clémentin. Best years: (reds) 2001 00 99 98 97 96 95 **90 89 88 86**; (white) 2001 00 99 98 **96**.

PARELLADA This Catalan exclusivity is the lightest of the trio of white grapes that go to make CAVA wines in north-eastern Spain. It also makes still wines, light, fresh and gently floral, with good acidity. Drink it as young as possible, while it still has the benefit of freshness.

PARKER COONAWARRA ESTATE *Coonawarra, South Australia* Red wine specialist now run by Andrew Pirie (ex-PIPERS BROOK). The top label, cheekily named First Growth★★ in imitation of illustrious BORDEAUX reds, has enjoyed much critical acclaim and auction success. It is released only in better years. Second label Terra Rossa Cabernet Sauvignon★ is lighter and leafier. The Merlot★★ is among the best produced in Australia. Best years: (First Growth) 1999 98 **96 93 91 90**.

C J PASK *Hawkes Bay, North Island, New Zealand* Chris Pask made the first wine in the now-famous Gimblett Gravels area of HAWKES BAY and remains one of the district's larger vineyard owners. Winemaker Kate Radburnd is best known for her Reserve reds, including a rich and powerful Reserve Merlot★★ and elegant, long-lived Reserve Cabernet Sauvignon★. Best years: (reds) (2002) **00 98**.

PASO ROBLES AVA *California, USA* A large AVA at the northern end of SAN LUIS OBISPO COUNTY. Cabernet Sauvignon and Zinfandel perform well in this warm region, and Syrah is now gaining a foothold as well. The Perrin family from Ch. de BEAUCASTEL selected this AVA to plant RHONE varieties for their California project, Tablas Creek, whose whites so far outshine the reds. Best producers: Adelaida★, Eberle★, Justin★, J Lohr★, Peachy Canyon★, Tablas Creek★, Wild Horse★.

LUIS PATO *Bairrada, Beira Litoral, Portugal* Leading 'modernist' in BAIRRADA, passionately convinced of the Baga grape's ability to make great reds on clay soil. He now labels wines as BEIRAS after arguing with Bairrada's bosses. Wines such as the Vinhas Velhas★, Vinha Barrosa★★, Vinha Pan★★ and the flagship Quinta do Ribeirinho Pé Franco★★ (from ungrafted vines) rank among Portugal's finest modern reds, and some can reach ★★★ with age. Homenagem★★ combines Baga with Touriga Nacional from Quinta de Cabriz (DÃO). Exciting white, Vinha Formal★★, is 100% Bical. Best years: (reds) 2001 00 97 **96 95 92**.

PAUILLAC AC *Haut-Médoc, Bordeaux, France* The deep gravel banks around the town of Pauillac in the HAUT-MEDOC are the heartland of Cabernet Sauvignon. For many wine lovers, the king of red wine grapes finds its ultimate expression in the 3 Pauillac First Growths (LATOUR, LAFITE-ROTHSCHILD and MOUTON-ROTHSCHILD). The large AC also contains 15 other Classed Growths. The uniting characteristic of Pauillac wines is their intense blackcurrant fruit flavour and heady cedar and pencil-shavings perfume. These are the longest-lived of Bordeaux's great red wines. Best producers: Armailhac★, BATAILLEY★, Clerc-Milon★, Duhart-Milon★, Fonbadet, GRAND-PUY-DUCASSE★, GRAND-PUY-LACOSTE★★, HAUT-BAGES-LIBERAL★, HAUT-BATAILLEY★, LAFITE-ROTHSCHILD★★★, LATOUR★★★, LYNCH-BAGES★★★, MOUTON-ROTHSCHILD★★★, Pibran★, PICHON-LONGUEVILLE★★★, PICHON-LONGUEVILLE-LALANDE★★★, PONTET-CANET★★. Best years: 2001 00 96 95 **90 89 88 86 85 83 82**.

CH. PAVIE★★ *St-Émilion Grand Cru AC, 1er Grand Cru Classé, Bordeaux, France* Pavie has had its ups and downs in recent years, but a change of ownership in 1998 (it is now part of the same team as Pavie-Decesse★ and MONBOUSQUET★) has put it in the top flight again. The wines are rich and concentrated, but for some a little *too* extracted. Best years: 2001 00 99 98 96 95 **90 89 88 86 85 83 82**.

CH. PAVIE-MACQUIN★★ *St-Émilion Grand Cru AC, Grand Cru Classé, Bordeaux, France* This has become one of the stars of the ST-EMILION GRAND CRU since the 1990s. Management and winemaking are in the hands of Nicolas Thienpont (of BORDEAUX-COTES DE FRANCS) and Stéphane Derenoncourt, who consults to CANON-LA-GAFFELIERE and PRIEURE-LICHINE, among others. Rich, firm and reserved, the wines need 7–8 years to open up and will age longer. Best years: 2001 00 99 98 97 96 95 **94 90**.

PÉCHARMANT AC *South-West France* Lovely red wines from this small AC north-east of BERGERAC. The wines are quite light in body but have a delicious, full, piercing flavour of blackcurrants and attractive grassy acidity. Good vintages will easily last 10 years and end up indistinguishable from a good HAUT-MEDOC. Best producers: Beauportail★, Bertranoux, Costes, Grand Jaure, Haut-Pécharmant★, la Tilleraie, Tiregand★. Best years: 2000 **98 96 95 90**.

PEDROSA *Ribera del Duero DO, Castilla y León, Spain* Delightful, elegant reds★ (Pérez Pascuas Gran Reserva★), both young and oak-aged, from a family winery in the little hill village of Pedrosa del Duero. The wines are not cheap, but far less pricy than some stars of this fashionable region. Best years: (Pérez Pascuas) 1996 **95 94 91 90**.

PEGASUS BAY *Waipara, Canterbury, New Zealand* Matthew Donaldson and Lynette Hudson fashion lush, mouthfilling Chardonnay★★, an almost chewy Pinot Noir★ and its even richer big brother Prima

Donna Pinot Noir★★, a powerful Sauvignon Blanc-Semillon★★ and a very stylish Riesling★★ – an impressive portfolio from this upcoming region. All will age well. Best years: (2002) **01 00 99 98**.

PEMBERTON *Western Australia* Exciting emergent region, deep in the karri forests of the south-west, full of promise for cool-climate Pinot Noir, Chardonnay, Merlot and Sauvignon Blanc. HOUGHTON lead the way thanks to the outstanding fruit coming from the vineyard they purchased a decade ago. Their regional range – sparkling Chardonnay-Pinot Noir★, Sauvignon Blanc★★, Chardonnay★★ and Merlot – has been highly successful. Best producers: Chestnut Grove, Mountford, Picardy, SALITAGE★, Smithbrook.

PEÑAFLOR *Mendoza, Argentina* The biggest wine producer in Argentina; BRIGHT BROTHERS make a good range of wines for export markets. Trapiche, Peñaflor's fine wine arm, with the expertise of Bordeaux enologist Michel Rolland, is beginning to deliver results. Iscay★, a Merlot-Malbec blend, is Trapiche's flagship red; there is also a punchy Sauvignon Blanc and melony Chardonnay.

PENEDÈS DO *Cataluña, Spain* The wealthy CAVA industry is based in Penedès, and the majority of the still wines are white, made from the Cava trio of Parellada, Macabeo and Xarel-lo, clean and fresh when young, but never exciting. Better whites are made from Chardonnay. The reds are variable, the best made from Cabernet Sauvignon and/or Tempranillo and Merlot. Best producers: Albet i Noya★, Can Feixes★, Can Ràfols dels Caus★ (Caus Lubis Merlot★★), Cavas Hill, JUVE Y CAMPS, Jean León★, Marques de Monistrol, Masía Bach★, Albert Milá i Mallofré, Puig y Roca★, TORRES★, Vallformosa, Jané Ventura★.

PENFOLDS *Barossa Valley, South Australia* Part of Australia's giant Southcorp group, Penfolds has always proved that quality *can* go in hand with quantity; but since merging with ROSEMOUNT there has been a discernible dulling of the Penfolds palate. Still makes the country's greatest red wine, GRANGE★★★, and a welter of other reds such as Magill Estate★★, St Henri★, Bin 707 Cabernet★★, Bin 389 Cabernet-Shiraz★, Bin 28 Kalimna★ and Bin 128 Coonawarra Shiraz, but as you go further down the range to previously reliable wines like Koonunga Hill and Rawson's Retreat a dispiriting blandness enters in. Whites are led by overpriced Yattarna Chardonnay★★. Also makes tasty wooded Semillon★★, citrus Eden Valley Riesling★ and Rawson's Retreat Riesling. Best years: (reds) 1998 96 **94 93 92 91 90 88 86 84 83 82**.

PENLEY ESTATE *Coonawarra, South Australia* Kym Tolley, a member of the PENFOLD family, combined the names when he left Southcorp and launched Penley Estate in 1991. From 1997 Cabernet Sauvignon★★ has been outstanding. Chardonnay and Hyland Shiraz can reach ★★; Merlot★ and fizz★ are also worth a try. Best years: (Cabernet) 2000 99 98 **96 94 93 92 91**.

PERNAND-VERGELESSES AC *Côte de Beaune, Burgundy, France* The little-known village of Pernand-Vergelesses contains a decent chunk of the great Corton hill, including much of the best white CORTON-CHARLEMAGNE Grand Cru vineyard. The red wines sold under the village name are very attractive when young with a nice raspberry pastille fruit and a slight earthiness, and will age for 6–10 years. As no one ever links poor old Pernand with the heady heights of Corton-Charlemagne, the whites sold under the village name can be a bargain. The wines can be a bit lean and dry to start with but fatten up beautifully after 2–4 years in bottle. Best producers: (reds) Champy, CHANDON DE BRIAILLES★★,

C Cornu★, Denis Père et Fils★, Dubreuil-Fontaine★, Laleure-Piot★, Rapet★, Rollin★; (whites) CHANDON DE BRIAILLES★★, Dubreuil-Fontaine★, Germain, A Guyon, JADOT, Laleure-Piot★, J-M Pavelot★, Rapet★, Rollin★★. Best years: (reds) (2002) 01 99 **98 97 96**; (whites) (2002) 01 **00 99 97 96**.

ANDRÉ PERRET *Condrieu AC, Rhône Valley, France* One of the few CONDRIEU growers. Clos Chanson★★ is direct and full, Coteau de Chéry★★★, made with some later-picked grapes, is musky, floral and rich. Very sound white and red ST-JOSEPH, notably Les Grisières★★ from old Syrah vines. Best years: (Condrieu) **2001 00 99 97**.

JOSEPH PERRIER *Champagne AC, Champagne, France* In 1998 Alain Thiénot took a controlling interest in this CHAMPAGNE house. The NV Cuvée★ is biscuity and creamy, Prestige Cuvée Josephine★★ has length and complexity, but the much cheaper Cuvée Royale Vintage★★ is the best deal. Best years: 1995 **90 89 88 85 82**.

PERRIER-JOUËT *Champagne AC, Champagne, France* Until 1999, Perrier-Jouët was owned by the Seagram group, and performance was generally lacklustre, although the vintage could be quite good, the Blason de France rosé★ charming and the de luxe cuvée Belle Époque★, white and rosé, was still classy. It is hoped that efforts to improve quality and consistency by winemaker Hervé Deschamps will continue under the ownership (since 2001) of Allied Domecq. Best years: (1997) 96 **95 92 90 89 85 82**.

PESQUERA *Ribera del Duero DO, Castilla y León, Spain* Tinto Pesquera reds, richly coloured, firm, fragrant and plummy-tobaccoey, are among Spain's best. Made by the small firm of Alejandro Fernández, they are 100% Tempranillo and sold as Crianza★★ and Reserva★★. Gran Reserva★★ and Janus★★★ are made in the best years. Condado de Haza (Alenza★) is a separate estate. New ventures have also been launched in Zamora (Dehesa La Granja★) and La MANCHA (Vínculo). Best years: (Pesquera Crianza) (1999) 96 **95 94 93 92 91 90 89 86 85**.

PESSAC-LÉOGNAN AC *Bordeaux, France* AC created in 1987 for the northern (and best) part of the GRAVES region and including all the Graves Classed Growths. The supremely gravelly soil tends to favour red wines over the rest of the Graves. Now, thanks to cool fermentation and the use of new oak barrels, this is also one of the most exciting areas of France for top-class white wines. Best producers: (reds) Brown, les Carmes Haut-Brion★, Dom. de CHEVALIER★★, FIEUZAL★, HAUT-BAILLY★★, HAUT-BRION★★★, Larrivet Haut-Brion★, LATOUR-MARTILLAC★, la LOUVIERE★★, MALARTIC-LAGRAVIERE★, la MISSION-HAUT-BRION★★★, PAPE-CLEMENT★★, SMITH-HAUT-LAFITTE★★, la Tour-Haut-Brion★; (whites) CARBONNIEUX★, Dom. de CHEVALIER★★★, Couhins-Lurton★★, FIEUZAL★★, HAUT-BRION★★★, LATOUR-MARTILLAC★, LAVILLE-HAUT-BRION★★★, la LOUVIERE★★, MALARTIC-LAGRAVIERE★, PAPE-CLEMENT★★, Rochemorin★, SMITH-HAUT-LAFITTE★★. Best years: (reds) 2001 00 99 98 96 95 **90 89 88**; (whites) 2001 00 99 **98 96 95 94 93 90**.

PETALUMA *Adelaide Hills, South Australia* This public company, which includes KNAPPSTEIN, MITCHELTON, STONIER and Smithbrook in WESTERN AUSTRALIA, was founded by Brian Croser, probably Australia's most influential winemaker. It was taken over by brewer Lion Nathan in 2001. Champagne-style Croser★ is stylish but lean. Chardonnay★★ and COONAWARRA (Cabernet-Merlot)★★ are consistently fine and CLARE Riesling★★ is at the fuller end of the spectrum and matures superbly. Vineyard Selection Tiers Chardonnay★★★ is ridiculously expensive but excellent. Best years: (Coonawarra) 2000 99 97 **94 91 90 88**.

211

PETIT VERDOT A rich, tannic variety, grown mainly in Bordeaux's HAUT-MEDOC to add depth, colour and violet fragrance to top wines. Late ripening and erratic yield limit its popularity, but warmer-climate plantings in Australia, California, Chile, Argentina, Spain and Italy are giving exciting results.

CH. PETIT-VILLAGE★★ *Pomerol AC, Bordeaux, France* This top POMEROL wine is sterner in style than its neighbours. In general it is worth aging the wine for 8–10 years at least. Best years: 2001 00 99 98 96 95 **94 90 89 88 85 82**.

PETITE ARVINE A Swiss variety from the VALAIS, Petite Arvine has a bouquet of peach and apricot, and develops a spicy, honeyed character with age. Dry, medium or sweet, the wines have good aging potential. Best producers: Chappaz★, Caves Imesch★, Dom. du Mont d'Or★.

PETITE SIRAH Long used as a blending grape in California but used also for varietal wines, Petite Sirah is often confused with the Durif of southern France. At its best in California and Mexico, the wine has great depth and strength; at worst it can be monstrously huge and unfriendly. Best producers: L A CETTO (Mexico), De Loach★, FETZER, Fife, Foppiano, RAVENSWOOD★★, RIDGE★★, Stags' Leap Winery★★, TURLEY★★.

CH. PÉTRUS★★★ *Pomerol AC, Bordeaux, France* Now one of the most expensive red wines in the world (alongside other superstars from POMEROL, such as le PIN), but only 50 years ago Pétrus was virtually unknown. The powerful, concentrated wine produced here is the result of the caring genius of Pétrus' owners, the MOUEIX family, who have maximized the potential of the vineyard of almost solid clay, although the impressive average age of the vines has been much reduced by recent replantings. Drinkable for its astonishingly rich, dizzying blend of fruit and spice flavours after a decade, but top years will age for much longer, developing exotic scents of tobacco and chocolate and truffles as they mature. Best years: 2001 00 99 98 96 95 90 **89 88 86 85**.

DOM. PEYRE ROSE *Coteaux du Languedoc AC, Languedoc, France* Organic viticulture, ultra-low yields and total absence of oak are all marks of the individuality of Marlène Soria's wines. Syrah is the dominant grape in both the raisin- and plum-scented Clos des Cistes★★ and the dense, velvety Clos Syrah Léone★★. Best years: (reds) 2000 99 98 **97 96 95 94 93**.

CH. DE PEZ★ *St-Estèphe AC, Cru Bourgeois, Haut-Médoc, Bordeaux, France* One of ST-ESTEPHE's leading non-Classed Growths, de Pez makes mouthfilling, satisfying claret with sturdy fruit. Slow to evolve, good vintages often need 10 years or more to mature. Now owned by Champagne house ROEDERER. Best years: 2001 00 99 98 96 95 **90 89 88**.

PFALZ *Germany* Germany's most productive wine region, with 23,420ha (57,870 acres), makes a lot of mediocre wine, but the quality estates are capable of matching the best that Germany has to offer. The Mittelhaardt has a reputation for Riesling, especially round the villages of WACHENHEIM, FORST and Deidesheim, though Freinsheim, KALLSTADT, Ungstein, Gimmeldingen and Haardt also produce fine Riesling as well as Scheurebe, Rieslaner and Pinot Gris. In the Südliche Weinstrasse the warm climate makes the area an ideal testing ground for Spät-, Weiss- and Grauburgunder (Pinots Noir, Blanc and Gris), as well as Gewürztraminer, Scheurebe, Muscat and red Dornfelder, the last often dark and tannic, sometimes with oak barrique influence. See also Bad Dürkheim, Burrweiler.

JOSEPH PHELPS *Napa Valley AVA, California, USA* Joseph Phelps' BORDEAUX-blend Insignia★★ is consistently one of California's top reds, strongly fruit-driven with a lively spicy background. Phelps' pure Cabernets include Napa Valley★ and Backus Vineyard★★, beautifully balanced with solid ripe fruit. The Vin du Mistral line of RHONE varietals includes an intensely fruity Viognier★ and a lightly spiced Syrah★ that improves with short-term cellaring. Best years: (Insignia) (2001) (00) 99 97 96 **95** 94 **93 91** 85.

CH. DE PIBARNON *Bandol AC, Provence, France* Blessed with excellently located vineyards, Pibarnon is one of BANDOL's leading properties. The reds★★, extremely attractive when young, develop a truffly, wild herb character with age. Average white and a ripe, strawberryish rosé. Best years: (red) 2001 00 99 98 **97 96 95 94 93 91 90 89 88** 85 82.

PIC ST-LOUP *Coteaux du Languedoc AC, Languedoc, France* This Cru, north of Montpellier, is one of the coolest growing zones in the MIDI and produces some of the best reds in the Languedoc. Syrah is the dominant variety, along with Grenache and Mourvèdre. Whites from Marsanne, Roussanne, Rolle and Viognier are showing promise. Best producers: Cazeneuve★, Clos Marie★, l'Euzière★, l'HORTUS★, Lancyre, Lascaux★, Lavabre★, MAS BRUGUIERE★, Mas de Mortiès★. Best years: (reds) 2001 **00 99 98 96 95 93 90**.

FRANZ X PICHLER *Wachau, Niederösterreich, Austria* Austria's most famous producer of dry wines. Demand for his Rieslings and Grüner Veltliners far outstrips supply. Top wines Grüner Veltliner and Riesling 'M'★★★ (for monumental) and Riesling Unendlich★★★ (endless), an alcoholically potent but perfectly balanced dry Riesling, are amazing. Since 1997 he has teamed up with Szemes and TEMENT in BURGENLAND to make red Arachon★★. Best years: (Riesling/Grüner Veltliner Smaragd) (2002) 01 00 99 98 **97 95 94 93 92** 90.

CH. PICHON-LONGUEVILLE★★★ *Pauillac AC, 2ème Cru Classé, Haut-Médoc, Bordeaux, France* Despite its superb vineyards with the potential for making great PAUILLAC, Pichon-Longueville (called Pichon-Baron until 1988) wines were 'also-rans' for a long time. In 1987 the management was taken over by Jean-Michel Cazes of LYNCH-BAGES and, since then, there has been a remarkable change in fortune. Most recent vintages have been of First Growth standard, with firm tannic structure and rich dark fruit. Cellar for at least 10 years, although it is likely to keep for 30. Second wine: les Tourelles de Pichon. Best years: 2001 **00** 99 98 97 96 95 **90 89 88 86 82**.

CH. PICHON-LONGUEVILLE-LALANDE★★★ *Pauillac AC, 2ème Cru Classé, Haut-Médoc, Bordeaux, France* Pichon-Longueville-Lalande has been run since 1978 by the inspirational figure of Madame de Lencquesaing, who has led the property ever upwards through her superlative vineyard management and winemaking sensitivity. Divinely scented and lush at 6–7 years, the wines usually last for 20

213

at least. Things dipped at the end of the 1980s, but recent efforts have been excellent. Second wine: Réserve de la Comtesse. Best years: 2001 00 99 98 97 96 95 **90 89 88 86 85 83 82 81**.

PIEDMONT *Italy* This is the most important Italian region for the tradition of quality wines. In the north, there is Carema, Ghemme and GATTINARA. To the south, in the LANGHE hills, there's BAROLO and BARBARESCO, both masterful examples of the Nebbiolo grape, and other wines from Dolcetto and Barbera grapes. In the Monferrato hills, in the provinces of Asti and Alessandria, the Barbera, Moscato and Cortese grapes hold sway. Recent changes in the system have created the broad DOCs of Langhe and Monferrato and the regionwide Piemonte appellation, designed to classify all wines of quality from a great range of grape varieties. See also Asti, Erbaluce di Caluso, Gavi, Moscato d'Asti, Nebbiolo d'Alba, Roero.

PIEROPAN *Veneto, Italy* Leonildo Pieropan produces exceptionally good SOAVE Classico★ and, from 2 single vineyards, Calvarino★★ and La Rocca★★. Excellent RECIOTO DI SOAVE Le Colombare★★, and opulent Passito della Rocca★★, a barrique-aged blend of Sauvignon, Riesling Italico and Trebbiano di Soave. Single-vineyard Soaves can improve for 5 years or more, as can the Recioto and other sweet styles.

PIERRO *Margaret River, Western Australia* Mike Peterkin makes Pierro Chardonnay★★★ by the hatful, yet still it is a masterpiece of power and complexity. The LTC Semillon-Sauvignon-Chardonnay blend★ is full with just a hint of leafiness, while Pinot Noir★ continues to improve as the vines age. Dark, dense Cabernets★★ is the serious, BORDEAUX-like member of the family. The Fire Gully range is sourced from a nearby vineyard, owned and managed by Peterkin. Best years: (Chardonnay) **1999 97 96 94 93**.

PIESPORT *Mosel, Germany* The generic Piesporter Michelsberg wines, soft, sweet and easy-drinking, have nothing to do with the excellent Rieslings from the top Goldtröpfchen site. With their intense peach and blackcurrant aromas they are unique among MOSEL wines. Best producers: GRANS-FASSIAN★, Reinhold HAART★★, Kurt Hain★, von KESSELSTATT★, St Urbans-Hof★, Weller-Lehnert. Best years: (Riesling Spätlese) (2002) 01 00 **99** 98 **97 96 95** 93 **92 90** 89.

CH. LE PIN★★★ *Pomerol AC, Bordeaux, France* Now one of the most expensive wines in the world, with prices at auction overtaking those for PETRUS. The 1979 was the first vintage and the wines, which are concentrated but elegant, are produced from 100% Merlot. The tiny 2ha (5-acre) vineyard lies close to those of TROTANOY and VIEUX-CH.-CERTAN. Best years: 2001 00 99 98 96 95 **94 90 89 88 86 85 83 82 81**.

PINE RIDGE WINERY *Stags Leap District AVA, California, USA* Pine Ridge offers wines from several NAPA AVAs, but its flagship Cabernet remains the supple, plummy Stags Leap District★★. Andrus Reserve★★, a BORDEAUX blend, has more richness and power. CARNEROS Merlot★★ is spicy and cherry fruited, and Carneros Chardonnay★ looks good. Best years: (Stags Leap Cabernet) (2001) 00 99 97 96 **95 94 91**.

PINGUS, DOMINIO DE *Ribera del Duero DO, Castilla y León, Spain* Peter Sisseck's tiny vineyards and winery have attracted worldwide attention since 1995 due to the extraordinary depth and character of the cult wine they produce, Pingus★★★. Second wine Flor de Pingus★★ is also super. Best years: (Pingus) (2001) 00 **99 98 97 96 95**.

PINOT BIANCO See Pinot Blanc.

PINOT BLANC Wine made from the Pinot Blanc grape has a clear, yeasty, appley taste, and good examples can age to a delicious honeyed fullness. In France its chief power-base is in ALSACE, where it is taking over the 'workhorse' role from Sylvaner and Chasselas. Most CRÉMANT D'ALSACE now uses it as the principal variety. Important in northern Italy as Pinot Bianco, but it is probably taken most seriously in southern Germany and Austria (as Weissburgunder), producing imposing wines with ripe pear and peach fruit and a distinct nutty character. Also successful in Hungary, Slovakia, Slovenia and the Czech Republic. Promising new plantings in CALIFORNIA, OREGON and Canada.

PINOT GRIGIO See Pinot Gris.

PINOT GRIS At its finest in France's ALSACE; with reasonable acidity and a deep colour the grape produces fat, rich wines that mature wonderfully. It is very occasionally used in BURGUNDY (called Pinot Beurot) to add fatness to a wine. As Pinot Grigio it is grown in northern Italy, where it produces some of the country's most popular yet boring dry whites, but also some of the most exciting. Also successful in Austria and Germany as Ruländer or Grauburgunder, and as Malvoisie in the Swiss VALAIS. There are some good Romanian and Czech examples, as well as spirited ones in Hungary (as Szürkebarát). In a crisp style, it is very successful in OREGON and showing some promise in CALIFORNIA and Canada's OKANAGAN VALLEY. Becoming fashionable in New Zealand and in the cooler regions of Australia.

PINOT MEUNIER The most widely planted grape in the CHAMPAGNE region. A vital ingredient in Champagne, along with Pinot Noir and Chardonnay – though it is the least well known of the 3.

PINOT NERO See Pinot Noir.
PINOT NOIR See pages 216–17.

PINOTAGE A Pinot Noir x Cinsaut cross, conceived in South Africa in 1925 but not widely planted until the 1950s. Today it covers 6.5% of the country's vineyards. Its versatility allows for success with styles as wide ranging as sparkling to fortified dessert, but the more classic versions are full-bodied, well-oaked with ripe plum, spice and maybe some mineral, banana or marshmallow flavours. New Zealand's limited plantings produce several examples – a few are interesting. California, too, is showing some good results. A little is also grown in New York, Virginia, Brazil and Zimbabwe. **Best producers (South Africa):** Graham BECK (sparkling★, Old Road★), Bellingham (Premium★), BEYERSKLOOF★, Clos Malverne★, Diemersfontein★, FAIRVIEW★, GRANGEHURST★, Kaapzicht★, KANONKOP★★, L'AVENIR★, Newton Johnson★, Simonsig★, SPICE ROUTE★★, Stony Brook★, Tukulu, Uiterwyk★ (Top of the Hill★★), WARWICK; (New Zealand): BABICH.

PIPER-HEIDSIECK *Champagne AC, Champagne, France* Traditionally one of CHAMPAGNE's least distinguished brands, though the owners, Rémy Cointreau, have made great improvements. The non-vintage★ is gentler and more biscuity than it used to be, and the vintage★★ has started to show real class. De luxe cuvée Champagne Rare★★ is pretty good. **Best years:** (1995) **90 89 85 82**.

PINOT NOIR

There's this myth about Pinot Noir that I think I'd better lay to rest. It goes something like this. Pinot Noir is an incredibly tricky grape to grow and even more difficult grape to vinify; in fact Pinot Noir is such a difficult customer that the only place that regularly achieves magical results is the thin stretch of land known as the Côte d'Or, between Dijon and Chagny in France, where mesoclimate, soil conditions and 2000 years of experience weave an inimitable web of pleasure.

This just isn't so. The thin-skinned, early-ripening Pinot Noir is undoubtedly more difficult to grow than other great varieties like Cabernet or Chardonnay, but that doesn't mean that it's impossible to grow elsewhere – you just have to work at it with more sensitivity and seek out the right growing conditions. And although great red Burgundy is a hauntingly beautiful wine, many Burgundians completely fail to deliver the magic, and the glorious thing about places like New Zealand, California, Oregon, Australia and Germany is that we are seeing an ever-increasing number of wines that are thrillingly different from anything produced in Burgundy, yet with flavours that are unique to Pinot Noir.

WINE STYLES

France All France's great Pinot Noir wines do come from Burgundy's Côte d'Or. Rarely deep in colour, they should nonetheless possess a wonderful fruit quality when young – raspberry, strawberry, cherry or plum – that becomes more scented and exotic with age, the plums turning to figs and pine, and the richness of chocolate mingling perilously with truffles and well-hung game. Strange, challenging, hedonistic. France's other Pinots – in north and south Burgundy, the Loire, Jura, Savoie, Alsace and now occasionally in the south of France – are lighter and milder, and in Champagne its pale, thin wine is used to make sparkling wine.

Other European regions Since the 1990s, helped by good vintages, German winemakers have made considerable efforts to produce serious Pinot Noir (generally called Spätburgunder). Italy, where it is called Pinot Nero, and Switzerland (as Blauburgunder) both have fair success with the variety. Austria and Spain have produced a couple of good examples, and Romania, the Czech Republic and Hungary produce significant amounts of Pinot Noir, though of generally low quality.

New World Light, fragrant wines have bestowed upon Oregon the reputation for being 'another Burgundy'; but I get more excited about the sensual wines of California. The cool, fog-affected areas stand out: the ripe, stylish Russian River Valley examples; the marvellously fruity, exotically scented wines of Carneros; and the startlingly original offerings from Santa Barbara County.

New Zealand is the most important southern hemisphere producer, with wines of thrilling fruit and individuality, most notably from Martinborough, Canterbury's Waipara district and Central Otago. In the cooler regions of Australia – including Yarra Valley, Adelaide Hills, North-East Victoria and Tasmania – producers are beginning to find their way with the variety. New Burgundian clones now reaching maturity bode well for South African Pinot Noir. Chile also has a few fine producers.

217

PIPERS BROOK VINEYARD *Northern Tasmania, Australia* Keenly sough wines combining highish prices, clever marketing and skillec winemaking. Steely Riesling★★, classically reserved Chardonnay★★ fragrant Gewürztraminer★ and refreshing Pinot Gris★ are highlights as well as increasingly good Pinot Noir (Reserve★, Blackwood★ anc Lyre★★). Its traditional-method sparkling wine, Pirie★★, may achieve ★★★ with a little extra age. Ninth Island, the second label, is good. Best years: (Riesling) 2001 **00 99 98 97 95 94 93 92 91 90**.

PLAIMONT, PRODUCTEURS *Madiran AC, Côtes de St-Mont VDQS and Vir de Pays des Côtes de Gascogne, South-West France* This grouping of 3 Gascon co-ops is the largest, most reliable and most go-ahead producer of COTES DE GASCOGNE and COTES DE ST-MONT. The whites, ful of crisp fruit, are reasonably priced and are best drunk young. The reds, especially Ch. St-Go★ and de Sabazan★, are very good too. Alsc good MADIRAN and PACHERENC DU VIC-BILH.

PLANETA *Sicily, Italy* Rapidly expanding, young and dynamic estate. Chardonnay★★ is already one of the best in southern Italy; Cabernet Sauvignon Burdese★ and Merlot★ are improving every year; and rich, peppery Santa Cecilia★★ (Nero d'Avola) is aiming for international stardom. The latest addition is a fascinating Sicilian version of FIANO, Cometa★★. Basic La Segreta red★ and white★ blends are marvellously fruity.

PLANTAGENET *Great Southern, Western Australia* Influential winery in the GREAT SOUTHERN region, contract-making wine for smaller outfits and producing its own flavourful range, notably spicy Shiraz★★ (at best, ★★★), limy Riesling★★, melony/nutty Chardonnay★★, plump Pinot Noir★ and classy Cabernet Sauvignon★★. Omrah is the second label, made from bought-in grapes – Sauvignon Blanc★, Chardonnay★ and Shiraz★ stand out. Best years: (Cabernet Sauvignon) 2001 98 97 **96 95 94 93 91 90 86 85**.

POL ROGER *Champagne AC, Champagne, France* Makers of Winston Churchill's favourite CHAMPAGNE and for many years a great favourite of the British market. The non-vintage White Foil★ (renamed Réserve as from December 2002) is biscuity and dependable rather than thrilling. Pol Roger also produces a vintage★★, a vintage rosé★★, a vintage Grand Cru Chardonnay★★ and a vintage Réserve Spécial★★ (50% Chardonnay). Its top Champagne, the Pinot-dominated Cuvée Sir Winston Churchill★★, is a deliciously refined drink. All vintage wines will improve with another 5 years' keeping or more. Best years: (1996) 95 **93 90 89 88 86 85 82**.

POLIZIANO *Vino Nobile di Montepulciano DOCG, Tuscany, Italy* A leading light in Montepulciano. VINO NOBILE★★ is far better than average, especially the Riserva Vigna Asinone★★. SUPER-TUSCAN Le Stanze★★★ (Cabernet Sauvignon-Merlot) has been outstanding in recent vintages – the fruit in part coming from owner Carletti's other estate, Lohsa, in MORELLINO DI SCANSANO. Best years: (Vino Nobile) (2001) (99) 98 97 **96 95 93 90**.

POLZ *Steiermark, Austria* Brothers Erich and Walter Polz are probably the most consistent producers of aromatic dry white wines in Styria. Few wines here fail to reach ★, and with Weissburgunder (Pinot Blanc), Morillon (Chardonnay) and Sauvignon Blanc the combination of intensity and elegance frequently deserves ★★. Steirische Klassik indicates wines vinified without any new oak. Best years: (Morillon, Sauvignon Blanc) (2002) 01 00 **99 97**.

POMEROL AC *Bordeaux, France* The Pomerol AC includes some of the world's most sought-after red wines. Pomerol's unique quality lies in its deep clay in which the Merlot grape flourishes. The result is seductively rich, almost creamy wine with wonderful mouthfilling fruit flavours. Best producers: Beauregard★, Bonalgue, le BON PASTEUR★★, Certan-de-May★★, Clinet★★, Clos l'Église★, Clos René★, la CONSEILLANTE★★, l'EGLISE-CLINET★★★, l'EVANGILE★★, la FLEUR-PETRUS★★, GAZIN★★, Hosanna★ (previously Certan-Guiraud), LAFLEUR★★★, LATOUR-A-POMEROL★★, Montviel, Nénin★ (since 1990), PETIT-VILLAGE★★, PETRUS★★★, Le PIN★★★, Sales★, TROTANOY★★, VIEUX-CHATEAU-CERTAN★★. Best years: 2000 98 96 95 **94 90** 89 88 86 85 83 82.

POMINO DOC See Chianti Rufina.

POMMARD AC *Côte de Beaune, Burgundy, France* The first village south of Beaune. At their best, the wines should have full, round, beefy flavours. Can age well, often for 10 years or more. There are no Grands Crus but les Rugiens Bas and les Épenots (both Premiers Crus) occupy the best sites. Best producers: Comte Armand★★★, J-M Boillot★, Carré-Courbin, Courcel★★, Dancer★, P Garaudet★, M Gaunoux★, V GIRARDIN★★★, LAFARGE★★, Lejeune★, Montille★★, J & A Parent★, Ch. de Pommard★, Pothier-Rieusset★. Best years: (2002) 99 98 97 96 95 **93 90 89 88**.

POMMERY *Champagne AC, Champagne, France* This warmly regarded CHAMPAGNE house has a new owner, Paul-François Vranken. Continuity of style should be assured under new winemaker Thierry Gasco, who worked with previous incumbent, Prince Alain de Polignac, a descendant of Madame Pommery, for nearly a decade. Restrained non-vintage Brut Royal is often surpassed by another non-vintage, Apanage★. Austere vintage Brut★ is delicious with maturity, and the prestige cuvée Louise, both white★★ and rosé★★, is the epitome of discreet, perfumed elegance. Best years: (1996) 95 **92 90** 89 88 85 82.

CH. PONTET-CANET★★ *Pauillac AC, 5ème Cru Classé, Haut-Médoc, Bordeaux, France* The vineyards of this property are located close to those of MOUTON-ROTHSCHILD. Since 1979, when the Tesserons of LAFON-ROCHET bought the property, there has been a gradual return to the typical PAUILLAC style of big, chewy, intense claret that develops a beautiful blackcurrant fruit. Now one of the best value of the Classed Growths. Best years: 2001 00 99 98 96 95 **94 90** 89 86 85 83 82.

PORT See pages 220–1.

CH. POTENSAC★★ *Médoc AC, Cru Bourgeois, Bordeaux, France* Potensac's fabulous success is based on quality, consistency and value for money. Owned and run by the Delon family, of LEOVILLE-LAS-CASES, the wine can be drunk at 4–5 years, but fine vintages will improve for at least 10 years. Best years: 2001 00 99 98 **96 95 90** 89 88 86.

POUILLY-FUISSÉ AC *Mâconnais, Burgundy, France* Chardonnay from 5 villages, including Pouilly and Fuissé. For several years high prices and low quality meant this was a wine to avoid, but now there are some committed growers producing buttery, creamy wines that can be delicious at 2 years but will often develop beautifully for up to 10. Best producers: D & M Barraud★★, Corsin★★, C & T Drouin★, J-A Ferret★★★, M Forest★★, Ch. Fuissé★, Guffens-Heynen (VERGET)★★★, R Lassarat★★, Léger-Plumet★, R Luquet★, O Merlin★★, Robert-Denogent★★, Saumaize-Michelin★★, Valette★★★. Best years: (2002) 01 00 **99 98 97 96 95**.

PORT DOC

Douro, Portugal

 The Douro region in northern Portugal, where the grapes for port are grown, is wild and beautiful. Steep hills covered in vineyard terraces plunge dramatically down to the Douro river. Grapes are one of the only crops that will grow in the inhospitable climate, which gets progressively drier the further inland you travel. But not all the Douro's grapes qualify to be made into increasingly good port. A quota is established every year, and the rest are made into table wines.

Red port grapes include Touriga Francesa, Tinta Roriz, Touriga Nacional, Tinta Barroca, Tinta Cão and Tinta Amarela. Grapes for white port include Malvasia Dorada, Malvasia Fina, Gouveio and Rabigato. The grapes are partially fermented, and then *aguardente* (grape spirit) is added – fortifying the wine, stopping the fermentation and leaving sweet, unfermented grape sugar in the finished port.

PORT STYLES

Vintage Finest of the ports matured in bottle, made from grapes from the best vineyards. Vintage port is not 'declared' every year (usually there are 3 or 4 declarations per decade), but only during the second year in cask, if the shipper thinks the standard is high enough. It is bottled after 2 years, and may be consumed soon afterwards, not uncommon in the USA; at this stage it packs quite a punch. The British custom of aging for 20 years or more can yield exceptional mellowness.

Single quinta A true single-quinta wine comes from an individual estate; however, many shippers sell their vintage port under a quinta name in years which are not declared as a vintage, even though it may be sourced from 2 or 3 different vineyards. It is quite possible for these 'off vintage' ports to equal or even surpass the vintage wines from the same house.

Aged tawny Matured in cask for 10, 20, 30 or even 40 years before bottling, older tawnies have delicious nut and fig flavours.

Colheita Tawny from a single vintage, matured in cask for at least 7 years – potentially the finest of the aged tawnies.

Late Bottled Vintage (LBV)/Late Bottled Port matured for 4–6 years in cask then usually filtered to avoid sediment forming in the bottle. Traditional unfiltered LBV has much more flavour and like vintage port requires decanting; it can generally be aged for another 5 years or more.

Crusted Rarely seen today, this is a blend of good ports from 2–3 vintages, bottled without filtration after 3–4 years in cask. A deposit (crust) forms in the bottle and the wine should be decanted.

Vintage Character (also known as Premium Ruby) has an average of 3–5 years' age. A handful represent good value.

Ruby The youngest red port with only 1–3 years' age. Ruby port should be bursting with young, almost peppery fruit, and there has been an improvement in quality of late, except at the cheapest level.

Tawny Cheap tawny is either an emaciated ruby, or a blend of ruby and white port, and is both dilute and raw.

White Only the best taste dry and nutty from wood-aging; most are coarse and alcoholic, best drunk chilled or with tonic water.

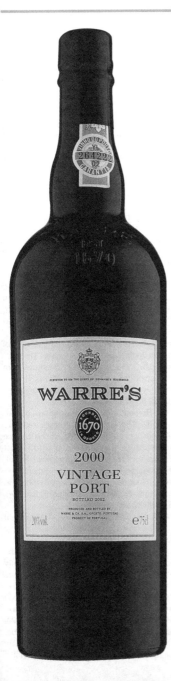

BEST PRODUCERS

Vintage BURMESTER, CHURCHILL, COCKBURN, CROFT, Delaforce, DOW, FERREIRA, FONSECA, GRAHAM, NIEPOORT, NOVAL (including Nacional), SMITH WOODHOUSE, TAYLOR, WARRE.

Single quinta BURMESTER (Quinta Nova de Nossa Senhora do Carmo), CHURCHILL (Agua Alta), COCKBURN (Quinta dos Canais), Quinta do CRASTO, CROFT (Quinta da Roêda), Delaforce (Quinta da Corte), DOW (Quinta do Bomfim), FONSECA (Guimaraens), GRAHAM (Malvedos), Martinez (Quinta da Eira Velha), NIEPOORT (Quinta do Passadouro), NOVAL (Silval), Quinta de la ROSA, SMITH WOODHOUSE (Madalena), TAYLOR (Quinta de Terra Feita, Quinta de Vargellas), Quinta Vale Dona Maria, Quinta do VESUVIO, WARRE (Quinta da Cavadinha).

Aged tawny Barros, BURMESTER, COCKBURN, DOW, FERREIRA, FONSECA, GRAHAM, Krohn, NIEPOORT, NOVAL, RAMOS PINTO, la ROSA, SANDEMAN, TAYLOR, WARRE.

Colheita Barros, BURMESTER, Feist, Krohn, NIEPOORT, NOVAL.

Traditional Late Bottled Vintage CHURCHILL, CRASTO, Infantado, NIEPOORT, NOVAL, RAMOS PINTO, la ROSA, SMITH WOODHOUSE, Vale da Mina, WARRE.

Crusted CHURCHILL, DOW.

Ruby COCKBURN, FERREIRA, FONSECA, GRAHAM, la ROSA, SANDEMAN, SMITH WOODHOUSE, TAYLOR, WARRE.

White CHURCHILL, NIEPOORT.

POUILLY-FUMÉ AC *Loire Valley, France* Fumé means 'smoked' in
French and a good Pouilly-Fumé has a pungent smell often likened to
gunflint. The only grape allowed is the Sauvignon Blanc, and the
extra smokiness comes from a flinty soil called silex. Despite the efforts
of a few producers, this is a disappointingly underperforming and
overpriced AC. Best producers: Berthiers★, G Blanchet★, Henri
Bourgeois★, A Cailbourdin★, J-C Chatelain★, Didier DAGUENEAU★★,
Serge Dagueneau★, M Deschamps★, Ladoucette★, Landrat-Guyollot★,
Masson-Blondelet★, M Redde★, Tinel-Blondelet★, Ch. de Tracy★. Best
years: (2002) **00 99 98 97 96 95 90**.

POUILLY-LOCHÉ AC See Pouilly-Vinzelles AC.

POUILLY-SUR-LOIRE AC *Loire Valley, France* Light appley wines from
the Chasselas grape from vineyards around Pouilly-sur-Loire, the town
which gave its name to POUILLY-FUME. Drink as young as possible.

POUILLY-VINZELLES AC *Mâconnais, Burgundy, France* A small AC
which, with its neighbour Pouilly-Loché (whose wines may be sold as
Pouilly-Vinzelles), lies somewhat in the shadow of big brother POUILLY-
FUISSE. Most of the wines come through the local co-operative, but
there are now some good domaines offering rich white wines from the
steep east-facing slopes. Best producers: Cave des Grands Crus Blancs,
la Soufrandière★★, Tripoz★, Valette★. Best years: (2002) 01 00 **99**.

CH. POUJEAUX★★ *Moulis AC, Cru Bourgeois, Haut-Médoc, Bordeaux,
France* Poujeaux is one reason why MOULIS AC is attracting attention:
the wines have a delicious chunky fruit and new-oak sweetness.
Attractive at 6–7 years old, good vintages can easily last for 20–30
years. Best years: 2001 00 98 96 **95 94 90 89 88 86 85 83 82**.

PRAGER *Wachau, Niederösterreich, Austria* Toni Bodenstein is one of
the pioneers of the region, producing the first Riesling Trocken-
beerenauslese★★★ in the WACHAU in 1993. Also top dry Rieslings from
the Achleiten and Klaus vineyards★★★ and excellent Grüner
Veltliners from the Achleiten vineyard★★. Best years: (Riesling/Grüner
Veltliner Smaragd) (2002) 01 00 99 98 **97 96 95 93 92 90 86**.

PREMIÈRES CÔTES DE BLAYE AC *Bordeaux, France* An improving AC
on the right bank of the Gironde. The fresh, Merlot-based reds are
ready at 2–3 years but will age for more. Top red wines can be
labelled under the new, quality-driven Blaye AC from 2002. Best
producers: (reds) Bel-Air la Royère★, Haut-Bertinerie★, Haut-Grelot,
Haut-Sociando, Jonqueyres★, Loumède, Mondésir-Gazin★, Rolande-la-
Garde, Segonzac★, Sociando, Tourtes; (whites) Haut-Bertinerie★,
Charron (Acacia★), Cave des Hauts de Gironde, Tourtes (Prestige★).
Best years: 2001 00 **98 96 95 94 90 89 88**.

PREMIÈRES CÔTES DE BORDEAUX AC *Bordeaux, France* Hilly region
overlooking GRAVES and SAUTERNES across the Garonne. For a long time
the AC was best known for its Sauternes-style sweet wines, particularly
from the communes of CADILLAC, LOUPIAC and STE-CROIX-DU-MONT, but
the juicy reds and rosés have now forged ahead. These are usually
delicious at 2–3 years old but should last for 5–6 years. Dry whites are
designated BORDEAUX AC. Best producers: (reds) Brethous★, CARSIN★,
Chelivette, Clos Ste-Anne, Grand-Mouëys★, Haux★, Jonchet, Juge
(Dupleich), Lamothe-de-Haux★, Langoiran, Melin, Puy-Bardens★,
REYNON★, le Sens, Suau, Tanesse. Best years: (reds) **2000 98 96 95 94 90**.

CH. PRIEURÉ-LICHINE★ *Margaux AC, 4ème Cru Classé, Haut-Médoc,
Bordeaux, France* Seriously underachieving property that saw
several false dawns before being sold in 1999. Right Bank specialist

Stéphane Derenoncourt of PAVIE-MACQUIN and CANON-LA-GAFFELIERE fame is now the consultant winemaker, and hopefully the wine will return at very least to its traditional gentle, perfumed style. Best years: 2001 00 99 98 96 **95 94 90 89 88 86 85 83 82**.

PRIEURÉ DE ST-JEAN DE BÉBIAN *Coteaux du Languedoc AC, Languedoc, France* One of the pioneering estates in the MIDI, now owned by former wine writer Chantal Lecouty and her husband. It took a dip in the early 1990s but is once more back on form, producing an intense, spicy, generous red★★. The second wine is La Chapelle de Bébian, and there is also a barrel-fermented white. Best years: (red) 2001 00 **99 98 97 96 95**.

PRIMITIVO DI MANDURIA DOC *Puglia, Italy* The most important appellation for PUGLIA's Primitivo grape, which has been enjoying a renaissance of interest since it was found to be identical to California's Zinfandel. The best wines combine outstanding ripeness and concentration with a knockout alcohol level. Good Primitivo is also sold as IGT Primitivo del Tarantino. Best producers: Felline★★, Pervini★★, Giovanni Soloperto. Best years: (2001) 00 **98 97**.

PRIMO ESTATE *Adelaide Plains, South Australia* Innovative Joe Grilli stuck his winery in one of Australia's hottest climates but works miracles with his own grapes and those from outlying areas. The premium label is Joseph: Grilli adapts the Italian *amarone* method for Moda Amarone Cabernet-Merlot★★ (★★★ with 10 years' age!) and makes a dense, eye-popping Joseph Red fizz★. He also does a sensuous Botrytis Riesling La Magia★★, fabulous honeyed fortified Fronti★★★, surprising dry white La Biondina Colombard★, and cherry-ripe Il Briccone★, a Shiraz-Sangiovese blend – and superb olive oils★★★. Best years: (Cabernet-Merlot Joseph) 2001 00 99 98 97 **96 95 94 93 91 90**.

PRIORAT DOC *Cataluña, Spain* A hilly, isolated district with very low-yielding vineyards planted on precipitous slopes of deep slate soil. Old-style fortified *rancio* wines used to attract little attention. Then in the 1990s a group of young winemakers revolutionized the area, bringing in state-of-the-art winemaking methods and grape varieties such as Cabernet Sauvignon to back up the native Garnacha and Cariñena. Their rare, expensive wines have taken the world by storm. Ready at 5 years old, the best will last much longer. The region was elevated to DOC status in 2001. Best producers: Bodegas B G (Gueta-Lupía★), Capafons-Ossó★, Cims de Porrera★★, CLOS ERASMUS★★★, CLOS MOGADOR★★★, La Conreria d'Scala Dei★, Costers del Siurana (Clos de l'Obac★★), J M Fuentes (Gran Clos★★), Mas Doix★★, Mas d'en Gil (Clos Fontà★★), Mas Martinet (Clos Martinet★★), Alvaro PALACIOS★★★, Pasanau Germans (Finca la Planeta★), Rotllan Torra★, Scala Dei★, VALL-LLACH★★. Best years: (reds) (2001) 00 99 98 **96 95 94 93 90**.

PROSECCO DI CONEGLIANO-VALDOBBIADENE DOC *Veneto, Italy* The Prosecco grape gives soft, scented wine made sparkling by a second fermentation in tank, though Prosecco can also be still, or *tranquillo*. Generally, however, it is a spumante or frizzante for drinking young. Cartizze, from a vineyard area of that name, is the most refined. Best producers: Adami★, Bernardi★, Bisol★, Carpenè Malvolti★, Le Colture, Col Vetoraz★, Nino Franco★, Ruggeri & C★, Tanorè★, Zardetto★.

PROVENCE *France* Provence is home to France's oldest vineyards but the region is better known for its beaches and arts festivals than for its wines. However, it seems even Provence is caught up in the revolution sweeping through the vineyards of southern France. The area has 5 small ACs (BANDOL, les BAUX-DE-PROVENCE, BELLET, CASSIS and PALETTE), but most of the wine comes from the much larger areas of the COTES DE PROVENCE, COTEAUX VAROIS, Coteaux de Pierrevert and COTEAUX D'AIX-EN-PROVENCE. VdP des BOUCHES-DU-RHONE is also becoming increasingly important. Provençal reds are generally better than whites and rosés.

J J PRÜM *Bernkastel, Mosel, Germany*   Estate making some of Germany's
♀ best Riesling in sites like the Sonnenuhr★★★ in WEHLEN, Himmelreich★★ in GRAACH and Lay★★ and Badstube★★ in BERNKASTEL. All have great aging potential. Best years: (2002) 01 99 98 **97** 96 95 **94 93 90 88 85 83 79 76 71**.

S A PRÜM *Wehlen, Mosel, Germany*   There are a confusing number of
♀ Prüms in the MOSEL – the best known is J J PRUM, but Raimund Prüm of S A Prüm comes a decent second. The estate's most interesting wines are Riesling from WEHLENer Sonnenuhr, especially Auslese★★, but it also makes good wine from sites in BERNKASTEL★, GRAACH★ and Zeltingen★. Best years: (2002) 01 99 **97 95 93 90 88 86 85**.

PRUNOTTO *Barolo DOCG, Piedmont, Italy*   One of the great BAROLO
♥ producers, now ably run by Albiera, the eldest of Piero ANTINORI's 3 daughters. Highlights include BARBERA D'ALBA Pian Romualdo★★, BARBERA D'ASTI Costamiòle★★, NEBBIOLO D'ALBA Occhetti★★, Barolo Bussia★★★ and Cannubi★★ and new BARBARESCO Bric Turot★★. Also produces good MOSCATO D'ASTI★, BARBERA D'ASTI Fiulot★ and ROERO Arneis★. Best years: (Barolo) (2001) (00) 99 98 97 96 **95 93 90 89 88 85**.

PUGLIA *Italy*   This southern region is a prolific source of blending wines, but exciting progress has been made with native varieties: Uva di Troia in CASTEL DEL MONTE; Negroamaro in SALICE SALENTINO and other reds and rosés of the Salento peninsula; white Greco for characterful Gravina, revived by Botromagno; and Verdeca and Bianco d'Alessano for Locorotondo. But it is the red Primitivo (CALIFORNIA's Zinfandel), led by examples from producers under the ACCADEMIA DEI RACEMI umbrella, that is set to make the biggest impact, whether under the PRIMITIVO DI MANDURIA DOC or more general IGTs.

PUISSEGUIN-ST-ÉMILION AC *Bordeaux, France*   Small ST-EMILION satellite
♥ AC. The wines are generally fairly solid but with an attractive chunky fruit and usually make good drinking at 3–5 years. Best producers: Bel-Air, Branda, Durand-Laplagne★, Fongaban, Guibeau-la-Fourvieille, Laurets, la Mauriane★, Producteurs Réunis, Soleil. Best years: 2001 00 **98 96 95**.

PULIGNY-MONTRACHET AC *Côte de Beaune, Burgundy, France*   Puligny
♀ is one of the finest white wine villages in the world and adds the name of its greatest Grand Cru, le MONTRACHET, to its own. There are 3 other Grands Crus (BATARD-MONTRACHET, Bienvenues-BATARD-MONTRACHET and Chevalier-MONTRACHET) and 11 Premiers Crus. The flatter vineyards use the Puligny-Montrachet AC. Good vintages really need 5 years' aging, while Premiers Crus and Grands Crus may need 10 years and can last for 20 or more. Only about 3% of the AC is red wine. Best producers: J-M Boillot★★, CARILLON★★★, J Chartron★, G Chavy★, DROUHIN★, A Ente★★, B Ente★, JADOT★★, Larue★★, LATOUR★★, Dom. LEFLAIVE★★★ (since 1994), O LEFLAIVE★, P Pernot★★, Ch. de Puligny-Montrachet★★, RAMONET★★, SAUZET★★. Best years: (2002) 01 00 99 **97 96 95 92**.

PYRENEES See Grampians and Pyrenees.

QUARTS DE CHAUME AC *Loire Valley, France* The Chenin Blanc grape finds one of its most rewarding mesoclimates here. Quarts de Chaume is a 40ha (100-acre) AC within the larger COTEAUX DU LAYON AC and, as autumn mists begin to curl off the river Layon, noble rot attacks the

grapes. The result is intense, sweet wines which can last for longer than almost any in the world – although many can be drunk after 5 years. Best producers: BAUMARD★★★, Bellerive★★, Laffourcade★, Pierre-Bise★★, J Pithon★★★, Plaisance★, Joseph Renou★★, Suronde★★. Best years: (2002) 01 99 **97 96 95 94 93 90 89 88 85 83 81 78 76 70 69 64 59 47**.

QUEENSLAND *Australia* Queensland still has the smallest production of all Australia's wine-producing states, but is catching up fast. About 30 wineries perch on rocky hills in the main region, the Granite Belt, near the NEW SOUTH WALES border. New regions South Burnett, north-west of Brisbane, Mount Cotton, Mount Tamborine and Toowoomba are showing some promise. Best producers: Albert River, Bald Mountain, Boireann, Robert Channon, Clovely Estate, Cody's, Kominos, Preston Peak, Robinsons Family, Sirromet, Wild Soul, Windermere.

QUERCIABELLA *Chianti Classico DOCG, Tuscany, Italy* This model of a modern CHIANTI producer serves up a gorgeously scented, rich-fruited Chianti Classico★★ and Riserva★★. But it has made an even greater splash with its three SUPER-TUSCANS: BURGUNDY-like white Batàr★★ from Pinot Bianco and Chardonnay; tobaccoey, spicy Sangiovese-Cabernet blend Camartina★★★; and newly launched Palofreno★ (Sangiovese-Merlot). Best years: (Camartina) (2001) (99) 97 95 **93 90 88**.

QUILCEDA CREEK *Washington State, USA* This tiny winery has built a cult following in Washington because of a big, rich Cabernet Sauvignon★★★. The wine can be a bit overpowering, but it does open up to stunning effect after a while in the glass and it has good aging potential. Since 1997 a less expensive Columbia Valley Red★★ has been produced from a blend of Cabernets Sauvignon and Franc and Merlot. Best years: (Cabernet) (2001) 00 99 98 97 **96 95**.

QUINCY AC *Loire Valley, France* Intensely flavoured, dry white wine from Sauvignon Blanc vineyards west of Bourges. Can age for a year or two but always keeps a rather aggressive gooseberry flavour. Best producers: Ballandors, H Bourgeois★, Mardon★, J Rouzé, Silices de Quincy, Troterau★. Best years: (2002) **01 00 99**.

QUINTARELLI *Valpolicella DOC, Veneto, Italy* Giuseppe Quintarelli is the great traditional winemaker of VALPOLICELLA. His philosophy is one of vinifying only the very best grapes and leaving nature to do the rest. His Classico Superiore★★ is left in cask for about 4 years and his famed AMARONE★★★ and RECIOTO★★ for 7 years or more before release. There is also Alzero★★, a spectacular Amarone-style wine made from Cabernets Franc and Sauvignon. Best years: (Amarone) (1997) **95 93 90 88 85 83**.

QUPÉ *Santa Maria Valley AVA, California, USA* Owner/winemaker Bob Lindquist makes a gorgeously tasty Bien Nacido Reserve Syrah★★. His Reserve Chardonnay★★ and Bien Nacido Cuvée★★ (two-thirds

Chardonnay, one-third Viognier) have sublime appley fruit and perfume. A leading exponent of RHONE-style wines, he also makes Viognier★, Mourvèdre★ and Marsanne★. Best years: (Reserve Syrah) (2001) (00) 99 98 97 **96 95 94 91 90**.

CH. DE LA RAGOTIÈRE *Muscadet Sèvre-et-Maine, Loire Valley, France*
The inexhaustibly inventive Couillaud brothers claim to have salvaged the reputation of Muscadet in US restaurants with M★★, an old-vines wine matured *sur lie* for over 2 years. The standard Muscadet★ is elegant and built to last, too; lighter ones come from the Couillauds' other property, Ch. la Morinière. Vin de pays Chardonnay is a speciality: top cuvée Auguste Couillaud★ is luxurious and Burgundian. Botrytized sweet Chardonnay doesn't work, but Melon-Chardonnay blend Chardet is very quaffable. Best years: (M) **1999 97**.

RAÏMAT *Costers del Segre DO, Cataluña, Spain* Owned by CODORNIU, this large, irrigated estate makes pleasant but surprisingly lean wines from Tempranillo, Cabernet Sauvignon (Mas Castell vineyard★) and Chardonnay. Fizz is lean but OK. 4 Varietales is a new upscale red blend. Best years: (reds) 2000 **99 98 97** 96 95 94 92 91 90.

RAMONET *Chassagne-Montrachet AC, Côte de Beaune, Burgundy, France*
The Ramonets (Noel and Claude) produce some of the most complex of all white Burgundies from 3 Grands Crus (BATARD-MONTRACHET★★★, Bienvenues-BATARD-MONTRACHET★★★ and le MONTRACHET★★★) and Premiers Crus including Ruchottes★★★, Caillerets★★★, Boudriotte★★, Vergers★★, Morgeot★★ and Chaumées★★★. If you want to spare your wallet try the ST-AUBIN★★ or the CHASSAGNE-MONTRACHET white★★ or red★★. Best years: (whites) (2002) 01 00 99 98 **97** 96 **95 92 90** 89.

JOÃO PORTUGAL RAMOS *Alentejo, Portugal* João Portugal Ramos is one of Portugal's foremost winemakers. He used to be a consultant to at least a dozen producers, including the fine Pegos Claros property in TERRAS DO SADO, but he is now making his mark with his own winery and vineyards. Smoky, peppery Trincadeira★★, spicy Aragonês (Tempranillo)★, powerful Syrah★ and intensely dark-fruited Vila Santa★★ (a blend of Trincadeira and Tempranillo topped up with Cabernet Sauvignon and Alicante Bouschet) are all superb. Marquês de Borba★ is the label for everyday red and white wines, though a small amount of a brilliant red Reserva★★ is also made. Best years: 2001 **00 99 97**.

RAMOS PINTO *Douro DOC and Port DOC, Douro, Portugal* Innovative PORT company now owned by ROEDERER, making complex, full-bodied Late Bottled Vintage★ and aged tawnies (10-year-old Quinta da Ervamoira★★ and 20-year-old Quinta do Bom Retiro★★). Vintage Ports★★ are rich and early maturing. Table wines Duas Quintas (Reserva★) and Bons Ares★ (Reserva★) are variable and no longer cheap. Best years: (Vintage) 2000 97 **95 94** 83.

RAMPOLLA, CASTELLO DEI *Chianti Classico DOCG, Tuscany, Italy* One of the outstanding CHIANTI CLASSICO★★ estates. SUPER-TUSCAN Sammarco, sometimes ★★★, is mostly Cabernet with some Sangiovese, while the extraordinary Vigna d'Alceo★★★ adds Petit Verdot to Cabernet Sauvignon. Best years: (Sammarco) (1999) 98 97 95 **90 88 85**; (Vigna d'Alceo) 1999 98 97 96.

RANDERSACKER *Franken, Germany* Important wine village in FRANKEN, producing excellent medium-bodied dry Rieslings, dry Silvaners, spicy Traminer and piercingly intense Rieslaner. Best producers: JULIUSSPITAL★, Robert Schmitt★, Schmitt's Kinder★. Best years: (Riesling Spätlese trocken) (2002) 01 00 99 **98 97 94 93 92 90**.

226

RAPEL, VALLE DEL *Valle Central, Chile*   One of Chile's most exciting red wine regions, Rapel is split between Valle del Cachapoal to the north and Valle de COLCHAGUA to the south. Both are excellent for Cabernet Sauvignon, Merlot and Carmenère. Best producers: Anakena, CASA LAPOSTOLLE★★, CONCHA Y TORO★★, CONO SUR★, Gracia, LA ROSA★, MONTES★, MONTGRAS★, Porta, Torreón de Paredes, Viu Manent★.

KENT RASMUSSEN *Carneros AVA, California, USA*   Tightly structured Burgundian-style Chardonnay★★ capable of considerable aging and a fascinating juicy Pinot Noir★★ are made by ultra-traditional methods. Also occasional delightful oddities like Pinotage, Alicante and Dolcetto under the Ramsay label. Best years: (Pinot Noir) (2002) (01) 00 99 98 97 **95 94 91 90**.

RASTEAU AC *Rhône Valley, France*   Rasteau is one of the original 16 villages entitled to the COTES DU RHONE-VILLAGES AC. The single-village AC is for a fortified red or white and a *rancio* version which is left in barrel for 2 or more years. Best producers: Beaurenard★, J Bressy★, Cave des Vignerons, Rabasse-Charavin, la Soumade★, du Trapadis★.

RENATO RATTI *Barolo DOCG, Piedmont, Italy*   The late Renato Ratti led the revolution in winemaking in the Alba area with BAROLO and BARBARESCO of better balance, colour and richness and softer in tannins than the traditional models. Today his son Pietro and nephew Massimo Martinelli produce sound Barolo★★ from the Marcenasco vineyards at La Morra, as well as good BARBERA D'ALBA (Torriglione★), Dolcetto d'Alba (Colombè★), NEBBIOLO D'ALBA (Ochetti★) and Monferrato DOC Villa Pattono★, a blend of Barbera and Freisa.

RAUENTHAL *Rheingau, Germany*   Sadly, only a few producers live up to the reputation earned by this RHEINGAU village's great Baiken and Gehrn sites, for intense, spicy Rieslings. Best producers: J B BECKER★, Georg BREUER★★, August Eser. Best years: (2002) 01 00 99 98 **97 96 94 93 90**.

CH. RAUZAN-SÉGLA★★ *Margaux AC, 2ème Cru Classé, Haut-Médoc, Bordeaux, France*   A dynamic change of winemaking regime in 1982 and the purchase of the property by Chanel in 1994 have propelled Rauzan-Ségla up the quality ladder. Now the wines have a rich blackcurrant fruit, almost tarry, thick tannins and weight, excellent woody spice and superb concentration. Second wine: Ségla. Best years: 2001 00 99 98 96 95 **94 90 89 88 86 85 83**.

JEAN-MARIE RAVENEAU *Chablis AC, Burgundy, France*   One of the outstanding growers in CHABLIS, producing beautifully nuanced wines from 3 Grands Crus (Blanchot★★★, les Clos★★★ and Valmur★★★) and 4 Premiers Crus (Montée de Tonnerre★★★, Vaillons★★, Butteaux★★★ and Chapelot★★), using a combination of old oak and stainless-steel fermentation. The wines can easily age for a decade or more. Best years: (top crus) (2002) 00 99 98 **97** 96 **95 92 90 89**.

RAVENSWOOD *Sonoma Valley AVA, California, USA*   Joel Peterson, one of California's best-known Zin experts, established Ravenswood in 1976. During the lean years, when most Zinfandel was pink and sweet, he added an intense Chardonnay, a sometimes very good Cabernet Sauvignon★ and several tasty Merlots (Sangiacomo★★). But Zinfandel remains the trump card. Peterson makes several, varying the menu from year to year, but recent offerings seem to have lost some of their depth and pungency – pleasant, but not memorable. Interestingly, Amador County★ and Lodi★ offerings showed more intensity than most of the Sonoma products. In 2001, Franciscan Estates purchased the winery. Best years: (Zins) (2001) (00) 99 **97 96 95 94 91 90**.

CH. RAYAS *Châteauneuf-du-Pape, Rhône Valley, France* The most famous estate in CHATEAUNEUF-DU-PAPE. Emmanuel Reynaud, nephew of the eccentric Jacques Reynaud, is running this estate in his uncle's inimitable rule-breaking style, producing big, alcoholic, exotically rich reds★★★ and whites★★ which also age well. Prices are not cheap and the wines are not consistent, but at its best Rayas is worth the money. The red is made entirely from low-yielding Grenache vines – the only such wine in the AC – while the white is a blend of Clairette, Grenache Blanc and (so rumour has it) Chardonnay. Second label Pignan can also be impressive. COTES DU RHONE Ch. de Fonsalette★★ is usually wonderful. Best years: (Châteauneuf-du-Pape) 2001 00 99 98 96 95 **94 93 91** 90 **89 88 86**; (whites) 2001 00 99 98 97 96 **95 94 93 91 90 89 86**.

REBHOLZ *Siebeldingen, Pfalz, Germany* This estate in the southern PFALZ produces fine dry Riesling★★, Weissburgunder★★ and Grauburgunder★, all crystalline in their clarity, with vibrant fruit aromas. Top of the range are intensely mineral dry Riesling★★★ from the Kastanienbusch vineyard, powerful dry Gewürztraminer★★ and extravagantly aromatic, crisp, dry Muskateller★★. Also produces Germany's finest barrel-fermented Chardonnay★★ and most serious Spätburgunder★★ (Pinot Noir) reds. Best years: (whites) (2002) 01 00 **99 98 97 96 94 93 92 90**; (reds) (2002) 01 00 99 98 97 **96 93**.

RECIOTO DELLA VALPOLICELLA DOC *Veneto, Italy* The great sweet wine of VALPOLICELLA, made from grapes picked earlier than usual and left to dry on straw mats until the end of January. The wines are deep in colour, with a rich, bitter-sweet cherryish fruit. Top wines age well for 10 years, but most are best drunk young. As with Valpolicella, the Classico tag is all important. Best producers: Accordini★, ALLEGRINI★★, Bolla (Spumante★★), Brigaldara★, Tommaso Bussola★★, Michele Castellani★★, DAL FORNO★★★, MASI★, QUINTARELLI★★, Le Ragose★, Le Salette★, Serègo Alighieri★★, Speri★, Tedeschi★, Tommasi★, Villa Monteleone★★, Viviani★. Best years: (2001) **00 98 97 95 93 90 88**.

RECIOTO DI SOAVE DOCG *Veneto, Italy* Sweet white wine made in the SOAVE zone from dried grapes, like RECIOTO DELLA VALPOLICELLA. Garganega grapes give wonderfully delicate yet intense wines that age well for up to a decade. The best, ANSELMI's I Capitelli, is now sold as IGT Veneto. Best producers: ANSELMI★★, La Cappuccina★★, Cà Rugate★, Coffele★, Gini★★, PIEROPAN★★, Bruno Sartori★, Tamellini★★. Best years: (2001) 00 **98 97 95 93 90**.

I CAPITELLI

ANSELMI

DOM. DE LA RECTORIE *Banyuls AC and Collioure AC, Roussillon, France* Marc and Thierry Parcé are producing some of the leading wines in BANYULS and COLLIOURE. Collioure cuvées Coume Pascole★★ and le Seris★★ are made for keeping, while Banyuls Cuvée Léon Parcé★★ can be enjoyed for its youthful fruit or kept for future pleasure. The vin de pays Grenache Gris, Cuvée l'Argile★, is one of the best whites in ROUSSILLON. Best years: (Coume Pascole) 2001 **00 99 98 97 96 95 93**.

RÉGNIÉ AC *Beaujolais, Burgundy, France* Most recent of the BEAUJOLAIS Crus, upgraded from BEAUJOLAIS-VILLAGES in 1988. In good years it is light, aromatic and enjoyable along the style of CHIROUBLES. A wine for drinking, not for keeping. Best producers: DUBOEUF★ (des Buyats★), H & J-P Dubost★, Gilles Roux (de la Plaigne★), Rochette★. Best years: (2002) **01 00**.

DOM. LA RÉMÉJEANNE *Côtes du Rhône AC, Rhône Valley, France*   First-class property on the west bank of the Rhône, making a range of strikingly individual wines. COTES DU RHONE-VILLAGES les Genèvriers★★ has the weight and texture of good CHATEAUNEUF-DU-PAPE, while COTES DU RHONE Syrah les Eglantiers★★ is superb. Both need at least 3–5 years' aging. Also good Côtes du Rhône les Chèvrefeuilles★ and les Arbousiers (red and white). Best years: (les Eglantiers) 2001 00 **99** 98 **96**.

REMELLURI *Rioja DOC, País Vasco, Spain*   Organic RIOJA estate producing red wines with far more fruit than usual and good concentration for aging – the best are ★★. There is also a delicate, barrel-fermented white blend★. Best years: (Reserva) 1998 **96 95 94 91 89**.

RETSINA *Greece*   Resinated white (and rosé) wine common all over Greece – although both production and sales are falling. Poor Retsina is diabolical but the best are deliciously oily and piny. Drink young.

REUILLY AC *Loire Valley, France*   Extremely dry but attractive Sauvignon from west of SANCERRE. Also some pale Pinot Noir red and Pinot Gris rosé. Best producers: H Beurdin★, Gerard Bigonneau. Best years: (2002) **01 00 99**.

REYNELL *McLaren Vale, South Australia*   Pioneer John Reynell established Chateau Reynella in 1838. Now HQ of the BRL HARDY empire, wines are labelled Reynell in Australia, although the Chateau Reynella name is still used for export. Prices have shot up lately, but they're not unreasonable given the quality. Basket Pressed Cabernet★★, Merlot★★ and Shiraz★★ are concentrated, tannic, ageworthy reds from low-yielding vines, some of which were planted in the 1930s. Best years: (reds) (2001) 00 98 **96 95 94**.

CH. REYNON *Premières Côtes de Bordeaux AC, Bordeaux, France*   Property of enology professor Denis Dubourdieu. The dry whites, particularly the barrel-fermented Vieilles Vignes★, are delightful and the red★ has come on tremendously since 1997. In the same stable is the quality Graves Clos Floridène★★, which is vinified at Reynon. Best years: (reds) 2001 00 99 **98 97 96 95**; (whites) 2001 00 **99 98 96 95**.

RHEINGAU *Germany*   3205ha (7920-acre) wine region on a south-facing stretch of the Rhine flanking the city of Wiesbaden, planted with 79% Riesling and 12% Spätburgunder (Pinot Noir). Traditionally considered Germany's most aristocratic wine region, both in terms of the racy, slow-maturing wines and because of the number of noble estate owners. But famous names here are no longer a guarantee of top quality, as a new generation now produces the best wines. See also Eltville, Erbach, Geisenheim, Hochheim, Johannisberg, Kiedrich, Rauenthal, Rüdesheim, Winkel. Best years: (Riesling Spätlese) (2002) 01 **99** 98 **97** 96 **93 90**.

RHEINHESSEN *Germany*   26,330ha (65,060-acre) wine region to the south and west of Mainz. On the Rheinterrasse between Mainz and Worms are a number of very famous top-quality estates, especially at Bodenheim, Nackenheim, NIERSTEIN and Oppenheim. BINGEN, to the north-west, also has a fine vineyard area along the left bank of the Rhine. Riesling accounts for only 10% of the vineyard area; Weissburgunder (Pinot Blanc) is the rising star. Best years: (Riesling Spätlese) (2002) 01 00 **99** 98 **97 96** 93 90.

RHÔNE VALLEY *France*   The Rhône starts out as a river in Switzerland, ambling through Lake Geneva before hurtling southwards into France. In the area south of Lyon, between Vienne and Avignon, the valley becomes one of France's great wine regions. In the northern part, where vertigo-inducing slopes overhang the river, there is not much wine produced but the little that is made is of remarkable individuality. The Syrah grape reigns here in COTE-ROTIE and on the great hill of HERMITAGE. ST-JOSEPH, CROZES-HERMITAGE and CORNAS also make excellent reds, while the white Viognier grape yields perfumed, musky wine at CONDRIEU and at the tiny AC CHATEAU-GRILLET. In the southern part the steep slopes give way to wide plains, where the vines swelter in the hot sun, with hills both in the west and east. Most of these vineyards are either COTES DU RHONE or COTES DU RHONE-VILLAGES, reds, whites and rosés, but there are also specific ACs. The most well known of these are CHATEAUNEUF-DU-PAPE and the luscious, golden dessert wine, MUSCAT DE BEAUMES-DE-VENISE. See also Clairette de Die, Coteaux de l'Ardèche, Coteaux du Tricastin, Côtes du Lubéron, Gigondas, Lirac, Rasteau, St-Péray, Tavel, Vacqueyras.

RÍAS BAIXAS DO *Galicia, Spain* The best of GALICIA's 5 DOs, Rías Baixas is making increasing quantities of Spain's best whites (apart from a few Chardonnays in the north-east). The magic ingredient is the characterful Albariño grape, making dry, fruity whites with a glorious fragrance and citrus tang. Drink young or with short aging. Best producers: Adegas Galegas★, Agro de Bazán★★, Quinta de Couselo★, Granxa Fillaboa★, Lagar de Fornelos★ (La RIOJA ALTA), Lusco do Miño★★, Martin Códax★, Gerardo Méndez Lázaro (Do Ferreiro Cepas Vellas★★), Pazo de Barrantes★ (MARQUES DE MURRIETA), Pazo de Señorans★★, Bodegas Salnesur (Condes de Albarei★), Santiago Ruiz★ (Lan), Terras Gauda★★.

RIBATEJO *Portugal* Portugal's second-largest wine region, now with its own DOC, straddles the river Tagus (Tejo). Hotter and drier than ESTREMADURA to the west, vineyards in the fertile flood plain are being uprooted in favour of less vigorous soils away from the river, though DFJ still believes in the quality of the original alluvial sites. There are several sub-regional DOCs. Best producers: (reds) Quinta da Alorna, BRIGHT BROTHERS, Casa Cadaval★, Quinta do Casal Branco (Falcoaria★), D F J VINHOS★, Caves Dom Teodosio, Quinta do Falcao, Falua (Reserva★), Fiuza, Quinta Grande, Horta da Nazaré, Quinta da Lagoalva★, Quinta de Santo Andre.

RIBERA DEL DUERO DO *Castilla y León, Spain* The dark, mouthfilling reds in this DO, from Tinto Fino (Tempranillo), sometimes with Cabernet Sauvignon and Merlot, are nowadays generally more exciting than those of RIOJA. But excessive expansion of vineyards and increase in yields may threaten its supremacy. Best producers: Alión★★, ARROYO★, Arzuaga★, Balbás★, Hijos de Antonio Barceló★, Briego★, Felix Callejo, Cillar de Silos★, Convento San Francisco★, Hermanos Cuadrado García★★, Dehesa de los Canónigos, Hacienda Monasterio★★, Emilio Moro★★, Pago de los Capellanes★★, Pago de Carraovejas★★, Parxet, PEDROSA★★, PESQUERA★★★, PINGUS★★★, Protos★, Teófilo Reyes, Rodero★, Telmo RODRIGUEZ★★, Hermanos Sastre★★, Tarsus★, Valduero★, Valtravieso, VEGA SICILIA★★★, Viñedos y Bodegas★, Winner Wines. Best years: (2001) 00 **99 96 95 94 91 90 89 86 85**.

BARONE RICASOLI *Chianti Classico DOCG, Tuscany, Italy* The estate where modern CHIANTI was perfected by Baron Bettino Ricasoli in the mid-19th century has recovered its lost form. 1993 saw the start of the renaissance under the guidance of Francesco Ricasoli. The flagship wine is Castello di Brolio Chianti Classico★★; that labelled simply

Brolio is effectively a second selection. Chianti Classico Riserva Guicciarda★ is good value. SUPER-TUSCAN Casalferro★★ is a Sangiovese-Merlot blend. Best years: (Casalferro) (2001) (00) 99 98 97 **95**.

DOM. RICHEAUME *Côtes de Provence AC, Provence, France* German-owned property, run on organic principles and producing impressively deep-coloured reds★ (Columelle★★) full of smoky spice and power. Best years: (Columelle) 2001 00 **99 98 97** 95.

RICHEBOURG AC *Grand Cru, Côte de Nuits, Burgundy, France* Rich, fleshy wine from the northern end of VOSNE-ROMANEE. Most domaine-bottlings are exceptional. Best producers: GRIVOT★★★, Anne GROS★★★, A-F GROS★★★, Hudelot-Noëllat★★, Dom. LEROY★★★, MEO-CAMUZET★★★, Dom. de la ROMANEE-CONTI★★★. Best years: (2002) 01 00 99 98 97 96 95 93 **91** 90 **89 88 85**.

DOM. RICHOU *Loire Valley, France* One of the leading domaines in the LOIRE, producing consistently good wines. Best are the ANJOU-VILLAGES Vieilles Vignes★★ and sweet COTEAUX DE L'AUBANCE les Trois Demoiselles★★. Best years: (les Trois Demoiselles) 1999 **97** 96 **95 94 93 90 89 88**.

MAX FERD RICHTER *Mülheim, Mosel-Saar-Ruwer, Germany* Racy Rieslings from some of the best sites in the MOSEL, including WEHLENer Sonnenuhr★★, BRAUNEBERGer Juffer★★ and GRAACHer Domprobst★★. Richter's Mülheimer Helenenkloster vineyard produces a magical Eiswein★★ virtually every year – although not in 1999. Best years: (Riesling Spätlese) (2002) 01 99 98 **97** 96 **95 94 93 90 89 88**.

RIDGE VINEYARDS *Santa Cruz Mountains AVA, California, USA* Paul Draper's Zinfandels★★★, made with grapes from various sources, have great intensity and long life. Other reds, led by Monte Bello Cabernet★★★, show impressive originality. There's fine Chardonnay★★, too. Best years: (Monte Bello) (2001) (00) 99 98 97 **95 94 93 92 91 90 87 85 84**.

RIDGEVIEW *West Sussex, England* Christine and Michael Roberts are emulating CHAMPAGNE every step of the way at their South Downs vineyard. Bloomsbury★ and Belgravia blends of Chardonnay, Pinot Noir and Pinot Meunier are produced under the Cuvée Merret label. Also delicious Fitzrovia rosé, Pinot Noir-based Cavendish and the new vintage Knightsbridge Blanc de Noirs.

RIECINE *Chianti DOCG, Tuscany, Italy* Small estate in Gaiole making exquisite CHIANTI. Yields are low, so there is a great intensity of fruit and a superb definition of spiced cherry flavours. New American owners have retained English winemaker Sean O'Callaghan, who continues to fashion still better CHIANTI CLASSICO★★, Riserva★★★ and barrique-aged La Gioia★★★. Best years: (La Gioia) (2001) (99) 98 97 **95 90 88 85**.

RIESLING See pages 232–3.

RIESLING ITALICO Unrelated to the great Riesling of the Rhine, this grape is widely planted in northern Italy, where it produces decent dry whites. As Olasz Rizling, it is highly esteemed in Hungary. Elsewhere in Europe it is known as Welschriesling; in Austria it makes some of the very best sweet wines, but tends to be rather dull as a dry wine.

CH. RIEUSSEC★★★ *Sauternes AC, 1er Cru Classé, Bordeaux, France* Apart from the peerless Ch. d'YQUEM, Rieussec is often the richest, most succulent wine of SAUTERNES. Cellar for at least 10 years. Dry white 'R' is often dull. Second wine: Clos Labère. Owned since 1984 by LAFITE-ROTHSCHILD. Best years: (2002) 01 99 98 97 **96 95** 90 89 88 86 85 83.

RIESLING

I'm sad to have to make this bald statement at the start, but I feel I must. If you have tasted wines with names like Laski Riesling, Olasz Riesling, Welschriesling, Gray Riesling, Riesling Italico and the like and found them bland or unappetizing – do not blame the Riesling grape. These wines have filched Riesling's name, but have nothing whatsoever to do with the great grape itself.

Riesling is Germany's finest contribution to the world of wine – and herein lies the second problem. German wines have fallen to such a low level of general esteem through the proliferation of wines like Liebfraumilch during the 1980s that Riesling, even true German Riesling, has been dragged down with it.

So what *is* true Riesling? It is a very ancient German grape, probably the descendant of wild vines growing in the Rhine Valley. It certainly performs best in the cool vineyard regions of Germany's Rhine and Mosel Valleys, and in Alsace and Austria. It also does well in Canada, New Zealand and both warm and cool parts of Australia, and it is widely planted in California and Italy. Plantings are declining in South Africa; in cooler areas dryish styles can be good, though dessert wines are often the most successful.

Young Rieslings often show a delightful floral perfume, sometimes blended with the crispness of green apples, often lime, peach, nectarine or apricot, sometimes even raisin, honey or spice depending upon the ripeness of the grapes. As the wines age, the lime often intensifies, and a flavour perhaps of slate, perhaps of petrol/kerosene intrudes. In general Rieslings may be drunk young, but top dry wines can improve for many years, and the truly sweet German styles can age for generations.

WINE STYLES

Germany These wines have a marvellous perfume and an ability to hold on to a piercing acidity, even at high ripeness levels, so long as the ripening period has been warm and gradual rather than broiling and rushed. German Rieslings can be bone dry, through to medium and even lusciously sweet, but if they are dry, they must be made from fully ripe grapes, otherwise the acidity is excessive and the wine's body insufficient. Styles range from crisp elegant Mosels to riper, fuller wines from the Pfalz and Baden regions in the south. The very sweet Trockenbeerenauslese (TBA) Rieslings are made from grapes affected by noble rot; for Eiswein (icewine), also intensely sweet, the grapes are picked and pressed while frozen.

Other regions In the valleys of the Danube in Austria, Riesling gives stunning dry wines that combine richness with elegance, but the most fragrant wines, apart from German examples, come from France's Alsace. The mountain vineyards of northern Italy, and the cool vineyards of the Czech Republic, Slovakia and Switzerland can show a floral sharp style. Australia is the southern hemisphere's world-class producer, with cool areas of South Australia, Victoria and Western Australia all offering superb – and different – examples. New Zealand's style is floral and fresh. South Africa's best examples are usually late-harvest or sweetly botrytized. The USA's finest are from the East Coast and the Pacific Northwest. California is best at sweet styles, as is Canada with its icewines.

BEST PRODUCERS

Germany

Dry BASSERMANN-JORDAN, Georg BREUER, Rudolf FURST, Heymann-Löwenstein, KOEHLER-RUPRECHT, KUNSTLER, J LEITZ, MULLER-CATOIR, REBHOLZ, ST ANTONY, SAUER, J L WOLF.

Non-dry DIEL, DONNHOFF, GUNDERLOCH, HAAG, HAART, Heymann-Löwenstein, JOST, KARTHAUSERHOF, von KESSELSTATT, KUNSTLER, C Loewen, Dr LOOSEN, MAXIMIN GRUNHAUS, MULLER-CATOIR, Egon MULLER-SCHARZHOF, J J PRUM, RICHTER, Willi SCHAEFER, WEIL.

Austria

Dry BRUNDLMAYER, HIRTZBERGER, J Högl, KNOLL, Nigl, NIKOLAIHOF, F X PICHLER, Rudi Pichler, PRAGER, Freie Weingärtner WACHAU.

France

(Alsace) *Dry* P BLANCK, A Boxler, DEISS, Dirler-Cadé, HUGEL, Kientzler, Kreydenweiss, Kuentz-Bas, A Mann, MURE, Ostertag, SCHOFFIT, TRIMBACH, WEINBACH, ZIND-HUMBRECHT.

Non-dry Léon Beyer, DEISS, HUGEL, Ostertag, TRIMBACH, WEINBACH, ZIND-HUMBRECHT.

Australia

Tim ADAMS, Leo Buring, DELATITE, Frankland Estate, GROSSET, HENSCHKE, HOWARD PARK, LEEUWIN, MITCHELL, MITCHELTON, Mount Horrocks, MOUNT LANGHI GHIRAN, ORLANDO, PETALUMA, PIPERS BROOK, PLANTAGENET, Skillogallee, Geoff WEAVER, YALUMBA.

New Zealand

CLOUDY BAY, DRY RIVER, FELTON ROAD, FROMM, GIESEN, MILLTON, PEGASUS BAY, VILLA MARIA, Waipara West.

South Africa

Avontuur (Above Royalty), Neethlingshof.

USA

(Washington) CHATEAU STE MICHELLE (Eroica), KIONA.

233

RIOJA DOC *Rioja, Navarra, País Vasco and Castilla y León, Spain* Rioja, in northern Spain, is not all oaky, creamy white wines and elegant, barrel-aged reds, combining oak flavours with wild strawberry and prune fruit. Over half Rioja's red wine is sold young, never having seen the inside of a barrel, and most of the white is fairly anonymous. Wine quality, as could be expected from such a large region with more than 300 producers, is inconsistent. There is far too much mediocre Rioja on the market as large producers and co-ops try to milk Rioja's reputation. However, a bevy of new producers with great ambitions is changing the regional hierarchy and they, at least, are taking quality seriously. Best producers: (reds) ALLENDE★★, Altos de Lanzaga★★ (Telmo RODRIGUEZ), Amézola de la Mora, ARTADI★★, Baron de Ley★, BERBERANA★, Bodegas Bilbaínas, CAMPILLO★, CAMPO VIEJO★, Luis Cañas, Contador★★, CONTINO★★, El Coto★, CVNE, DOMECQ★, FAUSTINO★, Lan (Culmen★), LOPEZ DE HEREDIA★, MARQUES DE CACERES★, MARQUES DE GRINON★, MARQUES DE MURRIETA★, MARQUES DE RISCAL★★, Marqués de Vargas★★, MARTINEZ BUJANDA★★, Montecillo★, MUGA★, Palacio, REMELLURI★★, Fernando Remírez de Ganuza★★, LA RIOJA ALTA★★, RIOJANAS★, Roda★★, Señorío de San Vicente★★, Viña Ijalba; (whites) CAMPO VIEJO★, CVNE★, LOPEZ DE HEREDIA★, MARQUES DE CACERES★, MARQUES DE MURRIETA★, MARTINEZ BUJANDA★★, Montecillo★, LA RIOJA ALTA★★, RIOJANAS★. Best years: (reds) (2001) **96 95 94 91 89 87 86 85 83 82 81 78**.

LA RIOJA ALTA *Rioja DOC, Rioja, Spain* One of the best of the older RIOJA producers, making mainly Reservas and Gran Reservas. Its only Crianza, Viña Alberdi, fulfils the minimum age requirements for a Reserva anyway. There is a little good, lemony-oaky Viña Ardanza Reserva★ white. Red Reservas, Viña Arana★ and Viña Ardanza★★, age splendidly, and Gran Reservas, Reserva 904★★ and Reserva 890★★★ (made only in exceptional years), are among the very best of Rioja wines. Best years: (Gran Reserva 890) **1987 85 82 81 78**.

RIOJANAS *Rioja DOC, Rioja, Spain* Quality winery producing Reservas and Gran Reservas in 2 styles – elegant Viña Albina★ and richer Monte Real★ – plus the new, refined Gran Albina★★. White Monte Real Blanco Crianza★ is one of RIOJA's best. The whites and Reservas can be kept for 5 years after release, Gran Reservas for 10 or more. Best years: (Monte Real Gran Reserva) 1996 **95 94 91 89 87 85 83 82 81**.

RION *Nuits-St-Georges AC, Côte de Nuits, Burgundy, France* Patrice Rion was the winemaker at Dom. Daniel Rion from 1979 to 2000, making consistently fine but often austere reds such as VOSNE-ROMANEE les Beauxmonts★★ and les Chaumes★★, NUITS-ST-GEORGES Clos des Argillières★★ and latterly ECHEZEAUX★★ and CLOS DE VOUGEOT★★★. Under his own Patrice Rion label he makes richly concentrated BOURGOGNE Rouge★★ and CHAMBOLLE-MUSIGNY les Cras★★ from his own vines as well as, since 2000, a small range of négociant wines. Best years: (top reds) (2002) 01 00 99 98 **97** 96 **95 93 90 88**.

RIVERA *Puglia, Italy* One of southern Italy's most dynamic producers. The CASTEL DEL MONTE Riserva Il Falcone★★ is an excellent, full-blooded southern red. Also a series of varietals under the Terre al Monte label, best of which are Aglianico★, Pinot Bianco and Sauvignon Blanc.

RIVERINA *New South Wales, Australia* Centred on the town of Griffith and irrigated by the waters of the Murrumbidgee River, the Riverina is an important source of reliable cheap quaffing wines. Many of Australia's best-known brands, from companies like HARDYS, MCWILLIAM'S, ORLANDO, ROSEMOUNT and PENFOLDS, though not mentioning either Riverina or

RIVERLAND on the label, are based on wines from these areas. The potential for quality is definitely there, but as yet no one has really determined to separate the characterful from the acceptable. The exception is the range of remarkable sweet wines made by all the region's producers to at least ★ level, but led by Noble One Botrytis Semillon★★★ from DE BORTOLI. Other leading producers are Casella, Cranswick Estate, Gramp's, Lillypilly, Miranda and West End★.

RIVERLAND *Australia* This important irrigated region, which is responsible for about a third of the national grape crush, lies along the Murray River in SOUTH AUSTRALIA near the border with VICTORIA. The region produces a great deal of cask wine and cheap quaffers. An increased awareness of quality has seen inferior varieties replaced and yields lowered; here and there, wines of real character are emerging. The Petit Verdot grape, for instance, has produced some remarkable reds. Best producers: Angove's, HARDYS (Banrock Station, Renmano), Kingston Estate, YALUMBA (Oxford Landing).

RIVESALTES AC *Languedoc-Roussillon, France* *Vin doux naturel* from a large area around the town of Rivesaltes. These fortified wines are some of southern France's best and can be made from an assortment of grapes, mainly white Muscat (when it is called MUSCAT DE RIVESALTES) and Grenache Noir, Gris and Blanc. A *rancio* style ages well. Best producers: la CASENOVE★, CAZES★★, Chênes★, Fontanel★, Força Réal★, GAUBY★, Ch. de Jau★, Joliette★, Laporte, Rivesaltes co-op, Sarda-Malet★, Terrats co-op, Trouillas co-op.

ROBERTSON WO *South Africa* Hot, dry inland area with lime-rich soils, uncommon in the Cape, that are ideal for vines. Chenin Blanc and Colombard are the major white wine varieties, and Chardonnay performs well (for both still and sparkling styles), as can Sauvignon in leafy, aggressive form. The traditional Muscadel (Muscat Blanc à Petits Grains) yields a benchmark fortified wine, usually unoaked and released young. A red revolution is currently under way; Shiraz, Merlot and Cabernet have made an excellent start. Best producers: Graham BECK★, Bon Courage, De Wetshof, Robertson Winery, SPRINGFIELD ESTATE★, Van Loveren, Zandvliet.

CH. ROC DE CAMBES★★ *Côtes de Bourg AC, Bordeaux, France* François Mitjavile of TERTRE-ROTEBOEUF has applied enthusiasm and diligence to this property since he acquired it in 1988. Full and concentrated, with ripe dark fruit, this wine takes the COTES DE BOURG appellation to new heights. Best years: 2001 00 99 98 **97 96 95 94 93 91 90 89**.

J ROCHIOLI *Russian River Valley AVA, California, USA* Meticulous growers still selling grapes, the Rochioli family are equally good at winemaking, offering silky, black cherry Pinot Noir★★ and a richer, dramatic West Block Reserve Pinot★★★. All wines stand out, including a fine Sauvignon Blanc★★ and a range of cult Chardonnays★★. Best years: (Pinot Noir) (2002) (01) 00 99 98 **97 95 94**.

ROCKFORD *Barossa Valley, South Australia* Wonderfully nostalgic wines from Robert O'Callaghan, a great respecter of the old vines so plentiful in the BAROSSA, who delights in using antique machinery. Masterful Basket Press Shiraz★★, Riesling★, Moppa Springs★ (a Grenache-Shiraz-Mourvèdre blend) and cult sparkling Black Shiraz★★★. Best years: (Basket Press Shiraz) 2001 00 99 98 96 **95 92 91 90 86**.

ANTONIN RODET *Mercurey AC, Côte Chalonnaise, Burgundy, France* Merchant based in the village of MERCUREY, specializing in COTE CHALONNAISE, but with an excellent range from throughout Burgundy.

Rodet owns or co-owns 5 domaines – Ch. de Rully★, Ch. de Chamirey★, Ch. de Mercey★, Dom. des Perdrix★ and Jacques Prieur★★ – which are the source of the best wines. BOURGOGNE Vieilles Vignes★ is one of the best inexpensive Chardonnays available Recently purchased Dom. de l'Aigle in LIMOUX. Best years: (reds) (2002) 99 **98 97 96 95**; (whites) (2002) 01 **00 99 97 96**.

TELMO RODRÍGUEZ *Spain*   The former winemaker for REMELLURI has now formed a 'wine company' that is active throughout Spain. With a team of enologists and viticulturists, it forms joint ventures with local growers and manages the whole winemaking process. The results are often spectacular. Top wines: Molino Real★★ (Sierras de MALAGA), Alto Matallana★★ (RIBERA DEL DUERO), Altos de Lanzaga★★ (RIOJA), Dehesa Gago Pago La Jara★★ (TORO), Viña 105★ (Cigales), Basa (RUEDA).

LOUIS ROEDERER *Champagne AC, Champagne, France*   Renowned firm making some of the best, full-flavoured CHAMPAGNES around. As well as the excellent non-vintage★★ and pale vintage rosé★★, it also makes a big, exciting vintage★★, delicious vintage Blanc de Blancs★★ and the famous Roederer Cristal★★★, a de luxe cuvée, much beloved of rappers, which is nearly always magnificent. Both the vintage wines and Cristal can usually be aged for 10 years or more; the non-vintage benefits from a bit of aging, too. Best years: 1996 95 **93 90 89 88 86 85**.

ROEDERER ESTATE *Anderson Valley AVA, California, USA*   Californian offshoot of Louis ROEDERER. The Brut★★ (sold in the UK as Quartet) is impressive though austere, a step back from the upfront fruit of many California sparklers, but it will age beautifully if you can wait. Lovely rosé★★, and the top bottling, L'Ermitage★★★, is a stunning addition to the range of California fizz. Best years: (L'Ermitage) (1997) (96) **94 92 91**.

ROERO DOC *Piedmont, Italy*   The Roero hills lie across the Tanaro river from the LANGHE hills, home of BAROLO and BARBARESCO. Long noted as a source of Nebbiolo in supple, fruity red wines to drink in 2–5 years, Roero has recently made its mark with the white Arneis grape. Best producers: (reds) G Almondo★, Ca' Rossa★, Cascina Chicco★, Correggia★, Deltetto★, Funtanin★, F Gallino★, Malvirà★, Monchiero Carbone★, Angelo Negro★, Porello★. Best years: (reds) (2001) **00 99 98 97 96**. See also Arneis.

ROMAGNA *Emilia-Romagna, Italy*   Romagna's wine production is centred on 4 DOCs and 1 DOCG. The whites are from Trebbiano (ineffably dull), Pagadebit (showing promise as both a dry and sweet wine) and Albana (ALBANA DI ROMAGNA can be dry or sweet). The reds are dominated by the Sangiovese grape, and range from young and fresh through to wines that can rival good CHIANTI CLASSICO. Best producers: (Sangiovese) La Berta★, Castelluccio★★, L Conti★, Drei Donà-La Palazza★, G Madonia★, San Patrignano co-op/Terre del Cedro★ (Avi★★), Tre Monti★, Zerbina★★.

LA ROMANÉE-CONTI AC *Grand Cru, Côte de Nuits, Burgundy, France*   For many extremely wealthy wine lovers this is the pinnacle of red Burgundy★★★. It is an incredibly complex wine with great structure and pure, clearly defined fruit flavour, but you've got to age it 15 years to see what all the fuss is about. The vineyard covers only 1.8ha (4½ acres), which is one reason for the high prices. Wholly owned by Dom. de la ROMANEE-CONTI. Best years: (2002) 01 00 99 98 97 96 95 93 **91** 90 **89** 88 **85** 78.

DOM. DE LA ROMANÉE-CONTI *Vosne-Romanée AC, Côte de Nuits, Burgundy, France* This famous red wine domaine owns a string of Grands Crus in VOSNE-ROMANEE (la TACHE★★★, RICHEBOURG★★★, ROMANEE-CONTI★★★, ROMANEE-ST-VIVANT★★★, ECHEZEAUX★★★ and Grands-Échézeaux★★★) as well as a small parcel of le MONTRACHET★★★. The wines are ludicrously expensive but can be quite sublime – full of fruit when young, but capable of aging for 15 years or more to an astonishing marriage made in the heaven and hell of richness and decay. Best years: (reds) (2002) 01 00 99 98 97 96 95 93 90 **89** 88 **85 78**.

ROMANÉE-ST-VIVANT AC *Grand Cru, Côte de Nuits, Burgundy, France* By far the largest of VOSNE-ROMANEE's 6 Grands Crus. At 10–15 years old the wines should reveal the keenly balanced brilliance of which the vineyard is capable, but a surly, rough edge sometimes gets in the way. Best producers: l'Arlot★★, R Arnoux★★★, S Cathiard★★★, J-J Confuron★★★, DROUHIN★★★, Hudelot-Noëllat★★★, JADOT★★★, Dom. LEROY★★★, Dom. de la ROMANEE-CONTI★★★, THOMAS-MOILLARD★★. Best years: (2002) 01 00 99 98 97 96 95 **93 91** 90 **89 88**.

ROQUES, QUINTA DOS *Dão DOC, Beira Alta, Portugal* Now the DAO's finest producer, the wines of 2 estates with quite different characters are made here. Quinta dos Roques red★ is ripe and supple, while Quinta das Maias★ is a smoky, peppery red. The top wines are the dos Roques Reserva★★, made from old vines and aged in 100% new oak, and Touriga Nacional★★. Both estates also have a decent dry white, especially Roques Encruzado★. Best years: 2001 00 **97 96**.

ROSA, QUINTA DE LA *Douro DOC and Port DOC, Douro, Portugal* The Bergqvist family have transformed this property into a small but serious producer of both PORT and DOURO★ (Reserve★★) table wines. The Vintage Port★★ is excellent, as is unfiltered LBV★★, while Finest Reserve and 10-year-old tawny★ are also good. A special selection vintage port, Vale do Inferno★★, was made in 1999 and shows a lovely old vine intensity. Best years: (Vintage) 2000 97 96 95 94 **92 91**.

ROSÉ DE LOIRE AC *Loire Valley, France* Dry rosé from ANJOU, SAUMUR and TOURAINE. It can be a lovely drink, full of red berry fruits, but drink as young as possible and chill well. It's far superior to Rosé d'Anjou AC, which is usually sweetish, without much flavour. Best producers: Hautes Ouches, Passavant, St-Arnoud, Trottières.

ROSÉ DES RICEYS AC *Champagne, France* This is a curiosity and an expensive one at that. It's a still, dark pink wine made from Pinot Noir grapes in the southern part of the CHAMPAGNE region. Best producers: Alexandre Bonnet★, Devaux★, Guy de Forez, Morel.

ROSEMOUNT ESTATE *Hunter Valley, New South Wales, Australia* Winery buying and growing grapes in several regions to produce some of Australia's most popular wines, but appears to have taken a new and unfortunate direction recently with many wines seeming sweeter and flatter than before. Sadly this doesn't just affect the cheaper wines: top-level Show Reserve wines are showing far less focus than they used to. The flagship Roxburgh Chardonnay★ is undergoing a dramatic style change at the moment, which may or may not return it to a position of eminence among Aussie whites. Best of the other whites is Orange Vineyard Chardonnay★, but even this has become sweeter and flatter. Show Reserve reds are generally a bit stodgy, but dense Balmoral

Syrah★★ and GSM★★ (Grenache, Syrah, Mourvèdre) can be good. After an inspiring start in MUDGEE, the quality of the Hill of Gold range has dropped, though Mountain Blue Shiraz-Cabernet★★ can still be excellent. Best years: (Balmoral Syrah) (2001) (00) 98 97 **96 94 92 91 90**.

ROSSO CÒNERO DOC *Marche, Italy* The best wines in this zone, on the Adriatic coast, are made solely from Montepulciano, and have a wonderfully spicy richness. Best producers: Fazi Battaglia★, Garofoli★ (Grosso Agontano★★), Lanari★ (Fibbio★★), Leopardi Dittajuti★, Malacari★, Mecella (Rubelliano★), Moroder★ (Dorico★★), Le Terrazze★ (Sassi Neri★★, Visions of J★★), Umani Ronchi★ (Cúmaro★★), La Vite (Adeodato★★). Best years: (2001) 00 **98 97 95 90**.

ROSSO DI MONTALCINO DOC *Tuscany, Italy* The little brother of BRUNELLO DI MONTALCINO spends much less time aging in wood, so enabling the wines to retain a wonderful exuberance of flavour that Brunello may lose through its longer cask-aging. Best producers: Altesino★, ARGIANO★, Caparzo★, Casanova di Neri★★, Ciacci Piccolomini d'Aragona★, Col d'Orcia★, Collemattoni★, COSTANTI★, Fuligni★, Gorelli-Due Portine★, M Lambardi★★, Lisini★, Siro Pacenti★★, Agostina Pieri★★, Poggio Antico★, Il Poggione★, Poggio Salvi★, Salicutti★★, San Filippo-Fanti★, Talenti★, Valdicava★. Best years: (2001) 00 **99 98 97 95**.

ROSSO DI MONTEPULCIANO DOC *Tuscany, Italy* Some VINO NOBILE producers use this DOC in order to improve selection for the main wine; the best Rossos deliver delightfully plummy, chocolaty flavours. Best producers: La Braccesca★/ANTINORI, La Ciarliana★, Contucci★, Dei★, Del Cerro★, Il Faggeto★, Fassati★, Nottola★, POLIZIANO★, Salcheto★★, Valdipiatta★, Villa Sant'Anna★. Best years: (2001) **99 98 97**.

ROSSO PICENO DOC *Marche, Italy* This red is often considered a poor relative of ROSSO CONERO, since Sangiovese tends to be lean and harsh in the Marche. But when the full complement (40%) of Montepulciano is used, Rosso Piceno can be rich and seductive. Best producers: Boccadigabbia★ (Villamagna★★), Le Caniette★, Laurentina★, Saladini Pilastri★, Velenosi★. Best years: (2001) 00 **99 98 97 95 94 93 90**.

RENÉ ROSTAING *Côte-Rôtie AC, Rhône Valley, France* René Rostaing produces modern, rich, ripe wines marked by their deep colour and soft fruit flavours. With vines in some of the best sites in COTE-ROTIE, he produces 4 wines: classic Côte-Rôtie★, la Viallère★★, Côte Blonde★★ and la Landonne★★. There's a very good CONDRIEU★★ too. Best years: (top crus) 2000 99 98 **95 94 91 90 88 85**.

ROTHBURY ESTATE *Hunter Valley, New South Wales, Australia* Len Evans' brainchild (now part of Beringer Blass) has struggled to find its way in recent years, but new winemaker Neil McGuigan is leading a quality charge (Neil McGuigan Shiraz★, Semillon★). The Hunter Valley Verdelho has life and zest; also inexpensive varietals from MUDGEE and COWRA (Chardonnay★).

GEORGES ROUMIER *Chambolle-Musigny AC, Côte de Nuits, Burgundy, France* Christophe Roumier is one of Burgundy's top winemakers, devoting as much attention to his vineyards as to cellar technique, believing in severe pruning, low yields and stringent grape selection. Roumier never uses more than one-third new oak. His best wine is often BONNES-MARES★★★, but his other Grands Crus include MUSIGNY★★★, Ruchottes-Chambertin★★ and CORTON-CHARLEMAGNE★★. The best value are usually the village Chambolle★★ and an exclusively owned Premier Cru in MOREY-ST-DENIS, Clos de la Bussière★★. Best years: (reds) (2002) 01 00 99 98 **97** 96 95 **93 90 89 88**.

ROUSSANNE The RHONE VALLEY's best white grape variety, frequently blended with Marsanne. Roussanne is the more aromatic and elegant of the two, less prone to oxidation and with better acidity, but growers usually prefer Marsanne due to its higher yields. Now being planted in the MIDI. There are some examples in Australia and, while much of the Roussanne planted in California has been identified as Viognier, there are a few true plantings that produce fascinating wines.

ARMAND ROUSSEAU *Gevrey-Chambertin AC, Côte de Nuits, Burgundy, France* One of the most highly respected and important CHAMBERTIN estates, with vineyards in Clos-de-Bèze★★★, Mazis-Chambertin★★ and Charmes-Chambertin★★ as well as CLOS DE LA ROCHE★★★ in MOREY-ST-DENIS and GEVREY-CHAMBERTIN Clos St-Jacques★★★. The outstandingly harmonious, elegant, yet rich wines are made in a traditional style and enjoy an enviable reputation for longevity. The Chambertin★★★ is exceptionally fine. Charles Rousseau has been at the helm since 1957, though recent vintages have been slightly inconsistent. Best years: (2002) 01 00 99 96 93 **91 90 89 88 85**.

ROUSSILLON *France* The snow-covered peaks of the Pyrenees form a spectacular backdrop to the ancient region of Roussillon, now the Pyrénées-Orientales *département*. The vineyards produce a wide range of fairly priced wines, mainly red, ranging from the ripe, raisin-rich *vins doux naturels* to light, fruity-fresh vins de pays, and there are now some really exciting table wines, both white and red, being made in Roussillon, especially by individual estates. See also Banyuls, Collioure, Côtes du Roussillon, Côtes du Roussillon-Villages, Maury, Muscat de Rivesaltes, Rivesaltes.

RUCHOTTES-CHAMBERTIN AC See Chambertin AC.

RÜDESHEIM *Rheingau, Germany* Village producing silky, aromatic wines from some steep terraced vineyards directly on the bank of the Rhein (Berg Schlossberg, Berg Rottland, Berg Roseneck and Bischofsberg). Not to be confused with the NAHE village of the same name. Best producers: Georg BREUER★★, Johannishof★, Josef LEITZ★★. Best years: (Riesling Spätlese) (2002) 01 00 **99** 98 **97** 96 **94 93 90**.

RUEDA DO *Castilla y León, Spain* The RIOJA firm of MARQUES DE RISCAL launched the reputation of this white-wine-only region in the 1970s, first by rescuing the almost extinct local grape, Verdejo, then by introducing Sauvignon Blanc. Fresh young whites have been joined by barrel-fermented wines aiming for a longer life, particularly those made at Castilla La Vieja and Belondrade y Lurton. Best producers: Alvarez y Diez★, Antaño (Viña Mocén★), Belondrade y Lurton, Cerrosol (Doña Beatriz), Hermanos Lurton★, MARQUES DE RISCAL★, Bodegas de Crianza Castilla La Vieja (Palacio de Bornos Vendimia Seleccionada★★), Javier Sanz Cantalapiedra★, Viñedos de Nieva★, Viños Sanz, Angel Rodríguez Vidal (Martinsancho★).

RUFFINO *Tuscany, Italy* Huge, long-established winemaking concern recently divided between two sides of the Folonari family. Brothers Marco and Paolo continue to produce CHIANTI CLASSICO from Santedame★ and the classic Riserva Ducale Oro★★. SUPER-TUSCANS include promising new Chardonnay, La Solatia★; new Sangiovese-Cabernet-Merlot blend Modus★; Pinot Noir Nero del Tondo★; and the unique blend of Colorino and Merlot (from 1997), Romitorio di Santedame★★. The Ruffino operation also includes VINO NOBILE estate

Lodola Nuova, BRUNELLO Il Greppone Mazzi and Borgo Conventi in COLLIO. The newly created Tenute Ambrogio & Giovanni Folonari includes the Cabreo (Sangiovese-Cabernet Il Borgo★, Chardonnay La Pietra★) and Nozzole (powerful, long-lived Cabernet Il Pareto★★) properties in Chianti Classico, but also extends to Vino Nobile estate Gracciano-Svetoni, BOLGHERI estate Campo del Mare and, since 2001, Brunello producer La Fuga.

RUINART *Champagne AC, Champagne, France* This is one of the oldest CHAMPAGNE houses. Ruinart has a surprisingly low profile, given the quality of its wines. The non-vintage★★ is very good, as is the Blanc de Blancs non-vintage★★, but the top wines here are the supremely classy Dom Ruinart Blanc de Blancs★★★ and the Dom Ruinart Rosé★★★. Best years: (1996) **95 93 92 90 88 86 85 83 82**.

RULLY AC *Côte Chalonnaise, Burgundy, France* One of Burgundy's most improved ACs with good-quality, reasonably priced wine. Once famous for sparkling wines, it is now best known for its still whites, often oak-aged. Reds are light, with a fleeting strawberry and cherry perfume. Best producers: (whites) Allaines★, J-C Brelière★, DROUHIN★, Dureuil-Janthial★, Duvernay, FAIVELEY★, V GIRARDIN★, JADOT★, JAFFELIN★, Olivier LEFLAIVE★, RODET★, Villaine★; (reds) A Delorme, Dureuil-Janthial★, Duvernay, la Folie, H & P Jacqueson★. Best years: (whites) (2002) 01 **00 99**; (reds) (2002) 01 **00 99**.

RUSSIAN RIVER VALLEY AVA *Sonoma County, California, USA* Beginning south of Healdsburg along the Russian River as it flows south-west, this valley cools as it meanders toward the Pacific. It is now challenging CARNEROS as the top spot for Pinot Noir and Chardonnay. Best producers: Davis Bynum★, DEHLINGER★★★, De Loach★, Dutton-Goldfield★, Gary Farrell★★, IRON HORSE★★, ROCHIOLI★★, SONOMA-CUTRER★, Rodney Strong★, Joseph SWAN★, Marimar TORRES★★, WILLIAMS SELYEM★★. Best years: (Pinot Noir) (2002) (01) 00 99 **97 95 94 93 91 90**.

RUST EN VREDE *Stellenbosch WO, South Africa* This red-only property is starting to reap the benefits of young, virus-free vines with fine, softer tannins and fresher fruit. Shiraz★ and Rust en Vrede★, a Cabernet-based blend designed to show off the *terroir*, are stars, but Merlot and Cabernet are catching up fast. Owner Jean Engelbrecht's joint venture with international golf star Ernie Els has resulted in a stylish BORDEAUX blend under the Ernie Els★ label, made by cellarmaster Louis Strydom. Best years: (Rust en Vrede estate wine) **1999 98 97 96 95 94 92**.

RUSTENBERG *Stellenbosch WO, South Africa* Premier-league producer, headed in the cellar by local youngster Adi Badenhorst. A massive vineyard overhaul – 53ha (130 acres) were planted with Rustenberg's imported vines in 2001 – will see other varieties, mainly Rhône-oriented, bearing shortly. Tradition is perpetuated in the majestic Peter Barlow Cabernet★★, BORDEAUX-style blend John X Merriman★★. Also new-look yet classically styled single-vineyard Five Soldiers★ (Chardonnay). The Brampton range represents good value. Best years: (Peter Barlow) 2001 **99 98 97 96**; (Five Soldiers) **2001 00 99 98 97**.

RUTHERFORD AVA *Napa Valley, California, USA* This viticultural area in mid-NAPA VALLEY has inspired hours of argument over whether it has a distinct identity. The heart of the area, the Rutherford Bench, does seem to be a prime Cabernet Sauvignon zone, and many traditional old Napa Cabernets have come from here and exhibit the 'Rutherford Dust' flavour. Best producers: BEAULIEU★★, Cakebread, FLORA SPRINGS★★, Freemark Abbey, NIEBAUM-COPPOLA★, Quintessa, Staglin★★. Best years: (Cabernet) (2001) (00) 99 97 96 **95 94 93 92 91 90 86**.

RUTHERGLEN *Victoria, Australia* This region in north-east VICTORIA is the home of heroic reds from Shiraz, Cabernet and Durif, and luscious, world-beating fortifieds from Muscat and Tokay (Muscadelle). Good sherry- and port-style wines. Best producers: (fortifieds) ALL SAINTS★★, Buller's★, Campbells★★, CHAMBERS★★, MORRIS★★, Stanton & Killeen★★.

SAALE-UNSTRUT *Germany* Located in the former East Germany, Saale-Unstrut's 650ha (1605 acres) of vineyards have been extensively replanted since 1989, but these vineyards must mature before first-class wines can be produced. Weissburgunder (Pinot Blanc) is the most important quality grape, with 12% of total vineyard area. Best producer: Lützkendorf★.

SACHSEN *Germany* Until recently one of Europe's forgotten wine regions (445ha/1100 acres) on the river Elbe in former East Germany. Now beginning to produce some good wines, the best being dry Riesling, Gewürztraminer, Weissburgunder (Pinot Blanc) and Grauburgunder (Pinot Gris) with surprisingly generous alcoholic content. Best producers: Schloss Proschwitz★, Schloss Wackerbarth★, Klaus Zimmerling★.

ST-AMOUR AC *Beaujolais, Burgundy, France* The most northerly of the BEAUJOLAIS crus, much in demand through the romantic connotation of its name. The granitic character of its vineyards produce wines with great intensity of colour that may be initially harsh, needing a few months to soften. Best producers: des Billards/Loron★, DUBOEUF★ (des Sablons★), des Duc★, J-P Ducoté. Best years: (2002) **00 99 98**.

ST ANTONY *Nierstein, Rheinhessen, Germany* Dr Alex Michalsky runs one of RHEINHESSEN's finest estates, making dry and off-dry Rieslings (frequently ★★) with unusual power and richness from the top sites of NIERSTEIN. Occasional sweet Auslese and higher Prädikat wines are always expansive and luscious. All wines except the regular dry Riesling★ have at least 5 years' aging potential. Best years: (Riesling Spätlese trocken) (2002) 01 00 99 98 **97 96 94 93 92 90 89**.

ST-AUBIN AC *Côte de Beaune, Burgundy, France* Some of Burgundy's best-value wines. Good reds, especially from Premiers Crus like les Frionnes and les Murgers des Dents de Chien. Also reasonably priced, oak-aged whites. Best producers: Allaines★, Bernard Bachelet, D & F Clair★★, M Colin★★, DROUHIN★, JADOT★, Lamy-Pillot★, Larue★★, Olivier LEFLAIVE★, B Morey★, H Prudhon★, RAMONET★★, Roux★, G Thomas★. Best years: (reds) (2002) 01 99 **98 96**; (whites) (2002) 01 **00 99**.

ST-CHINIAN AC *Languedoc, France* Large AC for strong, spicy red wines with more personality and fruit than run-of-the-mill HÉRAULT. Best producers: Berloup co-op, Borie la Vitarèle★, CANET-VALETTE★★, Cazal-Viel★, CLOS BAGATELLE, Combebelle, Jougla★, la Madura, Mas Champart★, Maurel Fonsalade★, Moulin de Ciffre, Moulinier, Navarre, Rimbert★, Roquebrun co-op. Best years: 2001 **00 99 98 96 95 94 93**.

SAINT CLAIR *Marlborough, South Island, New Zealand* A top performer thanks to some great vineyard sites and the help of talented consultant winemaker Kim Crawford. Intensely fruity Wairau Reserve Sauvignon Blanc★★ is almost a caricature of the MARLBOROUGH style. Omaka Reserve Chardonnay★ combines attractive citrus fruit flavours

and sensitive winemaking, while dense, rich Rapaura Road Reserve
Merlot★ is a consistent winner. Best years: (whites) (2002) **01 00 99**.

ST-DÉSIRAT, CAVE DE *St-Joseph, Rhône Valley, France* St-Désirat is
one of the best co-ops in the RHONE VALLEY. The intense, smoky red ST-
JOSEPH★ is a fantastic bargain, as are local vins de pays.

ST-ÉMILION AC *Bordeaux, France* The scenic Roman hill town of St-
Émilion is the centre of Bordeaux's most historic wine region. The
finest vineyards are on the plateau and *côtes*, or steep slopes, around
the town, although an area to the west, called the *graves*, contains 2
famous properties, CHEVAL BLANC and FIGEAC. It is a region of
smallholdings, with over 1000 properties, and consequently the co-
operative plays an important part. The dominant early-ripening
Merlot grape gives wines with a 'come hither' softness and sweetness
rare in red Bordeaux. St-Émilion AC is the basic generic AC, with 4
'satellites' (LUSSAC, MONTAGNE, PUISSEGUIN, ST-GEORGES) allowed to annex
their name to it. The best producers, including the Classed Growths,
are found in the more tightly controlled ST-EMILION GRAND CRU AC
category. Best years: 2001 00 **98 96 95 90 89 88 86 85**.

ST-ÉMILION GRAND CRU AC *Bordeaux, France* St-Émilion's top-quality
AC, which includes the estates classified as Grand Cru Classé and
Premier Grand Cru Classé. The 1996 Classification lists 55 Grands
Crus Classés. It also includes most of the new wave of limited edition
vins de garage. Best producers: (Grands Crus Classés) l'ARROSEE★★,
Balestard-la-Tonnelle★, CANON-LA-GAFFELIERE★★, Clos de l'Oratoire★, la
Clotte★, la Dominique★★, Grand Mayne★★, Grand Pontet★,
Larmande★, Pavie-Decesse★, PAVIE-MACQUIN★★, Soutard★, la Tour
Figeac★, TROPLONG-MONDOT★★; (others) Faugères★, Fleur Cardinale★,
Fombrauge★, la Gomerie★, Gracia★, MONBOUSQUET★★, La Mondotte★★,
Moulin St-Georges★, Quinault l'Enclos★, Rol Valentin★★, TERTRE-
ROTEBOEUF★★, Teyssier, VALANDRAUD★★. Best years: 2001 00 98 **96 95 90
89 88 86 85**. See also St-Émilion Premier Grand Cru Classé.

ST-ÉMILION PREMIER GRAND CRU CLASSÉ *Bordeaux, France* The St-
Émilion élite level, divided into 2 categories – 'A' and 'B' – with only
the much more expensive CHEVAL BLANC and AUSONE in category 'A'.
There are 11 'B' châteaux, with ANGELUS and BEAU-SEJOUR BECOT added
in the 1996 Classification. Best producers: ANGELUS★★★, AUSONE★★★,
BEAU-SEJOUR BECOT★★, Beauséjour★, BELAIR★, CANON★, CHEVAL BLANC★★★,
Clos Fourtet★, FIGEAC★★, la Gaffelière★, MAGDELAINE★★, PAVIE★★. Best
years: 2001 00 99 98 96 95 **90 89 88 86 85 83 82**.

ST-ESTÈPHE AC *Haut-Médoc, Bordeaux, France* Large AC north of
PAUILLAC with 5 Classed Growths. St-Estèphe wines have high tannin
levels, but given time (10–20 years) those sought-after flavours of
blackcurrant and cedarwood do peek out. More Merlot has been
planted to soften the wines and make them more accessible at an
earlier age. Best producers: CALON-SEGUR★★, COS D'ESTOURNEL★★, Cos
Labory, HAUT-MARBUZET★★, LAFON-ROCHET★, Lilian-Ladouys★,
Marbuzet★, MEYNEY★, MONTROSE★★, les Ormes-de-Pez★, PEZ★, Phélan
Ségur★. Best years: 2001 00 96 **95 94 90 89 88 86 85 83 82**.

DOM. ST-GAYAN *Gigondas AC, Rhône Valley, France* The Meffre family's
holdings include some very old vines, which lend power to the
GIGONDAS★ (★★ in top years) – but the extensive period of barrel-
aging really only suits the ripest vintages. COTES DU RHONE (red and
white) and Côtes du Rhône-Villages RASTEAU are usually good value.
Best years: (Gigondas) 2001 00 99 98 **97** 96 95 **93 90**.

ST-GEORGES-ST-ÉMILION AC *Bordeaux, France* The best satellite of
ST-EMILION, with lovely, soft wines that can nevertheless age for 6–10
years. Best producers: Calon, Griffe de Cap d'Or, Macquin St-Georges★,
St-André Corbin, Ch. St-Georges★, Tour-du-Pas-St-Georges★, Vieux-
Montaiguillon. Best years: 2001 00 **98 96 95 90 89 88 85**.

ST HALLETT *Barossa Valley, South Australia* Change is afoot at the home
of the venerable Old Block Shiraz★★ and its Shiraz siblings Blackwell★
and Faith★. Following a merger with MCLAREN VALE's Tatachilla, then a
joint takeover with ADELAIDE HILLS' Hillstowe, all 3 wineries have been
snapped up by brewer Lion Nathan (as has PETALUMA). Let's hope the
wines, including the bargain Gamekeeper's Reserve★ red, Poacher's
Blend★ white, EDEN VALLEY Riesling★ and The Reward Cabernet★★,
don't suffer. Best years: (Old Block) (2001) 99 98 **96 94 93 91 90**.

ST-JOSEPH AC *Rhône Valley, France* Large, mainly red AC, on the
opposite bank of the Rhône to HERMITAGE. Made from Syrah, the reds have
mouthfilling fruit with irresistible blackcurrant richness. Brilliant at 1–2
years, they can last for up to 10. Only a little white is made and, with up-
to-date winemaking, these are usually pleasant, flowery wines to drink
young, although an increasing number can age. Best producers: (reds)
CHAPOUTIER★, J-L CHAVE★★, Chêne★★, L Chèze★, COLOMBO★, Courbis★,
COURSODON★★, CUILLERON★★, DELAS★★, E & J Durand★, Florentin★, P
Gaillard★, Gonon★, GRAILLOT★★, B Gripa★★, GUIGAL★, JABOULET★,
Monteillet★★, Paret★, A PERRET★★, P Pichon★, ST-DESIRAT CO-OP★, TAIN
L'HERMITAGE CO-OP★, Tardieu-Laurent★★, Tunnel★, F Villard★★; (whites)
Chêne★★, L Chèze★, Courbis★, CUILLERON★★, DELAS★, E & J Durand★,
Ferraton★, P Finon★, Florentin★, P Gaillard★★, B Gripa★, GUIGAL,
JABOULET★, Monteillet★, A PERRET★, Trollat★, Villard★★. Best years: (reds)
2001 00 99 **98 97 96 95 94**; (whites) 2001 00 99 **98 97 96 95**.

ST-JULIEN AC *Haut-Médoc, Bordeaux, France* For many, St-Julien
produces perfect claret, with an ideal balance between opulence and
austerity and between the brashness of youth and the genius of
maturity. It is the smallest of the HAUT-MEDOC ACs but almost all is first-
rate vineyard land and quality is high. Best producers: BEYCHEVELLE★,
BRANAIRE★, DUCRU-BEAUCAILLOU★★★, GLORIA★, GRUAUD-LAROSE★★,
LAGRANGE★★, LANGOA-BARTON★★, LEOVILLE-BARTON★★★, LEOVILLE-LAS-
CASES★★★, LEOVILLE-POYFERRE★★, ST-PIERRE★★, TALBOT★. Best years:
2001 00 99 98 97 96 95 **94 90** 89 88 86 85 83 82.

ST-NICOLAS-DE-BOURGUEIL AC *Loire Valley, France* An enclave of
just under 500ha (1250 acres) within the larger BOURGUEIL AC. Almost
all the wine is red with the same piercing red fruit flavours of
Bourgueil, and much better after 7–10 years, especially in warm
vintages. Best producers: Y Amirault★, M Cognard★, P Jamet★,
F Mabileau★, J-C Mabileau★, Taluau-Foltzenlogel★, Vallée★. Best
years: (2002) 01 00 **97 96 95 90 89**.

ST-PÉRAY AC *Rhône Valley, France* Rather hefty, Champagne-method
fizz from Marsanne and Roussanne grapes. Still white is usually dry,
and improving. Best producers: CLAPE★, S Chaboud★, COLOMBO (La
Belle de Mai★★), DELAS, Fauterie★, B Gripa, J Lemenicier★, LIONNET★,
J-L Thiers★, A Voge★. Best years: 2001 **00 99 98 97 96 95**.

CH. ST-PIERRE ★★ *St-Julien AC, 4ème Cru Classé, Haut-Médoc, Bordeaux,*
France Small ST-JULIEN property making wines that have become a
byword for ripe, lush fruit wrapped round with the spice of new oak.
Drinkable early, but top vintages can improve for 20 years. Best years:
2001 00 99 98 97 96 95 **94 90** 89 88 86 83 82.

ST-ROMAIN AC *Côte de Beaune, Burgundy, France* Out-of-the-way village producing red wines with a firm, bittersweet cherrystone fruit and flinty-dry whites. Both are usually good value by Burgundian standards, but take a few years to open out. Best producers: (whites) Bazenet★, H & G Buisson, Chassorney★★, A Gras★★, JAFFELIN★, O LEFLAIVE★, P Taupenot, VERGET★★; (reds) A Gras★. Best years: (whites) (2002) **00 99 97**; (reds) (2002) **00 99 98 97 96**.

ST-VÉRAN AC *Mâconnais, Burgundy, France* Often thought of as a POUILLY-FUISSÉ understudy. This is gentle, fairly fruity, normally unoaked Mâconnais Chardonnay at its best, and the overall quality is good. The price is fair, too. Drink young. Best producers: D & M Barraud★, G Chagny, Corsin★★, Deux Roches★, B & J-M Drouin★, DUBOEUF★, G Guérin★, R Lassarat★, O Merlin★, Saumaize-Michelin★, J C Thévenet★★, J-L Tissier★, VERGET★, J-J Vincent★.

STE-CROIX-DU-MONT AC *Bordeaux, France* Best of the 3 sweet wine ACs that gaze jealously at SAUTERNES and BARSAC across the Garonne river (the others are CADILLAC and LOUPIAC). The wine is mildly sweet rather than splendidly rich. Top wines can age for at least a decade. Best producers: Crabitan-Bellevue, Loubens★, Lousteau-Vieil, Mailles, Mont, Pavillon★, la Rame★. Best years: 2001 **99 98 97 96 95 90 89 88**.

SAINTSBURY *Carneros AVA, California, USA* Deeply committed CARNEROS winery. Its Pinot Noirs★★ are brilliant examples of the perfume and fruit quality of Carneros; the Reserve★★ and the exquisite Brown Ranch★★★ are deeper and oakier, while Garnet★ is a delicious lighter style. The Chardonnays★★ are also impressive, best after 2–3 years. Best years: (Pinot Noir Reserve) (2001) (00) 99 98 **97 96 95 94 91**.

SALA, CASTELLO DELLA *Orvieto DOC, Umbria, Italy* Belongs to the ANTINORI family, making good ORVIETO★ and outstanding oak-aged Cervaro★★★ (Chardonnay and a little Grechetto). Also impressive Pinot Nero★ and sweet Muffato della Sala★★.

SALAPARUTA, DUCA DI *Sicily, Italy* Corvo is the brand name for Sicilian wines made by this firm. Red and white Corvo are pretty basic, but there are superior whites, Colomba Platino★ and Bianca di Valguarnera★, and 2 fine reds, Terre d'Agala★ and Duca Enrico★★.

SALICE SALENTINO DOC *Puglia, Italy* One of the better DOCs in the Salento peninsula, turning out wines (made with Negroamaro and tempered with a dash of perfumed Malvasia Nera) that are ripe and chocolaty, acquiring hints of roast chestnuts and prunes with age. Drink after 3–4 years, although they may last as long again. The DOCs of Alezio, Brindisi, Copertino, Leverano and Squinzano have similar Rosso and Rosato. Best producers: Candido★, Casale Bevagna★, Leone De Castris★, Due Palme★, Taurino★, Vallone★, Conti Zecca. Best years: (reds) (2001) 00 **98 97 96**.

SALITAGE *Pemberton, Western Australia* John Horgan established PEMBERTON's first and largest winery in 1989. The wines are good, sometimes excellent. There's a no-holds-barred barrel-fermented Chardonnay★★, an Unwooded Chardonnay★, Pinot Noir★ and Cabernet Blend★★ (Cabernet Sauvignon, Cabernet Franc, Merlot and Petit Verdot). A second label, Treehouse, produces good Chardonnay-Verdelho. Top reds will age for 3–7 years.

SAMOS *Greece* The island of Samos has a centuries-old reputation for producing rich, sweet dessert wines. The 2 wineries of the Samos co-op make similar Muscat-based wines. Pale green Samena dry white is made from early-picked Muscat; deep gold, honeyed Samos Nectar★★

is made from sun-dried grapes; the rarer apricotty Palaio is aged for up to 20 years; and seductively complex Samos Anthemis★ is fortified and cask-aged for up to 5 years.

SAN ANTONIO VALLEY *Chile* Situated 15km (9 miles) from the Pacific Ocean and influenced by the cold Humboldt Current, this zone was planted in 1998 and started to show its potential in the 2001 vintage, with mineral Chardonnay, crisp Sauvignon Blanc, fresh and fruity Pinot Noir and powerfully charged Syrah. Expect a new CASABLANCA in years to come. Best producers: Leyda, Matetic Vineyards.

SAN LUIS OBISPO COUNTY *California, USA* CENTRAL COAST county best known for Chardonnay, Pinot Noir, a bit of old-vine Zinfandel and Cabernet Sauvignon. There are 5 AVAs – Edna Valley, PASO ROBLES, SANTA MARIA VALLEY (shared with SANTA BARBARA COUNTY), Arroyo Grande Valley and York Mountain – each of which has already grown some outstanding grapes. Best producers: Claiborne & Churchill★, Creston★, Eberle★, Edna Valley★★, Justin★, J Lohr (Hilltop Cabernet Sauvignon★★), Meridian★★, Norman★, Saucelito Canyon★, Savannah-Chanelle★, Seven Peaks★★, Talley★★, Wild Horse★. Best years: (reds) (2001) (00) 99 **98 97 95 94**.

SAN PEDRO *Curicó, Chile* San Pedro is a giant operation and produced little of note before Jacques Lurton arrived as a consultant in 1994. He's now gone, but the French influence lingers in a new venture with ST-EMILION Ch. Dassault called Viña Totihue, aiming to produce top reds. 35 South range is quite good, Castillo de Molina Reservas are tasty, and 1865 Malbec★ and Cabernet★ are chunky and chewy.

SANCERRE AC *Loire Valley, France* Sancerre mania broke out in the 1970s, first with the white wine which can provide the perfect expression of the bright green tang of the Sauvignon grape, then with the reds and rosés, which are made from Pinot Noir. The whites, from a good grower, can be deliciously refreshing – as can the rare Pinot Noir rosé – but the very best also age well. Some growers produce a richer style using new oak. Reds are now being taken more seriously, but still really need fine, dry years to show best. The wines are now more consistent than

those of neighbouring POUILLY. Best producers: F & J Bailly★, Balland-Chapuis★, H Bourgeois★, H Brochard★, R Champault★, F Cotat★★, L Crochet★, Delaporte★, Gitton★, P Jolivet★, Serge Laloue★, A MELLOT★★, J Mellot★, P Millérioux★, H Natter★, A & F Neveu★, R Neveu★, V Pinard★★, H Reverdy★, J Reverdy★, Reverdy-Ducroux★, J-M Roger★, VACHERON★★, André Vatan★. Best years: (2002) **00 99 98 97 96 95 90**.

SANDEMAN *Port DOC, Douro, Portugal and Jerez y Manzanilla DO, Spain* Now owned by SOGRAPE, but run by George Sandeman (seventh-generation descendant of the founder). Excellent aged tawnies: Imperial Reserve★ and 20-year-old★★. Vintage ports are more patchy. Vau Vintage★★ is the second label, for early drinking. Formerly famous sherries are in need of improvement. Best years: (Vintage) 2000 97 94 **66 63 55**.

LUCIANO SANDRONE *Barolo DOCG, Piedmont, Italy* Luciano Sandrone has become one of PIEDMONT's leading wine stylists, renowned for his BAROLO Cannubi Boschis★★★ and Le Vigne★★★, as well as BARBERA D'ALBA★★ and Dolcetto d'Alba★★, which rank with the best.

SANFORD *Santa Rita Hills AVA, California, USA* Richard Sanford planted the great Benedict vineyard in the Santa Ynez Valley in 1971, thus establishing Santa Ynez and SANTA BARBARA as potentially top-quality vineyard regions. Sanford now makes sharply focused, dark-fruited Pinot Noir★★, Chardonnay★★ and Sauvignon Blanc★. Best years: (Pinot Noir) (2001) 00 99 98 **97 96 95 94**.

SANGIOVESE Sangiovese rivals Trebbiano as the most widely planted grape variety in Italy, but it reaches its greatest heights in central TUSCANY. This grape has produced a wide variety of clones that make generalization difficult. Much care is being taken in the current wave of replanting, whether in CHIANTI CLASSICO, BRUNELLO DI MONTALCINO or VINO NOBILE DI MONTEPULCIANO. Styles range from pale, lively and cherryish, through the vivacious, mid-range Chiantis, to excellent top Riservas and SUPER-TUSCANS. A number of fine examples are also produced in ROMAGNA. CALIFORNIA producers like ATLAS PEAK, SHAFER, Robert Pepi and SEGHESIO are now working some of their magic on this grape. Australia is taking a keen interest, with good examples from King Valley in VICTORIA (Gary Crittenden, Pizzini) and MCLAREN VALE (Coriole). Some interesting examples are also grown in Argentina, and both South Africa and New York's LONG ISLAND are trying it out.

SANTA BARBARA COUNTY *California, USA* CENTRAL COAST county, north-west of Los Angeles, known for Chardonnay, Riesling, Pinot Noir and Syrah. The main AVAs are Santa Ynez Valley and most of SANTA MARIA VALLEY (the remainder is in SAN LUIS OBISPO COUNTY), both leading areas for Pinot Noir. Best producers: AU BON CLIMAT★★, BABCOCK★, Beckmen★, BYRON★★, CAMBRIA★, Foxen★★, Hitching Post★★, Longoria★, Andrew MURRAY★★, Ojai★★, Fess Parker★, QUPE★★, SANFORD★★, Whitcraft★★, Zaca Mesa★. Best years: (Pinot Noir) (2001) (00) 99 98 **97 95 94**.

SANTA CAROLINA *Maipo, Chile* Long-established winery that is at last catching up with the modern world. You'll find fresh Reserva whites★ with good fruit definition, and substantial, ripe, if oaky, Barrica Selection reds★. Top of the range is the new Cabernet Sauvignon-based VSC★.

SANTA CRUZ MOUNTAINS AVA *California, USA* A sub-region of the CENTRAL COAST AVA. Long-lived Chardonnays and Cabernet Sauvignons are the most notable wines; the most famous is the stunning Monte Bello Cabernet from RIDGE. Small amounts of robust Pinot Noir are also produced here. Best producers: BONNY DOON★★, David Bruce★★, Clos La Chance★, Kathryn Kennedy★★, Mount Eden Vineyards★★, RIDGE★★★, Santa Cruz Mountain Vineyard★.

SANTA INÉS/DE MARTINO *Maipo, Chile* Old-established winery pulling itself up the quality scale. Important vineyard holdings in Maipo and new Marchihue region. Whites only fair, although good Marchihue Viognier★. Reds can be excellent under various labels: Nuevo Mondo Organic Cabernet Sauvignon-Malbec★★; Legado de Armida★ reds are good; and Enigma Reserve label reaches ★★ in Pinot Noir and Malbec.

SANTA MADDALENA *Alto Adige DOC, Italy* Light, delicate wine from the Schiava grape grown in the hills above Bolzano. It has a perfume of black cherries, cream and bacon smoke, and can be improved with the addition of up to 10% of Lagrein. Drink young, but some vintages will age. Best producers: Egger-Ramer★, Franz Gojer★, LAGEDER★, Josephus

Mayr★, Josef Niedermayr★, Plattner Waldgries★, Hans Rottensteiner★, Heinrich Rottensteiner★, Santa Maddalena co-op★.

SANTA MARIA VALLEY AVA *Santa Barbara County and San Luis Obispo County, California, USA*   Cool Santa Maria Valley is coming on strong as a producer of Chardonnay, Pinot Noir and Syrah. Look for wines made from grapes grown in Bien Nacido vineyards by several small wineries. Best producers: AU BON CLIMAT★★, BYRON★★, CAMBRIA★, Foxen★★, Lane Tanner (Pinot Noir★★), Longoria★, QUPE★★.

SANTA RITA *Maipo, Chile*   Long-established MAIPO giant, now revitalized under winemaker Andrés Ilabaca. Plummy red blends such as Triple C★★ (Cabernet Franc, Cabernet Sauvignon, Carmenère) and Syrah-Cabernet Sauvignon-Carmenère★ show real flair, and a trio of red blends in the Floresta★★ range are exciting and packed with flavour. Top-of-the-range Cabernet Sauvignon Casa Real★ is intentionally made in a more European style and lacks the fire of the other top reds.

SANTENAY AC *Côte de Beaune, Burgundy, France*   Red Santenay wines often promise good ripe flavour, though they don't always deliver it, but are worth aging for 4–6 years in the hope that the wine will open out. Many of the best wines, both red and white, come from les Gravières Premier Cru on the border with CHASSAGNE-MONTRACHET. Best producers: (reds) R Belland★★, D & F Clair★, M Colin★, J Girardin★, V GIRARDIN★★, Monnot★, B Morey★, L Muzard★★, Prieur-Brunet, Roux Père et Fils★; (whites) V GIRARDIN★, JAFFELIN, René Lequin-Colin★. Best years: (reds) (2002) 01 99 98 **97 96**; (whites) (2002) 01 **00 99**.

CASA SANTOS LIMA *Alenquer DOC, Estremadura, Portugal*   A beautiful estate with an expanding range. Espiga reds and whites are light, fruity and tasty, but for more character look to the spicy red★★ and creamy, perfumed white Palha Canas, or to red and white Quinta das Setencostas★. New reds sold under the Casa Santos Lima label include Touriz★ (from DOURO varieties) and varietal Touriga Nacional★, Touriga Francesa★, Trincadeira★ and Tinta Roriz★. Also a promising peachy, herby Chardonnay★.

SÃO JOÃO, CAVES *Beira Litoral, Portugal*   This company was a pioneer of cool-fermented, white BAIRRADA, and has made some very good Cabernet Sauvignons from its own vines. Rich, complex reds include outstanding Reserva★★ and Frei João★ from Bairrada and Porta dos Cavalheiros★★ from DAO – they demand at least 10 years' age to show their quality.

SARDINIA *Italy*   Grapes of Spanish origin, like the white Vermentino and Torbato and the red Monica, Cannonau and Carignano, dominate production on this huge, hilly Mediterranean island, but they vie with a Malvasia of Greek origin and natives like Nuragus and Vernaccia. The cooler northern part favours whites, especially Vermentino, while the southern and eastern parts are best suited to reds from Cannonau and Monica. The wines used to be powerful, alcoholic monsters, but the current trend is for a lighter, modern, more international style. Foremost among those in pursuit of quality are ARGIOLAS, SELLA & MOSCA and the Santadi co-op. See also Carignano del Sulcis, Vernaccia di Oristano.

SASSICAIA DOC★★★ *Tuscany, Italy*   This Cabernet Sauvignon-Cabernet Franc blend from the coast has done more than any other wine to gain credibility abroad for Italy. Vines were planted in 1944 to satisfy the Marchese Incisa della Rocchetta's thirst for fine red

247

Bordeaux, which was in short supply during the war. The wine remained purely for family consumption until nephew Piero Antinori (of ANTINORI) and winemaker Giacomo Tachis persuaded the Marchese to refine production practices and to release several thousand bottles from the 1968 vintage. Since then, Sassicaia's fame has increased as it proved itself, with a few weak vintage exceptions, to be one of the world's great Cabernets, combining a blackcurrant power of blistering intensity with a heavenly scent of cigars. It is the first Italian single-owner estate wine to have its own DOC, within the BOLGHERI appellation, from the 1995 vintage. Best years: (2001) (99) 98 97 95 **90 88 85 84 83 82 81 78 75 71 68**.

HORST SAUER *Escherndorf, Franken, Germany* His wines from the late 1990s shot Horst Sauer to stardom. His dry Rieslings★★ and Silvaners★ are unusually juicy and fresh for a region renowned for blunt, earthy wines. His late-harvest wines are unchallenged in the region and sometimes ★★★; they will easily live a decade, sometimes much more. Best years: (dry Riesling, Silvaner) (2002) 01 00 **99 98 97**.

SAUMUR AC *Loire Valley, France* Improving dry white wines, made mainly from Chenin Blanc, but up to 20% Chardonnay can be added. The reds are lighter than those of SAUMUR-CHAMPIGNY. Also dry to off-dry Cabernet rosé, and sweet Coteaux de Saumur in good years. Best producers: Château-Gaillard★, Clos Rougeard★★, Collier★, Filliatreau★, HUREAU★★, Langlois-Château★, R-N Legrand★, la Paleine★, Roches Neuves★, St-Just★, VILLENEUVE★★, Yvonne★. Best years: (whites) (2002) **01 00 99 97 96**.

SAUMUR-CHAMPIGNY AC *Loire Valley, France* Saumur's best red wine. Cabernet Franc is the main grape, and in hot years the wine can be superb, with a piercing scent of blackcurrants and raspberries easily overpowering the earthy finish. Delicious young, it can age for 6–10 years. Best producers: Clos Rougeard★★, Clos des Cordeliers★, Filliatreau★, des Galmoises★, HUREAU★, R-N Legrand★, Nerleux★, la Perruche★, Retiveau-Rétif★, Roches Neuves★★, de Targé★, St-Vincent★, VILLENEUVE★, Yvonne★. Best years: (2002) **01 00 97 96**.

SAUMUR MOUSSEUX AC *Loire Valley, France* Reasonable Champagne-method sparkling wines made mainly from Chenin Blanc. Adding Chardonnay and Cabernet Franc makes Saumur Mousseux softer and more interesting. Usually non-vintage. Small quantities of rosé are also made. Best producers: BOUVET-LADUBAY★, GRATIEN & MEYER★, Grenelle★, la Paleine★, la Perruche★, St-Cyr-en-Bourg co-op★.

SAUTERNES AC *Bordeaux, France* The name Sauternes is synonymous with the best sweet wines in the world. Sauternes and BARSAC both lie on the banks of the little river Ciron and are 2 of the very few areas in France where noble rot occurs naturally. Production of these intense, sweet, luscious wines from botrytized grapes is a risk-laden and extremely expensive affair, and the wines are never going to be cheap. From good producers (most of which are Crus Classés) the wines are worth their high price – as well as 14% alcohol they have a richness full of flavours of pineapples, peaches, syrup and spice. Good vintages should be aged for 5–10 years, and they can often last twice as long. Best producers: BASTOR-LAMONTAGNE★, Clos Haut-Peyraguey★★, Cru Barréjats★, DOISY-DAENE★★, DOISY-VEDRINES★★, FARGUES★★, GILETTE★★, GUIRAUD★★, Haut-Bergeron★, les Justices★, LAFAURIE-PEYRAGUEY★★★, Lamothe-Guignard★, Malle★, Rabaud-Promis★, Raymond-Lafon★★, Rayne-Vigneau★, RIEUSSEC★★★, Sigalas

Rabaud★★, SUDUIRAUT★★, la TOUR BLANCHE★★, YQUEM★★★. Best years: (2002) 01 99 **98 97 96 95 90** 89 88 86 83.

SAUVIGNON BLANC See pages 250–1.

SAUZET *Côte de Beaune, Burgundy, France* A producer with a reputation for classic, rich, full-flavoured white Burgundies, made in an opulent, fat style, but recently showing more classical restraint. Sauzet owns prime sites in PULIGNY-MONTRACHET★ and CHASSAGNE-MONTRACHET★, as well as small parcels of BATARD-MONTRACHET★★★ and Bienvenues-BATARD-MONTRACHET★★★.

SAVENNIÈRES AC *Loire Valley, France* Wines from Chenin Blanc, produced on steep vineyards south of Anjou. Usually steely and dry, although there's a spirit of experimentation abroad and some softer wines are being produced using new oak. The top wines usually need at least 8 years to mature, and can age for longer. There are 2 extremely good vineyards with their own ACs: la Coulée-de-Serrant and la Roche-aux-Moines. Best producers: BAUMARD★★, Clos de Coulaine★, CLOS DE LA COULEE-DE-SERRANT★★, Clos de Varennes★, Closel★★, Épiré★★, Forges★★, aux Moines★, Monnaie★, Pierre-Bise★★, P Soulez★, P-Y Tijou★★. Best years: (2002) 01 00 99 **97 96 95** 93 90 89 88 85 83 82.

SAVIGNY-LÈS-BEAUNE AC *Côte de Beaune, Burgundy, France* This large village concentrates on red wines; they are usually middle weight and best drunk 4–10 years after the vintage. The top Premiers Crus are more substantial. The white wines show a bit of dry, nutty class after 3–4 years. The wines are generally reasonably priced. Best producers: S Bize★, Camus-Bruchon★★, Champy★, CHANDON DE BRIAILLES★★, B CLAIR★★, M Écard★★, J J Girard★, P Girard★, V GIRARDIN★, L Jacob★★, D Laurent★★, LEROY★★, C Maréchal★, J-M Pavelot★★, TOLLOT-BEAUT★★. Best years: (reds) (2002) 01 99 98 **97 96 95** 93.

SAVOIE *France* Savoie's high Alpine vineyards, which are scattered between Lake Geneva and Grenoble and on the banks of the Rhône and Isère rivers, produce fresh, snappy white wines with loads of flavour, when made from the Altesse (or Roussette) grape. Drink them young. There are some attractive light reds and rosés, too, mainly from a group of villages south of Chambéry and, in hot years, some positively Rhône-like reds from the Mondeuse grape. Most of the better wines use the Vin de Savoie AC and should be drunk young or with 3–4 years' age. The 15 best villages, including Abymes, Apremont, Arbin, Chignin, Cruet and Montmélian, can add their own name to the AC name. Between Lyon and Savoie are the vineyards of the Vin du Bugey VDQS, which produce light, easy-drinking reds and whites. Best producers: Boniface★, Bouvet★, Dupasquier★, Jacquin★, Magnin★, C Marandon★, Monin, Neyroud, Perret★, A & M Quénard★, R Quénard★, Ripaille★, Rocailles★, C Trosset★. See also Seyssel.

SAXENBURG *Stellenbosch WO, South Africa* Red-wine specialist producing some of the Cape's most sought-after reds, led by the dense, burly Private Collection Shiraz★★ and an even richer, bigger Shiraz Select★★. These, plus excellent Cabernet★★ and Merlot★, benefit from new clones. Private Collection Sauvignon Blanc★★ and Chardonnay★ head the white range. Winemaker Nico van der Merwe produces equally good results at Swiss businessman Adrian Bührer's other estate, Ch. Capion in the LANGUEDOC. Drink whites young; reds will improve for 5–8 years. Best years: (premium reds) 2000 99 98 **97 96** 95 94 93.

SAUVIGNON BLANC

Of all the world's grapes, the Sauvignon Blanc is leader of the 'love it or loathe it' pack. It veers from being wildly fashionable to totally out of favour depending upon where it is grown and which country's consumers are being consulted. But Sauvignon is always at its best when full rein is allowed to its very particular talents because this grape does give intense, sometimes shocking flavours, and doesn't take kindly to being put into a straitjacket. One difficulty with the grape is that it must be picked perfectly ripe. Sometimes Loire Sauvignon Blanc is associated with a pungent 'catty' smell. This is a sure sign that the fruit was not fully ripe when picked. On the other hand, if the grapes are too ripe, they begin to lose the acidity that makes the wines so irresistibly snappy and refreshing.

WINE STYLES

Sancerre-style Sauvignon Although it had long been used as a blending grape in Bordeaux, where its characteristic green tang injected a bit of life into the blander, waxier Sémillon, Sauvignon first became trendy as the grape used for Sancerre, a bone-dry Loire white whose green gooseberry fruit and slightly smoky perfume inspired the winemakers of other countries to try to emulate, then often surpass the original model.

But Sauvignon is only successful where it is respected. The grape is not as easy to grow as Chardonnay, and the flavours are not so adaptable. Yet the range of styles Sauvignon produces is as wide, if less subtly nuanced, as those of Chardonnay. It is highly successful when picked not too ripe, fermented cool in stainless steel, and bottled early. This is the Sancerre model followed by growers elsewhere. New Zealand is now regarded as the top Sauvignon country, and most new producers in countries like Australia, South Africa, southern France, Hungary and Chile try to emulate this powerful mix of passionfruit, gooseberry and lime.

Using oak Sauvignon also lends itself to fermentation in barrel and aging in new oak, though less happily than does Chardonnay. This is the model of the Graves region of Bordeaux, although generally here Sémillon would be blended in with Sauvignon to good effect.

New Zealand again excels at this style, though there are good examples from California, Australia, northern Italy and South Africa. In Austria, a handful of producers in southern Styria (Steiermark) make powerful, aromatic versions with a touch of oak. In all these regions, the acidity that is Sauvignon's great strength should remain, with a dried apricots fruit and a spicy, biscuity softness from the oak. These oaky styles are best drunk either within about a year, or after aging for 5 years or so, and can produce remarkable, strongly individual flavours that you'll either love or loathe.

Sweet wines Sauvignon is also a crucial ingredient in the great sweet wines of Sauternes and Barsac from Bordeaux, though it is less susceptible than its partner Sémillon to the sweetness-enhancing 'noble rot' fungus, botrytis.

Sweet wines from the USA, South Africa, Australia and, inevitably, New Zealand range from the interesting to the out-standing – but the characteristic green tang of the Sauvignon should stay in the wine even at ultra-sweet levels.

BEST PRODUCERS

France

Pouilly-Fumé J-C Chatelain, Didier DAGUENEAU, Ladoucette, Masson-Blondelet, de Tracy; *Sancerre* H Bourgeois, F Cotat, L Crochet, A MELLOT, Pinard, Jean-Max Roger, VACHERON; *Pessac-Léognan* Dom. de CHEVALIER, Couhins-Lurton, FIEUZAL, HAUT-BRION, LAVILLE-HAUT-BRION, SMITH-HAUT-LAFITTE.

Other European Sauvignons

Austria Gross, Lackner-Tinnacher, POLZ, TEMENT.

Italy Colterenzio co-op, Peter Dipoli, GRAVNER, Edi Kante, LAGEDER, ORNELLAIA, SCHIOPETTO, Vie di Romans, Villa Russiz.

Spain (Rueda) MARQUES DE RISCAL, Hermanos Lurton, Javier Sanz; (Penedès) TORRES (Fransola).

New Zealand

Cairnbrae, CLOUDY BAY, Drylands, Forrest Estate, HUNTER'S, ISABEL, Lawson's Dry Hills, MONTANA, NEUDORF, NOBILO, PALLISER, SAINT CLAIR, SEIFRIED, Selaks, SERESIN, VAVASOUR, VILLA MARIA, WITHER HILLS.

Australia

Bridgewater Mill, Brookland Valley, HANGING ROCK, Hill Smith Estate, HOUGHTON (PEMBERTON), KATNOOK ESTATE, LENSWOOD VINEYARDS, Ravenswood Lane, SHAW & SMITH, Geoff WEAVER.

USA

California Abreu, ARAUJO, BABCOCK, FLORA SPRINGS (Soliloquy), KENWOOD, Mason, MATANZAS CREEK, Robert MONDAVI (Reserve Fumé), Murphy-Goode, Navarro, Quivira, ROCHIOLI, SPOTTSWOODE.

Chile

CASABLANCA, CONCHA Y TORO (Terrunyo).

South Africa

Cape Point Vineyards, Neil ELLIS, Flagstone, Havana Hills, MULDERBOSCH, SAXENBURG, SPRINGFIELD ESTATE, STEENBERG, THELEMA, VERGELEGEN, VILLIERA.

251

WILLI SCHAEFER *Graach, Mosel, Germany* Schaefer's naturally sweet
Riesling Spätlese and Auslese from the great Domprobst vineyard of
GRAACH are classic MOSEL wines. The balance of piercing acidity and
lavish fruit is every bit as dramatic as Domprobst's precipitous slope.
Made in tiny quantities and extremely long-lived, they're frequently
★★★, as is the sensational Beerenauslese Schaefer produces in good
vintages. Even his QbA wines are ★. Best years: (Riesling Spätlese,
Auslese) (2002) 01 00 99 98 97 96 95 **94 93 92 90 89 88 83 76 71**.

SCHEUREBE Very popular Silvaner x Riesling crossing most widespread
in Germany's RHEINHESSEN and PFALZ. Also planted in Austria, where it
is sometimes sold under the name Sämling 88. At its best in
Trockenbeerenauslese and Eiswein. When ripe, it has a marvellous
flavour of honey, exotic fruits and the pinkest of pink grapefruit.

SCHIOPETTO *Friuli-Venezia Giulia, Italy* One of the legends of Italian wine,
who pioneered the development of scented varietals and, above all,
high-quality, intensely concentrated white wines from COLLIO. Most
outstanding are Tocai★★, Pinot Bianco★★ and Sauvignon★★ which
open out with age to display fascinating flavours. New COLLI ORIENTALI
vineyards Poderi dei Blumeri can only add further prestige.

SCHLOSS LIESER *Lieser, Mosel, Germany* Since Thomas Haag (son of
Wilhelm, of the Fritz HAAG estate) took over the winemaking in 1992,
this small estate has shot to the top. MOSEL Rieslings★★ marry richness
with great elegance. Best years: (2002) 01 **99 98 97 96 95 94 93**.

SCHLOSS REINHARTSHAUSEN *Erbach, Rheingau, Germany* Estate
formerly owned by the Hohenzollern family, which ruled Prussia, then
Germany until 1918. There are several fine vineyard sites, including
the great ERBACHer Marcobrunn. Interesting organic Weissburgunder-
Chardonnay blend from its vines in Erbacher Rheinhell, an island in the
middle of the Rhine. Good Rieslings (Auslese, Beerenauslese, TBA
★★★) and Sekt★. Best years: (2002) 01 **99 98 97 96 95 94 93 92 90 89**.

SCHLOSS SAARSTEIN *Serrig, Mosel-Saar-Ruwer, Germany* Fine Saar
estate whose Riesling trocken can taste a little austere; better balanced
are wines like the Serriger Riesling Kabinett★ or Spätlese★ and
Auslese★★, which keep the startling acidity but coat it with fruit,
often with the aromas of slightly unripe white peaches. Saarstein
makes the occasional spectacular Eiswein★★★. Best years: (2002) 01
99 **97 95 93 92 90 89 88 86 85**.

SCHLOSS VOLLRADS *Oestrich-Winkel, Rheingau, Germany* Following
the sudden death of owner Erwein Graf Matuschka-Greiffenclau before
the 1997 harvest, the running of this historic estate was taken up by
its banker, Rowald Hepp, who continues to direct it. Quality seems to
have got back on track from the 1999 vintage.

SCHLOSSBÖCKELHEIM *Nahe, Germany* This NAHE village's top sites are
the Felsenberg and Kupfergrube, but good wines also come from
Mühlberg and Königsfels. Best producers: Dr CRUSIUS★, DONNHOFF★★★,
Gutsverwaltung Niederhausen-Schlossböckelheim★. Best years: (2002)
01 00 **99 98 96 95 94**.

DOM. SCHOFFIT *Alsace AC, Alsace, France* One of the two main owners
of the outstanding Rangen Grand Cru vineyard, also making a range
of deliciously fruity non-cru wines. Top-of-the-tree Clos St-Théobald
wines from Rangen are often ★★★ and will improve for at least 5–6
years after release, Rieslings for even longer. The Cuvée Alexandre

range is essentially declassified ALSACE VENDANGE TARDIVE. Best years: (Clos St-Théobald Riesling) 2001 00 99 98 **97 96 95 94**.

SCHRAMSBERG *Napa Valley AVA, California, USA*   The first CALIFORNIA winery to make really excellent Champagne-style sparklers from the classic grapes. Though all releases do not achieve the same heights, the best of these wines are among the best in California, and as good as most in Champagne. The Crémant★ is an attractive sweetish sparkler, the Blanc de Noirs★★ and the Blanc de Blancs★ are more classic. Top of the line is the Reserve Brut★★, which can be world class. In a bold, powerful style is J Schram★★ – rich and flavoursome and increasingly good. Vintage-dated wines can be drunk with up to 10 years' age.

SCREAMING EAGLE *Oakville AVA, California, USA*   Real estate agent Jean Phillips first produced a Cabernet Sauvignon from her OAKVILLE valley floor vineyard in 1992. Made in very limited quantities, the wine is one of California's most sought-after Cabernets each vintage. Made by Heidi Peterson Barrett, winemaker for Grace Family Vineyards and Paradigm, the Screaming Eagle Cabernet Sauvignon★★★ is a huge, brooding wine that displays all the lush fruit of Oakville.

SEGHESIO *Sonoma County, California, USA*   Having grown grapes in SONOMA COUNTY for a century, the Seghesio family is today known for its own Zinfandel. All bottlings, from Sonoma County★★ to the single-vineyard San Lorenzo★★ and Cortina★★, display textbook black fruit and peppery spice. Sangiovese from 1910 vines, known as Chianti Station★, is one of the best in the state. Also look for crisp Italian whites such as Pinot Grigio★ and Arneis★.

SEIFRIED *Nelson, South Island, New Zealand*   Estate founded in 1974 by Austrian Hermann Seifried and his New Zealand wife Agnes. The best wines include Sauvignon Blanc★, Gewürztraminer★ and botrytized Riesling★★. The Redwood Valley label is sometimes used in export markets. Best years: (whites) (2002) **01 00 99 98**.

SELBACH-OSTER *Zeltingen, Mosel, Germany*   Johannes Selbach is one of the MOSEL's new generation of star winemakers, producing very pure, elegant Riesling★ from the Zeltinger Sonnenuhr site. Also good wine from WEHLEN, GRAACH and BERNKASTEL. Best years: (Riesling Spätlese) (2002) 01 00 99 98 **97 96 95 94 93 92 91 90 89 88 85**.

SELLA & MOSCA *Sardinia, Italy*   Apart from the rich, port-like Anghelu Ruju★ made from semi-dried Cannonau grapes, this much-modernized old firm produces excellent dry whites, Terre Bianche★ (Torbato), La Cala★ (Vermentino) and oak-aged reds, Marchese di Villamarina★★ (Cabernet) and Tanca Farrà★★ (Cannonau-Cabernet). Best years: (Marchese di Villamarina) (2001) (00) 97 **95 93 92 90**.

SELVAPIANA *Chianti DOCG, Tuscany, Italy*   This estate in CHIANTI RUFINA has always produced excellent wines that are typical of the zone. But since 1990 it has vaulted into the top rank of Tuscan estates, particularly with the 2 single-vineyard Riservas, Vigneto Bucerchiale★★★ and Fornace★★. VIN SANTO★★ is very good. Best years: (Bucerchiale) (2001) (99) 98 96 95 **93 91 90 88 85**.

SÉMILLON   Found mainly in South-West France, especially in the sweet wines of SAUTERNES and BARSAC, because it is prone to noble rot (*Botrytis cinerea*). Also blended for its waxy texture with Sauvignon Blanc to make dry wine – almost all the great GRAVES Classed Growths are based on this blend. Performs well in Australia (aged Semillon from the

HUNTER, BAROSSA and CLARE VALLEY can be wonderful) on its own or as a blender with Chardonnay (the accent over the é is dropped on New World labels). Sémillon is also blended with Sauvignon in Australia, New Zealand, CALIFORNIA and WASHINGTON STATE. In South Africa it is primarily a bulk blender, but varietal wines, often barrel-fermented, and blends with Sauvignon are producing some outstanding results.

SEÑA★ *Valle del Aconcagua, Aconcagua, Chile* A MONDAVI and Chadwick family (ERRAZURIZ) partnership, currently sourced from Errázuriz's Don Maximiano vineyards – to the detriment of that label – Seña is a Cabernet-Carmenère blend. By 2005, it should be composed of 5 different varieties from a single estate west of Errázuriz. It has fruit intensity and quality is high, although not enough to justify the price. Cellar for 5–10 years. Best years: (2000) 99 **96 95**.

SEPPELT *Barossa Valley, South Australia and Grampians, Victoria* Historic Australian company, now part of Southcorp, best known for making classy fizz and fortifieds. Sparklers include tank-fermented crowd pleaser Great Western, through tasty Fleur de Lys★ up to the pristine, subtly yeasty Salinger★★, made by the Champagne method from Pinot Noir and Chardonnay. Also makes great sparkling red, including the wonderful Show Reserve Shiraz★★★. Top-notch fortifieds, from dry 'sherry' to aged 'port' styles, include the DP Show series★★★ and the legendary 100-year-old Para Liqueur Tawny★★★. Table wines are good, too, especially Great Western Shiraz★★ and Corella Ridge Chardonnay★, and wines from super-cool Drumborg.

SERESIN *Marlborough, South Island, New Zealand* Film producer Michael Seresin's winery is making a big impact on the MARLBOROUGH scene. Intense Sauvignon Blanc★★ is best within a year or two of the vintage, but creamy Chardonnay★★, succulent Pinot Gris★ and rich, oaky Pinot Noir★★ will age for up to 3 years.

SETÚBAL DOC *Terras do Sado, Portugal* Fortified wine from the Setúbal Peninsula south of Lisbon, which is called 'Moscatel de Setúbal' when made from at least 85% Moscatel, and 'Setúbal' when it's not. Best producers: José Maria da FONSECA★★, J P VINHOS★.

SEYSSEL AC *Savoie, France* Known for its feather-light, sparkling wine, Seyssel Mousseux. With the lovely sharp, peppery bite of the Molette and Altesse grapes smoothed out with a creamy yeast, it is an ideal summer gulper. The still white is light and floral, and made only from Altesse. Best producers: Mollex★, Varichon & Clerc★.

SEYVAL BLANC Hybrid grape (Seibel 5656 x Rayon d'Or) whose disease resistance and ability to continue ripening in a damp autumn make it a useful variety in England, Canada and NEW YORK STATE and other areas in the eastern US. Gives clean, sappy, grapefruit-edged wines that are sometimes a very passable imitation of bone-dry CHABLIS.

SHAFER *Stags Leap District AVA, California, USA* One of the best NAPA wineries, making unusually fruity Cabernet★★ and a Reserve-style Hillside Select★★★. Merlot★★ and Firebreak★★ (Sangiovese-Cabernet) are also important. Chardonnay★★★, from Red Shoulder Ranch, is classic CARNEROS style. Beginning with the 1999 vintage, estate-grown

Relentless (Syrah) has been added to the line-up. Best years: (Cabernet Hillside Select) (2001) (00) (99) 98 97 96 **95** 94 **93 92 91** 90 84.

SHAW & SMITH *Adelaide Hills, South Australia* Cousins Michael Hill Smith – Australia's first MW – and winemaker Martin Shaw had a runaway success with their tangy Sauvignon Blanc★ from the first vintage in 1989. They now release Unwooded Chardonnay★, single-vineyard M3 Chardonnay★ (originally Reserve★), Riesling and Merlot★, as well as a promising second label, Incognito, with Chardonnay, Riesling and Merlot. Best years: (M3 Chardonnay) **2001 00**; (Reserve Chardonnay) **99 98 97 96 95**.

SHERRY See Jerez y Manzanilla DO, pages 158–9.

SHIRAZ See Syrah, pages 266–7.

SICILY *Italy* Sicily is emerging with a renewed spirit and attitude to wine production. Those who lead the way, such as PLANETA, Duca di SALAPARUTA and TASCA D'ALMERITA, have been joined by others, including Donnafugata, the revitalized Spadafora and transformed Settesoli (headed by Diego Planeta). Other exciting estates include Abbazia Santa Anastasia, especially noted for its Cabernet Sauvignon-Nero d'Avola blend, Litra★★; Cottanera, for excellent varietal Merlot (Grammonte★★), Mondeuse (L'Ardenza★★) and Syrah (Sole di Sesta★★); Cusumano, for 100% Nero d'Avola (Sàgana★) and a Nero d'Avola-Cabernet-Merlot blend (Noà★); Morgante, for another pure Nero d'Avola (Don Antonio★★); Palari, for its Nerello Mascalese-Cappuccio blend (Faro Palari★★); and Ceuso, for a Nero d'Avola-Merlot-Cabernet blend (Ceuso Custera★). Firriato, aided by Kym Milne, also makes excellent reds★ and whites★. See also Marsala, Moscato Passito di Pantelleria.

SIEUR D'ARQUES, LES VIGNERONS DU *Limoux AC and Blanquette de Limoux AC, Languedoc, France* This modern co-op makes around 80% of the still and sparkling wines of LIMOUX. The BLANQUETTE DE LIMOUX★ and CREMANT DE LIMOUX★ are both reliable, but the real excitement comes with the Toques et Clochers Chardonnays★ (occasionally ★★). The co-op also makes a range of white and red varietal vins de pays.

SILENI *Hawkes Bay, North Island, New Zealand* Established by millionaire Graeme Avery, with a view to making nothing but the best, this modern winery brings a touch of the NAPA VALLEY to HAWKES BAY. A sleek and stylish Chardonnay★ and ripe, mouthfilling Semillon★ both impress. Best so far is the EV Merlot-Cabernet Franc★★, a dense yet elegant red with a classy oak influence.

SILVER OAK CELLARS *Napa Valley, California, USA* Only Cabernet Sauvignon is made here, with bottlings from ALEXANDER VALLEY★★ and NAPA VALLEY★★ grapes. Forward, generous, fruity wines, impossible not to enjoy young, yet with great staying power. Best years: (Napa Valley) (2001) (00) (99) 97 96 **95 94 93 92 91** 90 87 86 85 84.

SILVERADO VINEYARDS *Stags Leap District AVA, California, USA* The regular Cabernet Sauvignon★ has intense fruit and is drinkable fairly young; Limited Reserve★★ has more depth and is capable of some aging; a new STAGS LEAP DISTRICT Cabernet Sauvignon★★ displays the cherry fruit and supple tannins of this AVA. The Chardonnay★ has soft, inviting fruit and a silky finish. Also a fruity Merlot★ and a refreshing Sauvignon Blanc★. Best years: (Reserve Cabernet) (2001) 99 **95** 94 **91** 90.

SIMI *Alexander Valley AVA, California, USA* Historic winery bought by Constellation in 1999, although winemaker Nick Goldschmidt has stayed. The Cabernet Sauvignon★, Chardonnay★★ and Sauvignon Blanc★ (Sendal★★) attain high standards; Chardonnay Reserve occasionally reaches ★★★. Best years: (reds) (2001) (99) 97 **95 94 91 90**.

SIMONSIG *Stellenbosch WO, South Africa* Family-run estate known for pioneering new varieties, lately Verdelho. Winemaker Johan Malan's forte is reds: most notable are regular Shiraz and lavishly American-oaked Merindol Syrah; a delicious unwooded Pinotage and plusher Redhill Pinotage★; the svelte BORDEAUX-blend Tiara★; and bright-fruited Frans Malan Reserve★, a Cape blend of Pinotage, Cabernet Sauvignon and Merlot. Whites are sound if less exciting. Cap Classique sparklers, Kaapse Vonkel and Cuvée Royale, are biscuity and creamy.

CH. SIRAN★ *Margaux AC, Cru Bourgeois, Haut-Médoc, Bordeaux, France* Consistently good claret, approachable young, but with enough structure to last for as long as 20 years. Second wine: Ch. Bellegarde. Best years: 2001 00 98 96 **95 90 89 86 85 83 82**.

SKALLI-FORTANT DE FRANCE *Languedoc-Roussillon, France* Now one of the most important producers in the south of France, Robert Skalli was an early pioneer of varietal wines in the MIDI. Modern winemaking and the planting of international grape varieties were the keys to success. The Fortant de France brand includes a range of single-variety Vins de Pays d'OC. Grenache and Chardonnay are among the best, but I am yet to be fully convinced by the top reds.

CH. SMITH-HAUT-LAFITTE *Pessac-Léognan AC, Cru Classé de Graves, Bordeaux, France* Large property best known for its reds★★, now one of the most improved and innovative estates in PESSAC-LEOGNAN since a change of ownership in 1990. There is only a little white★★ (from 100% Sauvignon Blanc) but it is a shining example of tip-top modern white Bordeaux. Best years: (reds) 2001 00 99 98 96 **95 94 90 89**; (whites) 2001 00 99 **98 96 95 94 93 92**.

SMITH WOODHOUSE *Port DOC, Portugal* Underrated but consistently satisfying PORT from this shipper in the Symington group. The Vintage★★ is always worth looking out for, as is single-quinta Madalena (made since 1995), and its Late Bottled Vintage Port★★ is the rich and characterful, figgy, unfiltered type. Best years: (Vintage) 2000 97 94 **91 85 83 80 77 70 63**; (Madalena) 1999 98 95.

SOAVE DOC *Veneto, Italy* In the hilly Soave Classico zone near Verona, the Garganega and Trebbiano di Soave grapes can produce ripe, nutty, scented wines. However, 70% of all Soave comes from the flat fertile plains, and much of this is blended into a limp, tasteless white. Since 1992, the blend may include 30% Chardonnay, and good examples are definitely on the increase. Best producers: Bertani★, Ca' Rugate★, La Cappuccina★, Coffele★★, Gini★★, Inama★, MASI★, Pasqua/Cecilia Beretta★, PIEROPAN★★, Portinari★, Prà★, Suavia★, Tamellini★. See also Anselmi, Recioto di Soave DOCG.

CH. SOCIANDO-MALLET★★ *Haut-Médoc AC, Cru Bourgeois, Haut-Médoc, Bordeaux, France* Owner Jean Gautreau has made this one of BORDEAUX's star Crus Bourgeois. The wine shows every sign of great red Bordeaux flavours to come if you can hang on for 10–15 years. Best years: 2001 00 99 98 97 96 95 **94 93 90 89 88 86 85 83 82**.

SOGRAPE *Portugal* Portuguese giant Sogrape can be credited with revolutionizing quality in some of Portugal's most reactionary wine regions. Mateus Rosé is still the company's golden egg, but Sogrape makes good to very good wines in BAIRRADA (Reserva Branco★), DOURO (Reserva Tinto★) and VINHO VERDE as well. Subsidiaries FERREIRA, SANDEMAN and Offley provide top-flight PORTS and Casa Ferreirinha table wines. From the high-tech Quinta dos Carvalhais winery in DAO come improved Duque de Viseu★ and Grão Vasco reds and whites, and also premium wines under the Quinta dos Carvalhais label: varietal Encruzado★ (white) and reds Tinta Roriz★ and Touriga Nacional are promising but inconsistent. A (red) Reserva★★ is a further step up. Sogrape also makes Vinha do Monte and Herdade do Peso★★ from the ALENTEJO. Also owns Finca Flichman in Argentina.

SOLAIA★★★ *Tuscany, Italy* One of ANTINORI's SUPER-TUSCANS, sourced, like TIGNANELLO, from the Santa Cristina vineyard. Solaia is a blend of Cabernet Sauvignon, Sangiovese and Cabernet Franc. Intense, with rich fruit and a classic structure, it is not produced in every vintage. Best years: (2001) (99) 98 97 96 95 **94 93 91 90 88 86 85**.

SOMONTANO DO *Aragón, Spain* Up-and-coming region in the foothills of the Pyrenees. Reds and rosés from the local grapes (Moristel and Tempranillo) can be light, fresh and flavourful, and international varieties such as Chardonnay and Gewürztraminer are already yielding promising wines. An interesting development is the rediscovery of the powerful native red grape, Parraleta (RIOJA's Graciano). Best producers: Blecua★★, ENATE★★, Bodega Pirineos★, VINAS DEL VERO★. Best years: (reds) (2001) 99 **98 97 96 95 94**.

SONOMA COAST AVA *California, USA* A huge appellation, defined on its western boundary by the Pacific Ocean, that attempts to bring together the coolest regions of SONOMA COUNTY. It encompasses the Sonoma part of CARNEROS and overlaps parts of SONOMA VALLEY and RUSSIAN RIVER. The heart of the appellation are vineyards on the high coastal ridge only a few miles from the Pacific. Intense Chardonnays and Pinot Noirs are the focus. Best producers: FLOWERS (Camp Meeting Ridge★★★), HARTFORD COURT★★, KISTLER (Hirsch Pinot Noir★★★), Littorai (Hirsch Pinot Noir★★★), MARCASSIN★★, W H Smith★★, Wild Hog★.

SONOMA COUNTY *California, USA* Sonoma's vine-growing area is big and sprawling, with dozens of soil types and mesoclimates, from the fairly warm SONOMA VALLEY and ALEXANDER VALLEY regions to the cool Green Valley and lower RUSSIAN RIVER VALLEY. The best wines are from Chardonnay, Sauvignon Blanc, Cabernet Sauvignon, Pinot Noir and Zinfandel. Often the equal of rival NAPA in quality and originality of flavours. See also Carneros, Dry Creek Valley, Sonoma Coast.

SONOMA-CUTRER *Russian River Valley AVA, Sonoma County, California, USA* Crisp, pleasant but often overrated Chardonnay from 3 vineyards. Les Pierres is the most complex and richest of the 3, often worth ★★; Cutrer can also have a ★★ complexity worth waiting for. Russian River Ranches can be rather flat and ordinary, though much improved in recent releases. Best years: (2001) 00 99 **98 97 95 94**.

SONOMA VALLEY AVA *California, USA* The oldest wine region north of San Francisco, Sonoma Valley is situated on the western side of the Mayacamas Mountains, which separate it from NAPA VALLEY. Best varieties are Chardonnay and Zinfandel, with Cabernet and Merlot from hillside sites also good. Best producers: ARROWOOD★★, CARMENET★★, CHATEAU ST JEAN★, B R Cohn, Fisher★, GUNDLACH-BUNDSCHU★, KENWOOD★, KUNDE★, LANDMARK★★, LAUREL GLEN★★, MATANZAS CREEK★★, RAVENSWOOD★★, St Francis★, Sebastiani★. Best years: (Zinfandel) (2001) 00 99 **98 97 96 95 94**.

257

SPARKLING WINES OF THE WORLD ___

Made by the Traditional (Champagne) Method

Although Champagne is still the benchmark for top-class sparkling wines all over the world, the Champagne houses themselves have taken the message to California, Australia and New Zealand via wineries they've established in these regions. However, Champagne-method fizz doesn't necessarily have to feature the traditional Champagne grape varieties (Chardonnay, Pinot Noir and Pinot Meunier), and this allows a host of other places to join the party. Describing a wine as Champagne method is strictly speaking no longer allowed (only original Champagne from France is officially sanctioned to do this), but the use of a phrase like Traditional Method should not distract from the fact that these wines are still painstakingly produced using the complex system of secondary fermentation in the bottle itself.

STYLES OF SPARKLING WINE

France French fizz ranges from the sublime to the near-ridiculous. The best examples have great finesse and include grapy Crémant d'Alsace, produced from Pinot Blanc and Riesling; often inexpensive yet eminently drinkable Crémant de Bourgogne, based mainly on Chardonnay; and some stylish examples from the Loire, notably in Saumur and Vouvray. Clairette de Die and Blanquette de Limoux in the south confuse the issue by sometimes following their own idiosyncratic method of production, but the result is delicious.

Rest of Europe Franciacorta DOCG is a success story for Italy. Most metodo classico sparkling wine is confined to the north, where ripening conditions are closer to those of Champagne, but a few good examples do pop up in unexpected places – Sicily, for instance. Asti and Lambrusco are not Champagne-method wines. In Spain, the Cava wines of Cataluña offer an affordable style for everyday drinking. German Sekt comes in two basic styles: one made from Riesling grapes, the other using Champagne varieties. England is proving naturally suited to growing grapes for sparkling wine.

Australia and New Zealand Australia has a wide range of styles though there is still little overt varietal definition. Blends are still being produced using fruit from many areas, but regional characters are starting to emerge. Cool Tasmania is the star performer, making some top fizz from local grapes. Red sparklers, notably those made from Shiraz, are an irresistible Australian curiosity with an alcoholic kick. Cool-climate New Zealand is coming up fast for fizz with some premium and pricy examples; as in Australia, some have Champagne connections.

USA In California, some magnificent examples are produced – the best ones using grapes from Carneros or the Anderson Valley. Quality has been transformed by the efforts of French Champagne houses. Oregon is also a contender in the sparkling stakes.

South Africa Cap Classique is the local name for the Champagne method. Many producers are jumping on the fizz bandwagon and the best are very good, but there are problems with consistency.

See also individual producers.

BEST PRODUCERS

Australia BROWN BROTHERS, Cope-Williams, DOMAINE CHANDON (Green Point), HANGING ROCK, HARDYS, Stefano Lubiana, PETALUMA (Croser), PIPERS BROOK (Pirie), ROCKFORD (Black Shiraz), SEPPELT, TALTARNI (Clover Hill), Tamar Ridge, YALUMBA (Jansz), Yarrabank, Yellowglen.

Austria BRUNDLMAYER.

France (Alsace) Ostertag; (Burgundy) Caves de Bailly, Caves de Lugny; (Saumur) BOUVET-LADUBAY, GRATIEN & MEYER; (Die) Clairette de Die co-op; (Limoux) SIEUR D'ARQUES; (Vouvray) CLOS NAUDIN, HUET.

Germany (Franken) Rudolf FURST; (Pfalz) Bergdolt, KOEHLER-RUPRECHT; (Saar) Dr Heinz Wagner.

Italy (Franciacorta) BELLAVISTA, CA' DEL BOSCO; (Trento) FERRARI; (Sicily) TASCA D'ALMERITA.

New Zealand CELLIER LE BRUN, CLOUDY BAY (Pelorus), HUNTER'S, MONTANA (Deutz), MORTON ESTATE, Nautilus, PALLISER.

Portugal Caves ALIANCA, J P VINHOS.

South Africa Graham BECK, DISTELL (Pongrácz), Twee Jonge Gezellen, VILLIERA.

Spain (Cava) Can Ràfols dels Caus, CODORNIU, FREIXENET, JUVE Y CAMPS.

UK NEW WAVE (Chapel Down), NYETIMBER, RIDGEVIEW, VALLEY VINEYARDS.

USA (California) S Anderson, DOMAINE CARNEROS, DOMAINE CHANDON, HANDLEY, IRON HORSE, J Wine, Laetitia, MUMM NAPA, PACIFIC ECHO, ROEDERER ESTATE, SCHRAMSBERG; (Oregon) Argyle.

SOUTH AUSTRALIA Australia's biggest grape-growing state, with some 60,000ha (150,000 acres) of vineyards and almost half the country's total production. Covers many climates and most wine styles, from bulk wines to the very best. Established areas are ADELAIDE HILLS, Adelaide Plains, CLARE, BAROSSA and Eden Valleys, MCLAREN VALE, Langhorne Creek, COONAWARRA, PADTHAWAY and RIVERLAND. Newer districts creating excitement include Mount Benson and Wrattonbully, both in the LIMESTONE COAST zone.

SOUTH-WEST FRANCE As well as the world-famous wines of BORDEAUX, South-West France has many lesser-known, inexpensive ACs, VDQS and VdPs, over 10 *départements* from the Atlantic coast to LANGUEDOC-ROUSSILLON. Bordeaux grapes (Cabernet Sauvignon, Merlot and Cabernet Franc for reds; Sauvignon Blanc, Sémillon and Muscadelle for whites) are common, but there are lots of interesting local varieties as well, such as Tannat (in MADIRAN), Petit Manseng (in JURANÇON) and Mauzac (in GAILLAC). See also Bergerac, Cahors, Côtes de Duras, Côtes du Frontonnais, Irouléguy, Monbazillac, Montravel, Pacherenc du Vic-Bilh.

SPÄTBURGUNDER See Pinot Noir.

SPICE ROUTE WINE COMPANY *Swartland WO, South Africa* High-profile operation owned by Charles Back, of FAIRVIEW. The Flagship label features the big yet classically styled duo of Pinotage★★ and Syrah★★, and a Merlot that is not quite as successful. A Flagship white is also on the cards. Best years: (Flagship reds) 2000 **99 98**.

SPOTTSWOODE *Napa Valley AVA, California, USA* Replanted in the mid-1990s, this beautifully situated 16ha (40-acre) vineyard west of St Helena has not missed a beat since the winery opened in 1982. Deep, blackberry- and cherry-fruited Cabernet Sauvignon★★★ is wonderful to drink early, but is best at 5–10 years. Sauvignon Blanc★★ (blended with a little Semillon and barrel fermented) is a sophisticated treat. Best years: (Cabernet) (2001) (00) 99 98 97 96 **95 94 93 91**.

SPRINGFIELD ESTATE *Robertson WO, South Africa* Abrie Bruwer's approach is strictly hands-off in his efforts to capture his vineyard's *terroir*. Méthode Ancienne Chardonnay★★ is barrel fermented with vineyard yeasts and bottled without any fining or filtration. Not every vintage makes it! Cabernet Sauvignon is also made as Méthode Ancienne★. The unwooded Wild Yeast Chardonnay★ has expressive pineapple and pawpaw flavours. The farm's rocky soils are reflected in the flinty, lively Life from Stone Sauvignon Blanc★.

STAGS LEAP DISTRICT AVA *Napa County, California, USA* Created in 1989, this is one of California's best-defined appellations. Located in south-eastern NAPA VALLEY, it is cooler than OAKVILLE or RUTHERFORD to the north, so the red wines here are more elegant in nature. A little Sauvignon Blanc and Chardonnay are grown here, but the true stars are Cabernet Sauvignon and Merlot. Best producers: CHIMNEY ROCK★★, CLOS DU VAL★, Hartwell★★, PINE RIDGE★★, SHAFER★★★, SILVERADO★★, Robert Sinskey★★, STAG'S LEAP WINE CELLARS★★, Stags' Leap Winery★.

STAG'S LEAP WINE CELLARS *Stags Leap District AVA, California, USA* The winery rose to fame when its Cabernet Sauvignon came first at the Paris tasting of 1976. Cabernet Sauvignon★★ can be stunning, particularly the SLV★★★ from estate vineyards and the Fay★★; the Cask 23 Cabernet Sauvignon★ can be very good, but is overhyped. After a dip in quality, late 1990s vintages were back on form. A lot of work has gone into the Chardonnay★★ and the style is one of

NAPA's most successful. Sauvignon Blanc★ (Rancho Chimiles★★) is intensely flavoured, with brisk acidity. Best years: (Cabernet) (2001) (00) 99 98 97 96 **95 94 91 90 86**.

STEELE *Lake County, California, USA* Owner/winemaker Jed Steele is a master blender. He sources grapes from all over California and shapes them into exciting wines, usually featuring vivid fruit with supple mouthfeel. He also offers single-vineyard wines and has, in current release, 4–6 Chardonnays, most ★★. His Zinfandels★★ and Pinot Noirs★★ (CARNEROS, SANTA MARIA VALLEY) are often very good. Shooting Star label provides remarkable value in a ready-to-drink style.

STEENBERG *Constantia WO, South Africa* The oldest farm in the CONSTANTIA valley is seeing great results from total vineyard replanting in the early 1990s. Sauvignon Blanc Reserve★★, firmly established as one of South Africa's best, is smoky and flinty with underlying fruit richness; straight Sauvignon★ is upfront fruit. Semillon★★ is also impressive. An irresistible, minty Merlot★★ has been joined by BORDEAUX-blend Catharina★ and exciting, smoky Shiraz★★. Best years: (whites) **2002 01 00 99 98 97**.

STEIERMARK *Austria* Known as Styria in English, this 3290ha (8130-acre) wine region in south-east Austria formerly covered much of Slovenia's vineyards, too. It includes the areas of Süd-Oststeiermark, Süd-steiermark and Weststeiermark. It is the warmest of the 4 Austrian wine regions, but the best vineyards are in cool, high-altitude sites. The best wines are Morillon (unoaked Chardonnay, though oak is catching on here), Sauvignon Blanc and Gelber Muskateller (Muscat). Best producers: Gross★, Lackner-Tinnacher★★, POLZ★, TEMENT★★, Winkler-Hermaden★.

STELLENBOSCH WO *South Africa* This fine red wine district boasts the greatest concentration of wineries in the Cape, though is only third in vineyard area; the vineyards straddle valley floors and stretch up the many mountain slopes. Climates and soils are as diverse as wine styles; smaller units of origin – wards – are now being demarcated to more accurately reflect this diversity. The renowned reds are matched by some excellent Sauvignon Blanc and Chardonnay, as well as modern Chenin Blanc and Semillon. Best producers: BEYERSKLOOF★, Delaire★, De Trafford★★, Dornier★, EIKENDAL★, Neil ELLIS★★, Ken Forrester★, GRANGEHURST★★, HARTENBERG★, JORDAN★, KANONKOP★★, L'AVENIR★, Le Bonheur★, Le Riche★, Lievland★, Longridge★, MEERLUST★★, Meinert★, MORGENHOF★, MULDERBOSCH★★, Neethlingshof★, Overgaauw★, RUST EN VREDE★, RUSTENBERG★★, SAXENBURG★★, SIMONSIG★, Stellenbosch Vineyards, STELLENZICHT★, THELEMA★★, Uiterwyk★, VERGELEGEN★★, VILLIERA★, WARWICK★, Waterford★.

STELLENZICHT *Stellenbosch WO, South Africa* Winemaker Guy Webber aims for fruit and perfume rather than power in his wines. This is evident in his silky, lemony Semillon★, smoky, spicy Syrah★★, Sauvignon Blanc★ with gooseberry intensity and bold perfumed Golden Triangle Pinotage★. Best years: (Syrah) 2000 99 **98 97 95 94**.

STERLING VINEYARDS *Napa Valley AVA, California, USA* Merlot is the focus here, led by Three Palms★ and Reserve★★, both impressively packed with ripe, dense fruit. Reserve Cabernet★ is generally good, and the regular bottling is improving, as is Winery Lake Pinot Noir★. The Winery Lake Chardonnay★ delivers honey and apple fruit in an elegant package. Best years: (Three Palms) (2001) (00) 99 97 96 **95 94**.

SUPER-TUSCANS

Tuscany, Italy

The term 'Super-Tuscans', first used by English and American writers, has now been adopted by Italians themselves to describe the new-style red wines of Tuscany. The 1970s and 80s were a time when enormous strides were being made in Bordeaux, Australia and California, yet these changes threatened to bypass Italy completely because of its restrictive wine laws. A group of winemakers, led by Piero Antinori – who created the inspirational Tignanello and Solaia from vineyards within the Chianti Classico DOCG – abandoned tradition to put their best efforts and best grapes into creative wines styled for modern tastes.

Old large oak casks were replaced with French barriques, while Cabernet Sauvignon and other trendy varieties, such as Cabernet Franc, Merlot and Syrah, were planted alongside Sangiovese in vineyards that emerged with sudden grandeur as crus. Since the DOC specifically forbade such innovations, producers were forced to label their wines as plain Vino da Tavola. The 'Super-Tuscan' Vino da Tavolas, as they were quickly dubbed, were a phenomenal success: brilliant in flavour with an approachable, upfront style. Some found it hard to believe that table wines with no official credentials could outrank DOCG Chianti. A single mouthful was usually enough to convince them.

WINE STYLES

Sangiovese, the Cabernets and Merlot are the basis for most Super-Tuscans, usually in a blend. All also appear varietally, with Sangiovese forming the largest group of top-quality varietal Super-Tuscans. To some Sangiovese-based wines, a small percentage of other native varieties such as Colorino, Canaiolo or Malvasia Nera is added. Merlot for long played second fiddle to Cabernet Sauvignon but new plantings today are tending Merlot's way. Syrah is of growing importance, mostly varietally, but also in innovative new blends such as Argiano's Solengo. Super-Tuscan wines also show considerable differences in vinification and aging. Top wines are invariably based on ripe, concentrated grapes from a site with special attributes.

CLASSIFICATIONS

A law passed in 1992 has finally brought the Super-Tuscans into line with official classifications. Sassicaia now has its own DOC under Bolgheri. Chianti Classico's newly independent DOCG could cover many a Sangiovese-based Super-Tuscan, but the majority are currently sold under the region-wide IGT Toscana alongside wines made from international varieties. There are also 3 sub-regional IGTs, but only a few producers use these.

The situation for consumers remains confused in the short term because some examples labelled vino da tavola are still being sold.

See also BOLGHERI, CHIANTI CLASSICO, SASSICAIA, SOLAIA, SYRAH, TIGNANELLO; and individual producers.

(2001) 00 99 98 97 **95 93 90 88 85**

BEST PRODUCERS

Sangiovese and other Tuscan varieties Badia a Coltibuono (Sangioveto), BOSCARELLI, CASTELLARE (I Sodi di San Niccolò), FELSINA (Fontalloro), FONTODI (Flaccianello della Pieve), ISOLE E OLENA (Cepparello), Lilliano (Anagallis), MONTEVERTINE (Le Pergole Torte, Il Sodaccio), Paneretta (Quattrocentenario, Terrine), Poggio Scalette (Il Carbonaione), Poggiopiano (Rosso di Sera), Querceto (La Corte), RIECINE (La Gioia), RUFFINO (Romitorio di Santedame), San Giusto a Rentennano (Percarlo), VOLPAIA (Coltassala).

Sangiovese-Cabernet and Sangiovese-Merlot blends ARGIANO (Solengo), BANFI (Summus), Colombaio di Cencio (Il Futuro), FONTERUTOLI (Siepi), Gagliole, Montepeloso (Nardo), QUERCIABELLA (Camartina), RICASOLI (Casalferro), Sette Ponti (Oreno), TIGNANELLO.

Cabernet Col d'Orcia (Olmaia), Fossi (Sassoforte), ISOLE E OLENA (Collezione), Le Macchiole (Paléo Rosso), Nozzole (Il Pareto), RAMPOLLA (Sammarco, Vigna d'Alceo), SOLAIA.

Merlot AMA (L'Apparita), Le Macchiole (Messorio), ORNELLAIA (Masseto), Petrolo (Galatrona), Tua Rita (Redigaffi).

Cabernet-Merlot blends ANTINORI (Guado al Tasso), BANFI (Excelsus), Capezzana (Ghiaie della Furba), ORNELLAIA (Ornellaia), Poggio al Sole (Seraselva), POLIZIANO (Le Stanze), Le Pupille (Saffredi), Trinoro, Tua Rita (Giusto di Notri).

STONIER *Mornington Peninsula, Victoria, Australia* The peninsula's biggest winery and one of its best, and though Lion Nathan, via PETALUMA, now has a controlling interest, Tod Dexter is still at the winemaking helm. Reserve Chardonnay★★ and Reserve Pinot★★ are usually outstanding, and there are fine standard bottlings in warm vintages. Cabernet, in the rather herbaceous style typical of the region, continues to improve.

STONYRIDGE *Waiheke Island, Auckland, North Island, New Zealand* The leading winery on WAIHEKE ISLAND, Stonyridge specializes in reds made from Cabernet Sauvignon, Merlot, Petit Verdot, Malbec and Cabernet Franc. The top label, Larose★★★, is a remarkably BORDEAUX-like red of real intensity; it is one of New Zealand's most expensive wines. Best years: (Larose) (2002) 00 **99 98 96 94 93 91**.

CH. SUDUIRAUT★★ *Sauternes AC, 1er Cru Classé, Bordeaux, France* Together with RIEUSSEC, Suduiraut is regarded as a close runner-up to d'YQUEM. Although the wines are delicious at only a few years old, the richness and excitement increase enormously after a decade or so. Seemed to be under-performing in the 1980s and mid-90s but now owned by AXA (see PICHON-LONGUEVILLE) and back on song. Best years: (2002) 01 99 98 97 **96 95 90 89 88 86 82 81**.

SUHINDOL *Danube Plain Region, Bulgaria* Established in 1909, this former co-operative was privatized in 1991. With its 3 wineries, it is one of Bulgaria's largest producers. It also owns more than 40% of its own vineyards, which is rare in Bulgaria, with 1500ha (3700 acres) producing, and controls, through long-term contracts with growers, another 2500ha (6175 acres). New technology and judicious use of oak have improved quality enormously, as the Craftsman's Creek, Copper Crossing and regional wines show. The Gamza and Gamza-Merlot blends are worth trying, and it is now developing some premium Cabernet and Merlot reds.

SUMAC RIDGE *Okanagan Valley VQA, British Columbia, Canada* Winemaker Mark Wendenberg produces excellent Sauvignon Blanc★ and Gewürztraminer Reserve★, fine Pinot Blanc and one of Canada's best Champagne-method fizzes, Steller's Jay Brut★. Top reds include Cabernet Sauvignon, Cabernet Franc, Merlot, Pinot Noir and Meritage★.

SUNTORY *Japan* Red Tomi and sweet white Noble d'Or (made from botrytized grapes) are top brand names here for wine made exclusively from grapes grown in Japan; this is a rarity in a country where imported wine can legally be blended with Japanese and sold as Japanese. Classic varieties – Cabernet Sauvignon, Cabernet Franc, Chardonnay, Semillon and Sauvignon – are also having success.

SUPER-TUSCANS See pages 262–3.

SWAN DISTRICT *Western Australia* The original WESTERN AUSTRALIA wine region and the hottest stretch of vineyards in Australia, spread along the torrid, fertile silty flats of Perth's Swan River. It used to specialize in fortified wines, but SOUTH AUSTRALIA and north-east VICTORIA both do them better. New-wave whites and reds, especially from HOUGHTON and Moondah Brook, are fresh and generous. Best producers: Paul Conti, HOUGHTON★★, Lamont★, Sandalford★, Upper Reach, Westfield.

JOSEPH SWAN VINEYARDS *Russian River Valley AVA, California, USA* Joseph Swan made legendary Zinfandel in the 1970s and was one of the first to age Zinfandel★★ in French oak. In the 1980s he turned to Pinot Noir★★ which is now probably the winery's best offering. Since

Swan's death in 1989, his son-in-law, Rod Berglund, has proved a worthy successor. Best years: (Zinfandel) (2001) 99 98 97 **96 95 94 93 91**.

SYRAH See pages 266–7.

LA TÂCHE AC★★★ *Grand Cru, Côte de Nuits, Burgundy, France* Along with la ROMANÉE-CONTI, the greatest of the great VOSNE-ROMANÉE Grands Crus, owned by Dom. de la ROMANÉE-CONTI. The wine has the rare ability to provide layer on layer of flavours; keep it for 10 years or you'll only experience a fraction of the pleasure you paid big money for. Best years: (2002) 01 00 99 98 97 96 95 93 90 **89** 88 **85 78**.

TAHBILK *Goulburn Valley, Central Victoria, Australia* Wonderfully old-fashioned family company making traditionally big, gumleafy/minty reds, matured in old wood. Shiraz★ (1860 Vines★★) and Cabernet★ are full of character, even if they need years of cellaring. White Marsanne★★ is perfumed and attractive, as is a floral-scented Viognier★. Other whites tend to lack finesse. Best years: (1860 Vines) 1998 97 96 95 **94 92 91 90 87 86 82**.

TAIN L'HERMITAGE, CAVE DE *Hermitage, Rhône Valley, France* Progressive co-op producing an extensive range of good-value wines from throughout the northern Rhône. Go-ahead young winemaker produces surprisingly high quality, despite production of 500,000 cases annually. Top cuvées are marketed under the Nobles Rives label. Impressive CROZES-HERMITAGE les Hauts du Fief★, fine CORNAS★★ and both red and white ST-JOSEPH★ and HERMITAGE★★. Topping the range are an old-vine red Hermitage Gambert de Loche★★ and a fine Vin de Paille★★. Best years: (top reds) 2001 00 99 98 **97 95**.

TAITTINGER *Champagne AC, Champagne, France* The top wine, Comtes de Champagne Blanc de Blancs★★★, can be memorable for its creamy, foaming pleasures and the Comtes de Champagne rosé★★ is elegant and oozing class. Ordinary non-vintage is soft and honeyed but has been unusually inconsistent for a while now. Another de luxe cuvée, called Vintage Collection★, is simply the vintage Brut in a fancy bottle. Best years: (1996) **95 92 90 89 88 86 85 82 79**.

CH. TALBOT★ *St-Julien AC, 4ème Cru Classé, Haut-Médoc, Bordeaux, France* Chunky, soft-centred but sturdy, capable of aging well for 10–20 years. There is also an interesting and good-value white wine, Caillou Blanc de Talbot★. Second wine: Connétable Talbot. Best years: 2001 00 99 98 96 95 **90 89 88 86 85 83 82**.

TALBOTT *Monterey County, California, USA* Founded in 1980, this estate is known for its Chardonnays from vineyards near Gonzales and the Santa Lucia Highlands in MONTEREY COUNTY. Sleepy Hollow Vineyard★★, Cuvée Cynthia★★ and Diamond T Estate★★★ are all packed with ripe tropical fruit and ample oak. Chardonnay and Pinot Noir are also produced under the Logan label.

TALTARNI *Pyrenees, Victoria, Australia* Specializing in classic, deep-flavoured, European-style Cabernet★, Shiraz★ and Merlot; also a Malbec rosé and respected fizz, especially Clover Hill★★ and pink Brut Tâché★ from TASMANIA. Sauvignon Blanc★ is tangy and gooseberry-like. Best years: (Shiraz) 2001 00 99 98 96 **92 91 90 88 86**.

TARAPACÁ *Maipo, Chile* No expense has been spared in recent vineyard and winery improvements at this long-established company, and the wine, too, is improving under the guidance of Sergio Correa. New premium reds include Reserva Privada Syrah★ and Last Edition★ – an unusual blend of Cabernet, Merlot, Syrah and Mourvèdre. New CASABLANCA project should be good.

SYRAH/SHIRAZ

Syrah now produces world-class wines in 3 countries and its popularity is rising fast. In France, where Hermitage and Côte-Rôtie are 2 of the world's great reds; in Australia, where as Shiraz it produces some of the New World's most remarkable reds; and now in California, too. And wherever Syrah appears it trumpets a proud and wilful personality based on loads of flavour and unmistakable originality.

When the late-ripening Syrah grape is grown in the coolest, most marginal areas for full ripening, such as Côte-Rôtie, it is capable of producing wines of immense class and elegance. However, producers must ensure low yields if they are to produce high-quality wines.

Syrah's spread round the warmer wine regions of the world is at last accelerating. Syrah's heartland – Hermitage and Côte-Rôtie in the Rhône Valley – comprises a mere 290ha (715 acres) of steeply terraced vineyards, producing hardly enough wine to make more than a very rarefied reputation for themselves. This may be one reason for its relatively slow uptake by growers in other countries who simply had no idea as to what kind of flavour the Syrah grape produced, so didn't copy it. But the situation is rapidly changing.

WINE STYLES

French Syrah The flavours of Syrah are most individual, but with modern vineyard practices and modern winemaking techniques they are far less daunting than they used to be. Traditional Syrah had a savage, almost coarse, throaty roar of a flavour. And from the very low-yielding Hermitage vineyards, the small grapes often showed a bitter tannic quality. But better selections of clones in the vineyard and improved winemaking have revealed that Syrah in fact gives a wine with a majestic depth of fruit – all blackberry and damson, loganberry and plum – some quite strong tannin, and some tangy smoke, but also a warm creamy aftertaste, and a promise of chocolate and occasionally a scent of violets. It is these characteristics that have made Syrah popular throughout the south of France as an 'improving' variety for its rather rustic red wines.

Australian Shiraz Australia's most widely planted red variety has become, in many respects, its premium varietal. Shiraz gives spectacularly good results when taken seriously – especially in the Barossa, Clare, Eden Valley and McLaren Vale regions of South Australia. An increasingly diverse range of high-quality examples are also coming from Victoria's warmer vineyards, more traditional examples from New South Wales' Hunter Valley and Mudgee, and exciting, more restrained styles from Western Australia's Margaret River and Great Southern regions, as well as cooler high-country spots. Flavours are rich, intense, thick sweet fruit coated with chocolate, and seasoned with leather, herbs and spice. And here in Australia it is often blended with Cabernet Sauvignon.

Other regions In California producers are turning out superb Rhône blends as well as varietal Syrahs modelled closely on Côte-Rôtie or Hermitage. In South Africa, more exciting wines appear every vintage. Italy, Spain, Portugal, Argentina, Chile and New Zealand are also beginning to shine, and even North Africa is having a go.

266

267

TARRAWARRA *Yarra Valley, Victoria, Australia* Founder Marc Besen wanted to make a MONTRACHET, and hang the expense. The wine-makers are on the right track: Tarrawarra Chardonnay★★ is deep and multi-faceted. Pinot Noir★★ is just as good, with almost COTE DE NUITS flavour and concentration. Tin Cows is a less pricy brand for both these grapes, plus Shiraz and Merlot. Best years: (Pinot Noir) 2001 **00 99 98 97 96 94 92**.

TASCA D'ALMERITA *Sicily, Italy* The estate of the Conte Tasca d'Almerita in the highlands of central SICILY makes some of southern Italy's best wines. From native grape varieties come excellent Rosso del Conte★★ (based on Nero d'Avola) and white Nozze d'Oro★ (based on Inzolia), but the range extends to Chardonnay★★ and Cabernet Sauvignon★★ of extraordinary intensity and elegance. Almerita Brut★ (Chardonnay) is a fine Italian Champagne-method sparkler. Relatively simple Regaleali Bianco and Rosato are good value.

TASMANIA *Australia* Tasmania may be a minor state viticulturally, with only 925ha (2285 acres) of vines, but the island has a diverse range of mesoclimates and sub-regions. The generally cool climate has always attracted seekers of greatness in Pinot Noir and Chardonnay, and good results are becoming more consistent. Riesling, Gewürztraminer and Pinot Gris perform well, but the real star here is fabulous premium fizz. Best producers: Elsewhere Vineyard★, Freycinet★★, HARDYS (Bay of Fires★), Stefano Lubiana★, Moorilla★, Notley Gorge★, PIPERS BROOK★★, Spring Vale★, Wellington★. Best years: (Pinot Noir) 2001 00 99 **98 97 95 94 93 92 91**.

TAURASI DOCG *Campania, Italy* Remarkably, it was a single producer, MASTROBERARDINO, and a single vintage, 1968, that created the reputation for this red. Now the great potential of the Aglianico grape is being exploited by others, both within this DOCG and elsewhere in CAMPANIA. Drink at 5–10 years. Best producers: A Caggiano★★, Feudi di San Gregorio★★, MASTROBERARDINO★, S Molettieri★, Struzziero, Terre Dora di Paolo★. Best years: (2001) (00) 98 97 96 **94 93 92 90 89 88**.

TAVEL AC *Rhône Valley, France* Big, alcoholic rosé from north-west of Avignon. Grenache and Cinsaut are the main grapes. Drink Tavel at one year old if you want it cheerful, heady, yet refreshing. Best producers: Aquéria★, la Forcadière★, Genestière★, GUIGAL, Montézargues★, la Mordorée★, Vignerons de Tavel, Trinquevedel★.

TAYLOR *Port DOC, Douro, Portugal* The aristocrat of the PORT industry, 300 years old and still going strong. Now part of the Fladgate Partnership, along with FONSECA, CROFT and Delaforce. Its Vintage★★★ is superb; Quinta de Vargellas★★ is an elegant, cedary, single-quinta vintage port made in the best of the 'off-vintages'. Quinta de Terra Feita★★, the other main component of Taylor's Vintage, is also often released as a single-quinta in non-declared years. Taylor's 20-year-old★★ is a very fine aged tawny. First Estate is a successful premium ruby. The best vintage ports can be kept for at least 25 years. Best years: (Vintage) 2000 97 94 92 **85 83 80 77 75 70 66 63 60 55 48 45 27**; (Vargellas) 1998 96 95 91 **88 87 86 82 78 67 64 61**.

TE MATA *Hawkes Bay, North Island, New Zealand* HAWKES BAY's glamour winery, best known for its reds, Coleraine★★★ and Awatea★★, both based on Cabernet Sauvignon with varying proportions of Merlot and Cabernet Franc. Also outstanding is toasty Elston Chardonnay★★. Exceptional vintages of all 3 wines might be aged for 5–10 years.

Bullnose Syrah★ is an elegant, peppery red. Woodthorpe Viognier★ is a New Zealand first for the variety. Best years: (Coleraine) 1998 **96 95 94 91**.

TEMENT *Südsteiermark, Austria* Manfred Tement makes Austria's best Sauvignon Blanc★★ (single-site Zieregg★★★) and Morillon (Chardonnay)★★ in a spectacular new winery. Both varieties are fermented and aged in oak, giving power, depth and subtle oak character. Red Arachon★★ is a joint venture with F X PICHLER and Szemes in BURGENLAND. Best years: (Morillon Zieregg) (2002) 01 00 **99 97**.

DOM. TEMPIER *Bandol AC, Provence, France* Leading BANDOL estate, owned by the Peyraud family and making rich, ageworthy reds from a high percentage of Mourvèdre. The top wines are the single-vineyard Migoua★★, Cabassaou★★ and la Tourtine★★ – and they do need aging, otherwise the Mourvèdre can be overpowering. The rosé★ is one of Provence's best. Best years: 2001 00 99 98 **97 96 95 93 92 90 89 88**.

TEMPRANILLO Spain's best native red grape can make wonderful wine, with wild strawberry and spicy, tobaccoey flavours. It is important in RIOJA, PENEDES (as Ull de Llebre), RIBERA DEL DUERO (as Tinto Fino or Tinta del País), La MANCHA and VALDEPENAS (as Cencibel), NAVARRA, SOMONTANO, UTIEL-REQUENA and TORO (as Tinta de Toro). In Portugal it is found in the DOURO, DAO and ESTREMADURA (as Tinta Roriz) and in ALENTEJO (as Aragonez). Wines can be deliciously fruity for drinking young, but Tempranillo also matures well, and its flavours blend happily with oak. It is now being taken more seriously in Argentina, and new plantings have been made in CALIFORNIA, OREGON, Australia and South Africa.

TEROLDEGO ROTALIANO DOC *Trentino-Alto Adige, Italy* Teroldego is a native TRENTINO grape variety, producing mainly deep-coloured, grassy, blackberry-flavoured wine from the gravel soils of the Rotaliano plain. Best producers: Barone de Cles★, M Donati★, Dorigati★, Endrizzi★, FORADORI★★, Conti Martini★, Mezzacorona (Riserva★), Cantina Rotaliana★, A & R Zeni★. Best years: (2001) 00 99 **97 96 95 93 91 90**.

TERRAS DO SADO *Setúbal Peninsula, Portugal* Warm, maritime-influenced area south of Lisbon. SETUBAL produces fine sweet fortified wine. Many of the better reds, mostly based on Castelão, come from the Palmela DOC. A few good whites are also made. Best producers: (reds) Caves ALIANCA (Palmela Particular★), BRIGHT BROTHERS (Reserva★), D F J VINHOS★, José Maria da FONSECA★★, Hero do Castanheiro, J P VINHOS★, Pegões co-op★, Pegos Claros★★. Best years: 2001 00 **99 97 96 95**.

TERRICCIO, CASTELLO DEL *Tuscany, Italy* High in the hills south of Livorno, this estate has transformed itself from bulk wine producer to Tuscan superstar. However, changes in philosophy seem to have stripped both the top red Lupicaia★ (Cabernet-Merlot) and the less pricy Tassinaia★ (Sangiovese-Cabernet-Merlot) of much of their exciting scented personality. Hopefully things will revert to their potential ★★★ again. Rondinaia (Chardonnay)★★ and Con Vento (Sauvignon Blanc)★ are the most interesting whites. Best years: (Lupicaia) 1997 **96 95 94 93**.

CH. LE TERTRE-RÔTEBOEUF★★ *St-Émilion Grand Cru AC, Bordeaux, France* ST-EMILION's most exceptional unclassified estate. The richly seductive, Merlot-based wines sell at the same price as the Premiers Grands Crus Classés. Under the same ownership as the outstanding ROC DE CAMBES. Best years: 2001 00 99 98 **97 96 95 94 90 89 88 86 85**.

TEXAS *USA* Since the first experimental plantings in 1975, Texas has become one of the major US wine-producing states. The state has 7 AVAs, of which Texas High Plains is most significant, at least 46 wineries, and some fine Chardonnay and Riesling. Thunderstorms are a menace, capable of destroying entire crops in minutes. Best producers: Alamosa, Becker, Cap Rock, Fall Creek, Llano Estacado, Messina Hof, Pheasant Ridge.

THELEMA *Stellenbosch WO, South Africa* This mountainside farm is among the Cape's top wineries. Meticulous attention is paid to the vineyards, where California's Phil Freese helps with innovative ideas. Winemaker Gyles Webb's leafy yet blackcurrant Cabernet Sauvignon★★, ripe fleshy Merlot★, spicy, accessible Shiraz, barrel-fermented Chardonnay★★, vibrant Sauvignon Blanc★★ and Riesling★ continue to raise the quality bar. Best years: (Cabernet Sauvignon) **2000 99 98 97 96 95 94 93**; (Chardonnay) **2001 00 99 98 97 96**.

THERMENREGION *Niederösterreich, Austria* This warm, 2330ha (5760-acre) region, south of Vienna, takes its name from the thermal spa towns of Baden and Bad Vöslau. Near Vienna is the village of Gumpoldskirchen with its rich and often sweet white wines. The red wine area around Baden produces large amounts of Blauer Portugieser together with a couple of good examples of Pinot Noir and Cabernet. Best producers: Biegler, Fischer★, Hofer, Johanneshof★, Schellmann, Stadlmann★. Best years: (sweet whites) (2000) 99 **98 96 95**.

THIRTY BENCH *Niagara Peninsula VQA, Ontario, Canada* A collaboration of 3 winemakers, Thirty Bench is known for its excellent Rieslings, including Late Harvest and Icewine★, very good BORDEAUX-style red Reserve Red Blend and a fine barrel-fermented Chardonnay.

DOM. THOMAS-MOILLARD *Nuits-St-Georges AC, Côte de Nuits, Burgundy, France* This is the label for wines from the family-owned vineyards of négociant house Moillard-Grivot. The wines are not consistent across the range, but the best, including ROMANÉE-ST-VIVANT★★★ and BONNES-MARES★★★, are very fine, in an old-fashioned, long-lived, robust style. Other good reds include NUITS-ST-GEORGES Clos de Thorey★★, BEAUNE Grèves★ and VOSNE-ROMANÉE Malconsorts★★. Red and white HAUTES-COTES DE NUITS★ stand out at the simpler end of the range. Best years: (top reds) (2002) 01 00 99 98 **97** 96 95 **93 90**.

THREE CHOIRS *Gloucestershire, England* Martin Fowke makes an impressive range at this state-of-the-art winery set in a 28ha (70-acre) vineyard. Wines include lovely dry single varietals (Bacchus,  Madeleine Angevine, Schönburger and Phoenix), lightly oaked Estate Reserve white and a Pinot Noir-based red blend. A zingy white New Release appears in November at the same time as BEAUJOLAIS NOUVEAU. Sparkling wines, both non-vintage Classic Cuvée★ and Vintage Reserve, are based on Seyval Blanc but include Pinot Noir.

TICINO *Switzerland* Italian-speaking, southerly canton of Switzerland. The most important wine of the region is Merlot del Ticino, usually soft and gluggable, but sometimes more serious with some oak barrel-ageing. Best producers: Guido Brivio★, Gialdi (Sassi Grossi★★), Daniel Huber★, Werner Stucky★, Christian Zündel★. Best years: (2000) **97 96**.

TIGNANELLO★★ *Tuscany, Italy* The wine that broke the mould in Tuscany. Piero ANTINORI employed the previously unheard-of practice of aging in small French oak barrels and used Cabernet Sauvignon (20%)

in the blend with Sangiovese. Initially labelled as simple vino da tavola, the quality was superb and Tignanello's success sparked off the SUPER-TUSCAN movement that has produced many of Italy's most exciting wines. Top vintages are truly great: lesser years are of decent CHIANTI CLASSICO quality. Best years: (2001) (00) 99 98 97 **95 93 90 88 86 85**.

TINTA RORIZ See Tempranillo.

TOCAI FRIULANO Unrelated to Hungary's TOKAJI, Tocai Friulano is a north-east Italian grape producing dry, nutty, oily whites of great character in COLLIO and COLLI ORIENTALI and good wines in the Veneto's Colli Euganei, as well as lots of neutral stuff in Piave. Best producers: Borgo San Daniele★, Borgo del Tiglio★, Dorigo★, Drius★, Livio FELLUGA★, JERMANN★, Edi Keber★★, Miani★★, Princic★, Paolo Rodaro★, Ronchi di Manzano★, Ronco del Gelso★★, Russiz Superiore★★, SCHIOPETTO★★, Specogna★, Le Vigne di Zamò★★, Villa Russiz★.

TOKAJI *Hungary* Hungary's classic, liquorous wine of historical reputation, with its unique, sweet-and-sour, sherry-like tang, comes from 28 villages on the Hungarian–Slovak border. Mists from the Bodrog river ensure that noble rot on the Furmint, Hárslevelü and Muscotaly (Muscat Ottonel) grapes is a fairly common occurrence. Degrees of sweetness are measured in *puttunyos*. Discussions continue about traditional oxidized styles versus fresher modern versions. Best producers: Disznókö★★, Château Megyer★★, Oremus★, Château Pajzos★★, Royal Tokaji Wine Co★★, Istvan Szepsy (6 Puttonyos 95★★★, Essencia★★★), Tokaji Kereskedöház★. Best years: 2000 **99 97 93**.

TOLLOT-BEAUT *Chorey-lès-Beaune AC, Burgundy, France* High-quality COTE DE BEAUNE reds with lots of fruit and a pronounced new oak character. The village-level CHOREY-LES-BEAUNE★★, ALOXE-CORTON★★ and SAVIGNY-LES-BEAUNE★★ wines are all excellent, as is the top BEAUNE Premier Cru Clos du Roi★★. Whites are more variable. Best years: (reds) (2002) 01 99 98 **97 96 95**.

TORGIANO DOC & DOCG *Umbria, Italy* A zone near Perugia dominated by one producer, LUNGAROTTI. Lungarotti's basic Rubesco Torgiano★ is ripely fruity, the Riserva Vigna Monticchio★★ is a fine black cherry-flavoured wine. Torgiano Riserva Rosso has been accorded DOCG.

TORO DO *Castilla y León, Spain* Mainly red wines, which are robust, full of colour and tannin, and pretty high in alcohol. The main grape, Tinta de Toro, is a variant of Tempranillo, and there is some Garnacha. Whites from the Malvasía grape are generally heavy. Best producers: Alquiriz★★, Viña Bajoz★, Fariña★, Frutos Villar (Muruve★), Maurodos★★, Telmo RODRIGUEZ★★, Toresanas/Bodegas de Crianza Castilla la Vieja★, Vega Saúco★, Vega de Toro/Señorío de San Vicente (Numanthia★★).

TORRES *Penedès DO, Cataluña, Spain* Large family winery led by visionary Miguel Torres, making good wines with local grapes, (Parellada, Tempranillo) and international varieties. Viña Sol★ is a good, citrony quaffer, Viña Esmeralda★ (Muscat Blanc à Petits Grains and Gewürztraminer) is grapy and spicy, Fransola★★ (Sauvignon Blanc with some Parellada) is rich yet leafy, and Milmanda★★ is a delicate, expensive Chardonnay. Successful reds are Gran Coronas★, soft, oaky and blackcurranty (Tempranillo and Cabernet); fine, relatively rich Mas la Plana★ (Cabernet Sauvignon); floral, perfumed Mas Borrás (Pinot Noir); and raisiny Atrium★ (Merlot). The new top-line reds, Grans Muralles★, from a blend of

Catalan grapes, and Reserva Real★★, a BORDEAUX-style red blend, are interesting but expensive. Best years: (Mas la Plana) 1996 95 **94 91 90 88 87 83 81 79 76.**

MARIMAR TORRES ESTATE *Sonoma County, California, USA* The sister of Spanish winemaker Miguel TORRES has established her own winery in the cool Green Valley region of SONOMA COUNTY, only a few miles from the Pacific Ocean. She specializes in Chardonnay and Pinot Noir, the best of which are from the Don Miguel Vineyard. The Chardonnay★★ is big and intense, initially quite oaky, but able to age gracefully and interestingly for up to 10 years. Recent vintages of full-flavoured Pinot Noir★★ are the best yet. Best years: (2001) 00 99 98 **97 95 94.**

MIGUEL TORRES *Curicó, Chile* After a long period of under-achievement from the man who re-awoke the Chilean wine industry, we are once more seeing good snappy Sauvignon Blanc★, grassy, fruity Santa Digna rosé★ and a lean but blackcurranty Manso de Velasco Cabernet★, as well as exciting, sonorous old Carignan-based Cordillera★★. Best years: (Manso) (2000) **99 97 95.**

CH. LA TOUR BLANCHE★★ *Sauternes AC, 1er Cru Classé, Bordeaux, France* This estate regained top form in the 1980s with the introduction of new oak barrels for fermentation, lower yields and greater selection. Full-bodied, rich and aromatic, it now ranks with the best of the Classed Growths. Second wine: Les Charmilles. Best years: (2002) 01 99 98 97 **96 95 90 89 88 86.**

CH. TOUR BOISÉE *Minervois AC, Languedoc, France* Jean-Louis Poudou is one of the pioneering producers in MINERVOIS. Of most interest here is the red Cuvée Marie-Claude★, aged for 12 months in barrel, the white Cuvée Marie-Claude, which has a hint of Muscat Blanc à Petits Grains for added aroma, and the fruity Cuvée Marielle et Frédérique★, produced from Grenache and Syrah.

CH. TOUR DES GENDRES *Bergerac AC, South-West France* Luc de Conti's BERGERACS are made with as much sophistication as is found in the better Crus Classés of BORDEAUX. Generously fruity Moulin des Dames★ and the more earnest la Gloire de Mon Père★ reds are mostly Cabernet Sauvignon. Full, fruity and elegant Moulin des Dames★ white is a classic Bordeaux blend of Sémillon, Sauvignon Blanc and Muscadelle. Best years: (la Gloire de Mon Père) 2001 00 **99 98 97 96 95 94 90 89 88.**

TOURAINE AC *Loire Valley, France* General AC for Touraine wines in the central LOIRE. There are 5250ha (12,970 acres) of AC vineyards, divided half and half between red or rosé and white. Most of the reds are from the Gamay and in hot years these can be juicy, rustic-fruited wines. There is a fair amount of red from Cabernets Sauvignon and Franc, too, and some good Côt (Malbec). The reds are best drunk young. Fairly decent whites come from the Chenin Blanc but the best wines are from Sauvignon Blanc. These can be a good SANCERRE substitute at half the price. Drink at one year old, though Chenin wines can last longer. White and rosé sparkling wines are made by the traditional method, but are rarely as good as the best VOUVRAY and CREMANT DE LOIRE. Best producers: (reds and rosés) Ch. de Chenonceau★, Clos de la Briderie★, Corbillières★, J Delaunay★, Robert Denis★, Ch. Gaillard★, Marcadet★, Marionnet/la Charmoise★, Pavy★, Roche Blanche★; (whites) Acacias★, Ch. de Chenonceau★, Marcadet★, Marionnet/la Charmoise★, Michaud★, Octavie★, Oisly-et-Thésée co-op★, Pibaleau★, Pré Baron★, J Preys★, Roche Blanche★. Best years: (reds) (2002) **01 00 97 96.**

TOURIGA NACIONAL High-quality red Portuguese grape which is rich in aroma and fruit. It is prized for PORT production as it contributes deep colour and tannin to the blend, and is rapidly increasing in importance for table wines both in the DOURO and elsewhere in Portugal.

TOWER ESTATE *Hunter Valley, New South Wales, Australia* Len Evans' latest venture, in partnership with a syndicate that includes British super-chef Rick Stein, focuses on sourcing top-notch grapes from their ideal regions. So, there is powerful, stylish COONAWARRA Cabernet★★, top-flight BAROSSA Shiraz★★ (sourced via Peter LEHMANN), fine floral CLARE Riesling★★, fruity ADELAIDE HILLS Sauvignon Blanc★ and classic Semillon★★, Shiraz★ and Chardonnay★ from the HUNTER VALLEY.

TRÁS-OS-MONTES *Portugal* Impoverished north-eastern province with 3 IPRs, Valpaços, Chaves and Planalto-Mirandês, producing pretty rustic stuff. However, the Vinho Regional Trás-os-Montes/Terras Durienses covers a handful of very good DOURO-sourced reds. **Best producers: Quinta de Cidrô (Chardonnay★), RAMOS PINTO (Bons Ares★), Valle Pradinhos.**

TREBBIANO The most widely planted white Italian grape variety – far too widely, in fact, for Italy's good. As Trebbiano Toscano, it is the base for EST! EST!! EST!!! and any number of other neutral, dry whites, as well as in VIN SANTO. But there are also a number of grapes masquerading under the Trebbiano name that aren't anything like as neutral. The most notable are the Trebbianos from LUGANA and ABRUZZO – both grapes capable of full-bodied, fragrant wines. Called Ugni Blanc in France, and primarily used for distilling, as it should be.

TRENTINO *Italy* This northern region is officially linked with ALTO ADIGE, but they are completely different. The wines rarely have the verve or perfume of Alto Adige examples, but can make up for this with riper, softer flavours, where vineyard yields have been kept in check. The Trentino DOC covers 20 different styles of wine, including whites Pinot Bianco and Grigio, Chardonnay, Moscato Giallo, Müller-Thurgau and Nosiola, and reds Lagrein, Marzemino and Cabernet. Trento Classico is a special DOC for Champagne-method fizz. **Best producers: N Balter★, N Bolognani★, La Cadalora★, Castel Noarna★, Cavit co-op, Cesconi★★, De Tarczal★, Dorigati, FERRARI★★, Graziano Fontana★, FORADORI★★, Letrari★, Longariva★, Conti Martini★, Maso Cantanghel★★, Maso Furli★, Maso Roveri★, Mezzacorona, Pojer & Sandri★, Pravis★, San Leonardo★★, Simoncelli★, E Spagnolli★, Vallarom★, La Vis co-op.** See also Teroldego Rotaliano.

DOM. DE TRÉVALLON *Provence, France* Iconoclastic Parisian Eloi Dürrbach makes brilliant reds★★ (at best ★★★) – mixing herbal wildness with a sweetness of blackberry, blackcurrant and black, black plums – and a tiny quantity of white★★★. Dürrbach's tradition-busting blend of Cabernet Sauvignon and Syrah, no longer accepted by the appellation les BAUX-DE-PROVENCE, is now VdP des BOUCHES-DU-RHONE. The wines age extremely well, but are intriguingly drinkable in their youth. **Best years: (reds) 2001 00 99 98 97 96 95 94 93 90 89 88.**

TRIMBACH *Alsace AC, Alsace, France* An excellent grower/merchant whose trademark is beautifully structured, subtly perfumed elegance. Riesling and Gewurztraminer are the specialities, but the Pinot Gris and Pinot Blanc are first-rate too. Top wines are Gewurztraminer

Cuvée des Seigneurs de Ribeaupierre★★, Riesling Cuvée Frédéric Émile★★ and Riesling Clos St-Hune★★★. Also very good ALSACE VENDANGE TARDIVE★★ and Sélection de Grains Nobles★★. Best years: (Clos St-Hune) 1998 97 96 95 **93 92 90 89 88 85 83 81 76**.

TRITTENHEIM *Mosel, Germany* Important village with some excellent vineyard sites, notably the Apotheke (pharmacy) and Leiterchen (little ladder). The wines are sleek, with crisp acidity and plenty of fruit. Best producers: Ernst Clüsserath★, Clüsserath-Weiler★, GRANS-FASSIAN★, Milz-Laurentiushof★. Best years: (2002) 01 00 99 98 **97 95 93 90**.

CH. TROPLONG-MONDOT★★ *St-Émilion Grand Cru AC, Bordeaux, France* Consistently one of the best of ST-EMILION's Grands Crus Classés. The wines are beautifully structured and mouthfillingly textured for long aging. Best years: 2001 00 99 98 97 96 95 **94 90 89 88 86 85**.

CH. TROTANOY★★ *Pomerol AC, Pomerol, France* Another POMEROL estate (along with PETRUS, la FLEUR-PETRUS, LATOUR-A-POMEROL and others) which has benefited from the brilliant touch of the MOUEIX family. After a dip in the mid-1980s, recent vintages are getting back on form. Best years: 2001 00 99 98 97 96 95 **94 93 90 89 88 82**.

CAVE VINICOLE DE TURCKHEIM *Alsace AC, Alsace, France* Very important co-op with a reputation for good Pinot Blanc★, Pinot Gris★ and Gewurztraminer★. Brand★★ and Hengst★★ bottlings of the last two are rich and concentrated. Riesling is less reliable, but reds, rosés and CREMANT D'ALSACE★ are consistent. Best years: (Grand Cru Gewurztraminer) (2002) 01 00 **99 98 97 95 94 93 90 89**.

TURLEY *Napa Valley AVA, California, USA* Larry Turley specializes in powerful Zinfandel and Petite Sirah. After early assistance from his talented winemaking sister Helen (now based at MARCASSIN), Turley has gone on to produce ultra-ripe Zins★★ from a number of old vineyards. They are either praised for their profound power and depth or damned for their tannic, high-alcohol, PORT-like nature. Petite Sirah★★ is similarly built, and all the wines can last a decade or more. Best years: (Zins) (2001) (00) 99 **98 97 96 95 94**.

TURSAN VDQS *South-West France* Restaurateur Michel Guérard (3-star Michelin), with his Baron de Bachen label, has helped preserve and promote these wines, made on the edge of les Landes, the sandy coastal area south of Bordeaux. The white is the most interesting: made from the Baroque grape, it is clean, crisp and refreshing. Best producers: Baron de Bachen★, Dulucq, Tursan co-op.

TUSCANY *Italy* Tuscany's rolling hills, clad with vines, olive trees and cypresses, have produced wine since at least Etruscan times, and today Tuscany leads the way in promoting the new image of Italian wines. Its many DOC/DOCGs are based on the red Sangiovese grape and are led by CHIANTI CLASSICO, BRUNELLO DI MONTALCINO and VINO NOBILE DI MONTEPULCIANO, as well as famous SUPER-TUSCANS like ORNELLAIA and TIGNANELLO. White wines, despite sweet VIN SANTO, and the occasional excellent Chardonnay and Sauvignon, do not figure highly. See also Bolgheri, Carmignano, Montecarlo, Morellino di Scansano, Rosso di Montalcino, Rosso di Montepulciano, Sassicaia, Solaia, Vernaccia di San Gimignano.

TYRRELL'S *Hunter Valley, New South Wales, Australia* Stalwart family-owned company with prime Lower HUNTER vineyards. Comprehensive range from basic Long Flat quaffers through the Individual Vineyard range (★), up to the superb Vat 1 Semillon★★★, generally excellent

Vat 47 Chardonnay★★, and Vat 5★ and Vat 9★★ Shiraz. Old Winery★ range of easy drinkers is excellent. Best years: (Vat 1 Semillon) 2000 99 98 97 **96 95 94 93 92 91 90 89 87 86 77 76 75**; (Vat 47 Chardonnay) 2000 **99 98 97 96 95 94 91 89.**

UCO VALLEY *Mendoza, Argentina* This valley, in the foothills of the Andes, is an old secret of Argentine viticulture, newly rediscovered. With vineyards at 1000–1500m (3200–4900 ft) above sea level, it's Argentina's best spot for Chardonnays, especially from the Tupungato area. Reds are also showing fascinating flavours – especially Merlot, Malbec, Syrah and Pinot Noir. Best producers: Achaval-Ferrer★, CATENA★★, Finca La Celia★, Salentein★, Terrazas de los Andes★.

UGNI BLANC See Trebbiano.

UMBRIA *Italy* Wine production in this Italian region is dominated by ORVIETO, accounting for almost 70% of DOC wines. However, some of the most characterful wines are reds from TORGIANO and MONTEFALCO. Latest interest centres on remarkable new reds made by the outstanding Riccardo Cotarella at estates such as Pieve del Vescovo (Lucciaio★★), La Carraia (Fobiano★★), Lamborghini (Campoleone★★) and La Palazzola (Rubino★★).

ÜRZIG *Mosel, Germany* Middle MOSEL village with the famous red slate Würzgarten (spice garden) vineyard tumbling spectacularly down to the river and producing marvellously spicy Riesling. Drink young or with at least 5 years' age. Best producers: Bischöfliche Weingüter★, J J Christoffel★★, Dr LOOSEN★★★, Mönchhof★★, Peter Nicolay★. Best years: (2002) 01 00 99 98 **97** 96 95 **94 93**.

UTIEL-REQUENA DO *Valencia, Spain* Utiel-Requena is renowned for its rosés, mostly from the Bobal grape. Reds, increasingly based on Tempranillo, are improving. Best producers: Gandía, Bodegas Palmera (L'Angelet★), Schenk, Torre Oria, Vinival.

DOM. VACHERON *Sancerre AC, Loire Valley, France* Unusually for a SANCERRE domaine, Vacheron is more reputed for its Pinot Noir reds than for its whites, but the whole range is currently on top form. Intense and expensive Belle Dame★★ red and Les Romains★★ red and white lead the way. The basic Sancerres – a cherryish red★ and a grapefruity white★ – have reserves of complexity that set them above the crowd. Best years (Belle Dame) (2002) 01 **00 99 98 96 95**.

VACQUEYRAS AC *Rhône Valley, France* The most important of the COTES DU RHONE-VILLAGES communes was promoted to its own AC in 1990. Red wines account for 95% of production; dark in colour, they have a warm, spicy bouquet and a rich deep flavour that seems infused with the herbs and pine dust of the south. Lovely to drink at 2–3 years, though good wines will age for 7 years or more. Best producers: Amouriers★, la Charbonnière★, Clos des Cazaux★, Couroulu★, DELAS★, Font de Papier★, la Fourmone★, la Garrigue★, JABOULET★, Montmirail★, Montvac★, Sang des Cailloux★★, Tardieu-Laurent★, Ch. des Tours★, Vacqueyras co-op★, Verquière★. Best years: 2001 00 99 **98 97 96 95 94**.

VAL D'ORBIEU, LES VIGNERONS DU *Languedoc-Roussillon, France* This growers' association is France's largest wine exporting company, selling in excess of 20 million cases of wine a year. Membership includes several of the MIDI's best co-ops (Cucugnan, Cuxac, Montredon, Ribauté) and individual producers (Dom. de Fontsainte, Ch. la VOULTE-GASPARETS). It also owns Cordier (BORDEAUX) and Listel, and markets the wines of Ch. de Jau and the excellent BANYULS and COLLIOURE estate, Clos de Paulilles. Its range of blended wines (Cuvée Chouette★, Chorus★, Elysices★, Réserve St-Martin★, la Cuvée Mythique★) are a mix of traditional Mediterranean varieties with Cabernet or Merlot and show welcome signs of ambition to raise quality.

VALAIS *Switzerland* Swiss canton flanking the Rhône. Between Martigny and Sierre the valley turns north-east, creating an Alpine suntrap, and this short stretch of terraced vineyard land provides many of Switzerland's most individual wines from Fendant, Johannisberger (Silvaner), Pinot Noir and Gamay, and several stunning examples from Syrah, Chardonnay, Ermitage (Marsanne) and Petite Arvine. Best producers: M Clavien★, J Germanier★, R Gilliard, Caves Imesch, Didier Joris★, Mathier, Dom. du Mont d'Or★, Raymond, Zufferey.

CH. DE VALANDRAUD★★ *St-Émilion Grand Cru AC, Bordeaux, France* The precursor of the 'garage wine' sensation in ST-EMILION, a big, rich, extracted wine from low yields, from grapes mainly grown in different parcels around St-Émilion. The first vintage was in 1991 and since then prices have rocketed. Best years: 2001 00 99 98 97 96 95 **94 93**.

VALDEPEÑAS DO *Castilla-La Mancha, Spain* Valdepeñas offers some of Spain's best inexpensive oak-aged reds, but these are a small drop in a sea of less exciting stuff. In fact there are more whites than reds, at least some of them modern, fresh and fruity. Best producers: Miguel Calatayud, Los Llanos★, Luís Megía, Real, Félix Solís, Casa de la Viña.

VALDESPINO *Jerez y Manzanilla DO, Andalucía, Spain* The bodega has been sold and we await anxiously to see whether the superb quality of sherries such as Inocente Fino★★, Palo Cortado Cardenal★★ and dry amontillado Coliseo★★ is going to suffer.

VALDIVIESO *Curicó, Chile* Recipient of huge investment both in the Lontué winery and CURICO vineyards. Best known for smooth Pinot Noir★ and Chardonnay; there's also exciting Merlot★, Cabernet Franc★ and Malbec★★ in the single-vineyard Reserves, though both reds and whites can seem a little sweet at times. Multi-varietal blend Caballo Loco★★ is always fascinating but a long way from its goal of being Chile's answer to GRANGE. Although sparkling wines have been made here for 100 years, Champagne-method fizz is a recent introduction.

VALENCIA *Spain* The best wines from Valencia DO are the inexpensive, sweet, grapy Moscatels. Simple, fruity whites, reds and rosés are also good. Alicante DO to the south produces a little-known treasure, the Fondillón dry or semi-dry fortified wine, as well as a cluster of wines from native and foreign varieties made by a few quality-conscious modern wineries. Monastrell (Mourvèdre) is the main red grape variety. Best producers: (Valencia) Gandía, Los Pinos★, Celler del Roure★, Schenk, Cherubino Valsangiacomo (Marqués de Caro); (Alicante) Bocopa★, Gutiérrez de la Vega (Casta Diva Muscat★★), Enrique Mendoza★★, Salvador Poveda★, Primitivo Quiles★; (non-DO) Mustiguillo (Quincha Corral★★). See also Utiel-Requena.

VALL-LLACH *Priorat DOC, Spain* The tiny winery, owned by Catalan folk singer Lluís Llach, with young Sara Pérez as winemaker, has joined the ranks of the best PRIORAT producers with its powerful reds★★ dominated by old-vine Cariñena. Best years: 2000 99 **98**.

VALLE D'AOSTA *Italy*   Tiny Alpine valley sandwiched between PIEDMONT and the French Alps in northern Italy. The regional DOC covers 17 wine styles, referring either to a specific grape variety (like Gamay or Pinot Nero) or to a delimited region like Donnaz, a northern extension of Piedmont's Carema, producing a light red from the Nebbiolo grape. Perhaps the finest wine from these steep slopes is the sweet Chambave Moscato. Best producers: R Anselmet★, C Charrère★, Les Crêtes★, La Crotta di Vegneron★, Grosjean, Institut Agricole Regional★, Onze Communes co-op, Ezio Voyat★.

VALLEY VINEYARDS *Berkshire, England*   Eighteen grape varieties planted over 13ha (32 acres) from which 2 Aussies – viticulturist and owner Jon Leighton and consultant winemaker John Worontschak – produce full-flavoured wines, many with antipodean-style use of oak. Fumé★ is an excellent oaked white; Bacchus-based Regatta really refreshing; and the bottle-fermented sparkling wines Ascot, Heritage Brut and Heritage Rosé are all good and reasonably priced. Clocktower Pinot Noir and sparkling Clocktower Gamay Brut are produced in limited quantities in favourable years.

VALPOLICELLA DOC *Veneto, Italy*   This wine can range in style from a light, cherryish red to the rich, port-like RECIOTO and AMARONE Valpolicellas. Most of the better examples are Valpolicella Classico from the hills and are made predominantly from Corvina (the best grape). The most concentrated, ageworthy examples are made either from a particular vineyard, or by refermenting the wine on the skins and lees of the Amarone, a style called *ripasso*, or simply by using a portion of dried grapes. Best producers: Accordini★, ALLEGRINI★★, Bertani★, Brigaldara★, Brunelli★, Tommaso Bussola★★, M Castellani★, DAL FORNO★★, Guerrieri-Rizzardi★, MASI★, Mazzi★, Pasqua/Cecilia Beretta★, QUINTARELLI★★, Le Ragose★, Le Salette★, Serègo Alighieri★, Speri★, Tedeschi★, Villa Monteleone★, Viviani★★, Zenato★, Fratelli Zeni★. Best years: (2001) **00 97 95 93 90 88**.

VALTELLINA SUPERIORE DOCG *Lombardy, Italy*   Red wine produced on the precipitous slopes of northern LOMBARDY. There is a basic, light Valtellina DOC red, made from at least 70% Nebbiolo (here called Chiavennasca), but the best wines are made under the Valtellina Superiore DOCG as Grumello, Inferno, Sassella and Valgella. From top vintages the wines are attractively perfumed and approachable. Sfursat or Sforzato is a dense, high-alcohol red (up to 14.5%) made from semi-dried grapes. Best producers: La Castellina★, Enologica Valtellinese★, Fay★, Nino Negri★, Nera★, Rainoldi★, Conti Sertoli Salis★, Triacca★. Best years: (2001) (99) (98) 97 **95 93 90 88 85**.

VASSE FELIX *Margaret River, Western Australia*   One of the originals responsible for MARGARET RIVER rocketing to fame, with decadently rich, profound Cabernet Sauvignon★★ and oak-led Shiraz★. Flagship red is the powerful Heytesbury★★, with a Chardonnay★★ to match. But I'm still waiting for Vasse Felix consistently to reach the next level up. Best years: (Heytesbury) (2001) 99 98 97 96 **95**.

VAUD *Switzerland*   With the exception of the canton of Geneva, the Vaud accounts for the vineyards bordering Lake Geneva. There are 5 regions: la Côte, Lavaux, CHABLAIS, Côtes de l'Orbe-Bonvillars and Vully. Delightful light white wines are made from Chasselas; at DEZALEY it gains some real depth and character. Reds are from Gamay and Pinot Noir. Best producers: Henri Badoux, Louis Bovard★, Conne, Delarze, Dubois Fils, Grognuz, Massy, Obrist, Pinget, J & P Testuz.

VAVASOUR *Marlborough, South Island, New Zealand* First winery in
MARLBOROUGH's Awatere Valley, now enjoying spectacular success. One
of New Zealand's best Chardonnays★★, a fine Pinot Noir★★ and
palate-tingling oak-aged Sauvignon Blanc★★. Second label Dashwood
also impresses, particularly with the tangy Dashwood Sauvignon
Blanc★★. Best years: (Sauvignon Blanc) (2003) 02 **01 00**.

VEENWOUDEN *Paarl WO, South Africa* International opera singer Deon
van der Walt and his winemaker brother Marcel, an ex-golf pro, make
wines that regularly command top prices at auction. The 3 reds are
based on BORDEAUX varieties: sumptuous, well-oaked Merlot★★, firm
and silky-fruited Veenwouden Classic★★ and Vivat Bacchus★, with a
distinctive Malbec component. A tiny quantity of fine Chardonnay★ is
also made. Best years: (Merlot, Classic) 2000 **99 98 97 96 95 94 93**.

VEGA SICILIA *Ribera del Duero DO, Castilla y León, Spain* Among
Spain's most expensive red wines, rich, fragrant, complex and very
slow to mature, and by no means always easy to appreciate. This
estate was the first in Spain to introduce French varieties, and over a
quarter of the vines are now Cabernet Sauvignon, two-thirds are
Tempranillo and the rest Malbec and Merlot. Vega Sicilia Unico★★★ –
the top wine – was traditionally given about 10 years' wood aging,
but since 1982 this has been reduced to 5 or 6. Second wine:
Valbuena★★. A subsidiary winery produces the more modern-style
Alión★★, and the new Alquiriz★★ winery makes some of the most
distinctive wines in TORO. Best years: (Unico) **1990 89 86 85 83 82 81 80
79 76 75 74 70 68**.

VELICH *Neuseidlersee, Burgenland, Austria* Former casino croupiers
Roland and Heinz Velich make not only Austria's most mineral and
sophisticated Chardonnay★★ from old vines in the Tiglat vineyard,
but since 1995 also spectacular dessert wines of ★★ and ★★★ quality.
Best years: (Tiglat Chardonnay) (2002) 01 00 99 **97 95 93 92**; (sweet
whites) (2002) 00 99 98 **96 95 94 91**.

VENETO *Italy* This region takes in the wine zones of SOAVE, VALPOLICELLA,
BARDOLINO and Piave in north-east Italy. It is the source of a great deal of
inexpensive wine, but the Soave and Valpolicella hills are also capable of
producing small quantities of high-quality wine. Other hilly areas like Colli
Berici and Colli Euganei produce large quantities of dull staple varietal
wines, but can offer the odd flash of brilliance. The great dry red of this
zone is AMARONE. See also Bianco di Custoza, Prosecco di Conegliano-
Valdobbiadene, Recioto della Valpolicella, Recioto di Soave.

VERDICCHIO DEI CASTELLI DI JESI DOC *Marche, Italy* Verdicchio,
grown in the hills near the Adriatic around Jesi and in the Apennine
enclave of Matelica, has blossomed into central Italy's most promising
white variety. When fresh and fruity it is the ideal wine with fish, but
some Verdicchio can age into a white of surprising depth of flavours. A
few producers, notably Garofoli with Serra Fiorese★★, age it in oak, but
even without wood it can develop an almost Burgundy-like complexity.
Jesi is the classical zone, but the rarer Verdicchio di Matelica can be as
impressive. A little is made sparkling. Best producers: (Jesi) Brunori★,
Bucci★, Colonnara★, Coroncino★★, Fazi Battaglia★, Garofoli★★,
Mancinelli★, Terre Cortesi Moncaro★, Monte Schiavo★, Santa Barbara★,
Sartarelli★★, Tavignano★, Umani Ronchi★, Fratelli Zaccagnini★;
(Matelica) Belisario★, Bisci★, Mecella★, La Monacesca★★.

VERGELEGEN *Stellenbosch WO, South Africa*
Winemaker Andre van Rensburg is busy making this historic farm one of the greats of the new century. His Sauvignon Blancs are already considered benchmarks: the regular bottling★★ is aggressive and racy, streaked with sleek tropical fruit; the single-vineyard Reserve★★ flinty, dry and powerful. Topping both is a new barrel-

fermented white Vergelegen★★ – a Sauvignon Blanc-Semillon blend. There is also a ripe-textured, stylish Chardonnay Reserve★★. The reds are even more attention-grabbing. Vergelegen★★, the BORDEAUX-blend flagship, shows classic mineral restraint. Merlot★★ and Cabernet Sauvignon★★ are some of the best in South Africa. Van Rensburg has only been here since 1998; several of these wines will reach ★★★ in future vintages. Best years: (premium reds) **2000** 99 98 95 94; (Chardonnay Reserve) 2001 **00 99 98 97 96**.

VERGET *Mâconnais, Burgundy, France* A négociant house run by Jean-Marie Guffens-Heynen, an exuberant character with his own domaine. The Guffens-Heynen wines include excellent MACON-VILLAGES★ and POUILLY-FUISSE★★. The Verget range has outstanding Premiers Crus and Grands Crus from the COTE D'OR, notably CHASSAGNE-MONTRACHET★★ and BATARD-MONTRACHET★★★. But beware, the wines are made in a *very* individualistic style. Best years: (2002) 01 00 99 **97**.

VERITAS *Barossa, South Australia* *In vino veritas* (In wine there is truth), say the Binder family. There's certainly truth in the bottom of a bottle of Hanisch Vineyard Shiraz★★★ or Heysen Vineyard Shiraz★★★, both blindingly good wines. The Shiraz-Mourvèdre★★ (known locally as Bulls' Blood) and Shiraz-Grenache★★ blends are lovely big reds; Cabernet-Merlot★★ is also good. Under the Christa-Rolf label, Shiraz-Grenache★ is good and spicy with attractive, forward black fruit.

VERMENTINO The best dry white wines of SARDINIA generally come from the Vermentino grape. Light, dry, perfumed and nutty, the best examples tend to be from the north of the island, where the Vermentino di Gallura zone is located. Occasionally it is made sweet or sparkling. Vermentino is also grown in LIGURIA and TUSCANY, though its character is quite different. It is believed to be the same as Rolle, found in many blends in LANGUEDOC-ROUSSILLON. Best producers: (Sardinia) ARGIOLAS★, Capichera★, Cherchi★, Gallura co-op, Piero Mancini★, Pedra Majore★, Santadi co-op★, SELLA & MOSCA★, Vermentino co-op.

VERNACCIA DI ORISTANO DOC *Sardinia, Italy* Outstanding, oxidized, almost sherry-like wines from the west of the island, which acquire complexity and colour through long aging in wood. Amber-coloured and dry, nutty and long on the finish. Best producer: Contini★.

VERNACCIA DI SAN GIMIGNANO DOCG *Tuscany, Italy* Dry white wines – generally light quaffers – made from the Vernaccia grape grown in the hills around San Gimignano. It is debatable whether the allowance of up to 10% Chardonnay in the blend is a forward step. There is a San Gimignano DOC for the zone's up-and-coming reds, though the best SUPER-TUSCANS are sold as IGT wines. Best producers: Cà del Vispo★, Le Calcinaie★, Casale-Falchini★, V Cesani★, La Lastra (Riserva★), Melini (Le Grillaie★), Montenidoli★, G Panizzi★, Il Paradiso★,

Pietrafitta★, La Rampa di Fugnano★, Guicciardini Strozzi★, Teruzzi & Puthod (Terre di Tufi★★), Casa alle Vacche★, Vagnoni★.

NOËL VERSET *Cornas AC, Rhône Valley, France* Powerful, concentrated reds★ from some of the oldest and best-sited vines in CORNAS. Yields are tiny and it shows in the depth that Verset achieves. Worth aging for 10 years or more. Now retired, so watch this space for future developments. Best years: 1999 98 97 96 95 **94 91** 90 **88** 85.

VESUVIO DOC *Campania, Italy* Red wines based on Piedirosso and whites from Coda di Volpe and Verdeca. The evocative name Lacryma Christi del Vesuvio is now only for superior versions. Best producers: Cantine Caputo, Cantina Grotta del Sole, MASTROBERARDINO.

VESÚVIO, QUINTA DO★★★ *Port DOC, Douro, Portugal* A consistently top performer, it differs from Symington stablemates DOW, GRAHAM and WARRE in that it appears only when the high quality can be maintained (and not just in officially declared years). A brilliant port, best with at least 10 years' age. Best years: 2000 99 98 97 96 95 94 **92 91** 90.

VEUVE CLICQUOT *Champagne AC, Champagne, France* Produced by the LVMH luxury goods group, these Champagnes can still live up to the high standards set by the original Widow Clicquot at the beginning of the 19th century, although many are released too young. The non-vintage★ is full, toasty and satisfyingly weighty, or lean and raw, depending on your luck: the vintage★★ is fuller and the de luxe Grande Dame★★★ is both powerful and elegant. Grande Dame Rosé★★★ is exquisite. Best years: (1996) 95 **93 91** 90 89 88 85 82.

VICTORIA *Australia* Despite its relatively small area, Victoria has arguably more land suited to quality grape-growing than any other state in Australia, with climates ranging from hot Murray Darling and Swan Hill on the Murray River to cool MORNINGTON PENINSULA and GIPPSLAND in the south. The range of flavours is similarly wide and exciting. With more than 350 wineries, Victoria leads the boutique winery boom, particularly in Mornington Peninsula. See also Bendigo, Central Victoria, Geelong, Grampians and Pyrenees, Rutherglen, Yarra Valley.

VIEUX-CHÂTEAU-CERTAN★★ *Pomerol AC, Bordeaux, France* Slow-developing, tannic red with up to 30% Cabernet Franc and 10% Cabernet Sauvignon in the blend, which after 15–20 years finally resembles more a fragrant refined MEDOC than a hedonistic POMEROL. Best years: 2001 00 99 98 96 95 **90 89 88 86 85 83 82**.

VIEUX TÉLÉGRAPHE *Châteauneuf-du-Pape AC, Rhône Valley, France* One of the top names in the AC, less tannic than BEAUCASTEL perhaps, but with just as much aging potential. The vines are some of the oldest in CHATEAUNEUF and the Grenache-based red★★★ is among the best modern-style wines produced in the RHONE VALLEY. There is also a small amount of white★★, which is heavenly when very young. Good second wine, Vieux Mas des Papes. Also owns la Roquette (Châteauneuf-du-Pape★★) and les Pallières★ in GIGONDAS. Best years: (reds) 2001 00 99 98 **97 96 95** 93 90 89 88.

VILLA MARIA *Auckland and Marlborough, New Zealand* Founder George Fistonich also owns Esk Valley and Vidal (both in HAWKES BAY). Villa Maria Reserve Merlot-Cabernet★★★, Esk Valley The Terraces★★★ (a BORDEAUX-style blend) and Vidal Merlot-Cabernet★★ are superb. Reserve Chardonnay from Vidal★★ and Villa Maria★ are power-packed wines. The Villa Maria Reserve range also includes 2 outstanding examples of MARLBOROUGH Sauvignon Blanc: Wairau Valley★★ and even more concentrated Clifford Bay★★. Also from Marlborough, impressive Riesling★★ and stunning botrytized Noble Riesling★★★. Best years: (Hawkes Bay reds) (2002) **00 99 98**.

VILLARD ESTATE *Casablanca, Chile* Owner Thierry Villard (formerly of ORLANDO in South Australia) has created one of Chile's most successful boutique wineries. Big, buttery Chardonnay Reserve★ and clean, crisp Sauvignon Blanc★, both from CASABLANCA. Also good Casablanca Pinot Noir★, MAIPO Merlot★ and superb El Noble★★ sweetie.

CH. DE VILLENEUVE *Saumur-Champigny AC, Loire Valley, France* During the 1990s this property emerged as one of the very best in the region. The secret lies in low yields, picked when properly ripe. First-class SAUMUR-CHAMPIGNY★, with concentrated, mineral Vieilles Vignes★★ and le Grand Clos★★. Also good white, stainless steel-fermented SAUMUR★ and barrel-fermented Saumur Les Cormiers★★.

VILLIERA *Stellenbosch WO, South Africa* The speciality here is Cap Classique sparklers, offering all-round quality and value for money, led by the flagship vintage Monro Brut★, a Pinot Noir-Chardonnay blend with rich, biscuity flavours. Winemaker Jeff Grier is known for Sauvignon Blanc (Bush Vine★); there's also a consistent Riesling★ and 2 delicious Chenin Blancs with different degrees of oaking. Reds are equally good, especially the intense yet succulent BORDEAUX-style Cru Monro★ and newcomer Merlot-Pinotage★. Best years: (Cru Monro) (2001) 00 **99 98 97 96 95 94**.

VIN SANTO *Tuscany, Italy* The 'holy wine' of TUSCANY can be one of the world's great sweet wines – but it is also one of the most wantonly abused wine terms in Italy (in particular avoid anything called *liquoroso*). Made from grapes either hung from rafters or laid on mats to dry, the resulting wines, fermented and aged in small barrels (*caratelli*) for up to 7–8 years, should be nutty, oxidized, full of the flavours of dried apricots and crystallized orange peel, concentrated and long. Also produced in UMBRIA and TRENTINO as Vino Santo. Best producers: Castello di AMA★, AVIGNONESI★★★, Fattoria Basciano★, Bindella★★, Cacchiano★, Capezzana★★, Fattoria del Cerro★★, Corzano & Paterno★★, FONTODI★★, ISOLE E OLENA★★★, Romeo★★, San Felice★★, San Gervasio★★, San Giusto a Rentennano★★★, SELVAPIANA★★, Villa Sant'Anna★★, Villa di Vetrice★, VOLPAIA★.

VIÑAS DEL VERO *Somontano DO, Aragón, Spain* SOMONTANO's largest company, specializing in New World-inspired wines. A buttery but mineral unoaked Chardonnay and its toasty barrel-fermented counterpart★ are joined by more original whites such as Clarión★, a blend of Chardonnay, Gewürztraminer and Macabeo. Flavours have unfortunately been lightening up recently, but top reds – Gran Vos★ (Merlot-Cabernet-Pinot Noir) and the new red blend★★ made by its subsidiary Blecua – still deliver the goods.

VINHO VERDE DOC *Minho and Douro Litoral, Portugal* 'Vinho Verde' can be red *or* white. 'Green' only in the sense of being young, demarcated Vinhos Verde come from north-west Portugal. The whites are the most widely seen outside Portugal and range from sulphured and acidic to aromatic, flowery and fruity. One or two that fall outside the DOC regulations are sold as Vinho Regional Minho. Best producers: Quinta de Alderiz, Quinta da Aveleda, Quinta da Baguinha★, Encostas dos Castelos, Quinta da Franqueira★, Monção co-op (Deu la Deu Alvarinho★, Muralhas de Monção), Muros de Melgaço (Alvarinho★),

Quintas de Melgaço, Palácio de Brejoeira, Dom Salvador, Casa de Sezim★, Soalheiro, SOGRAPE (Gazela, Quinta de Azevedo★), Quinta do Tamariz (Loureiro★).

VINO NOBILE DI MONTEPULCIANO DOCG *Tuscany, Italy* The 'noble wine' from the hills around the town of Montepulciano is made from the Sangiovese grape, known locally as the Prugnolo, with the help of a little Canaiolo and Mammolo. At its best, it combines the power and structure of BRUNELLO DI MONTALCINO with the finesse and complexity found in top CHIANTI. Unfortunately, the best was a rare beast until relatively recently, though the rate of improvement has been impressive. The introduction of what is essentially a second wine, ROSSO DI MONTEPULCIANO, has certainly helped. **Best producers:** AVIGNONESI★★, Bindella★, BOSCARELLI★★, La Braccesca★★/ANTINORI, Le Casalte★, La Ciarliana★, Contucci★, Dei★★, Del Cerro★★, Fassati★★, Il Macchione★, Nottola★★, Palazzo Vecchio★, POLIZIANO★★, Redi★, Romeo★, Salcheto★★, Trerose★ (Angelini★★), Valdipiatta★. **Best years:** (2001) 00 99 **97 95 93 90 88**.

VIOGNIER A poor yielder, prone to disease and difficult to vinify. The wine can be delicious: peachy, apricotty with a soft, almost waxy texture, usually a fragrance of spring flowers and sometimes a taste like crème fraîche. Traditionally grown only in the northern RHONE, it is now found in LANGUEDOC-ROUSSILLON, Ardèche and the southern Rhône as well as in CALIFORNIA, Argentina, Chile, Australia and South Africa.

VIRÉ-CLESSÉ AC *Mâconnais, Burgundy, France* Appellation created in 1998 out of 2 of the best MACON-VILLAGES. Controversially, the rules have outlawed wines with residual sugar, thus excluding Jean Thévenet's extraordinary cuvées. **Best producers:** Bonhomme★★, Chazelles★, Cave de Viré★, Ch. de Viré★, Merlin★, Michel★★, Rijckaert★.

VIRGINIA *USA* Thomas Jefferson failed miserably at growing grapes at his Monticello estate, but his modern-day successors have created a rapidly growing and improving wine industry. Virginia now has more than 70 wineries and 6 AVAs. Aromatic Viognier and earthy Cabernet Franc show most promise. **Best producers:** Barboursville★, Chrysalis, Horton★, Linden★, Valhalla★, White Hall★.

ROBERTO VOERZIO *Barolo DOCG, Piedmont, Italy* One of the best of the new wave of BAROLO producers. Dolcetto (Priavino★) is successful, as is Vignaserra★★ – barrique-aged Nebbiolo with a little Cabernet – and the outstanding new BARBERA D'ALBA Riserva Vigneto Pozzo dell'Annunziata★★★. Barriques are also used for fashioning his Barolo, but such is the quality and concentration of fruit coming from densely planted vineyards that the oak does not overwhelm. Single-vineyard examples made in the best years are Brunate★★, Cerequio★★★, La Serra★★ and new Riserva Capalot★★★. **Best years:** (Barolo) (2001) (00) 99 98 97 96 **95 93 91 90 89 88 85**.

COMTE GEORGES DE VOGÜÉ *Chambolle-Musigny AC, Côte de Nuits, Burgundy, France* De Vogüé owns substantial holdings in 2 Grands Crus, BONNES-MARES★★★ and MUSIGNY★★★, as well as in Chambolle's top Premier Cru, les Amoureuses★★★. Since 1990 the domaine has been on magnificent form. It is the sole producer of minute quantities of Musigny Blanc★★★, but because of recent replanting the wine is now being sold as (very expensive) BOURGOGNE Blanc. Best years: (Musigny) (2002) 01 00 99 98 97 96 95 93 **92 91 90**.

VOLNAY AC *Côte de Beaune, Burgundy, France* Volnay is home to the finest red wines of the COTE DE BEAUNE in terms of elegance and class. Attractive when young, the best examples can age well. The top Premiers Crus are Caillerets, Champans, Clos des Chênes, Santenots (which actually lies in MEURSAULT) and Taillepieds. Best producers: R Ampeau★★, d'ANGERVILLE★★, J-M Boillot★★, J-M Bouley★★, Carré-Courbin★, COCHE-DURY★★, V GIRARDIN★★, LAFARGE★★★, LAFON★★★, Dom. Matrot★★, Montille★★, N Potel★★, J Prieur★★, Roblet-Monnot★, J Voillot★★. Best years: (2002) 99 98 **97 96 95 93 91 90**.

VOLPAIA, CASTELLO DI *Chianti Classico DOCG, Tuscany, Italy* Light, perfumed but refined CHIANTI CLASSICO★ (Riserva★★). Two stylish SUPER-TUSCANS, Balifico★★ and Coltassala★, are both predominantly Sangiovese. Sometimes good but not great VIN SANTO★.

VOSNE-ROMANÉE AC *Côte de Nuits, Burgundy, France* The greatest village in the COTE DE NUITS, with 6 Grands Crus and 13 Premiers Crus (notably les Malconsorts, aux Brûlées and les Suchots) which are often as good as other villages' Grands Crus. The quality of the village wine is also high. In good years the wines need at least 6 years' aging and 10–15 would be better. Best producers: R Arnoux★★★, Cacheux-Sirugue★★, Sylvain Cathiard★★, Champy★★, B CLAIR★★, B Clavelier★★, R Engel★★, GRIVOT★★★, Anne GROS★★★, A-F GROS★★, Haegelen-Jayer★★, F Lamarche★★, Dom. LEROY★★★, MEO-CAMUZET★★★, Mugneret-Gibourg★★, RION★★, Dom. de la ROMANEE-CONTI★★★, E Rouget★★★, THOMAS-MOILLARD★. Best years: (2001) 00 99 98 97 96 95 **93 91 90**.

VOUGEOT AC *Côte de Nuits, Burgundy, France* Outside the walls of CLOS DE VOUGEOT there are 11ha (27 acres) of Premier Cru and 5ha (12 acres) of other vines. Look out for Premier Cru Les Cras (red) and the Clos Blanc de Vougeot, first planted with white grapes in 1110. Best producers: Bertagna★★, Chopin-Groffier★★, C Clerget★, VOUGERAIE★★. Best years: (reds) (2002) 01 00 99 98 97 96 95 **93 91 90 89 88**.

DOM. DE LA VOUGERAIE *Burgundy, France* An estate created by Jean Claude BOISSET in 1999 out of the numerous vineyards – often excellent but under-achieving – which came with Burgundy merchant houses acquired during his inexorable rise to prominence since 1964. Under the inspired stewardship of Pascal Marchand, the wines are generally outstanding, notably Clos Blanc de VOUGEOT★★★, GEVREY-CHAMBERTIN les Évocelles★, le MUSIGNY★★ and VOUGEOT les Cras★★ reds.

CH. LA VOULTE-GASPARETS *Corbières AC, Languedoc, France* One of the MIDI's most consistent properties, producing CORBIERES with flavours of thyme and baked earth from old hillside vines. The Cuvée Réservée★ and Romain Pauc★★ are the most expensive wines, but the basic Voulte-Gasparets★ is also good. Can be drunk young, but ages well. Best years: (Romain Pauc) 2001 00 **98 96 95 93 91**.

VOUVRAY AC *Loire Valley, France* Dry, medium-dry, sweet and sparkling wines from Chenin grapes east of Tours. The dry wines acquire beautifully rounded flavours after 6–8 years. Medium-dry wines, when properly made from a single domaine, are worth aging for 20 years or more. Spectacular noble-rot-affected sweet wines can be produced in years such as 1995, 96 and 97. The fizz is some of the

LOIRE's best. Best producers: Aubuisières★★, Bourillon-Dorléans★★, Champalou★, CLOS NAUDIN★★, la Fontainerie★★, Ch. Gaudrelle★★, Gautier★★, Haute Borne★, HUET★★, Pichot★★, F Pinon★★, Taille aux Loups★, Vigneau Chevreau★. Best years: (2002) 01 **99 97 96 95 93 90 89 88 85 83 78 76 75 70**.

WACHAU *Niederösterreich, Austria* This stunning 1390ha (3435-acre) stretch of the Danube between Krems-Stein and the monastery of Melk is Austria's top region for dry whites, from Riesling and Grüner Veltliner. Best producers: F HIRTZBERGER★★★, Högl★★, Emmerich KNOLL★★★, NIKOLAIHOF★★, F X PICHLER★★★, PRAGER★★★, Freie Weingärtner WACHAU★★. Best years: (2002) 01 00 99 **98 97 95 94 93 92 90 88 86 83 79 77**.

WACHAU, FREIE WEINGÄRTNER *Wachau, Niederösterreich, Austria* Co-op long producing fine WACHAU white wines, especially vineyard-designated Grüner Veltliners and Rieslings★★. Now sells its top wines under the name Domäne Wachau. Best years: (2002) 01 99 **98 97 96 95 93 92 91 90**.

WACHENHEIM *Pfalz, Germany* Wine village made famous by the BÜRKLIN-WOLF estate, its best vineyards can produce rich yet beautifully balanced Rieslings. Best producers: Josef BIFFAR★, BÜRKLIN-WOLF★★, Karl Schaefer★, J L WOLF★★. Best years: (2002) 01 **99 98 97 96 94 93 90**.

WAIHEKE ISLAND *North Island, New Zealand* GOLDWATER pioneered winemaking on this island in Auckland harbour in the early 1980s, and this tiny, highly fashionable region is now home to over 30 winemakers. Hot, dry ripening conditions have made high-quality Cabernet-based reds that sell for high prices. An increasing quantity of Chardonnay is appearing, together with experimental plots of Shiraz and Viognier. Best producers: Fenton★★, GOLDWATER★★, Obsidian, STONYRIDGE★★★, Te Whau★. Best years: (reds) (2002) **00 99 98 96**.

WALLA WALLA VALLEY AVA *Washington State, USA* Walla Walla has more than 50 of WASHINGTON's wineries, but less than half of these were producing wine at the turn of the century. Vineyard acreage has trebled since 1999 – and is still growing. If you think there's a gold-rush feel about this clearly exciting area you wouldn't be far wrong. Best producers: CANOE RIDGE★, Dunham Cellars★, L'ECOLE NO 41★★, LEONETTI CELLAR★★★, Pepper Bridge Winery★, WOODWARD CANYON★★.

WARRE *Port DOC, Douro, Portugal* Top-quality Vintage PORT★★★, and a good 'off-vintage' port from Quinta da Cavadinha★★. LBV★★ is a very welcome traditional, full-bodied port. Warrior★ is a reliable ruby. Optima, an adequate 10-year-old tawny, is most remarkable for its unconventional clear bottle presentation. Age Vintage port for 15–30 years. Best years: (Vintage) 2000 97 94 **91 85 83 80 77 70 66 63**; (Cavadinha) 1999 98 95 **92 90 88 87 86 82 78**.

WARWICK *Stellenbosch WO, South Africa* This farm focuses on reds from the heart of the Cape's best red wine country. Traditional BORDEAUX varieties are responsible for the complex Trilogy★ blend, and a refined, fragrant, varietal Cabernet Franc★. Old Bush Vine Pinotage is less consistent but, at best, is plummy and perfumed; Pinotage also plays a role in the new red blend, Three Cape Ladies★, with Cabernet Sauvignon and Merlot. An attractive, unwooded Sauvignon Blanc partners the full-bodied yet lightly oaked Chardonnay★. Best years: (Trilogy) (2001) 00 **99 98 97 96 95 94**.

WASHINGTON STATE *USA* Second-largest premium wine-producing state in the US. The chief growing areas are in irrigated high desert, east of the Cascade Mountains, where the COLUMBIA VALLEY AVA encompasses the smaller AVAs of YAKIMA VALLEY, WALLA WALLA VALLEY and Red Mountain. Although the heat is not as intense as in CALIFORNIA, long summer days with extra hours of sunshine due to the northern latitude seem to increase the intensity of fruit flavours and result in both red and white wines of great depth. Cabernet, Merlot, Chardonnay, Sauvignon Blanc and Semillon produce very good wines here.

GEOFF WEAVER *Adelaide Hills, South Australia* Geoff Weaver crafts fine wines from grapes grown at his Lenswood vineyard. Quality fruit from low-yielding vines produces limy Riesling★★, crisply gooseberryish Sauvignon★★ and stylish cool-climate Chardonnay★★. Cabernet-Merlot★ is restrained but tasty, Pinot Noir promising.

WEGELER *Bernkastel, Mosel; Oestrich-Winkel, Rheingau; Deidesheim, Pfalz, Germany* The Wegeler family's 3 estates are dedicated primarily to Riesling, and today dry wines make up the bulk of production. Whether dry or naturally sweet Auslese, the best merit ★★ and will develop well with 5 or more years of aging. The MOSEL estate achieves the highest standard; nearly all the wines are ★. Best years: (Mosel-Saar-Ruwer) (2002) 01 99 98 **97 96 95 93 90 89 88 83 76**.

WEHLEN *Mosel, Germany* Village whose steep Sonnenuhr vineyard produces some of the most powerful Rieslings in Germany. Best producers: Kerpen, Dr LOOSEN★★★, J J PRUM★★★, S A PRUM★, Max Ferd RICHTER★★, SELBACH-OSTER★★, WEGELER★, Dr Weins-Prüm★. Best years: (2002) 01 **99** 98 **97** 95 **94 93 90 89 88 85 83 76**.

ROBERT WEIL *Kiedrich, Rheingau, Germany* This estate has enjoyed huge investment from Japanese drinks giant Suntory which, coupled with Wilhelm Weil's devotion to quality, has returned it to the RHEINGAU's premier division. Majestic sweet Auslese, Beerenauslese and Trockenbeerenauslese Rieslings★★★, and dry Rieslings★ are crisp and elegant, although the regular wines have been a little disappointing in recent vintages. Best years: (2002) 01 **99** 98 96 **95 94 93 90 89**.

WEINBACH *Alsace AC, Alsace, France* This Kaysersberg estate is run by Mme Colette Faller and her two daughters. The range is quite complicated. Some wines are named in honour of Mme Faller's late husband Théo★★; others are labelled Ste-Cathérine★★, and are late picked, though not technically Vendange Tardive. Also very fine are the Gewurztraminer Altenbourg Laurence★★ and the Pinot Gris Cuvée Laurence★★. The Riesling Grand Cru Schlossberg★★★ is the finest dry wine. In certain vintages the estate produces Quintessence – a super-concentrated Sélection de Grains Nobles – from Pinot Gris★★★ and Gewurztraminer★★★. All the wines are exceptionally balanced and can be aged for many years. Best years: (Grand Cru Riesling) 2001 00 99 98 **97 96 95 94 93 92 90 89**. See also Alsace Vendange Tardive.

WEISSBURGUNDER See Pinot Blanc.

WELSCHRIESLING See Riesling Italico.

WENDOUREE *Clare Valley, South Australia* Small winery using old-fashioned methods to make enormous, ageworthy reds★★★ from paltry yields off their own very old Shiraz, Cabernet, Malbec and Mataro (Mourvèdre) vines, plus tiny amounts of sweet Muscat★. Reds can, and do, age beautifully for 30 years or more. Best years: (reds) 2001 99 98 96 95 94 **92 91 90 86 83 82 81 80 78 76 75**.

WESTERN AUSTRALIA   Only the south-west corner of this vast state is suited to vines, the SWAN DISTRICT and Perth environs being the oldest and hottest area, with present attention (and more than 230 producers) focused on GREAT SOUTHERN, MARGARET RIVER, Geographe and PEMBERTON. The state produces just over 4% of Australia's grape crush but about 20% of its premium wines.

WIEN *Austria*   Region within the city limits of Wien (Vienna). The best wines come from south-facing sites in Grinzing, Nussdorf and Weiden; and the Bisamberg hill east of the Danube. Best producers: Bernreiter, Kierlinger, Mayer, Schilling, Wieninger★. Best years: (2002) 01 00 **99 97 95 94 93**. See also Heuriger.

WILLAMETTE VALLEY AVA *Oregon, USA*   This viticultural area is typical of OREGON's maritime climate. Wet winters, generally dry summers, and a good chance of long, cool autumn days provide sound growing conditions for cool-climate varieties such as Pinot Noir, Pinot Gris and Chardonnay. Dundee Hills, with its volcanic hillsides, is considered the best sub-region. Best producers: ADELSHEIM★, AMITY★, Argyle★, BEAUX FRERES★★, BETHEL HEIGHTS★, Cameron★, CRISTOM★, DOMAINE DROUHIN★★, ELK COVE★★, EYRIE★, KING ESTATE, PANTHER CREEK★, Ponzi, Rex Hill★, Sokol Blosser, Torii Mor★, WillaKenzie★, Ken WRIGHT★, Yamhill Valley★. Best years: (reds) (2002) 01 00 99 **98 96**.

WILLIAMS SELYEM *Russian River Valley AVA, California, USA*   Purchased in 1998 by John Dyson, a vineyard owner from New York, it looks as if the cult following for the Pinot Noirs★★, especially the J Rochioli Vineyard★★★, has diminished somewhat. Traditionally the wine is big, sometimes very fruity and sometimes just a bit off the wall. Best years: (Pinot Noir) (2001) (00) 99 98 **97 96 95 94**.

WINKEL *Rheingau, Germany*   RHEINGAU village whose best vineyard is the large Hasensprung but the most famous one is Schloss Vollrads – an ancient estate that does not use the village name on its label. Best producers: August Eser, Johannishof★★, SCHLOSS VOLLRADS★ (since 1999), WEGELER★. Best years: 2001 **99** 98 96 **93 90**.

WIRRA WIRRA *McLaren Vale, South Australia*   Consistent maker of whites with more finesse than is customary in the region; now reds are as good, too. Recent years have seen rapid expansion. Well-balanced Sauvignon Blanc★, ageworthy Semillon blend★, buttery Chardonnay★★ and soft reds led by delicious The Angelus Cabernet★★, chocolaty RSW Shiraz★★, decadent Original Blend Grenache-Shiraz★, and seductive Allawah BAROSSA Grenache★★. Best years: (The Angelus) 2001 00 99 98 97 **96 95 92 91 90**.

WITHER HILLS *Marlborough, South Island, New Zealand*   This quality-focused winery is one of the region's best. In 2002 it was bought by the Australian liquor group Lion Nathan; talented founder/winemaker Brent Marris stays until 2005. A trio of stylish MARLBOROUGH wines – concentrated, pungent Sauvignon Blanc★★, fine, fruit-focused Chardonnay★★ and vibrant Pinot Noir★★ – allows Wither Hills to concentrate only on wines that perform with distinction in this region. Expect little change, at least while Marris remains at the helm.

J L WOLF *Wachenheim, Pfalz, Germany*   Ernst Loosen, of Dr LOOSEN in the MOSEL, took over this underperforming estate in 1996. A string of concentrated dry and naturally sweet Rieslings★★ have won it a place among the region's top producers. Best years: (2002) 01 00 **99** 98 **97 96**.

WOODWARD CANYON *Walla Walla Valley AVA, Washington State, USA*
Big, barrel-fermented Chardonnays (Celilo Vineyard★) were the
trademark wines for many years, but today the focus is on reds, with a
fine Artist Series★ Cabernet Sauvignon and Old Vines★ (formerly
Dedication) Cabernet Sauvignon leading the line-up. Merlot can be
velvety and deeply perfumed. White and red★ BORDEAUX-style blends are
labelled Charbonneau, the name of the vineyard where the fruit is
grown. Best years: (Cabernet Sauvignon) (2001) 00 99 **98 97 96**.

KEN WRIGHT CELLARS *Willamette Valley AVA, Oregon, USA* Ken Wright
produces more than a dozen succulent, single-vineyard Pinot Noirs.
Bold and rich with new oak flavour, they range from good to ethereal,
led by the Carter★★★, Shea★★★, Arcus★★ and McCrone★★. Fine
WASHINGTON Chardonnay from the Celilo Vineyard★★, expressive
French clone OREGON Chardonnays from Carabella★ and McCrone★
and a zesty Pinot Blanc from Freedom Hill Vineyard★ make up the
portfolio of whites. Best years: (Pinot Noir) (2002) (01) 00 99 **98 97**.

WÜRTTEMBERG *Germany* Wine region centred on the river Neckar.
Two-thirds of the wine made is red, and the best comes from Lemberger
(Blaufränkisch), Dornfelder or Spätburgunder (Pinot Noir) grapes. Massive
yields are often responsible for pallid wines. However, a few of the many
marvellously steep sites are now producing perfumed reds and racy
Riesling. Best years: (reds) (2002) 01 **99 97 93 90**.

WÜRZBURG *Franken, Germany* The centre of FRANKEN wines. Some
Rieslings can be great, but the real star is Silvaner. Best producers:
Bürgerspital, JULIUSSPITAL★, Staatlicher Hofkeller, Weingut am Stein★.
Best years: (2002) 01 00 **99 97 94 93 92 90**.

WYNNS *Coonawarra, South Australia* Wynns' name is synonymous with
COONAWARRA. Now part of the giant Southcorp, its personality seems to
have suffered less than most of Southcorp's other brands and, except
at the top end, prices have remained fair. Attractive Chardonnay★
and consistently enjoyable Riesling★. However, Wynns is best known
for reds. The basic Cabernet-Shiraz-Merlot, Shiraz★ and Black Label
Cabernet Sauvignon★★ are all good. Top-end John Riddoch Cabernet
Sauvignon★★ and Michael Shiraz★★ are deep, ripe styles, but less
thrilling than they used to be. Best years: (John Riddoch) (2000) 99 98
96 94 **91 90 88 86 82**.

YAKIMA VALLEY AVA *Washington State, USA* This valley lies within the
much larger COLUMBIA VALLEY AVA. Yakima is planted mostly to
Chardonnay, Merlot and Cabernet Sauvignon and has around 30
wineries. Best producers: Bonair, Chinook★, Hedges Cellars★, HOGUE
CELLARS★, Kestrel★, KIONA★, Portteus★, Wineglass Cellars★.

YALUMBA *Barossa Valley, South Australia* Distinguished old firm, owned
by the Hill-Smith family, making a wide range of wines under its own
name, as well as Heggies Vineyard (restrained Riesling★, nice plump
Merlot★, opulent Viognier★ and botrytis Riesling★★), Hill-Smith Estate
(Sauvignon Blanc★) and Pewsey Vale (fine Riesling★ and Cabernet
Sauvignon★). Flagship reds are The Signature Cabernet-Shiraz★★,
Octavius Shiraz★★ and The Menzies Cabernet★★ and all cellar well.
New premiums include Old Vine Grenache★★, Contour Riesling★★,
Virgilius Viognier★★ and Shiraz-Viognier★. Reliable quaffers like
Galway Shiraz, Oxford Landing Chardonnay, Sauvignon★,
Viognier★★, Merlot and Cabernet-Shiraz are consistently impressive.

Angas Brut remains big-volume enjoyable fizz, while the acquisition of TASMANIA's Jansz★ (Vintage★★) has added a class act to the flight. Museum Release fortifieds (Muscat★★) are excellent, but rare. Best years: (The Signature red) (2000) 99 98 97 96 **95 93 92 91 90 88**.

YARRA VALLEY *Victoria, Australia* With its cool climate, the fashionable Yarra is asking to be judged as Australia's best Pinot Noir region. Exciting also for Chardonnay and Cabernet-Merlot blends and as a supplier of base wine for sparklers. Best producers: Arthur's Creek★★, COLDSTREAM HILLS★, DE BORTOLI★★, Diamond Valley★, DOMAINE CHANDON/Green Point★, Métier★, MOUNT MARY★★, St Huberts★, Seville Estate★, TARRAWARRA★★, Yarra Burn★, Yarra Ridge★, YARRA YERING★★, Yeringberg★, Yering Station★.

YARRA YERING *Yarra Valley, Victoria, Australia* Bailey Carrodus creates extraordinary wines from his exceptional vineyard. Dry Red No. 1★★ (Cabernet-based) and Dry Red No. 2★★ (Shiraz-based) are profound, concentrated, ageworthy, packed with unnervingly self-confident fruit and memorable perfume. Pinot Noir★ is expensive but can be fine and wild. Chardonnay★ is erratic, occasionally delicious. Best years: (No. 1) (2001) 00 99 98 97 96 **94 93 91 90 89 86**.

CH. D'YQUEM★★★ *Sauternes AC, 1er Cru Supérieur, Bordeaux, France* Often rated the most sublime sweet wine in the world, no one can question Yquem's total commitment to quality. Despite a large vineyard (100ha/250 acres), production is tiny. Only fully noble-rotted grapes are picked, often berry by berry, and low yield means each vine produces only a glass of wine! This precious liquid is then fermented in new oak barrels and left to mature for 3½ years before bottling. It is one of the world's most expensive wines, in constant demand because of its richness and exotic flavours. A dry white, Ygrec, is made in some years. In 1999 LVMH won a 3-year takeover battle with the Lur-Saluces family, owners for 406 years. Best years: 1997 96 95 94 **93 91** 90 **89 88 86 83 82 81 80 79 76 75 71 70 67 62**.

ZILLIKEN *Saarburg, Mosel-Saar-Ruwer, Germany* Estate specializing in Rieslings★★ (Auslese, Eiswein often ★★★) from the Saarburger Rausch vineyard. Best years: (2002) 01 99 97 95 **94 93 91 90 89 88 85 83 79 76**.

ZIND-HUMBRECHT *Alsace AC, Alsace, France* Olivier Humbrecht is one of France's outstanding winemakers. The family owns vines in 4 Grand Cru sites – Rangen, Goldert, Hengst and Brand – and these wines (Riesling★★, Gewurztraminer★★★, Pinot Gris★★★ and Muscat★★) are excellent, as is a range of wines from specific vineyards and *lieux dits*, such as Gewurztraminer or Riesling Clos Windsbuhl★★★ and Pinot Gris Clos Windsbuhl or Clos Jebsal★★. ALSACE VENDANGE TARDIVE wines are almost invariably of ★★★ quality. Even basic Sylvaners★ and Pinot Blancs★★ are fine. Best years: (Clos Windsbuhl Gewurztraminer) 2001 00 **99** 98 **97 96** 95 **94 93 92 90 89**.

ZINFANDEL CALIFORNIA's versatile red grape can make big, juicy, fruit-packed wine – or insipid, sweetish 'blush' or even late-harvest dessert wine. Some Zinfandel is now made in other countries, with notable examples in Australia and South Africa. Best producers: (California) Brown★★, Cline Cellars★★, Dashe★, DRY CREEK VINEYARD★, FETZER★, Martinelli★★, Nalle★★, Preston★, Rafanelli★★, RAVENSWOOD★, RIDGE★★★, Rosenblum★★, Saddleback★★, St Francis★★, SEGHESIO★★, TURLEY★★, WILLIAMS SELYEM★★; (Australia) CAPE MENTELLE★★, Kangarilla Road, Nepenthe. See also Primitivo di Manduria.

GLOSSARY OF WINE TERMS

AC/AOC (APPELLA-TION D'ORIGINE CONTRÔLÉE) The top category of French wines, defined by regulations covering vineyard yields, grape varieties, geographical boundaries, alcohol content and production method. Guarantees origin and style of a wine, but not its quality.

ACID/ACIDITY Naturally present in grapes and essential to wine, providing balance and stability and giving the refreshing tang in white wines and the appetizing grip in reds.

ADEGA Portuguese for winery.

AGING An alternative term for maturation.

ALCOHOLIC CONTENT The alcoholic strength of wine, expressed as a percentage of the total volume of the wine. Typically in the range of 7–15%.

ALCOHOLIC FERMENTATION The process whereby yeasts, natural or added, convert the grape sugars into alcohol (Ethyl alcohol, or Ethanol) and carbon dioxide.

AMONTILLADO Traditionally dry style of sherry. *See* Jerez and Manzanilla in main A–Z.

ANBAUGEBIET German for growing region; these names will appear on labels of all QbA and QmP wines. There are 13 *Anbaugebiete*: Ahr, Baden, Franken, Hessische Bergstrasse, Mittelrhein, Mosel-Saar-Ruwer, Nahe, Pfalz, Rheingau, Rheinhessen, Saale-Unstrut, Sachsen and Württemberg.

AUSBRUCH Austrian Prädikat category used for sweet wines.

AUSLESE German and Austrian Prädikat cat-

egory meaning that the grapes were 'selected' for their higher ripeness.

AVA (AMERICAN VITICULTURAL AREA) System of appellations of origin for US wines.

AZIENDA AGRICOLA Italian for estate or farm. It also indicates wine made from grapes grown by the proprietor.

BARREL AGING Time spent maturing in wood, usually oak, during which the wines take on flavours from the wood.

BARREL FERMENTA-TION Oak barrels may be used for fermentation instead of stainless steel to give a rich, oaky flavour to the wine.

BARRIQUE The *barrique bordelaise* is the traditional Bordeaux oak barrel of 225 litres (50 gallons) capacity.

BAUMÉ A scale measuring must weight (the amount of sugar in grape juice) to estimate potential alcohol content.

BEERENAUSLESE German and Austrian Prädikat category applied to wines made from 'individually selected' berries (i.e. grapes) affected by noble rot (*Edelfäule* in German). The wines are rich and sweet.

Beerenauslese wines are only produced in the best years in Germany, but in Austria they are a regular occurrence.

BEREICH German for region or district within a wine region or *Anbaugebiet*. Bereichs tend to be large, and the use of a Bereich name, such as Bereich Bingen, without qualification is seldom an indication of quality – in most cases, quite the reverse.

BIODYNAMIC VITI-CULTURE This approach works with the movement of the planets and cosmic forces to achieve health and balance in the soil and in the vine. Vines are treated with infusions of mineral, animal and plant materials, applied in homeopathic quantities.

BLANC DE BLANCS White wine made from one or more white grape varieties. Used especially for sparkling wines; in Champagne, denotes wine made entirely from the Chardonnay grape.

BLANC DE NOIRS White wine made from black grapes only – the juice is separated from

BOTTLE SIZES

CHAMPAGNE

Magnum	1.5 litres	2 bottles
Jeroboam	3 litres	4 bottles
Rehoboam	4.5 litres	6 bottles
Methuselah	6 litres	8 bottles
Salmanazar	9 litres	12 bottles
Balthazar	12 litres	16 bottles
Nebuchadnezzar	15 litres	20 bottles

BORDEAUX

Magnum	1.5 litres	2 bottles
Marie-Jeanne	2.25 litres	3 bottles
Double-magnum	3 litres	4 bottles
Jeroboam	4.5 litres	6 bottles
Imperial	6 litres	8 bottles

the skins to avoid extracting any colour. Most often seen in Champagne, where it describes wine made from Pinot Noir and/or Pinot Meunier.

BLENDING (assemblage) The art of mixing together wines of different origin, styles or age, often to balance out acidity, weight etc.

BODEGA Spanish for winery.

BOTRYTIS *See* noble rot.

BRUT French term for dry sparkling wines, especially Champagne.

CARBONIC MACERATION Winemaking method used to produce fresh fruity reds for drinking young. Whole (uncrushed) bunches of grapes are fermented in closed containers – a process that extracts lots of fruit and colour, but little tannin.

CAVE CO-OPÉRATIVE French for co-operative cellar, where members bring their grapes for vinification and bottling under a collective label. In terms of quantity, the French wine industry is dominated by co-ops. Often use less workaday titles, such as Caves des Vignerons, Producteurs Réunis, Union des Producteurs or Cellier des Vignerons.

CHAMPAGNE METHOD Traditional method used for all of the world's finest sparkling wines. A second fermentation takes place in the bottle, producing carbon dioxide which, kept in solution under pressure, gives the wine its fizz.

CHAPTALIZATION Legal addition of sugar during fermentation to raise a wine's alcoholic strength. More necessary in cool climates

where lack of sun produces insufficient natural sugar in the grape.

CHARTA A German organization founded to protect the image of the best Rheingau Rieslings in 1984, recognizable by a double-window motif on the bottle or label. The accent is on dry wines that go with food. Now merged with VDP to form VDP-Rheingau, but the Charta symbol remains in use.

CHÂTEAU French for castle, used to describe a variety of wine estates.

CHIARETTO Italian for a rosé wine of very light pink colour.

CLARET English for red Bordeaux wines, from the French *clairet*, which was traditionally used to describe a lighter style of red Bordeaux.

CLARIFICATION Term covering any winemaking process (such as filtering or fining) that involves the removal of solid matter either from the must or the wine.

CLONE Strain of grape species. The term is usually taken to mean laboratory-produced, virus-free clones, selected to produce higher or lower quantity, or selected for resistance to frost or disease.

CLOS French for a walled vineyard – as in Burgundy's Clos de Vougeot – also commonly incorporated into the names of estates (e.g. Clos des Papes), regardless of whether they are walled or not.

COLD FERMENTATION Long, slow fermentation at low temperature to extract maximum freshness from the grapes.

COLHEITA Aged tawny port from a single vintage. *See* Port in main A–Z.

COMMUNE A French village and its surrounding area or parish.

CORKED/CORKY Wine fault derived from a cork which has become contaminated, usually with Trichloroanisole or TCA, and nothing to do with pieces of cork in the wine. The mouldy, stale smell is unmistakable.

COSECHA Spanish for vintage.

CÔTE French word for a slope or hillside, which is where many, but not all, of the country's best vineyards are to be found.

CRÉMANT French term for traditional-method sparkling wine from Alsace, Bordeaux, Burgundy, Die, Jura, Limoux, Loire and Luxembourg.

CRIANZA Spanish term for the youngest official category of oak-matured wine. A red Crianza wine must have had at least 2 years' aging (1 in oak, 1 in bottle) before sale; a white or rosé, 1 year.

CRU French for growth, meaning a specific plot of land or particular estate. In Burgundy, growths are divided into Grands (great) and Premiers (first) Crus, and apply solely to the actual land. In Champagne the same terms are used for whole villages. In Bordeaux there are various hierarchical levels of Cru referring to estates rather than their vineyards.

CRU BOURGEOIS French term for wines from the Médoc and Sauternes that are ranked immediately below the Crus Classés. Many are excellent value for money.

CRU CLASSÉ The Classed Growths are the aristocracy of Bordeaux, ennobled by the Classifications of 1855 (for the Médoc, Barsac and Sauternes), 1955, 1969, 1986 and 1996 (for St-Émilion) and 1947, 1953 and 1959 (for Graves). Curiously, Pomerol has never been classified. The modern classifications are more reliable than the 1855 version, which was based solely on the price of the wines at the time of the Great Exhibition in Paris, but in terms of prestige the 1855 Classification remains the most important. With the exception of a single alteration in 1973, when Ch. Mouton-Rothschild was elevated to First Growth status, the list has not changed since 1855. It certainly needs revising.

CUVE CLOSE A bulk process used to produce inexpensive sparkling wines. The second fermentation, which produces the bubbles, takes place in tank rather than in the bottle.

CUVÉE French for the contents of a single vat or tank, but usually indicates a wine blended from either different grape varieties or the best barrels of wine.

DÉGORGEMENT Stage in the production of Champagne-method wines when the sediment, collected in the neck of the bottle during *remuage*, is removed.

DEMI-SEC French for medium-dry.

DO (DENOMINACIÓN DE ORIGEN) Spain's equivalent of the French AC quality category, regulating origin and production methods.

DOC (DENOMINAÇÃO DE ORIGEM CONTRO-LADA) The top regional classification for Portuguese wines.

DOC (DENOMI-NACIÓN DE ORIGEN CALIFICADA) Spanish quality wine category, intended to be one step up from DO. So far only Rioja and Priorat qualify.

DOC (DENOMI-NAZIONE DI ORIGINE CONTROLLATA) Italian quality wine category, regulating origin, grape varieties, yield and production methods.

DOCG (DENOMI-NAZIONE DI ORIGINE CONTROLLATA E GARANTITA) The top tier of the Italian classification system.

DOSAGE A sugar and wine mixture added to sparkling wine after *dégorgement* which affects how sweet or dry it will be.

EDELZWICKER Blended wine from Alsace in France, usually bland.

EINZELLAGE German for an individual vineyard site which is generally farmed by several growers. The name is preceded on the label by that of the village: for example, the Wehlener Sonnenuhr is the Sonnenuhr vineyard in Wehlen. The mention of a particular site should signify a superior wine. Sadly, this is not necessarily so.

EISWEIN Rare, chiefly German and Austrian, late-harvested wine made by picking the grapes and pressing them while frozen. This concentrates the sweetness of the grape as most of the liquid is removed as ice. *See also* Icewine.

ESCOLHA Portuguese for selection.

FILTERING Removal of yeasts, solids and any impurities from a wine before bottling.

FINING Method of clarifying wine by adding a coagulant (e.g. egg

whites, isinglass or bentonite) to remove soluble particles such as proteins and excessive tannins.

FINO The lightest, freshest style of sherry. *See* Jerez y Manzanilla in main A–Z.

FLOR A film of yeast which forms on the top of fino sherries (and some other wines), preventing oxidation and imparting a unique tangy, dry flavour.

FLYING WINEMAKER Term coined in the late 1980s to describe enologists, many Australian-trained, brought in to improve the quality of wines in many underperforming wine regions.

FORTIFIED WINE Wine which has high-alcohol grape spirit added, usually before the initial fermentation is completed, thereby preserving sweetness.

FRIZZANTE Italian for semi-sparkling wine, usually made dry, but sometimes sweet.

GARAGE WINE *See* vin de garage.

GARRAFEIRA Portuguese term for wine from an outstanding vintage, with 0.5% more alcohol than the minimum required, and 2 years' aging in vat or barrel followed by 1 year in bottle for reds, and 6 months of each for whites. Also used by merchants for their best blended and aged wines. Use of the term is in decline as producers opt for the more readily recognized Reserva as an alternative on the label.

GRAN RESERVA Top category of Spanish wines from a top vintage, with at least 5 years' aging (2 of them in cask) for reds and 4 for whites.

GRAND CRU French for great growth.

Supposedly the best vineyard sites in Alsace, Burgundy, Champagne and parts of Bordeaux and should produce the most exciting wines.

GRANDES MARQUES Great brands – the Syndicat des Grandes Marques was once Champagne's self-appointed élite. It disbanded in 1997.

GROSSLAGE German term for a grouping of vineyards. Some are not too big, and have the advantage of allowing small amounts of higher QmP wines to be made from the grapes from several vineyards. But sometimes the use of vast Grosslage names (e.g. Niersteiner Gutes Domtal) deceives consumers into believing they are buying something special.

HALBTROCKEN German for medium dry. In Germany and Austria medium-dry wine has 9–18g per litre of residual sugar, though sparkling wine is allowed up to 50g per litre. But the high acid levels in German wines can make them seem rather dry and lean.

ICEWINE A speciality of Canada, produced from juice squeezed from ripe grapes that have frozen on the vine. *See also* Eiswein.

IGT (INDICAZIONE GEOGRAFICA TIPICA) The Italian equivalent of the French vin de pays. As in the Midi, both premium and everyday wines may share the same appellation. Many of the Super-Tuscan vini da tavola are now sold under a regional IGT.

IPR (INDICAÇÃO DE PROVENIÊNCIA REGULAMENTADA) The second tier in the Portuguese wine classification regulations, covering grape varieties,

yields and aging requirements.

KABINETT Term used for the lowest level of QmP wines in Germany.

LANDWEIN German or Austrian country wine; the equivalent of French vin de pays. The wine must have a territorial definition and may be chaptalized to give it more alcohol.

LATE HARVEST *See* Vendange Tardive.

LAYING DOWN The storing of wine which will improve with age.

LEES Sediment – dead yeast cells, grape pips (seeds), pulp and tartrates – thrown by wine during fermentation and left behind after racking. Some wines are left on the fine lees for as long as possible to take on extra flavour.

MALOLACTIC FERMENTATION Secondary fermentation whereby harsh malic acid is converted into mild lactic acid and carbon dioxide. Normal in red wines but often prevented in whites to preserve a fresh, fruity taste.

MANZANILLA The tangiest style of sherry, similar to fino. *See* Jerez y Manzanilla in main A–Z.

MATURATION Positive term for the beneficial aging of wine.

MERITAGE American term for red or white wines made from a blend of Bordeaux grape varieties.

MESOCLIMATE The climate of a specific geographical area, be it a vineyard or simply a hillside or valley.

MOELLEUX French for soft or mellow, used to describe sweet or medium-sweet wines.

MOUSSEUX French for sparkling wine.

MUST The mixture of grape juice, skins, pips and pulp produced after crushing (but prior to completion of fermentation), which will eventually become wine.

MUST WEIGHT An indicator of the sugar content of juice – and therefore the ripeness of grapes.

NÉGOCIANT French term for a merchant who buys and sells wine. A négociant-éléveur is a merchant who buys, makes, ages and sells wine.

NEW WORLD When used as a geographical term, New World includes the Americas, South Africa, Australia and New Zealand. By extension, it is also a term used to describe the clean, fruity, upfront style now in evidence all over the world, but pioneered in the USA and Australia.

NOBLE ROT *(Botrytis cinerea)* Fungus which, when it attacks ripe white grapes, shrivels the fruit and intensifies their sugar while adding a distinctive flavour. A vital factor in creating many of the world's finest sweet wines, such as Sauternes and Trockenbeerenauslese.

OAK The wood used almost exclusively to make barrels for fermenting and aging fine wines.

OECHSLE German scale measuring must weight (sugar content).

OLOROSO The darkest, most heavily fortified style of sherry. *See* Jerez y Manzanilla in main A–Z.

OXIDATION Over-exposure to air, causing loss of fruit and flavour. Slight oxidation, such as occurs through the wood of a barrel or during racking, is part of the aging process and, in wines of sufficient structure, enhances flavour and complexity.

PASSITO Italian term for wine made from dried grapes. The result is usually a sweet wine with a raisiny intensity of fruit. *See also* Moscato Passito di Pantelleria, Recioto di Soave, Recioto della Valpolicella, and Vin Santo in main A–Z.

PERLWEIN German for a lightly sparkling wine.

PÉTILLANT French for a slightly sparkling wine.

PHYLLOXERA The vine aphid *Phylloxera vastatrix* attacks vine roots. It devastated European and consequently other vineyards around the world in the late 1800s soon after it arrived from America. Since then, the vulnerable *Vitis vinifera* has generally been grafted on to vinously inferior, but phylloxera-resistant, American rootstocks.

PRÄDIKAT Grades defining quality wines in Germany and Austria. These are (in ascending order) Kabinett (not considered as Prädikat in Austria) Spätlese, Auslese, Beerenauslese, the Austrian-only category Ausbruch, and Trockenbeerenauslese. Strohwein and Eiswein are also Prädikat wines. Some Spätleses and even a few Ausleses are now made as dry wines.

PREMIER CRU First Growth; the top quality classification in parts of Bordeaux, but second to Grand Cru in Burgundy. Used in Champagne to designate vineyards just below Grand Cru.

PRIMEUR French term for a young wine, often released for sale within a few weeks of the harvest. Beaujolais Nouveau is the best-known example.

QbA (QUALITÄTSWEIN BESTIMMTER ANBAUGEBIETE) German for quality wine from designated regions. Sugar can be added to increase the alcohol content. Usually pretty ordinary, but from top estates this category offers excellent value for money. In Austria *Qualitätswein* is equivalent to the German QbA.

QmP (QUALITÄTSWEIN MIT PRÄDIKAT) German for quality wine with distinction. A higher category than QbA, with controlled yields and no sugar addition. QmP covers 6 levels based on the ripeness of the grapes: *see* Prädikat.

QUINTA Portuguese for farm or estate.

RACKING Gradual clarification of a quality wine; the wine is transferred from one barrel or container to another, leaving the lees behind.

RANCIO A fortified wine deliberately exposed to the effects of oxidation, found mainly in Languedoc-Roussillon, Cataluña and southern Spain.

REMUAGE Process in Champagne-making whereby the bottles, stored on their sides and at a progressively steeper angle in *pupitres*, are twisted, or riddled, each day so that the sediment moves down the sides and collects in the neck of the bottle on the cap, ready for *dégorgement*.

RESERVA Spanish wines that have fulfilled certain aging requirements: reds must have at least 3 years' aging before sale, of which one must be in oak barrels; whites and rosés must have at least

2 years' age, of which 6 months must be in oak.

RÉSERVE French for what is, in theory at least, a winemaker's finest wine. The word has no legal definition in France.

RIPASSO A method used in Valpolicella to make wines with extra depth. Wine is passed over the lees of Recioto or Amarone della Valpolicella, adding extra alcohol and flavour, though also extra tannin and a risk of higher acidity and oxidation.

RISERVA An Italian term, recognized in many DOCs and DOCGs, for a special selection of wine that has been aged longer before release. It is only a promise of a more pleasurable drink if the wine had enough fruit and structure in the first place.

SEC French for dry. When applied to Champagne, it actually means medium-dry.

'SECOND' WINES A second selection from a designated vineyard, usually lighter and quicker-maturing than the main wine.

SEDIMENT Usually refers to residue thrown by a wine, particularly red, as it ages in bottle.

SEKT German for sparkling wine. The wine will be entirely German only if it is called Deutscher Sekt or Sekt bA. The best wines are traditional-method made from 100% Riesling or from 100% Weissburgunder (Pinot Blanc).

SÉLECTION DE GRAINS NOBLES A super-ripe category for sweet Alsace wines, now also being used by some producers of Coteaux du Layon in the Loire for the most concentrated wines. *See*

293

also Alsace Vendange Tardive in main A–Z.

SMARAGD The top of the three categories of wine from the Wachau in Austria, the lower two being Federspiel and Steinfeder. Made from very ripe and usually late-harvested grapes, the wines have a minimum of 12% alcohol, often 13–14%.

SOLERA Traditional Spanish system of blending fortified wines, especially sherry and Montilla-Moriles.

SPÄTLESE German for late-picked (therefore riper) grapes. Often moderately sweet, though there are dry versions.

SPUMANTE Italian for sparkling. Bottle-fermented wines are often referred to as *metodo classico* or *metodo tradizionale*.

SUPÉRIEUR French for a wine with a slightly higher alcohol content than the basic AC.

SUPERIORE Italian DOC wines with higher alcohol or more age potential.

SUR LIE French for on the lees, meaning wine bottled direct from the cask/fermentation vat to gain extra flavour from the lees. Common with quality Muscadet, white Burgundy, similar barrel-aged whites and, increasingly, commercial bulk whites.

TAFELWEIN German for table wine.

TANNIN Harsh, bitter, mouth-puckering element in red wine, derived from grape skins and stems, and from oak barrels. Tannins soften with age and are essential for long-term development in red wines.

TERROIR A French term used to denote the combination of soil, climate and exposure to the sun – that is, the natural physical environment of the vine.

TROCKEN German for dry. In most parts of Germany and Austria Trocken matches the standard EU definition of dryness – less than 9g per litre residual sugar.

TROCKENBEEREN-AUSLESE (TBA) German for 'dry berry selected', denoting grapes affected by noble rot (*Edelfäule* in German) – the wines will be lusciously sweet although low in alcohol.

VARIETAL Wine made from, and named after, a single or dominant grape variety.

VDP German organization recognizable on the label by a Prussian eagle bearing grapes. The quality of estates included is usually – but not always – high. Now merged with the Charta organization.

VDQS (VIN DÉLIMITÉ DE QUALITÉ SUPÉRIEURE) The second-highest classification for French wines, behind AC.

VELHO Portuguese for old. Legally applied only to wines with at least 3 years' aging for reds and 2 years for whites.

VENDANGE TARDIVE French for late harvest. Grapes are left on the vines beyond the normal harvest time to concentrate flavours and sugars. The term is traditional in Alsace. *See also* Alsace Vendange Tardive in main A–Z.

VIEILLES VIGNES French term for a wine made from vines at least 20 years old. Should have greater concentration than wine from younger vines.

VIÑA Spanish for vineyard.

VIN DE GARAGE Wines made on so small a scale they could be made in one's garage. Such wines may be made from vineyards of a couple of hectares or less, and are often of extreme concentration.

VIN DE PAILLE Sweet wine found mainly in the Jura region of France. Traditionally, the grapes are left for 2–3 months on straw (*paille*) mats before fermentation to dehydrate, thus concentrating the sugars. The wines are sweet but slightly nutty.

VIN DE PAYS The term gives a regional identity to wine from the country districts of France. It is a particularly useful category for adventurous winemakers who want to use good-quality grapes not allowed under the frequently restrictive AC regulations. Many are labelled with the grape variety.

VIN DE TABLE French for table wine, the lowest quality level.

VIN DOUX NATUREL (VDN) French for a fortified wine, where fermentation has been stopped by the addition of alcohol, leaving the wine 'naturally' sweet, although you could argue that stopping fermentation with a slug of powerful spirit is distinctly unnatural.

VIN JAUNE A speciality of the Jura region in France, made from the Savagnin grape. In Château-Chalon it is the only permitted style. Made in a similar way to fino sherry but not fortified. Unlike fino, *vin jaune* usually ages well.

VINIFICATION The process of turning grapes into wine.

VINO DA TAVOLA The Italian term for table wine, officially Italy's lowest level of production, is a catch-all that until recently applied to more than 80% of the nation's wine, with virtually no regulations controlling quality. Yet this category also provided the arena in the 1970s for the biggest revolution in quality that Italy has ever seen, with the creation of innovative, DOC-busting Super-Tuscans. *See* Super-Tuscans in main A–Z.

VINTAGE The year's grape harvest, also used to describe wines of a single year. 'Off-vintage' is a year not generally declared as vintage. *See* Port in main A–Z.

VITICULTURE Vine-growing and vineyard management.

VITIS VINIFERA Vine species, native to Europe and Central Asia, from which almost all the world's quality wine is made.

VQA (VINTNERS QUALITY ALLIANCE) Canadian equivalent of France's AC system, defining quality standards and designated viticultural areas.

WEISSHERBST German rosé wine, a speciality of Baden.

WO (WINE OF ORIGIN) South African system of appellations which certifies area of origin, grape variety and vintage.

YIELD The amount of fruit, and ultimately wine, produced from a vineyard. Measured in hectolitres per hectare (hl/ha) in most of Europe and in the New World as tons/acre or tonnes/hectare. Yield may vary from year to year, and depends on grape variety, age and density of the vines, and viticultural practices.

WHO OWNS WHAT

The world's major drinks companies are getting bigger and, frankly, I'm worried. As these vast wine conglomerates stride across continents, it seems highly likely that local traditions will – for purely business reasons – be pared away, along with individuality of flavour. It's not all bad news: in some cases wineries have benefited from the huge resources that come with corporate ownership, but I can't help feeling nervous knowing that the fate of a winery rests in the hands of distant institutional investors. Below I have listed some of the names that crop up again and again – and will no doubt continue to do so, as they aggressively pursue their grasp of market share.

Other wine companies – which bottle wines under their own names and therefore feature in the main A–Z – are gradually spreading their nets. KENDALL-JACKSON of California, for example, owns wineries in Chile, Argentina, Italy and Australia. GALLO, the second-biggest wine producer in the world, has an agreement with MCWILLIAM'S of Australia, and several areas report Gallo's interest in wineries. Robert MONDAVI is most famous for his wineries in California, but he also has interests in Italy and Chile, and, with the Rothschild family, co-owns OPUS ONE. The Rothschilds, in partnership with CONCHA Y TORO, produce ALMAVIVA in Chile, and have other interests in France besides the renowned Ch. MOUTON-ROTHSCHILD.

Cross-ownership is making it enormously difficult to know which companies remain independent, and the never-ending whirl of joint ventures, mergers and takeovers shows no signs of slowing down, which means that the following can only be a snapshot at the time of going to press. In 12 months time this list will probably look substantially different, as new players enter the arena and one giant gets gobbled up by another.

ALLIED DOMECQ UK-based group with a global wines and spirits portfolio. In 2001 it purchased New Zealand's MONTANA and Spain's Bodegas y Bebidas group (AGE/Siglo, CAMPO VIEJO and the prestigious Tarsus winery in Ribera del Duero). Brands include: ATLAS PEAK, Buena Vista, CLOS DU BOIS, William Hill and MUMM NAPA (California); Balbi and Graffigna (Argentina); COCKBURN (port); DOMECQ and Harveys (sherry); Marques de Arienzo (Rioja); MUMM and PERRIER-JOUET (Champagne). Allied Domecq has stakes in a number of Australian wineries, including Peter LEHMANN.

AXA-MILLESIMES The French insurance giant AXA's subsidiary owns Bordeaux châteaux PETIT-VILLAGE, PICHON-LONGUEVILLE, Pibran, Cantenac-Brown and SUDUIRAUT, plus TOKAJI producer Disznókö in Hungary and port producer Quinta do NOVAL.

BERINGER BLASS The wine division of Foster's, the brewers, takes its name from California's BERINGER and Australia's Wolf BLASS. In California it owns, among others, CARMENET, CHATEAU ST JEAN, Chateau Souverain, Meridian, St Clement, Stags' Leap Winery. Australian brands include Annie's Lane, BAILEYS of Glenrowan, Ingoldby, Jamiesons Run, Metala, Mildara, ROTHBURY ESTATE, Saltram (Mamre Brook), T'Gallant, Yellowglen. It also owns Castello di Gabbiano in Italy and MATUA VALLEY in New Zealand.

CONSTELLATION WINES The world's largest wine producer was created in 2003 by the merger of US-based wine, beer and spirits group Constellation Brands with Australia's BRL Hardy. California's Blackstone brand was the result of an earlier joint venture between the two giants. Other popular US brands include Paul Masson, Almaden, Inglenook and Covey Run. The FRANCISCAN Estates division makes wines from its Oakville estate and also owns Estancia, Mount Veeder Winery, RAVENSWOOD and Simi in California and Veramonte in Chile. BRL Hardy had already looked outside Australia, where brands include HARDYS, Banrock Station, BAROSSA VALLEY ESTATE, HOUGHTON, LEASINGHAM, Moondah Brook, REYNELL, Stonehaven and Yarra Burn, to New Zealand's NOBILO (Selaks, White Cloud) and Dom. de la BAUME in Languedoc – and in 2002 announced a joint venture with Stellenbosch Vineyards of South Africa. The UK's largest drinks wholesaler, Matthew Clark (which owns Stowells of Chelsea), is the UK division of Constellation Brands.

FREIXENET Spanish wine producer making a bid for global market share, with some of Spain's biggest names (including Castellblanch, Conde de Caralt, Segura Viudas, René Barbier) and wine companies in California and Mexico. It also owns the Champagne house of Henri Abelé, Bordeaux négociant/producer Yvon Mau and Australia's Wingara Wine Group (Deakin Estate, KATNOOK ESTATE, Riddoch Estate).

LVMH French luxury goods group Louis Vuitton-Moët Hennessy owns Champagne houses MOET & CHANDON (including Dom Pérignon), KRUG, Canard-Duchêne, Mercier, RUINART and VEUVE CLICQUOT, and has established DOMAINE CHANDON sparkling wine companies in California, Australia, Argentina and Spain. The purchase of Ch. d'YQUEM in 1999 was a major coup. It also owns CAPE MENTELLE and MOUNTADAM in Australia, CLOUDY BAY in New Zealand, NEWTON in California, and promising Argentinian winery Terrazas de los Andes.

PERNOD RICARD The French spirits giant owns the ORLANDO Wyndham Group (Australia), with Jacob's Creek; Etchart (Argentina); Long Mountain (South Africa); and has interests in wineries in China and Georgia.

SOUTHCORP Australia's biggest wine conglomerate, which merged with Rosemount in 2001. Brands include: Leo Buring, COLDSTREAM HILLS, Devil's Lair, James HERRICK (Languedoc-Roussillon), Kaiser Stuhl, Killawarra, Matthew Lang, LINDEMANS, PENFOLDS, Queen Adelaide, ROSEMOUNT ESTATE, Rouge Homme, Seaview, SEPPELT, Tollana, WYNNS.

NDEX OF PRODUCERS

303

305

306

311

319

ACKNOWLEDGEMENTS

Editor Maggie Ramsay; *Editorial Assistant* Kate Slotover;
Desktop Publishing Keith Bambury; *Cartographer* Andrew Thompson;
Proofreader Hugh Morgan; *Indexer* Angie Hipkin; *Production* Sara
Granger; *Art Director* Nigel O'Gorman; *Photography* Nigel James;
Managing Editor Anne Lawrance.

OLDER VINTAGE CHARTS *(top wines only)*

FRANCE

Alsace (vendanges tardives)										
90	89	88	85	83	81	76	71	69	61
10◆	9◆	8◆	8◆	9◆	7◇	10◆	9◇	8◇	9◇

Champagne (vintage)										
90	89	88	86	85	83	82	81	76	75
9◆	8◆	9◆	7◆	8◆	7◇	10◆	7◇	9◇	9◇

Bordeaux

	90	89	88	86	85	83	82	81	79	78
Margaux	10◇	8◇	7◆	8◆	8◆	9◆	8◆	7◇	6◇	7◆
St.-Jul., Pauillac, St-Est.	10◇	9◇	8◆	9◇	8◆	8◆	10◆	7◆	7◆	7◆
Graves/Pessac-L. (red)	8◇	8◇	8◆	6◆	8◆	8◆	9◆	7◆	7◇	8◆
St-Émilion, Pomerol	10◇	9◇	8◆	7◆	9◆	7◇	9◆	7◆	7◇	7◆

Bordeaux (cont.)

	75	70	66	62	61	59	55	53	49	47
Margaux (cont.)	6◇	8◆	7◇	8◇	10◆	8◇	6◇	8◇	9◇	8◇
St.-Jul. etc. (cont.)	8◇	8◆	8◆	9◇	10◆	9◇	8◇	9◇	10◇	9◇
Graves etc. (R) (cont.)	6◇	8◇	8◇	8◇	10◇	9◇	8◇	8◇	10◇	9◇
St-Émilion etc. (cont.)	8◇	8◆	6◇	8◇	10◇	7◇	7◇	8◇	9◇	10◇

Sauternes										
90	89	88	86	83	82	81	80	76	75
10◆	9◇	9◇	9◇	9◇	5◆	6◇	7◇	8◆	8◆

Sauternes (cont.)										
71	67	62	59	55	53	49	47	45	37
8◆	9◇	8◇	9◇	8◇	8◇	10◇	10◇	9◇	10◇

Burgundy

Chablis									
92	90	89	88	87	86	85
8◇	10◆	8◇	8◇	5◇	7◇	9◇

Côte de Beaune (wh.)									
92	90	89	88	86	85	82	79	78
8◆	7◇	9◆	6◇	8◇	9◇	6◇	8◇	8◇

Côte de Nuits (red)										
90	89	88	85	83	80	78	76	71	69
10◇	8◇	8◆	8◇	6◇	6◇	9◆	6◇	8◇	8◇

Oz Clarke's
Wine Buying Guide 2004

the essential companion to
Oz Clarke's Pocket Wine Book 2004

20TH
Anniversary
Edition

WEBSTERS

timewarner
b o o k s

A TIME WARNER/WEBSTERS BOOK

This edition first published in 2003 by
Time Warner Books UK
Brettenham House
Lancaster Place
LONDON WC2E 7EN
www.TimeWarnerBooks.co.uk

Created and designed by
Websters International Publishers Limited
Axe and Bottle Court
70 Newcomen Street
LONDON SE1 1YT
www.websters.co.uk
www.ozclarke.com

Oz Clarke's Wine Buying Guide 2004 edition
Copyright © 2003 Websters International Publishers
Text copyright © 1992–2003 Oz Clarke

A CIP catalogue for this book is available from the British Library

ISBN 0-316-72668-0

Printed and bound in Slovenia

The information and prices contained in the Guide were correct to the best of
our knowledge when we went to press.
Although every care has been taken in the preparation of the Guide, neither
the publishers nor the editors can accept any liability for any consequences
arising from the use of information contained herein.
Oz Clarke's Wine Buying Guide is an annual publication. We welcome any
suggestions you might have for the next edition.

Editor Maggie Ramsay
Art Director Nigel O'Gorman
Editorial Assistant Kate Slotover
DTP Consultant Keith Bambury
Production Sara Granger
Managing Editor Anne Lawrance

Cover photograph Nigel James
Cover painting David Dean

CORPORATE SALES
Companies, institutions and other organizations wishing to make
bulk purchases of this or any other Oz Clarke title published by
Time Warner Books UK should contact Special Sales on
+44 (0)20-7911 8933.

ADVERTISING SALES
Mongoose Media Limited
2 Lonsdale Road
LONDON NW6 6RD
tel (0)20-7306 0300, fax (0)20-7306 0301

Contents

Introduction

'There is no Coca-Cola of the winemaking world. We intend to be just that.' Sorry, did I hear that right? I sure did. This was the guy who is now in charge of the largest wine company in the world, giving his view of how he saw the future. It makes you want to weep.

It's especially depressing when you realize that inside the vast international behemoth that he heads there are such traditionally high-quality wineries as Hardys of Australia and the Franciscan Estates group in California. Both of these have always gone for flavour, character and a fair price in their wines. How does this guy square the global-domination-obsessed culture of something like Coke with the thrilling flavours of Eileen Hardy Shiraz, Franciscan Cuvée Sauvage Chardonnay, or Veramonte Sauvignon from their Chilean operation? How can a culture based on inexorable growth of dividends returned to shareholders and a relentless quest to increase market share at the expense of competitors also be sympathetic to the tribulations of vintage variation, voluntary reduction in yields to improve flavour, development of different high-quality terrains rather than of broad acres groomed for mechanization, preservation of ancient vines that yield little fruit but that are at the very heart of any fine wine culture? Has our wine world really come to this unsavoury pass?

COUNTING DOWN

Well, it's in real danger of doing so. The only wines such vast companies care about are their brands – big volume, heavily promoted and suicidally discounted brands. Just take a look around the wine aisles of some of our larger supermarkets, where for every shy cluster of good and interesting wines there's a barrage of brash brands crying buy one, get one free, three for the price of two, three for ten quid – and the rest. At first sight, it looks great – all this wine at such a discount. But think about it. Who's paying? Not the supermarkets. There's now such a glut of wine, particularly in places like Australia and California, that the supermarkets know the big companies have to shift their wine – at whatever cost. They know they've got millions of cases of wine they must move; there are tens, maybe hundreds, of thousands of tons of grapes about to turn up at the winery that will produce even more cases of wine in a few months time. And the supermarkets just sit there, waiting to be offered ridiculous promotional discounts. It's easy to blame the supermarkets, but as one head buyer said to me, 'It's a tap we can't turn off at the moment. Every Monday morning I have a queue of agents offering me massive discounts. What am I supposed to do? Say no?'

Of course not. And in the short term, we the consumers benefit from well-known names sold at silly prices. But do you actually like the taste of most of these heavily discounted wines? Isn't it becoming increasingly difficult to tell one brand from another, one country from another, one continent from another? You end up just buying whatever's the best deal. Brand loyalty goes out the window. The only brand you're faithful to is the supermarket itself. Almost 80% of the wine we buy is now from supermarkets. And one big New World brand ruefully admitted just recently that 98% of its wine is sold on deep discount! Take away the discount, lose the sale. But if you're big enough and aggressive enough, you'll be able to force smaller producers out of the market as you grind out your market share. Which in the long term will mean less choice, less quality and, once they've got rid of most of their competitors, higher prices.

David Williams, boss of Britain's biggest High Street wine group, Threshers, puts it bluntly. The New World brands 'have got themselves into a real bind with the supermarkets and they're being shagged to death.' Well put. And frankly, with the dilute, over-sweet quality of so much of their wine, should we really care, except to cast a brief sad glance backwards at what some of them, particularly the Australian brands, used to stand for?

GLOBAL WARNING
It's not just Australia. California is culpable, too – especially with its grape glut that has seen growers on the verge of insurrection and the price of Cabernet fall to $75 a ton: that represents about 7 cents for the juice in your £5 bottle of California Cab. No wonder the big companies who buy the grapes can afford deep discounts. But it's my long-term hero Australia who is causing me the most grief. Australia, at the end of the 1990s, brought out a grandi-loquent document labelling the first decade of the millennium the 'marketing' decade, outlining a strategy to make Australia the world's leading producer of branded wine – yes, just branded

wine – by 2025. Is this the same Australia which is losing hundreds of thousands of hectares of agricultural land to desertification every year? Is this the same Australia whose Murray River irrigates the majority of the nation's vineyards, and whose waters are now so damaged by land clearance on her banks and wanton irrigation that the river carries 5000 tonnes of salt leached from the land to the river mouth every single day – that's 18 tonnes every 5 minutes? If she took heed of the worried environmentalists on her own shores, Australia would realize that this feverish dash for volume growth can only bring long-term disaster.

As our tasting results show, the proud, determined, environmentally aware smaller growers are making some of Australia's best ever wine. This is the future for the parched acres of God's own country. Quality and individuality, not the crazed ambitions of marketing men. It was a Frenchman, Samuel Guibert de la Vaissière, of the Languedoc's outstanding Mas de Daumas Gassac winery, who put it best: 'Passion is the best brand.'

LOOKING UP

Happily, the good supermarkets do still have lots of interesting wines, and some, like Marks & Spencer and Waitrose, are going out of their way to avoid the herd mentality and actually improve their wine selections. This shows in increasingly interesting own labels, and in a really proactive attitude to areas like southern Portugal, inland Spain, southern France and southern Italy, where superb wines are available – usually for less than £5, sometimes for less than £4 – that should make the creators of pallid Australian Shiraz and limp Californian Chardonnay quake in their boots.

And then there are the Independent retailers. We had more independents entering their wines for our annual *Wine Buying Guide* tasting than ever before. There's a real sense of outrage at the dumbing down of our great British wine culture, and more and more men and women are taking up the challenge and starting wine companies. Well, this is our chance to show we won't be dumbed down, Coca Cola-ized. We have a great heritage of diversity and character in our wine world. Vote with your feet. Vote with your wallet. Wines of character and flavour – sold at a fair price, not artificially discounted – are in great profusion up and down the land. Let's keep it that way by buying them, or we may live to regret it.

Wine finder

RED WINES
VdP = Vin de Pays

Under £5
Argentinian Red, Milonga, Familia Zuccardi 68
Bonarda-Sangiovese, Santa Julia 82
Cabernet Sauvignon, Casillero del Diablo, Concha y Toro 38
Cabernet Sauvignon, Chilean, Viña Cornellana 65
Cabernet Sauvignon, Chilean, Viña San Pedro 69
Cabernet Sauvignon VdP d'Oc 71
Cabernet Sauvignon-Petit Verdot, Prospect Hill 67
Campo de Borja, Santo Cristo 65
Carignan, Ancient Vines, Les Marionettes, VdP de l'Aude 62
Carignan-Syrah, Nilia Estate 64
Carmenère, Peteroa 38
Castillo de Almansa 42
Chilean Red, Viña San Pedro 69
Cinsault-Ruby Cabernet, KWV 64
Claret, Patrice Calvet 69
Claret, Sainsbury's 70
Corbières, Ch. La Bastide 36
Corbières, Réserve de Reverend, Sichel 42
Cuvée Chasseur, VdP de l'Hérault 71
Cuvée de Richard, VdP de l'Aude 42
Estremadura, Cortello, Quinto do Gradil 65
Fitou, Mont Tauch 64
Garnacha, Calatayud, Viña Fuerte 64
Garnacha Old Vines, La Riada 34
Ch. Haut-Pradot 67
Jacques' French Organic Red, VdP du Gard 68
Merlot, The Society's Chilean, Concha y Toro 36

Mourvèdre-Shiraz, Tortoiseshell Bay 67
Navarra Crianza, Viña Sardasol 38
Nero d'Avola, Inycon 84
Petit Verdot, Kingston Estate 59
Pinot Noir, Recas 41, 83
Pinot Noir, Sainsbury's Romanian 70
Pinotage, Swartland 65
Ramada, DFJ Vinhos 41
Rioja, Sonsierra 37
Shiraz, Slinky 68
Shiraz, Snake Creek 41
Shiraz-Cabernet, Badgers Creek 70
Shiraz-Petit Verdot, Ransome's Vale 66
Shiraz-Pinotage, FirstCape 66
South African Red 68
Syrah VdP d'Oc, Mosaïque 41
Tempranillo, Cariñena 71
Tempranillo, Castillo de Alhambra 67
Touriga Franca & Tinta Roriz, Bela Fonte, DFJ Vinhos 36
Touriga Nacional & Touriga Franca, Estremadura, DFJ Vinhos 59
Trinacria Rosso Sicilia 71
Trincadeira-Cabernet Sauvignon, Sendo do Vale 84
Trincadeira-Castelão, Segada 37
Valdepeñas, Viña Albali Reserva, 39

£5–£10
The Advocate Red, David Owen, Bleasdale Wines 25
Les Alcusses 30
Beaujolais, Blaise Carron 82
Bobal-Tempranillo, Rozaleme 33
Cabernet Sauvignon, Chapel Hill 52
Cabernet Sauvignon, Neruda, Viñedos Sutil 31
Carmenère, Indomita Brio 30

Carmenère-Cabernet Sauvignon Reserve, Carmen 14
Carmènere-Cabernet Sauvignon, Novas, Viñedos Orgánicos Emiliana 28
Chianti Classico, Cafaggio 52
Chianti Rufina, Fattoria di Basciano 32
Chinon Vieilles Vignes, Dom. de la Chapelle 82
Côtes du Rhône, Mas de Libian 33
Côtes du Rhône Villages, Dom. de l'Enclos 32
Côtes du Rhône Villages Rasteau, Perrin 61
Côtes du Roussillon Villages, Dom. Gardiés 22
Coteaux du Languedoc, Ermitage du Pic St-Loup 56
Coteaux du Languedoc, Las Paures, Mas d'Auzières 30
Coteaux du Languedoc, Les Ruffes, La Sauvageonne 29
Coyam Red Wine, Viñedos Orgánicos Emiliana 19
Douro Reserva, Quinta de Fafide 54
Durif, Rutherglen Estates 60
The Fergus, Tim Adams 18
Garnacha Old Vine, Poema, Calatayud 54, 82
Gigondas, Cuvée de la Tour Sarrazine 21
Grenache-Shiraz-Mourvèdre, The Seven Surveys, Peter Lehmann 24
Grenache, Peter Lehmann 82
Lacrima di Morra d'Alba Rubico, Marotti Campi 83
Malbec, Anubis 29
Malbec-Corvina, Passo Doble, La Arboleda, Masi Tupungato 18, 84

7

Wine finder

Top twenty

The most encouraging thing about this year's tasting was how many more merchants were entering wines – and were winning through. In our top 20 there are 16 different merchants and only Oz Wines – biased? me? never! – managed three winners. And with ten of the top 20 wines, Australia continues to dominate this top end of the market by producing a whole range of thrilling wines at a fair price. Thank goodness the old Aussie individuality is still alive and kicking – at least among the smaller producers.

Please bear in mind that wine is not made in infinite quantities – some of these may well sell out, but the following year's vintage should then become available.

❶ 2000 Zinfandel, Nepenthe, Adelaide Hills, South Australia, ♟ £15.50, Vin du Van

What a wonderful, original, irresistible mouthful of Aussie red. I call it Aussie red, but they've used the great Californian grape, Zinfandel, to make it. Now, Zinfandel needs heat, and the Adelaide Hills are about the coolest, dampest place in South Australia, so I have no idea how they managed to ripen the grapes. But they did. They picked on 2 May (that's like 2 November up here) and produced a whopping 15.5% alcohol beautiful beast, rich with sultana and date sweetness, splashed with blackberry juice and smothered in custard and cream. The Californians will never forgive them.

JOINT WINNER

❶ 1999 Savennières, Clos du ♀ Papillon, Domaine des Baumard, Loire Valley, France, £11.95, La Réserve

This wine couldn't be more of a contrast with its co-holder of the top spot. This is coolness

personified – the haughty Chenin grape, the chill Loire Valley, the sombre, stern aspect of Savennières' vineyards and reputation. Fine, so it's not a barrel of laughs. But it *is* a truly delicious wine. Chenin wines are magnificent contradictions: harsh yet soft, forbidding yet calm, modern yet old. This is bone dry, but there's more to this wine than the initial taut slash of mineral taste, the biting lemon-lime acidity. If you're patient, a richness spreads across your tongue, of honey, of overweight bananas, peaches and brazil nuts dissolving into butter and cream. Above all, concentration, and a challenging individuality.

❸ 2000 Old Vine Zinfandel, Seghesio, Sonoma County, California, USA, £23.50, Liberty Wines

Zinfandel is a grape variety of excesses. All its personality is created during a last uproarious burst of sun-soaked ripening late in the season. Young vines picked early will make pallid rosé. Old vines picked late will give you a hedonists' fantasia of flavours – and 15.5% alcohol. The flavours here are so rich you think the wine has to be sweet. But the genius of Seghesio is that the wine is very, very dry. How can it be? The surge of blackberry and raspberry syrup, swirled with custard cream and dense dark chocolate has to be sweet. But it's not. *Also at Moriarty Vintners, Valvona & Crolla.*

❹ 2001 Shiraz, Tim Adams, Clare Valley, South Australia, £8.99, Tesco

This is the Adams 'basic' Shiraz, a term that sounds absurd when you taste how fine the wine is, with a texture like Viennese black chocolate melting in your palm on a hot summer's night, like double cream flowing thick and unwilling from a jug, like pepper, black cherries and fat red plums all laughing at each other's flavours, and as the morning sun carries rosehip on the breeze, the last stifling scents of midnight eucalyptus still linger in the air. £8.99 and it's all yours.

❺ 1997 Elmor's Ebenezer Old Vine Shiraz, Roehr Wines, Barossa Valley, South Australia, £19.90, Roger Harris

The Barossa keeps turning up sensational reds from producers whose ancestors cut the first sods of the valley vineyards back in the 19th century. Herr Roehr emigrated to Australia in 1841, his great-great-grandson farms the land today, and these vines are 80 years old. Who says Australia has no tradition? And this is brilliant, old-fashioned wine with a scented but haughty carapace of bark and polished cedar trying to restrain the rich beauty of dense black fruit and mint and eucalyptus gum that finally bursts out and floods your palate with pleasure.

For more wine recommendations see Oz Clarke's Wine Style Guide, pages 82–90

❻ 2000 Shiraz, Heartland Directors' Cut, Limestone Coast,
🍷 South Australia, £10.50, Great Western Wine
These are new guys on the block, and they're managing to
produce fantastic flavours at affordable prices. The wine is a
headspinning assault of licorice, chocolate and blackcurrant,
with refreshing acidity cutting through the thicket of
Harrogate toffee, peppermint and herbs. And at the end it's
almost as though someone has placed a drop of lime juice on
your tongue, just for a joke.

> *'...Harrogate toffee, peppermint and herbs...and a
> drop of lime juice on your tongue'*

❼ 2000 The Aberfeldy Shiraz, Tim Adams, Clare Valley,
🍷 South Australia, £18.50, Oz Wines
This is fantastic wine, but it is by no stretch of the
imagination beautiful. Yet. It will be, in 5 or 10 years time,
when it's tired of thumping its chest and baring its teeth and
roaring abuse to warn off misguided souls who might be
tempted to open a bottle, sort of... now? Well, if you're
misguided and brave, you can put some of this black liquid in
your mouth, and marvel at its rawhide leather chaps coated
with black prunes, black chocolate and black licorice
Pontefract cakes. And what's that? A soft, snowy scent wafts
by to lighten the darkness. It's gone. No, here it is again, like
crystallized violets on a chocolate cupcake – and it's gone
again. Wait 5 years. Wait 10, and the perfume will be in full
flow as this sumptuous rich black wine takes flight.

❽ 2000 Shiraz, Brothers in Arms, Langhorne Creek, South
🍷 Australia, £14, Tanners
Langhorne Creek has always been prized by the big
companies for providing succulent softness and sweet depth
to their top red wine blends, but there are a growing number
of independent producers showing just how good the fruit is
unblended. This has a sumptuous texture, fabulous burnt
toffee, chocolate, treacle and blackcurrant richness, as well as
a stern suggestion of pepper and licorice.

❾ 2000 Cabernet Sauvignon, Condé, Stark-Condé Wines,
🍷 Stellenbosch, South Africa, £17.95, H & H Bancroft
This Cabernet, from the gorgeous Jonkershoek Valley near
Stellenbosch, has a beauty to it the old Cape reds – hard and
mean and grumpy of mien – simply wouldn't be able to relate
to. It oozes blackcurrant ripeness and has a milk-fed fatty
flesh to it, but this is cut so sensitively by acidity and backed
by such a black depth that the balance is perfect.

❿ 1999 Carmenère-Cabernet Sauvignon Reserve, Carmen, Maipo Valley, Chile, £9.25, Wright Wine Co

Carmen, one of Chile's biggest wine companies, has wonderful vineyards near Santiago – some flat, some hilly – and top quality fruit. This wine is dark, fabulously ripe and awash with blueberry, black cherry and blackcurrant fruit, yet it also manages to cram in a violet scent, the rough resinous aroma of herbs, and a brilliant savoury depth halfway between coffee beans and a mouth-watering Sunday lunch mutton gravy. *Also at Berry Bros & Rudd.*

⓫ 2000 Cabernet Sauvignon, The Willows Vineyard, Barossa Valley, South Australia, £10.99, Philglas & Swiggot

Gosh, these guys are crowd-pleasers. I bet they flirted with all the girls when they were at school and broke every heart in the playground. For a Cabernet this wine is mesmerizingly smooth, with a peal of mint and eucalyptus laughter lightening up the fresh blackcurrant and black plum fruit. Lovely fruit, great balance.

⓬ 2000 Semillon, Tim Adams, Clare Valley, South Australia, £7.99, Tesco

The Clare Valley's Shiraz king is a pretty cool white wine guy too. He despises Chardonnay, but loves Semillon and makes it in a gloriously unashamed deep golden old-fashioned way. Old leather, old beeswax polish, old blowzy peach and quince and medlar fruit – all time-worn autumn flavours and absolutely magnificent with it.

⓭ 2000 Evo, Guelbenzu, Ribera del Queiles, Navarra, Spain, £14.99, Moreno Wines

Guelbenzu, one of the leading lights in the Navarra wine scene, have given up labelling their wines as Navarra out of disgust at what they see as the stifling effects of bureaucratic meddling. And freed from the shackles they're making their best wine ever. This is a tremendous, dense, deep red – or should I say purple – wine, with an almost overpowering pile of blackcurrant and black cherry fruit soused in chocolate and cream and topped off with the cool sweet scent of cedar.

⓮ 2000 Cabernet Sauvignon, Santa Isabel Estate, Casablanca, Casablanca Valley, Chile, £10.99, Moreno Wines

The word 'blackcurrant' comes up a lot in tasting notes. That's because the Cabernet Sauvignon grape, when it's ripe, positively reeks of mouth-watering blackcurrant and, to a lesser extent, so do Shiraz, Merlot and Tempranillo – and probably quite a few others as well. It is a lovely and unforgettable taste in a wine, and few wines have a purer taste of blackcurrant than this single-estate Chilean Cabernet, with a sophisticated whiff of cedar to add an extra touch of class.

⑮ 2001 Crozes Hermitage, Alain Graillot, Rhône Valley, France, £10.62, Anthony Byrne

Talk about elegance. *This* is elegance. Graillot is one of the most talented winemakers in France's Rhône Valley, but he doesn't have the best vineyards. So instead of trying to carve out an extra concentration that his grapes simply don't possess, he opts for elegance, quite unlike the overoaked Syrah pantechnicons that the northern Rhône Valley is currently spawning and totally unlike the fruit bomb Shirazes of Australia. Instead we get a wine with an ethereal lily-flower scent, pure fresh blackberry fruit and silky creamy texture, all in perfect balance. A delight.

Entirely Italian

SPARKLING
Brachetto d'Acqui, Contero (page 46)
Lambrusco, Concerto (page 46)
Prosecco, Ruggeri (page 45)

WHITE
Catarratto-Chardonnay, Firriato (page 68)
Pinot Bianco La Prendina, Cavalchina (page 36)
Soave Classico Superiore, Inama (page 55)
Trinacria Bianco Sicilia (page 69)
Verdicchio dei Castelli di Jesi Classico, Sartarelli (page 31)

RED
Barbera d'Alba, Serraboella, Cigliuti (page 21)
Chianti Classico, Basilica Caffagio (page 52)
Chianti Rufina, Fattoria di Basciano (page 32)
Graticciaia, Vallone (page 24)
Nero d'Avola, Abbazia Santa Anastasia (page 33)
Noà, Nero d'Avola-Cabernet Sauvignon-Merlot, Cusumano (page 15)
Squinzano Rosso, Cantine Due Palme (page 32)
Tassinaia, Castello del Terriccio (page 25)
Trinacria Rosso Sicilia (page 71)

⑯ 2000 Shiraz, The Willows Vineyard, Barossa Valley, South Australia, £10.99, Oz Wines

This beautiful rich red has a heady scent that starts out as pure mint and blackcurrant, and then adds the extra dimension of Benylin cough linctus. They couldn't have, could they? Well, I wouldn't put it past them – anything in the pursuit of pleasure. And this is pure pleasure: chocolate, blackcurrant and mint, freshened up with lime.

⑰ 2001 Noà, Nero d'Avola-Cabernet Sauvignon-Merlot, Cusumano, Sicily, Italy, £14.49, Oddbins

Sicily grows both local and international grapes very well, but the greatest excitement is with local varieties like Nero

An accurate tasting note on a wine label! The label also suggests tropical fruit – and again, I agree. A lovely scented peach and nectarine softness that is bound together by an acidity that has an almost rhubarb intensity. Delicious modern Sauvignon. *Also at James Nicholson.*

❺ 2000 The Fergus, Tim Adams, Clare Valley, South Australia, £9.99, Majestic

Powerful stuff. These are old Grenache vines, low yielding and planted in the sun-kissed Clare Valley, so expect a fair whack of alcohol – you get it – and a sensory battle royal as juicy ripe strawberries try desperately to keep their scented heads above a broiling cauldron full of herbs, black treacle and licorice.

❻ 1999 Malbec-Corvina, Passo Doble, La Arboleda, Masi Tupungato, Mendoza, Argentina, £8.99, Bring-a-Bottle and Berkmann

What a brilliant idea. Signor Masi, from Valpolicella in north-eastern Italy, takes the great Valpolicella grape, Corvina, combines it with the great Argentine grape, Malbec, makes the wine in the special 'double fermentation' method that produces the best Valpolicella, and comes up with this super-powered red redolent of Argentine soil but with a Venetian soul. It's a brawny, muscular mix of sultanas and cherry cake, chocolate and plums – but with a haunting mix of sweet sourness and bitterness like sour cherries squashed together with their kernels and licked with fish oil. Ah, fish oil – that's the Malbec's traditional (and curiously delicious) calling card.

❼ 1998 Riesling, Grand Cru Geisberg, Kientzler, Alsace, France, £15.50, H & H Bancroft

'Grand Cru' should mean the wine is from low-yielding vines in a tip-top vineyard. Well, that depends on the grower. But Kientzler is a serious operator and this wine is a delight, deftly managing to be both rich and austere, balancing honey with petrol and lime and then showing the power of the vineyard by producing a remarkable flavour of place, almost like double cream smeared over the pale golden stones.

❽ 2000 Joseph Cabernet Sauvignon-Merlot, Moda Amarone, Primo Estate, Fleurieu-Limestone Coast, South Australia, £18.99, Harvey Nichols

When this wine is mature, at 10, 15 years old, its astonishing mixture of profound richness and skeetering sourness turns it into one of Australia's greatest red wine achievements. At this young age it's so closed in and dark that it's difficult to discern anything more than the black weight of its power. But it's been made according to the traditional 'double fermentation' method of Valpolicella in Italy, and, like the great Italian Amarones, this dark beast of bitter herbs and black chocolate and black peppercorns all crushed together in a mesh of tannin and acidity will be rich, rare and brilliant in 10 years' time. Or maybe even longer.

9 **2001 Coyam Red Wine, Viñedos Orgánicos Emiliana, Valle Central, Chile, £8.95, Vintage Roots**

Organic wine from the inspired Alvaro Espinoza, making overdue use of the perfect vineyard conditions in Chile. This is expertly balanced ripe red wine full of deep, dark blackcurrant and black plum fruit, hardly tickled by the tannins and acidity that will allow it to age beautifully and gracefully.

Kiwi fruit

SPARKLING
Morton Premium Brut (page 44)

WHITE
Chardonnay, Stonecroft (page 16)
Pinot Gris, Villa Maria Private Bin (page 60)
Riesling, Waipara West (page 23)
Sauvignon Blanc, Craggy Range (page 56)
Sauvignon Blanc, Fairleigh Estate (page 29)
Sauvignon Blanc, Forrest Estate (page 17)
Sauvignon Blanc, Shepherds Ridge, Wither Hills (page 62)
Sauvignon Blanc, Tesco Finest (page 63)

RED
Pinot Noir, Bald Hills Vineyard, Valli (page 17)
Pinot Noir, Hope Vineyard, Greenhough (page 20)
Pinot Noir, Floating Mountain, Mark Rattray (page 21)

10 **2000 Pinot Gris, T'Gallant Tribute, Mornington Peninsula, Victoria, Australia, £11.95, Vin du Van**

Pinot Gris is becoming a very fashionable grape in the cooler parts of the world: Oregon in the USA, New Zealand, and places like Mornington Peninsula, south of Melbourne in Australia. I can see why. This manages to be appetizingly dry, but contentedly rich, the honey and dried peach fruit enjoying a very easy relationship with the savoury smack of freshly grilled and salted cashew nuts.

11 **2000 Gigondas, 'Les Blâches', Patrick Lesec Sélections, Rhône Valley, France, £13.45, Gauntley's**

Gigondas is one of those ancient vineyard areas of the southern Rhône where the sun literally bakes the grapes on the vine. Which explains the thick, churning power of its reds, high in alcohol and challenging on the tongue. However, the best wines avoid being too bumptiously aggressive, and this example has enough sultana, black chocolate and sweet plum richness to jostle along very good-naturedly with the resinous rasping scents of pepper, bay leaf and thyme.

Best buys

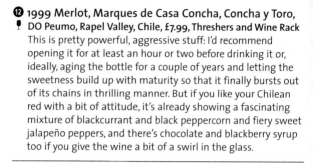

❶❷ 1999 Merlot, Marques de Casa Concha, Concha y Toro, DO Peumo, Rapel Valley, Chile, £7.99, Threshers and Wine Rack
This is pretty powerful, aggressive stuff: I'd recommend opening it for at least an hour or two before drinking it or, ideally, aging the bottle for a couple of years and letting the sweetness build up with maturity so that it finally bursts out of its chains in thrilling manner. But if you like your Chilean red with a bit of attitude, it's already showing a fascinating mixture of blackcurrant and black peppercorn and fiery sweet jalapeño peppers, and there's chocolate and blackberry syrup too if you give the wine a bit of a swirl in the glass.

---

❶❸ 2002 Chardonnay, Allandale, Hunter Valley, New South Wales, Australia, £7.99, Reid Wines
Delightful, characterful Aussie Chardonnay. This has gentle ripe peach fruit, stylishly set off by lemon acidity and grilled cashew smoke, and just enough of the traditional Hunter Valley lanolin and leather to let you know where it comes from. *Also at Australian Wine Club, Moriarty Vintners, Oz Wines.*

---

❶❹ 2001 Shiraz, Spear Gully, Limestone Coast-McLaren Vale-Yarra Valley, Australia, £13.99, Oz Wines
This Shiraz is blended from vineyards in warm McLaren Vale, cool Limestone Coast and even cooler Yarra Valley. The result is a wine of balance, finesse and decidedly original flavours: Victoria plums, bitter but rich chocolate, and a half-floral half-furious peppertree scent.

---

❶❺ 2000 Terroirs des Châteaux Forts, Rolly Gassmann, Alsace, France, £7.95, The Wine Society
There is a move in Alsace to place more emphasis on the *terroir* – the actual vineyard site – and less on the grape varieties. Ideally you'd catch the mineral excitement of many of the vineyards without losing the heavenly Alsace fruit. This manages it pretty well: a certain acid austerity runs like a dart through the wine, but it merely serves to emphasize the delightful rose petal scent and honeyed peach richness.

---

❶❻ 2001 Pinot Noir, Hope Vineyard, Greenhough, Nelson, New Zealand, £15.95, Lay & Wheeler
A seductively gentle, cooing kind of red with deep ripe strawberry fruit, some cherry syrup, a little toast and rather more of a creaminess like really good mum's rice pudding.

---

❶❼ 2000 Ancient Vines Mourvèdre, Cline, Contra Costa County, California, USA, £14.60, The Wine Treasury
I'm truly grateful for the band of California originals and eccentrics whose mission it is firstly to preserve these gnarled

old vines, miles away from trendy areas on the coast, and then lovingly to exploit their fruit. This isn't cheap, but the wine is fascinating, trading on a seam of bitterness that needs all the date and sultana viscosity the grapes can muster – and it gets it. *Also at Philglas & Swiggott, Virgin Wines.*

⑱ 2000 Carignane, Wild Hog Vineyard, Saini Farms, Dry Creek Valley, California, USA, £19.99, The Winery
If the smart alecs and marketing maestros of Californian wine had their way, curmudgeonly old grape varieties like Carignane would have been uprooted aeons ago. But there's a movement of anti-establishment grape growers who cosset and cherish these last pockets of California's vineyard history and make spectacular wines out of them – not subtle, not elegant, but bursting with old-time personality. This tastes almost sweet-sour, cherry and plum, like a Cantonese sauce – and it's rich, super-rich even, with a bit of cream sploshing about and some sprigs of hillside herbs.

> *'...sweet-sour, like a Cantonese sauce...with a bit of cream sploshing about and some hillside herbs'*

⑲ 2001 Pinot Noir, Floating Mountain, Mark Rattray Waipara, New Zealand, £10.25, Waterloo Wine Co
Mark Rattray is a bit of a wild man in the New Zealand wine world, definitely a free spirit, so I like the idea of him calling his Pinot Noir 'Floating Mountain'. It has an attractively nebulous, unchained feel to it, and the wine floats free too, on a magic carpet of strawberry and soft creamy contentment.

⑳ 1998 Gigondas, Cuvée de la Tour Sarrazine, Archimbaud-Vache, Rhône Valley, France, £8.95, The Wine Society
1998 was a heroic year in the southern Rhône, with the grapes bulging with sugar and just begging to be picked before they burst by the time harvest came. You can really taste the heat here – the mirage haze of hillside herbs, the superripe red fruit turning almost to sultana syrup, the meaty, beefy texture, and the shimmering heat of broad flat stones baked and scorched all summer long.

㉑ 2000 Barbera d'Alba, Serraboella, Cigliuti, Piedmont, Italy, £15.50, Morris & Verdin
Barbera is a smashing grape, with one great virtue rare in Italy: it's low in tannin and high in acidity, which means that not only does it make excellent food wine, but you can usually also get a lot of fun drinking the wine by itself. This is powerful stuff, but the relative absence of tannin frees the

floral and cedar scent and the rich plum sauce and cigar tobacco flavours so that they don't jangle on your unsuspecting palate, they dance.

㉒ 2001 Riesling, Howard Park, Great Southern,
♀ **Western Australia, £9.95, Lay & Wheeler**
For wine lovers tired of oak, this wine is pure fruit – Bramley apples, lemon and lime zest and passionfruit – it reminds me of the juice in the bottom of a bowl of fruit salad (though my mum always adds rosewater to hers – well, perhaps there is *something* floral here). It's really just a vibrant celebration of everything zesty and citrus with just a finger dip of honey.

㉓ 1999 Cabernet Sauvignon, Floresta, Santa Rita,
♥ **Fundo Apalta, Colchagua Valley, Chile, £14.99, Berkmann**
I know these Apalta vineyards – they're rocky, steep and difficult to tame. We've seen few wines from their daunting slopes as yet, but this turbo-charged red, roaring almost out of control across our palates – but with sweet blackberry fruit and thick chocolate cream hanging ragged in the jetstream – shows the kind of thing we can expect in the future.

㉔ 2000 Châteauneuf-du-Pape, Jean & Jean-Paul Versino,
♥ **Rhône Valley, France, £13.75, Jeroboams**
I don't know how Châteauneuf-du-Pape ever manages to produce perfumed wines, but it does. It's not all easy traffic: this wine is quite tannic, and you can taste the heat of the stones ready to blister the feet of anyone foolish enough to slip off their sandals, but through all this drives a magic caravan of lilies and blueberries and herbs – and there even seems to be a veil of violets acting as the fringe on top.

㉕ 2002 Colombard, La Biondina, Primo Estate,
♀ **Adelaide, South Australia, £7.50, Harvey Nichols**
The Colombard's main claim to fame is as one of the base wine producers for Armagnac brandy, and in hot countries it's normally used as a junk grape solely because it keeps some acidity in near-desert conditions. So this could well be the world's best Colombard. There may not be much competition, but that shouldn't stop you relishing this lovely, full, dry white, with lanolin weight, honeysuckle perfume, goldengage ripeness and green apple peel acidity nipping at its heels.

㉖ 2000 Côtes du Roussillon Villages, Les Millères,
♥ **Domaine Gardiés, Languedoc-Roussillon, France,**
£7.95, Jeroboams
This is a remarkable Roussillon red, because although it's easy to make big gutsy reds in this rocky hothouse region down

near the Pyrenees, perfume is a much bigger ask. But this wine has a positively swoony perfume of violets, floating above a turbulent red whirlpool of ripe damson fruit and chewy, grainy tannin.

㉗ 2000 Riesling, Waipara West, Tutton Sienko & Hill,
♀ **Canterbury, New Zealand, £8.49, Waterloo Wine Co**
New Zealand's Rieslings are usually very good, in a dry yet relatively soft, perfumed style. However, Waipara West grows their Riesling on harsh, barely tamed land well away from the region's other vineyards, and produces an uncompromising wine – very dry, initially a little severe, but quickly the compelling aroma of petrol and lime zest mixes with a rich but dry honeyed weight.

㉘ 2001 Pinot Noir, Shadowfax, Yarra Ranges & Geelong,
♂ **Victoria, Australia, £12.75, Wright Wine Co**
Pinot Noir likes cool conditions and Shadowfax has certainly gone cool to find the fruit for this: Yarra Ranges is one of the coolest bits of cool Yarra and Geelong is quite simply a tough place to get a crop at all. Well, the effort pays off, because this is smooth, mellow red, a soft-hearted mix of strawberry fruit, clean new leather perfume and bright vanilla cream with a tiny ripple of red cherry sweetness right at the end.

㉙ 1999 Old Vine Zinfandel, Clayton Estate Vineyard,
♂ **Lodi, California, USA, £19.99, The Winery**
They don't exactly give these old vine Zinfandels away, but you certainly get a great thick whack of taste for your buck. Old vines give more intense flavours and this is seriously intense – a thick deep superripe stew of caramel, dates and raisins and rich black plum sauce.

㉚ 2001 Saint-Véran, Les Vieilles Vignes, Domaine
♀ **Saumaize-Michelin, Burgundy, France, £9.99, Raeburn**
Old vines à la Française. This shows what a tasty and characterful grape Chardonnay can be if you don't mess about with it too much. It has a honeyed scent, a rich texture of syrup and honey, a dab of cream toffee and an appetizing acidity somewhere between apple flesh and lemon meringue pie lightly browned on the top under the grill.

㉛ 2001 Crozes Hermitage, Cuvée Albéric Bouvet, Gilles
♂ **Robin, Rhône Valley, France, £12.75, Great Western Wine**
There really is some very fragrant red being made in the northern Rhône right now, and the increasing number of independent growers in Crozes Hermitage are providing a fair few of them. This has a beguiling mix of lily perfume,

blackberry fruit and rosehip syrup richness that all tails off
contentedly to a lingering flavour of Turkish Delight.

**❸❷ 1996 Graticciaia, Agricole Vallone, Salento Rosso,
Puglia, Italy, £25, The Wine Society**
25 quid? – it's certainly good – but 25 quid? Even so, this is
powerful stuff: rich and deep, and it seems to get richer and
deeper the longer you leave it in your mouth. It manages to
combine the gooey dark brown flavours of sultana and raisin
and date without ever toppling backwards into overripeness.

**❸❸ 2000 Shiraz, Juniper Crossing, Juniper Estate,
Margaret River, Western Australia, £8.99, Adnams**
Very tasty Shiraz with loads of rich flavours that make you
sure the wine will be on the sweet side – but it isn't, it's
appetizingly dry. In fact it's the balance that makes the wine
so good: somehow the winemaker has had to try to keep
chocolate, coconut cream, plums, blackcurrant and vanilla all
in line – and he's managed it. Lovely.

**❸❹ 1999 The Seven Surveys, Grenache-Shiraz-Mourvèdre,
Peter Lehmann, Barossa Valley, South Australia,
£7.99, Threshers and Wine Rack**
The three great old red grapes of Australia all thrown into the
pot by Barossa supremo Peter Lehmann. It's not a blockbuster,
but it's really interesting stuff, full of strawberry and
blackberry fruit, licorice depth and a fairly aggressive thyme
and peppercorn scent and flavour that is most refreshing in a
Barossa red. *Also at Booths, Jeroboams, Mills Whitcombe.*

**❸❺ 2001 Lirac, Cuvée de la Reine des Bois, Domaine de la
Mordorée, Rhône Valley, France, £8, H & H Bancroft**
We hardly ever see Lirac over here, and the few we do see are
usually red or rosé (Lea & Sandeman have the very good
Mordorée red), but this is a serious white, with a honeysuckle
and pear blossom scent – bright, modern, come-hither – yet a
much more old-fashioned feel and flavour in the mouth, of
nut husks, apple purée and honey.

**❸❻ 2001 Montsant, La Planella, Joan d'Anguera,
Cataluña, Spain, £8.25, Laymont & Shaw**
Big, thick, dark, deep, stewy red – that sounds like Priorat,
currently the most overpriced wine in Spain. And this wine,
from Priorat's neighbour, Montsant, is a Priorat lookalike: a
rich fig and toffee core, with fistfuls of pepper and herbs
hurled in, mineral dust swirling about, tannin biting at your
gums and reprimanding the dark, deep, stewy fruit. This really
is the Priorat experience on the cheap.

㊲ 2000 Tassinaia, Castello del Terriccio, Tuscany, Italy,
£19.95, Lea & Sandeman
Fascinating wine from a relatively new but highly successful
vineyard on the Bolgheri coast of Tuscany. It's a mix of the
Tuscan Sangiovese grape variety with Bordeaux's Cabernet
Sauvignon and Merlot, and the result is a big, weighty wine
full of rich red fruit with red cherries to the fore. It's quite
tannic and has an unusual but delicious acidity rather like the
skin of a nectarine.

㊳ 2000 The Advocate Red, David Owen, Bleasdale Wines,
Langhorne Creek, South Australia, **£9.99,** Australian Wine Club
Fat, rich red, full of the typical ripe, round Langhorne Creek
fruit of stewed cherries and plums and blackcurrant abetted
by a little oak sweetness, but this one also has a dollop of
Petit Verdot – good idea! It adds a bright floral scent and lifts
the wine up to another level.

㊴ 2000 Merlot, Shottesbrooke, McLaren Vale, South
Australia, **£8.50,** Roger Harris
Merlot is a cool-climate grape that doesn't usually do all that
well in Australia. I certainly wouldn't expect it to do well in
McLaren Vale, an area south of Adelaide that can resemble a
cauldron on many summer days. But this one really works –
and it really tastes like Merlot – good, sweet, blackcurrant
fruit, a dab of soft oak and an uplifting perfume of fresh mint.

㊵ 2000 Shiraz, Classic McLaren, McLaren Vale, South
Australia, **£13.99,** Oz Wines
You certainly stand up to be counted when you start labelling
your wine 'classic'. But this Shiraz delivers. McLaren Vale heat
creates a rich, robust style of wine and this offers a satisfying
gobful of chocolate, black plum and blackcurrant seasoned
with a swatch of leather still smelling slightly of campfire
smoke. Good, typical McLaren.

*'...blackcurrant seasoned with a swatch of leather
still smelling slightly of campfire smoke'*

㊶ 2001 Shiraz, Rivermist Vineyards, Frankland Estate,
Western Australia, **£8,** Morris & Verdin
The far south of Western Australia is thought of as white
wine country, but I'm seeing more and more Shirazes that are
bursting with flavour, but have the balance and brightness of
the cool climate they're grown in. This is dry, but full of
blackberry and blackcurrant fruit, Fowler's Black Treacle depth
and a whiff of cedar. Lovely now, it'll age.

Oz Clarke's
Pocket Wine Book 2004
More information, more opinion, passion, facts, figures and
recommendations than any other comparable guide.
£10.00 h/b

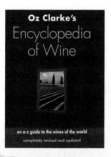

Oz Clarke's
Encyclopedia of Wine
Completely revised and updated

A comprehensive armchair
reference, with a truly vast amount
of up-to-date wine information.
£18.99 p/b

Oz Clarke
& Margaret Rand
Grapes and Wines

The definitive new guide to the
world's great grapes and the wines
they make.
£18.99 p/b

Oz Clarke's
Introducing Wine
Revised edition
The ultimate no-nonsense guide to wine. No jargon.
No frills. No previous knowledge assumed.
£8.99 p/b

Under £7

The UK's big operations, with tons of money and clout, can say to a producer – I'm selling this for £4.99 and I demand this much profit margin. Do you want to do business or don't you? The independent merchants generally prefer a more civilized method of doing business. They look for quality and individuality in their wines, they ask the producer for an honest price and then calculate whether or not they can afford to sell it and provide themselves with a profit margin. If they can't, they don't bully the producer, they simply don't deal in that wine. This price point is the heartland of the independent wine merchant, full of delicious, interesting wines, often from less trendy areas, less trendy grape varieties, but packed with character and worth every penny. We found a stunning array of wines, and at least as many again that were unlucky not to win through.

❶ 2001 Bergerac Sec, Cuvée des Conti, Château Tour des Gendres, South-West France, £6.50, Les Caves de Pyrène

This wine is so good it would have easily made it into the overall top ten, but since it *is* under seven quid, I thought – let it sit proudly and gloriously as this year's best wine at under £7. Luc de Conti, who owns this chateau, makes wines of seamless beauty, where colour and tannin, acidity and fruit are all bound together by gossamer, emotionally intertwined like life partners lucky in love. This is particularly evident in his red wines, but for a wine of sheer fruit-ripe beauty, like the most perfect white peach, the most glowing nectarine picked straight from the bough, so eager to be devoured you can suck the perfumed flesh from the stone, this is hard to beat.

❷ 2001 Carmenère-Cabernet Sauvignon, Novas, Viñedos Orgánicos Emiliana, Valle Central, Chile, £5.95, Vintage Roots

Alvaro Espinoza is one of Chile's trailblazers. Having masterminded the revival of the fine Carmen winery, he has struck out on his own, following an organic discipline. Organic vineyards are still rare in Chile, but the climate there is almost perfect for herbicide- and pesticide-free farming, so we will see a lot more organic wine in years to come. This is a brilliant marriage between the earthy, casserole-rich vegetal flavours of Carmenère and the black plum and blackcurrant sweetness of Cabernet. Add a little scented oak and a streak of mineral power, and you've got a fantastic bottle of red.

For more wine recommendations see Oz Clarke's Wine Style Guide, pages 82–90

❸ 2002 Verdelho, Chapel Hill, McLaren Vale, South Australia, £6.99, Waitrose

Verdelho is one of the original white wine grapes brought to Australia in the 19th century – *long* before Chardonnay found its way south. Verdelho is a Madeira grape, and was initially planted to make fortified wine in Australia, too. But as demand for that has waned, one or two growers have realized that Verdelho has the great ability to keep its freshness and vivacity even under the torrid cloudless skies of South Australia. Chapel Hill's brilliant winemaker Pam Dunsford has patiently worked on Verdelho for years, and this is her best effort yet – a thrillingly lemony style that isn't just lemon acidity but lemon flower and apple blossom too, and whose bite is massaged by honey and a nut softness that is delightful and marvellously refreshing. *Also at Oz Wines.*

❹ 2001 Coteaux du Languedoc, Les Ruffes, La Sauvageonne, Languedoc-Roussillon, France, £5.99, Virgin Wines

Les Ruffes, La Sauvageonne. Those French words imply that this wine is likely to apply fisticuffs to your palate. But the true savagery of the hillside vineyards of France's Languedoc lies not in bludgeoning power but uplifting scent and the glories of the warm open air and a broad blue sky. This is deep and dark, sure, but it's wonderfully scented with outdoor violets crushed greedily in your hand and cast into a cauldron of sweet dark fruits – damsons and blackcurrants and loganberries all flung together in the dervish dance.

❺ 2002 Sauvignon Blanc, Fairleigh Estate Single Vineyard, Marlborough, New Zealand, £6.99, Majestic

Kiwi Sauvignon Blanc has gone up in price rather alarmingly recently and after the small 2003 harvest we could see the price rise further still, so it is nice to find an example at £6.99 that is not only excellent, but is made by Brent Marris of Wither Hills, one of New Zealand's trendiest winemakers. What he's done here is to make a Sauvignon that is positively low key in New Zealand's rather ebullient terms, but it works because it is beautifully fresh, and somehow manages to be soft yet green – soft fluffy apple flesh blends easily with streaks of lime, passionfruit, capsicum and even gooseberry.

❻ 2002 Malbec, Anubis, Mendoza, Argentina, £5.99, Liberty Wines

Malbec is a grape variety that originated in Bordeaux, where it doesn't ripen properly; migrated up the Dordogne to Cahors – where it also rarely ripens – and finally got itself on a ship to Argentina, where it ripens so well that it is now the most valued variety in the country – but until the last few years, no-one seemed to know how to turn this luscious, scented grape into decent wine. They're getting there. Just try this big, spicy red, gorged with damson and blackberry fruit and blessed with a heady violet scent. Rich, dry, ridiculously approachable – and a fair price. *Also at Waitrose.*

---

❼ 2001 Mâcon-Farges, Cave Talmard, Burgundy, France, £6.95, The Wine Society

The Mâconnais region of Burgundy hasn't done itself many favours in recent years – uninspired co-operatives dominating the scene and growers allowed to get away with gross overproduction because no-one really cared. Well, the growers in the village of Uchizy, where this Mâcon comes from, are starting to make the best of their vines. This is perfectly ripe Chardonnay, full of honey and pineapple chunks, melon and angelica richness – all the natural flavours of really good Chardonnay, unsullied by the heavy thud of the oak barrel.

---

❽ 2000 Les Alcusses, Valencia, Spain, £6.99, Moreno Wines

This wine is a thudder. But it's supposed to be. It comes from the seriously hot vineyards of Valencia, where the grapes are bulging with ripeness. This is a powerful brew that almost goes too far, but the intense richness of dates and figs and a welcome scrape of tannin keep it on the right side of OTT.

---

❾ 2001 Las Paures, Mas d'Auzières, Coteaux du Languedoc, Laurent Vidal, Languedoc-Roussillon, France, £6.99, James Nicholson

Rich, powerful, hedonistic wine. The fruit positively explodes in the glass, and a sweet tide of raspberry and blackberry surges on to your palate on the coattails of a big old-fashioned wodge of date, fig and sultana ripeness.

---

❿ 1999 Grand' Arte Touriga Francesa, DFJ Vinhos, Estremadura, Portugal, £6.99, Sainsbury's

Intensely dark, deep wine, with fruit and herbs all piled on top of each other, fighting furiously for supremacy. The fruit wins out, indigo dark, black cherries coiled in embrace with sloes steeped in gin and blackberries stewed in syrup.

⓫ 2001 Carmenère, Indomita Brio, Rapel Valley, Chile, £5.83, Anthony Byrne

Carmenère is a grape variety – a fantastically good one – that gives wine of thrilling individuality, starting off in a blaze of ripe blackberry and black cherry fruit that almost immediately has to share centre stage with a positively shocking savoury intensity, like celery and beef casserole laced with black pepper, coffee beans and soy sauce, before a delightful aftertaste where the sweetness of the berry fruit returns and lingers for quite a while.

12 2002 Shiraz, Stellar Organics, South Africa, £6.50, Vintage Roots
This has rich plum and blackberry fruit made even richer by sultana sweetness, just enough tannin to keep the palate fresh, and a wisp or two of the coal smoke that often marks out a red as being from the Cape.

13 2001 Organic Pinot Noir, Barra Vineyards, California, USA, £6.75, Vintage Roots
Good Pinot Noir at less than £7 is not easy to find. Add to that the fact that this is organic (expensive) and it's from California (v. expensive), and this is beginning to look like a bit of a steal. It's gentle, ripe, beguiling, with soft strawberry fruit and a small smear of cream to soothe your palate.

> ## Rhône sharks
>
> **WHITE**
> Lirac, Cuvée de la Reine des Bois, Dom. de la Mordorée (page 24)
>
> **RED**
> Châteauneuf-du-Pape, J & J-P Versino (page 22)
> Côtes du Rhône, Mas de Libian (page 33)
> Côtes du Rhône Villages, Dom. de l'Enclos, Guy Dours (page 32)
> Côtes du Rhône Villages Rasteau, Perrin (page 61)
> Crozes Hermitage, Alain Graillot (page 15)
> Crozes Hermitage, Cuvée Albéric Bouvet, Gilles Robin (page 23)
> Gigondas, Cuvée de la Tour Sarrazine, Archimbaud-Vache (page 21)
> Gigondas, 'Les Blâches', Patrick Lesec (page 19)

---

14 2000 Cabernet Sauvignon, Estate Reserve, Neruda, Viñedos Sutil, Colchagua, Chile, £6.99, Army & Navy, Victoria, London SW1 (020) 7834 1234, and Unwins
Dark, toasty, black-fruited wine. Strong, serious, satisfying. On the label is the Chilean poet Neruda's *Ode to Wine*. It's rather good: 'Day-colored wine,/ Night-colored wine,/ wine with purple feet/ or wine with topaz blood,/ wine, starry child of earth,/ wine, smooth as a golden sword, /soft as lascivious velvet.' Well, he gets a bit carried away towards the end, but it does save the winemaker having to write a tasting note.

---

15 2001 Verdicchio dei Castelli di Jesi Classico, Sartarelli, Marche, Italy, £6.50, La Réserve
This year I've found several very interesting Verdicchio wines, mostly from the Castelli di Jesi Classico region on Italy's east coast. The wines aren't lean and dusty as they used to be, they're full and soft – dry, but with rich dry fruit, apples, honey and the crystallized sugar you sometimes get on top of a bun.

Under a fiver

As the pound weakens against currencies like the Euro, the Rand and the Australian dollar, the price/quality ratio at under £5 becomes more and more problematic. But this is a crucial area for all retailers, since most of our wine purchases are for less than a fiver a bottle. So I'd exhort our merchants to keep at it – look to less-well-known areas, less popular grape varieties, countries whose currencies are weaker than ours – but don't dumb down. We need the irresistible object of desire that is £4.99 worth of wine, not £4.99 worth of promotional gimmicks.

❶ 2000 La Riada Old Vines Garnacha, Spain, £4.99, Threshers and Wine Rack
This is smashing stuff – rich, deep, irresistibly juicy, packed with superripe cherry and strawberry fruit and gingered up with herbs. There are million upon million of old Garnacha vines in hinterland Spain. The more we drink of wines like this, the more they'll keep those ancient vines in the ground and not plant potatoes.

❷ 2002 Chardonnay, Casillero del Diablo, Concha y Toro, Casablanca Valley, Chile, £4.99, Waitrose
This is exactly what high-quality commercial Chardonnay should be like: loads of ripe but dry pineapple and melon fruit, a nice streak of lemon acidity, just a touch of oak spice and a beguiling honeysuckle finish. And this is made by the biggest winery in Chile. Quality and quantity *can* go hand in hand.

❸ 2002 Alvarinho & Chardonnay, DFJ Vinhos, Estremadura, Portugal, £4.99, Sainsbury's
The Portuguese haven't really fallen for this Chardonnay lark – they've got far too many good grapes of their own. But they do have *some* Chardonnay, which is pretty good but can be on the fat side. No problem. Alvarinho is a citrus, high-acid but fragrant grape native to the far north of the country. Blend these two together and you get all the honeysuckle and melon ripeness of the Chardonnay, a little clover honey richness too, but a faint apple-peel acidity from the Alvarinho.

❹ 2002 Viognier, Casillero del Diablo, Concha y Toro, Casablanca Valley, Chile, £4.99, Booths
Viognier is an exotic, perfumed grape, but if it's not picked at precisely the right time and vinified very carefully it tastes heavy and lumpen and you simply can't finish the bottle. Well, Concha y Toro have a talented young winemaking team

bottled passion

where else can you get
passion for only £4.99?

SANTA JULIA

Produced by the award winning Familia Zuccardi
ARGENTINA

SAUVIGNON BLANC ✦ VIOGNIER ✦ CHARDONNAY
BONARDA SANGIOVESE ✦ TEMPRANILLO ✦ SYRAH ROSÉ
MERLOT ✦ MALBEC ✦ CABERNET SAUVIGNON ✦ SHIRAZ

www.familiazuccardi.com

who relish all challenges; this wine has an unexpected
delicacy, with soft peach, apricot and pear fruit mingling
relaxedly with a touch of crystallized sugar richness and a
restrained nip of orange peel bitterness.

---

❺ 2000 The Society's Chilean Merlot, Concha y Toro,
Rapel Valley, Chile, £4.95, The Wine Society

The Wine Society has some of the canniest wine buyers in the
business, always seeking out the top suppliers. Concha y Toro
is on sparkling form just now and this is tremendous red –
deep, dark, ripe, yet with an aggressive power kept well under
control as the delicious Chilean Merlot fruit richness shadow-
boxes with fistfuls of pepper and herb and dark soy sauce.

---

❻ 2002 Pinot Bianco La Prendina, Cavalchina, Lombardy, Italy,
£4.99, Booths

You don't normally expect a north Italian Pinot Bianco to
taste all that exciting, so this one, from the lovely Lake Garda
region, is a welcome surprise. It has really good cooked apple
purée flavours, lanolin smoothness, a bit of summer-fresh
earth and a distinct suggestion of honey fudge.

---

❼ 2001 Bela Fonte, Touriga Franca & Tinta Roriz,
DFJ Vinhos, Beiras, Portugal, £4.99, Safeway

Portugal really does pack in more flavour to its reds at under a
fiver than any other European country. These two grapes marry
together blithely to produce a wine with such grainy tannic
power you can almost smell it – but you hardly notice the
bitterness in your mouth because your palate is awash with a
swirling sweet pudding of cherries and strawberries, toffee
and treacle, and the very slightest coy perfume of rose petals.

---

❽ 2001 Corbières, Château La Bastide, Languedoc-
Roussillon, France, £4.99, Booths

There's an old, unfashionable grape variety they grow in the
wild hills of the Corbières called the Carignan. This ancient
rough-diamond grape vine, capable of coarseness and
vulgarity as all old-timers are, is also able to squeeze out small
amounts of darkly individual juice. Add a little Syrah, as they
have here, and you get a brawny but almost beautiful blend of
rich black cherry and damson fruit, scratched by herbs.

---

❾ 2002 Sauvignon Blanc, Budai, Nyakashgy Ltd, Hungary,
£4.29, Wines of Westhorpe

Hungarian Sauvignon Blanc can be some of the best value for
money in Europe so long as you like your Sauvignons green 'n'

For more wine recommendations see Oz Clarke's Wine Style Guide, pages 82–90

mean. That's how I like them
– and this is a grapefruity
white with lots of piercing
citrus fruit as well as equally
tangy lime leaf and nettle
aggression.

**❿ 2001 Segada, Trincadeira-
Castelão, DFJ Vinhos,**
Ribatejano, Portugal,
£4.49, Budgens
This manages to be almost
gooey and chocolatey, with
more than a suggestion of
soft cake richness, and yet
this never extinguishes the
delightful red cherry fruit
and the lingering rose-petal
scent. *Also at Oddbins,
Sainsbury's, Unwins.*

**⓫ 2002 Averys French
Sauvignon Blanc,**
Bordeaux, France,
£4.95, Averys of Bristol
According to the label, this is
here to challenge the
Sauvignon hotspots of the
Loire Valley and New Zealand
– and by God it does, by
being swingeingly aggressive
yet ripe, so that the nettle,
lemon and blackcurrant leaf assault is softened but not
seduced by crisp apple fruit and a mildly syrupy sweet heart.

⓬ 2002 Rioja, Sonsierra, Spain, £4.95, Laymont & Shaw
Laymont & Shaw have been famous over the years for the
impeccable handling and shipping of some of the very grandest
of Spanish Riojas. But here they've found a co-op winery, talked
to them bluntly about what the British like to drink, and come
up with this delicious, rich, juicy redcurrants and strawberry and
white-pepper red that is infinitely more enjoyable than most
brand-name Riojas for a quid or two more.

⓭ 2002 Touraine Sauvignon, Domaine de la Renaudie,
Loire Valley, France, £4.95, The Wine Society
This positively pings with precisely the flavours you are pining
for at around a fiver – yet so rarely find. This is marvellously

Spanish acquisition

SPARKLING
Cava Brut (page 43)
1998 Cava Brut (page 73)

WHITE, ROSÉ
Castillo de Almansa (page 42)
Gran Feudo Rosé (page 39)

RED
Bobal-Tempranillo, Rozaleme
(page 33)
Calatayud, Poema, Old Vines
Garnacha (page 54)
Calatayud Garnacha, Viña
Fuerte (page 64)
Campo de Borja (page 65)
Evo, Guelbenzu (page 14)
Gran Tempranillo (page 71)
La Mancha, Castillo de
Alhambra (page 67)
Montsant, La Planella (page 24)
Navarra, Viña Sardasol (page 38)
La Riada, Old Vines Garnacha
(page 34)
Ribera del Duero, Bagús
(page 17)
Rioja Reserva, Elegia (page 62)
Rioja, Sonsierra (page 37)
Rioja, Tomas Blanco Crespo,
Telmo Rodríguez (page 57)
Valdepeñas, Viña Albali Reserva
(page 39)
Valencia, Les Alcusses (page 30)

rapier-like in its flavours of Granny Smith apples, trampled stinging nettles and lemon zest. It's just so refreshingly *green*, my mouth is already watering at the thought.

⓮ 1999 Navarra Crianza, Viña Sardasol, Bodegas Virgen Blanca, Spain, £4.95, Booths
This wine is from Navarra, Rioja's neighbour; it's made in the same way and from the same grape – Tempranillo – and it's a good couple of quid less than most Riojas. And as you sit contentedly mulling over its ripe strawberry fruit and its seductive vanilla cream softness, will you *really* care what it says on the label?

⓯ 2002 The Society's Australian Chardonnay, Wirra Wirra Vineyards, McLaren Vale, South Australia, £4.95, The Wine Society
The Wine Society know what we want from Aussie Chardonnay: full flavour, and that satisfying mouthfilling texture that talks of sun-ripened grapes. So they went to the first-rate Wirra Wirra winery and said – give us the Brits' idea of Aussie Chardie. And this is it – soft, fat but attractively so, lots of apple purée and banana fruit, lemon peel acidity and kitchen spice and just a touch of syrup.

⓰ 2002 Cabernet Sauvignon, Casillero del Diablo, Concha y Toro, Central Valley, Chile, £4.99, Threshers, Waitrose
It's dark, it's deep, it's so dense you'd need X-ray vision to see through it. The fruit is black and coiled in smoke, the tannins standing surly guard over the riches within. So you can do one of two things. Either open it well in advance and quaff it bravely with some Herculean barbecue or casserole. Or lay it down for 5 years, maybe 10, then revel in the sweet blackcurrant, bonfire smoke and mint beauty that it will reveal. And then remember that it only cost you £4.99.

⓱ Masterpeace Rosé, Australia, £4.99, Threshers
When the sun shines, there's nothing better than rosé to knock back with the seafood and salami. This one – an interesting mix between the juicy Shiraz and the more angular Sangiovese – has a fresh taste of apples and cream, just enough to make you take a second gulp, and a third...

⓲ 2001 Carmenère, Peteroa, Vinicola Montealegre, Central Valley, Chile, £4.99, Wines of Westhorpe
I love Carmenère's unashamed, blistering attack on the taste buds, and this powerful brew is burly, ripe, oozing black plum and black cherry richness at the same time as the savoury celery and soy sauce and pepper spread out their tendrils to

snatch your palate back from any flavour that was easy to comprehend.

---

⑲ 2002 Gran Feudo Rosé, Julian Chivite, Navarra, Spain, **£4.69, Oddbins**
Navarra has always made good rosé – pretty full-bodied as European rosés go – and this one's no exception, with nice strawberry fruit, creamy texture and a glycerine ripeness that tells you it could have been one helluva red.

---

⑳ 1999 Valdepeñas, Viña Albali Reserva, Castilla-La Mancha, Spain, **£4.49, Asda, Budgens, Co-Op, Sainsbury's**
Albali's were some of the first Valdepeñas wines I tasted, years ago, and we were all amazed by their oaky richness, their evident maturity – they were often 6 or 7 years old – and their low price. The wines are more modern now, and prices are up a bit, but this is still lovely, soft, oak-scented wine with a splash of blackcurrant juice.

㉑ 2002 Vin de Pays des Côtes de Gascogne, 'Les 4 cépages', Domaine de Pajot, South-West France, **£4.60, Vintage Roots**
This is called 'The 4 varieties', and it benefits from the Colombard and Sauvignon in particular by showing off a strong apple and white peach fruit to argue the toss with a serious splash of green leaf and lime juice. Aggressive but ripe. Fruity but taut with acidity. Perfick.

German wines

I wish I could persuade some of you to give German wines a try. Germany has a wine tradition as glorious as any in Europe, and flavours and sensations that no other country can match. So next time you're about to pick up your usual Chardonnay or Sauvignon, let your eye stray to the tall, thin bottle with the convoluted name on the label. Don't try to pronounce them. Just try the wine.

❶ 1996 Riesling Kabinett, Ürziger Würzgarten, Christoffel-Berres, Mosel-Saar-Ruwer, £5.49, Majestic

Set in a horseshoe curve steeply angled to the sun, the heavenly spice garden (*würzgarten*) is one of Germany's great vineyards. This wine is now 7 years old and has developed a remarkable custard creaminess just splashed with petrol, and a lime acidity that burns through the wine like electricity.

❷ 1994 Riesling Spätlese, Trittenheimer Apotheke, Josefinegrund, Mosel-Saar-Ruwer, £6.99, Wine Rack

The Apotheke vineyard is unbelievably steep, and loose shards of slate cascade to the roadway far below as you struggle to keep your footing. And from this exhilarating site come classic Rieslings – low in alcohol, but with a scintillating acid attack of lemon and grapefruit with lemon and lime blossom scent hovering over the glass and a remarkable buttercream and custard richness left on your palate after you swallow.

❸ 2002 Riesling QbA, 'Dr L', Ernst Loosen, Mosel-Saar-Ruwer, £5.99, Booths

Wonderfully snappy wine, with a mouth-watering not-quite-dry flavour of Cox's and Granny Smith apples, some extra lemony acidity, a touch of pastry softness – and a mineral streak to remind you that the vineyards are almost pure slate.

❹ 2002 Riesling, Dürkheimer Michelsberg, Darting Estate, Pfalz, £5.99, Marks & Spencer

Beautifully fresh and lively, with a streak of mineral and vivid acidity, but it also has endearing soft fatness like honey fudge.

❺ 2001 Riesling Kabinett, Piesporter Goldtröpfchen, Kurt Hain, Mosel-Saar-Ruwer, £8, Tanners

Another gorgeous vineyard, perfectly placed in a bend in the Mosel to capture every last ray of summer and autumn sun. Piesporter wines are slightly softer than most Mosels, and this one's lemon and lime acidity is almost mild, subtly losing itself among the honeybread, slate and custard cream softness.

Under £4

We don't really ask the independent wine merchants to excel here, yet this year we've expanded this section, largely because of the efforts of Oddbins and Booths.

❶ 2002 Ramada, DFJ Vinhos, Estremadura, Portugal, £3.49, Safeway, Tesco

If you want an intro wine showing why Portugal is such a fantastically original red wine country, start on Ramada. 2002 wasn't an easy vintage in Portugal, so the producers have given us a leaner version of the usual Ramada, but the flavours are still unbeatable for the money: bristling with hedgerow red fruits – rosehips, sloes and cranberries – and strewn with the resinous rasp of thyme and rosemary and the bite of black pepper. This isn't an easy-going glugging red, it's a challenging mealtime red with a real sense of where it came from. *Also at Sainsbury's, Threshers, Wine Rack.*

❷ 2002 Shiraz, Snake Creek, South-Eastern Australia, £3.99, Oddbins

Tasting some of the sweet sugary goo that passes for Australian Shiraz under a fiver nowadays, you could be forgiven for thinking that they'd lost the formula for Shiraz down under. They haven't lost it. The big companies that churn out the cheap stuff can no longer be bothered to make it properly. But this bushy-tailed red, packed with blackberry and plum fruit, thick with black treacle and smouldering with the smoky fumes of bacon and grilled nuts shows it can still be done.

> *'...bushy-tailed red packed with blackberry and plum, black treacle, smoky bacon and grilled nuts'*

❸ 2001 Mosaïque Syrah, Vin de Pays d'Oc, Jean d'Alibert, Languedoc-Roussillon, France, £3.99, Oddbins

Here's the French version of the Shiraz, or Syrah as they call it. Less rich, more austere than the Aussie version (above), it nonetheless has that same delightful plum and blackberry fruit but in lower key, and has added the slightly raw perfume of lily stems and a good streak of cocoa powder.

❹ 2002 Pinot Noir, Recas, Romania, £3.49, Wines of Westhorpe

Well done Wines of Westhorpe for locating the Recas winery and its 50-year-old wines high in the Carpathian mountains.

This delightfully spicy red with its gentle red plum fruit and its lush texture of strawberry syrup is a steal at £3.49.

❺ 2001 Corbières Réserve de Reverend, Sichel,
❢ Languedoc-Roussillon, France, £3.99, Booths
This speaks of the high hills and the lost, echoing valleys of the Corbières – full, firm, dry red fruit, swished with the rough perfume of bay leaf and thyme and splashed with the exotic mysteries of Angostura.

❻ 2002 Mosaïque Chardonnay, Vin de Pays d'Oc, Vincent

♀ Raganel, Languedoc-Roussillon, France, £3.99, Oddbins
Simple but delightful wine with a scent of honeycomb and a limpid flavour of melon and apple and lemon, showing Chardonnay in the nude, no mucking about, just the essence of the grape.

❼ 2002 Domaine de Pellehaut, Vin de Pays des Côtes de
♀ Gascogne, South-West France, £3.99, Booths
The most popular white wine flavour of today is the lipsmacking green-streaked tang of Sauvignon Blanc. But the Gascony area of South-West France grows white wine that is just as acidic as good Sauvignon. This positively crackles with cool green apple and lemon peel zesty fruit.

❽ 2003 Sauvignon Blanc, Van Loveren, Robertson,
♀ South Africa, £3.99, Somerfield
This is a nice fresh pear- and apple-tasting Sauvignon from the Cape. It's a 2003, so you get maximum freshness from the wine's youth, and it's from Robertson, whose limestone soils are proving to be ideal for white wines.

❾ 2002 Chardonnay-Semillon, Snake Creek,
♀ South-Eastern Australia, £3.99, Oddbins
Sunshine in a bottle for well under a fiver. There's not so much of that around these days, but this one's got soft banana and pear flesh fruit, a flicker of spice and balanced ripeness.

❿ 2002 Cuvée de Richard, Vin de Pays de l'Aude, Producteurs
❢ Réunis, Languedoc-Roussillon, France, £2.99, Majestic
Big solid chunky red with a fair dollop of fruit and a pleasing whiff of bayleaf. Buy it by the caseload.

⓫⓬ Castillo de Almansa, Spain, £3.99, Booths

This is a pair of very attractive easy drinkers. The white has lots of soft baked-apple fruit and is fresh and gluggable. The red's a bit more serious, dry but pretty full-bodied and whacked with herbs and fresh ground pepper.

Fizz

This is a bit of a turn-up for the books. With a few stunning exceptions we found many Champagnes a bit dull this year (the supermarket ones we tried, on the other hand, were rather good – see page 72), whereas we found loads of really good non-Champagne fizz. But hey, who's complaining? If the independent merchants are taking note of the tough times we're all experiencing and are helping us to trade down painlessly – thanks for being so thoughtful.

❶ Champagne Brut Pierre Vaudon, Union Champagne, France, £16.55, Haynes Hanson & Clark
Everything a house champagne should be. Not the kind of meagre green fizz that we've all suffered at poorly catered weddings and celebrations, but a drink that proud merchants can proudly offer. This is soft, foaming rather than spitting its bubbles at you, with a lovely soothing flavour of nuts baked in a brioche. Hmm. Nuts in brioche and a glass of this. That's what I'd call breakfast.

❷ Champagne Brut, The Wine Society's Private Cuvée, Alfred Gratien, France, £19, The Wine Society
Frankly, this is just as good as the Vaudon, but it really needs as much as 5 years to show how brilliant it can be whereas the Vaudon is spot-on right now. Gratien is a long-time favourite of mine: we launched the first edition of this guide with Gratien; I've still got a bottle, and I bet it's still good. This young pup has a lovely bright loft-apple fruit and a cascade of nut and cream flavours to soften the acidity – and long after I've swallowed, I can still taste a soothing savoury cashew nut richness. Now that's a mark of classy wine.

❸ Cava Brut, Private Cuvée Hicks & Don, Covides, Spain, £6.60, Hicks & Don
Hicks & Don is one of those wine merchant partnerships that seems to have been going ever since Adam was a boy. Here they've done a great job in sourcing a high-quality Cava, and also in demanding that it be aged properly. Cava rarely matures well, but this is a delight, gently foaming, attractively nutty, with appetizing apple and lime acidity wrapped in honey.

❹ Gaillac Brut, Bicary, Claude & Christine Rouquié, South-West France, £8.30, Devigne Wines
Anyone who grew up in the countryside must know the taste of a ripe Bramley apple – that wonderfully mouth-watering

acidity matched by a scented sweetness that somehow never loses sight of the vivid essential greenness that marks the Bramley's appeal – but for most people this side of Calais Bramleys are the world's greatest cooking apple. Well, imagine a fresh-picked Bramley, coated with icing sugar, dabbed with kitchen spice and dotted with lemon peel all ready to be popped into a pie and baked. Then add some bubbles. And you've got this wonderful Gaillac fizz.

> *'...the vivid essential greenness that marks the Bramley's appeal...dabbed with kitchen spice'*

---

❺ 1996 Blanquette de Limoux, Cuvée Exception, Antech, South-West France, £11.50, Devigne Wines
I'm not sure I've ever tasted a Blanquette de Limoux that anyone had aged on purpose. I've found the odd bottle under the bed, but this one is purposely aged. It's become a fascinating wine, full of layers of flavour: grilled nuts and toast – really crunchy toast like those rock-hard French biscottes – but also some brioche to soften things up, and someone's smeared Marmite on the brioche then left it in the loft next to the Christmas apples and a posy of lovage.

---

❻ Champagne Brut Brossault, P & C Heidsieck, £14.99, Majestic
Now that this wine is made by Charles Heidsieck it has changed from being a bit of a burly maverick to something verging on the suave – nicely flavoured with brioche and hazelnuts, surprisingly scented with pepper and leather.

---

❼ Morton Premium Brut, New Zealand, £9.99, Bring-a-Bottle
New Zealand is famous for making bubbly that is virtually indistinguishable from Champagne. Well, this one starts out with a heady smell of brioche smeared with butter and fresh grilled hazelnuts, but the ebullient fruit won't be silenced and the brioche and nuts get elbowed aside by a true southern seas flavour of kiwi fruit and green pea splashed with honey.

---

❽ 1995 Champagne Brut, Le Brun de Neuville, France, £20, Waterloo Wine Co
Last year the 1992 vintage was absolutely perfect and won this fizz section. The 1995 is from a more intense vintage – and it's much younger, which explains why it hasn't got such a high mark. It's still classy Champagne – powerful, with a richness of perfumed honey and a deep, dry, savoury quality rather like hazelnut husks – but if you want to drink it at its best you'll need to buy it and hoard it for a couple of years.

❾ Prosecco Ruggeri, Italy, £6.99, Valvona & Crolla

They drink bucketloads of Prosecco in Italy – usually out of tiny fluted glasses that are endlessly refilled by your host. And that's a nifty idea, because the joy of Prosecco is in the minute or so after it's been poured. It's not complex, it's not deep and discussion-worthy – it's just a bright, happy, flirtatious foaming wine with an apple- and pear-flesh softness coated in cream that demands no concentration and allows you to spend all your efforts on being inspirationally witty and irresistibly attractive to one and all.

❿ Graham Beck Brut, Robertson, South Africa, £7.99, Bibendum

The South Africans fancy themselves as pretty fair Champagne imitators. Well, carbon copies are thin on the ground, but Cape fizz *is* good. It doesn't have the nutty, creamy depth of good Champagne, but it's fairly dry, just oversoftened, perhaps, by icing sugar, and with faint apple fruit and some toffee depth.

⓫ 1996 Champagne Blanc de Blancs Brut, Ruelle-Pertois, France, £19.95, Roger Harris Wines

Good Champagne with a slightly severe look on its face, a touch of the Miss Jean Brodies when what you really want is more adolescent high jinks. It's actually quite mature, and has rather a nice leathery nutty flavour, but it is *genuinely* dry.

⓬ 2000 Chateau Vincent Extra Brut, Hungary, £5.98, Wines of Westhorpe

Wild, wild wine. It's got an amazing flavour of elderflower and cape gooseberries and a rather heady scent of lavender. I don't know if that's quite what all your party guests will hanker for, but some of the more intrepid surely will.

Red fizz

After a long day's tasting of serious wines, there is nothing to beat the sheer exuberant, irreverent burst of celebration and relief that surges through your veins as the first flood of purple potion splashes and foams into your glass. And if you're thinking – yuck! – you need to get out more and have some fun.

❶ Sparkling Durif, Emeri, De Bortoli, South-Eastern Australia, £6.99, Noble Rot, £7.50, Wright Wine Co

I first came across this cool crimson cordial after a heavy day's winetasting in baked vineyards about as close to the outback as the vine will grow in Australia. 'You need re-energizing', the guy said as he ripped the bottle from the fridge, banged out the cork and whooshed the dark purple foam into my glass. It's real rich red Durif wine – bubbling up with black cherry and black plum fruit just sweetened by muscovado sugar and sultanas – yet you just can't take it seriously. That flavour. That colour. Those bubbles. Get your glad rags on, as this is stampin', stompin' stuff.

② Sparkling Shiraz, Banrock Station, Australia, £7.99, Somerfield
This is the easiest red fizz to find: Banrock Station wines in general are widely available, and quite a few stockists do the fizz. It's about as irresistible as red wine gets – rich, ripe blackberry, toffee and chocolate flavours lurking behind the purple foam, just waiting their chance to leap out on you and haul you off to the party. Bruce juice with sequins and a tiara. *Also at Asda, Morrisons, Safeway, Tesco, Waitrose.*

③ Ardoisier demi-sec, Domaine de Montgilet, Victor et Vincent Lebreton, Loire Valley, France, £9.30, Devigne Wines
A bit more restrained than the Aussie pair – well, you'd expect the French to show a *little* more restraint. It's still a party animal, so treat it like one – not too seriously – but while you get high on the bubbles you'll realize the wine has the rather classy Loire red flavours of raspberry, pear and banana and a smooth dryness rather like pebbles at the bottom of a stream.

④ Lambrusco, Concerto, Emilia-Romagna, Italy, £6.49, Booths
I'm not sure I can write this and keep a straight face, but this is serious Lambrusco. The Real Thing. Not sickly sweet alcopop but biting, dry, foaming red, crackling with acidity and pumped up with chewy red cherry fruit. You'd never waste this on the back seat of a Ford Escort. Well, I dunno...

'...You'd never waste this on the back seat of a Ford Escort'

⑤ 2001 Brachetto d'Acqui, Contero, Piedmont, Italy, £9.95, Mills Whitcombe
Piedmont can be a very beetle-browed part of the world, with everyone trying to outdo everyone else in making the most daunting, gum-thwacking, lip-stripping red wine of the vintage. They should ease up and remember this jolly little number, all blossom and sweet-sour plummy fruit – and froth. Loads of crimson froth to flick playfully into a Barolo maker's eyes.

Fortified & sweet wines

There's still no real sign of a revival of interest in sweet wines. I can sort of understand this if we think of sweet wines as 'dessert' wines, implying that they come at the end of what might be a three- or four-course dinner. I mean, how many of us either give or go to dinner parties like that on a regular basis? So what we need to do is to find ways of drinking sweet wines by themselves or with savoury dishes – perfectly possible, but the sweetness means you don't always want more than a glass or so.

❶ Madeira, Verdelho, 15 Years Old, Henriques & Henriques, £16.99/50cl, Waitrose

A wonderful, original wine. Nothing in the world tastes even remotely like this. Madeira is a little island off the north African coast and its unique style of fortified wine has been in decline for decades, but you taste this and think – how can such fabulous flavours not find a market? Ah, but when should you drink it, people ask. When should you make love? Whenever the mood takes you. It's the same with this Verdelho, because despite the wealth of richness in its flavours it's actually highly acidic, and it's dry, almost sour – in the way that great balsamic or sherry vinegar is sour. Indeed it's the thrilling, searing acidity that is the defining factor in this wine, which has a smell as haunting as damp rose blooms trodden into the lawn by night-time revellers; yet it also seems to have dates and raisins floating in suspension, but even more it's the rich brown taste of treacle flapjacks, the strips of burnt jam left on the rim of a raspberry tart. *Also at Noel Young Wines.*

❷ Mavrodaphne of Patras, Nyx, B G Spiliopoulos, Greece, £7.79/50cl, Oddbins

What a wine! What haunting, unexpected flavours of decay and decadence. It's very rich, it's waxy too – the scented wax of beeswax candles dripping onto an ancient teak table. There are spices – kitchen spices like mace and allspice – and a coating of almond paste mashed up with dates and sultanas, maraschino cherries and crystallized violets from the top of a party cake, but hanging like a heavy-lidded mist over all this is a perfume, tired but lovely, like a world-weary courtesan's scent.

❸ Madeira, Malmsey, 15 Years Old, Henriques & Henriques, £16.99/50cl, Waitrose

Malmsey is the sweetest type of Madeira, but it's never as sweet as a sweet sherry or a port because of the trademark acidity that scythes through its heart like the whine of a lumberjack's saw in the dark depths of a silent forest. It is a marvellous mix of lushness and acidity, since any sugariness has been worn away by the 15 years spent aging in a barrel and you're left with dates and figs and nuts – like chewing on the bitter skin of a hazelnut before finally allowing yourself the crunchy, juicy, raw richness of the nut itself. *Also at Noel Young Wines.*

❹ Tanners Mariscal Manzanilla, Dolores Bustillo Delgado, **£6.55**
Really tasty dry sherry. It's a Manzanilla, from the seaside town of Sanlucar near Cadiz in southern Spain, and you really get a taste of the sea – I thought for a moment of ultra-fresh sardines splashed with salt. Ah yes, salt. Manzanillas are supposed to taste of salt. Well, above all else, this has a bracing flavour of old, old wood, like an ancient staircase kept carefully clean yet never quite free of dust, and that blends brilliantly with the slightly sour cream of bread yeast. Yes, but salt... mmm? And as you swallow the wine, an aftertaste floats up – of roasted almonds, and salt.

❺ The Society's Exhibition Manzanilla Pasada, Bodegas Hidalgo-La Gitana, **£6.95,** The Wine Society
What a fascinating idea. 'Pasada' on the label means that the wine has got a bit older and deeper in flavour than they originally intended it to. After all, Manzanilla is supposed to be keen and fresh as a sea breeze. But some barrels of sherry simply have a mind of their own and start to develop a richer, nuttier style by mistake. That's what's happened here. The wine is still bone dry, but there's just a little more old wood perfume than I'd expect, there's a hint of sweet nuttiness, a certain creamy warmth, a suggestion of the flavour of buttered brazils. These are just hints, but they add an intriguing extra dimension to a great glass of dry sherry.

❻ Palo Cortado Sherry, Vinícola Hidalgo, **£8.75,** Laymont & Shaw
Another fascinating dry sherry style. This is a sherry that never quite worked out whether it wanted to be pale Fino or brown Oloroso. It's properly dry, but fabulously full-flavoured too: there's not a hint of sugar here, but there's a richness of raisins like Garibaldi biscuits, of fig paste in fig rolls, of the caramel coating of buttered brazils, and someone's left a spoonful of Fowler's Black Treacle in the bottom of the vat. Superb, original stuff.

For more wine recommendations see Oz Clarke's Wine Style Guide, pages 82–90

7 Taylor's 10-Year-Old Tawny Port, £16.79, Sainsbury's

This isn't cheap, but it is exactly what a 10-year-old Tawny should look and taste like. it has a chestnut colour still tinged with russet red, a wonderfully ripe aroma – but gentle, not the purple blast of a young vintage port – and a flavour that is part texture part taste. The texture is syrup smooth, rich but mellow, and the taste has a delightful muscovado sugar and sultana intensity, but it also has the red fruit freshness of distant youth and the pink-cheeked perfume of rosehips. *Also at Asda, Booths, Majestic, Safeway, Unwins, Wimbledon Wine Cellar.*

8 Tanners Fino Superior, Pilar Aranda, £6.85

A lovely example of Fino sherry, bone dry but just a little weightier than the Manzanillas from the coast, because Finos are aged in the slightly warmer inland conditions of the town of Jerez. But you still get a deliciously cool wood perfume, the flawed richness of slightly sour cream – and a satisfying hazelnut flavour.

9 Dow's Crusted Port, Bottled 1998, Silva Cosens Ltd, £12.99, Waitrose

Crusted is a rare but excellent style of wine: you get a pretty decent dose of real Vintage port personality – and you do need to decant this – but you only pay half the money for it. What you don't get is the unbridled naked power and ferocious focus of a Vintage port, but you do get the rich dark flavours of damson and blackberry, a whack of peppery spirit and a rough brush of herbs – yet they don't hurt, they just serve to freshen up the fruit and keep your taste buds on full alert for a second glass.

> *'...a whack of peppery spirit and a rough brush of herbs – yet they don't hurt'*

10 2001 Moscatel, MR, Telmo Rodríguez, Málaga, Spain, £7.95/50cl, Adnams

This is not remotely like the dark, sweet, treacly Málaga that you might buy at the airport on the way home from a week sunning yourself on the Costa del Sol. This is Spanish wine genius Telmo Rodríguez's recreation of what he thinks real Málaga might have been like in the old days. If so, let's have more of it, because this is pale green gold, full and syrupy but the absolute essence of crunchy green Moscatel grapes slashed with lemon zest acidity and scoured by a distinctive minerality like a slippery grey slope of Cambrian shale. Old-timers might have drunk this with cake, but I think it's too good to share.

Best buys

⑪ 2000 Banyuls Rimage, Les Clos de Paulilles, Languedoc-Roussillon, France, £9.95, James Nicholson

Banyuls is made from grapes grown on the baking hillsides of southern France. And you can really taste the superripeness of the fruit in this medium-sweet but powerful red, packed with red plum and loganberry fruit, but streaked with an acidity like a loganberry coulis. It's the kind of rich red wine that would be an inspired choice to accompany wild boar or venison.

> *'...an inspired choice to accompany wild boar or venison'*

⑫ 1975 Montila-Moriles, Don PX Pedro Ximenez, Vino Dulce de Postre Gran Reserva, Bodegas Toro Albalá, Spain, £9.99/half bottle, Moreno Wines

Sweet. No, very sweet. No, intensely, ridiculously sweet. It's the sweetness of essence of fig, rich treacle, gooey raisins, thick as fudge. It's 28 years old – and it'll last another 28 – and that age has just begun to show in an intriguing flavour of beef tea starting to nudge the edge of this sea of sweetness.

⑬ 2000 Coteaux de l'Aubance, Domaine Richou, Loire Valley, France, £8.50, Waterloo Wine Co

This is classy wine, made by one of the most talented winemakers in Anjou, but it's not massively sweet. Aubance rarely gets the ultra-rich intensity of the most famous Loire sweet wines – but then it charges less than half the price. So enjoy this for its greengage and honey fruit, its metallic reserve and, strangely, just a hint of salt.

⑭ 1992 Warre's Traditional Late Bottled Vintage, £15.45, Waitrose

I'm extremely grateful to Warre's for persevering with the traditional and greatly superior unfiltered form of Late Bottled Vintage Port. 1992 is not as complex as some vintages, but it is the current one and it's a very attractive drink, with lovely blackberry fruit sprinkled with pepper and a little spirit. *Also at Oddbins, Safeway, Sainsbury's, Tesco, Wine Rack.*

⑮ 2000 Botrytis Semillon, Vat 5, Deen, De Bortoli, South-Eastern Australia, £5.35/half bottle, Wright Wine Co

This is the sort of baby brother of the world-famous De Bortoli Noble One, and is a pretty good mouthful at a fraction of the price. It's very sweet, full of bruised peach and pineapple fruit, it has a crucial streak of acidity, and it has a thick, waxy, lanolin texture that you can still feel coating your tongue long after you've swallowed the wine.

⓫ 1999 Shiraz, Alkoomi, Frankland River, Western Australia,
🍷 £9.99, Safeway

Not at all your average Aussie Shiraz. This is much drier and leaner than the general run, and it has a fantastic, shocking, peppercorn attack. It's like a mouthful of green peppercorns, incredibly fragrant but fiery so it hurts, and this is accentuated by another perfume – the green but floral scent of lily stems. Luckily the austere but focused blueberry and blackberry fruit is more than able to cope. *Also at Jeroboams.*

⓬ 2001 Syrah, Single-Vineyard, Errazuriz, Chile,
🍷 £9.99, Safeway

The Syrah is the same grape as the Shiraz – and the previous wine and this one show the impressive breadth of styles the grape can achieve. This one has none of the austerity and peppery attack of the Alkoomi. Instead, the first blast it gives out is of toasty, singed oak, sweet vanilla and chocolaty, plummy fruit. Austerity is just hinted at by a slightly unnerving sense of a strip of tarmac hidden in the heart of the wine.

⓭ 2001 Soave Classico Superiore, Inama, Italy,
🍷 £7.99, Sainsbury's

Now this is what I call imaginative and brave wine buying. Putting a Soave on at £7.99. Soave? Well, this Soave is from the Classico zone in the hills near Verona and it's a fascinating

55

wine, the subtle flavours ebbing and flowing, a smell of tobacco then a mellow sweetness like a French pear tart, raisins and honey too, before the texture fattens to waxiness and the scent drifts back to leather and unsmoked tobacco. So is it worth £7.99? It sure is. *Also at Bennetts, Fortnum & Mason, Christopher Piper, Sommelier Wine Co.*

⑭ 2001 Coteaux du Languedoc Pic St-Loup, Ermitage du ♥ Pic St Loup, Languedoc-Roussillon, France, £5.99, Waitrose
They call this vast area of southern France the Midi, and there are great historic wine sites down there, some planted as much as 2000 years ago, whose reputation was lost during the 19th century. The revitalization of the region through Vins de Pays encouraged many producers to pursue quality once more, and I believe the Midi is now the most exciting wine area in France. Pic St-Loup is one of the dozens of little zones with something special to prove, and one taste of this fabulous mouth-filling medley of sweet blackberry fruit, leather scent, powerful pepper rasp and a finish as soft as fudge should convince you too.

⑮ 2000 Montes Alpha Syrah, Apalta Vineyard, Colchagua, ♥ Chile, £11.99, Morrisons, Waitrose
Syrah, from the rockiest, roughest, steepest, most unfriendly vineyard yet planted in Chile. And Aurelio Montes adores it. This rugged site gives rugged fruit, aggressive texture and a forbidding character to the wine that warns the faint-hearted to stay well away, and cautions the wise that even they should leave the wine another 5 years to see if its cold carapace will dissolve, its pepper and tarmac smoke will mellow, and its sweet blackberry sauce fruit will finally burst its bonds and flow unfettered into the glass. *Also available at Berry Bros & Rudd, Christopher Piper, Wright Wine Co.*

⑯ 2001 The Lodge Hill Shiraz, Jim Barry, Clare Valley, South ♥ Australia, £9.99, Safeway
Jim Barry has been making better and better reds over the past few years, so I'm pleased to see this one on Safeway's shelves. It's as soft as a chocolate sponge pudding, rich, ripe, gooey, the chocolate spiced up with a little eucalyptus and a good deal more squashy plums, dried figs and prunes.

⑰ 2002 Sauvignon Blanc, Old Renwick Vineyard, Craggy ♀ Range, Marlborough, New Zealand, £9.99, Waitrose
This company is run by Steve Smith, who knows the Marlborough region like the back of his hand, so as soon as he started Craggy Range he knew exactly where to find old, low-yielding vineyards full of Sauvignon Blanc just bursting

with flavour. This is exceptional Sauvignon, packed with citrus fruit – lime zest and passionfruit – yet with a ripe apple softness before the tingle returns with stinging nettle intensity.

⓮ 2001 Chenin, Forrester Meinert, Ken Forrester, Stellenbosch, South Africa, £14.99, Waitrose

This is a pretty ambitious wine. Ken Forrester and Martin Meinert, two top Cape producers, decided they wanted to push the Chenin Blanc grape to its absolute limits, to try to create the ultimate Cape white. Well it's certainly a lot of money for a Chenin Blanc, but it is good and powerful. Not quite dry, it's like an annual convention of homemade jams – apricot jam, peach jam, pear jam, even marrow marmalade. Throw in some barley sugar and heather honey and rub it with toasty spice and you've got an unusual, but impressive, white.

> ### Pick of Portugal
>
> **WHITE**
> Alvarinho & Chardonnay, Estremadura, DFJ Vinhos (page 34)
>
> **RED**
> Bela Fonte, Touriga Franca & Tinta Roriz, Beiras, DFJ Vinhos (page 36)
> Douro Reserva, Quinta de Fafide (page 54)
> Estremadura, Cortello (page 65)
> Grand'Arte Touriga Francesa, Estremadura, DFJ Vinhos (page 30)
> Touriga Nacional & Touriga Franca, Estremadura, DFJ Vinhos (page 59)
> Ramada, Estremadura, DFJ Vinhos (page 41)
> Segada, Trincadeira-Castelão, Ribatejano, DFJ Vinhos (page 37)

⓳ 2001 Rioja, Tomas Blanco Crespo, Telmo Rodríguez, Spain, £6.99, Marks & Spencer

M&S have worked with Spanish wine wizard Telmo Rodríguez for several years and every year he comes up with some star wines from all over Spain. This one's from his home patch, Rioja, and it's a lush, generous wine, brimful of ripe red cherry and strawberry fruit, pinched with pepper and spice and barely perceptibly coated in custard and cream.

⓴ 2000 Minervois, Château de Landure, Cuvée de l'Abbé Frégouse, Languedoc-Roussillon, France, £6.99, Marks & Spencer

A really good example of this resurgent area in the south of France. It's got a bit of oaky sweetness but not too much, because the fruit itself is so wonderfully deep and ripe and scented the last thing it needs is to be hidden in a vanilla-ey oak shroud. The ripe blackberry and loganberry coulis fruit is made even more powerful by a meaty growl from the Mourvèdre grape and the revivifying medicinal fumes of Angostura and bay.

When
you choose
fairly traded
Co-op wines there's
no bitter after-taste. They
assure the world's
poorest crop
producers a
better
life.

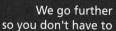

High street heroes

This section was absolutely blow for blow between France and Australia, with final honours even at six wines apiece. None of the Australian delights came from the big companies, but Aussie wine from the smaller producers has never been better. At this level of quality, you expect French wine to be from single estates – and indeed it is. France is trying to learn from Australia how to create big brands at the moment. Luckily there are enough people in Australia who are learning the old French arts of personal involvement with individual patches of land, and wines created in the image of their maker.

❶ **2001 Estremadura, Touriga Nacional & Touriga Franca**, DFJ Vinhos, Portugal, £4.99, Safeway
If you want original red wines with wild, exciting flavour combinations, the Portuguese really deliver. The grape varieties are not the ubiquitous international ones, but a whole gamut of indigenous numbers that bulge with fruit flavours and spice. This wine smells of eucalyptus and lavender and freshly baked buns. The eucalyptus is still there when you drink it, but now there's a mighty splat of rich damson and black plum fruit riotously churned up with black chocolate bitterness and pepper spice. See what I mean about original?

❷ **2001 Minervois, Les Vieilles Vignes de Château Marais**, Languedoc-Roussillon, France, £7.99, Waitrose
Minervois has been reinventing itself for a generation now, and it's brilliant wines like this that make all the effort worthwhile. What a scent! It's like a violet-scented Roger & Gallet soap! What fruit! Deep, ripe blueberry and damson which will turn richer and sweeter and more blackberryish in 2 or 3 years. And good grippy tannin too, before the violet scent wafts you off into red-wine reverie.

❸ **2001 Petit Verdot**, Kingston Estate Wines, Lower Murray, South Australia, £4.99, Sainsbury's
Petit Verdot is a rare Bordeaux grape that finds it really tough to ripen in Bordeaux's damp climate, but which reacts brilliantly to the eye-popping heat of inland Australia. Yet no-one seems to take it seriously. Well *I* do and so should you, because this is a fantastic mouthful of fruit – rich, syrupy black cherry scrunched up with Kendal mint cake and Fowler's Black Treacle – and somehow, gasping for air in the middle of all that, the perfume of violets. £4.99? You'd be mad not to.

Supermarket selection

❹ 2002 Durif, Rutherglen Estates, Australia, £6.99, Waitrose
Durif is an obscure grape that probably originates from somewhere in France's Rhône Valley – but take it to Rutherglen in the broiling north-east corner of Victoria and for just about the first time in its life it reveals its true character: tannin, certainly, but great gobs of rich blueberry and blackberry fruit to overwhelm any bitterness, and smoky oak toast from a brief stay in barrels. *Also at Asda, The Wine Society.*

❺ 2001 Nepenthe Tryst, Adelaide Hills, South Australia, £6.99, Waitrose
What a fascinating idea – take the red grapes of Bordeaux (Cabernet), Burgundy (Pinot Noir) and Rioja (Tempranillo), blend them together and try to work out what contributes what to the flavour. Well, the Cabernet dominates with its blackcurrant fruit and eucalyptus scent, but the other grapes have softened the tannins and added a full rich strawberry syrup and a touch of savoury herb to the wine, which is balanced, soft and very interesting. *Also at Oddbins.*

❻ 2002 Pinot Gris, Villa Maria Private Bin, Marlborough, New Zealand, £6.99, Booths
Pinot Gris is very different to the snappy nettly Sauvignon Blanc, and to the nutty, lush style of Chardonnay that New Zealand does so well. This one has a lovely bright Conference pear and Cox's apple acidity, and fruit just flecked with honey but then snapped awake with the citrus zest of cooked lemon peel and the slightly chewy toughness of Cox's apple peel.

❼ 1999 Fronsac, Château La Vieille Cure, Bordeaux, France, £13.99, Sainsbury's
A good old Bordeaux from an established property in the ancient region of Fronsac. Well, that's not quite fair. The vineyard may have been there for centuries but the current owners have made big efforts to upgrade the wine, and it's now a top example of Fronsac: oaky, toasty, a bit aggressive, but with splendid black chocolate and toffee depth and rich dark fruit.

❽ 2001 Gewurztraminer, Cave de Turckheim, Alsace, France, £5.99, Marks & Spencer
Ah, what a delight – a gorgeous, fragrant white, able to perfume a room at twenty paces. There have been a lot of rather disappointing High Street Alsace wines recently, so this Gewurztraminer from top co-op Turckheim is most welcome, and as good as any they've made for years. It has a heady

For more wine recommendations see Oz Clarke's Wine Style Guide, pages 82–90

scent of rose petals and lychees and a languorous sultry
flavour of custard apples and lychee jumbled together with
hothouse muscatels and a rebellious flash of peppercorn.

---

⑨ 2001 Rasteau Côtes du Rhône-Villages, Perrin, Rhône
Valley, France, £7.99, Marks & Spencer
When you see 'Rasteau' on the label of a Côtes du Rhône
Villages, you can expect a primal blast of tannins and herbs
and dark, sunbaked, cauldron-stewed fruit. The thing that
marks this one out is that along with the burly black plum
fruit and the mineral quarry tannin there's stewed fruit all
right – but it's apples and strawberries. And it *is* tannic – but
it's unfiltered. To get the real deal you have to give a little.

---

⑩ 2002 Novello Nero, Chain of Ponds, South Australia,
£5.99, Somerfield
Novello means new, and this is a kind of Aussie version of
Beaujolais Nouveau. The grapes aren't the same – southern
French Grenache and Italian Barbera and Sangiovese – and the
effect isn't the same – this is fantastically tasty, really original
and I'd definitely go back for a second bottle. And a third. It's a
wonderful welter of plum, blueberry and blackberry fruit, rich
and bright as can be, but with just a hint of cautionary (as in –
just *two* bottles now, let's not be silly) austerity.

---

⑪ 2001 Chardonnay Cuvée Alexandre, Casa Lapostolle,
Casablanca Valley, Chile, £9.99, Safeway
This is from Chile's top white wine area – the cool Casablanca
Valley – and the result is a powerful but delicious Chardonnay,
rich with nuts and syrup and cream but finely balanced by
lemon acidity and the lissom scent of fresh leather. *Also at
Friarwood, Philglas & Swiggot, Wright Wine Co.*

---

⑫ 2002 Chardonnay, Pirque Estate, Viña Haras de Pirque,
Maipo Valley, Chile, £6.99, Marks & Spencer
This is a serious Chardonnay, sort of half savage and half
refined. The savage flavours are – wait for it – like fresh sweat
and sausagemeat, but before you say 'Ugh, yuck', those are the
flavours of top white Burgundies and some say *they* are the
best dry whites in the world. OK, it's got lemony acidity and a
lovely nut and honey richness too. Does that help? You're just
going to have to try it.

---

⑬ 2001 Live Oak Road Old Bush Vine Zinfandel, California,
USA, £9.99, Marks & Spencer
Old Bush Vines, the label says. Don't be so coy. These vines are
a century old. The big One Hundred. And does it show! The
older the vine gets the more intense the juice gets – and if the

juice is intense it takes a really bad winemaker to make dull wine. Well, these guys aren't dull, they're a passionate crew who live, eat and drool flavour. This brew is seven-eighths of the way to being OTT – I mean, that great spludge of dates and raisins and blackberry, is it for real? Well, yes it is.

⑭ 2001 Ancient Vines Carignan, Les Marionettes, Vin de Pays de l'Aude, Languedoc-Roussillon, France, £4.99, Safeway
So, welcome to the Youth Club. The vines that grew this wine are a mere 90 years old. Why isn't the wine twice the price? Because Carignan is a very unsexy grape. That doesn't mean it's no good. When it's 90 years old, it's fantastic. Find me a rich, deep red piled full of rough-hewn strawberry and plum, slashed with green apple acidity and soused with the exotic spice of Angostura bitters. Well, it's here. And it's £4.99.

⑮ 2002 Sauvignon Blanc, Shepherds Ridge, Wither Hills, Marlborough, New Zealand, £7.99, Marks & Spencer
M&S are developing an enviable talent for persuading a region's best winemakers to produce special cuvées for them. Brent Marris of Wither Hills is the hottest winemaker in New Zealand's Sauvignon Blanc Nirvana of Marlborough. And this is spot-on: bright, snappy, bristling with kiwi fruit and lime, with passionfruit also determined to be heard.

⑯ 2001 Organic Shiraz, Kalleske Estate, Barossa Valley, South Australia, £8.99, Marks & Spencer
We really should see more organic wine coming out of Australia, given that it's the driest continent on earth and most vine diseases are strongly influenced by wet weather. But we see disappointingly few examples. So I'm glad M&S have unearthed this rich, rather old-style red packed with rather stewy plum and blackberry fruit, splashed with spice and wrapped in tannin.

⑰ 2001 Omrah Unoaked Chardonnay, Plantagenet Wines, Western Australia, £6.99, Somerfield
This wine shows that Chardonnay has a lovely flavour all its own of honeysuckle, apple purée, dates and quince – rich flavours, but flavours from the fruit, not from a bag of oak chips. *This* is true Chardonnay. Many of the other current cloddish examples from Australia are not.

⑱ 1998 Rioja Reserva, Elegia, La Rioja Alta, Spain, £7.99, Sainsbury's
Sainsbury's have dealt with La Rioja Alta for as long as I can remember. There are far cheaper Rioja companies, but there are none better, and it's thoroughly reassuring to note such

long-term relationships in the topsy-turvy world of supermarkets today. And this is wonderfully reassuring Rioja, too, with its ripe strawberries and cream flavour and its deft brush of something savoury dabbed across the fruit.

⑲ 2002 Tesco Finest Sauvignon Blanc, Marlborough, New Zealand, £7.49, Tesco
New Zealand Sauvignon, instantly recognizable, instantly enjoyable for its soft yet sharp apple flesh and lime leaf flavours. Citrus yet soft – that's difficult to do, but they've done it.

⑳ 2002 Cape Gewürztraminer, Limited Release, Bergsig Estate, Breede River Valley, South Africa, £4.49, Co-op
Deep gold, waxy, with a rose petal scent and squashy, juicy peach and pear fruit. It's full, it's fat, it's floral, but it's balanced – a very nice rich, OTT style.

㉑ 2001 Chablis Premier Cru Chantrerie, Michel Laroche, Burgundy, France, £7.82, Asda
Classy Chablis from the local leader. This one is a Premier Cru – a first growth – indicating one of the best vineyard sites, but it's only an ordinary Chablis price and the wine is good –

Chile factor

WHITE
Chardonnay, Cuvée Alexandre, Casa Lapostolle (page 61)
Chardonnay, Casillero del Diablo, Concha y Toro (page 34)
Chardonnay, Condor (page 66)
Chardonnay, Montes Alpha (page 52)
Chardonnay, Pirque Estate (page 61)
Viognier, Casillero del Diablo, Concha y Toro (page 34)

RED
Chilean Red, San Pedro (page 69)
Cabernet Sauvignon, Santa Isabel Estate, Casablanca (page 14)
Cabernet Sauvignon, Casillero del Diablo, Concha y Toro (page 38)
Chilean Cabernet Sauvignon, Cornellana (page 65)
Chilean Cabernet Sauvignon, San Pedro (page 69)
Cabernet Sauvignon, Floresta, Santa Rita (page 22)
Cabernet Sauvignon, Neruda, Viñedos Sutil (page 31)
Carmenère Indomita Brio (page 30)
Carmenère, Peteroa (page 38)
Carmenère-Cabernet Sauvignon Reserve, Carmen (page 14)
Carmenère-Cabernet Sauvignon Novas, Viñedos Orgánicos Emiliana (page 28)
Coyam Red, Viñedos Orgánicos Emiliana (page 19)
Merlot, Marques de Casa Concha, Concha y Toro (page 20)
Merlot, Visión, Cono Sur (page 51)
The Society's Chilean Merlot (page 36)
Syrah, Errazuriz (page 55)
Syrah, Montes Alpha (page 56)

gentle yet austere, mixing a slightly New World ripeness and flicker of honey with good Old World French minerally restraint.

Economy class

There's no question that you get much better flavours at £3.99 than £2.99. Well. Think about it. All that excise tax – currently £1.20 a bottle – that VAT at 17.5%, the supermarkets' profit – and some of them are after a 40% margin on their wines – and perhaps a tiny profit for the producer – what, after providing bottles, labels, transport, feeding the cat? There's not a lot left over from £4. Still, we've got quite a good spread here, New World and Old, though Australia's only here because people haven't yet caught on to the fact that Petit Verdot is a star grape. When they do, we won't be seeing any of it at this price again.

❶ **Fitou, Cuvée Rocher d'Embrée, Les Producteurs du Mont Tauch, Languedoc-Roussillon, France, £3.99, Somerfield**
This top red comes from the wild, wilful vineyards of Fitou, and it's made by a co-op, who have set out to preserve the character of their wonderful hills and cliffs by producing sturdy, aggressively self-confident wines. You taste the gorgeous ripe but brutal flavours of Fitou, set high in its fastness of crags and scree and forest, and although the raspberry fruit is ripe and inviting, the sweetness has been soaked with bay leaves and thyme and splashed with the heady bitterness of Angostura to make a memorable budget red.

❷ **2002 Calatayud Garnacha, Viña Fuerte, Aragón, Spain, £3.99, Waitrose**
Fantastic stuff from a parched, arid vineyard region way inland from the Catalonian coast. The wine is bursting with blueberry and blackberry fruit that struggles manfully to get the better of a welter of bay, thyme and pepper.

❸ **2001 Faircape Cinsaut-Ruby Cabernet, KWV, South Africa, £3.99, Morrisons**
Cinsaut and Ruby Cabernet are not two grapes that sing a particularly lovely song by themselves, but the bland Cinsaut and the brutish Ruby seem to set each other off very well in a blend. This is delightful rich red wine, almost mild to taste – that's got to be the Cinsaut – but with lovely fruit that reminds me of a crystallized cocktail cherry bouncing around on a bed of strawberry sauce.

❹ **2000 Mornag Carignan-Syrah, Nilia Estate, Tunisia, £3.99, Morrisons**
There's been a mini-revival in north Africa in the past year or two, but Tunisia's New Wave has so far been rather ambitious

oaky stuff at about 6 quid. I don't see that selling at an exactly spanking pace, but these flavours at around £4 suddenly make sense. You can really taste the heat of Africa with the rich date and sultana fruit, but there's also a strong surge of fresh black plums that make this a very ripe and very tasty red.

---

❺ 2002 **Campo de Borja**, Santo Cristo, Aragón, Spain, £3.55, Waitrose
Not quite such as mouthful as the Calatayud, above; this time we get loads of ripe, juicy red cherry and red plum fruit, a splash of strawberry sauce and that restrained autumn scent of rosehips. There's even a hint of grapiness, too, and the whole thing reminds me rather of a summer pudding before the blackcurrants and blackberries are ripe.

---

❻ 2001 **Estremadura**, Cortello, Quinta do Gradil, Portugal, £3.99, Safeway
Portuguese reds have fascinatingly different flavours and this is no exception, mixing a positively bright apple acidity and fresh strawberry fruit with a rich date and herbs potpourri that verges on the baked. But a lot of the best fruit puddings are baked, so why not this one?

---

❼ 2002 **South African Pinotage**, Swartland, £3.99, Tesco
This is a big rich ripe beauty of a wine, with all the fabulously original flavours that make Pinotage a 'love me or leave me' grape variety. Mulberry fruit, the toasty burnt sweetness of marshmallow dropped for a second into the bonfire, and a lovely, rather sophisticated rosehip aftertaste. The vines that gave this wine are old, and that's why the flavour is so good.

---

❽ 2002 **Chardonnay-Pinot Grigio**, Riverview, Tolna region, Hilltop Neszmely, Hungary, £3.99, Safeway
Lovely, soft, perfumed white showing what a brilliant combination Chardonnay and Pinot Grigio can be in the right hands, in this instance the ultra-modern Hilltop winery near the Danube. It has a beautiful white peach and angelica fruit, a subtle smell of orange blossom and a fascinating green perfume rather like sage. This is the new Hungary for you.

---

❾ 2001 **Chilean Cabernet Sauvignon**, Rapel region, Viña Cornellana, £3.99, Somerfield
I'd hoped for some more Chileans at £3.99, because the quality of their red wine especially is fantastic. Still, I'll take what I can get and this is a very good mouthful of ripe, squashy plum fruit, a good dollop of blackcurrant, and a couple of sprigs of thyme.

Supermarket selection

❿ 2002 FirstCape Shiraz-Pinotage, South Africa, £3.99, Safeway

Good, typical Cape red, by which I mean it's not just juicy fruit and silky texture: no, this one has an appetizing tannic rasp and a serious whiff of Cape coal dust smoke, but they don't get in the way of bright, very gluggable raspberry fruit.

⓫ 2002 Condor Chardonnay, Viña San Pedro, Lontue Valley, Chile, £4.09, Morrisons

Chilean Chardonnays often tread the dangerous path of giving you a bit more tropical fruit and syrupy ripeness than you really want. But this one's about right. You get some peach syrup ripeness, but it's balanced by a brighter, crisper pear and apple crunchy fruit and mouthwatering acidity.

⓬ 2002 Slinky Chardonnay, Famatina Valley, Argentina, £3.99, Morrisons

If you like the rich honeyed style of Chardonnay, look no further. This is piled high with honey; so much so that it has to be balanced by some quite assertive acidity and, I thought, intriguingly, by a touch of red wine tannin!

⓭ Shiraz-Petit Verdot, Ransome's Vale, South-Eastern Australia, £3.99, Aldi

This year we tasted no decent Aussie Shiraz at £3.99 – but beef the Shiraz up with the perfumed, rich, but as yet unappreciated flavours of Petit Verdot and we've got something really tasty. This is powerful, gutsy Aussie red: spicy, and with a ripe dark fruit that almost tastes like blueberry cheesecake.

⓮ 2002 Viognier Vin de Pays d'Oc, Domaine Mandeville, Languedoc-Roussillon, France, £3.99, Marks & Spencer

2002 was pretty cool down in the South of France. This meant that some of the reds are a bit mean, but the whites like the cool weather, and it shows in this Viognier – not as fat and lush as usual, but with good apricot and pear fruit, a hint of floral scent and, unusually, a refreshing grapefruit acidity.

⓯ 2002 Sémillon, Franschhoek, South Africa, £3.99, Co-op

The Franschhoek Valley has some of the oldest Sémillon plantations in South Africa and makes serious wine that takes a bit of getting used to. In fact this wine really needs another couple of years in bottle – and it's not often I say *that* about a £3.99 wine. Right now it's a powerful white tasting of cloves and carpenter's dust and lemon zest and just beginning to show a custardy richness that will grow with time.

Economy class

⑯ 2001 Mourvèdre-Shiraz, ▼ Tortoiseshell Bay, Casella Wines, South-Eastern Australia, £3.99, Somerfield

Mourvèdre is a top grape, but hardly known, even though it is a crucial part of the make-up of good Châteauneuf-du-Pape. But the one thing it absolutely demands is heat – loads of it. Well, you don't get much hotter than the inland Aussie vineyards this wine comes from, and the result is a very attractive, minerally wine with lots of gentle ripe red fruit and no hard edges at all.

⑰ 2002 La Mancha, ▼ Tempranillo, Castillo de Alhambra, Vinicola de Castilla, Spain, £3.79, Safeway

It's seriously hot down south of Madrid where this comes from, and there's just a hint of baked fruit here, along with some chewy tannin, but the fruit flavours are surprisingly fresh, even perfumed, with apple acidity cutting through a very pleasant cherry and strawberry core.

> ## Out of Africa
>
> **SPARKLING**
> Graham Beck Brut (page 45)
>
> **WHITE**
> Chardonnay, Neil Ellis (page 52)
> Chenin, Forrester Meinert (page 57)
> Chenin Blanc, KWV (page 70)
> Chenin Blanc, Villiera (page 33)
> Gewürztraminer, Bergsig Estate (page 63)
> Sauvignon Blanc, Van Loveren (page 42)
> Sémillon, Franschhoek (page 66)
>
> **RED**
> Cabernet Sauvignon, Condé (page 13)
> Mornag Carignan-Syrah, Nilia Estate, Tunisia (page 64)
> Cinsaut-Ruby Cabernet, KWV (page 64)
> Pinotage, Swartland (page 65)
> Shiraz, Stellar Organics (page 31)
> Shiraz-Pinotage (page 66)
> South African Red (page 68)

---

⑱ 2000 Cabernet Sauvignon-Petit Verdot, Prospect Hill, ▼ South-Eastern Australia, £3.99, Morrisons

Petit Verdot again provides the oomph here. I think the Cabernet by itself would have been a bit soft and flat, but Petit Verdot strides in and hurls a great wodge of black cherries and spice into the vat – and the wine is transformed.

---

⑲ 2002 Château Haut-Pradot, Bordeaux, France, ▼ £4, Asda

This is a smart piece of wine selection from Asda. 2002 wasn't an easy vintage in Bordeaux and decent Bordeaux from a single property is very difficult to source at this price. But this is proper claret: dry, rather earthy, but with a good, appetizing raspberry red fruit and just a nip of tannin at the end. 'Luncheon claret', the old guys used to call wines like this – enjoyable, but reasonably harmless if you've got an afternoon's work to do.

❽ Sainsbury's Claret, Bordeaux, France, £2.58

Another decent basic Bordeaux to make you ask why so many
other examples at a quid or two more are so poor. This is full,
soft, stewy stuff with some earthy tannin easily matched by
mouthfilling fruitcake flavours from the Merlot grape.

**❾ 2002 FairCape Chenin Blanc, KWV, South Africa,
£2.99, Morrisons**

This used to be a world-famous wine in the bad old days of
the Cape, nutty, honeyed, delicious. It's now a very nice mild
white, and you can still taste the honeysuckle.

**❿ 2000 Simply Gewürztraminer, Hilltop Neszmély,
Pannonhalma region, Hungary, £2.99, Tesco**

If you like mouthfilling whites redolent of flower gardens and
apple orchards, this'll do you nicely. It's so soft it reminds me
of a Bath bun, it's perfumed with rosepetals and hothouse
grapes and it's kept fresh with acidity as crisp as a bite of
English (not French) Golden Delicious.

**⓫ Chardonnay, Vin de Pays d'Oc, Languedoc-Roussillon,
France, £2.99, Budgens**

Attractive, clean, non-oaky Chardonnay with some banana
and pear freshness and a good crackling green apple acidity. If
all southern French Chardonnay were this easy to drink and
this approachable, we wouldn't feel compelled to turn to
other grape varieties with such enthusiasm.

**⓬ Romanian Pinot Noir, Prahova Winecellars, Dealul Mare
region, £3.09, Sainsbury's**

This used to be fantastic jammy stuff, then it went all green
and miserable, but it now looks as though it's getting back on
form in a more modern, up-front fruity kind of way. Which is
good, because when it's on form this is the best-value Pinot
Noir on the market – a little stewy, a little earthy, but with
enough loganberry and strawberry fruit and redcurrant
acidity for that not to matter.

**⓭ 2001 Chardonnay, Budavár, Danubiana,
Észak-Magyarországi region, Hungary, £2.49, Aldi**

Unbeatable value for penny-pinching Chardonnay lovers –
gentle, round, appley, with a touch of lemon acidity and some
honeysuckle scent.

**⓮ 2002 Shiraz-Cabernet, Badgers Creek, South-
Eastern Australia, £2.99, Aldi**

Bargain-priced Aussie blends are extremely erratic at the
moment, so let's hope this one keeps its decent chewy dark

spirit quietly transform into a beautiful, intense but lusciously smooth marriage of moist muscovado sugar, the richest of raisins and a surprising faint whiff of strawberries and cream.

---

❸ Morris Liqueur Muscat, Rutherglen, Australia, £5.49/50cl, Tesco

Don't expect subtle; this is seriously rich – great wodges of viscous grape syrup all churned up with muscovado sugar and sultanas and figs – and just when you think your palate's had enough, there's a sudden waft of tea rose perfume. Which is rather subtle, I suppose.

---

❹ 10-Year-Old Tawny Port, Smith Woodhouse, Portugal, £10.59, Tesco

This is good port, not thrilling, but a decent, solid mouthful of fat, rich fruit, and a seriously grapy texture that washes over your tongue and lingers for quite a while as you savour the flavour of hazelnuts and raisins – in syrup, of course.

---

❺ 2001 Elysium Black Muscat, Andrew Quady, California, USA, £7.49/half bottle, Budgens

This is pretty wild. Andrew Quady has made a kind of 'port': dark pink, slightly spirity, but awash with the flavours of loganberry, blackberry and sloes – and with a nip of acidity at the end. *Also at Berry Bros & Rudd, Lay & Wheeler, Unwins.*

---

❻ 1999 Tesco Finest Sauternes, Yvon Mau, Bordeaux, France, £9.99/half bottle

Don't expect a flood of super-rich flavours – Sauternes is rarely as out and out sweet as the stickies from New World countries – but this does have a seductive waxy texture almost like the beeswax from a honeycomb, and it does have a spiced fruit taste, like cinnamon sprinkled on top of an apricot cake, and it does have a deep pineapple syrup and barley-sugar maturity held in check by quite evident acidity. And I think all that is quite rich enough.

---

❼ Finest Reserve Vintage Character Port, Portugal, £7.99, Marks & Spencer

'Vintage Character' really only means a slightly beefier, slightly older and maybe slightly classier Ruby port. And that's what you get here. Nothing sophisticated, but a fair blast of fiery rich liquid, deep, ripe and packed with juicy plum fruit.

---

❽ Late Bottled Vintage Port, Smith Woodhouse, Portugal, £7.99, Safeway

This is made by one of my favourite port houses – Smith Woodhouse – but it's good rather than great. Full, deep and plummy, its ripeness tempered by a little wood bark dryness, but the flavour overall is a little indistinct.

❾ Muscat de Frontignan, Domaine d'Arain, Languedoc-Roussillon, France, £3.99, Somerfield

This is pretty good stuff and it really whacks your palate with grapy syrup. Unsubtle? Sure it is, but it heaps on the peaches in syrup, the rich orange marmalade and the Muscaty treacle, and that's exactly what I want.

❿ Fletcher's Fine Ruby Port, Portugal, £4.49, Aldi

As the evenings draw in, the fogs return and the gloom of winter spreads its baleful pall over the land, a slug of this rich, sweet red plum flavoured wine will seem like £4.49 well spent.

SHERRY

✪ Noé Very Old Pedro Ximénez, González Byass, £10.69, Tesco

Superb, inspiring sherry with flavours from another world. This is about as sweet a wine as you can get, yet the flavour is so thrilling it never cloys. Look at the colour first: dark, Stygian brown with a translucent green rim like a spirit level from Hades. It's so thick, it's unwilling to slither down the glass. You certainly can't drink anything else for a good half hour – and it's no good sluicing your mouth with water – this flavour embeds itself into your palate with crampons of luscious intensity. Molasses, Fowler's Black Treacle, Radio Malt – there's childhood memories for you, all so thick I could eat them – and piled in on top you get fistfuls of figs and moist muscovado sugar and Harrogate toffee burnt in the pan. But there's more. Running through this heavenly stew is a taut acidity, a wraith of smoke and a health-giving, savoury taste of Bovril beef tea.

✪ Extra Dry Manzanilla, Williams & Humbert, £4.99, Marks & Spencer

Good, bone dry wine – and I mean seriously bone dry – but there's also a delightfully soft texture and gentle dough and yeast taste, with just the merest hint of salt. Try this ice cold with tapas or salted roasted almonds and you'll wonder how you ever drank Chardonnay as an aperitif.ea.

✪ Sainsbury's Manzanilla, Francisco Gonzales Fernandez, £4.49

Another very nice, yeasty, slightly salty, bone dry sherry. If Marks & Spencer and Sainsbury's are prepared to pay for decent Manzanilla, let's encourage them by buying the stuff.

Storing, serving, tasting

Wine is all about enjoyment, so don't let anyone make you anxious about opening, serving, tasting and storing it – it's a doddle. Here are some tips to help you enjoy your wine all the more.

THE CORKSCREW

The first step in tasting any wine is to extract the cork. Look for a corkscrew with an open spiral, a comfortable handle and a mechanism that you like using. The Screwpull brand is still far and away the best, with a high-quality open spiral. 'Waiter's friend' corkscrews – the type you see used in restaurants – are good too, once you get the knack.

Corkscrews with a solid core that looks like a giant woodscrew tend to mash up delicate corks or get stuck in tough ones. A simple non-levered screw can require a heroic effort. And try to avoid those awful 'butterfly' corkscrews with the twin lever arms and a bottle opener on the end; they tend to leave cork crumbs floating in the wine.

CORKS

Don't be a cork snob. The only requirements for the seal on a bottle of wine are that it should be hygienic, airtight, long-lasting and removable. Real cork is environmentally friendly, but is prone to shrinkage and infection, which can taint the wine. Synthetic closures modelled on the traditional cork are common in budget wines and are increasingly used by high-quality producers, as are screwcaps, also known as Stelvin closures.

THE WINE GLASS

The ideal wine glass is a fairly large tulip shape, made of fine, clear glass, with a slender stem. This shape helps to concentrate the aromas of the wine and to show off its colours and texture. For sparkling wine choose a tall, slender glass, as it helps the bubbles to last longer.

Look after your glasses carefully. Detergent residues or grease can affect the flavour of any wine and reduce the bubbliness of sparkling wine. Always rinse glasses thoroughly after washing and allow them to air-dry. Ideally, wash them in very hot water and don't use detergent at all. Store your wine glasses upright to avoid trapping stale odours.

DECANTING

Transferring wine to a decanter brings it into contact with oxygen, which can open up the flavours. You don't need to do it ages before serving and you don't need a special decanter: a glass jug is just as good. And there's no reason why you shouldn't decant the wine to aerate it, then pour it back into its bottle to serve it.

Mature red wine is likely to contain sediment and needs careful handling. Stand the bottle upright for a day or two to let the sediment fall to the bottom. Open the wine carefully, and place a torch or candle beside the decanter. As you pour, stand so that you can see the light shining through the neck of the bottle. Pour the wine into the decanter in one steady motion and stop when you see the sediment reaching the neck of the bottle.

TEMPERATURE

The temperature of wine has a bearing on its flavour. Heavy reds are happy at room temperature – but not too warm, or they'll taste soupy and dull. The lighter the wine the cooler it should be: juicy, fruity young reds, such as wines from Beaujolais and the Loire Valley, are refreshing served lightly chilled; I'd serve Burgundy and other Pinot Noir reds at cool larder temperature.

Chilling white wines makes them taste fresher, but also subdues flavours, so bear this in mind if you're splashing out on a top-quality white and don't keep it in the fridge too long. Sparkling wines, however, *must* be well chilled to avoid exploding corks and fountains of foam.

For quick chilling fill a bucket with ice and cold water, plus a few spoonfuls of salt if you're in a real hurry. This is much more effective than a fridge or ice on its own. You can buy gel 'sleeves' to keep in the freezer for emergencies, or a domestic version of the chiller machine offered in some off-licences. If the wine is already cool a vacuum-walled cooler is ideal for maintaining the temperature.

KEEPING LEFTOVERS

Exposure to oxygen causes wine to deteriorate. It lasts fairly well if you just push the cork back in and stick the bottle in the fridge, but you can also buy a range of effective devices to help keep oxygen at bay. Vacuvin uses a rubber stopper and a vacuum pump to remove air from the bottle. Others inject inert gas into the bottle to shield the wine from the ravages of oxidation.

WINE STORAGE

The longer you keep a bottle of wine, the more important it is to store it with care. If you've got a cellar, lucky you; the Spiral Cellar makes the most of a small amount of space if you're able to excavate. If not, look around for a nook – under the stairs, a built-in cupboard or a disused fireplace – that is cool, relatively dark and vibration-free, in which you can store the bottles on their sides to keep the corks moist (if the cork dries out it will let air in – and spoil the wine).

Wine should be kept in a cool place – around 10–15°C/50–55°F – well away from central heating. It is even more important to avoid sudden temperature changes or extremes: a windowless garage or outhouse may be cool in summer but may freeze in winter. Exposure to light can very quickly ruin wine, but dark bottles go some way to protecting it from light.

SupremeCorq.® The closure that keeps wine as the winemaker *intended*.

The difference between a wine being "magnificent" and "musty" is often the length of the cork. Which is why hundreds of wineries have chosen to bottle their wines with SupremeCorq. SupremeCorq is a revolutionary closure that virtually eliminates the leakage and off-flavours associated with traditional closures. It opens with a regular corkscrew and is easy to reinsert. The SupremeCorq closure will not break or crumble and is recyclable. Look for them topping off bottles in pubs, fine restaurants and wine shops worldwide. Visit us at: www.supremecorq.com.

SUPREMECORQ®

Designed to keep fine wine fine.

How to taste wine

If you just knock your wine back like a cold beer, you'll be missing most of whatever flavour it has to offer. Take a bit of time to pay attention to what you're tasting and I guarantee you'll enjoy the wine more.

Read the label

There's no law that says you have to make life hard for yourself when tasting wine. So have a look at what you're drinking and read the notes on the back label if there is one. The label will tell you the vintage, the region and/or the grape variety, the producer and the alcohol level.

Look at the wine

Pour the wine into a glass so it is a third full and tilt it against a white background so you can enjoy the range of colours in the wine. Is it dark or light? Is it viscous or watery? As you gain experience the look of the wine will tell you one or two things about the age and the likely flavour and weight of the wine. As a wine ages, whites lose their springtime greenness and gather deeper, golden hues, whereas red wines trade the purple of youth for a paler brick red.

Swirl and sniff

Give the glass a vigorous swirl to wake up the aromas in the wine, stick your nose in and inhale gently. This is where you'll be hit by the amazing range of smells a wine can produce. Interpret them in any way that means something to you personally: it's only by reacting honestly to the taste and smell of a wine that you can build up a memory bank of flavours against which to judge future wines.

Take a sip

At last! It's time to drink the wine. So take a decent-sized slurp – enough to fill your mouth about a third full. The tongue can detect only very basic flavour elements: sweetness at the tip, acidity at the sides and bitterness at the back. The real business of tasting goes on in a cavity at the back of the mouth which is really part of the nose. The idea is to get the fumes from the wine to rise up into this nasal cavity. Note the toughness, acidity and sweetness of the wine then suck some air through the wine to help the flavours on their way. Gently 'chew' the wine and let it coat your tongue, teeth, cheeks and gums. Jot down a few notes as you form your opinion and then make the final decision... Do you like it or don't you?

Swallow or spit it out

If you are tasting a lot of wines, you will have to spit as you go if you want to remain upright and retain your judgement. Otherwise, go ahead and swallow and enjoy the lovely aftertaste of the wine.

WINE FAULTS

If you order wine in a restaurant and you find one of these faults you are entitled to a replacement. Many retailers will also replace a faulty bottle if you return it the day after you open it, with your receipt. Sometimes faults affect random bottles, others may ruin a whole case of wine.

- Cork taint – a horrible musty, mouldy smell indicates 'corked' wine, caused by a contaminated cork
- Volatile acidity – pronounced vinegary or acetone smells
- Oxidation – sherry-like smells are not appropriate in red and white wines
- Hydrogen sulphide – 'rotten eggs' smell.

WATCHPOINTS

- Sediment in red wines makes for a gritty, woody mouthful. To avoid this, either decant the wine or simply pour it gently, leaving the last few centimetres of wine in the bottle.
- White crystals, or tartrates, on the cork or at the bottom of bottles of white wine are both harmless and flavourless.
- Sticky bottle neck – if wine has seeped past the cork it probably hasn't been very well kept and air might have got in. This may mean oxidized wine.
- Excess sulphur dioxide is sometimes noticeable as a smell of a recently struck match; it should dissipate after a few minutes.

Wine style guide

When faced with a shelf – or a screen – packed with different wines from around the world, where do you start? Well, if you're after a particular flavour of wine, my guide to wine styles will point you in the right direction.

RED WINES
Juicy, fruity reds

The definitive modern style for easygoing reds. Tasty, refreshing and delicious with or without food, they pack in loads of crunchy fruit while minimizing the tough, gum-drying tannins that characterize most traditional red wine styles. Beaujolais (made from the Gamay grape) is the prototype, and Loire reds such as Chinon and Saumur (made from Cabernet Franc) pack in the fresh raspberries. Italy's Bardolino is light and refreshing. Nowadays, hi-tech producers all over the world are working the magic with a whole host of grape varieties. Carmenère and Merlot are always good bets, and Grenache/Garnacha and Tempranillo usually come up with the goods. Italian grapes like Bonarda, Barbera and Sangiovese seem to double in succulence under Argentina's blazing sun. And at around £5 even Cabernet Sauvignon – if it's from somewhere warm like Australia, South America, South Africa or Spain – or a vin de pays Syrah from southern France, will emphasize the fruit and hold back on the tannin.

- **2002 Santa Julia Bonarda-Sangiovese,** Familia Zuccardi, Mendoza, Argentina, £4.55, Waitrose
- **2001 Peter Lehmann Barossa Grenache,** Australia, £5.49, Oddbins
- **2001 Calatayud, Poema Garnacha Old Vine,** Bodegas Virgin del Mar y de la Cuesta, Aragón, Spain, £5.29, Morrisons
- **2002 Beaujolais, Blaise Carron,** Burgundy, France, £6.85, Roger Harris
- **2000 Chinon Vieilles Vignes, Domaine de la Chapelle,** Philippe Pichard, Loire Valley, France, £8.45, Christopher Piper

Silky, strawberryish reds

Here we're looking for some special qualities, specifically a gorgeously smooth texture and a heavenly fragrance of strawberries, raspberries or cherries. We're looking for soft, decadent, seductive wines. One grape – Pinot Noir – and one region – Burgundy – stand out and prices are high to astronomical. Good red

Burgundy is addictively hedonistic and all sorts of strange decaying aromas start to hover around the strawberries as the wine ages. Pinot Noirs from New Zealand, California, Oregon and, increasingly, Australia come close, but they're expensive, too; Chilean Pinots are far more affordable. You can get that strawberry perfume (though not the silky texture) from other grapes in Spain's Navarra or Rioja and up-coming regions like La Mancha and Murcia. Southern Rhône blends can deliver if you look for fairly light examples of Côtes du Rhône-Villages or Costières de Nîmes.

- 2002 **Pinot Noir, Recas,** Romania, £3.49, Wines of Westhorpe
- 2002 **Lacrima di Morra d'Alba Rubico,** Marotti Campi, Marche, Italy, £7.99, Oddbins
- 2002 **Ninth Island Pinot Noir,** Tasmania, Australia, £7.99, Waitrose
- 2000 **Cono Sur 20 Barrels Pinot Noir,** Chile, £11.49, Majestic
- 2000 **Ata Rangi Pinot Noir,** Martinborough, New Zealand, £26–28, Berry Bros & Rudd, Justerini & Brooks, Lea & Sandeman, New Zealand Wines Direct, Roberson, Frank Stainton, Tanners

Intense, blackcurranty reds

Firm, intense wines which often only reveal their softer side with a bit of age; Cabernet Sauvignon is the grape, on its own or blended with Merlot or other varieties. Bordeaux is the classic region but there are far too many overpriced underachievers there. And Cabernet's image has changed. You can still choose the austere, tannic style, in theory aging to a heavenly cassis and cedar maturity, but most of the world is taking a fruitier blackcurrant-and-mint approach. Chile does the fruity style par excellence. New Zealand can deliver Bordeaux-like flavours, but in a faster-maturing wine. Australia often adds a medicinal eucalyptus twist or a dollop of blackcurrant jam. Argentina and South Africa are making their mark too.

- 2001 **Steenberg Merlot,** Constantia, South Africa, about £11, John Armit, Waitrose, Wimbledon Wine Cellar
- 2001 **Esk Valley Reserve Merlot-Malbec-Cabernet Sauvignon,** Hawkes Bay, New Zealand, £14.99, Wimbledon Wine Cellar
- 2000 **Condé Cabernet Sauvignon,** Stark-Condé Wines, Stellenbosch, South Africa, £17.95, H & H Bancroft
- 1999 **Santa Rita Triple C,** Maipo Valley, Chile, about £14.99, Berkmann, Majestic
- 1999 **Terrazas Gran Cabernet Sauvignon,** Mendoza, Argentina, £19.50, Peter Green, Wimbledon Wine Cellar

Spicy, warm-hearted reds

Australian Shiraz is the epitome of this rumbustious, riproaring style: dense, rich, chocolaty, sometimes with a twist of pepper, a whiff of smoke, or a slap of leather. But it's not alone. There are southern Italy's Primitivo and Nero d'Avola, California's Zinfandel, Mexico's Petite Sirah, Argentina's Malbec, South Africa's Pinotage, Toro from Spain and some magnificent Greek reds. In southern France the wines of the Languedoc often show this kind of warmth, roughed up with hillside herbs. And if you want your spice more serious, more smoky and minerally, go for the classic wines of the northern Rhône Valley.

- **2001 Inycon Nero d'Avola,** Sicily, Italy, £4.99, Booths
- **2002 Diemersfontein Pinotage,** Wellington, South Africa, £6.99, Waitrose
- **2001 Nótios, Gaia,** Peloponnese, Greece, £7.39, Oddbins
- **2001 Heartland Wirrega Shiraz,** Limestone Coast, Australia, £7.29, Oddbins
- **2000 Ancient Vines Mourvèdre, Cline,** Contra Costa County, California, USA, £14.60, The Wine Treasury, Virgin Wines

Mouthwatering, sweet-sour reds

Sounds weird? This style is the preserve of Italy, and it's all about food: the rasp of sourness cuts through rich, meaty food, with a lip-smacking tingle that works equally well with pizza or tomato-based pasta dishes. But there's fruit in there too – cherries and plums – plus raisiny sweetness and a herby bite. The wines are now better made than ever, with more seductive fruit, but holding on to those fascinating flavours. You'll have to shell out up to a tenner for decent Chianti; more for Piedmont wines (especially Barolo and Barbaresco, so try Langhe instead). Valpolicella can be very good, but you need to choose with care. Portugal can deliver something of the same character with its sour-cherries reds. Oddball grapes like Chambourcin often have these flavours.

- **2001 Senda do Vale Trincadeira-Cabernet Sauvignon,** Ribatejano, Portugal, £4.99, Sainsbury's
- **2000 Valpolicella Classico Superiore Ripasso, La Casetta,** Veneto, Italy, £8.99, Majestic
- **1999 Malbec-Corvina, Passo Doble, La Arboleda, Masi Tupungato,** Argentina, £8.99, Berkmann, Bring-a-Bottle, Noel Young Wines
- **1997 Chianti Classico Riserva, Villa Cafaggio,** Tuscany, Italy, £14.99, Villeneuve Wines, Laithwaites
- **1998 Amarone della Valpolicella Classico, Allegrini,** Veneto, Italy, £30–35, Berry Bros, Philglas & Swiggot, Portland Wine Co, La Réserve, Frank Stainton, Valvona & Crolla, Noel Young Wines

Delicate (and not-so-delicate) rosé

Dry rosé can be wonderful, with flavours of strawberries and maybe herbs. Look for wines from sturdy grapes like Cabernet, Syrah or Merlot, or go for Grenache, the classic rosé grape of Spain and the Rhône Valley. South America is a good, flavoursome bet.

- **2002 Gran Feudo Rosé,** Julian Chivite, Navarra, Spain, £4.69, Oddbins
- **2003 Santa Julia Syrah Rosé,** Familia Zuccardi, Mendoza, Argentina, £4.99, Sainsbury's
- **2002 Goats do Roam Rosé,** Fairview, South Africa, £4.99, Oddbins, Tesco, Waitrose
- **Masterpeace Rosé,** Australia, £4.99, Threshers
- **2002 Santa Digna Cabernet Sauvignon Rosé,** Miguel Torres, Curicó, Chile, £5.69, Amey's Wines, Selfridges (London and Manchester), Tanners

Don't be a Nerd

𝕲𝖔𝖆𝖙𝖘 𝖉𝖔 𝕽𝖔𝖆𝖒

Join the Herd

THE WINES OF CHARLES BACK
SOUTH AFRICA

How to buy vegetarian and vegan wine

Virtually all wine is clarified with 'fining' agents, many of which are animal by-products. Although they are not present in the finished wine, they are clearly not acceptable for strict vegetarians and vegans. Non-animal alternatives such as bentonite clay are widely used and vegan wines rely solely on these; vegetarian wines can use egg whites or milk proteins.

• **Specialist merchants** Organic specialists such as Vinceremos and Vintage Roots assess every wine on their lists for its vegetarian or vegan status.

• **Supermarkets** Most supermarkets stock some vegetarian and vegan wines and identify own-label ones with a symbol, such as the 'V' logo used by Somerfield and Marks & Spencer. Also look for information on supermarket websites or contact the wine department at the head office. They should be able to send a list of all the vegetarian and vegan wines they sell.

• **Other outlets** Check the labels. Some producers, such as Chapoutier, use a 'V' symbol to indicate vegetarian wines.

WHITE WINES
Bone-dry, neutral whites

Neutral wines exist for the sake of
seafood or to avoid interrupting you
while you're eating. It's a question of
balance, rather than aromas and
flavours, but there will be a bit of lemon,
yeast and a mineral thrill in a good
Muscadet sur lie or a proper Chablis. Loads

of Italian whites do the same thing, but Italy is
increasingly picking up on the global shift towards fruit flavours
and maybe some oak. Cheaper French wines are often too raw,
whereas low-priced Italian whites tend to be insipid. Basic, cheap
South African whites are often a good bet.

- 2002 **Chardonnay Sur Lie, Danie de Wet**, Robertson, South
  Africa, £3.99–4.99, widely available
- 2001 **Chenin Blanc, Villiera**, South Africa, £5.99, Threshers
- 2002 **Muscadet, Domaine de l'Ecu**, Guy Bossard, Loire
  Valley, France, £6.49, everywine.co.uk
- 2001 **Soave Classico Superiore, Suavia**, Veneto, Italy, £6.95,
  Bibendum, £7.49 Oddbins
- 2001 **Pinot Blanc-Auxerrois, Albert Mann**, Alsace, France,
  £7.29, Oddbins

Green, tangy whites

For nerve-tingling refreshment, Sauvignon Blanc is the classic
grape, full of fresh grass, gooseberry and nettle flavours. I always
used to go for New Zealand versions, but I'm now more inclined
to reach for an inexpensive bottle from South Africa or Hungary.
Or even a simple white Bordeaux, because suddenly Bordeaux
Sauvignon is buzzing with life. Most Sancerre and the other
Loire Sauvignons are overpriced. Austria's Grüner Veltliner has a
peppery freshness. Alternatively, look at Riesling. Australia
serves it up with bountiful lime and toast flavours while classic
German versions are steelier and green-apple fresh, with
intriguing peach and smoke flavours in their youth.

- 2001 **Vin de Pays des Cotes du Tarn, Sauvignon Blanc,
  Domaine Vigné-Lourac**, £5.30, Hicks & Don
- 2002 **Neil Ellis Sauvignon Blanc**, Groenekloof, South Africa,
  £7.99, Safeway
- 2002 **Forrest Estate Sauvignon Blanc**, Marlborough, New
  Zealand, £8.75, Adnams
- 2001 **Howard Park Riesling**, Great Southern, Western
  Australia, £9.95, Lay & Wheeler
- 2000 **Escherndorfer Lump Riesling Kabinett, Horst
  Sauer**, Franken, Germany, £9.99, Noel Young Wines

Intense, nutty whites

The best white Burgundy from the Côte d'Or cannot be bettered for its combination of soft nut and oatmeal flavours, subtle, buttery oak and firm, dry structure. Prices are often hair-raising and the cheaper wines rarely offer much Burgundy style. For £6 or £7 your best bet is oaked Chardonnay from an innovative Spanish region such as Somontano or Navarra. You'll get a nutty, creamy taste and nectarine fruit with good oak-aged white Bordeaux or traditional white Rioja. Top Chardonnays from New World countries – and Italy for that matter – can emulate Burgundy, but once again we're looking at serious prices.

- **2001 Averys Fine White Burgundy,** France, £7.50, Averys
- **2001 Limoux Chardonnay,** Domaine Bégude, Languedoc-Roussillon, France, £7.99, Booths
- **2002 Neil Ellis Chardonnay,** South Africa, £8.99, Tesco
- **2001 Planeta Chardonnay,** Sicily, Italy, £17.50, Ballantynes, Roberson, Valvona & Crolla, Wimbledon Wine Cellar
- **2001 Piccadilly Chardonnay, Grosset,** Adelaide Hills, Australia, £18.50, Fortnum & Mason

Ripe, toasty whites

Aussie Chardonnay conquered the world with its upfront flavours of peaches, apricots and tropical fruits, spiced up by the vanilla, toast and butterscotch richness of new oak. This winning style has now become a standard-issue flavour produced by all sorts of countries, though I still love the original. You don't need to spend more than a fiver for a great big friendly wine, though a well-spent £8 or so will give you more to relish beyond the second glass. Oaked Australian Semillon can also give rich, ripe fruit flavours. If you see the words 'unoaked' or 'cool-climate' on an Aussie bottle, expect an altogether leaner drink.

- **2002 Marques de Casa Concha Chardonnay,** Chile, £6.99, Safeway, Threshers
- **2002 Allandale Chardonnay,** Hunter Valley, New South Wales, Australia, £7.99, Australian Wine Club, Moriarty, Oz Wines, Reid Wines
- **2001 Wither Hills Chardonnay,** Marlborough, New Zealand, £8.99, Booths, Waitrose
- **2003 D'Arenberg The Hermit Crab Marsanne-Viognier,** McLaren Vale, Australia, £7.29, Oddbins
- **2000 The Willows Vineyard Semillon,** Barossa Valley, Australia, £9.99, Australian Wine Club, Threshers

Wine style guide

Aromatic whites

Alsace has always been a plentiful source of perfumed, dry or off-dry whites: Gewürztraminer with its rose and lychee scent or Muscat with its floral, hothouse grape perfume. A few producers in New Zealand, Australia, Chile and South Africa are having some success with these grapes. Floral, apricotty Viognier, traditionally the grape of Condrieu in the northern Rhône, now appears in vins de pays from all over southern France and also from California and Australia. Condrieu is expensive (£20 will get you entry-level stuff and no guarantee that it will be fragrant); vin de pays wines start at around £5 and are just as patchy. Albariño from Rías Baixas in Spain is more reliable. For aroma on a budget grab some Hungarian Irsai Oliver or Argentinian Torrontes.

- 2002 **Torrontes La Nature (organic)**, Famatina Valley, Argentina, £4.49, Budgens
- 2002 **Casillero del Diablo Viognier, Concha y Toro**, Casablanca Valley, Chile, £4.99, Booths
- 2002 **Gewurztraminer**, Cave de Turckheim, Alsace, France, £5.99, Marks & Spencer
- 2001 **Pipers Brook Gewurztraminer**, Tasmania, Australia, £10–11, D Byrne, Connolly's, Noble Rot
- 2001 **Condrieu La Petite Côte, Cuilleron**, Rhône Valley, France, £29.99, Enotria (020 8963 4820)

Golden, sweet whites

Good sweet wines are difficult to make and therefore expensive: prices for Sauternes and Barsac (from Bordeaux) can go through the roof, but near-neighbours Monbazillac, Loupiac, Saussignac and Ste-Croix-du-Mont are more affordable. Sweet Loire wines such as Quarts de Chaume, Bonnezeaux and some Vouvrays have a quince aroma and a fresh acidity that can keep them lively for decades, as do sweet Rieslings, such as Alsace Vendange Tardive, German and Austrian Beerenauslese (BA), Trockenbeerenauslese (TBA) and Eiswein. Canadian icewine is quite rare over here, but we're seeing more of Hungary's Tokaji, with its sweet-sour, marmalade flavours.

- 1996 **Saussignac, Clos d'Yvigne**, Patricia Atkinson, South-West France, £17/50cl, Justerini & Brooks
- 1997 **Mission Hill Riesling Icewine**, Canada, £19.99/half bottle, Berkmann, James Nicholson, Valvona & Crolla, Wimbledon Wine
- 1999 **De Bortoli Noble One Botrytis Semillon**, New South Wales, Australia, £12.99/half bottle, Noble Rot
- 2000 **Scheurebe TBA No. 5, Kracher**, Austria, £22.99/half bottle, Noel Young Wines
- 2000 **Escherndorfer Lump Riesling BA, Horst Sauer**, Franken, Germany, £50/50 cl, Noel Young

SPARKLING WINES

Champagne can be the finest sparkling wine on the planet, but fizz made by the traditional Champagne method in Australia, New Zealand or California – often using the same grape varieties – is often just as good and cheaper. It might be a little more fruity, where Champagne concentrates on bready, yeasty or nutty aromas, but a few are dead ringers for the classic style. Fizz is also made in other parts of France: Crémant de Bourgogne is one of the best. England is beginning to show its potential. Spain's Cava is perfect party fizz available at bargain basement prices in all the big supermarkets.

CHAMPAGNE
BILLECART-SALMON
Maison Fondée en 1818

www.champagne-billecart.fr

- **NV Pelorus, Cloudy Bay,** New Zealand, £12.99, Threshers and Wine Rack
- **1999 Bloomsbury Cuvée Merret Brut, Ridgeview,** West Sussex, England, £14.99, Waitrose
- **1996 Pirie,** Tasmania, Australia, £19.50, Harvey Nichols (or direct from Boutinot Wines – 020 7357 7080)
- **Champagne Brut Réserve Charles Heidsieck Mis en Cave en 1996,** £23.49, Waitrose
- **1997 Champagne Billecart-Salmon Cuvée Nicolas François Billecart,** £38.99, Berry Bros & Rudd, Fortnum & Mason, James Nicholson, Oddbins, Portland Wine Co, Roberson

FORTIFIED WINES
Tangy, appetizing fortified wines

To set your taste buds tingling, fino and manzanilla sherries are pale, perfumed, bone-dry and bracingly tangy. True amontillado, dark and nutty, is also dry. Dry oloroso adds deep, raisiny flavours. Palo cortado falls somewhere between amontillado and oloroso, and manzanilla pasada is an older, nuttier style of manzanilla.

The driest style of Madeira, Sercial, is steely and smoky; Verdelho Madeira is a bit fuller and richer, but still tangy and dry.

- **Manzanilla La Gitana**, Hidalgo, about £6, widely available
- **Manzanilla Mariscal**, Dolores Bustillo Delgado, £6.55
- **Amontillado Del Duque**, González Byass, £10.99/half bottle, Harvey Nichols, Sainsbury's
- **Amontillado Principe de Barbadillo**, £19.99, Connolly's, Stevens Garnier
- **10 Year Old Sercial Madeira**, Henriques & Henriques, £11.99/50cl, Waitrose

Rich, warming fortified wines

Raisins and brown sugar, dried figs and caramelized nuts – do you like the sound of that? Port is the classic dark sweet wine, and it comes in several styles, from basic ruby, to tawny, matured in cask for 10 years or more, to vintage, which matures to mellowness in the bottle. The Portuguese island of Madeira produces fortified wines with rich brown smoky flavours and a startling bite of acidity: the sweet styles to look for are Bual and Malmsey.

Decent sweet sherries are rare; oloroso dulce is a style with stunningly concentrated flavours. In southern France, Banyuls and Maury are deeply fruity fortified wines. Marsala, from Sicily, has rich brown sugar flavours with a refreshing sliver of acidity. The versatile Muscat grape makes luscious golden wines all around the Mediterranean, but also pops up in orange, black, and the gloriously rich, treacly brown versions that Australia does superbly.

- **Nyx, Mavrodaphne of Patras**, B G Spiliopoulos, Greece, £7.79/50cl, Oddbins
- **Noé Very Old Pedro Ximénez**, González Byass, £10.69, Harvey Nichols, Tesco
- **15 Year Old Malmsey Madeira**, Henriques & Henriques, £16.99/50cl, Waitrose, Noel Young Wines
- **1999 Graham's Crusted Port**, Portugal, £13.04, Sainsbury's
- **Grand Rutherglen Muscat**, Chambers Rosewood Vineyards, Victoria, Australia, £16.95/half bottle, Lay & Wheeler

Buying for the long term

Most of this book is about wines to drink more or less immediately – that's how modern wines are made, and that's what you'll find in most high street retail outlets. If you're looking for a mature vintage of a great wine that's ready to drink – or are prepared to wait 10 years or more for a great vintage to reach its peak – specialist wine merchants will be able to help; the internet's another good place to look for mature wines. Here's my beginners' guide to buying wine at auction and *en primeur*.

AUCTIONS

A catalogue from either of the UK's top wine auction houses, Christie's and Sotheby's, will have wine enthusiasts drooling over the prestigious names that are virtually unobtainable elsewhere. Better still, the lots are often of mature vintages that are ready to drink. Before you go, find out all you can about the producer and vintages described in the catalogue. My *Pocket Wine Book* is a good place to start, or Michael Broadbent's *Vintage Wines* for old and rare wines, and the national wine magazines run regular features on the world's main wine regions and their vintages. This is important – some merchants take the opportunity to clear inferior vintages at auction.

The drawbacks? You have no guarantee that the wine has been well stored, and if it's faulty you have little chance of redress. But for expensive and mature wines, I have to say that the top auction houses nowadays make a considerable effort to check the provenance and integrity of the wines. As prices of the most sought-after wines have soared, so it has become profitable either to forge the bottles and their contents or to try to pass off stock that is clearly out of condition. And don't forget that there will be a commission to pay. Online wine auctions have similar pros and cons.

BUYING EN PRIMEUR

In the spring after the vintage the Bordeaux châteaux – and a few other wine-producing regions – make their opening offers. This means that their capital is not tied up in expensive stock for the next year or two, until the wines are bottled and ready to ship. In theory this also means that you can buy the wine at a preferential price – but do not forget that the cost of shipping, duties and VAT will appear on your final bill.

Traditionally merchants would buy *en primeur* for stock to be sold later at a higher price, while offering their customers the chance to take advantage of the opening prices as well. The idea of private individuals investing rather than institutions took off with a series of good Bordeaux vintages in the 1980s.

There is a lot to be said for buying *en primeur*. For one thing, in a great vintage you may be able to find the finest and rarest wines far more cheaply than they will ever appear again. This was especially true of the 1990 vintage; this, in turn, primed the market for the exceptional vintages of 1999 in Burgundy and 2000 in Bordeaux. Equally, when a wine – even a relatively inexpensive one – is made in very limited quantities, buying en primeur may be practically your only chance of getting hold of it.

But you should be aware of the risks. Some popular vintages are offered at ridiculously high prices – some unpopular ones too. It's only about twice a decade that the combination of high quality and fair prices offers the private buyer a chance of a good, guaranteed profit. Interestingly, if one highly touted vintage is followed by another, the prices for the second one often have to fall because the market simply will not accept two inflated price structures in a row. Recent Bordeaux examples of this are the excellent 1990 after the much hyped 1989 and the potentially fine 2001 after the understandably hyped 2000.

Prices can go down as well as up. They may easily not increase significantly in the few years after the campaign. The second risk is that a tasting assessment is difficult at an early date. There is a well-founded suspicion that many barrel samples are doctored (legally) to appeal to the most powerful consumer critics, in particular the American Robert Parker and The Wine Spectator magazine. The wine that is finally bottled may or may not bear a resemblance to what was tasted in the spring following the vintage. In any case, most serious red wines are in a difficult stage of their evolution in the spring, and with the best will in the world it is

possible to get one's evaluation wrong. However the aforementioned Americans, and magazines like Wine and Decanter will do their best to offer you accurate judgements on the newly offered wines, and most merchants who make a primeur offer also write a good assessment of the wines. You will find that many of them quote the Parker or Wine Spectator marks. Anything over 90 out of 100 risks being hyped and hiked in price. Many of the best bargains get marks between 85 and 89, since the 90+ marks are generally awarded for power rather than subtlety. Consideration can be given to the producer's reputation for consistency and to the general vintage assessment for the region.

Another risk is that the merchant you buy the wine from may not still be around to deliver it to you two years later. Buy from a merchant you trust, with a solid trading base in other wines.

Once the wines are shipped you may want your merchant to store the wine for you. If so, you should insist that (1) you receive a stock certificate; (2) your wines are stored separately from the merchant's own stocks; and (3) your cases are identifiable as your property and are labelled accordingly. All good merchants will offer these safeguards as a minimum service.

CHECK THE SMALL PRINT

Traditional wine merchants may quote prices exclusive of VAT and/or duty: wine may not be the bargain it first appears.

A wine quoted en primeur is usually offered on an ex-cellars (EC) basis; the price excludes shipping, duties and taxes such as VAT. A price quoted in bond (IB) in the UK includes shipping, but excludes duties and taxes.

Buying on the web

Nearly half of all British households can now access the internet from home, giving us the ability instantly to seek out the wines we want and compare up-to-the-minute prices. A recent survey found that in the first three months of this year, 80% of adult internet users had used the web to find information about goods or services, and 47% had ordered goods online. Have *you* bought wine over the internet yet?

Generally speaking, buying over the internet is much the same as buying from a traditional mail-order outlet – and many of our recommended retailers established their mail-order operation decades before the internet was even thought of, so their systems are pretty well tried and tested. Any serious online retailer will have invested in effective credit card security systems; e-way robbery is not a major threat to the public.

So, if you're in the mood to buy, consider the following: is this company offering the sort of wines I want? Will it deliver the wines swiftly and at my convenience? Are the prices (including delivery) competitive? What happens if I am dissatisfied with the wine? If you're happy with the answers, go ahead and net yourself a bargain.

If you just want to browse, my own website (www.ozclarke.com) has links to dozens of other wine- and food-related sites, online magazines, restaurant guides, auction houses and wine retailers.

CLICK ON THESE

○ If it's making news in the wine world, you'll find it in one of the UK's top wine magazines, all of which now have excellent websites: **www.decanter.com**, **www.harpers-wine.com** and **www.wineint.com**

○ **www.wine-pages.com** Tom Cannavan's website has lots of information and a weekly round-up of wines featured in the UK press.

○ **www.englishwineproducers.com** English wine is getting better and better; find your local vineyard and see for yourself.

○ **www.travelenvoy.com/wine/siteindex.htm** tells you just about everything you need to know about wine in the USA – and has plenty of links to wineries all around the world.

○ **www.wine-searcher.com** Can help locate unusual wines.

Retailers directory

All these retailers have been chosen on the basis of the quality and interest of their lists. If you want to find local suppliers, retailers are listed by region in the Who's Where directory on page 128.

> The following services are available where indicated:
> **C** = cellarage **G** = glass hire/loan
> **M** = mail order **T** = tastings and talks

A & B Vintners

Little Tawsden, Spout Lane, Brenchley, Kent TN12 7AS (01892) 724977 FAX (01892) 722673 E-MAIL info@abvintners.co.uk WEBSITE www.abvintners.co.uk HOURS Mon–Fri 9–6 CARDS MasterCard, Visa DELIVERY Free 5 cases or more, otherwise £10 per consignment UK mainland MINIMUM ORDER 1 mixed case EN PRIMEUR Bandol, Burgundy, Languedoc, Rhône. C M T

✪ Star attractions *Set up only in 1998, the impressive list includes a string of top-quality domaines from Burgundy and the Rhône, and little-known gems from the Languedoc.*

Free for complete cases, £7.50 part cases MINIMUM ORDER (Mail order) 1 mixed case EN PRIMEUR Bordeaux, Burgundy, Port, Rhône, Sauternes. G M T

✪ Star attractions *A fistful of top names from most regions of France; and characterful producers from the New World include Yarra Yering (Australia) and Forrest Estate and Martinborough Vineyards (NZ). Telmo Rodríguez, one of Spain's top winemakers, is well represented: his Dehesa Gago is superb value at £6.95. Or who could resist a bottle of 1997 Monte Bello Cabernet Sauvignon, from Ridge in California, at £85.00?*

Adnams

HEAD OFFICE & MAIL ORDER
Sole Bay Brewery, Southwold, Suffolk IP18 6JW (01502) 727222 FAX (01502) 727223 E-MAIL wines@adnams.co.uk WEBSITE www.adnams.co.uk SHOPS The Cellar & Kitchen Store, Victoria Street, Southwold, Suffolk IP18 6JW • The Wine Shop, Pinkney's Lane, Southwold, Suffolk IP18 6EW HOURS (Orderline) Mon–Fri 9–8, Sat 9–5, Sun 10–5; Cellar & Kitchen Store and Wine Shop: Mon–Sat 10–6 CARDS MasterCard, Switch, Visa DISCOUNTS 5% for 5 cases or more DELIVERY

Aldi Stores

PO Box 26, Atherstone, Warwickshire CV9 2SH; 268 stores STORE LOCATION LINE 08705 134262 WEBSITE www.aldi-stores.co.uk HOURS Mon–Wed 9–6, Thurs–Fri 9–7, Sat 8.30–5.30 CARDS Switch, Visa (debit only) DISCOUNTS Regular special offers

✪ Star attractions *Aldi have managed to snap up some terrific bargains from around the world, with lots still available under £3.*

Amey's Wines

83 Melford Road, Sudbury, Suffolk CO10 1JT (01787) 377144

95

HOURS Tue–Sat 9–5 **CARDS** AmEx, MasterCard, Switch, Visa **DISCOUNTS** 10% for a mixed dozen, 15% for 5 or more mixed cases **DELIVERY** Free within 10 miles of Sudbury for orders over £60. **G T**
✪ Star attractions *Expect the unexpected in this well-chosen list of characterful wines: O Fournier's Urban Oak, a Tempranillo/Malbec blend from Argentina (£6.49), and Gérard Depardieu's Condrieu (£19.99) rub shoulders with Pervini's Primitivo di Manduria (£7.49), Montes Alpha Syrah (£11.99) and Penfolds Grange (£99). France, Italy, Spain, Australia, New Zealand and South Africa look particularly inviting.*

John Armit Wines

5 Royalty Studios, 105 Lancaster Road, London W11 1QF (020) 7908 0600 **FAX** (020) 7908 0601 **E-MAIL** info@armit.co.uk **WEBSITE** www.armit.co.uk **HOURS** Mon–Fri 9–6 **CARDS** AmEx, MasterCard, Switch, Visa **DELIVERY** Orders of less than £180 will be subject to a £15 delivery charge **MINIMUM ORDER** 1 case **EN PRIMEUR** Bordeaux, Burgundy, Italy, Rhône. **C M T**
✪ Star attractions *Classy merchant with big names from Italy including Gaja, Sassicaia, Ornellaia and Bruno Giacosa – and stars from Burgundy, Bordeaux, Spain and California shine just as brightly. For everyday drinking the own-label range, from some great winemakers, is good value: NZ Sauvignon Blanc at £6.50, Italian red at £7.50.*

ASDA

HEAD OFFICE Asda House, Southbank, Great Wilson Street, Leeds LS11 5AD (0500) 100055 **FAX** (0113) 241 7766 **CUSTOMER SERVICE** (0113) 243 5435; 260 stores **WEBSITE** www.asda.co.uk **HOURS** Selected stores open 24-hrs, see local store for details **CARDS** MasterCard, Switch, Visa **DISCOUNTS** Buy 6 bottles, save 5%, case deals: 10% off price including delivery **DELIVERY** Selected stores. **T**
✪ Star attractions *Good-value basics – with lots under a fiver – from all over the world. There's a rather good (though quite short) list of clarets.*

Australian Wine Club

MAIL ORDER Regal House, 70 London Road, Twickenham TW1 3RS, 0800 856 2004 **FAX** 020 8843 8444 **E-MAIL** orders@austwine.co.uk **WEBSITE** www.austwine.co.uk **HOURS** Mon–Fri 8–7, Sat–Sun 9–4 **CARDS** AmEx, MasterCard, Switch, Visa **DELIVERY** £4.99 anywhere in UK mainland **MINIMUM ORDER** 1 mixed case **EN PRIMEUR** Australia. **M T**
✪ Star attractions *The original Aussie wine specialist. But no-longer alone, as operations like Vin du Van and Oz Wines are grabbing their share of the glory. They also represent*

a growing range of small boutique wineries from New Zealand, California and South America.

Averys of Bristol

Orchard House, Southfield Road, Nailsea, Bristol BS48 1JN **TEL** (01275) 811100 **FAX** (01275) 811101 **ORDERLINE** 08451 283797 **E-MAIL** sales@averys. com • Shop and Cellar, 9 Culver Street, Bristol, BS1 5LD (0117) 921 4146/5 **HOURS** Mon–Sat 10–7 **CARDS** AmEx, MasterCard, Switch, Visa **DISCOUNTS** Monthly mail order offers, Bin Club 10% off most list prices **DELIVERY** £4.95 per delivery address **EN PRIMEUR** Bordeaux, Burgundy, Port. **C G M**
✪ Star attractions *A small but very respectable selection from Bordeaux; ditto Burgundy, Rhône, Loire, Alsace and Germany. Italy runs to several pages, and there's some good New World stuff, such as Felton Road from New Zealand. From Canada, there's Inniskillin icewine, if you're willing to part with £42 for a half bottle.*

Bacchus Wine

Warrington House Farm Barn, Warrington, Olney, Bucks MK46 4HN (01234) 711140 **FAX** (01234) 711199 **E-MAIL** wine@bacchus.co.uk **WEBSITE** www.bacchus.co.uk **HOURS** Mon–Fri 10.30–6.30, Sat 10.30–2 **CARDS** AmEx, Diners, MasterCard, Switch, Visa **DELIVERY** Free within 10 miles of Olney; elsewhere £10 1 case; £5 subsequent cases (maximum charge £20) **MINIMUM ORDER** 1 mixed case. **G M T**
✪ Star attractions *One of the largest lists of Austrian wines, both red and white, in the UK. Splendid stuff from Italy, Burgundy – in fact from most of France – Spain, North and South America and South Africa. There are plenty of unusual choices. A 'revolutionary pricing policy' puts most wines between £6 and £20 – only a few are above the £20 mark.*

Ballantynes of Cowbridge

3 Westgate, Cowbridge, Vale of Glamorgan CF71 7AQ (01446) 774840 **FAX** (01446) 775253 **E-MAIL** richard@ballantynes.co.uk **WEBSITE** www.ballantynes.co.uk • 211–17 Cathedral Road, Cardiff, CF11 9PP (02920) 222202 **HOURS** Mon–Sat 9–5.30 **CARDS** MasterCard, Switch, Visa **DISCOUNTS** 8% per case **DELIVERY** £7.95 for first case; £3.95 for subsequent cases **EN PRIMEUR** Bordeaux, Burgundy, Italy, Rhône. **C G M**
✪ Star attractions *Italy, Burgundy and Languedoc-Roussillon are stunning, most regions of France are well represented, and there's some terrific stuff from Australia, New Zealand, Spain, California – even Oregon gets a look-in. There's a long list of fine malt whiskies, too.*

Balls Brothers

313 Cambridge Heath Road, London E2 9LQ (020) 7739 6466 **FAX** 0870 243 9775 **DIRECT SALES** (020) 7739 1642 **E-MAIL** wine@ballsbrothers.co.uk **WEBSITE** www.ballsbrothers.co.uk **HOURS** Mon–Fri 9–5.30 **CARDS** AmEx, Diners, MasterCard, Switch, Visa **DISCOUNTS** 10% off 5 cases or more **DELIVERY** Free 1 case or more locally; £7 1 case, free 2 cases or more, England, Wales and Scottish Lowlands; islands and Scottish Highlands phone for details. **G M T**
✪ Star attractions *French specialist – you'll find something of interest from most regions – with older vintages available. Spain and Australia are also very good. Many of the wines can be enjoyed in Balls Brothers' London wine bars.*

H & H Bancroft Wines

1 China Wharf, Mill Street, London SE1 2BQ (020) 7232 5450 **FAX** (020) 7232 5451 **E-MAIL** sales@handhbancroftwines.com **WEBSITE** www.handhbancroft wines.com **HOURS** Mon–Fri 9–5.30

CARDS MasterCard, Switch, Visa
DISCOUNTS Negotiable DELIVERY
£10 for 1–2 cases; free 3 cases
or more MINIMUM ORDER 1 case
EN PRIMEUR Bordeaux, Burgundy,
Rhône. C M T

✪ Star attractions *Bancroft are UK
agents for an impressive flotilla of
French winemakers: Burgundy,
Rhône, Loire and some interesting
wines from Cahors, Madiran, La
Clape and Pic St-Loup. Small, well-
chosen Bordeaux list goes back to
1945. Italy and Australia look
promising, and there's a healthy list
of half bottles, plus Churchill's ports.*

Bat & Bottle

MAIL ORDER 9 Ashwell Road,
Oakham, Rutland LE15 6QG (0845)
108 4407 FAX (0870) 458 2505
E-MAIL bohrobson@hotmail.com
HOURS Mon–Fri 8.30–5.30, out-of-
hours answering maching CARDS
MasterCard, Switch, Visa MINIMUM
ORDER 1 mixed case. M T G

✪ Star attractions *Ben and Emma
Robson 'would rather buy from
regions we know and visit regularly'.
They specialize in Italy and Portugal,
and in stylish and individual wines
from small producers, yet prices
don't look high: lots between £6
and £20, although if you want
Barolos and Brunellos you'll have
to pay more.*

Bennetts Fine Wines

High Street, Chipping Campden,
Glos GL55 6AG (01386) 840392
FAX (01386) 840974 E-MAIL
enquiries@bennettsfinewines.com
WEBSITE www.bennettsfinewines.
com HOURS Mon–Fri 10–6, Sat 9–6
CARDS MasterCard, Switch, Visa
DISCOUNTS On collected orders of 1
case or more DELIVERY £6 per case,
minimum charge £12 EN PRIMEUR
Burgundy, California, Rhône, Italy,
New Zealand. G M T

✪ Star attractions *I couldn't find
much under £5 here, but I wouldn't
really expect to, given the calibre of*
*the producers. France and Italy have
the lion's share, but Germany, Spain
and Portugal look good too. New
World wines are similarly high up
the quality scale, with the likes of
Kumeu River and Isabel Estate from
New Zealand, Plantagenet and
Cullen from Australia, Seghesio
from California and Domaine
Drouhin from Oregon.*

Berkmann Wine Cellars

10–12 Brewery Road, London N7
9NH (020) 7609 4711 FAX (020)
7607 0018 • Brian Coad Wine
Cellars, 41b Valley Road, Plympton,
Plymouth, Devon PL7 1RF (01752)
334970 • Pagendam Pratt Wine
Cellars, 16 Marston Moor Business
Park, Rudgate, Tockwith, N. Yorks
YO26 7QF (01423) 337567
• T M Robertson Wine Cellars,
10 Lower Gilmore Place, Edinburgh
EH3 9PA (0131) 229 4522
E-MAIL info@berkmann.co.uk
WEBSITE www.berkmann.co.uk
HOURS Mon–Fri 9–5.30 CARDS
MasterCard, Switch, Visa DISCOUNTS
£3 per unmixed case collected
DELIVERY Free for orders over £100
to UK mainland (excluding the
Highlands) MINIMUM ORDER 1
mixed case. C G M

✪ Star attractions *Berkmann is the
UK agent for, among others,
Antinori (which owns Prunotto in
Piedmont), Maculan, Masi,
Mastroberardino and Tasca
d'Almerita, so there are some fab
Italian wines here. Spain has
Marqués de Griñon, Portugal has
Casa Ferreirinha. New World wines
include some top stuff from
Australia, New Zealand and South
Africa, plus Stags' Leap from
California and Mission Hill from
Canada. But France hasn't been
forgotten: affordable claret and
Burgundy, Alsace from René Muré
and Beaujolais from Duboeuf. Loire
wines include Sancerre from
Crochet and Pouilly-Fumé from
Dagueneau at less than a tenner.*

Berry Bros. & Rudd

3 St James's Street, London SW1A
1EG (020) 7396 9600 **FAX** (020)
7396 9611 **ORDERS OFFICE** 0870 900
4300 (lines open Mon–Fri 9–6)
ORDERS FAX 0870 900 4301
• Berrys' Wine Shop, Hamilton
Close, Houndmills, Basingstoke,
Hants RG21 6YB (01256) 323566
• Terminal 3 departures, Heathrow
Airport, TW6 1JH (020) 8564 8361
• Terminal 4 departures, Heathrow,
TW6 3XA (020) 8754 1961 **E-MAIL**
orders@bbr.com **WEBSITE**
www.bbr.com **HOURS** St James's
Street: Mon–Fri 9–6, Sat 10–4;
Berrys' Wine Shop: Mon–Thur 10–6,
Fri 10–8, Sat 10–4; Heathrow: Daily
6am–10pm **CARDS** AmEx, Diners,
MasterCard, Switch, Visa **DISCOUNTS**
Variable **DELIVERY** Free for orders of
£150 or more, otherwise £10
EN PRIMEUR Bordeaux, Burgundy,
Rhône. **C G M T**
✪ **Star attractions** *The shop in
St James's is the very image of a
traditional wine merchant, but
Berry Bros. also has one of the best
websites around. The Blue List
covers old, rare fine wines while the
main list is both classy and wide-
ranging: there's an emphasis on
the classic regions of France; smaller
but equally tempting selections
from just about everywhere else.
I was certainly tempted by the
Gunderloch Nackenheimer
Rothenberg Spätlese (£14.95) and
Pierro Chardonnay (£22.95). Not
everything is expensive: Berrys' Own
Selection is extensive and includes,
for example, a Côtes du Rhône
(£5.95) made for them by Michel
Chapoutier.*

Bibendum Fine Wine

113 Regents Park Road, London
NW1 8UR (020) 7449 4120
FAX (020) 7449 4121 **E-MAIL**
sales@bibendum-wine.co.uk
WEBSITE www.bibendum-
wine.co.uk **HOURS** Mon–Fri 9–6
CARDS MasterCard, Switch, Visa

www.bbr.com
Website of the year 2002 & 2003
e-mail: orders@bbr.com
Tel: 0870 900 4300 Fax: 0870 900 4301

DELIVERY Free for London and Home
Counties for orders over £150,
otherwise £15; elsewhere on
application **MINIMUM ORDER** 1 case,
or £150 **EN PRIMEUR** Bordeaux,
Burgundy, New World, Rhône, Port.
G M T
✪ **Star attractions** *Bibendum
looks for wines that nobody else is
shipping – although that's not to
say you won't find them elsewhere,
since Bibendum supply the trade as
well as private customers. Equally
strong in the Old World and the
New: Huet in Vouvray, Lageder in
Alto Adige and Brundlmayer in
Austria are matched by d'Arenberg,
Chain of Ponds and Katnook from
Australia, and a full range from
Catena Zapata of Argentina.*

Booths Supermarkets

4 Fishergate, Preston PR1 3LJ (01772)
251701 **FAX** (01772) 204316; 27 stores
across the North of England

E-MAIL admin@booths-supermarkets.co.uk WEBSITE www.booths-supermarkets.co.uk, and www.booths-wine.co.uk HOURS Office: Mon–Fri 8.30–5; shop hours vary CARDS AmEx, Electron, MasterCard, Switch, Solo, Visa DISCOUNTS 5% off any 6 bottles. G T
✪ Star attractions *A list for any merchant to be proud of, never mind a supermarket. Wonderful Chablis from Defaix, Langhe Nebbiolo from Vajra and Rioja from Artadi. From Australia there's d'Arenberg Original Shiraz-Grenache at £7.99; and from South Africa, Jordan Estate Chardonnay at £8.49.*

Bordeaux Index

MAIL ORDER 6th Floor, 159–173 St John Street, London EC1V 4QJ (020) 7253 2110 FAX (020) 7490 1995 E-MAIL sales@bordeauxindex.com WEBSITE www.bordeauxindex.com HOURS Mon–Fri 8.30–6 CARDS AmEx, MasterCard, Switch, Visa, JCB (transaction fees apply) DELIVERY (Private sales only) free for orders over £2,000 UK mainland; others at cost MINIMUM ORDER £500 EN PRIMEUR Bordeaux, Burgundy, Rhône, Italy. C T
✪ Star attractions *A serious list for serious spenders. Pages and pages of red Bordeaux, dating back to 1964, and, in spite of the company name, stacks of top Burgundies. Rhône and Italy have smaller selections, with the focus on classic names. A sprinkling of wines from elsewhere includes Artadi and Pingus from Spain and Penfolds Grange from Australia.*

Bring-a-Bottle.com

MAIL ORDER 24b Albany Street, Edinburgh EH1 3QB TELEPHONE and FAX (0131) 557 5369 E-MAIL info@ bring-a-bottle.com WEBSITE www.bring-a-bottle.com HOURS Mon–Fri 10–5; Internet 24-hrs CARDS MasterCard, Switch, Visa DISCOUNTS Members discounts available after first purchase DELIVERY 24-hr service £6.99 UK mainland; £10.99 Northern Ireland and UK islands MINIMUM ORDER 1 mixed case. M (G Edinburgh only)
✪ Star attractions *Chatty, user-friendly website with an excellent selection of New World wines from small producers. Maximum price of any wine is currently £15.*

Budgens Stores

HEAD OFFICE PO Box 9, Stonefield Way, Ruislip, Middx HA4 0JR (020) 8422 9511 FAX (020) 8422 1596, for nearest store call 0800 526002; 210 stores mainly in South-East and Norfolk E-MAIL info@ budgens.co.uk WEBSITE www.budgens.com HOURS Usually Mon–Sat 8–8, Sun 10–4 CARDS MasterCard, Switch, Visa. G
✪ Star attractions *You can feel reasonably confident of going into a store and coming out with some wine you'd actually like to drink these days, at bargain-basement prices upwards.*

The Butlers Wine Cellar

247 Queens Park Road, Brighton BN2 9XJ (01273) 698724 FAX (01273) 622761 E-MAIL henry@butlers-winecellar.co.uk WEBSITE www.butlers-winecellar.co.uk HOURS Tue–Wed 10–6, Thur–Sat 10–7 CARDS AmEx, MasterCard, Switch, Visa DELIVERY Free locally 1 case or more; free UK mainland 3 cases or more EN PRIMEUR Bordeaux. G M T
✪ Star attractions *To get full value from this list you'll need to look at the website or join the mailing list: it's the odds and ends that are the main point, and they change all the time, but include French, Italian and Spanish vintages back to the 1960s. The main list is short but irresistible, with the likes of Anselmi from Italy, Isabel Pinot Noir from New Zealand, Quinta de la Rosa port and a sherry for all tastes. Lucky Brighton.*

Anthony Byrne

MAIL ORDER Ramsey Business Park, Stocking Fen Road, Ramsey, Cambs PE26 2UR (01487) 814555 FAX (01487) 814962 E-MAIL anthony@abfw.co.uk or claude@abfw.co.uk WEBSITE www.abfw.co.uk HOURS Mon–Fri 9–5.30 CARDS None DISCOUNTS available on cases DELIVERY Free 5 cases or more, or orders of £250 or more; otherwise £6 MINIMUM ORDER 1 case EN PRIMEUR Bordeaux, Burgundy, Champagne, Rhône. C M T
✪ Star attractions *A serious list of Burgundy; Loire from top growers such as Serge Dagueneau; and from Alsace there are enough Zind-Humbrecht wines to sink a ship. Interesting French wines also come from Provence (Ch. de Pibarnon) and the Rhône (Alain Graillot). Increasing coverage of South Africa.*

D Byrne & Co

Victoria Buildings, 12 King Street, Clitheroe, Lancs BB7 2EP (01200) 423152 HOURS Mon–Sat 8.30–6 CARDS MasterCard, Switch, Visa DELIVERY Free within 50 miles; nationally £10 1st case, £5 subsequent cases EN PRIMEUR Bordeaux, Burgundy, Rhône, Germany. G M T
✪ Star attractions *One of northern England's best wine merchants, with a hugely impressive range. Clarets back to 1978, stacks of Burgundy, faultless Loire and Rhône, Germany, Spain, USA (not just California) and many, many more. I urge you to go and see for yourself.*

Cape Province Wines

77 Laleham Road, Staines, Middx TW18 2EA (01784) 451860 FAX (01784) 469267 E-MAIL capewines@msn.com WEBSITE www.capewinestores.co.uk HOURS Mon–Sat 9–5.30 CARDS MasterCard, Switch, Visa DISCOUNTS 10% on 12 bottles DELIVERY £6.95 per case. G M T
✪ Star attractions *South African wines, mostly from established names rather than new discoveries.*

Cave Cru Classé

MAIL ORDER Unit 13 The Leathermarket, Weston Street, London SE1 3ER (020) 7378 8579 FAX (020) 7378 8544 and 7403 0607 E-MAIL enquiries@ccc.co.uk WEBSITE www.cave-cru-classe.com HOURS Mon–Fri 9–5.30 CARDS AmEx, MasterCard, Visa DELIVERY £20 per order in London and the South-East; at cost elsewhere MINIMUM ORDER 1 mixed case EN PRIMEUR Bordeaux. M T
✪ Star attractions *1945 was an excellent vintage for red Bordeaux, and if you'd like to plan ahead for a friend's sixtieth birthday Cave Cru Classé have a selection of excellent clarets, ranging from £150 to £995, plus VAT. If Burgundy or Rhône are your wines of choice, there are pages of top names to choose from. Italy and port look starry, too.*

Les Caves de Pyrene

Pew Corner, Old Portsmouth Road, Artington, Guildford GU3 1LP (office) (01483) 538820 (shop) (01483) 554750 FAX (01483) 455068 E-MAIL sales@lescaves.co.uk WEBSITE www.cavesdepyrene.com HOURS (office) Mon–Sat 9–5 (shop) Mon–Sat 9–7 CARDS MasterCard, Switch, Visa DELIVERY Free for orders over £200 witin M25, elsewhere at cost DISCOUNTS negotiable MINIMUM ORDER 1 mixed case EN PRIMEUR South-West France. G M T
✪ Star attractions *Excellent operation, devoted to seeking out the best wines in South-West France – Marcillac, Jurançon and Irouléguy as well as top stuff from Cahors and Madiran. Other areas of France, especially the Loire, are equally good. And there's Armagnac dating back to 1893!*

ChateauOnline

MAIL ORDER 29 rue Ganneron,
75018 Paris (0033) 1 55 30 31 41
FAX (0033) 1 55 30 31 41 **CUSTOMER
SERVICE** 0800 169 2736 **WEBSITE**
www.chateauonline.com **HOURS**
Mon–Fri 8–11.30, 12.30–4.30 **CARDS**
AmEx, MasterCard, Switch, Visa
DELIVERY £7.99 per consignment
EN PRIMEUR Bordeaux, Burgundy,
Languedoc-Roussillon.
✪ Star attractions *French specialist,
with an impressive list of over 3,000
wines. Easy-to-use website with a
well-thought-out range of mixed
cases, frequent special offers and
bin end sales.*

Cockburns of Leith
(incorporating J E Hogg)

The Wine Emporium, 7 Devon
Place, Haymarket, Edinburgh EH12
5HJ (0131) 346 1113 **FAX** (0131) 313
2607 **E-MAIL** sales@winelist.co.uk
WEBSITE www.winelist.co.uk
HOURS Mon–Fri 9–6; Sat 10–5
CARDS MasterCard, Switch, Visa
DELIVERY Free 12 or more bottles
within Edinburgh; elsewhere
£7 1–2 cases, free 3 cases or more
EN PRIMEUR Bordeaux, Burgundy. **G T**
✪ Star attractions *Clarets at
bargain prices, Burgundies from
Champy – in fact wines from all
over France, including plenty of vins
de pays. There are also well-chosen
wines from Italy, Chile, Argentina,
South Africa and New Zealand.*

Connolly's Wine Merchants

Arch 13, 220 Livery Street,
Birmingham B3 1EU (0121) 236
9269/3837 **FAX** (0121) 233 2339
E-MAIL sales@connollyswine.co.uk
WEBSITE www.connollyswine.co.uk
HOURS Mon–Fri 9–5.30, Sat 10–4
CARDS AmEx, MasterCard, Switch,
Visa **DELIVERY** Surcharge outside
Birmingham area **DISCOUNTS** 10%
for cash & carry **EN PRIMEUR**
Bordeaux, Burgundy, Port. **G M T**
✪ Star attractions *Bordeaux,
Burgundy and the Rhône all look
very good; a short German list
includes Dr Loosen; Italy has names
like Isole e Olena and Allegrini; and
from Spain there are Riojas from
Faustino and Artadi. Fizz includes
Pirie from Tasmania and Pelorus
from New Zealand.*

The Co-operative Group

HEAD OFFICE New Century House,
Manchester M60 4ES, freephone
0800 068 6727 for stock details
FAX (0161) 827 5117; approx. 2,430
licensed stores **E-MAIL** customer
relations@co-op.co.uk **WEBSITE**
www.co-op.co.uk **HOURS** Variable
CARDS Variable
• **ONLINE WINE STORE** www.co-
opdrinks2u.com **TELEPHONE** 0845
090 2222 **HOURS** 24-hrs **CARDS**
AmEx, MasterCard, Solo, Switch,
Visa **DISCOUNTS** regular special
offers **DELIVERY** Within 7 days
mainland UK £4.99 (UK islands
and N. Ireland £23.00); Saturday
delivery (major towns only) £26.00
MINIMUM ORDER Wine sold in
multiples of 3, can be mixed.
✪ Star attractions *Good modern
wines from Cyprus under the Island
Vines label, and champions of
English, organic and Fairtrade
wines. Plenty of good stuff for less
than a fiver, such as Argentinian
Torrontes, red and white Burgundy
from the Cave des Vignerons de
Buxy, Penfolds Rawson's Retreat
Riesling and organic Côtes du
Rhône-Villages Valréas.*

Corney & Barrow

HEAD OFFICE No. 1 Thomas More
Street, London EC1V 3TD (020) 7265
2400 **FAX** (020) 7265 2539
• 194 Kensington Park Road,
London W11 2ES (020) 7221 5122
• Corney & Barrow East Anglia,
Belvoir House, High Street,
Newmarket CB8 8DH (01638)
600000 • Corney & Barrow
(Scotland) with Whighams of Ayr,
8 Academy Street, Ayr KA7 1HT
(01292) 267000, and Oxenford

Castle, by Pathhead, Mid Lothian,
EH37 5UD (01875) 321921
E-MAIL wine@corbar.co.uk
WEBSITE www.corneyand
barrow.com **HOURS** Mon–Fri 9–6
(24-hr answering machine);
Kensington Mon–Fri 10.30–9, Sat
9.30–8; Newmarket Mon–Sat 9–6;
Edinburgh Mon–Fri 9–6; Ayr
Mon–Fri 9–6, Sat 9.30–5.30 **CARDS**
AmEx, MasterCard, Switch, Visa
DELIVERY Free 2 or more cases
within M25 boundary, elsewhere
free 3 or more cases or for orders
above £200. Otherwise £9 + VAT
per delivery. For Scotland and East
Anglia, please contact the relevant
office **EN PRIMEUR** Bordeaux,
Burgundy, Champagne, Italy, Spain,
South America, USA. **C G M T**
✿ **Star attractions** *If you want
certain Pomerols like Pétrus,
Trotanoy, la Fleur-Pétrus and Latour
à Pomerol, Corney & Barrow, by
Royal Appointment, is where you
have to come. At least, if you want
them en primeur. Burgundy kicks off
with Domaine de la Romanée-Conti
and proceeds via names like
Domaine Trapet and Domaine
Leflaive. The rest of Europe is
equally impressive; while there is
good stuff from the New World,
there's less of it.*

Croque-en-Bouche

221 Wells Road, Malvern Wells,
Worcestershire WR14 4HF (01684)
565612 **FAX** (08707) 066282 **E-MAIL**
mail@croque-en-bouche.co.uk
WEBSITE www.croque-en-bouche.
co.uk **HOURS** By appointment 7 days
a week **CARDS** MasterCard, Switch,
Visa **DISCOUNTS** 3% for orders over
£500 if paid in cash or by Switch
or Delta, 1.5% if paid by credit card
DELIVERY Free locally; elsewhere
£5 per consignment **MINIMUM
ORDER** 1 mixed case. **M**
✿ **Star attractions** *A wonderful list,
including older wines. Mature
Australian reds from the 1980s and
'90s; terrific stuff from the Rhône –*

*Château Beaucastel's Châteauneuf-
du-Pape going back to 1979; some
top clarets (1961 Ch. Léoville-Barton
for £200) and from Alsace, loads of
Zind-Humbrecht among others;
and a generous sprinkling from
other parts of the world. Sweet
wines include mature Sauternes
and Loire wines from the great
'47 vintage.*

Devigne Wines

Mas Y Coed, 13 Llanerchydol
Park, Welshpool SY21 9QE (01938)
553478 **FAX** (01938) 556831
E-MAIL info@devignewines.co.uk
WEBSITE www.devignewines.co.uk
HOURS Mon–Fri 10–6 (telephone 7
days) **CARDS** MasterCard, Switch,
Visa **DISCOUNTS** selected mixed
cases at introductory rate
DELIVERY free for orders over £300,
otherwise £6.50 per consignment
MINIMUM ORDER 1 mixed case. **M**
✿ **Star attractions** *Small list
specializing in French wines: 14
different rosés and 19 traditional-
(Champagne) method sparkling
wines from all over France as well as
red Gaillac from the South-West.*

Direct Wine Shipments

5–7 Corporation Square, Belfast,
Northern Ireland BT1 3AJ (028)
9050 8000 **FAX** (028) 9050 8004
E-MAIL enquiry@directwine.co.uk
WEBSITE www.directwine.co.uk
HOURS Mon–Fri 9–6.30 (Thur 10–8),
Sat 9.30–5.30 **CARDS** MasterCard,
Switch, Visa **DISCOUNTS** 10% in the
form of complimentary wine with
each case **DELIVERY** Free Northern
Ireland 1 case or more, £15 per 6-
bottle case, £20 per 12-bottle case
UK mainland **EN PRIMEUR**
Bordeaux, Rhône. **C M T**
✿ **Star attractions** *Rhône, Spain,
Australia and Burgundy look
outstanding, Italy and Germany are
not far behind, and from Chile
there's Santa Rita and Miguel Torres.
In fact there's good stuff from
pretty well everywhere.*

Domaine Direct

8 Cynthia Street, London N1 9JF
(020) 7837 1142 FAX (020) 7837
8605 E-MAIL mail@domainedirect.
co.uk WEBSITE www.domainedirect.
co.uk HOURS 8.30–6 or answering
machine CARDS MasterCard,
Switch, Visa DELIVERY Free London;
elsewhere in UK mainland 1 case
£11.16, 2 cases £14.69, 3 or more free
MINIMUM ORDER 1 mixed case
EN PRIMEUR Burgundy. M T
✪ Star attractions *Sensational
Burgundy list. From Australia you'll
find wines from the Leeuwin Estate;
from California there's Viader,
Spottswoode, Etude and Nalle.*

Farr Vintners

19 Sussex Street, London
SW1V 4RR (020) 7821 2000
FAX (020) 7821 2020 E-MAIL
sales@farr-vintners.com
WEBSITE www.farr-vintners.com
HOURS Mon–Fri 10–6 CARDS None
DELIVERY London £1 per case (min
£10); elsewhere £4 per case (min
£12) MINIMUM ORDER £500 + VAT
EN PRIMEUR Bordeaux. C M T
✪ Star attractions *A fantastic list of
the world's finest wines. The
majority is Bordeaux, but you'll also
find top stuff and older vintages
from Burgundy, the Rhône, Italy
(Gaja, Sassicaia), Australia and
California (Araujo, Dominus).*

Irma Fingal-Rock

64 Monnow Street, Monmouth
NP25 3EN TEL & FAX 01600 712372
E-MAIL irmafingalrock@msn.com
WEBSITE www.pinotnoir.co.uk
HOURS Mon & Wed 9.30–1.30, Thurs
& Fri 9.30–5.30, Sat 9.30–5 CARDS
MasterCard, Switch, Visa DISCOUNTS
5% for at least 12 bottles collected
from shop, 7.5% for collected orders
over £500, 10% for collected orders
over £1,200 DELIVERY Free locally
(within 30 miles); orders further
afield free if over £100. G M T
✪ Star attractions *The list's great
strength is Burgundy, from some
very good growers and priced
between £6 and £34. Small but
tempting selections from Bordeaux,
Loire, Rhône and other French
regions. Ditto Italy, Spain, Portugal
and the New World. Two local (yes,
Welsh) producers are also
represented.*

Le Fleming Wines

MAIL ORDER 19 Spenser Road,
Harpenden, Hertfordshire AL5 5NW
(01582) 760125 E-MAIL cherry@
leflemingwines.co.uk WEBSITE
www.leflemingwines.co.uk
HOURS 24-hour answering machine
DISCOUNTS 5% on large orders
DELIVERY Free locally MINIMUM
ORDER 1 case. G M T
✪ Star attractions *Australia looks
terrific here, with lots of serious and
not so serious wines. South Africa,
too, is good, with wines from
Hamilton Russell and Thelema. The
list is basically the New World and
France, plus short but focused
selections from Italy and Spain.*

Fortnum & Mason

181 Piccadilly, London W1A 1ER (020)
7734 8040 FAX (020) 7437 3278
ORDERING LINE 0845 300 1707
E-MAIL info@fortnumandmason.
co.uk WEBSITE www.fortnumand
mason.co.uk HOURS Mon–Sat
10–6.30, Sun 12–6 (Food Hall and
Patio Restaurant only) CARDS AmEx,
Diners, MasterCard, Switch, Visa
DISCOUNTS 1 free bottle per unmixed
dozen DELIVERY £6 per delivery
address EN PRIMEUR Bordeaux. M T
✪ Star attractions *Champagne,
Bordeaux and Burgundy are the
leaders of a very smart pack, but
there are names to impress from
just about everywhere: Ch. de
Pibarnon's Bandol, Egon Müller's
Scharzhofberger Rieslings, Willi
Opitz's dessert wines from Austria,
and the cream of the crop from
Italy, Australia, New Zealand, South
Africa and California. Impeccably
sourced own-label range.*

Friarwood

26 New King's Road, London SW6
4ST (020) 7736 2628 **FAX** (020)
7731 0411 • 16 Dock Street, Leith,
Edinburgh EH6 6EY (0131) 544 6703
E-MAIL sales@friarwood.com
WEBSITE www.friarwood.com
HOURS Mon–Sat 10–7 **CARDS** AmEx,
Diners, MasterCard, Switch, Visa,
Solo, Electron **DISCOUNTS** 5% on
mixed cases, 10% unmixed
DELIVERY (London) Free within
M25 and on orders over £250 in
mainland UK (Edinburgh) free
locally and for 2 cases or more
elsewhere (under 2 cases at cost)
EN PRIMEUR Bordeaux, Burgundy.
C G M T
✪ **Star attractions** *The focus is still
Bordeaux, including a good selection
of petits châteaux as well as classed
growths; vintages available go back
to 1982, or 1967 for Yquem.
Burgundy is mostly from Domaine
Antonin Guyon. New wines from
Italy, some good Californians,
Magnotta icewine from Canada
and a wide range of Armagnacs
round off this imaginative list.*

Gauntleys

4 High Street, Exchange Arcade,
Nottingham NG1 2ET (0115) 911
0555 **FAX** (0115) 911 0557
E-MAIL rhone@gauntleywine.com
WEBSITE www.gauntleywine.com
HOURS Mon–Sat 9–5.30 **CARDS**
MasterCard, Switch, Visa **DELIVERY**
Free within Nottingham area,
otherwise 1–3 cases £9.50, 4 or
more cases free **MINIMUM ORDER** 1
case **EN PRIMEUR** Alsace, Burgundy,
Italy, Loire, Rhône, southern France,
Spain. **M T**
✪ **Star attractions** *No Bordeaux,
but Rhône, Alsace, Loire, Burgundy,
southern France (Coteaux du
Languedoc, Bandol, Minervois),
Spain and Italy are all from top-
notch producers. Champagne is
Vilmart's wonderfully big, rich
wines. And after dinner? Malt
whisky heaven.*

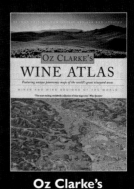

payable for smaller orders or other locations **MINIMUM ORDER** 1 mixed case **EN PRIMEUR** Bordeaux. **C G M T**
✿ **Star attractions** *A shortlist list with the focus on France. Madiran is from Alain Brumont, Sancerre from Gitton Père et Fils, and the red Bordeaux list looks interesting. Wines from lesser-known appellations like Costières de Nîmes can provide good drinking at lower prices. A sprinkling of wines from Spain and Italy, plus Grant Burge from Australia and Moreton Estate from New Zealand.*

Jeroboams (incorporating Laytons)

HEAD OFFICE 43 Portland Road, London W11 4LJ (020) 7685 1560 **FAX** (020) 7229 1085 **MAIL ORDER** Jeroboams, 6 Pont Street, London SW1X 9EL (020) 7259 6716 **FAX** (020) 7235 7246 **SHOPS** 50–52 Elizabeth Street, London SW1W 9PB (020) 7730 8108 • 51 Elizabeth Street, London SW1W 9PP (020) 7823 5623 • 20 Davies Street, London W1K 3DT (020) 7499 1015 • 77–78 Chancery Lane, London WC2A 1AE (020) 7405 0552 • 96 Holland Park Avenue, London W11 3RB (020) 7727 9359 • 6 Pont Street, London SW1X 9EL (020) 7235 1612 • 3 The Market Place, Cirencester, Glos GL7 2PE (01285) 655842 **E-MAIL** sales@jeroboams.co.uk **WEBSITE**s www.jeroboams.co.uk **HOURS** Offices Mon–Fri 9–6, shops Mon–Sat 9–7 (may vary) **CARDS** AmEx, MasterCard, Switch, Visa **DELIVERY** Shops: free for orders of £50 or over in central London; mail order free for orders over £200, otherwise £10 delivery charge **EN PRIMEUR** Bordeaux, Burgundy, Port, Rhône. **C G M T**
✿ **Star attractions** *Sensibly priced everyday clarets as well as classed growths, interesting Burgundies and a good list from the Rhône. Other regions of France – including Jura –*

are covered though in less depth. Italy and Australia – in particular Western Australia – are new specialities. A wide range of fine foods, especially cheeses and olive oils, is available in the shops.

S H Jones

27 High Street, Banbury, Oxfordshire OX16 5EW (01295) 251179 **FAX** (01295) 272352 • 9 Market Square, Bicester, Oxfordshire OX26 6AA (01869) 322448 • 121 Regent Street, Leamington Spa, Warwickshire CV32 4NU (01926) 315609 **E-MAIL** shjonesbanbury@aol.com **WEBSITE** www.shjones.com **HOURS** Mon–Sat 8.30–6 **CARDS** MasterCard, Switch, Visa **DELIVERY** Free within van delivery area for 1 case or more; 'small charge' otherwise. Elsewhere £7.50; free for orders over £250 **EN PRIMEUR** Bordeaux, Burgundy, Port. **C G M T**
✿ **Star attractions** *Wide-ranging list: good Burgundies; some top-name clarets, along with 'everyday' ones at around £10; Rhône from Vidal-Fleury and Perrin, and a comprehensive and affordable selection from southern France. Germany features Dr Loosen among others, Spain has Bodegas Muga, South Africa Rustenberg and Argentina Terrazas de los Andes.*

Justerini & Brooks

MAIL ORDER 61 St James's Street, London SW1A 1LZ (020) 7484 6400 **FAX** (020) 7484 6455 **E-MAIL** justorders@justerinis.com **HOURS** Mon–Fri 9–5.30 **CARDS** AmEx, MasterCard, Switch, Visa **DELIVERY** Free for orders over £250, otherwise £15 UK mainland **MINIMUM ORDER** 1 case **EN PRIMEUR** Bordeaux, Burgundy, Italy, Rhône. **C G M T**
✿ **Star attractions** *Superb list of top-quality wines from Europe's classic regions. The New World, though succinct, also has some*

excellent drinking. And while there are some very classy – and pricy – wines here, you'll find plenty of bottles under £7.

Kwiksave
See Somerfield.

Laithwaites
MAIL ORDER New Aquitaine House, Exeter Way, Theale, Reading, Berks RG7 4PL; ORDER LINE 0870 444 8383 FAX 0870 444 8182 E-MAIL orders@laithwaites.co.uk WEBSITE www.laithwaites.co.uk HOURS 24-hr answering machine CARDS AmEx, Diners, MasterCard, Switch, Visa DISCOUNTS On unmixed cases of 6 or 12 DELIVERY £4.99 per order EN PRIMEUR Australia, Bordeaux, Burgundy, Rhône. C M T
✪ Star attractions *Good selection including well-known names and interesting finds. The lists are generally the same as those for the Sunday Times Wine Club although some wines are exclusive to each. User-friendly website offers excellent mixed cases, while the bin ends and special offers are good value. Added extras include wine plans offering regular delivery of hand-picked cases, and a comprehensive database for matching wine and food – from cold fresh prawns to kangeroo steaks!*

The Lay & Wheeler Group
The Wine Centre, Gosbecks Park, Colchester CO2 9JT (01206) 764446 or 0845 330 1855 FAX (01206) 560002 E-MAIL sales@laywheeler. com WEBSITE www.laywheeler.com HOURS (order office) Mon–Fri 8.30–5.30, Sat 8.30–1; (wine centre) Mon–Sat 9–6 CARDS AmEx, MasterCard, Switch, Visa DISCOUNTS 10% on 5 or more mixed 12 bottle cases, £3 per case if collected DELIVERY £7.95; free for orders over £150 EN PRIMEUR Alsace, Australia, Bordeaux, Burgundy, California, Champagne, Germany, Italy, Loire, Rhône, Spain. C G M T

✪ Star attractions *There's enough first-class Bordeaux and Burgundy to satisfy the most demanding drinker here; indeed everything is excellent. Meyer-Fonné from Alsace, Jean-Luc Colombo from the Rhône, Henschke, Howard Park, Veritas, Penley Estate from Australia – and that's just for starters. A must-have list – and if you really can't make up your mind, their mixed cases are excellent too.*

Laymont & Shaw
The Old Chapel, Millpool, Truro, Cornwall TR1 1EX (01872) 270545 FAX (01872) 223005 E-MAIL info@laymont-shaw.co.uk WEBSITE www.laymont-shaw.co.uk HOURS Mon–Fri 9–5 CARDS MasterCard, Switch, Visa DISCOUNTS £5 per case if wines collected, also £1 per case for 2 cases, £2 for 3–5, £3 for 6 or more DELIVERY Free UK mainland MINIMUM ORDER 1 mixed case. C G M T
✪ Star attractions *An excellent, knowledgeable list that specializes in Spain, with Portugal, Uruguay and Argentina also featuring. And when I say 'specializes', I mean that they seek out wines that you won't find in supermarkets because the quantities are too small.*

Laytons
See Jeroboams.

Lea & Sandeman
170 Fulham Road, London SW10 9PR (020) 7244 0522 FAX (020) 7244 0533 • 211 Kensington Church Street, London W8 7LX (020) 7221 1982 • 51 High Street, Barnes, London SW13 9LN (020) 8878 8643 • 206 Haverstock Hill, London NW3 2AG (020) 7431 4412 E-MAIL info@leaandsandeman.co.uk WEBSITE www.londonfinewine.co.uk HOURS Mon–Sat 10–8 CARDS AmEx, MasterCard, Switch, Visa DISCOUNTS 5–15% by case, other discounts on 10 cases or more DELIVERY £5 for

less than 1 case; free 1 case or more London, and to UK mainland south of Perth on orders over £250 **EN PRIMEUR** Bordeaux, Burgundy, Italy. **C G M T**

✪ **Star attractions** *Burgundy and Italy take precedence here, and there's a succession of excellent names, chosen with great care. But L&S really do seek out unknown treasures wherever they go, so it's worth taking the time to study the list carefully. Bordeaux has wines at all price levels, and there are short but fascinating ranges from the US, Spain, Australia, New Zealand and South Africa.*

Liberty Wines

MAIL ORDER Unit D18, New Covent Garden Food Market, London SW8 5LL (020) 7720 5350 **FAX** (020) 7720 6158 **E-MAIL** info@libertywine.co.uk **HOURS** Mon–Fri 9–5.30 **CARDS** MasterCard, Switch, Visa **DELIVERY** Free to mainland UK **MINIMUM ORDER** 1 mixed case. **M**

✪ **Star attractions** *Italy rules, with superb wines and pretty well all the best producers from all over the country. Liberty are the UK agents for most of their producers, so if you're interested in Italian wines, this should be your first port of call. California features producers like Seghesio and Testarossa, and from Australia there's Cullen, Mount Horrocks, Charles Melton and Plantagenet. France, Germany and South America are not neglected.*

O W Loeb & Co

3 Archie Street, off Tanner Street, London SE1 3JT (020) 7234 0385 **FAX** (020) 7357 0440 **E-MAIL** finewine@owloeb.com **WEBSITE** www.owloeb.com **HOURS** Mon–Fri 8.30–5.30 **CARDS** MasterCard, Switch, Visa **DISCOUNTS** 5 cases and above **DELIVERY** Free 2 cases or more **MINIMUM ORDER** 1 case **EN PRIMEUR**

Burgundy, Rhône, Germany (Mosel), Bordeaux. **C M T**

✪ **Star attractions** *Burgundy, the Rhône, Loire and Germany stand out, with top producers galore. Then there are Loeb's new discoveries from Spain and the New World, especially New Zealand and South Africa.*

Majestic

(see also Wine and Beer World) **HEAD OFFICE** Majestic House, Otterspool Way, Watford, Herts WD25 8WW (01923) 298200 **FAX** (01923) 819105; 105 stores nationwide **E-MAIL** info@majestic. co.uk **WEBSITE** www.majestic.co.uk **HOURS** Mon–Fri 10–8, Sat 9–7, Sun 10–5 (may vary) **CARDS** AmEx, Diners, MasterCard, Switch, Visa **DELIVERY** Free UK mainland **MINIMUM ORDER** 1 mixed case **EN PRIMEUR** Bordeaux, Port. **G M T**

✪ **Star attractions** *This has long been one of the best places to come for Champagne, with a good range and good discounts for buying in quantity. Elsewhere you'll find real stars rubbing shoulders with some interesting oddballs. The Loire and Alsace are good, as are Germany, Italy and most of the New World.*

Marks & Spencer

HEAD OFFICE Michael House, Baker Street, London W1V 8EP (020) 7935 4422 **FAX** (020) 7487 2679; 293 licensed stores **WEBSITE** www.marksandspencer.com **HOURS** Variable **DISCOUNTS** 12 bottles for the price of 11. **T**

✪ **Star attractions** *M&S source their wines from top producers, so you can't go far wrong. I've always been keen on their sherries, and this year I especially liked the Shepherds Ridge Sauvignon Blanc – made by one of New Zealand's hottest young winemakers, Brent Marris, the man behind Wither Hills – and the top notch Chianti Classico, Basilica Cafaggio.*

Come and taste the Majestic experience

NATIONWIDE STORES
Over 100 stores across the UK, open 7 days a week

100's OF WINES ON SPECIAL OFFER

FREE HOME DELIVERY
Of a mixed case of wine *anywhere* in mainland UK*

AWARD WINNING SERVICE
From friendly, knowledgeable staff

FREE TASTING
Wines open to taste, all day, every day

ORDER ONLINE
Visit Majestic Online www.majestic.co.uk
E-mail us at info@majestic.co.uk

www.majestic.co.uk

Visiting France?
Wine & Beer World is Majestic Wine Warehouses French operation offering the best value wines in the Channel ports. Wines start from only 99p and include many Majestic favourites. With more than 100 products on Special Offer you can expect to save up to 50% on the UK price of your drinks bill. We offer a pre-ordering service, free tasting and a friendly, knowledgeable English speaking service.

Please call 01923 298297 or visit
www.wineandbeer.co.uk
for a free price list and
directions to our stores in Calais,
Coquelles and Cherbourg.

Martinez Wines

35 The Grove, Ilkley, Leeds, W. Yorks LS29 9NJ (01943) 603241 **FAX** 0870 922 3940 **E-MAIL** editor@martinez. co.uk **WEBSITE** www.martinez.co.uk **HOURS** Mon–Wed 10–6, Thurs–Fri 10–8, Sat 9.30–6, Sun 12–4 **CARDS** AmEx, MasterCard, Switch, Visa **DISCOUNTS** 5% on 6 bottles or more, 10% off orders over £150 **DELIVERY** Free local delivery, otherwise £9.95 per case mainland UK **EN PRIMEUR** Bordeaux, Burgundy, Port, Chateau Musar, South Africa. **C G M T**
✪ **Star attractions** *Starting at the beginning, Alsace and Beaujolais look spot-on. Bordeaux, Burgundy and Rhône are carefully chosen, and so I would trust their selections from other regions – sweeties and fortifieds are strong, too.*

Mayfair Cellars

203 Seagrave Road, London SW6 1ST (020) 7386 7999 **FAX** (020) 7386 0202 **E-MAIL** sales@mayfaircellars. co.uk **WEBSITE** www.mayfaircellars. co.uk **HOURS** Mon–Fri 9–6 **CARDS** AmEx, MasterCard, Switch, Visa **DELIVERY** England & Wales free; Scotland ring for details **MINIMUM ORDER** 1 mixed case **EN PRIMEUR** Bordeaux, Burgundy. **C M T**
✪ **Star attractions** *Mail-order specialist in the classic regions of Europe, from first-rate small producers not available in the high street. There are also wines from regions such as California and Tasmania and a full range of Jacquesson Champagnes.*

Millésima

87 Quai de Paludate, BP 89, F 33038 Bordeaux Cedex, France (0033) 5 57 80 88 13 **FAX** (0033) 5 57 80 88 19, Freephone 00800 26 73 32 89 or 0800 917 0352 **E-MAIL** cmyers@millesima.com **WEBSITE** www.millesima.com **HOURS** Mon–Fri 8–5.30 **CARDS** AmEx, MasterCard, Switch, Visa **DELIVERY** Free for orders over £500, otherwise £20 **EN PRIMEUR** Bordeaux, Burgundy, Rhône. **C M**
✪ **Star attractions** *Wines come direct from the châteaux to Millésima's cellars, where 3 million bottles are stored. A sprinkling of established names from other French regions – and from further afield there is Quinta do Crasto from Portugal, and Gaja and Sassicaia from Italy.*

Mills Whitcombe

New Lodge Farm, Peterchurch, Hereford HR3 6BJ (01981) 500028 **FAX** (01981) 550027 **E-MAIL** becky@millswhitcombe.co.uk **WEBSITE** www.floydonwine. com **HOURS** Mon–Fri 10–6, out-of-hours answering machine for orders **CARDS** MasterCard, Maestro, Visa **DISCOUNTS** 5% for wine collected from warehouse **DELIVERY** Free locally, £7.50 per consignment nationwide, free for orders over £140 **EN PRIMEUR** Bordeaux, Burgundy. **C G M T**
✪ **Star attractions** *Young company with an expanding list of quality wines in a host of styles from a wide range of regions, especially Australia, Italy, Portugal, southern France and South Africa.*

Montrachet

MAIL ORDER 59 Kennington Road, London SE1 7PZ (020) 7928 1990 **FAX** (020) 7928 3415 **E-MAIL** admin@montrachetwine.com **WEBSITE** www.montrachetwine. com **HOURS** (Office and mail order) Mon–Fri 8.30–5.30 **CARDS** MasterCard, Switch, Visa **DELIVERY** England and Wales £12 including VAT, free for 3 or more cases; Scotland ring for details **MINIMUM ORDER** 1 unmixed case **EN PRIMEUR** Bordeaux, Burgundy. **M T**
✪ **Star attractions** *Impressive Burgundies, some very good Rhônes, and Bordeaux is excellent at all price levels. A short but starry set of German wines.*

Moreno Wines

11 Marylands Road, London W9 2DU
(020) 7286 0678 **FAX** (020) 7286
0513 **E-MAIL** merchant@
moreno-wines.co.uk **WEBSITE**
www.morenowinedirect.co.uk
HOURS Mon–Fri 4–9, Sat 12–10
CARDS AmEx, MasterCard, Switch,
Visa **DISCOUNTS** 5% 1 or 2 cases, 10%
3 or more cases **DELIVERY** Free
locally. **M**
✪ Star attractions *Fine and rare
Spanish wines, with Rioja dating
back to the 19th century, but plenty
of everyday drinking too, from
upcoming regions like Aragon and
Castilla y León. Then there's weird
and wonderful stuff like Txomin
from the Basque country, or Don P X
Gran Reserva, a wonderful
Christmas pudding of a wine from
Montilla-Moriles in the sunny south
at only £9.99. Also wines from
South America.*

Moriarty Vintners

19 Wyndham Arcade, Cardiff CF10
1RH (02920) 229996 **FAX** (02920)
664814 **E-MAIL** sales@moriarty-
vintners.com **WEBSITE**
www.moriarty-vintners.com
HOURS Mon–Sat 10–6 **DISCOUNTS** 5%
off 6 bottles; 10% off 1 mixed case
and regular special offers **DELIVERY**
South Wales free, nationwide at
cost **MINIMUM ORDER** 1 mixed case
EN PRIMEUR Italy, Port, Rhône. **C G M T**
✪ Star attractions *This growing list
concentrates on exciting gems from
small producers. Italy is particularly
strong and other regions with good
coverage include the Languedoc,
Bordeaux, Australia and Spain.*

Morris & Verdin

MAIL ORDER Unit 2, Bankside
Industrial Estate, Sumner Street,
London SE1 9J2 (020) 7921 5300 **FAX**
(020) 7921 5333 **E-MAIL** sales@
m-v.co.uk **WEBSITE** www.morris-
verdin.co.uk **HOURS** Mon–Fri 8–6
DISCOUNTS 10% unmixed cases;
further discounts 10 or more cases

DELIVERY Free central London and
Oxford; elsewhere £10 up to 3 cases,
free 4 or more **MINIMUM ORDER** 1
mixed case **EN PRIMEUR** Bordeaux,
Burgundy, Rhône. **C G M T**
✪ Star attractions *Burgundy
specialist, with California coming on
strong. Top producers are also
cherry-picked from other areas: the
rest of France, Germany, Austria,
Spain, Portugal, Italy, Australia and
New Zealand, and Tokaji from
Hungary. From the US, besides no
fewer than 12 producers from
California, there's Domaine Drouhin
from Oregon and Washington
State's Andrew Will.*

William Morrison Supermarkets

HEAD OFFICE Hilmore House,
Thorton Road, Bradford,
W. Yorks BD8 9AX (01274)
494166 **FAX** (01274) 494831
CUSTOMER SERVICE (01274) 619703
120 licensed branches **HOURS**
Variable, generally Mon–Sat 8–8,
Sun 10–4 **CARDS** MasterCard,
Switch, Visa. **G T**
✪ Star attractions *A good range
of inexpensive, often tasty wines
and cropping up regularly in the
Supermarket Selection (see page
51). Southern France, Chile and
Argentina look particularly reliable.*

MR Wines (trading as Great Northern Wine)

The Warehouse, Blossomgate,
Ripon, N. Yorks HG4 2AJ (01765)
606767 **FAX** (01765) 609151
E-MAIL info@greatnorthern
wine.com **HOURS** Mon–Fri 9–6, Sat
9–5.30 **CARDS** AmEx, MasterCard,
Switch, Visa **DISCOUNTS** 10% on case
quantities **DELIVERY** Free locally,
elsewhere at cost, free 5 cases or
more **MINIMUM ORDER** (for
deliveries) £25 + VAT. **G M T**
✪ Star attractions *A sound list that
mixes well-known and less familiar
names: Australia (Campbells,
Tyrrell's), New Zealand (Alpha*

Domus, Trinity Hill), Portugal and Spain look terrific. France looks highly desirable too.

New Zealand Wines Direct

MAIL ORDER PO Box 476, London NW5 2NZ (020) 7482 0093 **FAX** (020) 7267 8400 **E-MAIL** sales@ fwnz.co.uk or margaret.harvey @btinternet.com **WEBSITE** www. fwnz.co.uk **HOURS** Mon–Sat 9–6 **CARDS** MasterCard, Visa **DISCOUNTS** 4 or more cases **DELIVERY** Free for 1 mixed case or more UK mainland, £15 per case N Ireland **MINIMUM ORDER** 1 mixed case. **M T**

✪ **Star attractions** *Some of New Zealand's great wines: the Bordeaux-style Larose from Stonyridge, plus wines from Ata Rangi, Hunter's, Kumeu River, Pegasus Bay, Palliser Estate, Quartz Reef, Redwood Valley and others.*

James Nicholson

27A Killyleagh Street, Crossgar, Co. Down, Northern Ireland BT30 9DQ (028) 4483 0091 **FAX** (028) 4483 0028 **E-MAIL** info@jnwine.com and shop@jnwine.com **WEBSITE** www.jnwine.com **HOURS** Mon–Sat 10–7 **CARDS** MasterCard, Switch, Visa **DISCOUNTS** 10% mixed case **DELIVERY** Free (1 case or more) in Eire and Northern Ireland; UK mainland £6.95 **EN PRIMEUR** Bordeaux, Burgundy, California. **G M T**

✪ **Star attractions** *Exceptionally appealing list: Bordeaux, Rhône and southern France are slightly ahead of the field, and there's a good selection of affordable Burgundy – as affordable as decent Burgundy ever is, anyway. Spain has new-wave wines from the likes of Artadi and Cellers de Capçanes, and there's excellent drinking from Germany, with names like von Buhl, Helmut Dönnhoff and Dr Loosen. Everything is well chosen, mainly from small, committed growers around the world.*

Noble Rot Wine Warehouses

18 Market Street, Bromsgrove, Worcestershire, B61 8DA (01527) 575606 **FAX** (01527) 833133 **E-MAIL** info@nrwinewarehouse. co.uk **WEBSITE** www.nrwineware house.co.uk **HOURS** Mon–Fri 10–7, Sat 9.30–6.30 **CARDS** MasterCard, Switch, Visa **DELIVERY** Free within 10 mile radius, otherwise, phone for prices. **G T**

✪ **Star attractions** *What Noble Rot's customers want is good wine for current drinking, at £3 to £10 a bottle. Australia, Italy, France and Spain feature most strongly in a frequently changing list. No minimum purchase.*

The Nobody Inn

Doddiscombsleigh, Nr Exeter, Devon EX6 7PS (01647) 252394 **FAX** (01647) 252978 **E-MAIL** info@nobodyinn.co.uk **WEBSITE** www.nobodyinn.co.uk **HOURS** Mon–Sat 12–2.30 & 6–11 (summer); 6–11 (winter), Sun 12–3 & 7–10.30; or by appointment **CARDS** AmEx, MasterCard, Switch, Visa **DISCOUNTS** 5% per case **DELIVERY** £8 for 1 case + £2 each additional case. **G M T**
• The Wine Company (01392) 477752 **FAX** (01392) 477759 **E-MAIL** sales@thewinecompany.biz **WEBSITE** www.thewinecompany.biz **HOURS** Mon–Fri 9.30–6, 24-hr ordering service **CARDS** AmEx, MasterCard, Switch, Visa **DELIVERY** Free for orders over £150.

✪ **Star attractions** *If you're going to eat here I advise you to turn up 2 hours early to browse through this extraordinary list. Australia rules, but there's something exciting from just about everywhere. Amazing range of sweet wines: Loire, of course, but also Greece's Samos Nectar Muscat and Vin de Constance from South Africa. The Wine Company is a new mail order venture for wines costing mainly between £5 and £10.*

Oddbins

HEAD OFFICE 31–33 Weir Road, London SW19 8UG (020) 8944 4400 **FAX** (020) 8944 4411 **MAIL ORDER** Oddbins Direct 0800 328 2323 **FAX** 0800 328 3848; 280 shops nationwide **WEBSITE** www.oddbins.com **HOURS** Generally Mon–Sat 10–10, Sun 10–8 in England & Wales, 12.30–8 Scotland **CARDS** AmEx, MasterCard, Switch, Visa **DISCOUNTS** regular offers on Champagne and sparkling wine, and general promotions **DELIVERY** (Stores) free locally for orders over £100; (online) £4.99 for 12 bottles or more, £6.99 for 1–11 bottles **EN PRIMEUR** Bordeaux. **G M T** • **CALAIS STORE** Cité Europe, 139 Rue de Douvres, 62901, Coquelles Cedex, France (0033) 3 21 82 07 32 **FAX** (0033) 3 21 82 05 83 **PRE-ORDER** www.oddbins.com/ storefinder/calais.asp

✿ **Star attractions** *New World pioneer or champion of the classics? Both, actually. Extensive Aussie selection, well-chosen Chileans and Argentinians; Spain, Italy, Greece, New Zealand, South Africa, Burgundy, Rhône and Germany all look good, and Languedoc is currently in the limelight. Great deals on Champagne. Now owned by French multinational group Castel who are also owners of the Nicolas chain of wine shops and so let's hope the range remains as eclectic as ever.*

Oz Wines

MAIL ORDER Freepost Lon 17656, London SW18 5BR, 0845 450 1261 **FAX** (020) 8870 8839 **E-MAIL** sales@ozwinesonline.co.uk **WEBSITE** www.ozwinesonline. co.uk **HOURS** Mon–Fri 9.30–7 **CARDS** Diners, MasterCard, Switch, Visa **DELIVERY** Free. **MINIMUM ORDER** 1 mixed case. **M** ✿ **Star attractions** *Australian wines made by small wineries and real people, which means wines with the kind of thrilling flavours that Australians do better than anyone else.*

Penistone Court Wine Cellars

The Railway Station, Penistone, Sheffield, South Yorkshire S36 6HP (01226) 766037 **FAX** (01226) 767310 **E-MAIL** pcwc@dircon.co.uk **HOURS** Tues–Fri 10–6, Sat 10–3 **CARDS** MasterCard, Switch, Visa **DELIVERY** Free locally, rest of UK mainland charged at cost 1 case or more **MINIMUM ORDER** 1 case. **G M** ✿ **Star attractions** *A well-balanced list, with something from just about everywhere, mostly from familiar names. So, you've got Champagne (Pol Roger, Bollinger, Roederer and others), Burgundy, Beaujolais, Alsace, Loire, Rhône and a short list of clarets. Outside France, there's quite a good list from Italy, plus Austria, Spain, Chile, the USA, New Zealand and Australia (Brown Brothers, Stonier, Penfolds and De Bortoli).*

Philglas & Swiggot

21 Northcote Road, Battersea, London SW11 1NG (020) 7924 4494 **FAX** (020) 7924 4736 • 64 Hill Rise, Richmond, London TW10 6UB (020) 8332 6081 **E-MAIL** info@philglas-swiggot.co.uk **WEBSITE** www.philglas-swiggot.co.uk **HOURS** (Battersea) Mon–Sat 11–7, Sun 12–5 (Richmond) Tue–Sat 11–7, Sun 12–5 **CARDS** AmEx, MasterCard, Switch, Visa **DISCOUNTS** 5% per case **DELIVERY** Free 1 case locally. **G M T** ✿ **Star attractions** *Excellent Aussie selection – subtle, interesting wines, not blockbuster brands. The same philosophy applies to wines they buy from elsewhere, so you'll find serious Italians and good French wines. Austria fits the bill nicely and dessert wines are good too.*

Christopher Piper Wines

1 Silver Street, Ottery St Mary, Devon EX11 1DB (01404) 814139

FAX (01404) 812100 HOURS Mon–Fri
8.30–5.30, Sat 9–4.30 CARDS
MasterCard, Switch, Visa DISCOUNTS
5% mixed case, 10% 3 or more
cases DELIVERY Free for orders over
£180, otherwise £5.25 per case
MINIMUM ORDER 1 mixed case
EN PRIMEUR Bordeaux, Burgundy,
Rhône. C G M T

✪ Star attractions *Oh, Oh, Oh what
a lovely list. There's nothing routine
here, just pages and pages of
interesting, well-chosen wines, with
lots of information to help you
make up your mind. Irresistible
Burgundies, Beaujolais, Bordeaux
and Rhônes; German wines from
Josef Leitz, von Kesselstatt, Bürklin-
Wolf and Dr Loosen; Italy, Spain and
Greece are here too, along with
California, Australia, New Zealand
and some terrific South Africans.*

Terry Platt Wine Merchants

Council Street West, Llandudno
LL30 1ED (01492) 874099 FAX
(01492) 874788 E-MAIL info@
terryplattwines.co.uk WEBSITE
www.terryplattwines.co.uk
HOURS Mon–Fri 8.30–5.30 CARDS
AmEx, MasterCard, Switch, Visa
DELIVERY Free locally and UK
mainland 5 cases or more
MINIMUM ORDER 1 mixed case. G M T

✪ Star attractions *A wide-ranging
list with a sprinkling of good
growers from most regions. New
World coverage has increased this
year: Argentina includes Terrazas de
los Andes and Humber to Canale
and Chile Casa Lapostolle and
Montes; Australia has Cape
Mentelle and Nepenthe among
others, and South Africa has
Grangehurst.*

Playford Ros

Middle Park House, Sowerby, Thirsk,
Yorkshire YO7 3AH (01845) 526777
FAX (01845) 526888 E-MAIL
sales@playfordros.com
WEBSITE www.playfordros.com
HOURS Mon–Fri 8–5 CARDS

MasterCard, Visa DISCOUNTS 2.5%
on orders over 6 cases DELIVERY
Free Yorkshire, Derbyshire, Durham,
Newcastle; elsewhere on UK
mainland (per case), £10 1 case,
£6.50 2 cases, £5 3 cases, £4 4 cases,
free 5 cases MINIMUM ORDER 1
mixed case EN PRIMEUR Bordeaux,
Burgundy. C G M T

✪ Star attractions *A carefully
chosen list, with reassuringly
recognizable representatives from
Bordeaux and Burgundy, Alsace, the
Rhône and the Loire. Australia looks
exceptional, with a range that
includes some top wines like St
Hallett's Old Block Shiraz at £16,65.
Similar standards apply in Spain,
Italy, Germany, New Zealand, North
and South America, and there is a
selection of 'everyday' wines at
around the £5 to £6 mark, from
every corner of the globe.*

Portland Wine Co

16 North Parade, off Norris Road,
Sale, Cheshire M33 3JS (0161) 962
8752 FAX (0161) 905 1291 • 152a
Ashley Road, Hale WA15 9SA (0161)
928 0357 • 82 Chester Road,
Macclesfield SK11 8DL (01625)
616147 E-MAIL sales@
portland-wine.co.uk WEBSITE
www.portlandwine.co.uk
HOURS Mon–Sat 10–10, Sun 12–3 &
7–9.30 CARDS MasterCard, Switch,
Visa DISCOUNTS 5% 2 cases or more,
10% 5 cases or more DELIVERY Free
locally 1 case or more, £10 + VAT
per consignment nationwide
EN PRIMEUR Bordeaux, Port. G M T

✪ Star attractions *Spain, Portugal
and Burgundy are the specialities
here and there is also a promising-
looking list of lesser clarets, as well
as more expensive, stunning older
vintages. This consumer-friendly list
has something at every price level
from around the world.*

Raeburn Fine Wines

21–23 Comely Bank Road,
Edinburgh EH4 1DS (0131) 343 1159

FAX (0131) 332 5166 **E-MAIL** sales@raeburnfinewines.com **WEBSITE** www.raeburnfine wines.com **HOURS** Mon–Sat 9.30–6, Sun 12.30–5 **CARDS** AmEx, MasterCard, Switch, Visa **DISCOUNTS** 5% unsplit case, 2.5% mixed **DELIVERY** Free local area 1 or more cases (usually); elsewhere at cost **EN PRIMEUR** Bordeaux, Burgundy, Germany, Languedoc-Roussillon, Rhône. **G M T**

✪ Star attractions *Everything here is carefully chosen, usually from small growers: if you want obvious choices you won't like this list, but if you want to try interesting wines from an impressive array of vintages you'll be more than happy. Burgundy is something of a speciality and in the Loire there are oodles of Vouvrays from Huet, in vintages going back to 1924. Italy, Germany, Austria, New Zealand, Australia and California all look fabulous. Ports from Niepoort.*

Reid Wines

The Mill, Marsh Lane, Hallatrow, Nr Bristol BS39 6EB (01761) 452645 **FAX** (01761) 453642 **HOURS** Mon–Fri 9–5.30 **CARDS** MasterCard, Visa (3% charge) **DELIVERY** Free within 25 miles of Hallatrow (Bristol), and in central London for orders over 2 cases **C G M T**

✪ Star attractions *Reid's is one of the lists I look forward to reading most: it's full of pithy comments alongside its fabulous array of older vintages. Five clarets from 1975 were 'heralded at birth, scorned in middle age, graceful and delicious (some of them) now.' A mix of great old wines, some old duds and splendid current stuff. Italy, USA, Australia, port and Madeira look tremendous.*

La Réserve

56 Walton Street, Knightsbridge, London SW3 1RB (020) 7589 2020 **FAX** (020) 7581 0250 • 7 Grant Road, London SW11 2NU (020) 7978 5601

• 29 Heath Street, Hampstead, London NW3 6TR (020) 7435 6845 • Milroys of Soho, 3 Greek Street, London W1V 6NX (020) 7437 9311 • 203 Munster Road, London SW6 6BX (020) 7381 6930 **E-MAIL** realwine@la-reserve.co.uk **WEBSITE** www.la-reserve.co.uk **HOURS** Vary from shop to shop **CARDS** AmEx, MasterCard, Switch, Visa **DISCOUNTS** 5% per case except accounts **DELIVERY** Free 1 case or more central London and orders over £200 on UK mainland. Otherwise £7.50 **EN PRIMEUR** Bordeaux, Burgundy, Italy, Rhône, Spain, Port. **C G M T**

✪ Star attractions *Varied, intelligent list. Burgundy, Bordeaux, the Loire, Alsace, Spain, Italy, North America, Australia, New Zealand and South Africa are all excellent, with well-chosen wines (Jermann, Gaja, Vajra and Argiano in Italy, for example).*

Richardson & Sons

2A Marlborough Street, Whitehaven, Cumbria CA28 7LL (01946) 65334 **FAX** (01946) 63545 **E-MAIL** mailwines@aol.com **HOURS** Mon–Sat 10–5.30 **CARDS** AmEx, Delta, MasterCard, Switch, Visa **DELIVERY** Free locally; UK mainland £10 first case and £2 each additional case; orders over £150 free. **G M T**

✪ Star attractions *It's the only place in Cumbria stocking Ch. Latour and Opus One, but in general Richardson & Sons carefully select from interesting small producers, preferring 'little hidden gems' to big-name brands. Rioja is chosen to represent various styles, and there's very good stuff from South Africa.*

Howard Ripley

25 Dingwall Road, London SW18 3AZ (020) 8877 3065 **FAX** (020) 8877 0029 **E-MAIL** info@howardripley.com **WEBSITE** www.howardripley.com **HOURS** Mon–Fri 9–8, Sat 9–1 **CARDS** MasterCard, Switch, Visa

Retailers directory

DELIVERY Minimum charge £9.50 + VAT, free UK mainland on orders over £500 ex-VAT MINIMUM ORDER 1 mixed case EN PRIMEUR Burgundy, Germany. C M T

✪ Star attractions *If you're serious about Burgundy, this is one of perhaps half a dozen lists that you need. Yes, the wines are expensive – great Burgundy is expensive – but they're not excessive. The German range is also excellent.*

Roberson

348 Kensington High Street, London W14 8NS (020) 7371 2121 FAX (020) 7371 4010 E-MAIL retail@roberson.co.uk WEBSITE www.roberson.co.uk HOURS Mon–Sat 10–8 CARDS AmEx, Diners, MasterCard, Switch, Visa DISCOUNTS MAIL ORDER 5% on unmixed cases; shop 10% unmixed cases, 5% mixed DELIVERY Free delivery within London, otherwise £15 per case EN PRIMEUR Bordeaux. C G M T

✪ Star attractions *Fine and rare wines, sold by the bottle. Clarets back to 1900, with plenty from the great 1989 and 1990 vintages. All of France is excellent; so is Italy and port, and if you fancy a bottle of 1945 Ch. Mouton-Rothschild at £5,500 you know where to look.*

The RSJ Wine Company

115 Wootton Street, London SE1 8LY (020) 7633 0881 FAX (020) 7401 2455 E-MAIL tom.king@rsj.uk.com WEBSITE www.rsj.uk.com HOURS Mon–Fri 9–6, answering machine at other times CARDS MasterCard, Visa DELIVERY Free central London, minimum 1 case; England and Wales (per case), £14.10 1 case, £10.25 2 cases or more. G M T

✪ Star attractions *A roll-call of great Loire names. From Savennières there is Domaine aux Moines, from Chinon J & C Baudry, Saumur from Domaine des Roches Neuves, to* mention just a few. And now there are wines from outside the Loire as well: Beaujolais, Alsace, Italy and even the odd wine from Australia and New Zealand.

Safeway

HEAD OFFICE 6 Millington Road, Hayes, Middlesex UB3 4AY (020) 8848 8744, FAX (020) 8573 1865 CUSTOMER SERVICE (01622) 712987; 480 stores nationwide WEBSITE www.safeway.co.uk HOURS Mon–Sat 8–10, Sun 10–4 (most stores) CARDS AmEx, MasterCard, Switch, Visa DISCOUNTS 5% on six or more bottles (except fortified wines and Montilla). G

✪ Star attractions *A list which swings weirdly between the cheap and the expensive, the routine and the fabulous. But this scatter-gun approach actually works rather well in most stores: you're sure to find an interesting bargain from the south of France or Hungary, for example, and I found plenty of wines to include in the Supermarket Selection (see page 51) but if money's no object there's a handful of good Burgundies and clarets, and some top stuff from the New World.*

Sainsbury's

HEAD OFFICE 33 Holborn, London EC1N 2HT (020) 7695 6000 CUSTOMER SERVICE 0800 636262; 501 stores nationwide (including Savacentres) WEBSITE www. sainsburys.co.uk HOURS Variable, some 24-hrs, locals generally Mon–Sat 7–11, Sun 10 or 11–4pm CARDS AmEx, MasterCard, Switch, Visa. G • CALAIS STORE La Boutique Sainsbury's, Centre Commercial Auchan, Route de Boulogne, 63100 Calais, France (0033) 3 21 82 38 48 FAX (0033) 3 21 36 01 91 PREORDER www.sainsburys.co.uk/calais

✪ Star attractions *Sainsbury's is doing rather well at the moment, catering for the sub-£3 bargain hunters, but also appealing to lovers of good-value wine higher up the scale. There's a short list of affordable clarets, improving Italians, and a willingness to venture into areas like Morocco and to give odd grape varieties like Petit Verdot and Nero d'Avola a go. Chile and Argentina remain good bets here.*

Savage Selection

The Ox House, Market Place, Northleach, Cheltenham, Glos GL54 3EG (01451) 860896 FAX (01451) 860996 • The Ox House Shop and Wine Bar at same address (01451) 860680 E-MAIL wine@savage selection.co.uk WEBSITE www.savageselection.co.uk HOURS Office: Mon–Fri 9–6; shop: Tue/Wed 10–7.30, Thur–Fri 10–10, Sat 10–3 CARDS AmEx, MasterCard, Switch, Visa DELIVERY Free locally 1 case, elsewhere on UK mainland free 3 cases, otherwise £10 per consignment EN PRIMEUR Bordeaux. **C G M T**
✿ Star attractions *Really well-chosen wines from names that you may never have heard of, covering 95 growers in 13 different countries – that's because Mark Savage takes the trouble to find wines himself rather than just buying them in from other people. So he lists wines from Oregon, Washington and Idaho, alongside Antonopoulos from Greece, Juris from Austria and the last 20 vintages from François Mitjavile at Ch. Tertre Rôteboeuf and Ch. Roc de Cambes in Bordeaux.*

Seckford Wines

Dock Lane, Melton, Suffolk IP12 1PE (01394) 446622 FAX (01394) 446633 E-MAIL sales@seckfordwines.co.uk WEBSITE www.seckfordwines.co.uk CARDS MasterCard, Switch, Visa DELIVERY £10 per consignment, UK mainland; elsewhere at cost. MINIMUM ORDER 1 mixed case. **C**
✿ Star attractions *Bordeaux,*

Burgundy and the Rhône are the stars of this list, and if you prefer older vintages, Seckford have got plenty of these, with Sauternes back to 1900. There's serious stuff from Italy, Spain and Austria, too.

Somerfield

HEAD OFFICE Somerfield House, Whitchurch Lane, Bristol BS14 0TJ (0117) 935 9359 FAX (0117) 935 6669; 593 Somerfield stores and 676 Kwiksave stores nationwide WEBSITE www.somerfield.co.uk HOURS Mon–Sat 8–8, Sun 10–4 CARDS MasterCard, Switch, Visa DISCOUNTS 5% off 6 bottles DELIVERY Free local delivery for orders over £25 in selected stores **M T**
✿ Star attractions *The focus is on wines under £5, and these tend to come from the Languedoc, South America, Spain and Portugal. Sparkling wines are generally good, from vintage Cava to the own-label Prince William Champagne.*

Sommelier Wine Co

23 St George's Esplanade, St Peter Port, Guernsey, Channel Islands, GY1 2BG (01481) 721677 FAX (01481) 716818 HOURS Mon–Thur 10–5.30, Fri 10–6, Sat 9.30–5.30 CARDS MasterCard, Switch, Visa DISCOUNTS 5% 1 case or more DELIVERY Free locally 1 unmixed case. Customs legislation restricts the shipping of wine to the UK mainland. **G T**
✿ Star attractions *An excellent list, with interesting, unusual wines. It's a big selection, too: there are yards of lovely subtle Italian whites and well-made reds, and lots of Loires and Beaujolais. Burgundy, South Africa, Chile and Argentina all look good, though Australia outdoes them all.*

Frank Stainton Wines

3 Berry's Yard, Finkle Street, Kendal, Cumbria LA9 4AB (01539) 731886 FAX (01539) 730396 E-MAIL admin@stainton-wines.co.uk

J. Straker, Chadwick & Sons

——— Established 1872 ———

conduct regular auctions of

FINE, RARE AND INTERESTING WINES

throughout the year.

We offer a personal, helpful and professional service to buyers and sellers alike of single bottles or complete cellars.

NO BUYERS PREMIUM

Further information from
The Wine Department,
Market Street Chambers,
Abergavenny, Mon. NP7 5SD

Tel: 01873 852624
Fax: 01873 857311
email: enquiries@strakerchadwick.co.uk
www.strakerchadwick.co.uk

HOURS Mon–Sat 9–5.30 **CARDS** MasterCard, Switch, Visa **DISCOUNTS** 5% mixed case **DELIVERY** Free Cumbria and North Lancashire; elsewhere (per case) £9 1 case, £6 2–4 cases, £4 5–9 cases, 10 cases free. **G M T**
✪ Star attractions *Some interesting Burgundy growers, but on the whole Bordeaux is better. Italy has a selection of leading names: among others, you'll find Allegrini's La Poja and Valpolicella, and Felsina Berardenga's Chianti Classico. Chile includes the wines of Casa Silva, which have real character and subtlety. Also Three Choirs wines from England.*

Stevens Garnier

47 West Way, Botley, Oxford OX2 OJF (01865) 263303 **FAX** (01865) 791594 **E-MAIL** shop@stevens garnier.co.uk **HOURS** Mon–Wed 10–6, Thur–Fri 10–7, Sat 9.30–6

CARDS AmEx, MasterCard, Switch, Visa, Solo **DISCOUNTS** 5% on an unmixed case **DELIVERY** Free locally; 'competitive rates' elsewhere. **G T**
✪ Star attractions *'Regional France' is a strength here, meaning there's at least one representative from most regions: this is one of the few places in the UK you can buy wine from Savoie. Portugal is from quality-conscious Sogrape. The New World has some pleasant surprises: Grant Burge and Willow Bridge from Australia, Carmen from Chile, Chateau des Charmes from Canada.*

Sunday Times Wine Club

New Aquitaine House, Exeter Way, Theale, Reading, Berks RG7 4PL **ORDER LINE** 0870 220 0010 **FAX** 0870 220 0030 **E-MAIL** orders@sundaytimeswineclub.co.uk **WEBSITE** www.sundaytimeswine club.co.uk **HOURS** 24-hr answering machine **CARDS** AmEx, Diners, MasterCard, Switch, Visa **DISCOUNTS** On special offers **DELIVERY** £4.99 per order **EN PRIMEUR** Australia, Bordeaux, Burgundy, Rhône.
C M T
✪ Star attractions *Essentially the same list as Laithwaites (see page 109), though the special offers come round at different times. The membership fee is £10 per annum. The club runs tours and tasting events for its members.*

T & W Wines

5 Station Way, Brandon, Suffolk IP27 OBH (01842) 814414 **FAX** (01842) 819967 **E-MAIL** contact@tw-wines.co.uk **WEBSITE** www.tw-wines.co.uk **HOURS** Mon–Fri 9.30–5.30, Sat 9.30–1.00 **CARDS** AmEx, Diners, MasterCard, Visa **DELIVERY** (most areas) 7–23 bottles £10.95 + VAT, 2 or more cases free **EN PRIMEUR** Burgundy. **C G M T**
✪ Star attractions *The list is a good one, particularly if you're looking for Burgundy, Rhône, Alsace or the Loire, but prices are not especially*

low, and when working out the final cost remember that they exclude VAT. There's an amazing list of over 240 half bottles, including the superb sweet wines of Willi Opitz, from Austria, and 25 biodynamic wines from France.

Tanners

26 Wyle Cop, Shrewsbury, Shropshire SY1 1XD (01743) 234500 **FAX** (01743) 234501 • 4 St Peter's Square, Hereford HR1 2PG (01432) 272044 **FAX** (01432) 263316 • 36 High Street, Bridgnorth WV16 4DB (01746) 763148 • Severn Farm Enterprise Park, Welshpool SY21 7DF (01938) 552542 **FAX** (01938) 556565 **E-MAIL** sales@tanners-wines.co.uk **WEBSITE** www.tanners-wines.co.uk **HOURS** Shrewsbury Mon–Sat 9–6, branches 9–5.30 **CARDS** AmEx, MasterCard, Switch, Visa **DISCOUNTS** 5% 1 mixed case (cash & collection); 2.5% for 3 mixed cases, 5% for 5, 7.5% for 10 (**MAIL ORDER**) **DELIVERY** Free 1 mixed case or more locally, or nationally over £90, otherwise £7.50 **EN PRIMEUR** Bordeaux, Burgundy, Rhône, Port. **G M T**
✪ **Star attractions** *The sort of list from which it's extremely difficult to choose, because you simply want everything on it. There are lots of lovely Rhônes; Bordeaux and Burgundy are both terrific; Germany is outstanding, and there are even a couple of wines from Switzerland and Lebanon. Spain and Italy look very good, and Australia, South Africa and California all show what these places can do.*

Tesco

HEAD OFFICE Delamare Road, Cheshunt, Herts EN8 9SL (01992) 632222 **FAX** (01992) 630794, **CUSTOMER SERVICE** 0800 505555; 566 licensed branches **E-MAIL** customer.services@tesco.co.uk **WEBSITE** www.tesco.co.uk **HOURS** Variable **CARDS** MasterCard, Switch, Visa **DISCOUNT** 5% on 6 bottles or more **EN PRIMEUR** Bordeaux. **G M T**
• **CALAIS STORE** Tesco Vin Plus, Cité Europe, 122 Boulevard du Kent, 62231 Coquelles, France (0033) 3 21 46 02 70 **WEBSITE** www.tesco.com/vinplus **HOURS** Mon–Sat 8.30–10pm
✪ **Star attractions** *This is looking increasingly like a place to do some serious wine shopping – for things like Tim Adams Shiraz (£8.99) and Riesling (£7.99) from Australia's Clare Valley and Babich Winemakers Reserve Syrah from Hawkes Bay (£7.49). And there are still lots of cheapies for when your budget is more of the baked beans on toast sort. Australia seems to inspire Tesco's excellent wine buyers the most. Well, I'm not about to argue with that.*

Thresher Group: Thresher Wine Shops and Wine Rack

HEAD OFFICE Enjoyment Hall, Bessemer Road, Welwyn Garden City, Herts AL7 1BL (01707) 387200 **FAX** (01707) 387350; 1,250 Thresher Wine Shops, 200 Wine Rack stores **HOURS** Mon–Sat 10–10 (some 10.30), Sun 11–10, Scotland 12.30–10.30 **CARDS** MasterCard, Switch, Visa **DELIVERY** Free locally, some branches. **G T**
✪ **Star attractions** *A major high street presence, Thresher wine shops are presumably a faithful reflection of everyday wine drinking in Britain. Threshers have a large number of stores and have undergone some justified criticism recently about cutting down their range of wines. But there's nothing inherently wrong with a reduced range – now down to 400–500 wines – so long as you take greater care in sourcing the wines you do decide to stock, and this they seem determined to do. Origins and superior Radcliffe, the new in-house brands, should be worth following.*

Retailers directory

Turville Valley Wines

The Firs, Potter Row, Great Missenden, Bucks HP16 9LT (01494) 868818 **FAX** (01494) 868832 **E-MAIL** info@turville-valley-wines.com **WEBSITE** www.turville-valley-wines.com **HOURS** Mon–Fri 9–5.30 **CARDS** None **DELIVERY** By arrangement **MINIMUM ORDER** £300/12 bottles. **C M**

✪ **Star attractions** *Serious wines for serious spenders. The Bordeaux is all classic, mostly mature stuff – no lesser wines here – and there are buckets of Domaine de la Romanée-Conti Burgundies. There are top names too from Spain, Italy, the Rhône, California (Dominus, Harlan Estate, Dalla Valle, Opus One) and odds and ends from all over.*

Unwins

HEAD OFFICE Birchwood House, Victoria Road, Dartford, Kent DA1 5AJ (01322) 272711 **FAX** (01322) 294469; 451 branches in southern and eastern England **E-MAIL** info@unwins.co.uk **WEBSITE** www.unwins.co.uk **HOURS** Variable, usually Mon–Sat 10–10, Sun 11–10 **CARDS** AmEx, Diners, MasterCard, Switch, Visa **DISCOUNTS** 10% on mixed case, 5% on 6 bottles and regular special offers **DELIVERY** Free locally **EN PRIMEUR** Bordeaux. **G T**

✪ **Star attractions** *Unwins was best known for its decent range of clarets and some interesting stuff from Italy, South America, South Africa and New Zealand, but who knows where the company is heading? The whole wine-buying team was made redundant in 2001 and since then it has been difficult to find out much about its future direction.*

Valvona & Crolla

19 Elm Row, Edinburgh EH7 4AA (0131) 556 6066 **FAX** (0131) 556 1668 **E-MAIL** wine@valvonacrolla.co.uk **WEBSITE** www.valvonacrolla.com **HOURS** Mon–Sat 8–6.30, Sun 11–5.30

CARDS AmEx, MasterCard, Switch, Visa **DISCOUNTS** 7% 1–3 cases, 10% 4 or more **DELIVERY** Free on orders over £125, £6 otherwise for 8 day service, £8 for next day service. **G M T**

✪ **Star attractions** *If you're fond of Italian wines you should be shopping here. The list has dozens and dozens of wines from Piedmont and Tuscany, and there are others from Lombardy, Basilicata, Calabria, the Marche, Sicily, Sardinia, the Veneto, and terrific dessert wines. It's a simply fabulous selection, and at all prices. There are wines from Australia, New Zealand, France, Argentina, Spain and Portugal and elsewhere, but they are not what V&C is really about.*

La Vigneronne

105 Old Brompton Road, London SW7 3LE (020) 7589 6113 **FAX** (020) 7581 2983 **E-MAIL** lavig@aol.com **WEBSITE** www.lavigneronne.co.uk **HOURS** Mon–Fri 10–8, Sat 10–6 **CARDS** AmEx, Diners, MasterCard, Switch, Visa **DISCOUNTS** 5% mixed case (collected) **DELIVERY** Free locally, £10 mainland England and Wales for orders under £250; mainland Scotland at cost **EN PRIMEUR** Bordeaux, Burgundy, Rhône. **M T**

✪ **Star attractions** *They do have fine and rare wines here – which you could guess from their tastings, which often take an in-depth look at a producer or region across a range of vintages. But one always associates the shop with the quirky and just-discovered, with names and properties they've found for themselves. The south of France is a particular love, and there are classics like Mas Jullien, Daumas Gassac, Domaine Tempier and Domaine de Trévallon, plus hard-to-find wines like Palette from Château Simone.*

Villeneuve Wines

1 Venlaw Court, Peebles, Scotland
EH45 8AE (01721) 722500 **FAX**
(01721) 729922 • 82 High Street,
Haddington EH41 3ET (01620)
822224 • 49A Broughton Street,
Edinburgh, EH1 3RJ (0131) 558 8441
E-MAIL wines@villeneuvewines.com
WEBSITE www.villeneuvewines.com
HOURS (Peebles) Mon–Sat 9–8, Sun
12.30–5.30; (Haddington) Mon–
Thur 10–7, Fri 10–8, Sat 9–8;
(Edinburgh) Mon–Sat 9–10, Sun
12.30–10 **CARDS** AmEx, MasterCard,
Switch, Visa **DISCOUNTS** 5% per case
DELIVERY 48-hour service. Free
locally, £7.50 per case elsewhere.
G M T
✪ Star attractions *Italy, California,
Australia and New Zealand are all
marvellous here. Italy has Pieropan,
Planeta, Aldo Conterno, Aldo Vajra,
Isole e Olena, Jermann, Allegrini and
many others. From California there
are wines from Duckhorn and
Shafer, Stag's Leap, Ridge and
Joseph Phelps. Australia includes
Brokenwood, Mount Langi Ghiran
and Plantagenet, New Zealand has
Mount Difficulty, Cloudy Bay and
Felton Road. Spain is clearly an
enthusiasm, Chile, Argentina and
South Africa are well chosen and
there are old vintages of Chateau
Musar in the Lebanon.*

Vinceremos

74 Kirkgate, Leeds LS2 7DJ (0113)
244 0002 **FAX** (0113) 288 4566
E-MAIL info@vinceremos.co.uk
WEBSITE www.vinceremos.co.uk
HOURS Mon–Sat 8.30–5.30
CARDS AmEx, Delta, MasterCard,
Switch, Visa, **DISCOUNTS** 5% on 5
cases or over, 10% on 10 cases or
over **DELIVERY** £5.95 per order, free 5
cases or more **MINIMUM ORDER** 1
mixed case **M**
✪ Star attractions *Organic
specialist, with a wide-ranging list
of wines that I'd actually like to
drink: Guy Bossard's Muscadet,
Huet's Vouvray, Domaine de
Riecheaume's Côtes de Provence,
Sedlescombe Vineyard in England,
Millton Vineyard in New Zealand,
Fetzer's Bonterra wines from
California and a whole page of reds
and whites from Morocco. Prices are
reasonable.*

Vin du Van

MAIL ORDER Colthups, The Street,
Appledore, Kent TN26 2BX (01233)
758727 **FAX** (01223) 758389 **HOURS**
Mon–Fri 9–5 **CARDS** Delta,
MasterCard, Switch, Visa **DELIVERY**
Free locally; elsewhere £5.95 for
first case, further cases free.
Highlands & islands ask for quote
MINIMUM ORDER 1 case. **G M**
✪ Star attractions *Star-studded
Australian list, with plenty of quirky,
boutique wines from a host of
grape varieties. But this is no
ordinary list. It's barking mad – read
it and weep. The new member of
staff this year is Harvey the Cat MW.*

Vintage Roots

Farley Farms, Reading Road,
Arborfield, Berkshire, RG2 9HT
(0118) 976 1999 **FAX** (0118) 976 1998
HOURS Mon–Fri 8.30–5.30,
Saturdays in December
E-MAIL info@vintageroots.co.uk
WEBSITE www.vintageroots.co.uk
CARDS Delta, MasterCard, Switch,
Visa **DISCOUNTS** 5% on 5 cases or
over **DELIVERY** £4.95 for single case,
£5.95 2–5 cases, free 6 cases or
more. **T**
✪ Star attractions *Everything on
this list is organic, beginning with a
choice of Champagnes and other
fizz and ending with beers and
cider. In between, most of the wines
are from France (Côtes de Bourg
from Ch. Falfas in Bordeaux, for
example), Spain and Italy.*

Vintage Wines

116 Derby Road, Nottingham
NG1 5FB (0115) 947 6565/941
9614 **FAX** (0115) 950 5276 **E-MAIL**
vintagewines@btconnect.com

WEBSITE www.vintagewinesltd.co.uk
HOURS Mon–Fri 9–5.15, Sat 9–5
CARDS AmEx, MasterCard, Solo,
Switch, Visa **DISCOUNTS** 10% for
6 or more bottles collected, other
discounts negotiable **DELIVERY** Free
locally **EN PRIMEUR** Bordeaux.
C G M T
✪ **Star attractions** *Champagne is
good here, and there's Chablis from
Vocoret. Most other countries and
regions here look a little routine,
though perfectly respectable.*

Virgin Wines

MAIL ORDER The Loft, St James' Mill,
Whitefriars, Norwich NR3 1TN
(01603) 614591 **FAX** (01603) 619277
CUSTOMER SERVICE 0870 164 9593
E-MAIL help@virginwines.co.uk
WEBSITE www.virginwines.com
HOURS (office) Mon–Fri 8–7,
Sat–Sun 10–5, Internet 24-hrs
CARDS AmEx, MasterCard, Switch,
Visa **DISCOUNTS** regular special
offers **DELIVERY** £4.99 for UK,
Northern Ireland and Scottish
Highlands, £6.99 for evening
delivery **MINIMUM ORDER** 1 case. **G M**
✪ **Star attractions** *Internet retailer
with hundreds of reasonably priced
wines from all around the world.
The list is organized by style rather
than by grape variety, region or
vintage and encourages the buyer
to branch out and try new wines.
Lots of customer comments, too.*

Waitrose

HEAD OFFICE Doncastle Road,
Southern Industrial Area, Bracknell,
Berks RG12 8YA, **CUSTOMER SERVICE**
0800 188884; 143 licensed stores
E-MAIL customerservice@waitrose.
co.uk **WEBSITE** www.waitrose.com
HOURS Mon–Tue 8.30–7 or 8,
Wed–Thur 8.30–8, Fri 8.30–9,
Sat 8.30–7, Sun 10–4 or 11–5
CARDS AmEx, Delta, MasterCard,
Switch, Visa **DISCOUNTS** 5% for 6
bottles or more **DELIVERY** Home
Delivery and Waitrosedeliver
available at selected branches

EN PRIMEUR Bordeaux, Port. **G T**
• **WAITROSE WINE DIRECT** 24-hr
freephone 0800 188881 or order
online at www.waitrose.com
E-MAIL winedirect@waitrose.co.uk
DISCOUNTS Vary monthly on
featured cases **DELIVERY** Free for
orders of £75 or more throughout
UK mainland and Isle of Wight,
otherwise £4.95 per delivery
address.
✪ **Star attractions** *Still ahead of the
other supermarkets in quality, value
and imagination. Waitrose brings
you the best from around the
world: their own-label wines are
sourced from top producers – see
Supermarket Selection (page 51) for
evidence. There are some very good
clarets, from the everyday right up
to Pomerol's Ch l'Évangile (£69) and
some serious Burgundies (Corton-
Charlemagne from Bouchard Père).
Italy, Germany and Spain all deliver
the goods, and Australia (Cape
Mentelle, Chapel Hill and Peter
Lehmann) and New Zealand
(Wither Hills, Villa Maria) have
wines to suit every pocket. Despite
its reputation for being a tad
expensive, we found some really
tasty stuff at under £5 (from Aragon
in Spain, for example). All Waitrose
wines are available from Waitrose
Wine Direct.*

Waterloo Wine Co

OFFICE AND WAREHOUSE 6 Vine Yard,
London SE1 1QL **SHOP** 59–61 Lant
Street, London SE1 1QN (020) 7403
7967 **FAX** (020) 7357 6976 **E-MAIL**
sales@waterloowine.co.uk **WEBSITE**
www.waterloowine.co.uk **HOURS**
Mon–Fri 10–6.30, Sat 10–5 **CARDS**
AmEx, MasterCard, Switch, Visa
DELIVERY Free 5 cases in central London
(otherwise £5); elsewhere, 1 case
£8.23, 2 cases £5.88, 3 cases £5.29, 4
cases £4.99, further reductions
according to quantity. **G T**
✪ **Star attractions** *A very quirky,
personal list, strong in the Loire
(1962 Vouvray Moelleux Clos de*

Bourg from Huet for £44, the utterly delicious Bourgueil Cuvée Prestige from Lame-Delisle for £8.25, Savennières from Domaine de Closel for £7.35) and making something of a speciality of the wines of the Waipara region of Canterbury, New Zealand (Waipara West, Waipara Springs and Mark Rattray). Waterloo are the UK agents for Minervois from Domaine de la Tour Boisée and Hewitson in South Australia, and this is one of the few places you'll find wines from Slovenia, Croatia and Montenegro. But there are finds in lots of regions, such as Sauternes and Germany.

Whitesides of Clitheroe

Shawbridge Street, Clitheroe, Lancs BB7 1NA (01200) 422281 **FAX** (01200) 427129 **E-MAIL** wine@whitesideswine.co.uk **HOURS** Mon–Fri 9–5.30, Sat 9–5 **CARDS** MasterCard, Switch, Visa **DISCOUNTS** 5% per case **DELIVERY** Free locally, elsewhere at cost. **G M T**

✪ **Star attractions** *A safe list of familiar names and flavours. I can find a reasonable number of wines I'd choose to drink here, especially from the New World, but also from Spain, Italy and Portugal.*

Wimbledon Wine Cellar

1 Gladstone Road, Wimbledon, London SW19 1QU (020) 8540 9979 **FAX** (020) 8540 9399 • 84 Chiswick High Road, London W4 1SY, 020 8994 7879 **E-MAIL** enquiries@ wimbledonwinecellar.com or chiswick@wimbledon winecellar.com **WEBSITE** www.wimbledonwine cellar.com **HOURS** (Wimbledon) Mon–Sat 10–9 (Chiswick) Mon–Sat 10–9, Sun 11–7 **CARDS** AmEx, MasterCard, Switch, Visa **DISCOUNTS** 10% off 1 case (with a few exceptions) **DELIVERY** Free within the M25. Courier charges elsewhere. **EN PRIMEUR** Burgundy, Bordeaux, Tuscany. **C G M T**

✪ **Star attractions** *Top names from Italy, Burgundy, Bordeaux, Rhône, Loire – and some of the best of the New World, especially Australia and California. They don't issue a list, as stock changes so frequently, so you'll just have to go along to one of the shops and dig out your own treasure or look at their website.*

Wine & Beer World (Majestic)

HEAD OFFICE Majestic House, Otterspool Way, Watford, Herts WD25 8WW (01923) 298200 **FAX** (01923) 819105 **PRE-ORDER** (01923) 298297 • Rue du Judée, Zone Marcel Doret, Calais 62100, France (0033) 3 21 97 63 00 • Centre Commercial Carrefour, Quai L'Entrepôt, Cherbourg 50100, France (0033) 2 33 22 23 22 • Unit 3A, Zone La Française, Coquelles 62331, France (0033) 3 21 82 93 64 **E-MAIL** info@wineandbeer.co.uk **WEBSITE** www.wineandbeer.co.uk **HOURS** (Calais) 7 days 7–10 (Cherbourg) Mon–Sat 8.30–8 (Coquelles) 7 days 9–8. All stores open bank holidays at the usual times **CARDS** MasterCard, Switch, Visa. **T**

✪ **Star attractions** *This is the French arm of Majestic, with three branches all handy for trips across the Channel. Calais is the largest branch, Coquelles the nearest to the Channel Tunnel terminal while Cherbourg has a more limited range of wines. English-speaking staff. Savings of up to 50% on UK prices.*

Winemark

3 Duncrue Place, Belfast BT3 9BU, 028 9074 6274 **FAX** 028 9075 1755; 71 branches **E-MAIL** info@ winemark.com **WEBSITE** www.winemark.com **HOURS** Branches vary, but in general Mon–Sat 10–10, Sun 12–8 **CARDS** Delta, MasterCard, Switch, Visa **DISCOUNTS** 5% on 6–11 bottles, 10% on 12 bottles or more. **G M T**

✪ **Star attractions** *Winemark is strong in the New World: there is lots to choose from in Australia (Peter Lehmann, Chateau Reynella and Hardys right up to Eileen Shiraz at £49.99), New Zealand (Esk Valley and Villa Maria), California (Geyser Peak and Byron, among others), Chile (Errázuriz Wild Ferment Chardonnay for £9.99 and Carmen Nativa Cabernet Sauvignon for £9.69), and there's a good list of Bordeaux from older vintages.*

Wine Rack

See Thresher Group.

The Wine Society

Gunnels Wood Road, Stevenage, Herts SG1 2BG (01438) 741177 **FAX** (01438) 761167 **ORDER LINE** (01438) 740222 **E-MAIL** memberservices@ thewinesociety.com **WEBSITE** www.thewinesociety.com **HOURS** Mon–Fri 8.30–9, Sat 9–2; showroom: Mon–Thurs 10–6, Fri 10–7, Sat 9.30–5.30 **CARDS** MasterCard, Switch, Visa **DISCOUNTS** (per case) £1 for 5–9, £2 for 10 or more, £3 for collection **DELIVERY** Free 1 case or more UK mainland and Northern Ireland. Collection facility at Hesdin, France at French rates of duty and VAT **EN PRIMEUR** Bordeaux, Burgundy, Germany, Port, Rhône. **C G M T**
✪ **Star attractions** *The Wine Society has an inspired wine-buying team and this is an outstanding list. Bordeaux is excellent, with masses of well-chosen affordable wines as well as big names; Burgundy ditto; Rhône ditto; Loire, Italy, Spain, Portugal, all ditto, and lovely, classy New World wines. If you close your eyes and choose wines from this list with a pin, you'll always get something wonderful. The own label wines are as good as ever. You have to be a member to buy wine, but it costs only £40 for life and although it is necessary to be proposed by an existing member to join, the secretary of the society will propose you if you don't happen to know any members.*

Wine Treasury

MAIL ORDER 69–71 Bondway, London SW8 1SQ (020) 7793 9999 **FAX** (020) 7793 8080 **E-MAIL** quality@winetreasury.com **WEBSITE** www.winetreasury.com **HOURS** Mon–Fri 9.30–6.30 **CARDS** MasterCard, Switch, Visa **DISCOUNTS** 10% for unmixed dozens **DELIVERY** £10 per case, free 2 or more cases over £100, England and Wales; Scotland phone for more details **MINIMUM ORDER** 1 mixed case. **M T**
✪ **Star attractions** *California is a speciality here. There are the stunning Cabernet Sauvignons and Chardonnays from Stag's Leap Wine Cellars, Zinfandel from Cline Cellars, lots of tasty stuff from Joseph Phelps and much, much more. Italy looks just as good, with stars such as Sandrone and Roberto Voerzio from Piedmont, Tuscany's Castello di Ama and Sicily's Cusumano. But these top names don't come cheap.*

The Winery

4 Clifton Road, London W9 1SS (020) 7286 6475 **FAX** (020) 7286 2733 **E-MAIL** dmotion@globalnet. co.uk **HOURS** Mon–Sat 11–9.30, Sun and public holidays 12–8 **CARDS** MasterCard, Switch, Visa **DISCOUNTS** 5% on a mixed case **DELIVERY** Free locally or for 3 cases or more, otherwise £8.50 per case. **G M T**
✪ **Star attractions** *Burgundy, Rhône, Italy and California are the specialities, and there's also a range of grower Champagnes. From California there is Green & Red, Robert Sinskey, Bacio Divino and other seldom-seen names, and from Burgundy a list of very respectable names that begins at £9.99 and goes up to £114.99. The company sources its own wines, so it's a list to linger over – and a shop to linger in.*

Wines of Westthorpe

Coxmoor Road, Sutton-in-Ashfield, Notts, NG17 5LA (01623) 516001 FAX (01623) 510910 E-MAIL wines@westhorpe.co.uk WEBSITE www.westhorpe.co.uk HOURS Mon-Sat 8.30-6 CARDS MasterCard, Switch, Visa DISCOUNTS Variable on 1 case or more DELIVERY Free UK mainland (except northern Scotland) MINIMUM ORDER 1 mixed case. M

✪ Star attractions An excellent list for devotees of Eastern European wines – especially Hungarian and Romanian, as well as some Chile, Australia and South Africa, all at reasonable prices. From Hungary there's Kékfrankos, Kékoportó and Tokaji, as well as Szekszárdi Cabernet Franc and Budai Sauvignon Blanc, both at £3.99.

Wright Wine Co

The Old Smithy, Raikes Road, Skipton, N. Yorks BD23 1NP (01756) 700886 (01756) 794175 FAX (01756) 798580 E-MAIL bob@wineand whisky.co.uk WEBSITE wwwwine andwhisky.co.uk HOURS Mon-Sat 9-6; open Sundays in December 10.30-4 CARDS MasterCard, Switch, Visa DISCOUNTS Wholesale price unspilt case, 5% mixed case DELIVERY Free within 30 miles, elsewhere at cost. G

✪ Star attractions South Africa, Australia and Alsace look good, but it's a pretty comprehensive list, so you'll also find short(ish) but well-chosen selections from Burgundy, the Loire, Portugal, Italy, Argentina – and everywhere else.

Peter Wylie Fine Wines

Plymtree Manor, Plymtree, Cullompton, Devon EX15 2LE (01884) 277555 FAX (01884) 277557 E-MAIL peter@wylie-fine-wines. demon.co.uk WEBSITE wwwwylie finewines.co.uk HOURS Mon-Fri 9-6.30 CARDS None DISCOUNTS Unspilt cases DELIVERY 1 case £20; 2 cases £11; 3-4 £6; 5 or more £4.50

EN PRIMEUR Bordeaux. C M

✪ Star attractions Fascinating list of very old wines. Bordeaux from throughout the 20th century – there are umpteen 1961 clarets and a decent selection of serious wines from every vintage since. Red and white Bordeaux are the top performers on this list, but there are also a few Rhônes and Burgundies, plus ports going back to 1912, Madeiras to 1870.

Yapp Brothers

The Old Brewery, Mere, Wilts BA12 6DY (01747) 860423 FAX (01747) 860929 E-MAIL sales@yapp.co.uk WEBSITE wwwyapp.co.uk HOURS Mon-Sat 9-6 CARDS MasterCard, Switch, Visa DISCOUNTS £5 per case on collection DELIVERY £5 one case, 2 or more cases free. C G M

✪ Star attractions Rhône and Loire specialists who really know their way around these regions. They also have some of the hard-to-find wines of Provence (Bunan, Ch. de la Rouvière, Richeaume, Trevallon), plus Charles Schleret from Alsace – oh, and two interlopers from Australia (Jasper Hill and Neagles Rock).

Noel Young Wines

56 High Street, Trumpington, Cambridge CB2 2LS (01223) 844744 FAX (01223) 844736 E-MAIL admin@nywines.co.uk WEBSITE www.nywines.co.uk HOURS Mon-Sat 10-8, Sun 12-2 CARDS AmEx, MasterCard, Switch, Visa DISCOUNTS 5% for orders over £500 DELIVERY £7 first case, £4 subsequent cases, larger orders negotiable EN PRIMEUR Australia, Burgundy, Italy, Rhône. G M T

✪ Star attractions Fantastic wines from just about everywhere. Think of a region and you'll find the best wines on Noel Young's list. Australia is a particular passion. There's a famously good Austrian list, some terrific Germans, plus beautiful Burgundies and Italians.

Who's where

COUNTRYWIDE
Aldi
Asda
Australian Wine Club
Bat & Bottle
Bottoms Up
Bordeaux Index
Bring-a-Bottle
Anthony Byrne
Cave Cru Classé
Chateau Online
Co-op
Le Fleming Wines
Justerini & Brooks
Laithwaites
Liberty Wines
Majestic
Marks & Spencer
New Zealand Wines
    Direct
Oddbins
Oz Wines
Safeway
Sainsbury's
Somerfield
Sunday Times Wine
    Club
Tesco
Thresher
Victoria Wine
Vin du Van
Vintage Roots
Virgin Wines
Waitrose
Wine Rack
The Wine Society
Wine Treasury

LONDON
John Armit
Balls Brothers
H & H Bancroft Wines
Berkmann Wine
    Cellars
Berry Bros. & Rudd
Bibendum Fine Wine
Budgens
Corney & Barrow
Domaine Direct
Farr Vintners
Fortnum & Mason
Friarwood
Goedhuis & Co
Haynes Hanson &
    Clark
Harvey Nichols
High Breck Vintners
Jeroboams
Lea & Sandeman
O W Loeb
Mayfair Cellars
Montrachet
Moreno Wines
Morris & Verdin

Philglas & Swiggot
La Reserve
Howard Ripley
Roberson
RSJ Wine Company
Unwins
La Vigneronne
Waterloo Wine Co
Wimbledon Wine
    Cellar
The Winery

SOUTH-EAST AND
HOME COUNTIES
Bacchus Wine
Berry Bros. & Rudd
Budgens Stores Ltd
Butlers Wine Cellar
Cape Province Wines
Les Caves de Pyrene
Hedley Wright
Turville Valley Wines
Unwins

WEST AND
SOUTH-WEST
Averys of Bristol
Bennetts Fine
    Wines
Croque-en-Bouche
Great Western Wine
Haynes Hanson &
    Clark
Hicks & Don
Jeroboams
Laymont & Shaw
Mills Whitcombe
The Nobody Inn
Christopher Piper
Reid Wines
Savage Selection
Peter Wylie Fine
    Wines
Yapp Brothers

EAST ANGLIA
A&B Vintners
Adnams
Amey's Wines
Corney & Barrow
Roger Harris Wines
Hicks & Don
Lay & Wheeler
Seckford Wines
T & W Wines
Unwins
Noel Young Wines

MIDLANDS
Bat & Bottle
Connolly's
Gauntleys
SH Jones
Morrisons

Noble Rot Wine
    Warehouses
Portland Wine Co
Stevens Garnier
Tanners
Vintage Wines
Wines of Westhorpe

WALES
Ballantynes of
    Cowbridge
Irma Fingal-Rock
Mills Whitcombe
Moriarty Vintners
Terry Platt
Tanners

NORTH
Berkmann Wine
    Cellars
Booths
D Byrne
Harvey Nichols
Martinez Wines
Morrisons
MR Wines (Great
    Northern Wine)
Penistone Court
Playford Ros
Richardson & Sons
Frank Stainton
    Wines
Vinceremos
Whitesides of
    Clitheroe
Wright Wine Co

SCOTLAND
Berkmann Wine
    Cellars
Cockburns of Leith
Corney & Barrow
Friarwood
Harvey Nichols
Peter Green & Co
Raeburn Fine Wines
Valvona & Crolla
Villeneuve Wines

NORTHERN IRELAND
Direct Wine
    Shipments
James Nicholson
Winemark

CHANNEL ISLANDS
Sommelier Wine Co

FRANCE
Millésima
Oddbins
Sainsbury's
Tesco Vin Plus
Wine & Beer World